MW01033190

THE BIRTH OF WESTERN CANADA

Louis "David" Riel

THE BIRTH OF WESTERN CANADA

CANADA

A History of the Riel Rebellions

By

GEORGE F. G. STANLEY, D.Phil.

With Illustrations

Maps by C. C. J. Bond

UNIVERSITY OF TORONTO PRESS

TORONTO BUFFALO LONDON

Copyright Canada 1961 by
University of Toronto Press
Toronto   Buffalo   London
Reprinted 1963, 1966, 1970, 1973, 1975, 1978

Printed in the United States of America

ISBN 0-8020-6010-2
LC 61-1393

First published June 1936
by Longmans, Green and Co. Ltd.

In piam memoriam
JOHANNIS HENRICI STANLEY
patris mei
qui Canadae suae amantissimus
ut studio pari annales eius evolverem
me stimulavit
hunc librum
dedico.

PREFACE

THE Riel Rebellions were the most dramatic episodes in the history of Western Canada. Their historical significance has, however, been distorted and even lost sight of in the political, racial and religious controversy which their events engendered. Many writers, steeped in the immediacy of the events, have read into the conflict of the half-breeds and Indians with the Canadians in 1869–70 and 1885, the prejudices of Old Canada; others, developing this theme, have regarded the valleys of the Red and the Saskatchewan rivers as the western battle ground of the traditional hostilities of French Catholic Quebec and English Protestant Ontario. I feel that the significance of those troubles which marked the early history of Western Canada is to be found rather in their connexion with the general history of the frontier than with the ethnic relationships of Quebec and Ontario. Both the Manitoba insurrection and the Saskatchewan rebellion were the manifestation in Western Canada of the problem of the frontier, namely the clash between primitive and civilized peoples. In all parts of the world, in South Africa, New Zealand and North America, the penetration of white settlement into territories inhabited by native peoples has led to friction and wars; Canadian expansion into the North-West led to a similar result. Here both the half-breed population and the Indian tribes rose in arms against Canadian intrusion and the imposition of an alien civilization.

Fundamentally there was little difference between the half-breed and the Indian question. Both were aspects of the same general problem. By character and upbringing the half-breeds, no less than the Indians, were unfitted to compete with the whites in the competitive individualism of white civilization, or to share with them the duties and responsibilities of citizenship. They did not want to be civilized; they only wanted to survive. To the half-breeds and Indians, unable even to maintain the advantage of numbers, civilization meant demoralization, decline and

vii

ultimate extinction. Bishop Grandin, writing in 1887, placed his finger on the underlying cause of the half-breed rising when he wrote : " Les métis . . . ont grandement souffert des changements arrivés dans leur pays.   Ils n'étaient pas assez préparés à cette civilisation qui tout à coup est venue fondre sur eux . . . Je pourrais dire que c'est là toute l'explication de la guerre civile." And Hayter Reed, Assistant Indian Commissioner, in 1885, " I have now formed, I think, a pretty correct idea as to our rebel Indians, they all look upon the whites as interlopers and would get rid of them if they saw their way clear."

The dates of the two Riel risings are significant.   The first, 1869–70, coincided with the passing of the Hudson's Bay Company as the governing power of the North-West.   The second, 1885, coincided with the completion of the Canadian Pacific Railway, an event which definitely marked the end of the old order in the North-West.   The rebellion of 1885 was the last effort of the primitive peoples in Canada to withstand the inexorable advance of white civilization.   With the suppression of the rebellion white dominance was assured.   Henceforth the history of the Canadian West was to be that of the white man, not that of the red man or the bois brulé.

In writing this volume I have endeavoured to provide a more accurate and fuller history of the birth of Western Canada than has hitherto been written.   New details have been added to the history of the transfer of the Hudson's Bay Company Territories to Canada, the immediate causes which made possible—even inevitable—the insurrection, Riel's Provisional Government, and the amnesty controversy of the 'seventies ; also to the Government's Indian policy, the grievances of the half-breeds and Indians in 1885, and particularly to the part played by many of the white settlers in the District of Lorne during the Riel agitation ; and lastly to the effect of the racial, religious controversy of 1885–6 upon the political life of the Dominion.   The book is fully documented.   It has been my object to bring the reader into direct contact with the original materials, the letters and records of those who were themselves principals or eye-witnesses, and thus enable him to form his own independent judgment.

I have, therefore, examined the contemporary sources, many of which had not been examined before in this respect, studied both sides of controversies, and endeavoured to eliminate—as far as is possible to the historian relating events, the fire of which has not yet been extinguished by time—all partisan or personal bias. I have also read widely the works of others on the same subject. For any unwitting or unacknowledged appropiation I ask pardon ; it is difficult for those who have read and made notes from innumerable sources over a period of years to be at all certain of the originality of their ideas or phrases. In this work I have made a serious effort to reach the truth and feel that the justification of this book lies in its thorough treatment and its contribution of a new interpretation to a story which, however familiar in outline, has not hitherto been the subject of serious research.

During the preparation of this work assistance has been received from many sources. For placing materials at my disposal and assisting my research, I am indebted to the Governor and Committee of the Hudson's Bay Company, Dr. V. T. Harlow, Keeper of the Rhodes House Library, the Royal Empire Society and the Public Record Office ; also to Sir Arthur Doughty and the Public Archives of Canada, the Commissioner of the Royal Canadian Mounted Police, the Deputy Minister of Indian Affairs, and the Librarians of the University of Ottawa and the Bibliothèque St. Sulpice ; also to the officials of the State Department, Washington, D.C. I am under obligation to Miss D. G. Lent for preparing and forwarding me transcripts from the *New Nation* at Winnipeg. Sir Francis Wylie and J. G. Legge, Esq., kindly read the manuscript, and R. Leveson Gower, Esq., made many important corrections in the proofs. Professor R. Coupland was a source of constant encouragement. For their very generous assistance in making this publication possible, I am deeply indebted to the Rhodes Trustees, the Beit Trustees and the Committee for Advanced Studies of the University of Oxford. Lastly I wish to acknowledge my debt of gratitude to my Mother for her patience, interest and helpful criticism during the writing of this book.

G.F.G.S.

Keble College, Oxford.
    April 20th, 1936.

PREFACE TO THE SECOND EDITION

ON THE night of December 29–30, 1940, enemy air attacks reduced a great part of the city of London in the vicinity of St. Paul's Cathedral to flames and rubble. One of the minor casualties of this raid was the destruction of the premises of Longmans, Green and Company on Paternoster Row, and the loss of the remaining copies of the original edition of this book. Formidable as it may now seem to readers accustomed to pocket books, *The Birth of Western Canada* could not withstand the impact of German bombs. The book thus became, by accident of war rather than by deliberate policy on the part of the publishers, a very limited edition.

Although the work appeared first in 1936 its general thesis is still accepted by Canadian historians. There have been challenges, it is true, but these were no more than efforts to revive the traditional explanation of the métis question as a manifestation of the Franco-English quarrel in Canada. For this reason, if for no other, the reappearance of this book is justified. Admittedly new materials have been made available to historians, and had it been possible for the author to have done so, he would gladly have made additions and alterations and—dare I admit it?—a few corrections in the text. But such changes would in no way have altered the original thesis and would have made reproduction by the offset process impracticable. Thus the text remains unaltered with whatever virtues and imperfections it may originally have possessed. There are, however, new maps and several new illustrations which have not hitherto been published.

Acknowledgments of gratitude are owing to Longmans, Green and Company of London, the first publishers, for surrendering the copyright, and to The University of Toronto Press for assuming it. In particular I thank Miss Francess G. Halpenny for her interest, encouragement, and assistance in bringing out a new edition of an old book. My thanks go also to Major C. C. J. Bond for preparing the maps and to the Commandant of The Royal Military College for permission to use photographs belonging to the College Library.

G.F.G.S.

The Royal Military College of Canada,
    Kingston, Ontario,
       July 1st, 1960.

CONTENTS

CHAPTER   PAGE

PREFACE   vii

BOOK ONE

THE RED RIVER REBELLION

I. The Old Order of Red River · · · 3
II. The End of Company Rule · · · · 19
III. Half-Breed Unrest in the Red River Settlement · · · · · · 44
IV. The Red River Rebellion : Part I · · 67
V. The Red River Rebellion : Part II · · 87
VI. The Manitoba Act · · · · · 107
VII. The Military Expedition 1870 · · · 126
VIII. The Amnesty Question · · · · 144

BOOK TWO

THE NORTH-WEST REBELLION

IX. The Growth of Settlement in the North-West · · · · · · · 177
X. The Indian Problem : The Treaties · · 194
XI. The Indian Problem : The Reserves · · 216
XII. The Growth of Political Discontent in the North-West Territories · · · · 243
XIII. The Growth of Discontent among the Indians 269
XIV. The Return of Riel and the Development of the Agitation · · · · · 295
XV. The North-West Rebellion : Part I · · 327

xi

CHAPTER   PAGE

XVI. THE NORTH-WEST REBELLION : PART II   .   . 350

XVII. THE POLITICAL RESULTS OF THE NORTH-WEST
        REBELLION 380

        BIBLIOGRAPHICAL NOTE   408

        NOTES   411

        INDEX 453

ILLUSTRATIONS

Louis "David" Riel . . . . . . *frontispiece*
    By permission of the late Rev. A. G. Morice, O.M.I.

FACING PAGE

A Métis Encampment on the Prairies, 1874 . 8
    By permission of George Shepherd, Esq.

Fort Garry 72
    By permission of the Governor and Committee of the
      Hudson's Bay Company

Cartoon, A Case of Riel Distress! . . . 168
    From "Grip," by permission of Thomas Bengough, Esq.

Cartoon, Loyalty in a Quandary . . . 172
    From "Grip," by permission of Thomas Bengough, Esq.

Crowfoot 230
    From MacInnes, "In the Shadow of the Rockies," by
      permission of Messrs. Rivington and Co. Ltd.

Cartoon, Merely a Hum-Bug-Bear . . . 264
    From "Grip," by permission of Thomas Bengough, Esq.

Big Bear 280
    By permission of the Public Archives of Canada

Poundmaker 284
    By permission of H. A. Kennedy, Esq.

Imasees 338
    From Cameron, "The War Trail of Big Bear," by
      permission of Messrs. Gerald Duckworth and Co. Ltd.

FACING PAGE

GABRIEL DUMONT 358
    From Ouimet, "La Verité sur la question métisse"

CANADIAN ARTILLERY IN ACTION AT BATOCHE . 368
    By permission of the Royal Military College of Canada

THE SURRENDER OF POUNDMAKER 372
    By permission of the Royal Military College of Canada

THE SURRENDER OF MISERABLE MAN . . . 376
    By permission of the Royal Military College of Canada

MAPS

THE RED RIVER SETTLEMENT, 1870 . . . 14

BRITISH NORTH AMERICA, 1869–70 . . . 42

THE INDIAN TREATIES, 1871–77 210

THE NORTH SASKATCHEWAN VALLEY, 1885 . . 243

THE NORTH-WEST TERRITORIES, MILITARY COLUMNS 355

BOOK ONE

THE RED RIVER REBELLION

CHAPTER I

THE OLD ORDER OF RED RIVER

On May 2nd, 1670, Charles II granted to the Governor and Company of Adventurers of England Trading into Hudson's Bay "the sole Trade and Commerce of all those Seas, Streightes, Bayes, Rivers, Lakes, Creekes and Soundes in whatsoever Latitude they shall bee, that lie within the entrance of the Streightes, commonly called Hudsons Streightes together with all the Landes and Territoryes upon the Countryes, Coastes and Confynes of the Seas, Bayes, Lakes, Rivers, Creekes and Soundes aforesaid that are not already actually possessed by or granted to any of our Subjectes, or possessed by the Subjectes of any other Christian Prince or State" : and constituted them "the true and absolute Lordes and Proprietors of the same Territory, lymittes and places."[1]   Of the extent of this vast territory, henceforth called Rupert's Land after the cavalier prince, neither the King nor the Company had any conception.   Yet an area as large as Europe, bounded on the north by the "Barren Lands," on the west by the snow-capped Rockies, and on the south by the arid plains, was transferred by Charles's sweeping gesture to the overlordship of the Hudson's Bay Company.

Scattered throughout this area were thousands of aborigines, or Indians, as they had been miscalled by Columbus.   It is almost impossible to compute their numbers at this period, but it is possible that the native inhabitants of Rupert's Land at the beginning of the nineteenth century numbered about 50,000.[2] These Indians were made up of three great linguistic groups, the Algonkin, the Athapascan and the Siouan.   Each group was split up into tribes.   The Algonkin included the Crees, Ojibways, Saulteaux, Blackfeet, Bloods and Piegans : the Athapascan included the Sarcees, Beavers, Chipewyans and other northern tribes : the Siouan, predominantly American in habitat, were represented in British territory by the Assiniboines or Stonies and a few wandering Sioux.   These tribes were again divided

3

into sub-tribes or bands, and even into families, often dispersed over a wide extent of wilderness.

The aboriginal inhabitants were not left in undisturbed possession of the western plains. Although the Hudson's Bay Company wasted little time on exploration or " the discovery of a new Passage into the South Sea,"[3] several expeditions were despatched inland to draw the remote tribes to the trading posts on the Bay. As early as 1690 Henry Kelsey was sent to visit some of the tribes of the interior. From his *Journal*[4] it would appear that he reached the country of the Assiniboines and Crees in what is now the south-eastern region of the province of Saskatchewan. In 1754-5 Anthony Henday travelled over the prairies and wintered among the Blackfeet in the western foothills. Matthew Cocking made a similar journey in 1772.

While the English were thus penetrating Rupert's Land from Hudson Bay, the French, impelled by a spirit of adventure and a desire for furs, were pushing up the St. Lawrence Valley and the Great Lakes. Dulhut is said to have built a post on the shores of Lake Superior about 1678 : ten years later Jacques de Noyon reached the Lake of the Woods : and in 1717 La Noüe followed in his footsteps. But the man who really opened the door to the North-West was Pierre Gaultier, Sieur de la Vérendrye, whose explorations from 1732 to 1743, carried on in the face of extraordinary difficulties, render his name " one of the most honoured names in Canadian exploration."[5] Accompanied by his sons, Vérendrye discovered the Red River of the North and built Fort Rouge on the site of the present city of Winnipeg. Pressing further west in his search for " the western sea " he reached the Saskatchewan River ; but, harassed by creditors whose interests were economic rather than scientific, Vérendrye was finally obliged to abandon his explorations. Trade entered the gateway which exploration had opened and by 1757 the French had built a chain of forts from Montreal to the Rockies.

The conquest of Canada by Wolfe and Amherst changed, for a time, the course of events. Within five years of Henday's journey the French had disappeared from the west. Engaged in a struggle for the defence of Canada, the French withdrew their officers and men from the fur trade with the Indians to combat the English. But within a year of the capitulation of Montreal the fur trade was resumed, and French and English merchants were again sending goods to the western Indians. The evils of unrestricted competition soon urged upon individual traders the advisability of co-operation, and during the winter of 1783–4 competing interests in Canada united to form the North-West Company.

Spurred on by a bitter commercial rivalry the North-West Company and the Hudson's Bay Company pushed further and further into the Indian country, until, within the space of ten years, the whole region from Lake Superior to Lake Athabasca and from Hudson Bay to the Rocky Mountains was dotted with trading posts. By 1800 it is estimated that the rival fur companies must have had from 1,500 to 2,000 white men permanently in the North-West. These men were apprenticed for a definite period to serve in the interior and were known as the " winterers." They ranged from the humblest guide to the highest officer, Chief Factor or Bourgeois. In the English company the apprentice clerk served five years before becoming a clerk ; this was followed by a longer period before promotion to the position of Chief Trader and by another period before promotion to the rank of Chief Factor. Each of these was entitled to share in the profits of the company's trade. In the Canadian company the gradations of rank were similar, the highest being that of Bourgeois or partner. In addition there was an army of guides, labourers, and voyageurs, attached to each company. As a general rule the employees of the Hudson's Bay Company were drawn from Scotland and the Orkney Islands, while those of the North-West Company were Scots and French Canadians.

It was inevitable that these men, living in the midst of a savage society far from their own kind, should unite with the Indian women of the plains. When Henry Kelsey returned to Fort York in 1692, accompanied by an Indian woman, he only began among the Hudson's Bay Company employees the practice which had been customary among the French traders and coureurs de bois since the early days of Canadian history. The Hudson's Bay Company at first viewed these unions with displeasure, but eventually favoured them as having a steadying effect upon the men and establishing useful trading connexions with the Indians. Accordingly, during the next century and a half, there were few employees of either fur company who did not contract alliances with the Indian women in the neighbourhood of the Companies' forts.

Most of these alliances were " according to the custom of the country." Daniel Harmon, a Bourgeois of the North-West Company, writing in 1800, described the procedure followed :

" When a person is desirous of taking one of the daughters of the Natives, as a companion, he makes a present to the parents of the damsel, of such articles as he supposes will be most acceptable ; and, among them, rum is indispensable ; for of that all the savages are fond, to excess.   Should the parents accept the articles offered, the girl remains at the fort with her suitor, and is clothed in the Canadian fashion.   The greater part of these women, as I am informed, are better pleased to remain with the white people, than with their own relations.   Should the couple, newly joined, not agree, they are at liberty, at any time, to separate ; but no part of the property, given to the parents of the girl, will be refunded."[6]

Many of these marriages were only temporary.   When her white consort returned to civilization, the Indian woman, of necessity, rejoined her tribe, to remain in widowhood until she caught the fancy of some other voyageur or trader.   Some, however, proved permanent.   The Indian women readily adapted themselves to the life of the whites and " the tenderness existing between them and their husbands presents one great reason for that attachment which the respective classes of whites cherish for the Indian countries."[7]   After many years spent in the free life of the wilds, men found the ways of civilization cramping and preferred to settle down in the country with their native wives.   Harmon, in spite of his early scorn for these unions, not only married, but became so attached to his Indian wife that he took her with him when he returned to civilization.

From this intermingling of natives and Europeans developed a race of people known as half-breeds, métis, or bois brulés. In the century following the penetration of the North-West by the fur traders these people increased rapidly in numbers, and, separate alike from whites and Indians, they became the chief actors in the political troubles which mark the history of Western Canada to 1885.

The greater number of these half-breeds, or métis, were of French-Canadian origin, the offspring of the hardy voyageurs

who served the North-West Company.   Their skin was dark—
hence the name brulé—but beyond that they carried few traces of
their savage origin.   They dressed like the whites in common
blue capote, red belt, and corduroy trousers : the belt was the
simple badge of distinction, the métis wearing it under and the
whites generally over the capote. "Too many at home," wrote
Southesk in January 1860, " have formed a false idea of the half-
breeds, imagining them to be a race little removed from barbarians
in habits and appearance. . . . I doubt if a half-breed, dressed and
educated like an Englishman, would seem at all remarkable in
London society.   They build and farm like other people, they go
to church and to courts of law, they recognize no chiefs (except
when they elect a leader for their great hunting expeditions), and
in all respects they are like civilized men, not more uneducated,
immoral, or disorderly, than many communities in the Old
World."[8]
    Of the physical characteristics of the métis the same observer
wrote :
    " Physically they are a fine race, tall, straight, and well pro-
portioned, lightly formed but strong and extremely active and
enduring.   Their chests, shoulders, and waists are of that
symmetrical shape so seldom found among the broad-waisted,
short-necked English, or the flat-chested, long-necked Scotch."[9]
W. B. Cheadle, on his journey across the North American continent
in 1862, found them unequalled as guides and voyageurs :
    " Of more powerful build, as a rule, than the pure Indian, they
combine his endurance and readiness of resource with the greater
muscular strength and perseverance of the white man.   Day after
day, with plenty of food, or none at all, whether pack on back,
trapping in the woods, treading out a path with snowshoes in the
deep snow for the sleigh-dogs, or running after them at a racing
pace from morning to night, when there is a well-beaten track,
they will travel fifty or sixty miles a day for a week together
without showing any sign of fatigue."[10]
    The métis were a hospitable people ; all comers and goers
were welcome guests at their board.[11] Theft seems to have been
uncommon among them.   Upon one occasion a gentleman
travelling over the plains left at his camping place a box containing
gold and notes to the value of £1030.   The following evening a
French half-breed, camping at the same spot, found the box, and,

in spite of his own poverty, followed the owner a day's journey to return it.   Alexander Ross, who cannot be suspected of undue sympathy for the métis, nevertheless recorded that " this act might be taken as an index of the integrity of the whole body, generally speaking."[12] They were, moreover, very religious and devoted to their clergy.   The hunter always reserved the best cut of meat for the priest, while the trader kept aside his best piece of cloth for the Church.

At the same time the French half-breeds were indolent, thoughtless and improvident, unrestrained in their desires, restless, clannish and vain.   Life held no thought of the morrow. To become the envied possessor of a new suit, rifle, or horse, they would readily deprive themselves and their families of the necessities of life.   " A half-breed able to exhibit a fine horse, and gay cariole," wrote Ross, " is in his glory ; this achievement is at once the height of his ambition, and his ruin.   Possessed of these, the thriftless fellow's habitation goes to ruin ; he is never at home, but driving and caricoling in all places, and every opportunity ; blustering and bantering every one he meets."[13] Another observer gave the following description of their care-free life of pleasure :

" They are a merry, light-hearted, obliging race, recklessly generous, hospitable, and extravagant.   Dancing goes on nearly every night throughout the winter, and a wedding, or ' noce ' as it is called, is celebrated by keeping open house, and relays of fiddlers are busily employed playing for the dancers all through the night and often far on into the next day.   By that time most of the guests are incapacitated from saltatory exercise ; for rum flows freely on these occasions, and when a half-breed drinks he does it, as he says, *comme il faut*—that is, until he obtains the desired happiness of complete intoxication."[14]

With few exceptions the French half-breeds were neither extensive nor successful farmers.   Brought up in the open prairies they preferred the excitement of the chase to the monotony of cultivating the soil.   They might have envied the lot of the more industrious and regretted their own poverty, but so strong was their attachment to the roving life of the hunter that " the greater part of them depend entirely on the chase for a living, and even the few who attend to farming take a trip to the plains, to feast on buffalo humps and marrow fat."[15] These métis were not a savage,

A Métis Encampment on the Prairies, 1874

vicious, or immoral people, but honest, hospitable and religious, rather improvident and happy-go-lucky, without care and without restraint, true sons of the prairie, as free as the air they breathed and by nature as independent as the land which gave them birth.

As a rule the English-speaking half-breeds formed a contrast to the French. The greater number were of Scotch origin. Many of the officers of the Hudson's Bay Company came from Scotland and their half-breed children inherited the steadier disposition of their fathers, as the métis inclined to the roving life of the *coureurs de bois*. They were, for the most part, economical, industrious and prosperous. Cheadle declared that the English and Scotch half-breeds " form a pleasing contrast to their French neighbours, being thrifty, industrious, and many of them wealthy, in their way . . . we met but few who equalled the French half-breeds in idleness and frivolity."[16] John McLean in his *Notes of a Twenty-five Years' Service in the Hudson's Bay Territory* also stated :

" The English half-breeds, as the mixed progeny of the British are designated, possess many of the characteristics of their fathers ; they generally prefer the more certain pursuit of husbandry to the chase, and follow close on the heels of the Scotch in the path of industry and moral rectitude. Very few of them resort to the plains, unless for the purpose of trafficking the produce of their farms for the produce of the chase ; and it is said that they frequently return home better supplied with meat than the hunters themselves."[17]

It often happened that, as the Scots and English held the rank of gentlemen in the fur trade, their half-breed sons were given a better start in life and a training which did not oblige them to seek their living with their rifle like the sons of the poor voyageurs. If they indicated any aptitude for learning these sons might be sent to schools in England or Scotland. On their return, some, like Moses Norton, rose in the service of the fur trade, others settled down to farm and to take a leading part in the life of their community. But to say that the English half-breeds cultivated more land, were better educated and possessed more of the world's goods, is not to speak slightingly of the French, nor to say that they were more honest or loyal. Each possessed distinct characteristics and each played a part in the history of the half-breed race.

In spite of these differences there was a common bond between the English and the French half-breeds. Both sprang from a common race; both claimed territorial rights to the North-West through their Indian ancestry; both, in a large measure, spoke their mother tongue in addition to French or English. The half-breeds as a race never considered themselves as humble hangers-on to the white population, but were proud of their blood and their deeds. Cut off, as they were, from European expansion by the accident of geography and by the deliberate policy of the Hudson's Bay Company, they developed a resolute feeling of independence and a keen sense of their own identity which led them to regard themselves as a separate racial and national unit, and which found expression in their name, " The New Nation." Louis Riel, the métis leader, gave expression to this national feeling when he wrote :

" C'est vrai que notre origine sauvage est humble, mais il est juste que nous honorions nos mères aussi bien que nos pères. Pourquoi nous occuperions-nous à quel degré de mélange nous possédons le sang européen et le sang indien ? Pour peu que nous ayons de l'un ou de l'autre, la reconnaissance et l'amour filial, ne nous font-ils pas une loi de dire : Nous sommes Métis."[18]

This consciousness of community and strong racial feeling dominated the half-breed " nation " for almost a century : it was the basic factor in the frontier problem of Western Canadian history.

Colonization naturally followed the opening of Rupert's Land by the fur trade. In 1812 the first attempt to found a white settlement in the North-West was made under the patronage of Lord Selkirk. Four years previously Selkirk had begun to buy up the stock of the Hudson's Bay Company in an effort to secure a controlling share, and, although he was unable to interest the Company in his project, he was thus able to secure from them a grant of 116,000 square miles in the Red River valley, covering what is now the southern part of Manitoba and a portion of Minnesota, for the purposes of a colony. In July 1811, the first band of Scottish settlers, led by Miles Macdonnell, a Canadian highlander, sailed for the New World. They passed the winter at York Factory and in the following spring made their way south to the site of the proposed settlement.

The Hudson's Bay Company viewed Selkirk's efforts with

indifference; but the North-West Company regarded them with undisguised hostility. Selkirk's grant of land lay directly across the route from Montreal to the interior of Rupert's Land and the Nor' Westers believed its settlement was merely a move upon the part of their rivals to stifle their trade. With their economic interests at stake they set out to destroy the Selkirk colony by fair means or foul. At first an attempt was made to bribe the colonists to abandon the settlement. But sugary promises of free passages and assistance to fertile lands in Upper Canada failed to lure the stubborn Scots from Red River, and so the Nor' Westers turned to the half-breeds.

At the door of the North-West Company must be laid the responsibility for rousing the racial consciousness of the métis. The Nor' Westers carefully fostered the idea of half-breed territorial rights and informed the credulous métis that the white settlers were interlopers who had come to steal the land from them. The métis were easily convinced. They had already been estranged by two ill-advised acts of Miles Macdonnell—the one a proclamation forbidding the sale of pemmican to the North-West Company, and the other an attempt to prohibit the running of the buffalo on horseback—and readily construed every act of coercion against the fur company as unjustifiable tyranny over their race. Under the leadership of Cuthbert Grant and Peter Pangman, two half-breed employees of the North-West Company, they began to assert their claim to an aboriginal title to the country and to demand compensation from the white settlers.

In 1816 the situation reached a climax. Grant was appointed " Captain General of all the half-breeds in the country," and in March it was reported that " the new nation under their leaders are coming forward to clear their native soil of intruders and assassins."[19] In May, Grant and fifty half-breeds surprised the brigade descending the Assiniboine River towards the settlement, confiscated the goods and took several prisoners. Early in June they seized Brandon House and set out to join a party from Fort William for a combined attack on the Red River Settlement. Passing Fort Douglas, the centre of the colony, on the 19th, they were accosted by Robert Semple, the newly-appointed Governor. A gun was fired and in the exchange of shots which followed, Semple and twenty-one of his men were killed, Grant losing only a single follower.

This massacre of Seven Oaks, or La Grenouillère as it is known to the French half-breeds, is important in the history of the western frontier, not so much in itself, as in its portents. By stirring up the natives of the country, imbuing them with the idea that they were the true owners of the soil and that the whites—" les jardinières "—were intruders, the North-West Company sowed the seeds of that métis unrest which manifested itself at intervals for the next seventy years. Seven Oaks was only the first of several demonstrations by the half-breeds against the settlement of their country by the whites, and was, in consequence, the forerunner of the Riel Rebellions of 1869–70 and 1885. On each of these occasions the underlying cause of trouble was this spirit of half-breed nationalism and the conviction, expressed in the " chanson " of Pierre Falcon, a métis folk-song, that the white strangers had come " pour piller notre pays."[20]

Seven Oaks did not mean the end of the Red River Settlement. Lord Selkirk at once sent military assistance, made prisoners of the North-West Company leaders in their stronghold of Fort William, restored the settlers to their lands and continued the struggle in the courts. In 1820 Lord Selkirk died, discouraged by the failure of his colony and crushed by the persecution of his enemies. His death removed the principal obstacle to a reconciliation between the two fur companies whose opposition to colonization was mutual, and in 1821 they were united under the name of the Hudson's Bay Company. This union was significant. Both companies were convinced of the incompatibility of colonization and the successful prosecution of the fur trade, and for the next two generations the interests of the latter predominated in Rupert's Land. No further attempts at colonization were made and the Red River Settlement entered upon a period of quiet and obscure development.

The outstanding feature of this development during the years from 1820 to 1860 was the transformation of the colony from a white settlement into a half-breed settlement. When Miles Macdonnell selected the site on the Red River in 1812, his little band numbered seventy. In 1817, the year after Seven Oaks, the number of the Scottish settlers at Kildonan had increased to 200, while across the river at St. Boniface were a few Canadians and about 100 Swiss mercenaries whom Selkirk had brought to the country during his struggle with the North-West Company.

The Swiss, however, had little love for Red River and when that little was devoured by the grasshoppers and washed away by the floods they abandoned the country for the United States. In spite of this defection the colony grew in numbers, not by accessions from Canada or Europe, but by the settlement of the employees, half-breed and white, of the fur companies. It had been a condition of Selkirk's grant that one-tenth of the area should be set apart " to the use of such person or persons being or having been in the service or employ of the said Governor and Company for a term not less than three years,"[21] and Red River became the favourite retreat of the Company's servants with their squaws and half-breed progeny. Moreover, the union of the rival fur concerns in 1821 threw many clerks and voyageurs out of employment, with the result that the numbers of the colony were practically doubled in a few years. In 1831 the population numbered 2,417, and nine years later, 4,369.[22] As evidence of the rapid change in the racial composition of the Red River Settlement, H. Y. Hind reported that although the population had increased by 1,232 souls between 1849 and 1856, the number of European and Canadian families had decreased by 102.[23] Finally, in 1871, the official census stated that there were in the country 5,720 French-speaking half-breeds, 4,080 English-speaking half-breeds and 1,600 white settlers.[24] This transformation is significant, for it explains why Canadian annexation, with its implied white predominance, failed to gain many adherents in the Red River colony.

The economic life of the Settlement was primitive in character. The principal occupation was the buffalo hunt. The following figures indicate its growing importance. In 1820, 540 buffalo carts were sent out from Red River to the western plains; in 1830, 820 carts; and in 1840, 1,210: the total value of the hunt, in the last year amounting to £24,000.[25] Next in importance were freighting and farming. The Hudson's Bay Company employed a number of half-breeds to transport goods from the posts on Hudson Bay to the valley of Lake Winnipeg. Fifty-five boats, of three to five tons burden, were engaged in this service in 1856.[26] As the western states of America were opened to settlement the occupation of freighting increased in importance and St. Paul, Minnesota, became a distributing point for the Red River Settlement. Donald Gunn wrote in 1857 that there were 300 carts with an average load valued at £25 to £30 engaged in the overland transport from St. Paul.[27] Beyond these occupations there was no industry or distinct trade in the Settlement. Every man was his own wheelwright, carpenter or mason, as well as hunter, farmer or freighter.

When the Settlement was first established land was sold at five shillings an acre. This price gradually increased until, in 1834, it reached twelve shillings and sixpence.[28] The transfer of the territory from Lord Selkirk's heirs to the Hudson's Bay Company in 1836, was made without prejudice to those who held good title from the Earl. The price was reduced and the Company resumed the policy of selling land at five shillings or seven and six an acre, generally leasehold for 999 years.[29] In return they demanded from the lessee that he should bring at least one-tenth of his land under cultivation within five years, refrain from trading or dealing with the Indians or trafficking in furs and peltries except under licence, obey the Company's laws, contribute to the public expenses, and neither dispose of nor assign the lease without the Company's assent.[30] The Hudson's Bay Company, however, made few sales under these terms. In 1857 Sir George Simpson made the statement that not more than £2,000 to £3,000 had been received from the settlers in payment for their lands.[31] This may be accounted for by the fact that the majority of the settlers were half-breed squatters, who maintained the view that the land was theirs by natural law and that there was no need to bother about the Company's title. As the latter never made any effort to disturb them in the peaceful enjoyment of their lands, this lack of title was not a great source of anxiety. Governor Simpson informed the Select Committee of the House of Commons in 1857 that the Company's title was held of little value and that " nineteen-twentieths of the people have no title "[32]; while Henry Youle Hind wrote that " in no single instance could I find any half-breed, in possession of a farm, acquainted with its existence. In very many instances the settlers did not know the number of their lots, and had no paper or document of any kind to show that they held possession of their land from the Company, or any other authority."[33] This complete absence of a systematic land tenure, although it aroused no apprehensions at that time, was, however, to prove an important cause of unrest among the half-breed squatters

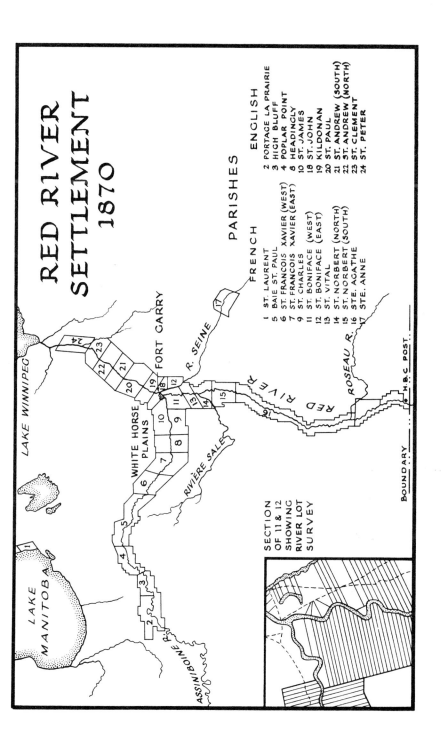

RED RIVER SETTLEMENT 1870

PARISHES

FRENCH
1 ST. LAURENT
5 BAIE ST. PAUL
6 ST. FRANCOIS XAVIER (WEST)
7 ST. FRANCOIS XAVIER (EAST)
9 ST. CHARLES
11 ST. BONIFACE (WEST)
12 ST. BONIFACE (EAST)
13 ST. VITAL
14 ST. NORBERT (NORTH)
15 ST. NORBERT (SOUTH)
16 STE. AGATHE
17 STE. ANNE

ENGLISH
2 PORTAGE LA PRAIRIE
3 HIGH BLUFF
4 POPLAR POINT
8 HEADINGLY
10 ST. JAMES
18 ST. JOHN
19 KILDONAN
20 ST. PAUL
21 ST. ANDREW (SOUTH)
22 ST. ANDREW (NORTH)
23 ST. CLEMENT
24 ST. PETER

LAKE MANITOBA

LAKE WINNIPEG

WHITE HORSE PLAINS

FORT GARRY

ASSINIBOINE R.

RIVIÈRE SALE

R. SEINE

RED RIVER

ROSEAU R.

BOUNDARY .... H.B.C. POST.

SECTION OF 11 & 12 SHOWING RIVER LOT SURVEY

when Rupert's Land was transferred to the Dominion of Canada.

The system of survey,[34] by which the Settlement was divided, was similar to that adopted in French Canada. The farms were long and narrow and at right angles to the general course of the river. They all had frontage on the water, after the fashion of farms in Quebec—a system which had grown up from the times when rivers were the principal routes of communication. At first the farms ran back ninety to one hundred chains, but subsequently they were extended to two miles. There was no uniformity of width and holdings were divided and subdivided at will. There was, in addition, a valuable privilege recognized by the Company—and which, apparently, had always been exercised by the owners of these river farms—namely, the exclusive right of cutting hay on the outer two miles immediately in the rear of the river lot. This outer portion came to be known as the "hay privilege" and was jealously guarded by local laws, infringements of which were visited with punishment.

For the first few years of its existence the Red River colony was governed directly by a Governor appointed by Lord Selkirk. After the Earl's death in 1820, the Settlement remained nominally under the care of his executors, but actually was administered through the Hudson's Bay Company. This anomalous position became each year more evident, and the sixth Earl, lacking his predecessor's interest in colonization, finally surrendered, in 1836, the territory granted to his father in 1811. From 1836 to 1869 the Company ruled at Red River.

Little change was made in the system of government in the colony. The Hudson's Bay Company followed the practice of Lord Selkirk and appointed a local Governor and Council to conduct the affairs of Red River, or Assiniboia, as it was known during the Company régime. Although the interests of the Company naturally predominated, nevertheless there was a deliberate attempt to make the Council fairly representative of all the interests in the colony. The clergy, Roman Catholic and Protestant, were represented, as were the half-breeds, French and English. In the first Council, after the reconveyance of the Selkirk grant, sat John Bunn, an English half-breed, and Cuthbert Grant, who had led the métis at Seven Oaks. The representative character of the Council was attested by no less an authority

B

than the Roman Catholic Bishop of St. Boniface, who wrote to Governor Dallas in 1862 :

" It is well known that these Nominees are chosen among the most respectable and the most intelligent of the place. Moreover the Company has, even in this choice, evinced generosity, as several of the Members of the Council have personal interests diametrically opposed to the commercial interests of the Company. To my knowledge the Company went so far as to consult those interested, and the greater number of the Councillors have been appointed because such appeared to be the desire of the population in general."[35]

The Anglican Bishop expressed a similar view, namely, that the members of the Council

" have been generally selected on the spot, as those possessing weight and influence, and generally acceptable with the settlement at large. . . . All cannot be Councillors, but I feel confident that the voice of each District would have elected for the most part the very individual recommended for a seat in Council."[36]

At first the duties of the Council were largely judicial, but from 1835 they tended to become more and more legislative and executive in character. A great variety of local measures were passed, relating to fires, animals, hay, roads, sale of intoxicating liquors to the Indians, police, debtors, contracts for services, surveys, administration of justice and other matters. To assist in carrying out these regulations the Council organized a Board of Works, a Committee of Economy, legal and judicial machinery, customs and postal facilities, and appointed various public officials. The work of the Council covered the whole life of the colony, from the issue of marriage licences to the encouragement of local industries.[37]

The jurisdiction of the Governor and Council of Assiniboia covered only an area of fifty miles' radius around the Red River Settlement. For administrative purposes this area was divided into four judicial districts, each under a magistrate or Justice of the Peace competent to try petty cases. In 1837 this judicial machinery was altered. The settlement was divided into three judicial districts, each under two magistrates. Two years later further changes were made. A special officer, the Recorder of Rupert's Land, was appointed as head of the legal affairs of the colony, and the number of magistrates over each district was increased to three, one of whom, at least, was to reside in the district, and one, at least, outside it. Owing to the growth of the colony this number was increased again in 1850. These magistrates held quarterly courts—after 1850, twice monthly—of summary jurisdiction, with final judgment in cases of debt not exceeding forty shillings. Cases of doubt or difficulty were referred to the supreme tribunal, the Quarterly Court of the Governor and Council of Assiniboia.[38]

The Canadian courts had concurrent jurisdiction with those of the Company. In 1803 an Act was passed " for extending the Jurisdiction of the Courts of Justice in the Provinces of *Lower* and *Upper Canada*, to the Trial and Punishment of Persons guilty of Crimes and Offences within certain parts of *North America* adjoining to the said Provinces."[39] This Act, assuming that crimes committed in the Indian territories were not cognizable by any jurisdiction, brought such crimes within the jurisdiction of Canadian courts, and empowered the Governor of Lower Canada to appoint Justices to commit offenders until conveyed to Canada for trial. As doubt arose as to whether this Act extended to the territories of the Hudson's Bay Company, since crimes committed in them could hardly be said to be " not cognizable by any Jurisdiction whatever," another Act was passed in 1821[40] to clarify the position. After reciting the doubts referred to and the necessity of removing them, this Act declared that the provisions of the previous Act should be deemed " to extend to and over, and to be in full force in and through all the Territories heretobefore granted to the Company of Adventurers of *England* trading into *Hudson's Bay*." Nothing in the Act, however, was to be construed to affect the rights, privileges, authority, or jurisdiction of the Company. But, while this concurrent jurisdiction was granted to the Canadian courts, there is no record of any persons having been authorized to act as magistrates or Justices of the Peace, nor any courts constituted under either Act.

Such is the picture of the primitive society which existed in the Red River Settlement during the last century. Economically and politically it was a simple society and filled the needs of a simple people for nearly two generations. Cut off from the outside world by the opposition of the Hudson's Bay Company to colonization, and by the physical barrier of geography to immigration, the half-breeds of Red River " were without the vexation and the heart-burning of active politics . . . their simple life . . . had nothing of that fierce element of competition into which the newer civilization was to hurl them."[41] But there could be no place for this almost static society in the competitive civilization of the North American continent. The half-breeds, particularly the hunting class, were doomed to economic absorption. Neither their racial consciousness, nor their primitive economy was strong enough to maintain the separate identity of the half-breed " nation " in the midst of an overwhelming white immigration and a competitive nineteenth-century civilization. Herein lay the basic cause of the half-breed rising in 1869. The métis leaders and their clergy realized that the rapid influx of settlers, which was bound to follow the transfer of the country to the Dominion of Canada, would lead to the loss of their lands and their livelihood, the breakdown of their society, and the eventual effacement of their race. Resistance was therefore inevitable.

CHAPTER II

TOWARDS the middle of the nineteenth century it became increasingly evident that the days of Company rule in British North America were numbered. With the ascendancy of the doctrines of economic liberalism the outlook for the great trading and governing monopolies was decidedly unfavourable. It is true that many Englishmen had ceased to believe in the economic advantages of the great chartered monopolies long before the adoption of free trade, but it was not until the 'fifties and 'sixties that the principles of the Manchester School began to dominate British colonial policy. The influence of that school of thought was much greater than its parliamentary voting power. But, although it never became a governing body, its ideas suffused the policies of both the great political parties.

The mid-Victorian attack upon the chartered companies was not confined to their alleged economic fallacies, but was also directed against their political status. In the pursuit of commercial advantages these companies had often extended their activities over widespread areas, and in doing so were invariably obliged to assume administrative responsibilities for which their character as trading corporations scarcely fitted them. Adam Smith had emphasized the fundamental contradiction of this position, namely, the clash between the interests of trade and the responsibilities of government. "As sovereigns," he wrote of the East India Company, their "interest is exactly the same with that of the country which they govern. As merchants, their interest is directly opposite to that interest."[1] Even in the case of companies like the Virginia Company, whose first interest was colonization, the necessity of operating at a profit conflicted with the aspirations of the colonists and the needs of administration. This conflict of interests was all the more apparent in the case of those companies which, like the Hudson's Bay Company and the East India Company, were primarily trading corporations. The great chartered companies of the seventeenth century had been the pioneers of Britain's Empire in the East and in the West, but by the nineteenth they were regarded as anachronisms, a mere transitory phase in Imperial expansion.

It cannot be denied that economic rather than political considerations dominated the policy of the Hudson's Bay Company in Red River. Every effort was made to discourage the idea of colonization and Sir George Simpson sought to keep a Chinese Wall around the Company's fur preserve. *Pro Pelle Cutem* was the Company's motto, and the fur trade, not the settlement of their vast territories, was the Company's object. Old " Bear " Ellice, who, more than any other man, had been responsible for the union of the North-West and the Hudson's Bay Company, openly stated that " a fur company have very little to do with colonization . . . the Hudson's Bay Company would have done much better if they had never had anything to do with colonization."[2] They feared that an inrush of immigrants would drive away the fur-bearing animals—a fear which was fully justified in the light of experience—and that a chain of settlements would not only deprive the Company of their supply of buffalo meat, but would so interfere with their trade as to lead to the inevitable extinction of the Company.

It was impossible, however, for the Company to keep Red River and Rupert's Land in a state of perpetual isolation. The prejudice of the fur traders, the charter rights of the Company and the rocky barrier of geography were not insuperable obstacles, and from the early part of the nineteenth century to the transfer of the country to Canada, the question of the colonization of the North-West and the extinction of the Company's territorial rights occupied a position of increasing importance in the politics of both Great Britain and Canada.

The first evidence of official interest in the idea of colonization in the North-West appeared in 1837, when the Hudson's Bay Company applied to the British Government for a renewal of the licence of exclusive trade granted to the combined companies in 1821. Lord Glenelg was not, apparently, convinced by the Company's repeated assertions of the sterility of their territories and their unfitness to sustain any considerable population. Instead he was " disposed to regard them with distrust " and urged upon the Board of Trade that a renewal of the licence should be accompanied by " such conditions as may enable Her

Majesty to grant, for the purpose of settlement or colonization, any of the lands comprised in it, and with that view . . . a power should be reserved even of establishing new colonies or provinces within the limits comprised in the Charter."[3] This amendment was accepted by the Company, and when the licence of exclusive trade was renewed in 1838 for twenty-one years, a special clause was inserted granting the Crown authority to annex any portion of the Company's chartered territories for the purpose of establishing a Crown colony.

No action was, however, taken to implement this provision until 1857. During these years the agitation in the Red River colony against the Company's fur monopoly and the difficulties in Vancouver Island focused attention upon the position of the Hudson's Bay Company, and it was generally realized that a state of things in which vast tracts of land were withheld from colonization in the interest of a trading monopoly could not continue indefinitely. The approaching expiry of the exclusive trade privilege provided the British Government with the opportunity of reviewing the political status of the Company and the question of North-West colonization. Early in 1857, therefore, a Select Committee was appointed " to consider the State of those British Possessions in North America which are under the Administration of the Hudson's Bay Company, or over which they possess a Licence to Trade."[4]

From February to July this committee conducted their investigations. The whole economy of the Hudson's Bay Company was thoroughly discussed. Twenty-four witnesses were examined, 6,098 questions were asked, and evidence to the total of over 450 printed folio pages was compiled. The Company was charged with exercising an obnoxious monopoly in a tyrannical manner and with placing every obstacle in the way of colonization and settlement. The Company replied with a denial of the first charge and a justification of the second. Their witnesses declared that the Red River Settlement had been " an unwise speculation " and " had failed." According to Sir George Simpson, who had for thirty-seven years been engaged in the fur trade, the North-West was quite unfit for settlement, the soil was poor and beyond a mile from the river even the native grass grew only " in detached spots." When asked whether a colony could be self supporting in what is now Manitoba, he replied, " A population thinly scattered along the banks might support themselves, but a dense population could not live in that country, the country would not afford the means of subsistence," while in some regions there were " deep morasses which never thaw." This, oddly enough, was how he described in 1857 the country which, only ten years before, he had compared to the beautiful country in the neighbourhood of the Thames at Richmond, and concerning which he had prophesied, " Is it too much for the eye of philanthropy to discern through the vista of futurity this noble stream . . . with crowded steamboats on its bosom and populous towns on its borders."[5]

In spite of the labours of the Select Committee and its brilliant personnel[6] the report was quite colourless. It postponed decision upon the question of the Company's political status and left the question of the boundary of Rupert's Land and Canada " to be solved by amicable adjustment." Nevertheless it indicated the trend of popular opinion. Gladstone had moved " that the country capable of colonization should be withdrawn from the jurisdiction of the Hudson's Bay Company " which should thus rest upon a statutory foundation, and his proposal was negatived only by the deciding vote of the chairman. The final report of the Committee conceded the principle by recommending that the Red River and Saskatchewan districts be ceded to Canada " on equitable principles," or, if " Canada should not be willing at a very early period to undertake the government of the Red River District, it may be proper to consider whether some temporary provisions for its administration may not be advisable."

The recommendation that the colonizable portions of the Company's territories might be annexed to Canada represented a new departure in British policy. Hitherto the intention had been eventually to erect these districts into Crown Colonies. Sir James Stephen, the Under-Secretary of State for the Colonies, wrote in 1837 that Glenelg was " of opinion that the public interest may not improbably require the erection of some part of the territory comprised in the Company's Charter into one or more colonies, independent of and distinct from either Upper or Lower Canada."[7] As time went on and the settled provinces of Canada grew in population and importance it became evident that the political status of the Company's territories could not be settled without reference to Canada's future relations with the

North-Western territory. Moreover, British interest in colonization was on the wane.   The adherents of *laissez-aller* and the
Manchester School regarded with distrust the adoption of further
colonial responsibilities by the mother country, and the desire
of Canada for westward expansion was a welcome alternative.

Canada did not begin to take an active interest in the North-
West until the middle of the century.   It is true that prior to
1821 explorers and traders had pushed as far west as the Rocky
Mountains and the western fur trade had been an important
factor in the economic life of the country, but after the union of the
English and Canadian fur companies and the abandonment of the
old North-West canoe route, Canadians no longer gazed with
adventurous eyes towards the *Terra Incognita* on the western
horizon.   For the next three decades their attention and energies
were absorbed in the political struggles accompanying the attain-
ment of self-government, and it was not until the late 'forties that
the *Globe* and the *North American,* edited respectively by George
Brown and William McDougall, began to attack the Hudson's
Bay Company and to urge the acquisition of the North-West by
Canada.

At first the *Globe's* campaign met with little public response.
The Company's territories were still looked upon by many as an
inaccessible region in the centre of the continent, locked in
eternal frost and snow, in which no one could live except the
Indians and a few hardy individuals from the north of Scotland
who were inured to the cold.   The Canadian press deprecated
the value of the territory.   Even as late as 1855 the Montreal
Transcript stated that the climate of the North-West was " altogether unfavourable to the growth of grain " and that the summer
season was too short to " mature even a small potato or cabbage."[8]
The Hudson's Bay Company assiduously cultivated this erroneous
conception, and in a series of letters to the Hamilton *Spectator,*
Edward Ermatinger emphasized the small value of the country,
its inhospitable climate, its inaccessibility, and the legal authority
by which it was held.   Nevertheless, the need for action became
increasingly apparent during the 'fifties, and Chief Justice Draper
was commissioned by the Canadian Government to watch the
investigations of the Select Committee in 1857 and generally to
press upon the British Government the rights and interests of
Canada relative to the North-West.

It was the north-westerly movement of the American frontier of settlement that brought home to Canadians the urgency of securing the north-western territories for British rule.   In 1849 there had been fewer than 5,000 people in the territory of Minnesota, south of Assiniboia, but by 1860 there were more than 172,000.   St. Paul had become the distributing centre for the Red River Settlement and the overland route via the United States had displaced Hudson Bay as the principal trade route to the interior of the British North-West.   The natural direction in which further expansion would take place appeared to be the Red River valley, and it was evident that, unless Rupert's Land was in the hands of a power stronger than a trading monopoly, American frontiersmen would pay little heed to the existence of an imaginary boundary line.   It was not difficult to foresee the serious international complications which might arise from a sudden and unauthorized influx of immigrants from the United States.   The Americans were, as a rule, anti-British and strongly biased in favour of republican institutions, and the doctrine of " manifest destiny " was a powerful force in American politics. Peaceable American penetration had been the preliminary step to the annexation of Oregon and Texas, and it was not beyond the bounds of possibility that Rupert's Land and the North-West might go the same way.

Great anxiety was, therefore, felt in Canada.   Chief Justice Draper said that he was " speaking the sentiments of large numbers of the inhabitants " when he informed the Select Committee that in Canada there was " a very serious apprehension that if something is not done that territory will in some way or another cease to be British Territory."[9]   A Minute of Council in January 1857 stated that this was a question of paramount importance :

" The rapid settlement of Minnesota, shortly to be admitted a state of the American Union renders this the more necessary, for as civilization approaches the boundary so will be increased the difficulty of maintaining the distinction between the rights of the two nations on the frontier."[10]

Opinion in Red River was also apprehensive of the danger which threatened from the south.   American agents were already in the country " tampering and meddling with our people " with the result that among many " everything American is praised, everything British dispraised."[11] Petitions were sent both to Great Britain and to Canada calling attention to " the immediate danger which threatens the integrity of the present Imperial rule in British America " from the " subtle ingression of a foreign power into its very centre " ;[12] and A. K. Isbister urged before the Select Committee that Great Britain should take over the North-West " because the United States are fast peopling the territory along the frontier, and they will have that territory from us unless we do people it."[13]

American westward expansion not only emphasized the danger to British interests in the North-West ; it also inspired Canadians with the spirit of emulation. Events in the United States are scarcely ever without their reaction in Canada and in this instance American expansion led to the vision of a greater Canada extending " *A mari usque ad mare.*" Canadian people began to regard the vast unpeopled territories to the west as the natural outlet for their surplus population and as the necessary complement for the full development of their commerce and nationality. " I hope you will not laugh at me as very visionary," said Chief Justice Draper to the Select Committee in 1857, " but I hope to see the time, or that my children may live to see the time, when there is a railway going all across that country and ending at the Pacific ; and so far as individual opinion goes, I entertain no doubt that the time will arrive when that will be accomplished."[14]

The revival of Canadian interest in the North-West was influenced by economic as well as by political considerations. The idea of linking up the British possessions on the Atlantic with those on the Pacific by a North-West passage by land had long been in the minds of promoters and statesmen.[15] As early as 1845, Warre and Vavasour were sent out to report upon the the practicability of such a project, and in 1851 Allan Macdonnell, of Toronto, sought a charter for the incorporation of the Lake Superior and Pacific Railway Company. Macdonnell's application was refused by the Legislature. The railways of Canada were hardly a financial success, and the idea of constructing a road through an Indian-infested wilderness and over a mountain range to the small settlements on the Pacific coast was not such as would appeal either to the private investor or to the Government Treasury. Nevertheless the project was not abandoned.

By 1858 the outlook had undergone a change. Macdonnell was granted a charter for his North-West Transportation, Navigation and Railway Company, to construct railways linking the navigable waterways ; Sandford Fleming, later Engineer-in-Chief of the Canadian Pacific Railway, expressed his belief in the feasibility of a Pacific railway ; and the Canadian Legislature resolved :

" In view of the speedy opening up of the territories now occupied by the Hudson's Bay Company, and of the development and settlement of the vast regions between Canada and the Pacific Ocean. it is essential to the interests of the Empire at large, that a highway extending from the Atlantic Ocean westward should exist, which should at once place the whole British possessions in America within the ready access and easy protection of Great Britain, whilst, by the facilities for internal communication thus afforded, the prosperity of those great dependencies would be promoted, their strength consolidated and added to the strength of the Empire, and their permanent union with the Mother Country secured."[16]

There were a few individuals in Canada whose interest in the future of the North-West was inspired by purely selfish motives. Sir George Simpson believed that with many of the leaders of the Canadian annexation movement " the chief incentive undoubtedly is the desire of participating in the Indian Fur Trade," and informed the Governor and Committee of the Hudson's Bay Company that " several persons who have rendered themselves conspicuous in this movement . . . have proceeded from Toronto to Red River Settlement with a view, it is stated, of taking advantage of the present juncture, pending the negotiations for the renewal of the Company's Licence of trade—to incite the inhabitants to resist the constituted authorities, and to embark in the Indian trade in disregard of the Company's rights. In these objects they' will no doubt receive willing support from the American traders on the frontier, who have a common interest in the matter with the Canadian agitators."[17] There were, indeed, many who held exaggerated notions as to the profits to be derived from the fur trade, and both John Ross and Chief Justice Draper testified before the Select Committee that there were "certain gentlemen at Toronto very anxious to get up a second North-West Company."[18]

By 1857 the acquisition of the North-West appears to have been a generally recognized ideal in Canada. In March the

municipal Council of Lanark and Renfrew petitioned the legislature that measures might be adopted to impress upon the
British Government the necessity and expediency " of at once
assuming possession of the Hudson's Bay Territory . . . and
incorporating it with Canada."[19] The Toronto Board of Trade,
although interested more in the commercial than in the political
aspects of Canadian expansion, urged the Legislative Council of
Canada to " take into consideration the subject of how far the
assumption of power on the part of the Hudson's Bay Company
interferes with Canadian rights, and as to the necessity of more
particularly declaring the boundaries of Canada on the westward
and on the northward, and of extending throughout the protection of Canadian laws, and the benefits of Canadian institutions."[20]
The Legislature voted £5,000 towards the opening of communications with Red River, and parties under Hind, Gladman
and Dawson, were sent to explore the southern regions of the
Hudson's Bay Company's territories in order to report upon a
feasible route.

The principal obstacle in the way of Canadian westward
expansion was the royal charter granted to the " Adventurers " in
1670. The validity of this charter had been challenged upon
several occasions but the law officers of the Crown had always
upheld it and the question had never been referred to a legal
tribunal. This course was suggested to Isbister and his fellow
petitioners in 1849 but they had refused the responsibility. In
1857 the question was taken up by Canada. When asked whether
" Canada would be disposed . . . to raise the question of the
validity of the charter of the Hudson's Bay Company, either in
whole or in part, before either the Judicial Committee of the
Privy Council, or some other tribunal," Chief Justice Draper
replied, " I can best answer that question by stating that I have
express instructions and authority to retain counsel to represent
the province, whenever, in my judgment, it is necessary . . . .
If Her Majesty's Government were broadly to say that Canada
must appear before the Judicial Committee of the Privy Council
for the purpose of determining her boundaries, I apprehend that
my instructions go the full length of enabling me to do so."[21]

Canada based her case upon early exploration. Draper was
instructed to bring forward " any claims of a legal equitable
kind which this province may possess on account of its territorial

position or its past history,"[22] and was provided with an elaborate historical statement[23] prepared by the Honourable Joseph Cauchon, Commissioner for Crown Lands. This stated that the territory occupied by the Hudson's Bay Company had, in 1670, belonged to New France, and was thus specifically excluded from the grant of Charles II by the words " not already actually . . . possessed by the Subjectes of any other Christian Prince or State." In regard to those regions which were at that time unknown, Cauchon argued that Charles II could not reasonably convey any right to property which might afterwards become his or anothers by the right of prior discovery :

" The right of discovery is and was so well established, and wherever considered of any importance, has been so jealously watched that volumes of diplomatic controversy have been written on single cases of dispute, that the King of Great Britain could not by his Charter annul the recognized law of nations, or limit in any degree the right of other States to discover and possess countries then unknown."

The greater part of the territories claimed by the Hudson's Bay Company had been discovered by those intrepid French Canadians who had travelled overland from New France into the North-West hinterland. Therefore, Cauchon concluded, the utmost to which the Company had a clear title was a strip of territory in the neighbourhood of Hudson Bay ; the vast North-West, including the Red River and Saskatchewan valleys, belonged to New France, and hence to Canada, by right of prior discovery and occupation.

To determine the validity of the charter of Charles II, Henry Labouchere, the Colonial Secretary, referred the question to the law officers, early in June 1857. They replied in July that " the Crown could not now with justice raise the question of the general validity of the Charter " which could not " be considered apart from the enjoyment that has been had under it during nearly two centuries, and the recognition of the rights of the Company in various acts, both of the Government and the Legislature. Nothing could be more unjust, or more opposed to the spirit of our law, than to try this Charter as a thing of yesterday, upon principles which might be deemed applicable to it, if it had been granted within the last ten or twenty years."[24] Accordingly Labouchere informed the Canadian Government in January 1858 that while the question of the boundary between Canada and the Company's territories might be referred to the Privy Council for decision, he could not challenge the general validity of the charter " without departing from those principles of equity by which their conduct ought to be guided."[25] The Colonial Office was, however, anxious to meet any reasonable demands upon the part of Canada. At the same time that he wrote the above to the Governor-General, Labouchere also wrote to the Hudson's Bay Company urging upon them the necessity of ascertaining the boundary between Canada and Rupert's Land, or, preferably, of surrendering to the Crown " such portions of the Territory now claimed . . . under the Charter, as may be available to and required by Canada for purposes of settlement," and suggesting the appointment of a board of three commissioners representing the Imperial and the Canadian Governments and the Hudson's Bay Company, to consider when the proposed annexation should take place, the amount of compensation to be awarded and other details of the transfer.[26] The Company replied accepting these proposals, but before further action could be taken, Labouchere surrendered the seals of office.

The change of government was followed by a change in the policy of the Colonial Office. Sir Edward Bulwer Lytton, Labouchere's successor, was not inclined to temporize with the Hudson's Bay Company. He abandoned Labouchere's idea of negotiations by means of a commission, and informed Shepherd and Berens, the Company's representatives, that he intended to take the opinion of the law officers as to the best method of ascertaining the validity of the Company's charter.[27] The Canadian Legislature also favoured this mode of procedure. In August they forwarded to the British Government an address praying for " a final decision on the validity of the Charter of the Company, and the boundary of Canada on the north and west."[28]

The Company regarded this address as a direct challenge. They reasserted their right to the privileges granted by the contested charter and informed the Colonial Office that they would refuse to become " a consenting party to any proceeding which is to call in question rights so long established and recognized ; but . . . will . . . be prepared to protect themselves against any attempt that may be made on the part of the Canadian Authorities to deprive them, without compensation, of any portion of the territory they have so long been in possession of."[29]

Lytton did not conceal his " disappointment and regret " at this rebuff. He again stressed the necessity of an inquiry before the Judicial Committee of the Privy Council and threatened to take " the necessary steps for closing a controversy too long open, and securing a definite decision, which is due to the material development of British North America, and the requirements of an advancing civilization."[30] The Company, however, were not to be intimidated. They expressed their willingness to surrender any of their rights or territory, but refused to consent to an inquiry to call those rights into question. The matter was then referred to the law officers, who replied in December that, under the circumstances, the only course open was for Canada to proceed by a writ of *scire facias*.[31] Lytton hastened to inform the Canadian Government, who, after a delay of several months, refused to avail themselves of this opportunity, and claimed that the responsibility of litigation should be assumed by the Imperial rather than by the Colonial Government.[32] Before any steps could be taken in this respect Lytton was out of office, the net result of his secretaryship being the development of a spirit of acrimony between the Colonial Office and the Hudson's Bay Company and the expiry, without renewal, of the Company's licence of exclusive trade.

The Duke of Newcastle reopened negotiations in 1860 with much vigour. He adopted the principle of negotiation expressed in Labouchere's letter of January 1858, reminded Berens of the Company's expressed willingness to surrender portions of their territory for settlement, and forwarded him a draft of a " Bill to Facilitate Colonization in parts of the British Territories in North America " for comment.[33] This Bill called for the surrender of Red River and the Saskatchewan within five years and provided for compensation for loss incurred for immovable improvements, live stock, chattels and loss of profit or monopoly of trade—the amount of compensation to be settled by arbitration. These proposals were a great advance on those of Lytton, the validity of the charter and the principle of compensation, although from what source is not evident, being readily admitted. Berens replied at the end of May.[34] He acknowledged Newcastle's offer but suggested certain modifications, including compensation

for land held in fee simple and provision for no interference
with the Company's rights until the date of the actual payment.
No mutually satisfactory agreement was, however, reached, and
the proposed Bill was never introduced into Parliament.

In the meantime public demand in Canada for the opening of
overland communication with the colony of British Columbia and
for the settlement of the fertile western plains was becoming
more insistent, as the knowledge of the interior was increased by
the reports of surveyors, scientists and travellers. By 1860
an irregular postal service by canoe, courier and dog-sled, had
been inaugurated between Canada and Red River. A steamer
was placed on the Great Lakes to ply between Collingwood and
Fort William and a group of Toronto men promoted the " North-
West Transit Company " to carry mails and passengers by
steamboat and waggon across British North America. This
project did not meet with an immediate response, but in 1861 it
received a decided fillip as a result of Edward Watkin's visit to
Canada in connexion with the Grand Trunk and the Intercolonial
Railways. The capitalists with whom he was associated took up
the project and the Duke of Newcastle considered it " a grand
conception."[35]

The Hudson's Bay Company regarded the North-West Transit
Company without enthusiasm. Berens wrote to the Colonial
Secretary that the whole scheme was impracticable, that the land
west of Lake Superior was one of rocks and swamps, and that
the region west of Red River was " a vast desert." The Company
refused to risk any capital in what they characterized as " a doubtful undertaking " but promised, if the Duke should insist upon
making the experiment, to give it all " the moral support " in
their power.[36] The Transit Company was in greater need of
practical assistance than of moral support and Newcastle urged
the Company to make a grant of land to help the proposed road
and telegraph. In response to this demand Berens replied,
almost in terror, " What! sequester our very tap-root! Take
away the fertile lands where our buffaloes feed! Let in all kinds
of people to squat and settle, and frighten away the fur-bearing
animals they don't hunt and kill! Impossible. Destruction—
extinction of our time-honoured industry. If these gentlemen
are so patriotic, why don't they buy us out ? " To this outburst
the Duke quietly replied, " What is your price ? " Thus pushed

to the wall the Governor of the Hudson's Bay Company answered, "Well, about a million and a half."[37]

Watkin appears to have made every effort to persuade the British Government to accept Berens' price and to purchase the assets of the Hudson's Bay Company. He assured Newcastle that at the figure named there could be no risk of loss, that the fur trade could be separated from the proprietorship of the soil, that a new company could be formed to take over the old company's posts and trade, and that it could pay a rental of three and a half per cent on £800,000, leaving only £700,000 as the price of a territory larger than Russia. The Government was, however, opposed to the scheme. As we have observed earlier, the trend of political opinion was against the assumption of further colonial responsibilities by the mother country, and Newcastle could only reply, "Were I minister of Russia I should buy the land. It is the right thing to do for many, for all reasons; but ministers here must subordinate their views to the Cabinet."[38]

Accordingly Watkin and his associates came to the conclusion that, if the project was to be carried through, the Hudson's Bay Company would have to be bought out by private enterprise. The Company's offer of a mere site for the road and ground for the telegraph was of little value, and finally, after several months of bickering, a satisfactory agreement was reached. Throughout the negotiations the Duke of Newcastle lent his unofficial assistance to the promoters of the "Pacific Scheme." In March 1863, Berens wrote privately to Dallas "there can be no doubt that the Duke of Newcastle is most anxious to get rid of us, and would, I believe, do all he can to further this purpose. He is certainly encouraging other parties to move vigorously in the promotion of his views and no one can foretell what the result may be."[39] The result was the purchase, three months later, by the International Financial Society, of the stock of the Hudson's Bay Company, and its redistribution among a new body of proprietors who were to carry on the fur trade under the original charter of Charles II, but who would administer the affairs of the re-organized company "on such principles as to allow the gradual settlement of such portions of the Territory as admit of it, and facilitate the communication across British North America by telegraph or otherwise."[40]

The solution of the North-West question now appeared to be

only a matter of formal negotiation. The proprietors who had been hostile to the idea of colonization had disposed of their interest in the Hudson's Bay Company and the new proprietors were fully alive to the necessity of surrendering the Company's territorial and governing privileges to promote the settlement of the western plains. Looking forward to this happy state of affairs the new Governor and Committee entered into a lengthy correspondence with the Colonial Office. On August 28th, 1863, a resolution to the effect that " the time has come when, in the opinion of this Committee, it is expedient that the authority, executive and judicial, over the Red River Settlement and South-Western portion of Rupert's Land should be vested in officers deriving such authority directly from the Crown and exercising it in the name of Her Majesty," was forwarded to the Duke of Newcastle.[41]

In reply Newcastle signified his readiness to consider any proposal made by the Company. Whereupon the Company made what they considered " a fair and advantageous offer," offering to surrender all the land south of the Saskatchewan River and east of the Rockies for a money compensation for the value of the territory and the Company's charter interest in all gold and silver found therein, or, alternatively, for the ownership in fee simple of half the lands surrendered, one-third royalty for mineral rights, and the sole right to erect and operate a telegraph under Government guarantee.[42] The Duke was unable to consent to these demands, but, desirous of keeping the negotiations alive, he submitted counter proposals, offering the Company one shilling for every acre of the surrendered lands sold by the Crown but limited to £150,000 in all, and to fifty years in duration, one-fourth of any revenue from gold or silver, but limited to £100,000, and fifty years, and one square mile of adjacent land for every lineal mile of road and telegraph constructed to British Columbia.[43] These proposals were carefully considered by the Committee of the Hudson's Bay Company who accepted the principle but not the details of the offer. They demanded, instead, that either the payments should not be limited to fifty years or should total one million sterling, and that the land to be granted to the Company should amount to five thousand acres for every fifty thousand sold.[44] In the meantime, however, Newcastle had been obliged to relinquish his position at the Colonial Office by the illness which resulted in his death. Edward Cardwell, his successor, was not disposed to accept the Company's terms " without considerable modifications,"[45] and for several months no further correspondence took place on this question.

The change in the directorate of the Hudson's Bay Company did not alter the attitude of the Canadian Government. They were suspicious of any corporation which succeeded to the territorial rights granted by the charter and put little faith in the Company's professed interest in colonization and their plan to construct a transcontinental telegraph. Watkin's " heads of proposals " submitted to the Canadian Government on behalf of the " Atlantic and Pacific Transit and Telegraph Company " were rejected, and Canada revived her claim to the North-West territory by virtue of French discovery. This meant the virtual end of the road and telegraph project. The Hudson's Bay Company refused to build it without substantial assistance and a guaranteed profit of not less than four per cent, and countered the Canadian historical claim with the venerable charter of Charles II. In words that might have come from Shepherd or Berens, Sir Edmund Head informed the Colonial Office that " it is not precisely as a boon to themselves " that the Hudson's Bay Company had encouraged the surrender of their territories, that " their commercial interest would be equally served if things remained as they are,"[46] and that the Company would never institute proceedings against their charter but would defend it to the utmost.[47]

In 1865 the first real progress was made towards breaking the deadlock between Canada and the Company. The Hudson's Bay authorities had always expressed their willingness to surrender their territorial claims for equitable compensation, and every Colonial Secretary since 1857, with the possible exception of Lytton, had endeavoured to reach an agreement on that principle. Accordingly, when John A. Macdonald, George Cartier, George Brown and Alexander Galt visited England in the spring of 1865, to confer on matters relating to Canada, Mr. Edward Cardwell urged upon them the advisability of a modification in the Canadian attitude. He pointed out the vital necessity of opening the North-West to Canadian enterprise and emigration, and the risk that recent gold discoveries on the eastern slopes of the Rockies might attract to the country large numbers of settlers unaccustomed to British institutions. In the end the Canadian delegates concluded that " the quickest solution of the question would be the best," and proposed that the whole of Rupert's Land should be annexed to Canada, " subject to such rights as the Hudson's Bay Company might be able to establish ; and that the compensation to that Company (if any were found to be due) should be met by a loan guaranteed by Great Britain."[48] Cardwell at once informed the Hudson's Bay authorities that Canada would undertake negotiations with them. A settlement of the North-West question was now in sight. Canada having accepted —although in ungracious terms—the principle of compensation, subsequent negotiations should only have been a matter of agreeing upon the amount.

Canada did not, however, undertake immediate negotiations with the Hudson's Bay Company. The task of Confederation occupied the attention and energies of Canadian statesmen during the next two years, and it was not until December 1867 that the legislature of the newly constituted Dominion picked up the threads of negotiation where the provincial legislature of Canada had dropped them.

In the meantime the position of British rule in the North-West was growing ever more precarious. The political leaders of the frontier states openly encouraged American expansion into British territory, and there is strong evidence that this movement was tolerated if not directly encouraged by Washington. One reason suggested for the abrogation of Reciprocity was the hope that Canada's economic life being so bound up with that of the United States, the colony would be forced to seek admission into the American union.[49] In July 1866 a Bill, providing for " the admission of the States of Nova Scotia, New Brunswick, Canada East and Canada West, and for the organization of the Territories of Selkirk, Saskatchewan and Columbia," was intro- duced into the House of Representatives at Washington.[50] Seward's covetous interest in British Columbia and his purchase of Alaska in 1867 were acclaimed and defended as a brilliant stroke of policy shutting off the new Dominion from the Pacific. " It was, in short," wrote the New York *Tribune* of April 1st,[51] " a flank movement " upon Canada ; soon the world would see in the north-west of the continent " a hostile cockney with a watch- ful Yankee on each side of him " and John Bull would be made to understand that his only course would be the disposal of his

North American interests to Brother Jonathan.   Typical of the American jingoism of this period was the expressed wish of Ignatius Donnelly that American territories " abut only on the everlasting seas," and the fears of Mr. Shellabarger, that the United States might become so large " that we could only love half at a time."[52]

The north-western states were those directly interested in the annexation of the Hudson's Bay Company territory.   As early as 1859, J. W. Taylor, later consul at Winnipeg, whose life-long ambition was to bring about the peaceful annexation of British territory to the United States, had been sent to report on the route from Pembina, via Red River and the Saskatchewan, to the Fraser river gold-fields—a question which Governor Ramsey of Minnesota declared concerned " in a great degree the future growth and development of our State."[53]   Public opinion was strongly in favour of the acquisition of the British North-West. The newspapers were full of blustering patriotism concerning " the integrity of American territory between St. Paul and Sitka." The St. Paul *Daily Press* urged that a protest should be sent to Washington against the proposed transfer of that region to Canada and stated " We trust that Mr. Seward and Congress will not be slow in giving the London Cabinet a gentle hint that the course talked of over there is not at all compatible with the common understanding of good neighbourhood."[54]   In March 1868, the Minnesota Legislature—at Taylor's instigation[55]— followed this advice.   It protested against the transfer of the Hudson's Bay Company Territories to Canada without a vote of the settlers, and passed a resolution to the effect that it " would rejoice to be assured that the cession of North-West British America to the United States " was " regarded by Great Britain and Canada as satisfactory provisions of a treaty which shall remove all grounds of controversy between the respective countries."[56]

The absence in the colony of any defensive force constituted a potential danger.   In 1861 the Royal Canadian Regiment, then stationed at Fort Garry in the Red River Settlement, was withdrawn in spite of the Company's protests, just at a time when the increased knowledge of the territory, the rumours of the discovery of gold on the Saskatchewan and the news of the negotiations for the transfer of the country to Canada, would attract crowds of adventurers and settlers to a colony which had no force save moral suasion to back its authority. With a sufficient number of troops the Company might have held their rights secure, but they were like a king without an army, helpless in the face of defiant opposition. The Americans were fully aware of this weakness and Taylor reported to the Secretary of the Treasury that " in case of a collision with England, Minnesota is competent to ' hold, occupy, and possess ' the valley of Red River to Lake Winnipeg."[57]

There is no doubt that the United States would have welcomed overtures from the Hudson's Bay Company. The presumptuous Bill of 1866 contained the following clause :

" Article XI.   The United States will pay ten millions of dollars to the Hudson's Bay Company in full discharge of all claims to territory or jurisdiction in North America, whether founded on the charter of the Company, or any treaty, law or usage."

In the same year a group of Anglo-American capitalists offered to purchase the Company's territories in order to " colonize the same on a system similar to that in operation in the United States in respect to the organization of territories and states " ;[58] while in 1869 Taylor wrote to the Company's agent at St. Paul :

" I know that President Grant is anxious for a treaty with England which shall transfer the country between Minnesota and Alaska in settlement of the *Alabama* controversy, and as a consideration for the establishment of complete reciprocal trade with Canada.   I have no doubt that a clause would be inserted in such a treaty giving $5,000,000 to the Hudson's Bay Company in satisfaction of the title to one-twentieth of the land in central British America."[59]

This " awful swallow for territory," together with the bellicose attitude of the United States, their ill-concealed hostility towards Great Britain as a result of the *Alabama* affair, the danger of international complications arising out of the Indian troubles south of the frontier, and the weakness of the colony from a military standpoint, rendered the political future of the North-West uncertain.

The federation of the four British provinces in North America concluded in 1867, negotiations for the acquisition of the North-West were resumed.   The British North America Act had made special provision for the admission of Rupert's Land and the

North-Western Territories into the federal union, and on December 4th, William McDougall, one of the foremost apostles of national expansion, introduced into the Canadian House of Commons a series of resolutions which formed the basis of an Address to the Crown praying for the transfer of the Hudson's Bay Company territories to Canada. This address did not, however, follow the course urged by Cardwell in 1865. Instead it requested that the transfer should precede the settlement of the Company's claims which might then be submitted for adjudication to the Canadian courts.

The Hudson's Bay Company had ample reason to protest against this course. In 1865 the Canadian delegates had undertaken to negotiate with the Company and the fact of this undertaking was recited by the Colonial Office as a reason why the Company should not consider proposals from other sources. Now, after the conclusion of Confederation, the Canadian Government suggested a mode of proceeding entirely contrary to the expectations raised by the acts of their delegates and the communications which had passed between the Colonial Office and the Company. It had always been understood that the negotiations should precede and not follow the transfer of the territory. If the latter course were adopted the Company could only rely upon the honesty and considerate disinterestedness of the Canadian Parliament and the impartiality and competence of Canadian courts—a doubtful support in view of the long expressed hostility to the Hudson's Bay Company in Parliament and press. That this was fully realized is shown by a passage in a speech by the Honourable Mr. Holton and by John A. Macdonald himself, who admitted that the procedure advocated in the address would render the Company's title practically worthless.[60]

The Colonial Office were unwilling to accept the Canadian suggestion. The law officers had assured the Duke of Buckingham and Chandos, the latest Colonial Secretary, that the Crown could not, in view of the charter, transfer Rupert's Land to Canada without the consent of the Company, and the Duke informed Sir Curtis Lampson, the Deputy Governor of the Hudson's Bay Company, that he favoured direct negotiations for an arrangement to be confirmed by Parliament.[61] The Newcastle negotiations were advanced as a possible basis for discussion, with the difference that the whole of Rupert's Land, rather than certain specified areas, should be the object of surrender. On May 13th, 1868, the Governor outlined the Company's terms.[62] They demanded one shilling per acre for every acre sold, leased or granted by the Government, and one-fourth of any export duty on gold or silver, the total to be fixed at £1,000,000 ; a land grant on the basis of 5,000 acres for every 50,000 disposed of by the Government ; 6,000 acres around each Company post except at Red River ; Canada to take over the telegraph materials at cost plus interest ; the Company to be exempt taxes on undeveloped land and to be free to carry on trade.

The Duke of Buckingham could hardly accede to these demands. The Colonial Office considered them unreasonable and in a draft reply the Duke wrote :

" If . . . the Company adhere to the terms indicated in their letter, Her Majesty's Government must be understood distinctly to decline to assent to those terms, which they conceive it would be inexpedient for the Crown to concede in the event of retaining the territory as a Crown Colony, and which they would not therefore suggest for the concurrence of the Canadian Government."[63]

Nevertheless he went ahead with arrangements for the eventual transfer. In July, an Act, known as the Rupert's Land Act, was passed by the Imperial Parliament to enable the Crown to accept, upon terms, a surrender of the lands and privileges of the Hudson's Bay Company, and, within a month of this acceptance, to transfer them to Canada.[64] During the next few months private discussions took place between the representatives of the Colonial Office and those of the Company. Buckingham suggested several modifications, such as the reduction of the land reserves around the posts, and land grants of five lots, of not less than 200 acres, in each township. No definite answer was made to these counter proposals until January 13th, 1869, when Sir Stafford Northcote, the new Governor of the Company, without accepting Buckingham's suggestions, offered certain amendments of his own.[65]

In the meantime the Canadian Government had intimated their desire to have some voice in the settlement of the North-West question, and requested that the negotiations then in progress be suspended until the arrival of a Canadian delegation.[66] In October Sir George Cartier and William McDougall sailed for

England. On their arrival they were invited by the Duke to Stowe " for the purpose of discussing freely and fully the numerous and difficult questions involved in the transfer of these great territories to Canada."[67] It was Buckingham's object to arrange a compromise to which both parties would consent and he impressed upon the Canadian delegates the determination of the British Government to treat with the Company as " lords proprietors," not as a body with a defective title. Before he was able to accomplish his aim, however, the Duke quitted office on the fall of the Derby-Disraeli administration in December.

Lord Granville, the Duke's successor, abandoned the policy of direct negotiation between the Colonial Office and the Hudson's Bay Company. He regarded the Company's letter of January 13th, 1869, as a definite rejection of Buckingham's proposals and considered the matter as closed. He insisted that further negotiations " for the purchase " were a matter for " the seller and the buyer, the Company and the Colony." He refused to frame or suggest further terms of accommodation, but offered to act " as a channel of communication between these two real parties to the transaction, using its best endeavours to remove any difficulties not inherent in the nature of the case."[68] Accordingly he forwarded Northcote's letter of January to Cartier and McDougall for comment. On February 8th the Canadian delegates returned their answer. It displayed[69] a sharpness of tone and an unwillingness to treat with the Company in a spirit of compromise. The delegates reiterated their challenge to the Company's chartered rights ; declared that they had been hitherto merely " spectators of a negotiation begun and carried on upon principles and under conditions to which we are strangers, rather than that of assenting principals, responsible for its initiation and bound by its results " ; offered £106,431 as the highest amount which could be properly demanded by the Company ; and concluded with a request that, as no money offer deemed reasonable by Canada would be accepted by the Company, Great Britain should authorize a transfer of the North-West to Canada without further loss of time !

The Hudson's Bay Company felt that the uncompromising attitude taken in this letter left little hope for a satisfactory settlement, but the Colonial Office were, nevertheless, determined to carry matters through to a conclusion. The negotiations were continued, Granville using his position as go-between to exert pressure upon both parties. Interviews were held with the Canadian delegates and with the representatives of the Company and finally, on March 9th, Granville presented his ultimatum with the remark :

" If the proposal is really an impartial one, Lord Granville cannot expect that it will be otherwise than unacceptable to both of the parties concerned. But he is not without hope that both may find, on consideration, that if it does not give them all that they conceive to be their due, it secures to them what is politically or commercially necessary, and places them at once in a position of greater advantage with respect to their peculiar objects than that which they at present occupy."[70]

The main provisions were : the surrender by the Hudson's Bay Company of all its rights and privileges in Rupert's Land ; the payment by Canada to the Company of £300,000 ; a land grant of one-twentieth of the land within the Fertile Belt, and certain blocks of land in the vicinity of the Company's trading posts totalling 50,000 acres ; the right of the Company to continue its trade without hindrance or "exceptional " taxation ; and the purchase by Canada of the materials for the neglected telegraph.

The Company were in a difficult position. Events at Red River had made it apparent that they could not much longer carry on the civil government in the absence of a military force, and Lord Granville had coupled his offer with a shadowy threat :

" At present the very foundations of the Company's title are not undisputed. The boundaries of its territory are open to questions of which it is impossible to ignore the importance. Its legal rights, whatever these may be, are liable to be invaded without law by a mass of Canadian and American settlers, whose occupation of the country on any terms they will be little able to resist ; while it can hardly be alleged that either the terms of the charter, or their internal constitution, are such as qualify them under all these disadvantages for maintaining order and performing the internal and external duties of government."[71]

A final effort was made to secure more favourable terms, the Company offering to accept Granville's proposals with certain modifications. But Cartier and McDougall were determined to make no concession. They replied to Northcote that they had accepted Granville's terms " pure et simple " and would go no

further.[72]   The Company had, therefore, no alternative save to
accept.   In April the terms were submitted to a General Court
of the Proprietors.   Northcote moved their acceptance, but a
considerable body of proprietors opposed them " as obviously
involving too great a sacrifice of their interests."[73]   The meeting
was a stormy one, but, after a long discussion, the motion was
carried by a show of hands.   The minority shareholders protested
to the Committee and even to the Colonial Office that Northcote's
motion had not been carried constitutionally, but the deal was
closed and the date for the surrender fixed.

The terms of the transfer were, perhaps, the best that the
Company could have obtained at the time, although there is
evidence to show that the Canadian delegates might have paid the
million pounds specified in Buckingham's proposals.[74]   The
cession was, in any event, inevitable, and time was on the side
of the Canadian Government.   There is no doubt that the
Company always believed that a Crown Colony would be the
best solution, but with the spirit of expansion dominant in
Canada and *laissez-aller* in England, this was never seriously
considered by the Colonial Office.   Nevertheless, in view of the
recognition of the validity of the Company's charter and the
territorial jurisdiction granted by it, for two hundred years, the
extent and value of the rights surrendered, and the beneficial
rule of the Company over the Indians, the price paid was not
over-generous.

The terms agreed upon at London were ratified by the Canadian
Parliament and the date of the transfer was fixed for October
1st, 1869.[75]   This date was, however, altered to December 1st,
owing to a delay in making the necessary financial arrangements.
In the meantime the Canadian Government, in anticipation of the
transfer, passed " An Act for the Temporary Government of
Rupert's Land,"[76] which provided for the administration by a
Lieutenant-Governor and Council not exceeding fifteen and not
less than seven persons, and the retention of all the laws then in
force in the territory not inconsistent with the British North
America Act or the terms of the transfer.   The choice for the
position of Lieutenant-Governor fell upon the Honourable
William McDougall.   It was regarded by many as a fitting
reward for his public services in bringing about the acquisition
of the North-West—although his enemies suggested that the

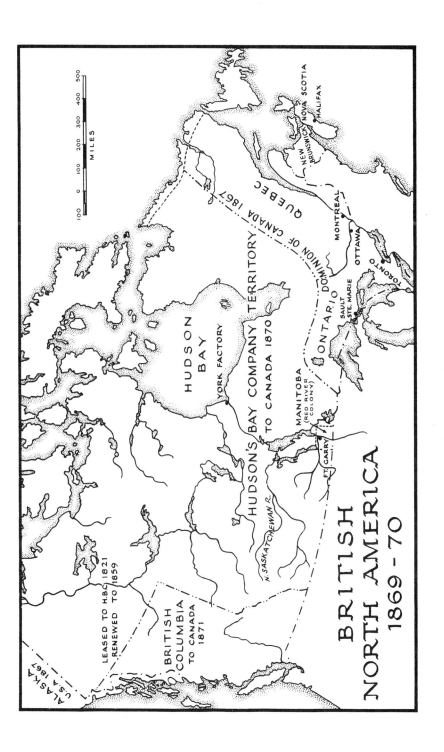

BRITISH
NORTH AMERICA
1869 - 70

ALASKA
U.S.A. 1867

LEASED TO H.B.C. 1821
RENEWED TO 1859

BRITISH COLUMBIA
TO CANADA
1871

N. SASKATCHEWAN R.

HUDSON'S BAY COMPANY TERRITORY
TO CANADA 1870

FT. GARRY

MANITOBA
(RED RIVER
COLONY)

HUDSON
BAY

YORK FACTORY

ONTARIO

DOMINION OF CANADA 1867

QUEBEC

SAULT
STE. MARIE

TORONTO

OTTAWA

MONTREAL

NEW
BRUNSWICK

NOVA SCOTIA

HALIFAX

MILES

100   0   100   200   300   400   500

Government were anxious to disembarrass themselves of an unpopular colleague.

In order to be present at Red River when the long-negotiated transfer should finally take place, the Governor-designate, accompanied by his prospective Provincial Secretary, his Attorney General, his Collector of Customs and his Chief of Police, set out, by way of the United States, for the seat of his prairie government. Towards the end of October he arrived at the frontier village of Pembina where he was greeted, not by the expected address of welcome, but by

" A Monsieur McDougall.

" Monsieur—Le Comité National des Métis de la Rivière Rouge intime à Monsieur McDougall l'ordre de ne pas entrer sur le Territoire du Nord-Ouest sans une permission spéciale de ce Comité.

        Par ordre du président.

JOHN BRUCE
LOUIS RIEL, Secrétaire.

Daté à St. Norbert, Rivière Rouge,
ce 21e jour d'octobre, 1869."

CHAPTER III

In outlining the history of the transfer of Rupert's Land to the Dominion of Canada we have travelled ahead and must now return to examine the events which led to the erection of the barricade at St. Norbert in 1869. During the years between 1830 and 1870 there were two distinct and separate periods of unrest in Red River, each marked by an agitation on the part of the half-breed inhabitants of the colony. The one, covering the years to 1850, was economic in origin; the other, racial and political. The first was a movement against the Hudson's Bay Company for commercial freedom; the second, a movement against the Dominion of Canada for national and economic security. This distinction is important, for, while the first movement led to the breakdown of the Hudson's Bay Company monopoly of the fur trade, the second led to the insurrection, alliteratively called the Red River Rebellion.

By 1837 the walls of the Hudson's Bay Company's monopoly, buttressed though they were by a parliamentary licence of exclusive trade, were beginning to crumble. The settlers were restless. The fur-trading restrictions were resented by the free spirits of the colony, brulé and white, and a mischievous adventurer named Dickson, who styled himself " Liberator of the Indian Race," endeavoured to take advantage of this resentment by inciting the half-breeds and Indians to seize the trading posts and depots and to take possession of the fur trade and the country.[1] Dickson's efforts were unsuccessful, and the Company, taking time by the forelock, secured from the British Government a renewal, for twenty-one years, of their trade licence. Thus assured of their legal position the Hudson's Bay Company authorities determined to take active measures to suppress the illicit trade in furs which had by this time developed between the Red River Settlement and the American State of Minnesota. In 1840 the officers of the Company at Fort Garry, armed with muskets and bayonets, broke open a half-breed cabin and confiscated all the furs that it contained. This punitive measure failed to deter the offenders and in 1844 Governor Christie took the drastic step of ordering all letters sent by importers to their agents in England via the Company's ships, to be sent to Fort Garry open for perusal by the officials of the Hudson's Bay Company; exemption from this regulation was only to be granted to those willing to sign a declaration that they had not engaged in the fur trade. This regulation was much resented by the inhabitants of the Settlement, most of whom were not averse to making a few pounds by quietly trading in furs when the opportunity presented itself. Leading settlers, like James Sinclair and Andrew McDermott, unhesitatingly avowed their intention of carrying on their illicit trade without regard for the Company's chartered privileges. "Over and above the direct results of their own operations," wrote Sir George Simpson, "the example of these two persons has proved to be peculiarly pernicious, inasmuch as their superior standing and comparative intelligence gave considerable weight to their opinions."[2]

To counter this move by the settlers and "to the utmost extent of our means, to avert the blow thus aimed at the very vitals of the Company's trade and power,"[3] the Council of Rupert's Land endeavoured to exert financial pressure upon the traders of the colony. A special duty of twenty per cent was placed upon maritime importations, but, as before, the Governor of Assiniboia was authorized to exempt from payment all those who did not traffic in furs. The result was a storm of indignation. In August 1845, a number of half-breeds led by James Sinclair, who, as early as 1837, had been a leader of the free trade in furs movement, presented an address to the Governor of Assiniboia, asking for a statement of their position and that of the Company. The Governor replied, a week later, that the half-breeds possessed no rights superior to those of other British subjects, and that they had ample opportunity of knowing the law of the land as laid down in the charter and in the enactments of the Council of Rupert's Land.[4] This answer was hardly satisfactory and the agitation continued.

It is interesting to note that Sir George Simpson believed that American influence was to a large extent responsible for the unrest prevalent in Red River over the question of the fur trade. In a letter to the Governor-General of Canada, dated November 1845, he wrote:

c

" The half-breeds, who, from their volatile character, are ever fascinated by novelty, seem . . . elated by the advantages they are led to believe would be derived from a more intimate connexion with the United States ; and when the canoe came away, a petition was being sent round among the settlers for signature, praying Congress to assist and protect them in the formation of a settlement at Pembina.   The petition appears to have been drawn up by one McLaughlin, a British subject, who last year went to the Settlement from St. Louis . . . and who, together with a relative of his (named McDermott) who has for many years been settled at Red River, and a partner of McDermott's named Sinclair, I have no doubt, have been employed by some of the United States authorities, as secret emissaries among our half-breed settlers and the neighbouring Indians, with a view of sowing the seeds of disaffection, as a preliminary measure to the overtures that have now been made, in which they appear to have been very successful, if I am at liberty to judge from the tone of discontent towards the Mother Country which has recently obtained among those people. McLaughlin, I understand, has been entrusted with this petition, which has been signed by 1,250 half-breed and Canadian settlers, and is now on his way to Washington for the purpose of laying it before the authorities there."[5]

The prompter behind the scenes of this foreign interference appears in a subsequent letter of Simpson's, in which he encloses a letter from the agent of Messrs. P. Chouteau, Jr. and Company of New York, a large American fur company, to McDermott and McLaughlin, promising to take all the furs they could supply, and arranging for the establishment of the American company's trading posts on the boundary.[6]

In 1847 the unrest in the Red River Settlement was brought to the attention of the British Government by the Memorial and Petition against the Hudson's Bay Company, presented by A. K. Isbister to the Colonial Secretary on February 17th.[7]   There was also a petition drawn up by a committee of French métis bearing 977 signatures. This petition, among other things, demanded that:

" Comme sujets Britanniques, nous désirons ardemment être gouvernés d'après les principes de cette constitution qui rend heureux tous les nombreux sujets de notre auguste Souveraine."

This was the only demand on the part of the settlers for a system of representative or responsible government.   Neither the Memorial nor the instructions to the delegates in England made any mention of a desire for representative institutions ; nor was it likely that the French half-breeds who signed the petition had the slightest conception of the political implications of their demand. The real issue was not one of self government, but of freedom of trade in furs. Isbister's mission was not a success. His refusal to contest the validity of the charter, coupled with the favourable reports of Colonel Crofton and Lord Elgin on the government of the Hudson's Bay Company, persuaded the British Government to drop the matter. But the handwriting was on the wall and the destruction of the monopoly was close at hand.

The whole question was brought to a head in 1849, when Guillaume Sayer and three others were arrested and imprisoned for trafficking in furs. Although convicted by a jury of his own selection, Sayer was merely dismissed with an admonition, in view of the hostile manifestations of the métis, three hundred of whom, led by the fiery " miller of the Seine," Louis Riel père, and armed with rifles and buffalo guns, surrounded the Court House. The métis hailed the decision as a virtual victory for their cause and greeted the break up of the court with a *feu de joie* and shouts of " Le commerce est libre, le commerce est libre, vive la liberté."[8] The Council of Assiniboia discussed the half-breed demands a few days later, but the control of events had been taken from their hands, and henceforth the fur trade was carried on openly, and in increasing amount by private parties.

The release of Sayer marked the end of the first period of unrest and the Red River Settlement quickly settled down to its early state of Arcadian simplicity. For the next ten years there was little or no discontent manifest in the colony. The " smoothing " influence of Sir George Simpson, and the tacit concession of free trade in furs resulted in a period of amity and tranquillity. The half-breeds gradually acquired an increasing voice in the government by the admission of leading half-breeds to the Council of Assiniboia. In spite of the complete absence of any military force to enforce the law, crimes were " perhaps, less frequent in proportion than in any other community, while the more atrocious offences are altogether unknown ; and as to the general condition of the people, there is not . . . any country where industry is more independent of the accidents of fortune or where idleness is less likely to lead to want or to prompt to dishonesty."[9] According to R. G. MacBeth, the settlers, half-breed and white, lived in harmony together " contented and happy under the régime of the Hudson's Bay Company, especially as that company did not latterly insist on monopoly in trade."[10]   Riel told the Council of Assiniboia in October 1869 " that his party were perfectly satisfied with the present Government, and wanted no other."[11] But this happy state of affairs was not to last.   In less than two decades the " invidious bar " of isolation was broken down, and the simple, peaceful, contented community of Red River was thrown into political and racial strife.

The second period of unrest in the Red River valley began with the westward advance of Canadian expansion.   Following the awakening in Canada of an interest in the political future of the Hudson's Bay Company territory, adventurers and settlers began to follow the historic advice of Horace Greeley " go west, young man."   With them they carried their national prejudices, their ideas of political liberty, and their printing press, and like their American prototype in Texas, they soon began to agitate and to advocate annexation to the land from which they had come. Although this " Canadian Party," as they were known in the Settlement, were few in number, they made up in vigour and vocality what they lacked in numerical strength.   Of all the anti-Hudson's Bay Company and pro-Canadian element, the most prominent was Dr. John Christian Schultz, a young physician from Kingston, whose interests turned more to politics than to the practice of his profession.   He it was who led the small band of storm troops who, from 1860, constantly assailed the crumbling political breastworks of the great corporation.

The native population viewed this development with growing concern.   Much of what has been attributed, on the one hand, to the unsatisfactory government of the Hudson's Bay Company, and on the other to a traditional Franco-English hostility brought to Red River from the banks of the St. Lawrence, was, in reality, a social and economic antagonism to the advancing army of white immigrants and settlers.   There was in the half-breed mentality an inherent opposition to any political or economic change in Rupert's Land.   The half-breeds had been the first inhabitants of the country, and, unreasonable as the claim may appear in view of their small numbers, they felt that the country was theirs.   This feeling of ownership and nationality had been fostered by the North-West Company and had manifested itself against the Selkirk colony in 1816. This same feeling of ownership and nationality was the underlying cause of the half-breed opposition to Canadian expansion in Red River. It must be remembered that at no time had there ever existed any particular attachment on the part of the inhabitants of the Red River Settlement for Canada. Their racial origin was different from that of the Canadians, their historical life was distinct from that of Canada, and all intercourse, social or economic, between the two peoples had been prevented by natural obstacles. It was only natural, therefore, that the half-breeds should view with alarm the expansion of what was to them almost a foreign country —particularly when this expansion meant the disorganization of their economic existence. With the advent of the Canadians in Red River the day of the buffalo hunter and the small freighter was at an end. A primitive people, the half-breeds were bound to give way before the march of a more progressive people. It was the recognition of this fact and the gradual realization of their inability to adjust themselves to the new order that kindled the spark of half-breed resentment which unfortunate circumstances fanned into the flame of insurrection. Louis Riel stated the basic cause of the Red River Rebellion when he told the Council of Assiniboia in 1869 that the half-breeds " were uneducated, and only half civilized, and felt, if a large immigration were to take place, they would probably be crowded out of a country which they claimed as their own."[12] Their fears were justified. In spite of their victory in the rising of 1869–70, the half-breeds were soon forced back by the advancing frontier of civilization into the valley of the Saskatchewan, where, fifteen years later, they made their last stand.

Under these circumstances it is not surprising that the agitation of the Canadian party made little headway among the half-breed settlers. There developed, instead, a feeling of distrust regarding the motives of the agitators. In 1863 and 1866 efforts were made by the Canadians to secure popular approval to petitions favouring annexation to Canada, but they met with little success. On the first occasion a memorial, praying for the establishment of means of communication between Canada and British Columbia via Red River and the Saskatchewan, was drawn up and sent to Sandford Fleming, a civil engineer in Canada, who, although he had never visited the colony, had been for some time the warm advocate of the construction of a railway across British North America. This petition was forwarded by Fleming to the Canadian Government and later to the Colonial Office, but no action was taken either at Ottawa or London. It is interesting to note that, according to the Governor of Rupert's Land, the origin of Fleming's petition lay, not in the grievances of the settlers, but in the desire of that gentleman to win public notice. " In the course of last winter (1862–63)," wrote Dallas to the London Committee, " we were rather surprised to observe in the columns of our only paper, the *Nor'Wester*, an announcement that at *large* and *influential* public meetings Mr. Sandford Fleming had been appointed Delegate to represent the wishes and opinions of the people of the Red River Settlement in Canada and England. As no such meetings had been held, we were rather at a loss to make out the precise object of the Editor of the paper, and by a curious coincidence (the paper having now changed hands) I have ascertained that the whole affair originated in a douceur of one hundred dollars paid by Mr. Fleming to the Editor to *secure* his appointment as Delegate, Mr. Fleming's object being I believe solely to bring himself into notice. If opportunity offers it may be well to make the Duke of Newcastle aware of the imposition which has been practised upon him. Mr. Fleming virtually appointed himself to represent a country and a people whom he had never seen. Many of the statements of his memorial are incorrect, and the views and opinions set forth, open to much question and of no value whatever."[13] In 1866 a meeting was called by Thomas Spence, a Canadian newly arrived in the Settlement, at which a series of resolutions were drawn up amidst uproarious expression of enthusiasm by five people ![14] while a petition, drawn up by Dr. Schultz, demanding an entire change of government, not only " met with no support " but " in consequence of its appearance a counter petition to the Governor and Committee has been got up."[15] This lack of support was probably due, as the Governor of Assiniboia wrote, to the fact that " there is a pretty general suspicion among the people that their foreign Friends are simply following the course that they think will best serve their own interests."[16]

In spite of the fact that the native population held aloof from the Canadian party, the Government of the colony was, however, quite incapable of coping either with the agitation or with the agitators. The Company lacked an adequate force to back its administration of the law and depended greatly upon the peaceful, law-abiding and contented nature of the Settlement for a strict observance of law and order. After 1860 the Company experienced increasing difficulty in enforcing respect for its authority, largely because of the aggressive attitude of the immigrants from Canada. In 1863 its authority was openly flouted when the Rev. James Corbett, who had been imprisoned for a serious offence, was released from the little prison outside the walls of Fort Garry, by a small but determined band of men. The leader himself was imprisoned for this breach of the law, but was forcibly released by his friends.[17] A few years later there was a recurrence of jail-breaking. This time Dr. Schultz was the central figure. Imprisoned for assault in resisting a seizure for debt, he was freed by a band of fifteen or eighteen men led by his fearless wife, who overpowered the constables on duty and broke open the prison door.[18] As a result of this episode the Council of Assiniboia proposed to enlist the services of one hundred special constables, but the proposal was, for some reason or another, never carried into effect.

The principal weapon of the Canadian Party was the press. In December 1859 the *Nor'Wester* was founded at Winnipeg by two Canadian journalists, William Coldwell and William Buckingham. The avowed purpose of the paper was to attack the Company rule and to further the cause of Canadian annexation. At first the tone of the paper was relatively mild, but from 1865, when it became the sole property of Dr. Schultz, it became more fiery and abusive. Its articles were reprinted in the Canadian press and the impression was conveyed to the people of Canada that the North-West was groaning under the yoke of an obnoxious tyranny and pleading to the outside world for assistance. The refusal of the Council of Assiniboia to appoint Dr. Schultz to that body as representative of the Canadians in Red River was the object of a special outburst. The colony was represented as standing alone on the face of the British globe in being denied the rights of representative government, and vague threats were made that some of the people were " openly discussing the propriety of taking the Government from its present hands into that of their own."[19]

To the native inhabitants the political agitation of the *Nor'* *Wester* was decidedly disturbing. The first copy contained the significant remark that " such a colony cannot now remain unpeopled " and in 1860 the paper began to predict ominous changes : " The wise and prudent will be prepared to receive and to benefit by them ; whilst the indolent and the careless, like the native tribes of the country, will fall back before the march of a superior intelligence."[20] This was exactly what the French half-breeds feared, and during the ten years prior to the Red River Insurrection these fears were sufficiently justified to produce a deep unrest. Many of the white people living in the Settlement also resented the lawlessness of the Canadian Party and the mis-representations and threats which marked the columns of their paper.   A. G. B. Bannatyne, one of the most substantial of the English-speaking settlers, wrote a friend :

" Old Red River is going to the devil faster than ever, and God only knows what is to become of us if the English Government or some other friendly soul does not take us by the hand.   Between James Ross and Corbitt they have managed to make the place too hot to live in."[21]

Finally, after the Schultz jail-breaking of 1868, there was an outburst of feeling against the Canadians and the *Nor'Wester*. A petition was drawn up and signed by some eight hundred people protesting against the unlawful liberation of Dr. Schultz and misstatements concerning it in the little newspaper.[22]

Had the *Nor'Wester* been less violent and more truthful it might have exercised a salutary influence on public affairs in Red River, but instead it only served to discredit the Canadian Party and the country they claimed to represent.   Writing after the outbreak of insurrection, J. J. Hargrave, secretary to the Governor of Assiniboia, said :

" The way was prepared for these disorders by a party in the colony, the representative of which was the *Nor'Wester* news-paper.   It was simply a disreputable clique which has in many ways for a long time past excited sedition against existing authority under pretence of loyalty to Canada."[23]

Whether or not we accept this—not wholly unbiased—descrip-tion of the Canadian Party, the fact remains clear that their con-tinued war upon the Hudson's Bay Company government in Red River contributed in no small measure to the unrest which finally broke out in insurrection. Illustrative of the unsettled feeling in the colony is the following quotation from a contemporary source :

" Dans la colonie elle-même il règne une certaine agitation et inquiétude au sujet de son avenir. Les uns, en très petit nombre, qui espèrent gagner par un changement quelconque, le demandent à grands cris ; d'autres considérant plus les systèmes que leur application voudraient pouvoir tenter un changement, ne se doutant pas qu'on ne revient plus à l'état primitif d'òu ils veulent s'écarter ; le plus grand nombre, la majorité redoute ce changement."[24]

To add to the troubles of Red River, the whole country was visited in the autumn of 1867 by a horde of locusts. These deposited their eggs and in the spring the young insects devoured everything that was green in the Settlement. The colony was at once faced with starvation. Taché wrote to the *Nor'Wester* that " within the whole colony not one bushel will be harvested. . . . Moreover the buffalo hunters instead of furnishing their large share of provisions . . . arrived starving from their usual hunting grounds."[25] The distress was appalling. The Rev. George Young wrote to a friend, " I heard of one family last week who had killed and eaten their house cat, and others in the distance have eaten their horses."[26] The Council of Assiniboia immediately voted £1,600 for provisions and seed wheat. Lord Kimberley's letter to *The Times*[27] brought a generous response, while the Hudson's Bay Company, the Dominion of Canada and the United States all contributed generously.

At this crucial moment there arrived in the colony a party of Canadian Government employees under J. A. Snow, for the purpose of building a road from the Lake of the Woods to the Red River Settlement. This action on the part of Canada, was somewhat premature in view of the fact that negotiations with the Hudson's Bay Company had not yet been concluded. The Company authorities in London protested against this trespass, but offered to grant permission for the work to proceed.[28] The Canadian delegates in England replied that the Canadian Government intended it as a relief work, thus providing the indigent settlers with employment and provisions.[29] The Canadian Government were committing no injustice in demanding work in return for supplies and Snow's party was at first welcomed in the colony. Unfortunately, however, subsequent events made it appear as if Canada had merely taken advantage of the distress in Red River to gain a foothold in the country. Moreover, Snow and his party were guilty of sharp practice in the matter of provisions. The men were engaged at the rate of £3 a month in provisions, but were charged a higher rate than that prevailing in the Settlement. The men were charged £3 12s. od. for a barrel of flour that could be purchased elsewhere in the colony for £3.[30]   This naturally aroused resentment, which was increased by paying the wages in orders on Schultz's store, a procedure particularly offensive to the French half-breeds.

This association of the Canadian Government employees with John Schultz and his unpopular companions was a serious blunder. On many occasions hostilities between the half-breeds and Schultz's clique had been prevented only through the personal influence of Governor Mactavish and Bishop Taché. The English-speaking community too, according to Hargrave, " fully understood the character of these people ; but the Canadians, belonging to the surveying and road-making parties lately arrived, lived among them, and to the scandal of the well-disposed, appeared to support them in their disorders. The result has been that Canadians have made no progress in gaining the goodwill of the people."[31]   Mactavish considered this one of the principal causes of the troubles which followed :

" The chief cause of hostility on the part of the half-breeds appears to be that they thought every Canadian official as he arrived was too intimate with Doctor Schultz and his party, and they suspected were acting under the Doctor's influence, which they suppose would not be in their favour."[32]

With Snow came Charles Mair, who succeeded in making himself and other Canadians extremely unpopular in Red River. Mair wrote to his friends in Ontario a series of letters which contained, in rather ungracious terms, his opinions of the people of the North-West. These letters were, unfortunately, published in the Toronto *Globe*[33] and other newspapers in eastern Canada, and in the colony they aroused considerable resentment. " The indignation against Mr. Mair is going on furiously," wrote a friend to Hargrave.[34]   The female part of the population, about whom Mair had made many uncomplimentary remarks, was particularly angry. One pulled his nose, another his ears, while a third, the wife of a leading citizen of the Settlement, drove him from the Post Office with a horse whip ![35] The indignation was so great that Mair was ordered to leave the Settlement and was only allowed to return upon the personal intervention of Governor Mactavish and on apologizing to the people concerned.[36]

To this growing resentment against the Canadians upon the part of the half-breeds was added the fear, dormant since the tumultuous days of Cuthbert Grant, Bostonnais Pangman and the North-West Company, that the whites had come " pour piller notre pays." The majority of the population, it will be remembered, were only squatters who had cultivated for years lands to which they held no title. Moreover, lands had passed from hand to hand and little account had ever been kept of the transactions. Governor Mactavish had foreseen trouble in this regard. As early as 1860 he wrote, " The land business here is anything but in a satisfactory state."[37] The news of the negotiations with Canada aroused feelings of apprehension as regards the land question, feelings which were aggravated by the thoughtless threats of the Canadian Party as to what would happen to the country when it belonged to Canada. The fears of the half-breeds seemed justified when it was learned that certain of the Canadian Government employees had been purchasing from the Indians—who had no right to sell—land in the neighbourhood of the métis settlement at Oak Point. Snow himself was fined £10 in the Petty Court for supplying liquor to the Indians in connexion with these questionable land deals.[38] Moreover, the rumour was spread about that these lands were actually those belonging to the métis. Colonel Dennis swore on oath, in 1874, that Dr. Schultz had told him that he and Snow had staked off and bought from the Indians lands near Oak Point to which the French half-breeds had laid claim, and asked Dennis if he thought that the Canadian Government would recognize his right to them.[39] But, whether these lands were métis lands or not, the effect of the news was electric, and the men in charge of the road operations at that point were compelled by the incensed inhabitants to quit the neighbourhood forthwith.

The temper of the native population, now thoroughly aroused, was scarcely improved by the tactless decision upon the part of the Minister of Public Works to begin at once the survey of the territory which was to be transferred to Canada in accordance with the agreement with the Hudson's Bay Company. In July 1869, Colonel Stoughton Dennis was sent to superintend the new surveys at Oak Point and Red River. Although the London Office of the Company granted permission for this undertaking to proceed, the local Governor, William Mactavish, considered the move ill-advised. " It is unfortunate," he wrote, " that any survey should be commenced till the Canadian Government was in authority here, as the whole land question is fruitful of future trouble which it will take much time and great labour to settle. I expect that as soon as the survey commences the half-breeds and Indians will at once come forward and assert their right to the land and possibly stop the work till their claim is satisfied."[40]

The most serious blunder, however, was the system of survey adopted by the Department of Public Works. It was suggested to Dennis that the American system, with certain modifications, was best suited to the country. This system divided the country into square townships of sixty-four sections of eight hundred acres each, and cut across the long ribbon-like farms which bordered on the river. The result would have been chaotic ; not a half-breed farm would have fitted into the proposed system. Dennis soon learned that these surveys were not regarded with any degree of goodwill by the inhabitants. He accordingly wrote to the Minister, the Honourable William McDougall, that great skill would be required in reconciling the proposed system with the prevailing irregularity and confusion ; and " that a considerable degree of irritation exists among the native popula- tion in view of surveys and settlements being made," particularly among the French half-breeds, who " have gone so far as to threaten violence should the surveys be attempted to be made."[41] A few days later Dennis wrote again to McDougall that he hesitated to proceed with the surveys in view of " the present temper of the half-breeds " and stated, " I have again to remark the uneasy feeling which exists in the half-breeds and Indian element with regard to what they conceive to be premature action taken by the Government in proceeding to effect a survey without having first extinguished the Indian title."[42] Dennis' warnings were, however, dismissed with the curt order to " proceed with the surveys on the plan proposed."[43] The result was, a few days later, that Mr. Webb, who had charge of the surveys in the neighbourhood of the French half-breed settlement of St. Vital, on the Red River, was ordered to desist by a party of métis who claimed the region " as the property of the French half-breeds, and which they would not allow to be surveyed by the Canadian Government."[44]   The surveyors were withdrawn from that district, but the temper and irritation of the people was such that Dennis did not consider it advisable to take any measures against the offenders.

Under these circumstances it was regrettable that the Dominion Government completely ignored the people of Assiniboia in the negotiations with the Hudson's Bay Company.   Many of the difficulties consequent upon the transfer might have been obviated by consulting the wishes of the inhabitants and guaranteeing legislative security for their national preservation.   As early as 1857 the Canadian explorer, Hind, had penned the warning that " There is a strong and growing feeling among the few who have turned their attention to such matters, that in the event of an organic change occurring in the Government of the country, the ' native ' or half-breed population should not be neglected, or thrust on one side."[45]   Moreover, the experience of Nova Scotia was fresh in the memory of the Government.   But at the very time when the Federal Government were legislating away two million dollars as a douceur to reconcile that refractory province to Confederation, they were legislating to annex the North-West without consulting the inhabitants in any way.   Even the authorities at Red River were kept in complete ignorance of the proposed arrangements.   As late as November 1869, Governor Mactavish declared that he was still without any official instruction, either from Canada or from England, of the fact, conditions or date of the proposed transfer.   It is not surprising, therefore, that the half-breeds, feeling that they had been sold " like dumb driven cattle," determined to dictate their own terms to the Dominion of Canada.   Writing after the stopping of the surveyors the Governor of Assiniboia placed his finger on the direct cause of the outbreak :

" The men who have thus interfered say they know the survey could proceed without injury to anyone, but that stopping it is always a beginning ; and they are desirous to let the Canadian Government know that it is not wanted by them ; that they consider, if the Canadians wished to come here, the terms on which they were to enter should have been arranged with the local government here, as it is acknowledged by the people in the country."[46]

To secure their own terms and thus erect a barrier around their racial and religious privileges became the motive force behind the half-breed rising in 1869.

Foreign influences were also at work upon the native population of Red River. With the opening of the western states of America and the linking of the economic interests of the colony of Assiniboia with those of the State of Minnesota, a small, but aggressive, American element grew up in the Settlement. " Some of those gentlemen," says Garrioch, " took a lively interest in the Transfer, and were outspoken enough to try and persuade the people that Garry, as they called it, was the lawful and natural prey of the American eagle."[47] The New York *Times* stated after the outbreak of the insurrection that " A mistake will be committed if, in considering the causes and scope of the insurrection, some allowance be not made for the variety and strength of the American influences which have long been in operation in the Red River region," and hinted that the insurgents might be able to " draw aid and comfort of a very practical kind from the bold adventurous element which forms so large a proportion of our frontier population."[48] Bryce, in his *Remarkable History of the Hudson's Bay Company*, wrote that he had it " on the information of a man high in the service of Canada " that " there was a large sum of money, of which an amount was named as high as one million dollars, which was available in St. Paul for the purpose of securing a hold by the Americans on the fertile plains of Rupert's Land "[49]; while Bishop Taché wrote to the Governor-General during the course of the troubles that " des sommes à un montant de plus de quatre millions de dollars, des hommes et des armes " had been offered by interested American parties to the half-breed leaders.[50] Corroborative evidence of this offer was given by the Archbishop of St. Paul. Speaking before the Catholic Club of Winnipeg in 1908 he said, " Ce que je vous dis là n'est pas une légende ni une rumeur vague. . . . J'étais alors en relation directe avec quelques uns des hommes qui firent cette offre, et c'est d'eux que je tiens le fait."[51]

More important, however, than the actions of adventurers of the stamp of Enos Stuttsman, J. Rolette and Major H. N. Robinson, was the active interest displayed by the American

Government in the events at Red River. We have already observed the expansionist sympathies of Seward and Ramsey and the provocative resolutions of 1866 and 1868, and there can be little doubt that a certain amount of underhand work for American annexation was countenanced if not directly encouraged by official circles at Washington and St. Paul during the half-breed rising of 1869–70. From 1867, J. W. Taylor, who had inspired the resolutions, acted as special agent for the United States at Red River, and worked actively in the cause of voluntary union. In June 1869 Taylor learned of the terms of the transfer and the details of the proposed government for the colony, and, feeling certain that they would prove unsatisfactory to the inhabitants, he requested the Governor of Minnesota to obtain for him a commission from the State Department, in which his services might be used in connexion with the impending trouble. The State Department were watching development in the Hudson's Bay Company territories with keen interest. As early as September 11th they had been informed by the American consul at Winnipeg that " the mass of settlers are strongly inclined . . . to get up a riot to expel the new Governor on his arrival here about October 15th," and that " in case of insurrection . . . if the settlers . . . should raise from among themselves a small regularly armed force of say 1,000 troops, it would form a nucleus around which volunteers from the North Western States might collect."[52] In November the consul again reported, " Should this revolution be successful it may, I think, be safely predicted that in less than two years' time all the British colonies on this continent will apply for admission into the Union."[53] As a result of this encouraging information the State Department appointed Taylor, United States Secret Agent, with instructions to investigate and report upon the following subjects :

" 1. Full details of the revolt by the inhabitants of Selkirk Settlement against the Canadian Confederation and the expulsion of Honorable William McDougall on his way to assume the office of Governor.

" 2. The geographical features and commercial affinities of the Selkirk, Saskatchewan and Columbia districts.

" 3. The character and disposition of the population.

" 4. Existing routes of communication from Canada and the United States and what changes or improvements in this respect are proposed.

" 5. The political relations of the several British possessions between Minnesota and Alaska.

" 6. The general question of commercial and political relations between the United States and Canada.

" 7. The political relations between the Dominion of Canada and the several states and provinces composing it."[54]

The United States were thus kept fully informed as to the march of events. On December 8th the American Senate passed a resolution requesting the president to communicate to them information " relating to the presence of the Honorable William McDougall at Pembina in Dakota Territory, and the opposition by the inhabitants of Selkirk Settlement to his assumption of the office of Governor of the North-West Territory."[55] These papers were not brought down until several years after the insurrection, but the resolution and the actions of the American authorities at this time were significant of the attitude of mind at Washington.

The French half-breeds could never have carried out their successful resistance had they not had the advice and tacit support of their clergy. The part played by the Roman Catholic clergy in the Red River Rebellion has often been misunderstood and sometimes misrepresented. Dr. George Bryce, with an obvious bias, speaks of them as " ecclesiastics from old France," with " no love for Canada, no love for any country, no love for society, no love for peace ! "[56] To understand the rôle that they played in the rising, we have only to turn to the history of Canada. From the fall of Quebec to the present day, the French Canadian, with the assistance of his curé, has clung strenuously to his laws, his language, his religion and his institutions. Cut off from France, the French Canadians have, nevertheless, maintained inviolate their separate identity ; wherever we may go in Canada we find communities of French Canadians maintaining the nationality of their fathers, true to the watchword of old Quebec, " Je me Souviens." Anyone who is acquainted with the French Canadian in Western Canada is struck by the tenacity with which he holds to his language and his nationality in the face of overwhelming odds and difficulties. One of the greatest forces which has assisted this tenacious survival has been the influence exercised by the Roman Catholic Church. From the time of the Conquest it has been the curé who has held the citadel of French Canadian nationalism against the assaults of the Anglo-Saxon.

The Church realized that the French Canadian who lost his language might also lose his faith. It was the strong organization of the Catholic parish which saved the French Canadian as such after 1670, and which maintains him to this day in the midst of the English-speaking provinces of Canada.

This same influence was exercised by the Church in Red River. The Roman Catholic clergy saw that unless some definite guarantee was secured from the Canadian Government, unless some breakwater could be raised against the tide of Protestant English immigration, the French Catholic métis would suffer the same fate as the French Catholic Louisianian. Bishop Taché had returned from Canada in 1857 full of apprehension for the future of his race and his religion in the North-West, and expressed his fear in a letter to Sir George Cartier :

" J'ai toujours redouté l'entrée du Nord-Ouest dans la Confédération parceque j'ai toujours cru que l'élément français catholique serait sacrifié . . . Le nouveau système me semble de nature à amener la ruine de ce qui nous a coûté si cher."[57]

Accordingly, certain members of the French Canadian Catholic clergy, particularly the Abbé Ritchot, identifying the cause of the métis with that of the French Canadian, threw the weight of their influence on the side of the half-breeds rather than upon that of Canada. Thus the Red River Rebellion, which was fundamentally the revolt of a semi-primitive society against the imposition of a more progressive, alien culture, assumed a religious and racial aspect which was to have unfortunate repercussions in Eastern Canada.

The situation in Red River in the autumn of 1869 was critical. Constituted authority had been weakened by the actions of the turbulent element, and the continued attacks of the *Nor' Wester*; while the half-breeds, who otherwise would have been its strongest adherents, unaware of the Company's helplessness in the matter, felt that in selling Rupert's Land to Canada the Company had abandoned them, and thus forfeited its claim to their allegiance. The métis, forming the largest and most homogeneous section of the population were strongly suspicious by nature of a change, exasperated by the actions of an aggressive Canadian minority, and left in complete uncertainty as to the future of their nationality and their livelihood. This feeling was naturally strongest among the French half-breeds. Their social and economic interests were more affected by

Canadian expansion than those of their English-speaking kindred. Not only were the latter English speaking and Protestant, but they were, as we have observed in Chapter One, for the most part agriculturists, not hunters, and, therefore, less likely to suffer from the economic dislocation which was bound to follow any rapid influx of white settlers. Nevertheless, the Scotch and English half-breeds expressed anxiety regarding their rights, and Thomas Bunn, a prominent English half-breed member of the Council of Assiniboia, declared that, had the surveys taken place among the English half-breeds instead of among the French, they would have acted as the French had done.[58]

The attitude of the white inhabitants of Red River—with the exception of the aggressive Canadians and the interested Americans—was one of complete indifference to the proposed transfer. The Hudson's Bay Company employees, like the métis, were hardly enthusiastic for the change. The sale of the Company in 1863 had aroused considerable feeling among the " wintering partners " who felt that they were entitled to receive some share of the purchase money. There is little doubt that the transaction of 1869 was viewed in the same light. " The younger men in the service never disguised their indignation and disgust," and Dr. Cowan, the Chief Factor at Fort Garry, complained bitterly to Mair that the Company in England had ignored their interests.[59] If anything, these men preferred a crown colony to political connexion with Canada. The Selkirk settlers and their descendants were also little inclined to look with favour upon the transfer of Red River to the Canadian Confederation[60] and were, as a result, branded as " cowards, one and all of them."[61] Although they " never entertained a doubt that in due time everything that would be advantageous for the country would be granted by Canada,"[62] the English-speaking population felt that they had been treated discourteously by the Canadian Government, and informed Dennis that " when you present to us the issue of a conflict with the French party, with whom we have hitherto lived in friendship, . . . we feel disinclined to enter upon it, and think that the Dominion should assume the responsibility of establishing amongst us what it, and it alone, has decided upon."[63] It was largely owing to this passive sympathy on the part of the English-speaking population, and to the active co-operation of certain of the Scotch and English half-breeds, that the French métis, " united and effective . . . obedient to daring leaders of their own race . . . proved capable of dominating for ten months a community in which, in moral and social influence, they were perhaps the least considerable element."[64]

Joseph Pope, in his biography of Sir John Macdonald says :

" it does not appear that the Hudson's Bay Company took any steps to prepare the settlers for the change of government. Nor did they give any hint to the Dominion authorities of the state of feeling afterwards known to have prevailed at the time, among the half-breeds of the Red River."[65]

It was true that the Company did not officially warn Canada of the impending political storm; nevertheless, the Dominion authorities were scarcely ignorant of the unsettled state of affairs in the Red River colony. In 1868, Machray, the Anglican Bishop of Rupert's Land, in interviews with leading Canadian statesmen, told them of the state of the colony and offered his services in arranging a harmonious settlement. Although they listened to him with courtesy, the Government took advantage neither of his information, nor of his offer. Later Machray wrote to Buckingham and Chandos that there was " imminent risk any day of some outbreak leading to the utter prostration of law and order,"[66] and urged that some military force should be sent, and liberal provisions should be made for the securing to the settlers of titles to the lands which they had acquired from the Hudson's Bay Company or by squatters' rights. But this letter, like so many others, was merely acknowledged, pigeon-holed, and in all probability forgotten. Another warning was given by Mactavish, the Governor of Assiniboia. Thinking that the prospective rulers of Rupert's Land might wish to consult him, he visited Ottawa on his return from London in 1869. Mactavish's account of his reception indicates the complacency of the Canadian politicians. He was " left waiting for an interview for some days " and when it was obtained his " advice was not asked for as to the mode in which the government should be assumed or carried on." The Governor was usually " cautious and dip-lomatic," but on this occasion he plainly intimated " that they would not find it child's play to rule the North-West. It had been in the past no easy place to govern, and under new rulers he thought the difficulties would increase."[67] Speaking to Bishop Taché, Mactavish described his rebuff :

" I have just returned from Ottawa, and although I have been for forty years in the country, and Governor for fifteen years, I have not been able to cause any of my recommendations to be accepted by the Government. Those gentlemen are of opinion that they know a great deal more about this country than we do."[68]

Still a third and more important warning was given to the Canadian authorities by Bishop Taché. On his way to the Oecumenical Council at Rome, Taché warned Sir George Cartier that there was considerable unrest in the North-West over the proposed transfer. Cartier, however, replied that " he knew it all a great deal better than I did, and did not want any information."[69] In spite of this snub, Taché repeated his warning, but no notice was apparently taken of it, save to despatch a few rifles and rounds of ammunition to the North-West with Lieutenant-Governor McDougall !

There seems to be very little excuse, in the light of these repeated warnings, for the conduct of the Canadian Government. Had some effort been made to use these men who had great influence in the colony to reassure the inhabitants as to the policy that Canada intended to follow, and to guarantee the tenure of their lands and the protection of the half-breed element, the insurrection, with its bloodshed, might have been averted.   It is true that Joseph Howe, as Secretary of State for the Provinces, paid a flying visit to the colony and wrote to Macdonald that his visit had been opportune in removing a number of " absurd rumours " and much " strong prejudice."[70] Mactavish wrote hopefully of Howe : " a shrewd clear headed man—he very soon made out his whereabouts and steadily avoided Dr. Schultz's offers of accommodation. He told me to-day that he was perfectly astonished to find the state of matters here and that without any means it was most wonderful how things had been kept together. . . . I have no doubt from his observations he will be able to set some of his colleagues right in their ideas about Red River."[71]   Others, however, expressed the opinion that Howe's journey did more harm than good.   McDougall, in a masterpiece of invective, accused Howe of being " the chief abettor, if not the chief instigator " of the Red River insurrection ;[72] while the *Globe*, rejoicing in an opportunity to belabour the Government, stated that Howe had urged the settlers to follow the example of Nova Scotia and fight for " better terms."[73] There is no authority for these statements which were the result of personal vindictiveness and political partisanship. If any encouragement was given to the Red River population, it was probably due to the fact that Howe did not identity himself with the objectionable Canadian Party, and that his successful opposition to Confederation was not unknown in the colony. Beyond Howe's short and unofficial visit, no person of any official position was sent to the colony to prepare the way for the new government, and even in November Mactavish declared " up to this moment we have no official intimation from England, or the Dominion of Canada, of the fact of the transfer, or of its conditions, or of the date at which they were to take practical effect upon the Government of this Country."[74]

The final blunder of this chapter of blunders was the form of government devised, temporary though it was meant to be, and the selection of William McDougall as the first Lieutenant-Governor. The white settlers, at least, had hoped for some representative form of government and feared that the continuation of the nominated council would lead to the appointment of those who professed to be the friends of Canada. The *Globe*, in a rare prophetic moment, stated :

" If Wm. McDougall is sent up to Fort Garry with a ready-made council composed of men utterly ignorant of the country and the people, the strongest feelings of discontent will be aroused."[75]

Although McDougall intended to include some of the more prominent inhabitants in his council, the appointment of A. N. Richards and J. A. N. Provencher to the leading positions, and the presence of Cameron, Wallace, Begg and others in the Governor's suite, appeared to the people of Red River as " a whole government appointed and despatched to their destination before the people at Ottawa had taken the first steps to obtain legislation for their guidance, and before the necessary measures had been taken to get possession."[76]

The choice of Lieutenant-Governor was most unfortunate. Had Canada desired to stir up trouble in the North-West she could not have chosen a more suitable man. Cold and intractable in his dealings with his colleagues, McDougall was not the man to handle a difficult situation with patience and understanding. He did not know the half-breeds at all, but they knew him only too well : McDougall, more than anyone else, had been the consistent advocate of Canadian expansion and the implacable enemy of the Hudson's Bay Company. He was, moreover, the Minister of Public Works who was held responsible for the conduct of the road workers and the surveyors at Red River. It was believed by some that many of the difficulties consequent upon McDougall's appointment might have been precluded by the appointment of Governor Mactavish as his own successor. This course was suggested both by Bishop Taché[77] and Sir Alexander Galt,[78] but was ignored ; and William McDougall, C.B., was appointed to usher in the new order at Red River.

CHAPTER IV

It was in the latter part of the summer of 1869 that the first steps were taken by the half-breeds to organize their opposition to the transfer of Red River to the Dominion of Canada. In 1868 Louis Schmidt found " un grand changement parmi le peuple. On commençait à parler *politique*, même parmi nos gens " ;[1] but after the return of Louis Riel to the colony events moved rapidly. An ardent patriot of his people, Riel was destined to become one of the stormy characters upon the Western Canadian scene. Upon two occasions, in 1869 and in 1885, he led the half-breeds in a futile protest against the inevitability of their national extinction, and perished upon the scaffold for unfurling the standard of armed rebellion.

Louis Riel was born at St. Boniface in the district of Assiniboia, on October 22nd, 1844. His mother, Julie Lagimodière, was the daughter of the first white woman in the North-West, and his father, one of the leaders of the free trade in furs movement of the 'forties, was a French Canadian with a dash of Indian blood in his veins. Bishop Taché, early impressed by Riel's success in the school at St. Boniface, arranged for his education in Eastern Canada ; and for several years Riel attended the College of Montreal. In 1866 he completed his classical education and spent the following year with an uncle, John Lee, near Montreal. In 1867 financial reasons compelled him to return to the West where he secured employment in St. Paul. A year later he returned to Red River, where he was joined by Louis Schmidt, both " bien résolus toutefois de nous occuper des affaires publiques quand le moment en sera venu."[2]

Louis Riel did not stir up the métis to the insurrection which occurred in 1869 ; he only assumed the leadership of the discontent, which we have observed in the previous chapter, and guided it according to his judgment or his impulse. His education, his eloquence in both French and English, and his ability marked him at once as the natural leader of the half-breed malcontents; but his lack of experience, and inability to brook opposition, unfitted him for the responsibilities of leadership. Even as a youth he was unable to tolerate criticism. "Pas trop de contradictions avec le jeune Louis qui aimait bien à discuter pourvu qu'il gagnât toujours son point de discussion:" wrote a contemporary, "lui offrir une opinion contraire à sienne c'était l'irriter; il ne comprenait pas qu'on ne put partager son opinion tant qu'il croyait à son infaillibilité personelle."[3] Nevertheless, it is only fair to state, that in spite of his quick temper and his love of popular adulation, Riel was inspired by feelings of racial patriotism and a genuine belief in the justice of the half-breed cause.

Riel found the people ready for the kind of leadership which he was able to give and his fiery speeches fell upon inflammatory material. Louis Schmidt, the companion of his boyhood years and later secretary of the insurgent government, remarked in his reminiscences upon "l'effet qu'il faisait sur ces natures simples et honnêtes comme l'étaient les métis, lorsqu'il leur démontrait leurs droits les plus sacrés foulés aux pieds par l'envahissement de leur pays par le Canada."[4] Thoroughly aroused to a realization of the danger which they believed to threaten them, the half-breeds began to hold secret gatherings among themselves to discuss the political situation. These small gatherings soon developed into large assemblies, and it was resolved in August, or early in September 1869, that every means should be taken to oppose the entry of the Canadian Governor until adequate guarantees had been given for the safeguarding of half-breed rights.[5]

The first actual resistance to the new order occurred on October 11th, when Captain Webb began to run his survey lines across the "hay privilege" of André Nault, about two and a half miles from Red River. Nault protested, but as the surveyors did not understand French, he was obliged to seek the aid of his cousin, Louis Riel.[6] Riel and a band of some eighteen men accordingly informed Webb that the country south of the Assiniboine belonged to the French half-breeds, and that they would allow no survey to be made. No arms were seen with the party. They merely stood upon the chain but made it clear that if the surveys were persisted in trouble would ensue. Colonel Dennis complained to Dr. Cowan, the magistrate at Fort Garry, but neither his efforts nor those of Roger Goulet[7] or Governor Mactavish were able to extract anything from Riel save the determined statement that " the Canadian Government had no right to make surveys in the Territory without the express permission of the people of the Settlement."[8] Application was made to Father Lestanc, administrator of the Diocese of St. Boniface during the absence of Bishop Taché at Rome, but the Reverend Father, fearing that once the métis began to believe " that the Church also was in sympathy with the Government " of Canada, it " might lead to weakening their influence over the people in a religious point of view,"[9] refused to do anything, adding " let the Canadian Government convince them that their rights shall not be interfered with and the métis will of themselves go for Mr. McDougall and triumphantly bring him here."[10]

The news of McDougall's approach with his ready-made government and his cases of rifles accelerated events. On October 16th a meeting of the French half-breeds was held at the house of Abbé Ritchot at St. Norbert. What passed at this gathering is not known, but the métis apparently determined to organize the entire French-speaking population on the semimilitary lines of the buffalo hunt. John Bruce was chosen as president and Louis Riel as secretary. Bruce was, however, president in name only[11] ; the real leaders were Louis Riel and the curé of St. Norbert.[12] Steps to prevent McDougall's entry into the Red River Settlement were undertaken at once. On the day following the organization of the " Comité National des Métis " some forty horsemen assembled at St. Norbert and erected a barricade across the road, a short distance from the point where it crosses la Rivière Sale ; and, on October 21st, a warning was despatched to the prospective Lieutenant-Governor, not to attempt to enter the country without the permission of the National Committee.

Learning of these summary proceedings the Council of Assiniboia met on the 25th to consider the situation. The Council unanimously expressed " their indignant reprobation of the outrageous proceedings . . . but, feeling strongly impressed with the idea that the parties concerned in them must be acting in utter forgetfulness, . . . of the very serious consequences," it was thought that " by calm reasoning and advice they might be induced to abandon their dangerous schemes."[13] With this object in view, Riel and Bruce were invited to present themselves at the Council board. Riel expressed his satisfaction with the Hudson's Bay Government, but stated that the métis " objected to any Governor coming from Canada without their being consulted in the matter ; that they would never admit any Governor . . . unless delegates were previously sent, with whom they might negotiate as to the terms and conditions under which they would acknowledge him . . . that they consider that they are acting not only for their own good, but for the good of the whole Settlement, that they did not feel that they were breaking any law, but were simply acting in defence of their own liberty and that they were determined to prevent Mr. McDougall from coming into the Settlement at all hazards." The Council failed to convince Riel that his views were erroneous and at length decided to send two influential French half-breeds to procure the peaceable dispersion of the party intending to intercept McDougall. Owing to Ritchot's determined attitude this mission was a failure, and all that could be reported to the Council was that the assembly of malcontents " appeared to be even more fully bent on their purpose."[14] The Council, lacking any police or military force to prevent a breach of the peace, were unable to do anything more save to advise McDougall, in view of the temper of the people, to remain at Pembina.[15] McDougall, however, pushed on to the Hudson's Bay Company post on the Canadian side of the border. Several days later he was obliged to return to the United States by a body of armed half-breeds.

The thoroughness with which Riel carried out his organization of the French métis is astonishing. The number of his men increased rapidly. On November 1st " the muster roll . . . was answered by 402 men, all bearing arms," later " about 100 more came into camp."[16] Strict discipline was maintained. The men were obliged to take an oath against drinking intoxicating liquors and seem to have kept it. Scouts were posted on the prairie and along the road to cut McDougall off from his adherents in Red River, and all parties and mails entering the colony were subject to examination by the métis at the barricade.

The half-breed movement, which had begun as a riotous assembly, assumed the serious proportions of an insurrection when, on November 2nd, Louis Riel, accompanied by some

hundred or more of his followers, entered Fort Garry and
informed Dr. Cowan, the Company officer in charge, that they
had come to guard the Fort from an impending danger.[17] It
was not without difficulty that Riel persuaded his followers to
carry out this daring act, but the move was decisive. Situated
at the junction of the Red and the Assiniboine Rivers, about a
mile from the village of Winnipeg, provisioned with stores of
food and munitions, and defended by high stone walls and
cannon, Fort Garry was the geographical and strategical centre of
the Red River Settlement. The party that controlled the Fort
controlled the colony. The Canadian sympathizers were not
unaware of this fact, an old pensioner having offered to raise a
force " which . . . could hold the Fort against all the Rebels who
would be likely to attack it."[18] This was precisely what Riel
feared, and, realizing that if the Canadians took possession of
Fort Garry the movement of the métis would be completely
paralysed and their position rendered untenable, he decided to
forestall his adversaries, and " to keep Mr. McDougall at a
distance, in order that his party, which were so hostile to our
interests, might not, under such circumstances, get possession of
the Government of our native country."[19]

Now in possession of Fort Garry, Riel turned his attention to
the English-speaking settlers, half-breed and white, who had so
far taken no part in the insurrection. His aim was not to fight
Canada, but, with the whole body of settlers, French and English,
behind him, to force the Canadian Government to negotiate
with the half-breeds the terms of their entry into Confederation.
This was Riel's constant objective from the beginning to the
conclusion of the insurrection. Their own terms, embodied in a
Canadian statute and confirmed by the Imperial Parliament, were
regarded by the half-breed leaders as the only safeguard for the
interests of a people soon to find themselves on the defensive.
Prior to the capture of Fort Garry Bruce had informed Provencher
that " if the Canadian Government was willing to do it, they were
ready to open negotiations with them, or any person vested with
full powers, in view of settling the terms of their coming into the
Dominion of Canada."[20] Such a concession by Canada was not,
however, likely as long as the half-breeds failed to present a
united front. Accordingly, on November 6th, Riel issued a
" Public Notice to the Inhabitants of Rupert's Land "[21] inviting

the English-speaking people of the colony to " send twelve representatives . . . in order to form one body," with the French
Council, " to consider the present political state of this country,
and to adopt such measures as may be deemed best for the future
welfare of the same." The delegates were to meet in convention
" in the Court House at Fort Garry, on Tuesday, November 16th."

The English half-breeds and the whites, not understanding
Riel's motives, were inclined to regard his overtures with suspicion. It was the universal opinion that the métis had over-
stepped the mark. The stoppage of the mails, the retention of
private goods in transit, and the seizure of the public books
" were acts uncalled for in their cause, and have raised a great
deal of indignation against them ; but as yet it will be only an
act of extraordinary provocation or the spilling of blood that will
raise a fight among the settlers."[22] Desiring, however, to co-
operate in finding a peaceful solution of the difficulties which had
arisen, the English parishes, notwithstanding the assurances of
Snow and others to the contrary, decided to elect representatives
to meet the French in council.

The Convention opened on a discordant note. The English
demanded the election of a new president and secretary, a demand
to which the French refused to accede until there was evidence
of agreement among the delegates upon a common course of
action. The English then voiced their opposition to the
occupation of the Fort and to the ejection of McDougall from
British soil. Despite this they were impressed—at least so Riel
wrote—by the métis protestations of loyalty to the Crown and by
the plea for the protection of their common rights and liberties
from the ingress of a " foreign power." At this moment, Hargrave,
secretary to Governor Mactavish, presented to the Convention a
Proclamation by the Governor which protested against the
unlawful actions of the French party. Whereupon James Ross,
the leader of the English-speaking delegates, declared that the
métis must now evacuate the Fort or be considered guilty of
rebellion. Riel protested. " Si nous rebellons contre la
Compagnie qui nous vend et veut nous livrer, et contre le Canada
qui veut nous acheter," he declared, " nous ne nous rebellons
pas contre la suprématie anglaise, qui n'a pas encore donnée son
approbation pour le transfert définitif de ce pays . . . de plus nous
sommes fidèles à notre patrie. . . . Nous voulons que le peuple de

FORT GARRY

la Rivière Rouge soit un peuple libre. Aidons-nous les uns les autres. Nous sommes tous frères et des parents, dit Monsieur Ross, et c'est vrai. Ne nous séparons pas. Voyez ce que Monsieur Mactavish dit. Il dit que de cette assemblée peut venir un bien incalculable. Unissons-nous, le mal qu'il a redouté n'aura pas lieu."[23]

In spite of the fact that the Convention was entirely unofficial in character, it continued to sit with the tacit approval of Governor Mactavish. Its labours, however, did not result in that unanimity of opinion for which Riel had hoped. The English, with a greater knowledge of constitutional procedure, stubbornly contended that the proper course was to permit McDougall to enter the territory and for the settlers to place their grievances before him; while the French obdurately declared that McDougall could only be brought in over their dead bodies. The Convention, therefore, remained at a deadlock, and Mactavish wrote on November 23rd that he believed that the French would consent to nothing short of the establishment of a Provisional Government.[24]

Riel had already satisfied himself that this step was not only necessary, but was, under the circumstances, justifiable. Finding that the English and Scotch colonists would not go as far as he desired, Riel decided that, if the métis were not to lose all the advantage they had gained, he must consolidate their position and form a Provisional Government which could treat with Canada on equal terms. Accordingly, at the risk of alienating all the English speaking and moderate opinion, he forced the Hudson's Bay Company accountant to surrender the public accounts, carefully assuring Governor Mactavish " that there was not only no desire to meddle with private funds, but every desire to respect them." " How far this resolution will be carried out," wrote the Governor, " it is very difficult to say, though at the time it was made I have no doubt it was sincere."[25] In the Convention Riel argued that the formation of a Provisional Government was indispensable on the grounds that the Council of Assiniboia " a vraiment montré une faiblesse extrême dans ces derniers jours . . . Qu'en conséquence il est temps que les habitants de la colonie songent à la formation d'un gouvernement provisoire pour une protection et pour traiter avec le Canada et forcer celui-ci à nous donner un mode de gouvernement responsable." This suggestion was even less acceptable to the English, who hinted that Canada was more likely to send troops than delegates. The meeting thus concluded, as Riel noted, with " pas d'entente, peu d'espoir d'entente."

Fundamentally a conservative people, the French half-breeds, like their English-speaking kindred, were reluctant to go the full distance proposed by Riel, and it was not without some difficulty that he finally carried his point. The night of November 23rd was spent by the French party in heated debate on this question. Riel, himself, is said to have argued for seven hours to bring the faltering " National Committee " to agree to his plan of procedure. " Que de craintes et d'hésitations à vaincre," he wrote, " c'est incroyable les répugnances que j'ai eu à leur faire surmonter." The métis objected to the Provisional Government as constituting an act of rebellion against the British Crown, and it was only as a result of Riel's repeated declarations of loyalty and his arguments " que le gouvernement d'Assiniboia en se vendant s'est tellement affaibli . . . que s'il lui reste encore quelque chose d'un gouvernement c'est le nom . . . que si la Reine savait ce que nous voulons, elle nous écouterait " that they accepted his proposal.

On November 24th the Convention sat again. The proposal to form a Provisional Government was once more put before the delegates, this time backed by the unanimous voice of the French. The English regarded this proposal as beyond the scope of their authority and declared that they would be obliged to consult their constituents before taking such a radical step. The unfortunate result was that nothing was accomplished, and the Convention adjourned until December 1st, the date on which Canada had provisionally agreed to accept the transfer of the North-West to the Dominion.

McDougall's instructions had requested him to proceed with all convenient speed to Fort Garry, and there to make the necessary preliminary arrangements for the completion of the transfer. En route he passed Joseph Howe, returning from his flying visit to Red River, but " as the weather was stormy " they " had only a very short interview."[26] Howe promised to advise McDougall by post of the situation in the colony, but " apparently did not anticipate, that there was any danger of an armed insurrection before my arrival at Fort Garry." The promised letter, with the salutary advice that " it would be a great mistake to patronize a little clique of persons at war with the more influential elements of society " which was " sufficiently mixed and heterogeneous to require delicate handling,"[27] did not reach McDougall until after he had met with his rebuff at the hands of the militant French half-breeds. He was not, however, totally unaware of the dissatisfaction which prevailed in Red River, but confidently anticipated that, with the aid of J. A. N. Provencher, a nephew of the late Bishop of the North-West, he would be able to pacify the malcontents. Arriving at Pembina McDougall was surprised at the extent of the métis opposition, but hoping to assure the insurgents that the Government would " deal justly with all classes . . . without reference to race or religion,"[28] he sent his prospective provincial secretary to interview the métis at the barricade. At the same time, Captain Cameron, the dashing prospective Chief of Police, in spite of McDougall's expressed wishes, determined to proceed to Fort Garry on his own responsibility. But neither the persuasion of Provencher's name, nor the command of Cameron to " remove that blasted fence " accomplished anything. Both were escorted back to Pembina and McDougall suffered the humiliation of being expelled from the territory which he had expected to govern. The American press were jubilant at his discomfiture ; a newspaper of St. Paul wrote :

" A King without a Kingdom is said to be poorer than a peasant. And I can assure you that a live Governor with a full complement of officials and menials from Attorney-General down to cooks and scullions without one poor foot of territory is a spectacle sufficiently sad to move the hardest heart."[29]

Confident that an exposition of his designs would induce a reaction in his favour, McDougall wrote to Mactavish asking him to issue a Proclamation explaining the nature of the proposed transfer and warning the malcontents of the serious nature of their actions.[30] Mactavish consulted the Council of Assiniboia and replied that in view of the fact that no official word had yet come to the colony of the fact or date of the transfer, they doubted the value of the suggested Proclamation, and advised McDougall, in the interests of " the peace of the country " and " the establishment in the future of the Canadian Government," to return to Canada.[31] This would probably have been the wisest course, as McDougall's presence on the frontier was a constant provocation to the French half-breeds, while the English-speaking settlers were obviously not prepared to support him. Unfortunately he preferred to listen to the more congenial, but misleading advice of the Canadian Party, with whom, in spite of Riel's precautions, he was in secret communication. Snow advised " Issue Proclamation, and then you may come fearlessly down. Hudson's Bay Company evidently shaking. By no means leave Pembina."[32] Mair, even more blindly optimistic, declared that the only reason the English had not yet risen was because they had not been called upon to do so. " Issue your Proclamation," he wrote, " and it will be responded to by five hundred men."[33] Although Mactavish's intervention had been unable to induce the English-speaking half-breeds and Selkirk settlers to adopt the Canadian cause, McDougall, encouraged by the false reports of his adherents in the colony, determined to issue, on December 1st, a proclamation in the Queen's name, announcing the transfer of the North-West territory to Canada and his appointment as Lieutenant-Governor.

The proclamation of December 1st was a very serious blunder from the Canadian standpoint. McDougall's commission appointed him Lieutenant-Governor only " from and after the day to be named by Us for the admission of Rupert's Land and the North-Western Territory into the Union or Dominion of Canada." That McDougall was fully cognizant of his position is apparent from his correspondence. Shortly after his arrival at Pembina he had written to Mactavish :

" As you are aware, the transfer of the Territory and the powers of government entrusted to you, is to take effect on a day to be named in Her Majesty's Royal Proclamation, until that day arrives (which I am informed will be about the 1st day of December next), you are the legal ruler of the country, and responsible for the preservation of the public peace. My commission authorizes and commands me to assume and exercise the powers of government from and after that day."[34]

On November 7th he wrote again :

" I shall remain here until I hear officially of the transfer of authority, and shall then be guided by circumstances as to what I shall say and do."[35]

Again on the 14th, referring to Snow's suggestion to issue a proclamation, McDougall wrote to Howe :

" The recommendation that I should issue a Proclamation at once, is not made for the first time, but I have uniformly replied that until the transfer of the Territory has taken place, and I am notified of the fact I shall not assume any of the responsibilities of Government."

but, he added :

" I expected to hear, by this time, that the ' transfer ' had been agreed to, and the Imperial Order in Council passed. If I do not receive notice of this ' Order ' in a few days, I shall be much embarrassed in my plans, and the leaders of the insurrection will be emboldened and strengthened. They understand perfectly that I have no legal authority to act, or to command obedience, till the Queen's Proclamation is issued."[36]

On November 25th he complained that he was " still without any official notice of the Imperial Order in Council, and must act, if at all, upon the information contained in the private letters from Sir Curtis Lampson, which announces the date of the transfer agreed to by the Imperial Government to be December 1st next."[37] Notwithstanding the fact that he had received no official confirmation of the transfer which he knew he must await, McDougall informed the Canadian Government, on the 29th, that he had " prepared a Proclamation to be issued the first day of December . . . stating . . . the fact of surrender by the Hudson's Bay Company, acceptance by Her Majesty, and transfer to Canada, from and after December 1st, A.D. 1869. These facts I gather from the newspapers, from a private letter to me of the Deputy Governor of the Company, and my own knowledge before I left Ottawa, that December 1st had been agreed upon as the date of the transfer."[38] McDougall realized the weakness of his position. Writing after the issuance of the questionable proclamation he said :

" I hope I am right in using the name of Her Majesty as prominently as I have done."[39]

This action was all the more regrettable as, on December 6th, McDougall received a despatch from Howe, dated November 19th, reminding him that " as matters stand, you can claim or assert no authority in the Hudson's Bay Territory, until the Queen's Proclamation, annexing the country to Canada, reaches you through this office."[40] At the same time a private letter from the Prime Minister warned him :

D

" Never forget . . . that you are now approaching a foreign country, under the government of the Hudson's Bay Company. . . . You cannot force your way in."[41]

And another a few days later :

" A Proclamation such as you suggest . . . would be very well if it were sure to be obeyed. If, however, it were disobeyed, your weakness and inability to enforce the authority of the Dominion would be painfully exhibited, not only to the people of Red River, but to the people and Government of the United States."[42]

This letter concluded with the startling information that the Canadian Government had refused to complete the transfer :

" We have thrown the responsibility on the Imperial Government."

The decision to withhold the acceptance of the territory was made by the Dominion Government following the receipt of McDougall's letters reporting the active opposition of the French half-breeds and his expulsion from the Red River Settlement. On November 25th, Sir John Rose, the confidential agent of the Canadian Government at London, was instructed to refrain from paying over the £300,000 to the Hudson's Bay Company, and on the 26th the Governor-General telegraphed to Lord Granville that " the responsibility of administration of affairs " would " rest on Imperial Government " if the surrender were accepted by Great Britain as " Canada cannot accept transfer unless quiet possession can be given."[43] The Colonial Office were, to say the least, annoyed. Granville's comment on receiving this news was :

" I see no grounds for the Dominion to repudiate the agreement which has been formally made. They had no business to send a Governor-designate to Red River unless they considered the agreement as substantially concluded. Delay, moreover, will now be most inconvenient and injurious to all parties."[44]

He accordingly replied to Young's telegram that the transfer must follow the surrender to the Imperial Government in order to make the latter legal as the Rupert's Land Act required the act of transfer to follow the surrender within one month ; otherwise the territory would remain under the jurisdiction of the Hudson's Bay Company " liable to all the disorders which are to be expected when the prestige of a Government long known to be inadequate, is shaken by the knowledge that it is also expiring, and by the appearance, however well intended, of its successor."[45]

There can be no doubt that Canada was under a legal obligation to complete the transfer once the Deed of Surrender, which had already been prepared by the Hudson's Bay Company, was accepted by the British Government. Such was the opinion of the law officers to whom Granville referred the question.

" We are of opinion that if the surrender is accepted by the Crown and the proposed Order in Council is passed within a month of that acceptance, Canada is bound to accept the territory, to pay the price of it as specified in the Second Address, and to provide for its government. . . . The Executive Government of Canada have, in our views, no power to invalidate a proceeding of the Canadian Legislature which has been acted upon by the Hudson's Bay Company and by the Crown in pursuance of powers conferred by the Imperial Legislature."[46]

Nevertheless, there was a certain political justification for the action of the Canadian Government. As a minute of the Cabinet pointed out :

" Any hasty attempt by the Canadian Government to force their rule upon the Insurgents would probably result in armed resistance and bloodshed. Every other course should be tried before resort is had to force. If life were once lost in an encounter between a Canadian force and the inhabitants, the seeds of hostility to Canada and Canadian rule would be sown, and might create an ineradicable hatred to the union of the Countries, and thus mar the future prosperity of British America. If anything like hostilities should commence, the temptation to the wild Indian tribes, and to the restless adventurers, who abound in the United States (many of them with military experience gained in the late Civil War) to join the Insurgents, would be almost irresistible. . . . No one can see the end of the complications that might thus be occasioned, not only as between Canada and the North-West, but between the United States and England. From a sincere conviction of the gravity of the situation, and not from any desire to repudiate or postpone the performance of any of their engagements, the Canadian Government have urged a temporary delay of the transfer."[47]

Granville too recognized the force of this argument and did not push legality to the limit. " We have two objects," he wrote in an office minute, " First, in common with Canada, and, if they are wise, the Hudson's Bay Company, to give Canada the time really necessary for getting peaceably into the saddle. Second, in common with the Hudson's Bay Company, and, if they are honest, the Canadian Government, to prevent any waste of time in so doing. . . . For the moment we ought all to agree to a moderate delay."[48]   But this " moderate delay," whether judicious or not, cut the ground from under McDougall's feet, and rendered his proclamation not only worthless but illegal.

Both Howe and Macdonald condemned McDougall's ill-considered, hasty action. Howe reminded McDougall that he had used the Queen's name without Her authority, and had attributed to Her Majesty acts which she had not yet performed.[49] McDougall, obstinately optimistic, declared that results would justify his policy. " I feel very confident," he wrote, " that this prompt display of vigour, and the determination to assert, and maintain by force, if need be, the authority of the new Government, from the day and hour of its expected birth, will inspire all the inhabitants of the Territory with respect for your Representative, and compel the traitors and conspirators to cry ' God Save the Queen ' or beat a hasty retreat."[50]

Events in the Settlement, however, showed no indication of bearing out McDougall's view. The French were frankly sceptical of the authenticity of the Queen's Proclamation ; the English accepted it without enthusiasm ; only the Canadians were jubilant. At this moment the French party brought forward a " Bill of Rights " embodying their demands. The Bill was discussed by the Convention, and the English, finding nothing unreasonable in the demands of their French-speaking compatriots, agreed to its adoption by the Convention. It was then proposed that delegates, two French and two English, should be sent to McDougall to learn if he was empowered, by virtue of his commission, either to accept this " Bill of Rights " or to guarantee its acceptance by the Canadian Parliament. The English, believing in the validity of McDougall's Proclamation, considered a delegation useless on the terms suggested, and the Convention came to an indecisive conclusion. At the close of the sitting Riel addressed the English-speaking delegation in scathing terms :

" Allez, retournez-vous en paisiblement sur vos fermes. Restez dans les bras de vos femmes. Donnez cet exemple à vos enfants. Mais regardez-nous agir. Nous allons travailler et obtenir la garantie de nos droits et des vôtres.   Vous viendrez à la fin partager."

The Convention had accomplished little in the way of promoting English and French co-operation, but that little had been sufficient to persuade the English-speaking inhabitants that the French demands were both reasonable and justifiable, and to cool any ardour that might have developed for the Canadian cause.

During his sojourn at Pembina McDougall was responsible for several blunders, but the most serious in its consequences was the determination, expressed in his letter to Howe " to assert and maintain by force . . . the authority of the new government." On December 1st, McDougall issued to Colonel Dennis a commission as " Lieutenant and Conservator of the Peace " authorizing him, in the Queen's name, to " raise, organize, arm, equip and provision, a sufficient force " to " attack, arrest, disarm, or disperse the . . . armed men so unlawfully assembled and disturbing the public peace ; and for that purpose, and with the force aforesaid, to assault, fire upon, pull down, or break into any fort, house, stronghold, or other place in which the said armed men may be found."[51]   Armed with this redoubtable commission and with the illegal proclamation referred to earlier, Dennis eluded the vigilance of the métis guards and made his way into the Settlement.   At Winnipeg he discussed the situation with two representative leaders of the party opposed to Riel and then proceeded to the Stone Fort, twenty miles below Fort Garry, which he made the headquarters of the counter-insurrectionary movement.   He then divided the colony into company districts, appointed volunteer drill instructors for each, and entrusted Major Boulton, a former member of his surveying party, with the task of enrolling volunteers.

The response fell far short of what Dennis or McDougall had hoped.   Although Henry Prince and the Saulteaux Indians in the neighbourhood of the Stone Fort turned out in full war paint, eager to fight the métis or anyone else, the white and half-breed settlers held back.   " You speak of enthusiasm," Dennis complained to Dr. Schultz, "I have not seen it yet with anybody but ' Prince's ' men."[52]   Boulton, while attempting to enlist recruits at the Scotch settlement of Kildonan, found that even they were beginning to question the validity of McDougall's proclamation ;   and one disgusted " loyalist " wrote to the expectant Lieutenant-Governor that "even among our English-speaking population, we have to contend with worse characters than the French half-breeds . . . The Scotch Settlement won't join us or any other Parish of the Protestant population, so that it would be the height of folly for us to take any aggressive steps."[53] As a last resort Dennis issued a " call " by virtue of his commission, to " all loyal men of the North-West Territories to assist me, by every means in their power . . . and thereby restore public peace and order, and uphold the supremacy of the Queen in this part of Her Majesty's Dominions."[54] This, however, proved of little value, and the next day Dennis was forced to admit that he had not sufficient men to relieve a small band of Canadians who had succeeded in precipitating hostilities with the métis at Winnipeg.

McDougall's appeal for armed support had been doomed to failure. The English-speaking inhabitants, as we have seen, had little in common with the Canadians, and both Dennis and Wallace had previously reported that they were opposed to the idea of a conflict with " those who have been born and brought up among us, ate with us, slept with us, hunted with us, traded with us, and are our own flesh and blood."[55] Moreover, the discord which had been apparent at the proceedings of the Convention became less pronounced, a fact which Dennis informed McDougall, " might probably be accounted for by the distribution through the parishes . . . of the French ' List of Rights.' It was stated, that, up to the time of the dissemination of this document, no one but themselves knew what the demands of the malcontents were ; and now that they had been published, some of them proving reasonable in their character . . . it might easily be conceived that the effect upon the rest of the people would be to make them less jealous of French domination, and more hopeful of seeing peace brought about by other means than by a resort to arms."[56] Hence, after a letter from Bishop Machray deprecating the use of force, Dennis issued a proclamation on December 9th, calling upon " the loyal party in the North-West Territory, to cease further action under the appeal to arms made by me,"[57] and rejoined McDougall at Pembina. Howe was genuinely alarmed at the report of Colonel Dennis' actions. He wrote to McDougall, "the proceedings of Colonel Dennis, as reported by himself, are so reckless and extraordinary, that there can be no relief from solicitude here while an officer so imprudent is acting under your authority."[58]   Although Dennis acted in perfect sincerity that his commission was legal, his actions were both illegal and unwise; illegal, because he had no lawful authority to resort to force, and unwise, because the only consequence of his attempt was the imprisonment in Fort Garry of a number of Canadians.

Dennis had found the Canadians, at least, eager to enlist. After enrolling at the Stone Fort they were sent back to Winnipeg, where the majority of them were living, with orders to remain quietly in their usual lodgings until further orders. " Their presence there in that way, having fully instructed them to avoid being any cause of offence to the French," wrote Dennis, " seemed to me could be no cause of irritation, and the knowledge that they were there, might tend to prevent any outrage on person or property of loyal people in the town."[59]   Unfortunately these orders were not strictly obeyed.   Instead of remaining at their lodgings, the Canadians at Winnipeg assembled at the storehouse of Dr. Schultz, where a considerable quantity of Canadian Government provisions, intended for the use of the road and survey parties, was stored.   Officers was elected, sentries posted, and all preparations made to withstand an attack.[60]   This move was ostensibly to protect the provisions and prevent them from falling into the hands of the insurgents; but it appeared to the half-breeds as the spearhead of attack against Riel when the occasion should be deemed opportune.   As soon as he learned of these hostile manifestations, Colonel Dennis wrote both to Boulton and to Schultz that the Canadians were to avoid any conflict with the métis and should retire to Kildonan.   They refused.   Boulton boldly replied to Dennis that " under the circumstances (that we have seventy men and sixty-five good arms on the premises), we have a strong position, and could resist successfully a strong attack."[61]

Under the circumstances this attitude was one of sheer bravado and absolute foolhardiness.   Fearing a sudden assault by the assembled Canadians, the French half-breeds poured into Fort Garry.   Bishop Machray assured Dennis on December 6th that Riel had " over six hundred men . . . in arms and . . . well armed."[62]   At the same time Riel appropriated provisions, guns and ball from the Hudson's Bay Company and " cleared all the

Stores of the merchants in the village of Winnipeg of all their guns and ammunition."[63]   Realizing the danger in which the small band of Canadians stood, far more than they apparently did themselves, Dennis wrote to Boulton repeating his orders of December 4th.   Riel, however, had posted his men about the warehouse and retreat was impossible.   The following day Snow went to Fort Garry on behalf of the besieged party and informed Riel that they had assembled only to protect themselves and their property and would retire quietly to their homes if allowed to do so.   A. G. B. Bannatyne and the Reverend George Young likewise tried to dissuade Riel from any act that might lead to bloodshed.   But Riel's men were impatient with keeping guard during the cold winter days and urged that the Canadians should be taken prisoners and confined in the Fort.[64]   Riel therefore demanded an unconditional surrender within fifteen minutes, offering only to secure their lives if they would comply.[65] There was no alternative save to fight, and Riel had posted two hundred men with cannon around the house.   Preferring to live to fight another day the Canadians accepted Riel's terms, and forty-five prisoners were marched between the files of Riel's nondescript soldiers to the cells of Fort Garry.

The next day, December 8th, Riel issued a grandiloquent " Declaration of the People of Rupert's Land and the North-West,"[66] declaring " that a people, when it has no Government, is free to adopt one form of Government, in preference to another, to give or to refuse allegiance to that which is proposed."   It continued further that the Hudson's Bay Company having abandoned the people, without their consent, to a " foreign power," the people were free to establish a Provisional Government " and hold it to be the only and lawful authority now in existence in Rupert's Land and the North-West, which claims the obedience and respect of the people " ; but, nevertheless, expressed the readiness of the new government " to enter into such negotiations with the Canadian Government as may be favourable for the good government and prosperity of this people."   Macdonald had feared that this would be the outcome when writing to McDougall on November 27th :[67]

" An assumption of the Government by you, of course, puts an end to that of the Hudson's Bay Company authorities. . . . There would then be, if you were not admitted into the country, no legal Government existing and anarchy must follow. In such a case . . . it is quite open by the Law of Nations for the inhabitants to form a Government *ex necessitate* for the protection of life and property, and such a Government has certain sovereign rights by the *jus gentium* which might be very convenient for the United States but exceedingly inconvenient for you. The temptation to an acknowledgment of such a Government by the United States, would be very great and ought not to be lightly risked."

Again, in a minute of the Privy Council,[68] he wrote :

" While the issue of the Proclamation would put an end to the Government of the Hudson's Bay Company, it would not substitute the Government by Canada, therefore such a Government is physically impossible until the armed resistance is ended ; and thus a state of anarchy and confusion would ensue, and a legal status might be given to any Government *de facto* formed by the inhabitants for the protection of their lives and property."

Although the law officers in Great Britain expressed the opinion " that the apprehensions of the Canadian Government are unfounded, and the insurgents or rioters (by which term they may be properly designated) will not be improved or strengthened by the transference of the territory from the Hudson's Bay Company to the Canadian Government,"[69] nevertheless it must be admitted that McDougall's ill-advised act in ending the Hudson's Bay Company government without being able to impose his own, gave a colour of justification, if not legality, to Riel's Provisional Government.

To celebrate the proclamation of the new government Riel hoisted, on December 10th, the flag of the Provisional Government, a fleur de lys and shamrock on a white back, and allowed his men for the first time " de trinquer en l'honneur du nouveau drapeau."[70] At the same time the *Nor'Wester* and its embryo successor, the *Red River Pioneer*, were suppressed, reappearing in January under the significant title of *The New Nation*, as the organ of the Provisional Government. On the 13th McDougall sent a letter to Riel suggesting an interview, but receiving no reply, he wrote once more to Mactavish informing him that " if, in consequence of the action of the Dominion Government, the surrender and transfer of the country did not take place on the first day of December, as previously agreed upon, then you are the Chief Executive officer as before, and responsible for the preservation of the Peace and enforcement of the Law. If, on the other hand, the Transfer *did* take place on the first day of December, then, I take it, my Commission came into force, and the notice, in the form of a Proclamation, issued by my authority on that day, correctly recited the facts, and disclosed the legal *status* of the respective parties."[71] On December 18th McDougall quitted the inhospitable village of Pembina and proceeded with his party to St. Paul.   In the Settlement Riel took the final steps to power.   On the 22nd he confiscated the money in possession of the Hudson's Bay Company at Fort Garry,[72] and five days later was elected to succeed John Bruce, who had resigned, as president.[73]

Thus, by the close of the year 1869, Louis Riel and the métis were, without striking a blow or shedding one drop of blood, complete masters of the Red River Settlement.   The Fort, with large supplies of ammunition, stores and money, was in their hands ; the English half-breeds were either indifferent or mildly sympathetic ; the Canadian appeal to arms had failed ; sixty-five political prisoners were in close confinement ; the Provisional Government had been proclaimed ; and the disappointed Lieutenant-Governor with his discomfited " Conservator of the Peace " was returning over the snows to Canada.

CHAPTER V

HAD the Imperial Government or the Dominion Government imitated the rash and reckless conduct of those claiming to represent the Queen's authority in Rupert's Land, civil war and bloodshed might have followed, and the Settlement would have become the prey of the warlike Indian tribes of the North-West. Fortunately calmer counsels prevailed both in London and in Ottawa. On learning by telegram of the fact of the outbreak, Lord Granville hastened to send the following reply to the Governor-General of Canada :

" 25 November 1869.
" Make what use you think best of the following :

" The Queen has heard with surprise and regret that certain misguided persons have banded together to oppose by force the entry of the future Lieutenant-Governor into Her Majesty's settlements on the Red River.

" Her Majesty does not distrust the loyalty of Her subjects in these settlements, and can only ascribe to misunderstanding or misrepresentation their opposition to a change which is plainly for their advantage.

" She relies on your Government for using every effort to explain whatever is misunderstood, to ascertain the wants and to conciliate the good will of the Red River settlers. But meantime She authorizes you to signify to them the sorrow and dis-pleasure with which she views their unreasonable and lawless proceedings, and her expectation that if any parties have desires to express, or complaints to make respecting their condition and prospects, they will address themselves to the Governor-General of the Dominion of Canada.

" The Queen expects from Her Representative that as he will always be ready to receive well founded grievances so he will exercise all the power and authority with which She has entrusted him, in the support of order and for the suppression of unlawful disturbance."[1]

This telegram was the basis of a Proclamation issued by Sir John Young on December 6th, which concluded with the words, " I do lastly inform you, that in case of your immediate and peaceable obedience and dispersion, I shall order that no legal proceedings be taken against any parties implicated in these unfortunate breaches of the law."[2]

As soon as the Canadian Government was informed of the resistance to the entry of the Honourable William McDougall, the Cabinet, " as a preliminary, decided upon sending up emissaries well known to, and personally liked by these French half-breeds, to confer with them, and, if possible, disabuse their minds of the erroneous impressions that have been made upon them."[3] Accordingly the Very Reverend Grand Vicar Thibault and Colonel de Salaberry were instructed to proceed to Red River with the Governor-General's Proclamation, to explain to the people the liberal intentions of the Canadian Government, and to remove the existing apprehensions of danger consequent upon the transition of the little colony into the Canadian Confederation. The choice of emissaries was one calculated to bring to a successful conclusion this " mission of peace and conciliation." The Grand Vicar had lived and laboured amongst the people of the North-West for more than thirty-six years. " He has much influence," wrote Young, " being greatly beloved, and holding a high position in the Roman Catholic Church."[4] Colonel de Salaberry was the son of the distinguished French Canadian officer who had repelled the American invaders at Châteauguay in 1813. He also had passed several years in the North-West Territory and was looked up to as a leader and a friend by the French half-breeds.

Unfortunately, the real nature of the trouble in Red River was misunderstood by the Canadian authorities. The half-breed rising was not merely a French ebullition, to be calmed by the presence and promises of two prominent French Canadians ; it was the rising of a small, primitive, native community against economic and racial absorption by an unfamiliar, aggressive civilization. The mission of peace was thus handicapped from the beginning. No authority was given the Commissioners to conclude any definite arrangements with the insurgents, conceding them the guarantees they demanded ; they were authorized merely to use their influence to persuade the métis to lay down arms. Yet Riel and his adherents were determined to accept no settlement which was not based upon negotiations and guaranteed by Parliament. It was unlikely, therefore, that success would attend the efforts of Thibault and de Salaberry.

At the same time a third Commissioner was chosen to follow the two French Canadians who had departed for the North-West. On November 24th, Donald A. Smith, the chief representative of the Hudson's Bay Company in Canada, offered to the Canadian Government, the loyal co-operation of all the officers of the service " to restore and maintain order throughout the territory."[5] At the request of George Stephen, afterwards Lord Mount Stephen, Sir John A. Macdonald consulted Smith, who suggested that a " Protestant, unconnected with office, and known to be an independent man of business, might be exceedingly useful " and intimated that Stephen might prove a suitable appointment as Commissioner.[6] Stephen, however, refused and Smith himself finally accepted Macdonald's offer to undertake the difficult mission to the North-West. Colonel Wolseley, then Deputy Quartermaster-General in Canada, expressed a desire to accompany Smith,[7] but Macdonald wisely saw that there was no place in a mission of peace for a military officer like Wolseley. " Smith goes to carry the olive branch," he wrote to his intimate friend Stephen, " and were it known at Red River that he was accompanied by an officer high in rank in military service, he would be looked upon as having the olive branch in one hand and a revolver in the other."[8] On December 10th the Secretary of State for the Provinces officially informed Smith that the Governor-General had been pleased to appoint him a " Special Commissioner, to inquire into and report upon the causes and extent of the armed obstruction offered at the Red River . . . to the peaceful ingress of the Hon. Wm. McDougall," and to " explain to the inhabitants the principles on which the Government of Canada intends to govern the country and to remove any misapprehensions that may exist on the subject. And also to take such steps, in concert with Mr. McDougall and Governor Mactavish, as may seem most proper for effecting the peaceable transfer of the country and the Government, from the Hudson's Bay authorities to the Government of the Dominion."[9] This commission, like that issued to Thibault and de Salaberry, did not give Smith authority to negotiate or to come to terms with the insurgents ; it only authorized him to probe the causes of the trouble, to explain away misapprehensions and to report upon the best mode of effecting the speedy transfer of the North-West to Canada.

The selection of Donald A. Smith as Commissioner was opportune. He was a man of personality, ability, and resource. Entering the service of the Hudson's Bay Company as a boy of seventeen he had made rapid strides, until, in 1868, he attained the position of the Company's Resident Governor in Montreal. This, however, was only the beginning of his career. Knighted in 1886 and elevated to the peerage in 1897, he was, from 1870, one of the most important figures in the public life of the Dominion of Canada. One biographer[10] has stated—albeit in prejudice—that so great was Smith's influence that Parliament, upon many occasions, without being aware of the fact, simply registered his decrees ! This was the man, with whose personality, courage, tact, and "invaluable knack of turning everything to account" Louis Riel, the métis leader, was to contend.

On December 24th, Thibault and de Salaberry arrived at Pembina, the border village lately quitted by the frustrated McDougall. Here they found the people full of distrust against all persons coming from Canada, "in fact, even against us," wrote Thibault, "notwithstanding that they had been for a long time aware of our entire devotion to the interests of the country."[11] At Fort Garry the hostility was so great that Mactavish doubted whether Thibault would be able to win any support among the métis. "I believe Bishop Taché alone has influence sufficient to detach the men from their present leaders," he wrote to the London Office, "and even he might fail."[12] In view of this fact, and acting upon the advice of Cameron and Provencher, it was decided that de Salaberry should remain at Pembina with the official papers while Father Thibault alone proceeded to the Settlement. Thibault was not, however, permitted to carry out his political mission in Red River, but was kept a virtual prisoner in the Bishop's house. As a result of the intervention of Dr. Tupper, who had gone to Fort Garry to escort his daughter back to Canada, Thibault was given his liberty, and he and Colonel de Salaberry were given an opportunity to represent the views of the Canadian Government to the disaffected leaders.[13] This interview took place on January 6th. A few days later Riel informed the Commissioners that "he was sorry to see that our papers gave us no authority to treat with them," but he appeared to hold out hopes of a satisfactory settlement.[14] Nevertheless the two Commissioners were not allowed to move freely among the people, nor were their official papers, including the Governor-General's Proclamation of December 6th, which had been entrusted to Riel, ever made public.

On December 27th, Donald A. Smith arrived by sleigh at Fort Garry. He was immediately taken before Riel and the insurgent Council who demanded the purport of his visit. Smith replied that he was connected with the Hudson's Bay Company, but mentioned also that he held a commission from the Canadian Government. He was then requested to take an oath to do nothing to undermine the " Government, legally established." This Smith peremptorily declined to do, but gave his word to do nothing to upset the Government " legal or illegal, as it might be," without first announcing his intention of so doing.[15] This was interpreted by some of the half-breeds as an official recognition by the Canadian Government, through their Commissioner, of the Provisional Government; but Smith's letter, written to Macdonald immediately after the event,[16] and his subsequent correspondence, leaves no doubt that he scrupulously avoided doing anything that might constitute a recognition of the legality of the insurgent government.

Once established in the colony, Smith turned his attention to the task of " effecting the peaceable transfer of the country." On January 6th he again interviewed Riel, but " came to the conclusion that no good could arise from entering into any negotiations with his ' Council,' even were we to admit their authority, which I was not prepared to do."[17] Accordingly he adopted the suggestion of Governor Mactavish of working quietly and individually among some of the less enthusiastic of Riel's supporters. In spite of the fact that he was kept a virtual prisoner in the Fort, Smith recorded that he " had frequent visits in the Fort from some of the most influential and most reliable men in the Settlement, who gladly made known to the people generally, the liberal intentions of the Canadian Government " ; and in 1874 he informed the Select Committee that he had spent £500 among the French métis " whose assistance had been absolutely necessary in my position as Canadian Commissioner in 1869 and 1870."[18] De Salaberry likewise made use of his opportunities to present a favourable picture of Canada's intentions, even going so far—if we may believe the American consul at Winnipeg—of trying to bribe Riel " by the offer of a considerable amount of money which was contemptuously refused."[19]   The result of this active campaign of promises and money, combined with a reaction against the pro-Yankee sentiments of the *New Nation*, was that " one after another of Riel's Councillors seceded from him " and were joined " by many of their compatriots and co-religionists who had throughout held aloof from the insurgents."[20]   Finding his position undermined by these defections, Riel abandoned his attitude of no compromise, and expressed his desire to see the credentials which the shrewd Commissioner had left with Provencher.   Refusing to give a written order for the papers, Smith sent his brother-in-law, Richard Hardisty, who had accompanied him on his mission, with one of Riel's men to bring the papers from Pembina.   It was believed that Riel intended to intercept the messengers at St. Norbert, but Mactavish, anticipating this move, sent several stalwart half-breeds to bring the papers straight to Smith.   At St. Norbert, Father Ritchot was pushed irreverently aside and told " not to interfere any further with matters unconnected with his spiritual duties,"[21] while one of Mactavish's men, Pierre Léveillé, threatened Riel with his pistol ! The final outcome of this manœuvre was that a mass meeting of the whole settlement was fixed for January 19th, at Fort Garry, at which Smith's commission and other official papers would be read publicly to the people of Red River.

It was a bold policy which Smith had adopted.   Owing to his and de Salaberry's intrigues " feeling is very high on both sides,"[22] and the convening of these conflicting elements might well have led to trouble.   A rash oration, a misunderstood word or allusion, a heated retort, or an imagined affront, might quickly have precipitated a conflict.   The possibilities of trouble were infinite.

The mass meetings of the 19th and 20th were, however, a complete vindication of Smith's policy.   Inside the walls of the old stone fort, in the small snow-covered square, with the temperature at twenty below zero, upwards of a thousand people gathered to hear what Canada had to offer them.   French métis, English half-breeds, and Scotch settlers, each with a common interest in the welfare of Red River Settlement, but differing in language, education and political outlook, stood for five hours in the biting wind and conducted their open air meeting with a respect for constitutional procedure surprising in a frontier community. On the motion of Louis Riel, seconded by Pierre Léveillé, Thomas Bunn, an English half-breed, was called to the chair,[23] and de Salaberry, although he had promised Smith to act as interpreter, nominated Riel for that position. Judge Black, the Recorder of Assiniboia, was appointed secretary. Donald A. Smith was then introduced and proceeded at once to read to the assembled multitude the official documents which had been entrusted to his care. This was not accomplished without some opposition, but " les mesures de précaution adoptées par le gouvernement provisoire réussirent à réprimer tous les désordres."[24] Smith carried his audience with him, and, in spite of an altercation which threatened trouble over the documents taken from Thibault and de Salaberry, the meeting adjourned until the next day.

At noon the following day a still larger assembly gathered at Fort Garry to hear the Commissioner complete the reading of his papers. Smith appeared to have won the confidence of his listeners and his assurances that his only object was to " contribute to bring about peaceably union and entire accord among all the classes of people of this land " was greeted with cheers. After the reading of the documents an adjournment of half an hour was proposed. Business being resumed, Louis Riel, seconded by A. G. B. Bannatyne, moved that twenty representatives should be elected by the English-speaking parishes to meet twenty representatives chosen by the French, " with the object of considering the subject of Mr. Smith's commission and to decide what would be best for the welfare of the country." The meeting was brought to a close with speeches by Father Ritchot, Bishop Machray, and Louis Riel. *The New Nation* reported the last as follows :

" Before this Assembly breaks up, I cannot but express my feelings, however briefly. I came here with fear. We are not yet enemies (loud cheers) but we came very near being so. As soon as we understood each other, we joined in demanding what our English fellow subjects in common with us believe to be our just rights (loud cheers). I am not afraid to say *our* rights, for we all have rights (renewed cheers). We claim no half rights, mind you, but all the rights we are entitled to. Those rights will be set forth by our representatives, and what is more, Gentlemen, we will get them (loud cheers)."[25]

The utmost good feeling existed among all classes. Caps were thrown into the air, cheers were given, and French and English shook hands over what was considered the happy auguries of a satisfactory settlement. " Les choses," wrote Thibault to Howe, " avaient l'air de prendre une bonne tournure . . . nous avons l'espoir de réussir . . . tout le peuple en général parait donner ses sympathies au Canada et finira certainment par se donner à lui s'il consent (le Canada) à lui faire des concessions."[26]

The new Convention met on January 25th pursuant to the resolution adopted at the mass meeting. The next day the delegates proceeded to business. Riel, seconded by John Sutherland, nominated Judge Black as chairman, W. Coldwell and Louis Schmidt were chosen as secretaries, and Louis Riel and James Ross as interpreters. The meetings were conducted behind closed doors at the request of the English, only the reporter for The New Nation and the clergy being present in addition to the delegates. The presence of the clergy was significant, for there is little doubt that they were anxious for " un arrangement prompt avec le Canada."[27] During the course of the discussion on Smith's papers, Riel moved that the Canadian Commissioner " be requested to come before the Convention . . . in order to say what he can do for us . . . and what according to the best of his judgement ought to be done under present circumstances to secure us our rights." Smith was " received with much cordiality " and " gave assurances that on entering confederation, they would be secured in the possession of all rights, privileges, and immunities enjoyed by British subjects in other parts of the Dominion."[28] Riel raised the question of the " Bill of Rights " drawn up by the first Convention in November, but it was decided, amidst the customary cheers, to nominate a committee to draw up a new list of " rights " to be presented to Commissioner Smith. Louis Riel, Louis Schmidt, Charles Nolin, James Ross, Thomas Bunn and Dr. Bird, all of whom were natives of the country, were selected for the task.

The committee worked almost continuously for forty-eight hours and on January 29th presented a draft " List of Rights," based to a certain extent, probably, upon a number of suggestions which Father Lestanc had forwarded to Riel on the 26th.[29] This list was thoroughly discussed and amended by the Convention. On February 4th Riel made the startling proposal that the colony should enter Confederation, not as a territory, but as a province. He had discussed the question with Smith on the previous day, but the latter had held out little hope of the realization of this demand for several years. This was what Riel feared, for it was openly avowed that, by that time, the country would be flooded with Canadians and the native element swamped. " These impulsive half-breeds have got spoiled by this *émeute*," wrote Sir John Macdonald, "and must be kept down by a strong hand until they are swamped by the influx of settlers."[30]   It had been to forestall this very contingency that Riel first organized the métis resistance and the same motive lay behind his demand for provincial status.   As a province the half-breeds would be able to erect the legislative safeguards necessary to protect their rights and those of the Church against the time when they would be in the minority.   The Convention debated the question but Riel's motion was lost by twenty-four votes to fifteen.

Riel suffered another reverse when he moved " that all bargains with the Hudson's Bay Company, for the transfer of this Territory, be considered null and void ; and that any arrangements, with reference to the transfer of this country, shall be carried on only with the people of this country."   Three of the French representatives voted with the English against the motion.   Riel, who could seldom brook opposition, strode the Council Chamber and shouted with animation, " The devil take it ; we must win. The vote may go as it likes ; but the measure which has now been defeated must be carried.   It is a shame to have lost it ; and it was a greater shame, because it was lost by those traitors."   Hot words flew across the floor, but order was finally restored.   Riel, however, went to see Dr. Cowan and Governor Mactavish, and threatened to have them both shot within three hours if they did not order the immediate departure from Fort Garry of ten French half-breeds who belonged to the party opposed to Riel, the head of which, Pierre Léveillé, Riel asserted, was being kept there in the Company's pay.[31]   At the same time he demanded that Mactavish and Cowan should take the oath of allegiance to the Provisional Government, and, upon their refusal, placed the former under guard and confined the latter in prison with the Canadians taken in December.[32]

In spite of Riel's display of violence, the delegates met again on February 7th.   Colonel de Salaberry, Father Thibault and

Donald A. Smith were invited to be present, Smith to express his opinion upon the " List of Rights." Riel tried to force Smith to admit that his commission did not give him the authority to guarantee a single article on the list, but the Commissioner adroitly covered this weakness by pointing out that Parliament, in any event, must have the final say. In the end his answers were considered satisfactory by the majority of the delegates, and entire confidence was expressed in Canada. Smith then brought his mission to a close by extending, on behalf of the Canadian Government, an invitation to the Convention to send " a delegation of the residents of Red River, to meet and confer with them at Ottawa . . . to explain the wants and wishes of the Red River people, as well as to discuss and arrange for the representation of the country in Parliament." This invitation was received with cheers, and James Ross, seconded by Louis Riel, moved that " as the Canadian Commissioners have invited a delegation from this country to Canada, to confer with the Canadian Government, as to the affairs of this country ; and as a cordial reception has been promised to said delegates, be it therefore resolved that the invitation be accepted, and that the same be signified to the Commissioners."[33]

Smith's mission was thus brought to an end. He had succeeded where Thibault and de Salaberry had failed. He had acquainted the people with Canada's favourable disposition towards them, and implanted a new feeling of unity and accord in Assiniboia. But this very success played into Riel's hand. From the beginning of the outbreak Riel had aimed at securing a united front of the different racial elements in the colony and the co-operation of the French and English-speaking people in a Provisional Government, which should treat with Canada the terms upon which they would enter the Canadian Confederation. Hitherto he had been unable to find a workable basis for united action, and was, accordingly, not slow to take advantage of that union which Smith had diplomatically brought about. Riel's first success had been the drafting of the " List of Rights " by the Convention ; his second, and more important, was the formation of the Second Provisional Government with the approval and support of the English speaking half-breeds and white settlers.

The Provisional Government was Riel's *idée maîtresse*. He had established one in December upon his own initiative, but, during the sitting of the Convention, its authority appears to have lapsed, and on February 8th Riel raised the question of forming another upon the broader basis of popular approval. To the delegates he declared :

" We have arrived at the point, or very near it, where we must consider the nature of the Convention, notwithstanding our differences of opinion we have been friendly to this point. But we are yet in a loose, unsatisfactory way. It is now necessary for us to place ourselves in a more suitable position. We must have a more fixed existence before proceeding much further. Unquestionably our position can be improved by drawing closer together than at present ; and it is equally unquestionable that we ought to be bound together by bonds of friendship and self-interest. Union is strength. United we command a hearing from Canada, where our rights are to come from, which we can command no other way (cheers). It is also to be borne in mind that a feeling of insecurity reigns in the minds of people which can be successfully combated in no other way than by a union. This feeling of insecurity, I need hardly say, is unsatisfactory, and all the more so, when it is in our power to remove it. Here is a large Convention of representatives, able, honest and good men, the choice of their people, men who are needed at a crisis like this. Here we have the elements from which the people look for something good. Why not throw them into a shape in which we can act effectually, and work in a more satisfactory manner ? We must recognize the fact that perhaps in pushing opinion too far, we may go a long way to repeal the work we have done. We have worked carefully and wisely, and consequently believe we have done a good work. Let us not spoil it by pressing our peculiar opinions too far. For myself, I feel the last four months' work to be a good one, and to be consistent, I feel called on to work to the end for the interests of the people. Still the Convention must not for the moment imagine that there is any disposition on our part to disown, or not to acknowledge others, in wishing to maintain what has been accomplished. If matters had been pushed to the extreme there would in all possibility have been something disastrous before now. But there has been a spirit of moderation and friendship under all this earnest working to secure the rights of the people. One of these days, then, manifestly we have to form a Government in order to secure the safety of life and property, and establish a feeling of security in men's minds, and remove a feeling of apprehension which it is not desirable should continue for a moment. How often have we not, on our side, expressed a fear as to the security of property and life. It is our duty to put an end to this, and it will be our glory as well as our duty. As for the past, it can never be admitted that a proceeding which has saved the country is a thing to be despised. The result shows it to be a meritorious and a good thing. Should this Convention separate without coming to an understanding, we leave matters worse than ever ; we leave a gap in which all our people may be engulfed and in the angry waves of the flood which might sweep over the Settlement we may find reason for regret, that a wiser course had not been adopted when it lay in our power."[34]

The question was now fairly before the Convention. Discussion followed. Riel and O'Donoghue urged that the Provisional Government was an established fact and should be recognized. The English delegates, however, remained as reluctant as upon the previous occasion in December, to form a Government opposed to the Hudson's Bay Company or the Council of Assiniboia whom they still regarded as the legal rulers of the country ; others considered that their powers as delegates did not extend to the recognition or formation of a Provisional Government. Finally, Sutherland and Fraser, two of the English-speaking delegates, accompanied by Lépine and Pagée, went to consult Governor Mactavish upon the question. When asked his opinion as to the advisability of forming a Provisional Government Mactavish replied, " Form a Government for God's sake, and restore peace and order in the Settlement."[35] Thus reassured, the English and Scotch no longer hesitated. On the following day, Fraser, seconded by Donald Gunn, moved that " the Committee previously appointed to draw up the List of Rights, be reappointed to discuss and decide on the basis and details of the Provisional Government which we have agreed is to be formed for Rupert's Land and the North-West Territory."[36] At the evening session, the same day, the Committee handed in a draft resolution outlining the details of the proposed Provisional Government. After a considerable discussion, during which Riel gave several displays of temper, Ross moved the adoption of the draft resolution or report sent down by the Committee, which was seconded by Charles Nolin. Xavier Pagée then moved in amendment that the name of Mr. Riel be added to the report as President of the Provisional Government. Neither of these motions appear to have been put to a vote. Finally, combining the two, Pagée, seconded by P. Thibert, another métis, moved that the report of the committee be adopted and that the name of Mr. Riel be included as president. The English, now committed to the principle of a Provisional Government, were unwilling to oppose Pagée's motion merely to spite Riel, and the motion was carried without a dissenting voice. Judge Black, Mr. Boyd, and Mr. Cummings did not vote.[37] The final item of business was the nomination of the following delegates to proceed to Canada in accordance with the invitation extended by Donald A. Smith ; Reverend Father Ritchot, Judge Black and A. H. Scott.

Riel's star had now reached its zenith. The people were united, the Provisional Government established and recognized by the French and English half-breeds and the white settlers, and Riel's vanity satisfied by his election as president. The prospects for an early and a peaceful settlement were bright. Thibault wrote to Langevin, " J'ai le plaisir de vous annoncer aujourd'hui que les affaires prennent une bonne tournure et que sous peu nous pouvons soumettre à l'examen du Gouvernement du Canada, les conditions auxquelles les habitants du pays consentiront à entrer dans la Confédération."[38] Unfortunately, however, an event occurred which brought discord to the Settlement, discredit to the Provisional Government and disrepute to Louis Riel.

It will be remembered that Riel had imprisoned, in December, some sixty or more Canadians, as a result of Dennis' " call to arms." Several of these had been released early in January, after promising either to quit the country or to take the oath of allegiance to the Provisional Government. A few days later several more escaped, including Charles Mair and Thomas Scott, an Irish Canadian who was to play so prominent and so sad a part in later events. Encouraged by this success, Dr. Schultz, the leader of the prisoners, determined to effect his escape. A knife and a gimlet concealed in a pudding, by his wife, provided him with the necessary tools, and on the night of the 23rd he let himself out of his window and dropped to the ground. Although injured by the fall, he made his way to the house of Robert MacBeth at Kildonan, where he was sheltered for several days from the prying eyes of Riel's guards.[39]

Meanwhile the other prisoners were detained at the Fort. A

suggestion was made by one of the settlers at the mass meeting on January 20th that the prisoners should be released, but Riel had summarily refused, and the matter was not pressed.[40] However, after the acceptance of the Provisional Government by the English-speaking inhabitants, all reason for the detention of the prisoners had passed away, and on February 10th Riel gave a categorical statement to the Convention " that all the prisoners are to be released. . . . A few will have to leave the country as men considered dangerous to the public peace . . . in respect to Dr. Schultz the position is this, he is exiled for ever and if found in the country is liable to be shot."[41]   On February 12th sixteen of the prisoners were released in accordance with this promise and the remainder would have unquestionably been released had not events taken an unexpected turn.

On February 10th, Riel mentioned in the Convention " I have heard a rumour as to armed men gathering in the Lower Settlement. I do not believe it."[42] These rumours were, unfortunately, true.   The Canadian Party, with their predilection for trouble, were at work again, this time in Portage la Prairie.   The settlement at the Portage was situated on the banks of the Assiniboine, about sixty miles from Fort Garry, and was thus beyond the jurisdiction of the government of Red River.   It had been settled largely by immigrants from Ontario and was, therefore, English by tongue and Canadian by sympathy.   It was natural that Portage should become the haven of refuge for the Canadian Party after the outbreak of the insurrection.   Here the prisoners who had made good their escape from Riel received a warm welcome from their former associates and friends, and here, in spite of the fiasco of the previous call to arms, the Canadians began to discuss the possibility of organizing an armed force to effect the release of the remaining prisoners.   Major Boulton, who had been Dennis' chief assistant in December, claims that he endeavoured to dissuade the Canadians from any hostile action " knowing that commissioners had been appointed by the Canadian Government on a mission of peace " ;[43] but the enthusiasm over Scott's bold escape and the indignation at his sufferings, were such that Boulton could no longer restrain them, and, feeling it his duty " to keep them to the legitimate object for which they had organized," he consented to act as the leader of a force of " Liberators."

On February 12th, the Portage party, numbering about sixty, and indifferently armed with rifles and clubs, set off from Portage la Prairie. At Headingly they were met by their delegate to the Convention, Kenneth Mackenzie, who informed them that the prisoners were about to be released, and strongly advised them to turn back.[44] Notwithstanding this sound advice the Portage party decided to continue, and after making certain that Major Boulton "meant fight," emissaries were sent to the English-speaking settlements below Fort Garry to inform them of the counter-insurrection. Here Dr. Schultz had been endeavouring to stir up the people and when the Portage party arrived at Kildonan they were joined by a force of several hundred settlers and Indians led by the redoubtable Doctor.

The promised gaol-delivery had been slow, owing to the reluctance of some of the prisoners to take the oath of obedience to the Provisional Government, but by the 15th the last prisoner had been released. Several writers have declared that this release was the result of negotiations between Schultz's force and Riel.[45] It may have been that the presence of the hostile force hastened the release of the prisoners, but it was not until the next day, the 16th, that John Norquay arrived with a list of demands from the counter-insurrectionaries. Their demands included the release of the prisoners, a general amnesty for all, including Dr. Schultz : at the same time they announced the refusal of several of the English-speaking parishes to recognize the Provisional Government. Riel replied by the same messenger :

" Gentlemen,
" The prisoners are out, they have sworn to keep the peace. We have taken the responsibility of our past acts. Mr. William Mactavish has asked you, for the sake of God, to form and complete the Provisional Government. Your representatives have joined us on that ground. Who will now come and destroy Red River Settlement ?

" I am,
" Your humble, poor, fair, and confident public servant,
Louis Riel."[46]

This message cooled the bellicose ardour of the English, the majority of whom were only half-hearted in their opposition and had joined the expedition merely to effect the release of the prisoners. The Canadians, however, led by Schultz, urged that they should attack the fort and overthrow Riel.[47]   Fortunately wiser counsels prevailed.   Bishop Machray and other clergymen informed them, unpalatable though it was, that they were no match for Riel, who had five hundred men under his command, and that any operation against the Fort could only result in disaster.[48]   One disgusted " loyalist," not appreciating the wisdom of this advice, complained bitterly to the *Globe* that " this settlement is as completely priest-ridden as ever unfortunate Ireland was," and had " the Reverend Quartette quietly studied their sermons, or in their closets offered a prayer for our success instead of going through our ranks discouraging our men " the counter-insurrection might have been a success.[49]   Lacking the inclination to indulge in fratricidal strife the men departed to their homes and the hostile demonstration collapsed.   The Portage Canadians, in view of the fact that their road led past Fort Garry, were advised not to proceed home in a body by the usual route; nevertheless a large number set off on February 17th.

In the face of danger the French half-breeds immediately concentrated their forces and every preparation was made to withstand an attack upon the Fort.   The *New Nation* facetiously describes their activity :

" the women and children were translated to a more peaceful region, and the men prepared for the coming engagement. Shops were shut.   Six-shooters looked up, and preparations made for a general barricade.   Mr. O'Donoghue and his men busied themselves taking the arms in town and exploring for powder.   Mr. Bannatyne's magazine was unroofed, as he refused to give up the keys, and such a clean sweep made of its contents, that not a solitary keg was left to the disgusted proprietor. . . . Men were gathering in hot haste.   Cannons mounted, grape and cannister laid in order.   Five hundred men and more, we are informed, were told off to man the bastions, ramparts, etc.   Shot and shell were piled around promiscuously.   Everything that could be done was done to make a bold stand and strike terror into the hearts of les Anglais."[50]

The war fever mounted and when the little Portage party were seen pushing their way through the heavy snowdrifts outside the Fort, a band of horsemen led by O'Donoghue and Lépine, followed by about fifty men on foot, plunged through the snow to intercept them.   Everyone expected a fight.   Major Boulton, however, ordered his men not to provoke hostilities, and they were, accordingly, taken to the Fort and thrust into the prison rooms so lately vacated by the first group of prisoners. Boulton was placed in irons and later informed that he was to be executed at twelve o'clock on the morrow.[51]

This counter movement was both futile and ill-advised. For more than three weeks the English and French of Red River had striven to promote unity and friendship in the Settlement; but scarcely was this achieved when the whole edifice of peace was imperilled by the actions of a few political firebrands. The movement did not originate with the English half-breeds or with the Selkirk settlers; it was arranged and carried through largely by the Canadian Party and the members of Colonel Dennis' surveying party who had remained behind at the Portage when the " Conservator of the Peace " accompanied McDougall back to Canada. Smith wrote in his Report that the movement was " discountenanced " by the majority of the settlers, who " bitterly complained of those who had set it on foot," and Sir John A. Macdonald did not hesitate to stamp the expedition as both " foolish " and " criminal."[52] The immediate results were deplorable. Two men were killed at Kildonan as the result of a misunderstanding, forty-eight were imprisoned, and their leader was placed under sentence of death : all the arrangements for negotiation with Canada were jeopardized, and the mission of the delegates indefinitely postponed. To make matters worse, Louis Riel, who had now the opportunity to show his statesmanship in reuniting the colony, committed the greatest blunder of his career.

Two alternatives presented themselves to Riel, conciliation or coercion. He chose the latter. Exasperated at the ever-recurring hostility and lack of good faith towards the government which he regarded as legitimate—and which, as we have seen, had been recognized by the representatives of both English and French-speaking parishes—Riel felt there could be no peace until the malcontents were convinced of the determination and power of the Provisional Government to defend itself from seditious attacks. This was Riel's motive in imprisoning the Portage party and condemning Boulton. Riel informed Smith that he " bitterly . . . deplored the necessity " of the action, but that the Canadians " had laughed at and despised the French half-breeds, believing that they would not dare to take the life of anyone, and that, under these circumstances, it would be impossible to have peace and establish order in the country ; an example must therefore be made, and he had firmly resolved that Boulton's execution should be carried out."[53]   At the earnest entreaty of Bishop Machray, Archdeacon McLean, Père Lestanc and other people of influence, the execution was delayed for a day.   In the meantime Smith reasoned " long and earnestly " with Riel until the latter finally yielded, and " apparently with much feeling " asked Smith to use his influence to reunite the Settlement and to persuade the English to rejoin the French in demanding their rights.   Smith agreed to visit the English parishes to persuade them to elect their representatives to the Assembly of the Provisional Government.   Riel then, not only spared Boulton's life, but even invited him to join the Provisional Government as the leader of the Canadian party![54]

Among the Portage prisoners was a young Irish Canadian to whom we have referred previously, Thomas Scott.   Physically, Scott was strong and sinewy, and by temperament, self-willed and " indisposed . . . to be trodden upon."[55]   Coming to Red River as a road worker he soon quarrelled with his employer, Snow, over a matter of wages, and when Snow refused to pay him for time lost during a strike, Scott and several others " dragged me," wrote Snow, " violently from the house towards the River Seine, in which they declared they would drown me unless I payed their unjust demand."[56]   The sum was paid under protest, and Snow laid a charge of robbery against the men—a charge which was subsequently changed to one of violent assault.[57]   A Canadian and an Orangeman, Scott incurred the enmity of the métis " by associating with the agitators Schultz and Company,"[58] and was made prisoner on December 6th, " comme l'un des plus dangereux partisans du Dr. Schultz, de McDougall, et de Dennis."[59]   He escaped with the others on the night of January 9th, and made his way to Portage la Prairie, where he helped stir up the people to the disastrous expedition of February.   Passing Winnipeg with the Portage expedition of the night of the 13th–14th, Scott entered the house of one Coutu, a cousin of Riel, where the latter was accustomed to stay, and demanded to know if the President were there, " with the intention, according to some, of killing him, or according to others of seizing him as a hostage."[60]   Taken prisoner a second time, it is said that he violently attacked his guards, incited his companions to do likewise and threatened the life of Riel if he ever escaped.[61]   Indeed his alleged insolence and aggressiveness were such that it was difficult to restrain the guards.[62]   Riel visited Scott and entreated him to be peaceful under pain of punishment ; but Scott, no more willing to temporize than his captor, and never believing that the métis would dare to go to extremities, took little heed.

Finally, on March 3rd, Scott was brought before a Council of War composed of seven French half-breeds, presided over by " Adjutant-General " Ambroise Lépine, and charged with " d'avoir pris les armes contre le Gouvernement Provisoire et frappé l'un des capitaines des gardes."[63]   Three witnesses, Riel, Joseph Delorme and Edward Turner, were examined ; but Scott, although given an opportunity to answer " quelque chose . . . pour se justifier " was not, apparently, allowed to call witnesses in rebuttal.   The question of his guilt, when put before the Council, was carried by a majority vote.

" Janvier Ritchot proposa, secondé par André Nault la condamnation à la peine de mort, et Elzéar Goulet et Joseph Delorme votèrent avec le moteur et le secondeur de cette motion.   Mais Lagemonière déclara que le Gouvernement Provisoire avait bien existé jusque là sans effusion de sang, et qu'il valait mieux ne pas recourir à de pareilles mesures.   En s'inscrivant contre cette condamnation il suggéra l'exil.   J. Bte Lépine vota également contre la motion. . . . Ambroise Lépine présidait le Conseil et ne parla ni dans un sens ni dans l'autre.   Seulement, lorsque le vote eut été pris, il dit : Puisque la majorité se rallie à la proposition, Scott sera executé."

When it became known that Scott was to be shot, the Reverend George Young, D. A. Smith, Père Lestanc and others pleaded with Riel for Scott's life ; but to no avail.   At twelve o'clock on March 4th, Scott, after bidding farewell to his companions, was conducted outside the Fort, and in the presence of some one hundred and fifty to two hundred people, knelt before the firing squad.   The first discharge did not kill the unfortunate man, and one of the firing squad discharged his revolver at the sufferer as he lay upon the ground.

What was the motive for this cruel act of bloodshed ?   The charges brought against Scott, namely, that he was guilty of disorderly conduct in the autumn, had twice been involved in hostilities against the Provisional Government, had been abusive to his guards and incited the prisoners to insubordination, were hardly offences that demanded the death penalty.   That two of the French half-breed members of the Council of War voted against the death penalty emphasized this fact.   The charges supply only the excuse, not the reason.   Scott's death was a deliberate act of policy.   To Donald A. Smith, Riel said " we must make Canada respect us."[64]   Riel was convinced that unless the Provisional Government struck fear into the hearts of those likely to attack this government, peace would be impossible.   To Riel the question was not one of legality but one of political expediency ; " Les complications des affaires politiques de la Rivière Rouge rendirent sa mort inévitable."[65]   It is, moreover, undeniable that the immediate object of his policy was attained, and that the settlement from a state of extreme excitement, suddenly seemed to have dropped into one of thorough tranquillity.   The English and Scotch half-breeds, and even the white settlers, continued to co-operate with Riel and the Provisional Government.   Indeed, only five days after the execution, W. Garrioch, the representative of Portage la Prairie, whence the rising that had indirectly led to the death of Scott had emanated, stated in the Assembly of the Provisional Government " Except in one instance, we have done our utmost to keep the peace.   We feel that we are in duty bound to come under the Provisional Government, and are now on perfectly good terms with all the people of Red River."[66]

Nevertheless the execution of Scott cannot be condoned. Speaking of the assassination of the Duc d'Enghien by Napoleon in 1804, Talleyrand is reputed to have said, " C'est plus qu'une crime, c'est une sottise."   The execution of Scott was both. There can be no doubt that Riel and the French métis had higher motives than mere vindictiveness, but it was a grave error to have recourse to a form of punishment used only as a last resort in civilized communities.   The rebellion had been almost bloodless, but this regrettable event aroused those latent racial and religious passions which have been so deplorable a feature of Canadian history, and left bitter memories that were not soon forgotten.

CHAPTER VI

W HILE these events were taking place, Bishop Taché was hurrying home from Rome whither he had gone in October, 1869, to attend the Oecumenical Council. Alexandre Antonin Taché, the first Archbishop of St. Boniface, was one of the outstanding men of the North-West, as a missionary, author and scholar. Born in Quebec in 1823, he felt himself called, like many of his compatriots, to the service of the Roman Catholic Church, and in 1844 he began his noviciate in the Order of the Oblates of Mary Immaculate. One year later he began his mission work in the West under Bishop Provencher, whom he succeeded as Bishop on the latter's death in 1853. By his long residence in the North-West and by his devotion to the welfare of the people, Taché acquired an almost unbounded influence over the métis : it was to be regretted that the Canadian Government did not take advantage of this to facilitate the peaceful transfer of the Hudson's Bay Company Territories to Canada. Unfortunately, not only were Taché's warnings disregarded, but the prelate himself was in Rome when the troubles broke out.

Before leaving Canada, Taché had promised, in spite of the snub received from Sir George Cartier,[1] that he would return should the Government consider his services necessary.[2] At Paris he heard the first news of the troubles in his diocese, and at Rome the critical proportions which they had attained. On Christmas day Taché was informed that his presence would probably be required at Ottawa, and a few days later a positive request to this effect was made through Bishop Langevin. Taché was reluctant to return, in view of his earlier treatment at the hands of the Canadian Government and " l'immense consolation que je goûte au Concile,"[3] but, putting personal considerations to one side, he replied by telegram to Sir Hector Langevin that, at the request of the Government, he would leave for Canada as soon as possible.[4] Having secured Papal permission to absent himself from the Council, Taché left Rome on January

13th. En route he stopped in England where he had an interview with Sir Stafford Northcote, to whom he stated that he " went down to Canada last autumn especially to confer with the Canadian Government on the approaching change, but that his remarks and advice met with little response on their part—in fact they ridiculed him, and said that he had been bought by the Hudson's Bay Company," but declared that while " he had heard that the Rev. Mr. Ritchot was reported to be supporting the half-breeds . . . as regards himself no efforts would be wanting on his part to support order and use his influence with others to that effect."[5]

At Portland, where he arrived on February 2nd, he received a letter from Cartier conveying the thanks of the Canadian Government and requesting him to come at once to the capital. On Taché's arrival Cartier frankly admitted the Government's previous errors and introduced Taché to the leading members of the administration with whom interviews and conversations were held. The question of an Imperial Commission to the North-West was discussed but discarded,[6] and Taché himself, having been taken fully and unreservedly into the Government's confidence, undertook the mission. Armed with the Proclamation of December 6th, with letters from Sir John Young, Sir John A. Macdonald and Joseph Howe,[7] and with the promise of a general amnesty, Bishop Taché set out for the North-West.

The prelate's arrival was eagerly awaited in the Settlement. Critical days were at hand. On February 26th Smith reported that he was expected at any moment,[8] but, unfortunately, it was not until March 9th, five days after the regrettable shooting of Scott, that Taché reached the scene of the insurrection. Riel was suspicious of the Bishop's intentions : " Ce n'est pas Mgr. Taché qui passe, ce n'est pas l'Evêque de Saint Boniface, c'est le Canada qui passe."[9] Thus, while Taché was free to come and go as he pleased, a guard was placed at his door.[10] On the 11th the Bishop made his first report to the Canadian Government. In a long letter to Howe he analysed the whole situation and explained the antagonism of the métis to Canada.[11] Taché was fully aware of the fear of racial and economic absorption underlying the rising and he suggested that it might be wise to delay immigration for the time being. He also announced the prospective departure of the North-West delegates and begged the Canadian Government " to do justice to their demands."

The temper of the people at Red River seems to have been comparatively quiet when Taché arrived in the Settlement. It is true that Taché later declared that he had found matters much worse than either he or the Canadian Government had anticipated, but he appears to have been unduly alarmed. Contemporary evidence shows that the execution of Scott was followed, not by a storm, but by a calm. The American Consul in his despatches to the State Department made no reference to the Scott affair, and was apparently sufficiently impressed by the Government's determination to assert its authority to inquire " whether in my official intercourse with the officers of the so-called Provisional Government I shall recognize them as *de facto* officers or not."[12] Riel's speech on March 9th to the partially gathered Assembly was marked by conciliation and moderation. He made an earnest plea for mutual concession and unity : " If we were so united—as was said long ago—the people of the Red River could make their own terms with Canada."[13]   The half-breed secretary, Louis Schmidt, declared that Taché was merely preaching to converts.[14]   There was a complete absence of political tension in the columns of the *New Nation* which, on the 11th, stated that " the departure of the delegates for Ottawa, which was to have taken place last week, was deferred until the arrival of His Lordship, Bishop Taché, in the expectation of some additional powers for the adjustment of political matters having been delegated to him.   Thus far, nothing has occurred which justified the belief that further delay is necessary and so the delegates will take their departure early in the ensuing week."[15]

Although the situation was not so critical as has been supposed, Taché's beneficent influence was bound to make itself felt.   The excitement in the colony gradually disappeared, and gave place to calmer judgment in dealing with the troubles of the country. On March 11th the Bishop interviewed Riel, Lépine, O'Donoghue and others, and explained that the Canadian Government was favourably disposed towards the people of Red River, and that he was the bearer of a Proclamation from the Governor-General. This appeared to produce a favourable impression, and the leaders of the Provisional Government protested " that they had never intended to rise against the Crown, that their sole intention was to come to an understanding with the Canadian authorities

E

previous to joining Confederation."[16]   On the following day
Taché preached " an eloquent sermon " on " the state of affairs
in the country," urging " moderation and union amongst the
people " and promising that " Canada was prepared to grant
them everything that was right."[17]   Two days later a special
meeting of the newly-elected " Legislative Assembly " was
summoned to hear what the Bishop, in his capacity as Commissioner, had to say.   He pointed out that Canada was expecting
a delegation from the North-West, and quoted Macdonald's
words that " in case a delegation is appointed to proceed to
Ottawa, you can assure them that they will be kindly received,
and their suggestions fully considered.   Their expenses, coming
here and returning, and whilst staying in Ottawa, will be defrayed
by us."[18]   Taché also read a telegram, which he had received
from Joseph Howe, in which the latter described the " List of
Rights " promulgated by the Convention as " Propositions in the
main satisfactory ; but let the delegation come here to settle the
details."[19]   The happy conclusion was the unanimous decision to
send the delegates who had been nominated for the mission, and
the release, upon Bishop Taché's request, of the Portage prisoners.[20]

The delegates, however, did not depart immediately.   Judge
Black had informed Riel, as early as February 16th that " the
obstacles being considered insurmountable, he is under the
necessity of declining to accept the office of Delegate to Canada."[21]
Ritchot, likewise, was reluctant to serve, and it was only after
Taché's " repeated entreaties in private conversations with those
gentlemen "that they finally agreed " to accept the delicate mission
that had been offered them more than a month before."[22]   The
question of credentials and instructions now arose.   The " List
of Rights " approved by the Convention in February was
considered unsatisfactory as a final basis of negotiation with
Canada.   Riel had never given up the idea of provincial status
and Taché himself was said " to incline to the erection by the
people of a *provincial* government."[23]   Accordingly the Executive
of the Provisional Government, assisted, no doubt, by the Bishop,
drew up the following " List of Rights " which was printed,
both in English and in French, and given to the delegates on
March 22nd.

" 1. That the Territories, heretofore known as Rupert's Land
and North-West, shall not enter into the Confederation of the

Dominion of Canada, except as a Province, to be styled and known as the Province of Assiniboia, and with all the rights and privileges common to the different Provinces of the Dominion.

" 2. That we have two Representatives in the Senate, and four in the House of Commons of Canada, until such time as an increase of population entitle the Province to a greater representation.

" 3. That the Province of Assiniboia shall not be held liable, at any time, for any portion of the public debt of the Dominion contracted before the date the said Province shall have entered the Confederation, unless the said Province shall have first received from the Dominion the full amount for which the said Province is to be held liable.

" 4. That the sum of eighty thousand dollars ($80,000) be paid annually by the Dominion Government to the Local Legislature of this Province.

" 5. That all properties, rights and privileges enjoyed by the people of this Province, up to the date of our entering into the Confederation, be respected, and that the arrangement and confirmation of all customs, usages, and privileges be left exclusively to the Local Legislature.

" 6. That during the term of five years, the Province of Assiniboia shall not be subjected to any direct taxation except such as may be imposed by the Local Legislature for municipal or local purposes.

" 7. That a sum of money equal to eighty cents per head of the population of this Province be paid annually by the Canadian Government to the Local Legislature of the said Province, until such time as the said population shall have increased to six hundred thousand (600,000).

" 8. That the Local Legislature shall have the right to determine the qualifications of members to represent this Province in the Parliament of Canada, and the Local Legislature.

" 9. That, in this Province, with the exception of uncivilized and unsettled Indians, every male native citizen who has attained the age of twenty-one years, and every foreigner, being a British subject, who has attained the same age, and has resided three years in the Province, and is a householder ; and every foreigner other than a British subject who has resided here during the same period, being a householder, and having taken the oath of allegiance, shall be entitled to vote at the election of members for the Local Legislature and for the Canadian Parliament. It being understood that this Article be subject to amendment exclusively by the Local Legislature.

" 10. That the bargain of the Hudson's Bay Company with respect to the transfer of the Government of this country to the Dominion of Canada be annulled, so far as it interferes with the rights of the people of Assiniboia, and so far as it would affect our future relations with Canada.

" 11. That the Local Legislature of the Province of Assiniboia shall have full control over all the public lands of the Province, and the right to amend all acts or arrangements made or entered into with reference to the public lands of Rupert's Land and the North-West, now called the Province of Assiniboia.

" 12. That the Government of Canada appoint a Commission of Engineers to explore the various districts of the Province of Assiniboia, and to lay before the Local Legislature a report of the mineral wealth of the Province within five years from the date of our entering into Confederation.

" 13. That treaties be concluded between Canada and the different Indian tribes of the Province of Assiniboia, by and with the advice and co-operation of the Local Legislature of this Province.

" 14. That an uninterrupted steam communication from Lake Superior to Fort Garry be guaranteed to be completed within the space of five years.

" 15. That all public buildings, bridges, roads, and other public works be at the cost of the Dominion Treasury.

" 16. That the English and French languages be common in the Legislature and in the Courts and that all public documents, as well as Acts of the Legislature, be published in both languages.

" 17. That whereas the French and English-speaking people of Assiniboia are so equally divided as to number, yet so united in their interests and so connected by commerce, family connections, and other political and social relations, that it has happily been found impossible to bring them into hostile collision, although repeated attempts have been made by designing strangers, for reasons known to themselves, to bring about so ruinous and disastrous an event.

" And whereas after all the troubles and apparent dissensions of the past, the result of misunderstanding among themselves, they have, as soon as the evil agencies referred to above were removed, become as united and friendly as ever.

" Therefore as a means to strengthen this union and friendly feeling among all classes we deem it expedient and advisable—

" That the Lieutenant-Governor who may be appointed for the Province of Assiniboia should be familiar with both the French and English languages.

"18. That the Judge of the Supreme Court speak the English and French languages.

"19. That all debts contracted by the Provisional Government of the Territory of the North-West, now called Assiniboia, in consequence of the illegal and inconsiderate measures adopted by Canadian officials to bring about a civil war in our midst, be paid out of the Dominion Treasury; and that none of the members of the Provisional Government, or any of those acting under them, be in any way held liable or responsible with regard to the movement or any of the actions which led to the present negotiations.

"20. That in view of the present exceptional position of Assiniboia, duties upon goods imported into the Province shall, except in the case of spiritous liquors, continue as at present for at least three years from the date of our entering the Confederation, and for such further time as may elapse until there be uninterrupted railroad communication between Winnipeg and St. Paul; and also steam communication between Winnipeg and Lake Superior."24

This list was, unfortunately, not submitted to the "Legislative Assembly," which had been in session since March 9th, until some weeks after the departure of the delegates. Time was pressing and it may possibly have been that Riel feared the rejection by the Assembly of those terms which had not appeared in the previous list.

The essential differences between this list and that adopted by the Convention are to be found in Clauses 1 and 19, namely, the demand for provincial status, the payment of the debts of the Provisional Government by the Dominion, and an amnesty for all acts committed during the insurrection. The Convention had rejected the demand for provincial status in February, but Riel had clung to the idea and Taché wrote to Cartier, "Je crois qu'il vaut mieux que nous entrions de suite dans la Confédération comme *province*."25 The demand for an amnesty was inserted to protect the half-breeds from the legal consequences of their levies upon the Hudson's Bay Company and private individuals, and from criminal proceedings arising out of the death of Thomas Scott. The other clauses, although for the most part similar to those drawn up for Smith, were more exacting. The financial demands were increased from £25,000 to £80,000 and eighty cents per head of the population; four representatives in the

House of Commons and two in the Senate instead of two and one respectively were asked for ; and the annulment of the " bargain " with the Hudson's Bay Company, in place of exemption from liability " for any portion of the £300,000 paid to the Hudson's Bay Company." The remaining clauses were virtual repetitions of those of the previous list : while the demands relative to the inviolability of local customs, usages and privileges, the equality of the French and English languages, and the necessity for steam and rail communication with Eastern Canada and the United States, had appeared, not only in the February List, but also in the December " Bill of Rights." On the whole the third list of rights was not an impracticable document. Some of the demands were, in view of the small population of the Red River Settlement, unreasonable ; nevertheless the terms of the list were astonishing evidence of the political understanding of Louis Riel and his half-breed associates.

It is important, however, to note that this third list of Rights was not the only list used during the negotiations at Ottawa. Ritchot, at least, carried with him another list identical in every respect with that quoted above, with the exception of clause 7 which ran as follows :

" Que les écoles soient separées, et que les argents pour écoles soient divisés entre les différentes dénominations religeuses, au pro rata de leurs populations respectives."[26]

Whether this change was made on the authority of the Executive of the Provisional Government, or by Riel and·his clerical advisers, is not known. It is not improbable that either Ritchot or Taché, realizing the inevitability of Protestant predominance in Assiniboia, and feeling that Section 5 of the list was not sufficiently definite, requested the insertion, at the last moment, of the clause cited above. One thing, at least, is certain, namely, that the demand for separate schools was made and was conceded during the North-West negotiations at Ottawa, although, for reasons which are not apparent, this fact was not made known generally until 1874.[27]

The question of the credentials of the delegates was also a controversial one. The Canadian Government took the stand that Ritchot, Black, and Scott, were the accredited delegates of the Convention rather than of the Provisional Government. Lord Dufferin stated in 1875 that " they were selected, and the terms they were instructed to demand were settled, before the election of Riel to the so-called Presidency."[28]   This was not, strictly speaking, what actually occurred.   As related above, the delegates had declined to accept their appointment from the Convention and were not persuaded to undertake the task of negotiation until after Taché's return.   In view of the fact that the Provisional Government had been established by and with the approval of the majority of the different racial elements in the colony, it would appear that the delegates were justified in accepting their commission directly from the Secretary of that Government.   The following is a copy of the commission forwarded to Ritchot on March 22nd.[29]

" To Revd. N. J. Ritchot Ptre.
" Sir—The President of the Provisional Government of Assiniboia in Council, by these presents grants authority and commission to you, the Reverend N. J. Ritchot, jointly with John Black, Esquire, and the Honorable A. Scott, to the end that you betake yourselves to Ottawa, in Canada ; and that when there you should lay before the Canadian Parliament the list entrusted to your keeping with these presents, which list contains the conditions and propositions under which the people of Assiniboia would consent to enter into Confederation with the other Provinces of Canada.
" Signed, this twenty-second day of March, in the year of Our Lord, one thousand eight hundred and seventy.
                    " By Order,
                         " (Sgd.) THOMAS BUNN,
                                   " Secretary of State.
" Seat of Government,
   " Winnipeg,
      " Assiniboia."

Armed with this commission, a letter of instructions, and a copy of the List of Rights, the delegates set out for Canada.   On the 23rd the Reverend Father Ritchot and Alfred H. Scott departed in company with Colonel de Salaberry, followed the next day by Judge Black and Major Boulton.

In the meantime a storm of indignation was sweeping over Ontario as a result of the execution of Thomas Scott.   Early events at Red River had aroused the spirit of the expansionists and the " Canada First " party—a group of vigorous young nationalists of whom Dr. Schultz was one—but among the majority of the people of the province the actions of the half-breeds created only a passing interest or a mild amusement. The execution of Scott, an Ontarian, was, however, a different matter from the mishaps of McDougall, and the " Canada First " party were not slow to seize the opportunity to whip up public opinion. A great demonstration was planned for the " refugees " of Red River in order to draw attention to the event, and the widespread denunciation of the execution as a murder was expected to " foment a public opinion that would force the Government to send up an armed expedition to restore order."[30]   The passionate editorials of W. A. Foster in the Toronto *Telegraph*, and the fiery denunciations of the *Globe* set Ontario aflame. When Schultz, Mair, Lynch, Monkman and Dreever, arrived in Toronto on April 7th, they were greeted by a large crowd of demonstrators and conducted to the Market Square where a huge open-air meeting was held. Six thousand or more people were present. This vast multitude was addressed by Schultz and the other " refugees," and a series of resolutions passed endorsing the actions of the " loyalists," advocating decisive measures to quell the " revolt," and declaring that " it would be a gross injustice to the loyal inhabitants of Red River, humiliating to our national honour, and contrary to all British traditions for our Government to receive, negotiate, or treat with the emissaries of those who have robbed, imprisoned and murdered loyal Canadians, whose only fault was zeal for British institutions, whose only crime was devotion to the old flag."[31]

The agitation was carried on with vigour.   Conferences were held with Schultz, Mair, and Lynch, and it was decided that local demonstrations should be held all over the country and pressure brought to bear upon the Prime Minister.   Numerous " indignation meetings " were held in Ontario and even in Montreal ; a petition was forwarded by Lynch to the Governor-General ; and the *Telegraph*, in an article, entitled, " The Messengers of the Murderer, Are they to be received ? " urged that no truck should be had with " rebels," no treaty with " traitors," and no intercourse with " murderers."   The matter was taken up in Parliament.   The Prime Minister was asked if he was prepared " to treat with men who come here with their hands red with blood . . . knowing . . . that the feelings of the people of the country is (sic) excited to a red hot heat."[32]   Alexander Mackenzie, the leader of the Opposition, maintained that the delegation should not be received,[33] and in the Senate the Honourable David Reesor was with difficulty persuaded to withdraw his motion that " If the Government met or recognized any delegation of persons, sharing the reponsibility of this murder, they would compromise themselves and shock the moral sense of the people of Canada."[34]

The next move of the " Canada First " group was to effect the detention of the Red River delegates. Hugh Scott, a brother of the " murdered " man, swore out a warrant for the arrest of Ritchot and A. H. Scott on a charge of aiding and abetting the " murder." The warrant was despatched to Ottawa with the request that the prisoners should be sent to Toronto for trial.[35] On April 14th the two delegates, who had travelled from Prescott to Ottawa under police protection, were arrested on the above warrant. They were almost immediately released as the warrant was held to have no power in Ottawa, but were soon re-arrested upon another warrant issued in that city. Ritchot protested vigorously to the Governor-General against this breach of diplomatic inviolability.[36] The Canadian Government, however, could take no action in the matter, the information having been sworn by private parties, but they retained the Honourable J. H. Cameron as counsel for the defence and assured the anxious Colonial Office that the arrest had been in no way authorized by them.[37] When the case came before the court it was found that there was no evidence to support the charge, and the two delegates were honourably discharged. Shortly afterwards, the negotiations which had begun in such an inauspicious manner, were resumed in spite of the fulminations of the disappointed " loyalists."[38]

The Colonial Office attached considerable importance to these pourparlers, although it was at first doubted if any good would come of them,[39] and Sir Clinton Murdoch, who was being sent on a mission to New York and Ottawa regarding emigration, was directed to proceed first to the Canadian capital in order that the Canadian Government might be in close touch with the views of Her Majesty's Government on the Red River difficulty.[40] Sir Stafford Northcote, the Governor of the Hudson's Bay Company, also offered his services, but acceptance was not deemed advisable by the Canadian Government.[41]

The negotiations opened with preliminary conversations with Judge Black, but on the release of Ritchot and Scott, the three delegates officially notified the Canadian Government of their mission. Macdonald, in the face of Ontario's manifest hostility, did not wish either to recognize the delegates in any official capacity, or to make any concession which might further inflame Canadian opinion. He at first made a set upon Judge Black, " as the party to be flattered and influenced," inducing him to stand firmly on the original Bill of Rights in opposition to any new demands made by Ritchot and Scott.[42]   Ritchot, however, was adamant, and threatened to return to Red River if the delegates were not given official recognition. Howe accordingly addressed the following letter [43] to the delegates.

" Ottawa, April 26th, 1870.

" Gentlemen—I have to acknowledge the receipt of your letter of the 22nd instant, stating that as delegates from the North-West to the Government of the Dominion of Canada, you are desirous of having an early audience with the Government, and am to inform you in reply that the Hon. Sir John A. Macdonald and Sir Geo. Et. Cartier have been authorized by the Government to confer with you on the subject of your mission and will be ready to receive you at eleven o'clock.   I have the honour to be

" Gentlemen,
" Your most obdt. servant,
"(Signed) JOSEPH HOWE."

" To the Revd. N. J. Ritchot, Ptr.,
" J. Black, Esq.,
" Alfred Scott, Esq."

Thenceforth the negotiations proceeded upon the basis of the instructions given to the delegates by the Provisional Government.

The path of the negotiations was by no means a smooth one. Many of the half-breed demands were considered " extravagant and inadmissable,"[44] and Ritchot was little inclined to compromise. Moreover, Macdonald and Cartier were faced with the difficult task of preserving the balance between Ontario and Quebec. In the English province the agitation was vociferous and the cry for vengeance was heard everywhere. In the French province sentiment was inclined to find apologies for Riel's violence. The situation was such that the American Secret

Agent, who was watching the progress of the discussions at Ottawa, wrote to Washington " there seems a gloomy prospect for the Ministry unless Hon. Joseph Howe and the members of the Eastern Provinces can interpose for the adoption of a moderate measure."[45]   In the end, a satisfactory compromise was arrived at.   To appease Ontario an armed force was to be sent to the North-West, not as a punitive expedition, but as a constabulary and a defence against the Indians.   To satisfy the half-breeds—and incidentally, Quebec—a Bill was drawn up incorporating the general features of the " List of Rights," and introduced into the House of Commons by Sir John A. Macdonald on May 2nd.

The Manitoba Bill provided for a province of some eleven thousand square miles, governed by a Lieutenant-Governor appointed by the Dominion, a nominated Upper House of seven members, and an elected Assembly of twenty-four.   The little province was to be granted two senators and four representatives in the House of Commons, this number to increase in proportion to the growth of the population.   Separate schools and the official equality of the French and English languages were guaranteed.   The province was to be granted, in lieu of debt, $27.27 per head, plus an annual subsidy at the rate of eighty cents per head, until the population, then estimated at 17,000, numbered 400,000.   An additional $30,000 was allowed for the expenses of government.   The lands were to be under the control of the Dominion, but 1,400,000 acres were reserved for the half-breeds and their children and all existing titles and occupancies were to be respected.

The Bill met with considerable criticism from the Liberal Opposition benches.   McDougall condemned the granting of a responsible representative government, and drew attention to the omission of the " Canadian " settlement of Portage la Prairie from the new province, allegedly at the instance of the French Roman Catholics.[46]   The Honourable Alexander Mackenzie, forgetting for the moment Simcoe's Lilliputian Legislature in Upper Canada, characterized the Bill as so " ludicrous . . . that it only put one in mind of some of the incidents in Gulliver's Travels."[47]   After an amendment in accordance with Mc-Dougall's suggestion, incorporating the Portage settlement in the Province of Manitoba, the Bill was introduced for the second reading by Sir George Cartier—Macdonald having been seized by an illness which for some time threatened his life. The debate was long and heated, and was marked by bitter clashes between McDougall and Howe. The size of the province, the expensive system of government, and the large reserve of land for the half-breeds, all came under the fire of the Liberal benches ; but the Government would accept no further amendments. Finally, on May 9th, McDougall moved the rejection of the Bill. The result was an anti-climax to the debate. McDougall's motion was defeated by the decisive vote of 120 to 11,[48] and on May 12th the Manitoba Bill was given the Royal Assent.

In view of the fact that the Manitoba Act departed very radically in some respects from the British North America Act of 1867, it was considered necessary to place it upon the footing of an Imperial statute. The provisions in regard to the representation of the province in the Federal Parliament were, technically at least, *ultra vires* of the Federal Government ; while the retention of the control of crown lands in the province by the Dominion, was a distinct violation of section 92 of the British North America Act which reserved to the province the management and sale of public lands. Hence, in December 1870, Sir John A. Macdonald drew up a memorandum[49] on the question, in which he pointed out that it was advisable that there should be an Imperial Act confirming the Manitoba Act, empowering the Dominion to establish new provinces in the North-West, and giving the Federal Government power to increase or diminish the size of the provinces with their consent. In accordance with this request the British Parliament passed the British North America Act of 1871, confirming the Manitoba Act " for all purposes whatsoever."[50]

The selection of a new Lieutenant-Governor was a matter of considerable importance. An error of judgment in this respect had previously resulted in unpleasant complications ; another might prove fatal. The Honourable William McDougall, on his return, had promptly resigned the office of Lieutenant-Governor and devoted his energies to the defence and justification of his conduct. He was attacked in the press and in Parliament, but he struck back with vigour and passion, and addressed to Howe a series of open letters " which for heat, pungency, and invective, are not excelled in the political literature of Canada."[51]   As

McDougall's successor several possibilities presented themselves. Judge Black was suggested by Father Thibault as agreeable to the settlers.[52] Mactavish and Donald A. Smith were also considered by Macdonald, and even Colonel Garnet Wolseley intimated his desire for the position.[53] But the appointment of a military man was not deemed advisable, and the Prime Minister's choice fell upon the Honourable A. G. Archibald of Nova Scotia, who fully justified the confidence thus placed in him, and who, by his tact and conciliation, tided over a difficult period in Manitoban history.

The Red River insurrection virtually at an end, the Canadian Government concluded arrangements for the acceptance of the transfer of Rupert's Land, which had, in December, been indefinitely postponed. Immediately upon the conclusion of the negotiations with the Red River delegates, Sir John Rose was authorised to pay the agreed indemnity to the Company,[54] and upon the delivery of the Deed of Surrender to Lord Granville, the Canadian financial agents in London paid over the £300,000. The process of surrender completed, the Imperial Government, on June 23rd, 1870, passed an Order in Council that " from and after the fifteenth day of July, 1870, the . . . North-Western Territory shall be admitted into and become part of the Dominion of Canada . . . and that the Parliament of Canada shall from the day aforesaid have full power and authority to legislate for the future welfare and good government of the said Territory."[55] July 15th, 1870, thus became the natal day of the Province of Manitoba.

In the meantime the Provisional Government had continued to administer the political affairs of the Red River Settlement. On March 18th, the following resolutions were adopted :[56]

" 1. That we, the people of Assiniboia, without disregard to the Crown of England, under whose authority we live, have deemed it necessary for the protection of life and property and the securing of those rights and privileges we have seen in danger, to form a Provisional Government, which is the only acting authority in this country ; and we do hereby ordain and establish the following Constitution :

" 2. That the country hitherto known as Rupert's Land and the North-West be henceforth known and styled ' Assiniboia.'

" 3. That our Assembly of Representatives be henceforth styled the ' Legislative Assembly of Assiniboia.'

" 4. That all legislative authority be vested in a President and Legislative Assembly composed of members elected by the people ; and that at any future time another house, called a Senate, shall be established when deemed necessary by the President and Legislature.

" 5. That the only qualification necessary for a member to serve in the Legislature be, that he shall have attained the age of twenty-three years ; and he be a citizen of Assiniboia and a resident of the country for a term of at least five years ; and he shall be a householder and have rateable property to the amount of £200 sterling ; and that if an alien, he shall have first taken the oath of allegiance."

On March 23rd, Louis Riel took the oath as President of the Provisional Government and the elected deputies were sworn in as members of the " Legislative Assembly of Assiniboia."

A few days later Riel entered into negotiations with Governor Mactavish of the Hudson's Bay Company for the resumption of business by the Company. The terms were severe. Riel demanded :[57]

" 1. Que toute la Compagnie de la Baie d'Hudson dans le Nord-Ouest reconnaisse le Gouvernement Provisoire.

" 2. Que vous souscrivez, au nom de la Compagnie de la Baie d'Hudson, à un emprunt au Gouvernement Provisoire pour la somme de £3,000 sterling.

" 3. Que sur la demande du Gouvernement Provisoire, dans le cas où les arrangements avec le Canada seraient entravés, vous garantissiez un supplément de £2,000 sterling à la somme sus-mentionée.

" 4. Qu'il soit octroyé par la Compagnie de la Baie d'Hudson à l'administration militaire du Gouvernement Provisoire, pour la valeur de £4,000 en provisions de bouche et en marchandises au prix courant.

" 5. Que la Compagnie de la Baie d'Hudson remettra immédiatement ses bills en circulation.

" 6. Que la Compagnie de la Baie d'Hudson se désiste d'une quantité spécifiée de marchandises que le Gouvernement Provisoire se réserverait, en cas d'arrangements."

In return he promised to open Fort Garry and the other Company stores, and to grant them the protection of the Provisional Government. Mactavish had no alternative but to accept. On April 2nd, he signified his acquiescence, and a week later began to grant bills of exchange on London.

The whole aspect of the Settlement was now in a process of change. The *New Nation* dropped its pro-Yankee tone, and, under the editorship of an erstwhile supporter of the Canadian Party, Thomas Spence, became very loyal. On April 23rd the Union Jack was raised over Fort Garry by the order of Louis Riel. W. B. O'Donoghue, who represented the American and Fenian interest during the insurrection, resented these pro-British manifestations ; he tore down the Union Jack which Riel had raised and replaced it with the flag of the Provisional Government. The American vice-consul reported the incident in the following manner : " Quite a war of words ensued between the two leaders, and the two flags alternated with great rapidity for some days, the matter being finally compromised by the hoisting of both flags. The dispute between them, however, has not yet healed and their friendship is very Platonic."[58] Riel stationed André Nault at the foot of the British flag with strict orders to shoot anyone who should endeavour to remove it.[59] As a result of this action " Riel rose greatly in the public opinion."[60] In all of these things we can see the moderating influence of Bishop Taché, who was, according to report, " virtually, although not in name, the Government of the country."[61]

Bright as the prospects for a peaceful settlement appeared, there were, still, threatening clouds upon the political horizon. The arrest of the delegates, the fulminations of the Ontario press, and the uncertainty as regards a general amnesty, all contributed to produce a feeling of unrest, which was further aggravated by the fear of the Indians, the Fenians, and the offers of men and money from interested American sources to oppose the troops which Canada was sending to the Settlement. It was even reported that " there is a strong disposition evinced by many members of the Provisional Government to commence hostilities upon any pretext whatever."[62] It is probable that this was an overstatement, but, nevertheless, the situation was such that only the definite assurance by Bishop Taché of a general amnesty,[63] the corroborative promises of Father Ritchot, and the favourable terms of the Manitoba Act relieved the tension.

In June, Ritchot returned to Red River with the result of his efforts at Ottawa. The Canadian Government had studiously avoided any recognition of the right of the Provisional Government to ratify the terms of the settlement, as this would have involved a recognition of Riel and his associates for which the British and the Canadian Governments were not prepared; nevertheless the Provisional Government proceeded to a formal ratification. A special session of the " Legislative Assembly " was summoned, to which Ritchot, as an official accredited delegate of the Provisional Government, made his report. This report was received with much satisfaction, and on the motion of Thomas Bunn and A. G. B. Bannatyne, a cordial vote " for the straight-forward, courageous, and successful way " in which Father Ritchot had discharged his duty was adopted. It was then moved by Louis Schmidt and Pierre Poitras, and carried with enthusiastic applause, " that the Legislative Assembly of this country do now, in the name of the people, accept the Manitoba Act."[64] Thomas Bunn accordingly despatched the following letter to Joseph Howe notifying him of the ratification of the terms agreed upon at Ottawa :[65]

" I have the honour to inform you that one of our delegates to your Government has returned and has reported on the result of his mission.

" In considering that report, the first point which presented itself, was the insulting and undignified reception which our invited delegates met with on their arrival in Canada, a circumstance which, I need hardly say, is very much to be deplored.

" In view, however, of the liberal policy adopted in the interest of the people of the North-West by the Canadian Ministry, and recommended by the Imperial Government, a policy necessarily based on the principles for which they have fought, the Provisional Government and the Legislative Assembly, in the name of the people of the North-West, do accept the ' Manitoba Act,' and consent to enter into Confederation on the terms entered into with our delegates.

" I have further the honour to inform you that the Provisional Government and the Legislative Assembly have consented to enter into Confederation in the belief, and on the understanding, that in the above-mentioned terms a general amnesty is contemplated to all the parties who had to meet the difficulties with which the Provisional Government had to deal, without which amnesty the people of the North-West could not consider themselves treated as a peaceable and a loyal people ought to be, but would feel themselves unjustly forced into Confederation.

"I have, etc.,

"(Sgd.) THOMAS BUNN."

Riel concluded the proceedings with a characteristic speech :[66]

" I congratulate the people of the North-West on the happy issue of their undertakings (cheers). I congratulate them on having trust enough in the Crown of England to believe that ultimately they would obtain their rights (cheers). I must, too, congratulate the country on passing from under this Provisional rule to one of a more permanent and satisfactory character. From all that can be learned, also, there is great room for con-gratulation in the selection of Lieutenant-Governor which has been made. For myself, it will be my duty and pleasure, more than any other, to bid the new Governor welcome on his arrival (loud cheers). I would like to be the first to pay him the respect due to his position as Representative of the Crown (cheers). Something yet remains to be done. Many people are yet anxious and doubtful. Let us still pursue the work in which we have been lately engaged . . . the cultivation of peace and friendship, and doing what can be done to convince these people that we never designed to wrong them (cheers), but that what has been done was as much in their interest as our own (cheers)."

Assured by Ritchot that Cartier had instructed him to carry on the government until the arrival of Lieutenant-Governor Archibald,[67] Riel remained, until August 24th, at the helm of the government which he had launched. Everything appeared to have reached a peaceful and satisfactory conclusion. The Pro-visional Government proceeded to disband their troops, all necessity for their existence having passed away. The half-breeds had been protected, by Act of Parliament, from the worst dangers of an alien immigration ; the Roman Catholic Church had been guaranteed the privileges it had sought ; the Red River Settle-ment appeared about to enter upon a new era of unity and self-government ; and Riel was only waiting to surrender the government into the hands of the Canadian Lieutenant-Governor, when the arrival of the military force threw the colony once more into a state of turmoil.

CHAPTER VII

THE despatch of a military force to the North-West was an undertaking confronted with many formidable obstacles. The objective, Fort Garry, was cut off from Canada by a land of rocky rivers, swampy valleys, tangled forests, and treacherous muskegs, which provided neither supplies nor provisions, but afforded excellent cover for guerrillas. There were only three possible routes, the first, via Hudson Bay ; the second, through the United States ; and the third, over the old North-West canoe route from Lake Superior to Lake Winnipeg.

The first route had been used in 1846 and 1848 when a few troops and pensioners were sent to Red River during the Oregon alarm. But upon each occasion the force had been a peaceful one. For a force whose intent against the colony might be considered hostile, the Hudson Bay route was of small value. From the Bay, which was closed by ice for the greater part of the year, the only channel of access to the Settlement was a canoe or bateau route seven hundred miles long, through a series of lakes and rivers broken by innumerable portages, which a few hundred sharpshooters might defend against an army of several thousand. The second alternative was out of the question. No troops could be sent over American soil in view of the prevailing anti-British feeling current in the United States. The Washington *National Republican* probably voiced the opinion of the majority of the American people when it declared " if . . . any attempt should be made to bring the North-West colony into subjection by a resort to arms there can be but one opinion throughout the American Union, as to the duty of the United States Government in the matter, and that is to adopt the most decisive method to prevent an Indian war of extermination and protect the colony in the spirit of the Monroe Doctrine and under the claims of our common humanity against the oppression of a foreign power."[1] Senator Chandler, of Michigan, moving an insolent resolution for the annexation of Red River by the United States, declared that for Canada to send five or ten thousand men was " simply to sacrifice them." Only one hundred thousand men, he maintained, could hope to make a stand, and then only with the permission of the United States, for, should the great Republic protest, " one hundred thousand would be no better than one hundred."[2]   The third route, through the chain of lakes and rivers which lie partly along the international boundary between Lake Superior and Lake Winnipeg, was the shortest.   It was a water route, practicable only for boats and canoes.   In winter, however, it was useless, and in summer its innumerable portages, deep morasses, and thick forests, afforded excellent cover for irregular troops, a few of whom might render the passage of an expeditionary force practically impossible.

While nature and politics thus provided serious obstacles to the advance of an invading army, the vast prairies to the west, like the plains of Russia and the veldts of South Africa, provided an unlimited retreat for the inhabitants of the colony.   The adventures of General Christian de Wet in the South African War are sufficient proof of the extreme difficulty, even with modern facilities, roads, railways and telegraphs, of making a clean sweep of mobile columns operating in wide spaces.   Of the half-breeds as soldiers Colonel Crofton wrote :

" The half-breed hunters with their splendid organization when on the prairies, their matchless power of providing themselves with all necessary wants for many months together, and now since a trade with the Americans has sprung up, if they should choose, for years, their perfect knowledge of the country and their full appreciation and enjoyment of a home in the prairie wilds, winter or summer, would render them a very formidable enemy in case of disturbance or open rebellion against constituted authorities.   The half-breed hunters of Red River could pass into the open prairies at a day's notice, and find themselves perfectly at home and secure, where white men, not accustomed to such a life would soon become powerless against them and exposed to continued peril.

" The physical appearance of the half-breeds is much in their favour.   They are a tall, strong, and active race of men.   They are the best horsemen and marksmen in the country.   If it should ever be considered expedient by Her Majesty to raise a body of irregular cavalry in this country, there exists in the half-breed the most eligible material I have ever seen in any country and I have seen the Risalus of India and the Arabs."[3]

Under these circumstances it is not surprising that Riel felt himself secure from any attempts at military coercion. During the first Convention he replied to the suggestion that Canada would probably send troops :

"l'hiver nous protège avec ses neiges et ses tempêtes . . . la Baie d'Hudson, la Baie de Tonnerre, et le térritoire Americain ne sont pas aisés à franchir pour nous atteindre d'ici au printemps . . . pendant ce temps nous aurons des arrangements avec le Canada."[4]

To add to the difficulties of sending a military expedition to the North-West, the British Government, in 1870, announced that all British troops in Canada, with the exception of small garrisons at Quebec and Halifax, were to be withdrawn. The whole question of Imperial defence had been carefully considered in 1861 with the almost unanimous conclusion that the main object of British policy should be to ncourage local efforts and local organization, instead of dependence upon the mother country ; and that the responsibility and cost of military defence should, in future, be assumed by the self-governing colonies themselves. Although this policy did not meet with unqualified approval in the colonies, nevertheless the trend of colonial development was national rather than Imperial, and the presence of Imperial troops in Canada was inconsistent with the growth of Dominion autonomy. To attain the status of nationhood the colonies had to assume the responsibilities of nationhood, the greatest of which was self defence. Accordingly, in 1862, the British House of Commons resolved that " Colonies exercising the rights of self-government ought to undertake the main responsibility of providing for their own internal order and security, and ought to assist in their own external defence."[5] Thenceforward this principle was adopted by every successive ministry until, in 1873, the Under-Secretary for the Colonies was able to announce " that the military expenditure for the colonies is now almost entirely for Imperial purposes."[6]

From the beginning of the outbreak in Red River, it was apparent that the Canadian Government considered the possibility of sending troops to the colony, urging as a reason for the delay of the transfer that " troops cannot be sent through British territory until May. United States will not allow troops through their country."[7] The British Government were not, however, anxious to become involved in the North-West imbroglio, and Granville noted in an office minute " the more I think of it the more I doubt the expediency of sending Imperial troops to Red River."[8] Canadian public opinion, more or less indifferent to the events in the far west, did not demand the despatch of a military force during the early months of the rising.   Until the death of Scott aroused the public wrath the *Globe* made only a passing suggestion that a military man with wide discretionary powers and an adequate force should be sent to Red River " as soon as ever it is seen that there is no other way."[9] Sir John Macdonald, however, while pursuing a policy of conciliation and concession, was quietly making preparations for the sending of an expedition over the old North-West canoe route in the spring.   S. J. Dawson, who had virtually rediscovered the route in his explorations in 1868, was placed in charge of the construction of a road from Lake Superior to the navigable waters of the interior.   This road was part of the scheme of communication with Red River of which Snow's road was to form the western link.   Early in January Dawson was instructed to have the road from Lake Superior to Lake Shebandowan ready by May 1st so as to admit of the passage of horses and waggons.[10]   The portages were ordered to be cleared and contracts were let for the building of one hundred boats.   The *Algoma* and the *Chicora* were chartered to convey men and boats through the Sault Ste. Marie canal as soon as it was open, about the middle of April, and agents were sent to prepare the way for the expedition among the Indians who lived along the route to be traversed.

Although British policy was to leave questions of internal order and security to the Dominion alone, Sir John Macdonald made these preparations with every hope of Imperial assistance. Writing to Granville on January 26th, he expressed the hope " that Her Majesty's Government will co-operate liberally with us in the way of a Regular Force. I think the best plan will be to send a mixed expeditionary force of a small body of Regulars with some light artillery so as to shell the Forts in case they are held.   It is of great importance that a part of the force should be Regular troops as it will convince the United States Government and people that Her Majesty's Government have no intention of abandoning this continent."[11]   This letter was followed early in February by a confidential Cabinet minute urging the expediency of immediate preparations for an expeditionary force and the necessity of Imperial co-operation :

" First, a belief exists not only in Rupert's Land but in the United States, extending even to their leading statesmen, that England does not care for the retention of her North American Colonies as a portion of the Empire, and that she will not make any effort to retain them.

" Secondly, because the prestige of an Expedition composed partly of Regular troops will be much greater than if it consisted of untried volunteers only ; and

" Thirdly, because a feeling of hostility to Canada having unfortunately arisen which does not exist with regard to England, the insurgents would more readily lay down their arms to a British force than one entirely Canadian—and even in the case of actual resistance, the conflict would not be attended with the same animosity, and after the rising was put down would not leave behind it such feelings of bitterness and humiliation.

" It is hoped, then, that H.M. Government will readily assent to send a small body of Regular troops, with an officer of reputa-tion in command.   Canada will supplement that Force to any extent that may be necessary to quell the insurrection and restore peace and order."[12]

The British Government was not prepared to authorize the use of Imperial troops to suppress a rather nebulous political disturbance in the far off North-West, and Granville replied to the above memorandum that the Imperial Government would give the required assistance only on condition that reasonable terms were granted to the Red River settlers, and the transfer of the territory proclaimed simultaneously with the movement of the force.[13]   The Canadian authorities accepted these conditions, and on March 24th the Honourable James Lindsay left for Canada to replace Sir John Michel as Lieutenant-General, and to take charge of the arrangements for the Red River Expedition.

The proposed expedition was not regarded with complete approval in military circles.   The retiring commander, Sir John Michel, in a memorandum on the military and political aspects of an expedition of British troops to the Red River Settlement asked " is it too much to say that England is risking a disgrace for an apparently small cause ?   If it be a pecuniary matter England can better afford to pay her millions than suffer a partial failure, much more a disgrace."[14]   Again in a private letter[15]

Michel voiced his opinion that " our War Office should be as clear of this reckless expedition as circumstances will now admit," emphasizing the danger of Fenian and American complications :

" It must always be borne in mind that at Fort Garry you are in a trap, from whence in case of any difficulty on the part of the United States you can only escape by Hudson Bay, of which the waters are only open six weeks in the year and then only with a perfectly friendly free state in your rear . . . Will not the American Government succumb to the love, as well as the electioneering necessity of popularity, by holding their hands in reference to Fenian or Minnesota sympathy, and by tacitly permitting aid to be sent to what is termed a free expression of the will of the people ? "

With the arrival of General Lindsay, on April 5th, the organization of the proposed expedition was undertaken with a military efficiency to which the Canadian Government was unaccustomed. Feeling that the force, though mixed, was essentially an Imperial one, Lindsay endeavoured to centralize control in his own hands. All details of equipment, commissariat, transport, and supplies, were taken out of the hands of the officers employed by the Ministry of Militia, and placed under a Control Department. It was impossible, however, to dispense with some form of dual control, a fact which led to delay, indecision, mistrust, and ill-feeling. Despite the early purchases by the Canadian Government, preparations were far from complete, and Lindsay complained to the War Office of the vexing necessity of making frequent trips to Ottawa to spur on the Canadian authorities,[16] who, even as late as April 11th, were apparently undecided as to whether troops would definitely be sent to Red River or not.[17] Under Lindsay's pressure preparations moved more quickly. On the 15th a plan for the enlistment of two militia regiments was drawn up by the Canadian Adjutant-General, and on May 6th Granville informed Young that the troops might proceed.[18]

The force was composed of small detachments from the Royal Artillery, Royal Engineers, Army Service Corps and Army Hospital Corps, 373 men and officers of the 60th Rifles (Regulars), and two battalions of Militia from Ontario (382 men) and Quebec (389 men). There were, in addition, a large number of teamsters, guides, Indians and voyageurs under S. J. Dawson, attached to the force to assist its transportation to Red River. The Imperial

Regulars were under strict orders to return after the successful completion of the expedition, in order to be withdrawn from North American soil before the New Year. The Militia were enlisted for one year's service. Only men of the strongest and hardiest constitutions were selected, as, on an expedition of this nature, every sick man would be more than an ordinary encumbrance. Moreover, General Lindsay decided that none of those who had had any connexion with the Honourable William McDougall or with the recent disturbances in Red River were to accompany the expedition. In spite of this wise precaution many of those who enlisted in the Ontario battalion did so with the object of revenging the death of Thomas Scott—a fact which was pregnant with future discord in the newly-formed province. On the other hand the Quebec battalion was slow to fill its ranks, and, in the end, had to be completed with English-speaking volunteers. Almost the entire Quebec press was opposed to the expedition and to French Canadian enlistment in a force, which, they claimed, was directed against their kindred in the North-West; with the unfortunate result that of the 362 volunteers of the Quebec battalion (exclusive of officers), only seventy-seven were of French Canadian parentage.[19]

The officer selected to lead the expeditionary force was Colonel—later Field Marshal and Viscount—G. J. Wolseley, who was, at that time, Deputy Quartermaster-General in Canada. Although it is said that the Militia Department would have preferred the selection of Colonel Robertson Ross,[20] then Adjutant-General of the Canadian Militia, Wolseley's appointment received wide approval. "I consider it very fortunate," wrote Lindsay, "that an officer who knows Canada and its Volunteers so well, and who has so much ability and experience, should have been available for this service."[21]

While the military force was in the process of organization, the Canadian Government, it will be remembered, had been negotiating with the delegates of the Provisional Government. Political expediency and the British Government had insisted upon this course and the successful conclusion of the negotiations removed whatever necessity there may have been for punitive measures. But to abandon the expedition was impossible. The refugee Canadians loudly demanded " a conquest and a military rule, until a Canadian immigration can outvote the present inhabitants,"[22] and public opinion in Ontario, now at a white heat over the Scott affair, would never have tolerated such a concession to the French of Quebec and the half-breeds of Manitoba.   On the other hand, Quebec opinion regarded the expedition as an instrument of English Protestant coercion and a menace to the peaceful settlement of the Red River troubles ; and a resolution was moved in Parliament, by a French Canadian Conservative, that the duty of restoring order rested only with the Imperial Government.[23]   The position of the colony, however, demanded the presence of some form of police or military force, if only to protect the people from possible inroads by filibustering Fenians or irresponsible Indians.   Sir John Young wrote to Granville to this effect early in May :[24]

" Preparations are being pushed on with vigour to start the expedition at an early date.   The Government are very confident that no attempt at opposition will be made, but the events of the last six months make it indispensable to send a force to support the civil authority established by law, and guarantee the preservation of order to the industrious and peaceable portion of the settlers against any riot or violence on the part of others, and against any troubles which might arise from the ignorance or possible discontent of the Indian tribes whose minds have been shaken and disturbed by recent events at Fort Garry."

Thus, to satisfy the demands of necessity in the North-West and expediency in Ontario the military expedition was proceeded with ; but to reassure the half-breeds and Quebec all appearance of a punitive force was avoided.   The Governor-General explained the nature of the compromise in his speech closing the session of Parliament on May 12th :[25]

" Her Majesty's troops go forth on an errand of peace, and will serve as an assurance to the inhabitants of the Red River Settlement and the numerous Indian tribes that occupy the North-West, that they have a place in the regard and counsels of England, and may rely upon the impartial protection of the British sceptre."

The expedition was from the first confronted with vexatious delays.   At Collingwood two steamers had been provided, and by means of these, troops, stores, waggons, horses, etc., were carried to Sault Ste. Marie.   To pass into Lake Superior it was necessary to make use of the canal built on the American side. Acting in a manner which was both discourteous and unfriendly,

in view of the fact that Canada had permitted the United States
to send armed revenue cutters through Canadian canals, Secretary
Fish, without making any inquiry, gave orders that ".no military
expedition of any foreign power, whether of troops or boats
intended for the purpose of taking part in any military or warlike
expedition, or of warlike material be allowed to pass through
Sault Ste. Marie canal without express instructions . . . from the
Government at Washington."[26]   The result was, that although
the *Algoma* slipped through the canal unsuspected, the Superintendent of the canal refused to allow any other boats to pass
through, even when empty.   Immediate representations were
made by the Governor-General to the British Minister at
Washington.[27]

" My Government has learned with great surprise that Canadian
steamer *Chicora* has been stopped from passing through Sault
Ste. Marie canal.   She had on board ordinary commercial freight
and no warlike stores.   The Canadians at all times have allowed
free use of Welland and other canals to American vessels, even
to armed revenue cutters when the Government of the United
States desired during war to transfer some of those cutters to the
Atlantic.   Persecution considered very unfriendly.   My ministers trust United States Government will interfere and let Ste.
Marie canal remain on same footing as regards Canadian vessels
as Welland is as regards United States vessels.   No munitions of
war will be sent through canal in any event, not even tents."

The British Minister, Sir Edward Thornton, communicated
the views of the Governor-General to the American Government,
and although the *Globe* considered his protest as unnecessarily
weak and humiliating,[28] he was able to reply on May 17th that
official instructions had been sent to permit the passage of the
Chicora and other vessels through the Sault canal.[29]   This unnecessary act of discourtesy brought forth a strong minute from
the Canadian Government, but it must be admitted that the whole
affair might have been obviated had the Canadian Government
taken Lindsay's advice and requested the necessary permission
before the expedition had embarked.

The second delay was encountered in the early stages of the land
journey.   It had been expected that by the time the expedition
landed at Prince Arthur's Landing, near Fort William, a
practicable road would be completed from that place to Lake

Shebandowan where the troops were to embark in canoes and boats for Fort Garry. Superintendent Dawson had positively assured the Canadian Government that the road would be ready by the opening of navigation,[30] and upon that assurance Colonel Wolseley had based his calculations. Unfortunately the forest fires and the heavy rains had so delayed the construction of the road that by the time of Wolseley's arrival on May 25th, only thirty miles had been finished and many miles were still uncut through primeval forests. To expedite matters the troops and voyageurs were put to work, and throughout the month of June and half of July, Wolseley's army struggled with the tools of the road builder instead of the weapons of the soldier.

To relieve the deficiency of the land transports Wolseley directed his attention to the possibility of sending boats by way of the Kaministiquia, a neighbouring river full of rocks and rapids. Such a course was deemed impossible by S. J. Dawson, but the Hudson's Bay Company officer at Fort William pronounced it possible, although very difficult. Wolseley was willing to take the risks involved and Captain Young was directed to proceed with the boats to Lake Shebandowan. The experiment, although successful, was too costly. The work was of such a difficult nature that many of the Indians hired as boatmen deserted, and considerable discontent manifested itself among the voyageurs, who considered that the boats could more easily have been taken overland by waggon. Moreover, the boats were badly damaged, and rowlocks and oars lost or broken.[31]

A month and a half of this heavy and uncongenial labour of constructing a road through an inhospitable country, and the reiterated hints in both the French and the English Canadian press that the expedition would eventually be abandoned, dampened the spirits of the troops. Wolseley himself became discouraged, and went so far as to accuse Cartier and Langevin—the latter, Minister of Public Works—of attempting to sabotage the expedition.[32] The timely visit of General Lindsay inspired the waning enthusiasm, and by July 16th the first boatload of troops was despatched from the shores of Lake Shebandowan.

Further delays might have ensued had the Indians of the region made any effort to oppose the passage of the troops through their country. The Government had foreseen this possibility and W. M. Simpson and R. Pither were despatched in advance to prepare the way for the expedition. This was a wise precaution, for, as Captain Huyshe admitted, " there is no doubt that a hundred determined men might have inflicted termendous loss on the troops with comparative impunity ; for, thoroughly acquainted with the vast network of lakes, they could have fired on the boats as they passed through narrow channels, or blocked up the portages, and done much mischief in a variety of ways, while to have attempted to pursue them through the woods and lakes would have been madness."[33] At Fort Frances several pow-wows were held with the Indians. These occupied several days. Old Crooked Neck, the principal chief, made exorbitant demands in stating the terms on which they would allow the troops free passage through their territory, but finally compromised on a few presents of flour and pork.[34]

In order to instruct Colonel Wolseley as to the progress of events in the North-West, and more particularly regarding the rumoured Fenian activity south of the frontier, Captain Butler—later Sir William Butler—was sent to Red River via the United States. After proceeding through Minnesota to Fort Garry, where he had an interview with Louis Riel, Butler returned up the Winnipeg river by canoe to meet the expedition. Arriving at Fort Frances on August 4th, he learned that Wolseley was close at hand. Paddling to meet him, Butler met the large North-West canoes, sweeping along with their Iroquois paddlers timing their strokes to an old French boat song. In the foremost canoe sat Colonel Wolseley, who, on recognizing Butler, called out " Where on earth have you dropped from ? " " Fort Garry, twelve days out, sir," was the reply.[35]

Colonel Wolseley had also despatched a Proclamation to the Red River Settlement explaining the peaceful nature and objects of his force. At the same time he sent letters to J. H. McTavish, the Hudson's Bay Company agent at Fort Garry, and to the Roman Catholic and Anglican Bishops, requesting them to take measures for pushing forward the partially completed Snow road to the Lake of the Woods. In accordance with this request the following notice appeared in the colony:[36]

" Department of Public Works.

" Laborers Wanted :

" Notice is hereby given, that from two hundred to two hundred and fifty men are immediately required to make a cart road

from the east end of Mr. Snow's road to the north-west angle of
the Lake of the Woods.

"Engagements made at the Office of the Hudson's Bay
Company, Upper Fort Garry.

"Five shillings sterling per day, and board, will be given to
axe men and laborers.

"By order of

"G. J. WOLSELEY,
"Colonel, commanding Red River
Expeditionary Force.
"J. H. McTAVISH,
"Hudson's Bay Company."

By the time Wolseley reached the Lake of the Woods this road
was reported as feasible, but the Colonel had determined to have
no more to do with partially completed roads. Instead he
continued down the Winnipeg river, a route considered by many
as the most dangerous part of the journey.

The navigation of the Winnipeg river by boat or canoe was an
extremely difficult task, except for very experienced men. In its
course to the lake, the river falls many hundreds of feet over a
succession of rocky cataracts. It was possible to run many
rapids, but the greater number had to be passed over by long and
arduous portages. Fortunately the expedition managed to over-
come all the perils of the route without serious misadventure,
and although several boats were wrecked, no lives were lost.

Colonel Wolseley gives a vivid description of running a
rapid:[37]

"The pleasurable excitement of danger is always an agreeable
experience, but the enthralling delight of feeling your frail canoe
or boat bound under you, as it were, down a steep incline of
wildly rushing waters into what looks like a boiling, steaming
cauldron of bubbling and confused waters, exceeds most of the
other maddening delights that man can dream of. Each man
strains for his life at oar or paddle, for no steerage-way can be
kept upon your boat unless it be made to run quicker than the
water. All depends upon the nerve and skill of the bowsman
and steersman, who take you skilfully through the outcropping
rocks around you. But the acme of excitement is of short
duration, and the pace is too quick to admit of self-examination.
No words can describe the rapid change of sensation when the
boat jumps through the last narrow and perhaps twisted passage

between rocks, into an eddy of slack water below! You had—perhaps unknowingly—held your breath, whilst every nerve was nigh to breaking point, during the moments of supreme danger; but in a few seconds of time afterwards, a long breath of relief comes that enables you to say ' Thank God! ' with all heartfelt sincerity."

The whole story of the expedition was by no means such a narrative of sport and adventure. The portages involved considerable labour. As the troops were obliged to cross some forty-seven portages, it may be useful to describe the method of portaging employed. The bulkiest articles were the boats, which were about thirty feet long and built in proportion. Each carried eight or nine soldiers and two or three voyageurs or Indians, together with sixty days' provisions for all. There was, in addition, artillery, ammunition, and camp equipment. The boats were distributed into brigades of six, each brigade carrying all its own extra supplies and replacements. As each brigade reached the rapid or waterfall over which it was necessary to portage, the boats were unloaded and a road was cut over the portage, which might vary in length from several hundred yards to more than a mile. Rollers of six or eight inch poplar trees were then cut and laid on the road, over which the boats were hauled by the soldiers. The stores were carried by men and officers alike. The system adopted was that used by the Indians and the voyageurs; a long strap, of several inches in width, was passed around the forehead and attached to the barrel or load on the back, the head and neck thus bearing the greater part of the strain. Men accustomed to this work were able to carry weights from three to four hundred pounds. Steele, in his *Reminiscences*,[38] related that one of the guides carried two barrels of pork and one thousand rounds of ammunition, a load of five hundred and twenty-eight pounds of awkward bulk; while Captain Redvers Buller always took at least two hundred pounds and sometimes three hundred pounds at a trip. Some of the portages were very rocky, others excessively steep, and others of considerable height and very long, still others were barred by streams or marshland and had to be corduroyed or bridged. Some idea of the amount of work involved in a portage is shown by the fact that, on a portage one mile long, each man, heavily burdened, might be required to make ten trips across it, thus walking at least

nineteen miles.[39]   It is not surprising, therefore, that when the
men returned to Canada, they were in splendid condition, expert
axe men, and all more or less skilled in the craft of the voyageur
and woodsman.

At Rat Portage Wolseley was met by letters from Fort Garry,
and, what was more important, by several guides and skilled
rivermen brought from the Red River Settlement by the Reverend
Mr. Gardiner.   Without the assistance of these men the passage
of the Winnipeg river would probably have been much slower
and more perilous.   As it was, the advance guard of the force
arrived safely, on August 20th, at Fort Alexander at the mouth
of the Winnipeg river, where they were welcomed by Donald A.
Smith.

From this place Wolseley pushed south towards Fort Garry.
He had received no information from the neighbouring parishes
as to the state of affairs in the capital of the colony, and was
apparently uncertain as to whether the half-breeds would make a
show of resistance.   On August 23rd, the army encamped a
few miles from the Fort.   Forgetful that they were bound " on
an errand of peace " the soldiers were eager for battle, hoping
that the morrow would see " a pretty little field day when our
line of skirmishers should enclose Fort Garry and its rebel
garrison, as in a net."[40]   The next morning, their enthusiasm
undampened by the drenching downpour during the night, they
marched towards their objective.   An eye-witness account of the
taking of the fort is given by Captain Huyshe :[41]

" Passing round the flank of the village, the fort appeared in
sight about seven hundred yards off, across the open prairie.   A
few stray inhabitants in the village declared that Riel and his
party still held possession of the fort and meant to fight.   The
gates were shut, no flag was flying from the flag-staff, and guns
were visible, mounted in the bastions and over the gateway that
commanded the approach from the village and the prairie over
which the troops were advancing.   It certainly looked as if our
labours were not to be altogether in vain.   ' Riel is going to
fight ! ' ran along the line, and the men quickened their pace and
strode cheerily forward, regardless of mud and rain.   M. Riel
rose in their estimation immensely.   The gun over the gateway
was expected every moment to open fire, but we got nearer and
nearer and still no sign ; at last we could see that there were no
men standing to the guns, and, unless it were a trap to get us

close up before they opened fire, it was evident that there would be no fight at all. ' By God ! he's bolted ! ' was the cry. Colonel Wolseley sent forward some of his staff to see if the south gate were also shut ; they galloped all round the fort, and brought back word that the gate opening on to the bridge over the Assiniboine River was wide open, and men bolting away over the bridge. The troops then marched in by this gateway, and took possession of Fort Garry after a bloodless victory."

The half-breeds had long since abandoned any idea of resistance. The first news of the approach of the military expedition had, indeed, caused considerable uneasiness, but the successful conclusion of the negotiations at Ottawa, the repeated declarations of the Canadian Government that the expedition was not a warlike one—" the expedition is an expedition of peace, and the Quebec battalion comprises a large number of your friends "[42] —and the assurances of Bishop Taché that a general amnesty had been promised, persuaded Riel and his adherents that no hostile movement was being directed against them. Moreover, Wolseley's proclamation,[43] which had been sent to Red River at the end of June and circulated throughout the Settlement by Riel himself,[44] was likewise reassuring to the erstwhile insurgents.

" To the Loyal Inhabitants of Manitoba.

" Her Majesty's Government having determined upon stationing some troops amongst you, I have been instructed by the Lieutenant-General Commanding in British North America to proceed to Fort Garry with the force under my command.

" Our mission is one of peace, and the sole object of the expedition is to secure Her Majesty's sovereign authority.

"(Courts of Law such as are common to every portion of Her Majesty's Empire will be duly established, and justice will be impartially administered to all races and all classes. The loyal Indians or half-breeds being as dear to our Queen as any others of Her loyal subjects.")[45]

" The force which I have the honour of commanding will enter your province representing no party either in religion or politics, and will afford equal protection to the lives and property of all races and of all creeds.

" The strictest order and discipline will be maintained, and private property will be carefully respected. All supplies furnished by the inhabitants to the troops will be duly paid for. Should anyone consider himself injured by any individual belonging to the force, his grievance shall be promptly enquired into.

" All loyal people are earnestly invited to aid in carrying out the above-mentioned objects.

"G. J. WOLSELEY, Colonel, Commanding the Red River Force.

" Prince Arthur's Landing,
   "Thunder Bay, 30th June, 1870."

Had the half-breeds determined to make a stand, and taken advantage of their knowledge of the country and their kinship with the Indians, there is a strong possibility that the dramatic ambush of Braddock at Fort Duquesne might have been re-enacted in the North-West. The conciliatory policy of the Government and the sympathetic statements of Cartier had, however, completely disarmed the malcontents in Red River, and, instead of sending men to oppose Wolseley's advance, many of those who had taken part in the insurrection were out with no more formidable weapons than axes and shovels, making a road for Her Majesty's troops ! In the " Legislative Assembly " Riel declared that " it will be my duty and pleasure more than any other to bid the new Governor welcome on his arrival," and informed Butler, " I only wish to retain power until I can resign it to a proper Government. I have done everything for the sake of peace, and to prevent bloodshed amongst the people of this land."[46] Even as late as August 23rd Riel was told by Bishop Taché that he had nothing to fear from the military expedition. But, warned at the last moment that his life would be in danger if he remained at Fort Garry, Riel, considering discretion the better part of valour, fled.

Nine days after the fall of the Fort and the flight of Riel, Governor Archibald arrived at Fort Garry. It had been the Government's intention that, as the military force was not a punitive expedition, Archibald should so time his arrival as to reach Red River immediately after the troops in order to take charge of the civil government.[47] This precaution was necessary, for, in spite of the reiterated statements of the peaceful nature of the force, Canadian malcontents hoped " that as soon as the troops arrive, martial law will be proclaimed, to be followed by the hanging of a few of the French party."[48] J. H. McTavish of the Hudson's Bay Company was aware of this feeling and wrote to Taché in Eastern Canada " knowing what I do of the intentions of the Canadian Government, and fully understanding those of

F

the Provisional Government, I consider it highly advisable that Mr. Archibald should be on the spot at least as soon as the troops."[49]   Bishop Taché, it appears, hoped to expedite Archibald's arrival by sending a number of half-breeds to meet and conduct him to the Settlement via the Snow road.[50]   Unfortunately, the Governor was unable to find the place where he was to meet the escort and was obliged to continue his journey down the Winnipeg river, arriving in Winnipeg on September 2nd. In the meantime, the Provisional Government having vanished and the new Government not having yet assumed authority, the civil affairs of the colony were administered by Donald A. Smith, as the representative of the Hudson's Bay Company, at the request of Colonel Wolseley.   On Archibald's arrival Smith surrendered his authority to the Lieutenant-Governor.   " I yield up my responsibilities with pleasure," Smith declared. " Yes," returned the Governor, "I really don't anticipate much pleasure on my own account."[51]

Archibald did not find the organization of the new province an easy task.   Racial feeling continued to run high in view of the actions of those whose only thought was of revenge.   In the end, however, owing to the Governor's moderate, but firm course, the clouds began to lift and the political horizon of Manitoba took on a brighter hue.   Proceeding at once to form a new government, Archibald appointed Alfred Boyd, an English-speaking resident of Red River and member of the second Convention, and Marc Girard, lately arrived from Montreal, as the first members of his executive council.   A census of the Settlement was taken and the province divided into twenty-four electoral districts.   On December 30th, the first provincial elections were held.   The results of these were significant.   Dr. Schultz was defeated by D. A. Smith and many of those returned, both English and French, had participated in the Convention or the Provisional Government in some capacity or other—a fact which refutes any charge that the insurrection was entirely a minority movement, the work of Louis Riel and a few French-speaking adherents.   Reporting the returns to Howe, Archibald wrote, " I am happy in being able to add that the elections were conducted all over the province in perfect good humour.   I do not believe a blow was struck or violence of any kind attempted at any hustings in the province during the progress of the elections.   The returns give a large majority sustaining the policy of the Government."[52]

It was the desire of the British Government that the British troops should be withdrawn as soon as order had been restored, and following the arrival of the two regiments of Canadian militia, arrangements were made for the return of the Regulars. On August 29th, the first detachment started down the Red River and by September 3rd the last of the Imperial troops had waved farewell to the grey stone fort at the junction of the Red and Assiniboine rivers.   On their arrival in Eastern Canada they at once embarked for England, and were the last Regular troops to serve in Canada.

CHAPTER VIII

THE first Riel Rebellion had now come to an end, but it left as its legacy a question which, for the next five years, became the shuttlecock of Canadian party politics, namely, the question of an amnesty to those involved in the Red River troubles. The history of this question is one of assertions and denials, of hopeless appeals and nugatory correspondence, but it raised questions of paramount importance to the young Dominion. Although of little importance in itself, the amnesty question not only revealed the fundamental weakness of Canadian unity, the absence of a fully developed nationalism ; it also went to the root of Imperial constitutional relations.

" La politique canadien," wrote André Siegfried, " est un champ clos de rivalités passionées."[1] An immemorial struggle has marked the pages of Canadian history from 1760 to the present day, a struggle of race and of religion. When Great Britain conquered the French in Canada she failed either to annihilate or to assimilate them, with the result that Canada has been faced with the problem of reconciling the diverse interests of two races divided by nationality, language, and religion. Various constitutional experiments have been made and cast aside as failures. Both the Constitution of 1791 and the Act of Union were rendered unworkable by racial conflict. The Confederation of 1867 was a conscious effort to provide a solution for this deadlock and to promote unity among the divergent elements which fate and circumstance had brought together. Sir George Cartier saw in the federal union the possible development of a super-nationality in which the differences of race, language, and religion, should lose their disintegrating power. Under these circumstances it was imperative that no crisis should arise until the Confederation, which was, in Macdonald's words " only yet in the gristle,"[2] had hardened into bone. It was this consideration which guided the policy of Sir John A. Macdonald and the Honourable Alexander Mackenzie when the amnesty question forced itself upon them. The amnesty question was the first serious racial controversy which the new Dominion was called upon to face, and with which, for national reasons, it was reluctant to grapple.

Had there been no bloodshed during the insurrection an amnesty for the insurgents would probably have followed as a matter of political expediency. But the execution of Thomas Scott, an English-speaking Orangeman, by Louis Riel, a French-speaking Roman Catholic, kindled all those racial and religious passions, which, however common to Canadian history, were the outcome rather than the cause of the half-breed troubles of 1869–70. In Red River the death of Scott aroused no bitter feelings or racial recriminations, but in Canada it was the spark which relighted the latent embers of sectarian controversy. Ontario regarded the execution as a cold-blooded murder of an English Protestant loyalist by a French Catholic rebel : Quebec, believing that the métis were fighting for the rights of French-speaking Canadians, regarded the shooting of Scott as a necessary, although regrettable, incident. What was to be the attitude of the Dominion Government, composed as it was of representatives of both races, and dependent for its life upon the caprice or passion of a democratic electorate ? To take either one side or the other might be fatal, both to the young Confederation and to the Conservative Government. Macdonald and Cartier, therefore, compromised. To please Quebec they negotiated with the Red River delegates ; to placate Ontario they despatched the military force ; to save the Government they endeavoured to shift to the Colonial Office the responsibility for the proclamation of a general amnesty.

This last policy, namely, the refusal to accept the responsibility for an unpopular though necessary course of action—now a common feature of federal and provincial relations—raised an issue of Imperial importance. The granting of responsible government had placed in the hands of the colonial executive the whole responsibility for the exercise of the prerogative formerly exercised by the Crown through the Governor-General. This, together with the fact that Canadian courts had concurrent jurisdiction with the Hudson's Bay Company in the North-West, gave the Canadian Government undoubted authority to grant an amnesty to the Red River insurgents, if it so desired. At the same time it may be argued that, although the Hudson's Bay Company possessed virtual sovereignty in Rupert's Land, this giant was held of the Crown, which could, accordingly, resume what it had granted, and assume direct sovereignty over the Company's territories.   As a matter of law the Crown had the authority to promulgate an amnesty for the insurgents, directly, or through the Governor-General of Canada.   It was not, however, advisable that the Crown should thus act independently in a matter which was of paramount interest to the Dominion of Canada.   For Great Britain to have taken the matter into her own hands and to have acted without ascertaining the collective opinion of the Canadian Government, would have been contrary to the general tendency of Imperial policy.   It would have removed an awkward burden from the shoulders of the Canadian Government, but it would have created an undesirable precedent for referring internal racial controversies to an outside authority for judgment.   If Canada was to advance along the path leading to nationhood, it was imperative that she should assume the responsibility of finding a solution for her own difficulties, not resort to the mother country upon every occasion that her government might be faced with an embarrassing racial and religious issue.   Canada owes much to Lord Granville and to Lord Kimberley for refusing to accept the responsibility which the Canadian Government endeavoured to foist upon them.   With this in mind we may review the apparently futile correspondence between Canada and the Colonial Office, with an appreciation of the policy of the latter in forcing Canada to recognize the implications and to assume the burdens of her new juridical status.

The first reference to an amnesty was contained in Sir John Young's proclamation of December 6th, 1869, which stated:

" And I do lastly inform you, that in case of your immediate and peaceable obedience and dispersion, I shall order that no legal proceeding be taken against any parties implicated in these unfortunate breaches of the law."[3]

Five hundred copies of this proclamation were given to Commissioners Thibault and de Salaberry, but were taken, along with Thibault's other official papers, by Riel's Council, and were never published.   Donald A. Smith, although he had in his possession a copy of the proclamation, did not read it before the mass meet-

ings of January. Thus, while the members of Riel's Council
must have been aware of its contents, the terms of the Governor-
General's proclamation were never made public to the people of
Red River until the arrival of Bishop Taché in March.

At Ottawa Bishop Taché was taken fully into the confidence of
the Canadian Government and was requested to lend his invaluable services to the work of pacification.   In the course of these
conversations Taché brought up the question of an amnesty for
the offences committed during the troubles ; but he was assured
that if the people of Red River would consent to enter Confederation the past would be forgotten, and " they should not be
troubled in any way on account of the past."[4]   The proclamation
of the Governor-General was given to the Bishop as official proof
of the intentions of the Canadian Government and he was
assured that it would have, from the date of his arrival at Red
River, all the force that it had on the day of issue.   " Tout fut
dit et fait," wrote Taché, " de façon à convaincre le prélat que
s'il réussissait à calmer les esprits, on serait heureux d'oublier
les faits malheureux qui avaient pu se produire avant son arrivée
au Fort Garry."[5]   Immediately after the conversations in question
Macdonald wrote to Rose, " Bishop Taché has been here and has
left for the Red River, after exceedingly full and unreserved
communication with him as to our policy and requirements, all
of which he approves."[6]   There was, however, an unfortunate
misunderstanding concerning the extent of the promises made.
While Taché was apparently convinced of the definite intention
of the Canadian Government to grant an amnesty covering all
offences up to the time of his arrival at Red River,[7] Macdonald
apparently did not expect any particular change in the situation in
the colony, such as the execution of Thomas Scott involved.   In
fact, Taché later declared that the Canadian Government, during
their conversations with him, had no real idea as to the state of
affairs in Red River.

On his departure for the North-West Taché was given several
letters, all of which leave little doubt that, in view of the situation
as it was understood at Ottawa, an amnesty was intended by
the Canadian Government.   In his letter to the Bishop, the
Governor-General wrote :[8]

" You are fully in possession of the views of my Government,
and the Imperial Government, as I informed you, is earnest in the

desire to see the North-West Territory united to the dominion on equitable conditions. . . . In declaring the desire and determination of Her Majesty's Cabinet you may safely use the terms of the ancient formula, that right shall be done in all cases."

Further evidence is furnished by Macdonald's letter :[9]

" Should the question arise as to the consumption of any stores or goods belonging to the Hudson's Bay Company by the insurgents, you are authorized to inform the leaders that if the Company's Government is restored, not only will there be a general amnesty granted ; but in case the Company should claim the payment for such stores, that the Canadian Government will stand between the insurgents and all harm."

On March 11th Taché interviewed Riel, Lépine and the other leaders of the Provisional Government. He explained to them the favourable disposition of Canada and, in response to their demand for an amnesty, produced the Governor-General's proclamation, which, he assured them, covered all offences up to that date. English Canadian feeling was hardly in accord with these professions of good will. The outburst of religious and racial fanaticism in the Ontario press, the arrest of the Red River delegates, the threat of military coercion, and above all the absence of any definite promise of an amnesty, created a feeling of unrest and suspicion which was rendered all the more dangerous by offers of assistance to the insurgents, from interested parties in the United States. Realizing the danger, convinced that nothing else could save the situation, and supported by the opinions of Thibault, Mactavish and de Salaberry, Taché gave his solemn word of honour and promised in the name of the Canadian Government " that all the irregularities of the past will be totally overlooked or forgiven ; that nobody will be annoyed for having been either leader or member of the Provisional Government, or for having acted under its guidance. In a word, that a complete and entire amnesty (if not already bestowed) will surely be granted before the arrival of the troops."[10] Taché felt no compunctions in making this promise in view of the impression left upon him by his conversations with the members of the Canadian Government in February. Nevertheless he exceeded his authority in so doing. Unlike the other Commissioners, the Bishop was not armed with any formal commission from the Canadian Government. He did not, however, claim to bind the Government as a plenipotentiary, but gave the assurances above in the hope that the Canadian Government, realizing the exigencies of the case, would, as a matter of policy, honour his promises.[11]

The Canadian ministers, whatever their private opinions as to the advisability of an amnesty, could not, in the face of English-speaking opinion in Canada, proclaim it. Howe immediately replied to Taché[12] informing him that the amnesty was a matter exclusively for the Queen, and that the Canadian Government did not possess the power as a government to grant it. He added, however :

" Though I have felt it my duty to be thus explicit in dealing with the principal subject of your letter, I trust I need not assure you that your zealous and valuable exertions to calm the public mind in the North-West are duly appreciated here, and I am confident that when you regard the obstructions which have been interposed to the adoption of a liberal and enlightened policy for Manitoba, you will not be disposed to relax your exertions until that policy is formally established."

This letter contained no direct disavowal of Taché's promise, nor a command to correct a misinformed people, but requested him to continue his rôle of pacificator. This concluding portion of Howe's letter must have been, to say the least, very reassuring to the Bishop. The more so when it was followed the next day by a letter from Sir George Cartier, who was leader of the Government during Macdonald's illness. This letter gave undoubted colour to the assertion made at the time that Howe's letter was for the public eye and Sir George's was for the prelate alone. The following are a few extracts from Cartier's letter relative to the amnesty question :[13]

" This letter is written to you, my Lord, with the intention that it is to be strictly confidential, as I have to speak with you of the delicate question of the amnesty. You must be convinced from what you have seen in the newspapers, that Ontario and part of the Province of Quebec and of the Maritime Provinces are keenly opposed to an amnesty. But happily for the people of Red River the question of the amnesty rests with Her Majesty the Queen, and not with the Canadian Government. . . . If the amnesty rested with and were the province of the Canadian Government, composed with heterogeneous elements, it would be in great danger. But it is, I repeat, fortunate that it is Her Majesty, aided by the advice of Her Ministers, who will have to decide this question. Her Majesty has already, by the proclamation of December 6th last, which She caused to be issued by Sir John Young, so to speak, promised an amnesty. This fact was mentioned in Father Ritchot's petition to the Queen. I must now intimate to you that the surest way of securing this amnesty is that the whole population of Red River should accept the new order of things. . . . The Queen will perhaps await this result before making known her clemency. The expedition is an expedition of peace, and the Quebec battalion comprises a large number of your friends. . . . The soldiers will not be instruments of Dr. Schultz or anyone else, to arrest or drag to prison any person whomsoever. . . .

" Note the fact that copies of all your letters received here have been sent by Sir John Young to Lord Granville, in order to shew the position of the amnesty question, if it should happen, which I do not apprehend, that opposition were offered on the arrival of the troops and of the new Governor, those who took part in it would incur the risk of finding themselves excluded from the amnesty Her Majesty may have in view, and which She will sooner or later make known."

Coming from the leader of the Government this letter appeared to be a definite committal of the Canadian Government in favour of the principle of an amnesty.

On March 23rd and 24th, the delegates, charged by the Provisional Government to arrange the terms of the union with Canada, left for Ottawa, bearing with them a List of Rights which was to serve as the basis for negotiations. Clause nineteen read in part as follows :

" that none of the members of the Provisional Government, or any of those acting under them, be in any way held liable or responsible with regard to the movement or any of the actions which led to the present negotiations."

From April 22nd to May 6th negotiations were—as we have seen in Chapter VI—carried on between the delegates of Red River and the representatives of the Canadian Government. Unfortunately only one of these delegates has given any evidence as to the history of these negotiations, but that delegate, Father Ritchot, deposed before the Select Committee in 1874, that he had insisted upon Clause 19 as the *sine qua non* of any definite arrangement between the people of Red River and the Dominion Government.[14] Other evidence seems to show that Ritchot was not alone in this demand. On April 28th, Taylor, the United States Secret Agent, after a conversation with Judge Black, reported :

" I am inclined to think that the Red River Delegates will unite in a demand for a full and unqualified amnesty for all acts in Winnipeg prior to the passage of the proposed territorial Act."[15]

It does not appear that Macdonald and Cartier positively conceded this demand, but there is no doubt that they conveyed to the delegates the impression " that there would be no difficulty whatever, with regard to the amnesty."[16] Ritchot stated this emphatically in his deposition in 1874, and A. H. Scott informed Taylor during the course of the negotiations that " the civil amnesty would be full and proceed from Canada ; while the Imperial Government would assume the responsibility of a pardon for criminal offences."[17]

On May 3rd an official audience was granted Ritchot by the Governor-General, Sir Clinton Murdoch also being present. Ritchot expressed his satisfaction with the terms of the proposed Manitoba Bill, but referred again to the absence of any definite assurances with regard to the amnesty. His Excellency then pointed to Sir Clinton Murdoch, and said, " He knows it is the intention of Her Majesty to declare a general amnesty in order to establish peace in the country. Besides you have seen my proclamation." Murdoch repeated these assurances : " You have nothing to fear, Her Majesty wishes but one thing, and that is to pass the sponge over all that has happened in the North-West, and establish peace. She wishes to place that Province in a position to attain prosperity like the other English provinces."[18] Another interview was held on the 19th at which similar assurances were made.

In considering this question it is important to note that the Governor-General subsequently denied that any definite promises had been made at either of these interviews. Writing in 1872 to Lord Kimberley, the Secretary of State for the Colonies, he said :

" I am clear that I never made any such promise of an amnesty as that which they allege. . . . In reply to the earnest and repeated instances of the delegates, I uniformly answered that the question of amnesty should be duly submitted for the consideration both of the Dominion Government and of Her Majesty's Ministers, and that I had no doubt it would receive from them that serious attention in all its bearings which it merited, but I guarded myself by adding that I was not in a position to make any promise or give any assurances whatever on the subject."[19]

Additional evidence to this effect is furnished by the fact that in his official despatch of May 19th to Lord Granville, Young made no mention of any promise of an amnesty.   Likewise Sir Clinton Murdoch's letters contained no reference to any such promise.   Sir George Cartier, who was present at the interviews, confirmed the Governor-General's statement in a letter to Sir John A. Macdonald :

" Bear in mind that with Father Ritchot and the Archbishop I always took the same ground—we both did—namely that the question of amnesty was not for our decision, but for the Queen and Imperial Government."[20]

These assertions and denials make it abundantly clear that while no definite promise of an amnesty was made to the delegates, nevertheless the impression left upon the minds of Ritchot and his colleagues, both by the conversations and letters of the Canadian ministers, was that an amnesty would be granted by the Queen and the Imperial Government as a matter of public policy.

Assured, although not wholly convinced, Ritchot left for Red River.   On his arrival he immediately communicated with Riel, informed him of the happy conclusion of the Ottawa negotiations, and assured him that the amnesty would be proclaimed, " that it was promised me as a *sine qua non* condition of our arrangements."[21]   The same assurances were repeated to Bishop Taché, " The Canadian authorities . . . had done all in their power to secure the amnesty, and they were in a position to assure the delegates, not only that it would be granted, but that it would arrive probably before they had returned home, certainly before the arrival of the Lieutenant-Governor."[22]

In spite of these numerous assurances, the absence of anything in writing and the delay in implementing the oral promises were disquieting both to the half-breeds and to Bishop Taché.   Accordingly, the Bishop, without awaiting an answer to his despatch of June 9th, left for Ottawa in order to satisfy himself as to the full authority behind Ritchot's assertions.   Arriving there about July 11th or 12th, he immediately conferred with Sir George

Cartier, who agreed that " the report of Father Ritchot was correct,"[23] and insisted that he should himself see Sir John Young. In company with Sir George, Bishop Taché proceeded to Niagara where the Governor-General was staying. Although his reception was not a cordial one, Taché once more drew the Governor's attention to the necessity of the amnesty, whereupon the latter pointed to his proclamation of December 6th, which lay upon the table, and said, " Here is my proclamation ; it covers the whole case . . . See Sir George Cartier ; he knows my views upon the subject, and he will tell you all."[24] Thus assured, Taché hastened to send a telegram to Father Lestanc at Red River, informing him that all was well, and that in spite of the bellicose statements to the contrary in the Ontario press, the amnesty would be granted. On August 8th he left for St. Boniface where he arrived on the day before the eventful capture of Fort Garry by Colonel Wolseley.

In view of this evidence the question arises, why was the amnesty not granted ? There can be no doubt that an amnesty was fully intended by certain members at least of the Canadian Government. Macdonald's claim that Cartier and the delegates regarded the amnesty from two different points of view—the one considering only an amnesty from which those responsible for the death of Scott were excluded, the others desiring an amnesty embracing all offenders—is clearly untenable. Cartier's correspondence leaves no doubt that he fully understood and sympathized with the demand for a complete and general amnesty. In particular his Secret Memorandum to the Governor-General of June 8th,[25] is explicit :

" If the undersigned had any suggestion to make in the matter it would be his opinion that the best policy to pursue in case Her Majesty should be graciously inclined to grant a general amnesty for any acts amounting to high treason, levying of war, rebellion and treasonable practices during the period mentioned . . . would be that such amnesty should except no one."

The evidence also shows that while Cartier always insisted that the amnesty was a matter for the Queen alone, he fully believed that there would be no difficulty in obtaining it ; and assured Taché, Ritchot and others, by word of mouth and by his correspondence that an amnesty would be granted. The evidence of the two clergy is fully corroborated by other evidence. A. H.

Scott, Ritchot's co-delegate, joined him in a petition to the Queen which stated :[26]

" That the Honourable Sir John A. Macdonald and Sir G. E. Cartier declared to the delegates that they were in measure to assure them that such was the intention of Your Majesty, that they could consequently proceed with the negotiations, being satisfied that the Royal Prerogative of Mercy would be exercised by the grant of a general amnesty."

J. W. Taylor reported to Washington[27] that :

" everything now confirms the opinion expressed in former communications that long before the expedition reaches Red River the Queen's proclamation of complete amnesty will be issued."

The Honourable Joseph Royal, a Minister of the Crown in the Province of Manitoba and later Lieutenant-Governor of the North-West Territories, deposed :[28]

" I said to Sir George, I intend to go to Manitoba if the amnesty is to be proclaimed. He advised me very strongly to go, for several reasons. . . . He told me to tell Riel, and to write to him ' L'amnistie est une affaire decidée, c'est une affaire faite.' "

The Honourable Marc Girard, a former Prime Minister of Manitoba, deposed as follows :[29]

" As one of the Ministers of the Province, and feeling that it would be impossible to do much good in the Province without an amnesty, I wrote to Sir George Cartier, whom I regarded as one of my particular friends, on two or three different occasions, drawing his attention to that amnesty and the promise which I understood from the whole of the people had been made of an amnesty. In these letters I described the condition of the country, and urged strongly upon Sir George the necessity of an amnesty. . . . His answer was to request me to be sure that the amnesty would come.   ' Soyez certain que l'amnistie viendra avant longtemps.' "

Major Futvoye, Cartier's deputy minister, and Benjamin Sulte, his secretary, made similar statements, namely, that Sir George Cartier had repeatedly promised that an amnesty would be granted by the Queen.

But, while Cartier was taking this definite stand, other members of the Cabinet, in view of the rising storm of public agitation in the English-speaking provinces, were hardly inclined to view the situation with sympathy. " I must state to you," wrote Cartier to Taché in July, " that your letter of June 9th last to Mr. Howe, relative to the amnesty, caused a little fear and dismay amongst several of my colleagues, who stand in fear and dread of public opinion in Ontario and other parts of the Dominion on this question."[30] Herein lay the danger. The country had now become divided into two antagonistic camps over the shooting of Scott and the amnesty question, and the calm reason of statesmanship was unable to resist the mass emotionalism of an overwrought democracy.

We have related above the early agitation fostered by the " Canada First " group during March and April, but this was only the beginning. Once started the movement gathered force and the old religious and racial strife of former decades was renewed with new battlecries. The rumour that the visit of Cartier and Taché to the Governor-General at Niagara was to discuss the promulgation of an amnesty, incited the agitators to violent demonstrations. Colonel Denison, a member of the " Canada First " group, threatened to take possession of the arsenal and fight it out in the Toronto streets ! [31] Indeed the fear of mob violence was such that Taché was obliged to journey to Niagara over foreign soil. The fact that the unfortunate Scott was a member of the Orange Order provided the anti-French-Catholic forces with a powerful bludgeon. The city of Toronto was placarded with inflammatory notices : " Shall French Rebels Rule our Dominion ? Orangemen, is Brother Scott Forgotten Already ? Men of Ontario, Shall Scott's Blood cry in Vain for Vengeance ? " A formal petition to the Governor-General,[32] prepared by Dr. Lynch, urging that to grant an amnesty would be " injudicious, impolitic, and dangerous . . . destructive of all confidence in law and order " and an " encouragement to rebellion," was given wide publicity in the press. Great meetings were held to voice the popular disapproval of the Government's conduct.

To add to the Government's embarrassment, the Liberal party politicians eagerly grasped the opportunity to turn to political account the popular indignation, and to turn the normally Conservative Orange vote against Sir John and Sandfield Macdonald at the next elections. On the defeat of Edward Blake's tactical motion in the Ontario Assembly deploring " the cold-blooded murder, for his outspoken loyalty to the Queen, of *Thomas Scott*, lately a resident of this Province " and urging that " every effort should be made to bring to trial the perpetrators of this great crime, who, as yet, go unwhipt of justice,"[33] the *Globe* unfurled the banner of " loyalty " over the Liberal cause.

Stung by the taunts, and incited by the agitation of the *Globe* and the Reform press, the wrath of the Orange Order was aroused. The Honourable J. H. Cameron was voted out as Grand Master for having undertaken, in April, the defence of Ritchot and Scott; and, as the chief Liberal organ gleefully related, "expression was also given to the determination that the body should use its influence to defeat the Government at the ensuing general election, and an uncompromising tone of dissent was given to the position occupied by Sir John A. Macdonald in his humiliating subservience to Sir G. E. Cartier."[34] In Montreal the *Witness* belaboured the Orangemen for their continued adherence to the Conservative party :

" The Orangemen, who foamed at the mouth with wild hysterical demands for vengeance and the extermination of all French rebels, follow their party leaders like whipped spaniels, and dare not raise their voices to protest against the manner in which the affairs of the new Province are being engineered in the French and rebel interest."[35]

An attempt by D'Alton McCarthy and other dignitaries of the Orange brotherhood to deprecate the making of political capital out of the execution of Scott was denounced as " unwarrantable," " unprotestant," and " unorange."[36] The Conservatives were accused of having betrayed English-speaking and Orange interests, and George Brown of the *Globe* declared that their defeat in Ontario would serve to end " the French domination in Manitoba."[37] This appeal to prejudice was not unsuccessful. Partly at least as a result of Orange votes and Blake's pre-election strategy, the Government of Sandfield Macdonald fell from power on December 15th, 1871.

On the other hand, the population of Quebec, linked by ties of blood and speech to the métis of the west, were quick to resent the attacks upon the Red River " rebels." They interpreted it as an attack upon French Canadian Catholic nationalism. What one side looked upon as a dastardly crime, the other extolled as

a patriotic deed.   Ontario was full of righteous indignation at
the murder of a " loyal " Ontario Orangeman by a French
Catholic " rebel " ;   Quebec, at the challenge to her dearly
earned privileges of faith and language.   Taché's letter was
typical of the whole French Canadian feeling :

" it is obvious to every one that the pretended loyalty of those
who speak the loudest is entirely due to the deception they
experienced on not having succeeded, as quickly as they desired,
in assuming for themselves all power in the North-West, making
it, as they now so openly avow, ' Another Ontario in creed and
politics.' "[38]

At first the French opinion was inclined to be moderate.
L'Opinion Publique declared that it was difficult to consider the
execution as other than a murder.[39]   Even *Le Nouveau Monde*
expressed its regret that Riel would not listen to the counsels
and prayers of the Catholic clergy who had asked grace for the
condemned man :   " Pourquoi mettre un cadavre sur le chemin
glorieux parcouru jusqu'ici ? "[40]   But the challenge to race
and religion was soon to receive its answer.   *Le Journal de Québec*
characterized the Toronto demonstration as an assemblage of
Orange fanatics brought together, not so much to deprecate
Scott's murder, as to give vent to their anti-French passions.
The *Globe* and *Telegraph* were accused of working for " l'extermination des métis français à la Rivière Rouge " and the people
of the neighbouring province were branded as " ces Prussiens
du Canada qui veulent tout absorber à leur profit."[41]   It was
declared that " Si Louis Riel s'appelait John Jones ou Duncan
McDougall, et si le défunt Scott, fût-il simplement J. Bte.
Papineau, il n'y aurait jamais eu de *meeting* d'indignation à
Toronto."   The more radical newspapers, led by *Le Nouveau
Monde*, *Le Canadien*, and *L'Ordre*, vigorously denounced the
Government for not granting an unconditional amnesty for the
illegal acts of a conflict for which the Government was itself
responsible.   The most extreme illustration of the French
Canadian attitude was a poem printed in *Le Canadien* by Pamphile
Lemay.   In it Riel was described as " a man frank, just and noble,
whom it is desired to crucify, a sovereign by the voice of the people
who have asked protection from his tutelary arms."   On the
other hand Scott was spoken of as an " ignoble victim, who was
about to plunge the steel during the night into the heart of his

sovereign." The whole production was addressed to those
" who demand Riel's head " and had for title, " Crucify him !
Crucify him ! " As to the persons thus apostrophized the poem
called upon them " to cease to shout " and declared that what
they regretted most was not the " blood of their venal and traitor-
ous friend, but the sceptre which has passed into the hands of
a fortunate rival," and what they demanded " is that the Catholics
who have always treated them so well should expire on the cross
like Christ at Golgotha." Although some of the milder papers
criticized this blasphemous work as " indigne d'un homme de
sens," *Le Nouveau Monde* declared that it contained " dans des
iambes énergiques et vrais le sentiment de ses compatriotes sur le
ʼort de ce misérable Scott dont les Orangistes font en ce moment
leur héros."[42]

As a result of this clash of nationalities the Federal Government was placed upon the horns of a dilemma. To grant the
amnesty would be to commit political suicide in Ontario ; to
refuse would be to imperil the traditional Conservative hold on
Quebec ; while in either case the fabric of Confederation would be
subjected to a great strain. The Colonial Government, therefore,
endeavoured to shift the responsibility to the shoulders of the
mother country. Cartier and Macdonald both assured the Red
River delegates that they must look to the Queen solely and
directly for the exercise of the royal clemency. In Parliament
the ministers took the same stand, namely, that the amnesty
belonged exclusively to the jurisdiction of the Imperial authorities,
and could not be dealt with by Canada. Cartier wrote to the
Colonial Office that " it would have been impossible for this
administration to agree among themselves on that question " and
that the amnesty was for " the decision of Her Majesty advised
by the Imperial ministers themselves, inasmuch as no decision
could have been otherwise arrived at."[43] The question was
fully discussed in the Cabinet chamber, and the official view was
embodied in the letter to Taché on July 4th, which, while not
actually repudiating his promise to the people, disclaimed any
authority to rule upon the matter. For the Dominion to have
passed judgment either one way or the other might have been
harmful both to the party and to the State ; nevertheless, for the
Government to refuse all responsibility for a question which was
primarily one of Canadian interest and to pass it on to the

Imperial Government, cannot be considered as other than a retrograde step, a precedent contrary to the spirit of self-government.

In Great Britain the Red River Rebellion aroused little or no interest. It received scant mention either in press or parliament. *Laissez-aller* was still the order of the day, and with Sir Frederic Rogers and his conviction that " the destiny of our Colonies is independence "[44] dominating the Colonial Office, the principal object of that department was to get the North-West question off their hands as soon as possible. Once the transfer was completed the North-West was regarded as entirely a Canadian problem, to be dealt with, in all its ramifications, by the Canadian Government alone. Accordingly, throughout the next five years, the British Government steadily refused to assume any Imperial responsibility for the question of an amnesty for the Red River insurgents.

The first evidence of any suggestion to the Colonial Office of an amnesty appeared at the time of the *Chicora* incident, when the American President expressed his hope " that an amnesty will be proclaimed for Riel and his followers."[45] This request brought forth an important minute[46] by Sir Frederic Rogers outlining the principles which were to govern the actions of the British Government throughout the entire controversy :

" The point is respecting Riel and amnesty. It appears to me that in case of a rising of this kind the mere having taken part in it, under passion or misconception ; and having been party to such acts of treason or seizure of property, or personal violence as are necessarily incident to such a political movement, conducted with reasonable moderation and care for human life, cannot be too completely and promptly condoned under such circumstances as exist.

" But it is a great evil if a Government is forced to make itself party, by giving avowed impunity to seizure of property which is mere plunder and tyranny, and to destruction of life which is mere brutal passion, unjust, irregular, and unnecessary, to an extent which could not be overlooked in the case of a lawful authority.

" This is the objection in the abstract to an amnesty.

" But further, the United States Government seems to expect that we shall aid them in endeavouring to get credit with their countrymen for establishing in our Territories a kind of protectorate over those persons who engage in the overthrow of our institutions. It seems to me that this is a position in which it is unwise and ridiculous for us to place ourselves, and that we should take some pains to show that Riel, Lynch (sic) etc., owe their lives and liberties—if they retain them—to British leniency and not to American protection—or at least should not encourage the opposite belief.

"Politically I suppose that to 'amnesty' Riel and Lépine would make the Upper Canadians furious and to proceed against them with the weapon of the law would make the Lower Canadians furious.

" Therefore it appears to me that the best course for Canada, and for us, is to make it evident that there is no idea of treating the insurrection as an offence or of subjecting any person to punishment for having been concerned in it.

" With regard to persons who under colour of the insurrection have taken away the property or lives of individuals the best course is to say nothing—but if something must be said, to declare that such cases must necessarily be dealt with on their particular circumstances and that it is impossible to put forth any general promise or any general threat respecting them.

" As we get near Red River it may be hoped that the very few persons who have been concerned in the great outrages will be wise enough (after the warning derivable from the arrest of Scott and Ritchot) to take themselves off.

" The only material matter, if that is so, appears to be that we and the Canadians should understand each other.

" It seems to me that if anything is sent or said to the Canadian Government which might be taken as a hint to do this or that, it should be accompanied by an intimation that in the opinion of Her Majesty's Government it would be most unfortunate if any more blood were shed, either in the field or by process of law— that it would also be a bad example if the Government formally condoned any outrage of such gravity that it could not be excused as one of the unhappy accidents of civil disturbances—that under the circumstances the proclamation of an indiscriminate amnesty seemed impolitic—but that if there existed any apprehension that persons would be disquieted for being concerned in the insurrectionary movement, it would be most desirable that such apprehension should be, if possible, dispelled—and that it was much to be hoped that the persons who had been the principals in any grave outrage would consult their own safety and the public peace by removing from British jurisdiction."

On the basis of this minute Lord Granville, the Colonial

Secretary, wrote confidentially to Young to learn the views of the Canadian Government, requesting that he should forward immediately the instructions given to Lieutenant-Governor Archibald " with respect to the persons immediately concerned in the recent insurrection in the Red River Settlement." He added, " I wish especially to be informed of the course which the Canadian Government would propose should be taken."[47] Sir John Young had, in the meantime, forwarded the petition of Ritchot and a secret despatch which stated that the Canadian Cabinet were not of one mind on the question of an amnesty, and expressed the hope that " in prospect of the jealousies and animosities which the discussion of the subject is certain to give rise to here, I trust Her Majesty's Government will not remit the question to the Dominion Government, but will pronounce an opinion upon it themselves."[48] A few days later Sir George Cartier's secret memorandum, giving his personal opinion in favour of a complete and general amnesty, was forwarded to the Colonial Office. The British Government, however, were not prepared to act upon the question without the collective approval of the Canadian Government. To have done so, while not unconstitutional, would have been inexpedient. It was above all necessary, as Rogers had noted, that the Canadian and Imperial Governments should be in agreement upon the policy to be followed. Accordingly Lord Granville replied to the Governor-General by a confidential despatch on June 30th that Cartier's memorandum, not having been submitted to his colleagues, gave Her Majesty's Government no authority from Canada to assume the responsibility for the settlement of the question.[49] Granville was succeeded at the Colonial Office by Lord Kimberley a few days after the sending of this despatch, but the official attitude of the Government remained unchanged. To Young's repeated request that the British Government should rule upon this question, Kimberley merely replied, " I have to refer you on this subject to my predecessor's despatch of June 30th."[50]

For the Canadian Government to speak with a united voice on the amnesty question was impossible. Young again emphasized this point when forwarding Bunn's letter signifying the Provisional Government's willingness to enter the Canadian Confederation on the understanding that an amnesty would be granted. He also intimated that both Cartier and Macdonald were of

opinion that the Imperial Government must assume the responsibility of dealing with the amnesty question, on the ground that
the illegal acts were committed prior to the acquisition of the
North-West by Canada.[51]   Kimberley observed on receipt of
this despatch " it is for the Canadian Government to determine
what course they would recommend.   We must have their
opinion as a Government, not the separate views of different
ministers."[52]   To explain the utter impossibility of the Canadian
Government determining any course, Cartier prepared another
memorandum.[53] After pointing out that the Canadian authorities
had insisted both in Parliament and out " that the inhabitants of
Red River Settlement must necessarily look to Her Majesty the
Queen, solely and directly, for the exercise of the Royal clemency
in favour of the participators in the disturbances referred to,
and must trust to the merciful disposition ever evinced by Her
Majesty in all cases in which She felt warranted in exercising her
Prerogative of Pardon," Cartier emphasized the dilemma with
which the Canadian Government was faced :

" Irrespective of the reasons given above for leaving the
question of amnesty to be dealt with by the Imperial authorities
without the advice or interference of the Canadian Government,
Your Excellency knows as a fact that it would be impossible for
this Administration to agree among themselves on that question,
and it was within the spirit and purport of that paragraph to
reserve the question for the decision of Her Majesty advised by
Her Imperial Ministers, inasmuch as no decision could have
been otherwise arrived at.   It may, moreover, be observed that
had the views of the Delegates with regard to the question of
amnesty, as a preliminary step towards negotiation been at all
entertained, it would have been manifestly impossible to arrive
at any conclusion with them and the passing of the Manitoba
Act would have been an impossibility.

" If Your Excellency were to refer that question for the consideration of Your Council, the answer would necessarily be that
it was not one for the action or advice of the Canadian Government but for that of Her Majesty in Her Imperial Council ; and
further, that in view of the explanations offered by Your Ministers
in the House of Commons, Parliament and the country expect a
solution of that question directly by Her Majesty advised by Her
Imperial Ministers. . . .

" Notwithstanding the transfer to Canada of the North-West
Territory on July 15th instant ; that transfer cannot alter the

legal aspect of the question as regards offences committed by the people of that territory anterior to that date, the pardoning of which offences resting now as well as then properly with Her Majesty under the advice of Her Imperial Ministers.

" As regards the merits of the question of amnesty the undersigned persists in the views which he has already individually expressed to Your Excellency, and in which Sir Francis Hincks has stated his concurrence."

Kimberley, however, refused to consider the question in this light. He wrote "It is for your responsible ministers to determine what advice shall be tendered to you as the Representative of the Crown, respecting this as well as other questions affecting the Government of the Dominion of which Manitoba now forms a part."[54] A fortnight later, on August 11th, the Colonial Secretary sent another despatch to Ottawa outlining the considered opinion of the British Government :[55]

" Her Majesty's Government cannot act in so grave a matter upon the authority of any individual member of the Canadian Government, however eminent. If your Ministers should resolve that this is a question which they cannot undertake to decide and that they must refer its decision to the Imperial Government, this resolution must be conveyed through you as the opinion of the Government of the Dominion, and Her Majesty's Government must be distinctly requested to assume the responsibility of dealing with the question."

From this position the Imperial authorities refused to recede. The British Government fully appreciated the difficulty in which the Canadian Ministers were placed, but constantly refused to assume, on their own responsibility, the unpleasant task of settling the amnesty issue. The whole trend of colonial policy for the previous ten years was against the assumption of further colonial responsibilities, and the Imperial authorities were hardly anxious to bear the unpopularity which a decision, one way or the other, was bound to create. Kimberley was well aware that if the Imperial authorities were to deal with the amnesty question without a definite understanding with Canada, such a procedure would serve as a precedent for the reference of politically dangerous questions to the mother country for solution. " The issue of an amnesty by the Queen directly," he wrote in a minute in 1873, " may be used by the Dominion Government to cast an undue responsibility on the Imperial Government, and it may be an inconvenient precedent."[56]

In Manitoba the promised amnesty had been anxiously awaited by Riel. But in spite of the promises of Taché and the assurances of Ritchot, the half-breed leader had been obliged to seek safety in flight. This was, as Rogers had suggested, probably the most satisfactory solution for the moment, especially as it was openly admitted that no amnesty could have protected Riel from the wrath of the Ontarians. Lieutenant-Governor Archibald wrote with relief, " it is perhaps the best solution of the question that these men have taken to flight. Their presence here in the meantime would have been a source of incessant trouble."[57] The flight of Riel, however, was only a temporary respite at best, for the whole controversy regarding the amnesty was resumed a year later after the attempt of O'Donoghue to revive the Provisional Government and the half-breed insurrection.

The half-breed leaders were not long in exile. They returned quietly to the Red River Settlement, and on September 17th, a gathering was held at the Rivière Sale. Riel denounced the Canadian Government for refusing to carry out its " solemn pledges " and a petition was drawn up by the meeting, addressed to " His Excellency U. S. Grant, President of the United States," praying for his intercession on their behalf.[58] An appeal to the United States was not regarded with unqualified approval by Louis Riel. He had not yet renounced his allegiance to the British Crown, and, probably under clerical advice, refused to tolerate any proposals for annexation to the American Republic. This led to an open breach with W. B. O'Donoghue, the former Treasurer of the Provisional Government, who had never disguised his Irish antagonism to things British and his sympathy with the Yankee annexationists.

Henceforth O'Donoghue worked actively to revive the Provisional Government and the half-breed insurrection as an instrument of American annexation. Early in October he redrafted the Rivière Sale petition on annexationist lines and forwarded it to the President of the United States. At Washington he had the active support of Senator Ramsey of Minnesota, but, receiving little encouragement from other sources, he turned to enlist the aid of the Fenian Brotherhood, which had already demonstrated their anti-British proclivities by two unsuccessful armed raids into Canadian territory. It does not appear that O'Donoghue was officially sponsored by the Brotherhood, but no obstacle was placed in the way of his enlisting their members. Finally on October 5th, 1871, O'Donoghue, accompanied by "General" O'Neill and other well-known Fenian filibusters, crossed the frontier at Pembina and took possession of the Hudson's Bay Company Fort.

The success of the venture depended upon the spontaneous rising of the discontented half-breeds. Certainly O'Donoghue had ample reason to expect that they might adhere to a movement which he claimed to be carrying on under the banner of the Provisional Government. Everything seemed to point in that direction. The métis were sullen and discontented. The coming of the volunteers—many of whom had openly stated " that they had taken a vow before leaving home to pay off all scores by shooting down any Frenchman " who was in any way connected with the execution of Scott[59]—opened an era of persecution. In spite of the fact that Wolseley, in his proclamation, had declared that his force represented " no party, either in religion or politics," one of the first actions of the Ontario volunteers was to establish an Orange Lodge.[60] Conflicts between the métis and the Canadians became common occurrences. Shortly after the establishment of the Provincial Government, Elzéar Goulet, who had been a member of the court-martial which had sentenced Scott, was drowned while endeavouring to escape from a hostile crowd of pursuers. An investigation was held, but, owing to the prevailing excitement, no arrests were made.[61] A month later an English half-breed, James Tanner, who had gained the enmity of the ultra-Orange and Ontario faction, was killed by a fall when his horse was deliberately frightened by his enemies.[62] André Nault, who had commanded the firing squad and later protected the British flag against O'Donoghue, was chased across the American boundary, kicked, stabbed and left for dead.[63]

A more serious situation arose when the métis found their lands were being taken forcible possession of by newcomers from Ontario. Although a métis settlement had been established at the Rivière aux Ilets de Bois, Canadian immigrants squatted in this region and even upon lands claimed by the half-breeds, declaring that they would defend them against all comers.   To add insult to injury they ignored the name by which the district was known and called the river the Boyne.   The métis organized to drive out the intruders, and it was only with the greatest difficulty that a collision was avoided.   Governor Archibald summed up the dangerous situation in the following words :

" Had blood been shed on that occasion we should have had a civil war in which every French half-breed would have been an active participator ;   while from the English half-breeds, in accord on this question of property with the French, neutrality was the utmost that we could have counted on, and at this moment we had a garrison of only eighty men to defend all our military stores at Fort Garry, and to preserve the peace of half a continent besides."[64]

It is unnecessary to go into the details of O'Donoghue's raid which was suppressed by the American troops at Pembina.   The ease with which the " Fenians " were scattered and the complete and sudden collapse of the movement have served to bring out the ridiculous rather than the serious aspects of the raid.   When we consider the military potentialities of the métis organization, their success in 1885, and the support which a general rising might have obtained from the several thousand unemployed railway workers in the northern States, we realize the great danger in which the little province with its miniature army lay. Had O'Donoghue received the active support of the half-breeds upon which he was relying, the Fenian incursion might have been crowned with at least temporary success.

That the métis did not join O'Donoghue was largely due to the stand taken by Louis Riel.   He had a magnetic hold upon his people and had he supported his erstwhile colleague, they would doubtless have followed him.   Riel, however, not only held aloof from the new movement, but, on October 7th, forwarded the following communication to Lieutenant-Governor Archibald.[65]

" St. Vital, 7 October, 1871.
" May it please Your Excellency,—We have the honour of informing you that we highly appreciate what Your Excellency has been pleased to communicate to the Reverend Mr. Ritchot, in order that we might be better able to assist the people, in the exceptional position they have been placed in, to answer your appeal.   As several trustworthy persons have been requested to

inform you, the answer of the métis has been that of faithful subjects. Several companies have already been organized, and others are in process of formation. Your Excellency may rest assured that, without being enthusiastic, we have been devoted. So long as our services continue to be required, you may rely on us.

" We have the honour, etc., etc.

" LOUIS RIEL
" A. D. LEPINE
" PIERRE X PARENTEAU
(his mark) "

Realizing the great moral value of the stand taken by Riel and the French métis, as well as the practical value of their force, Archibald crossed to St. Boniface, publicly thanked the métis for their assistance, and shook hands with Louis Riel.[66]

It is probable that Riel was inspired more by motives of personal advantage than by an abstract sense of loyalty in his stand upon this occasion. He hoped, by offering his services, to place the Dominion Government under some obligation towards him and thus to secure the promised amnesty. In any event these services rendered to the Crown at a critical moment added further complications to an already vexing question. Riel used the occasion to obtain from the Lieutenant-Governor a written promise of immunity. Archibald, whose fears may have been exaggerated, and who was not unsympathetic to the demand for an amnesty, not only promised him immunity " pour la circonstance actuelle "[67] but urged that it " was a good time for Riel to prove his loyalty " and " that it would be a further occasion for the hastening of the granting of an amnesty."[68] This promise of temporary immunity, while it could not be construed as binding upon the Federal Government, together with Riel's active support in a time of crisis, greatly strengthened the métis leader's claim for a general amnesty.

Thus placed under a certain moral obligation to Riel, the Dominion Government could only regard the situation with increasing trepidation, especially in view of the success of Blake in Ontario, who, having attained power at the expense of the Conservatives, was now offering $5,000 reward for Riel's apprehension. Sir John Macdonald was equal to the occasion. To forestall the crisis which Riel's arrest would bring and to spare the Government the embarrassment of having to rule upon the amnesty question, Sir John forwarded $1,000 to Bishop Taché to induce Riel and Lépine to remain outside Canadian jurisdiction until the political storm had blown over : to appease the wrathful feelings of Ontario he publicly declared " Where is Riel ? God knows ; I wish I could lay my hands on him ! "

The situation was further complicated by the defeat of Sir George Cartier in the federal elections of 1872, by an alliance of the volunteers and the English-speaking element of Montreal with the French Canadian nationalists. On learning of Cartier's defeat, Sir John Macdonald at once telegraphed to Archibald, " Get Sir George elected in your Province."[69] Archibald consulted Bishop Taché on the matter, and, at the Lieutenant-Governor's request, Taché undertook to persuade Louis Riel, who had been nominated for Provencher, to withdraw his candidature to permit the unopposed return of Sir George. Riel demanded certain guarantees respecting the métis lands. Macdonald did not relish the idea of a cabinet minister giving pledges, but finally telegraphed " Sir George will do all he can to meet the wishes of the parties."[70]   Although Cartier unfortunately died before he was able to take his seat in Parliament for his Manitoba constituency, the Federal Government were, by his election, once more tacitly placed under an obligation to Louis Riel.

In the Red River Settlement popular sympathy was in favour of an amnesty.   Many of the native settlers had participated one way or another in the insurrection and with the exception of the Canadians, few were hostile to its leaders.   Archibald wrote to Cartier in February 1872, that the feelings of the great body of the English-speaking population were such " that it is difficult to find a magistrate who does not hesitate to issue warrants which may lead to fatal consequences ; and several Justices, who were themselves sufferers at the time of the troubles, and who a year ago were urging all kinds of vindictive proceedings, have refused to issue warrants now."[71]   Riel was twice elected by acclamation for Provencher in the Province of Manitoba after the death of Cartier, but did not take his seat in Parliament.   In the local legislature a resolution was passed condemning the interference of the Province of Ontario in Red River affairs and an Address was drawn up by both houses praying the Imperial Parliament " that in the interests of peace and good order it is

MACKENZIE   RIEL   MACDONALD

A CASE OF RIEL DISTRESS!

(*Grip*, Oct. 25th, 1873)

not only desirable but requisite that steps should be taken to settle and set at rest all questions connected with such troubles."[72]

The Manitoba Address re-opened the amnesty question in Ottawa and London. On forwarding it to the Governor-General, Macdonald again referred to the excitable state of the population but suggested to Lord Lisgar that " an amnesty for all offences, except murder, would be advisable."[73] This Address and a petition from Ritchot and Scott were sent to Lord Kimberley in April 1872. There was nothing, however, in either document to alter the attitude of the Colonial Secretary, and the Under Secretary merely observed " The Canadian Government have not yet fulfilled the conditions upon which Her Majesty's Government would be willing to act in this awkward business, and it appears to me that the position of the two governments should be made clear before any answer is given to this petition."[74] Accordingly, Kimberley replied by referring again to his despatch of August 11th, 1870; but he added that the idea of a partial amnesty was one which might very well be entertained.[75] Here the matter rested for another year despite the untiring efforts of Bishop Taché who continually agitated in the press and to the Government for the promulgation of the general amnesty which he had promised.

The matter was rapidly approaching a crisis in the Dominion Cabinet. The French Canadian members had long been the foremost protagonists of an amnesty, and in 1873 the French-speaking ministers threatened to disrupt the Government unless some action was taken. Langevin and Robitaille both offered to surrender their portfolios,[76] while Masson, who had become Riel's defender in the House of Commons, not only refused to enter the Cabinet at Macdonald's request, but threatened to lead the Quebec Conservatives into opposition.[77] Faced with this ultimatum Macdonald, with his customary adroitness, avoided the unpleasant complications which might arise from a direct decision by promising to go personally to England to arrange a definite settlement. Nevertheless it is obvious that Macdonald never contemplated anything more than a partial amnesty excluding those responsible for the death of Scott—a solution which the Imperial Government favoured and which, they hoped, might prove acceptable to both the French and English-speaking Canadians. Nothing was done to implement this promise,

Macdonald's Government going down to defeat in the autumn of 1873.

For several years the Liberals, secure in the irresponsibility of Opposition, had used the alleged promises of an amnesty to belabour the Government, but now thrust into office by the Pacific Scandal, they were no less unprepared to deal with the question than were their predecessors. The question was not long in abeyance, and was brought to Mackenzie's attention by two unexpected events ; the arrival in Ottawa of Louis Riel, and the trial and conviction of his lieutenant, Ambroise Lépine.

In 1873 Riel had been elected to the Federal Parliament. He had made no effort to assume the responsibilities consequent upon his election, but so strong was his hold over the French half-breeds that he was a second time chosen to represent them at Ottawa. In the spring of 1874 he proceeded to the Dominion capital and, with the assistance of a Quebec colleague, appeared in the Parliament Buildings to sign the members' register. He did not, however, venture to take his seat in the Commons Chamber. Blake was still offering the $5,000 reward for Riel's apprehension and warrants had been issued for his arrest. In the House the Ontario and Orange faction were not slow to act. In spite of the fact that a Select Committee had been appointed to inquire into the causes of the insurrection of 1869–70 and into the alleged promises of amnesty given to the insurgents, Mackenzie Bowell, the Grand Master of the Orange Association and a prominent Conservative, seconded by Dr. Schultz, now member for Lisgar, moved :

" That *Louis Riel*, a Member of this House for the Electoral District of *Provencher*, in the Province of *Manitoba*, having been charged with murder, and a Bill of Indictment for the said offence having been found against him, and Warrants issued for his apprehension, and the said *Louis Riel* having fled from justice and having failed to obey an Order of this House that he should attend in his place on Thursday, the 9th day of April, 1874, be expelled this House."[78]

Holton and Cameron, two Liberals, moved an amendment to stay proceedings until the report of the Select Committee had been received ; while Mousseau and Baby, two Quebec Conservatives, moved for an Address asking for a complete and immediate amnesty. The question thus cut across party lines.

Even members of the Administration opposed one another on purely racial lines. Only two Ontario members ventured to vote against the motion for Riel's expulsion. Mousseau's motion was defeated by 164 votes to 27, Holton's by 117 to 76, and the original motion was carried by a majority of 56 votes.[79]

Riel's flight and expulsion from the Commons' Chamber in no way solved the amnesty question, which was becoming more and more urgent owing to the arrest, trial and conviction for murder, of Ambroise Lépine. From all parts of the Dominion no less than 252 petitions bearing 58,568 names flooded the embarrassed executive. The Archbishop and six Bishops of the Province of Quebec added their prayers to those of Archbishop Taché for a pardon and a general amnesty, and the Provincial Legislature, led by Adolphe Chapleau, who had defended the convicted man, passed a unanimous resolution requesting the Governor-General " de vouloir bien exercer en faveur du condamné Ambroise Lépine, la royale prérogative de miséricorde, en lui octroyant grâce et pardon."[80] Unwilling to offend his English-speaking supporters and yet unable to resist the appeals of the French, Mackenzie sought to throw the responsibility of a decision upon the Imperial Government, urging, in words that might have come from Macdonald's pen, that he was compelled to adopt this course " by the obvious embarrassments attending the settlement of a controversy, whose aspects are alleged to have been already modified by the intervention of Imperial authority, and which are so seriously complicated by the vehement international antagonism which they have excited in this country."[81]

Accompanying this request Lord Dufferin, the new Governor-General, sent to the Colonial Office a despatch of great value, examining the whole amnesty question, weighing the evidence for and against, and concluding with the decision to commute, upon his own responsibility, the sentence of death passed upon Lépine.[82] The Earl of Carnarvon replied on January 7th, 1875, fully approving of Dufferin's analysis, and suggesting in addition to the proposed commutation, forfeiture of political rights.[83] Accordingly, on January 15th, the Governor-General commuted the capital sentence passed upon Lépine to two years' imprisonment and permanent forfeiture of political rights.

This commutation, on his Lordship's own responsibility, raised an issue of constitutional importance. Had Lord Dufferin

G

remitted Lépine's sentence after formally consulting his Ministers, he would only have done what every Governor had a right to do in capital cases ; but if, as his despatches and the absence of any formal minute of Council imply, he acted in this manner in order to relieve his Ministers from the responsibility of offering advice upon a delicate issue, the commutation of Lépine was an act inconsistent with the whole theory and practice of responsible government.   The Canadian press vigorously assailed the refusal of the Ministers to give advice.   The Hamilton *Spectator* declared, " It was generous, no doubt, on His Excellency's part, to endeavour to settle on his own responsibility a question which the thirteen trembling cowards were afraid to face ; but he has no power—and there is no power in the Constitution to relieve Ministers of the responsibility for an executive act, unless they signify their disapproval by resigning.   This is taught by the plainest maxims of the Constitution."[84]   The *Gazette* of Montreal took the same stand : " For a ministry to have no opinion on such a subject is virtually to abdicate.   A parliamentary ministry must advise, it is appointed for no other purpose.   If its advice is rejected it must resign.   This is the very essence of Responsible Government.   Some person must be found who is accountable for every act of the Government, even the exercise of the royal prerogative."[85]   The Ottawa *Citizen* concluded an article of a similar nature with the words " O Reform ! O Responsible Government ! Where are thy glories now ? "[86]

Divested of its local details, the Lépine question brought to the front the question of how the prerogative of mercy was to be exercised in future in the self-governing colonies.   Was the prerogative to be exercised by the Governor by virtue of his responsibility to the Crown, or by the colonial government responsible to the people of the country ?   The Colonial Secretary held the view that the Governor was personally selected by the Crown as the depository of the Crown's prerogative of mercy ; this prerogative was not alienated from the Crown by any general delegation, but was confided as a matter of high trust to those individuals whom the Crown commissioned for the purpose. Thus, while the colonial ministers were responsible for advising the Governor, the latter could not divest himself of the personal responsibility which had been specially entrusted to him.   The peculiar circumstances of the Lépine case, however, unfitted it

MACDONALD   MACKENZIE

LOYALTY IN A QUANDARY; or THE "LEPINE CASE" MADE
PLAIN.

(*Grip*, Feb. 6th, 1875)

for the purpose of a test case—the Colonial Ministry being only too willing to have the perplexing question settled by an external authority—and when the question was discussed in the House of Lords in April 1875, Dufferin's action was defended, not on the ground that it was compatible with ministerial responsibility, but that the case of Lépine was exceptional. Carnarvon stated that " it touches on most delicate ground " and justified the commutation as politically expedient.[87] Kimberley admitted that " the general question of the exercise of the Prerogative of mercy by Colonial Governors . . . certainly does involve . . . one of the most delicate functions of the machinery of Colonial Government " but argued that " in matters of this kind, we ought not to be too logical. Constitutional Government in this country has not grown up by means of a rigorous application of the principles of logic, but rather by a happy application of good sense on the part of the men who proved themselves equal to deal with emergencies."[88]

Nevertheless the Lépine question led to a more precise definition of the relation of the Governor-General to the Crown and to the colonial ministry. In June 1876, the Honourable Edward Blake visited England and discussed with Carnarvon the advisability of recasting the Governor-General's instructions. In July Blake forwarded an important memorandum[89] to the Colonial Secretary which stated :

" Canada is not merely a Colony or a Province : she is a Dominion composed of an aggregate of seven large provinces federally united under an Imperial Charter, which expressly recites that her constitution is to be similar in principles to that of the United Kingdom."

After pointing out that the Queen exercised the prerogative of pardon in Great Britain on the advice of her Ministers, the memorandum continued :

" While the Canadian Parliament makes laws for the punishment of crimes committed by the inhabitants of Canada, the Sovereign should exercise the prerogative of mercy towards such criminals under the advice of her Privy Council for Canada, or of her Minister there, chosen as her other Canadian Ministers are chosen, and responsible to the Canadian Parliament for his advice."

As a result of Blake's mission a new commission and letter of instructions were issued to the Governor-General at the expiry of Dufferin's term of office, which vindicated the doctrine of ministerial responsibility and placed the prerogative of pardon on the same footing as the other royal prerogatives, namely, to be exercised only upon the advice of responsible Ministers. In this way another stage was passed in the evolution of the self-governing colonies from Colonial to Dominion status.

The commutation of the sentence of death passed upon Lépine, together with the expulsion of Louis Riel, forced the attention of the Canadian Government to the anomalous condition of affairs in regard to others implicated in the insurrection. The action of Lord Dufferin had provided the virtual solution of the question. In February 1875, the Honourable Alexander Mackenzie moved :

" That in the opinion of this House it would be proper, considering the said facts, that a full amnesty should be granted to all persons concerned in the North-West troubles for all acts committed by them during the said troubles, saving only L. Riel, A. D. Lépine and W. B. O'Donoghue. That in the opinion of this House it would be proper . . . that a like amnesty should be granted to L. Riel and A. D. Lépine, conditional on five years' banishment from Her Majesty's Dominions."[90]

The debate was long and bitter. Macdonald accused Mackenzie of playing politics. Mousseau and Masson called for a complete amnesty. Cauchon, however, contended that half a loaf was better than none and Laurier, the rising star of the Liberal party, gave his full support to the Government motion. Mousseau's amendment was lost by 152 votes to 23 and the original motion carried by 126 to 50.[91] Immediately following this Mackenzie moved the banishment of Riel, which was carried by a substantial majority. Two years later the last vestige of· the Red River Rebellion was buried in official oblivion when O'Donoghue was included in the amnesty on the same terms as Riel.[92] In this manner, the amnesty question, which had for a time threatened to split the fabric of Confederation and retard the development of colonial autonomy, was finally settled.

BOOK TWO

THE NORTH-WEST REBELLION

CHAPTER IX

THE GROWTH OF SETTLEMENT IN THE NORTH-WEST

ON July 15th, 1870, Rupert's Land and the North-Western territory were formally transferred from the Hudson's Bay Company to the Dominion of Canada. Out of this extensive area, a small district, approximately one hundred miles square, and inhabited by a handful of settlers, was organized into the Province of Manitoba. The remaining territory was a vast wilderness. To the north lay a forbidding land of rivers, lakes, rocks and forest; to the west, a monotonous vision of grass and sky, the prairies. For centuries past the western prairies had been the hunting grounds of the wandering Indian tribes, and, apart from the few fur-trading posts and mission stations, there were no settlements outside the Province of Manitoba. Writing as late as 1872 Sir William Butler, then Captain Butler, after a visit to the North-West, declared :

" The ' Great Lone Land ' is no sensational name. The North-West fulfils, at the present time, every essential of that title. There is no other portion of the globe in which travel is possible where loneliness can be said to dwell so thoroughly. One may wander five hundred miles in a direct line without seeing a human being, or an animal larger than a wolf. And if vastness of plain, and magnitude of lake, mountain and river can mark a land as great, then no region possesses higher claims to that distinction."[1]

The first white men to penetrate this western wilderness and native fastness were the explorers and fur traders. But neither regarded the North-West as a home, and, by the time this region was acquired by Canada, settlement can scarcely be said to have begun. In 1871 Butler, after an investigation into the conditions prevailing in the North-West, reported only six embryonic colonies.[2] All were of mission origin ; Prince Albert, White Fish Lake and Victoria for the English half-breeds, and St. Albert, Lac la Biche and Lac Ste. Anne for the French métis. There were, in addition, a few adventurous whites to be found at

Prince Albert, and at the Hudson's Bay Company posts at Fort Qu'Appelle, Fort Pelly, Touchwood Hills, Cumberland House, Fort à la Corne, Fort Carlton, Fort Pitt and Fort Edmonton.   It is impossible, however, to determine the extent of the population of the North-West at this time owing to the unsettled nature of some of the communities and the nomadic habits of their half-breed members.

The half-breeds, as in Manitoba, were the first to settle in the North-West Territory.   Many of them were born in the country and grew up around the fur-trading posts.   Others moved west-wards from Red River.   For many years the métis had set out from the Red River valley upon their great hunts over the western prairies, but the gradual withdrawal of the buffalo further and further from the eastern plains made these long journeys unprofit-able.   The Red River métis were then faced with two alternatives, to follow the wild animals westwards, or to settle down to a life of agriculture.   The métis had a horror of a sedentary existence. The chase was to them a necessity as well as a pleasure, and many, choosing the easier road, followed the well-defined buffalo trails into the interior.

These hunting expeditions were seldom disordered, isolated efforts.   The métis gathered in large bands under the command of chosen leaders and self-imposed regulations, a practice which undoubtedly facilitated Riel's organization of the French half-breeds in 1869.   Early in their history they had learned that only by union could they cope with hostile bands of marauding Indians. Experience and necessity had evolved a loose code of rules and restrictions which, tightened by the bonds of tradition, governed the conduct of the hunt.   As a rule, these expeditions were accompanied by a missionary priest, who, with his portable altar, daily celebrated mass in his tent, taught the children their catechism, visited the sick and injured, and formed the nucleus of a fervent, though nomadic parish.   During the winter those who did not return to their homes in the Red River Settlement were obliged to seek provisional quarters.   Their winter camps were chosen with care.   They had to be near a wood for building purposes and fuel, close to a stream or river, and not too far from the favourite haunts of the buffalo for the next spring's hunt. The construction of log huts gave these camps an air of solidity and permanency, which indicated the possibilities of a definite settlement.[3] Winter after winter the métis returned to the same districts and gradually, through the efforts of the missionaries and the diminution of the chase, these became the sites of permanent villages. The most important of these hunting communities were to be found between the lower reaches of the North and South Saskatchewan Rivers near Duck Lake and Fort Carlton, and in the Qu'Appelle valley.

After the stormy career of the Provisional Government and the political disturbances at Fort Garry in 1870, a half-breed trek to the North-West began. Sullen, suspicious and estranged from their white neighbours by the actions of the Canadians and the non-promulgation of the amnesty, almost immediately many métis began to look for new homes. The failure of their first struggle with a superior civilization, and the ill-disguised contempt with which they, the original inhabitants, were treated by the newcomers, destroyed the self-confidence of the métis. They held aloof from their neighbours and turned to the North-West to find their former state of unrestricted liberty. Some of the more restless spirits had already joined the buffalo camps in the interior, and many others began to follow.

It was to these irreconcilables, who, like the Boer Voortrekkers of South Africa, trekked to escape the consequences of their inability to adjust themselves to a new order, that the colony of St. Laurent owed its foundation. This fact is significant in view of the subsequent history of the North-West. For, although the métis settlement of St. Albert, near Edmonton, was both older and larger, it was the colony of St. Laurent in the Saskatchewan valley which became the scene of the second métis attempt to stem the inexorable tide of European civilization, the Riel Rebellion of 1885.

A buffalo camp of small importance seems to have made the neighbourhood of Duck Lake its winter headquarters. In 1868 Father André, who became the mentor of the colony, visited the region for the first time, " visiter quelques familles patriarcales de métis."[4] The events of 1870 soon brought an addition to their numbers. In 1871, Father Légeard wrote, " un certain nombre de familles métisses venues de la Rivière Rouge voulant passer l'hiver près du Fort Carlton sur une des branches de la Saskatchewan avaient demandé à Mgr. de leur donner un Père pour rester avec eux."[5] In accordance with this request, a permanent mission was established there on October 8th, 1871, bearing the name of St. Laurent.[6]

This colony quickly grew in numbers and importance. At first it differed little from the other métis buffalo camps. The new-comers quickly reverted from their more restricted life at Red River to the carefree life of the plains. Father Leduc, writing to his Superior-General concerning the mission at St. Laurent, declared :

"La population du Père André est toujours considérable. Elle formerait une belle et prospère Mission si elle promettait de se fixer irrévocablement dans une localité. Malheureusement la plupart de ces métis n'ont quitté la Rivière Rouge que pour courir plus aisément après les buffles de la Prairie. Il est bien à craindre qu'ils ne laissent la Mission du Père André pour s'avancer davantage encore dans les prairies où les buffles s'éloignent de plus en plus, et finiront par disparaître tout à fait, dans un avenir qui paraît prochain."[7]

Steps were, however, taken to establish the colony upon a permanent basis. On December 10th, 1873, a great assembly of all the métis living in the district was held at St. Laurent. The absence of any effective government in the North-West and the necessity for some form of law suggested the adoption of regulations similar to those governing the hunt, in order to protect the community and to enforce justice. Prompted by public interest and guided by Father André, the métis unanimously resolved to form a provisional government and to submit to the laws and regulations imposed by it. Gabriel Dumont was elected "president" for one year, assisted by eight "councillors." It is important to note that the métis protested their loyalty to Canada, and stated that "en faisant ces lois et ces règlements, les habitants de St. Laurent ne prétendent nullement constituer pour eux un état indépendant . . . mais en formant ces lois ils se reconnaissent les sujets loyaux et fidèles du Canada et se sont preparés à abandonner leur propre organisation et à se soumettre aux lois de la Dominion aussitôt que le Canada aura établi au milieu d'eux des magistrats réguliers avec une force suffisante pour maintenir dans le pays l'autorité de la loi."[8]

A Provisional Government elected, and the oath "d'accomplir fidèlement leur devoir et de juger dans la droiture de leur con-science sans acceptation de personne, les causes qui seraient referées à leur tribunal" administered to the "President" and "Councillors," the assembled gathering proceeded to adopt a code of "Lois et Régulations . . . pour la Colonie de St. Laurent sur la Saskatchewan." These provided for monthly meetings of the "President" and "Council," the punishment of offences against property and person, the sanctity of contract, the prevention of prairie fires, the observance of Sunday, the obligations of employers and employees, the fees and costs of adjudication, and for fines and penalties for wilful disregard of the newly-established authorities. The enforcing of these regulations were placed in the hands of selected "captains" and "soldiers," after the custom of the buffalo hunt. Considering the nomadic nature of the métis, their lack of education and intolerance of restraint, this simple code of laws was a bold attempt to meet the needs of a primitive community.

The experiment in self-government was a complete success. The code drawn up by the assembled métis and the periodical regulations of the "Council" were productive of the greatest benefits to the people. Peace was maintained and tranquillity marked the relationships of man to man. The re-election of Dumont and six of his "Councillors" a year later strikingly confirmed the advantages of the new organization.

The history of St. Laurent does not appear to have been paralleled by the other métis settlements in the North-West. Neither at Red River—if we except Riel's Provisional Government—St. Albert, nor St. Florent de Lebret, did they rise to the same stage of independent political development. It is quite evident that the métis attained at St. Laurent, during this period, their highest development, politically, as a distinct race.[9]

The attempt, however, in the spring of 1875 by "President" Dumont and his "soldiers" to enforce the laws of St. Laurent upon independent parties quickly brought about official intervention. Alarmed by a letter from the Hudson's Bay Company Factor at Carlton referring to a state of affairs which sounded ominously familiar,[10] the Canadian Government ordered Commissioner French of the North-West Mounted Police at Swan River, Manitoba, to take action against any repetition of the unpleasant events of 1869–70. A party of fifty Mounted Police, commanded by Colonel French and accompanied by Major-General Selby Smythe, the officer commanding the Canadian

Militia, then on a tour of inspection of the Mounted Police, was despatched by a forced march to Fort Carlton. In spite of the alarming rumours which were circulating in Manitoba, " Another stand against Canadian authority in the North-West; a Provisional Government at Carlton; M. Louis Riel again to the front; 10,000 Crees on the war-path; Fort Carlton in possession of the Rebels; a number of Mounted Police killed; "[11] Colonel French reported on August 7th, " The outrages by half-breeds in this vicinity are of a trivial nature."[12] At first it was proposed to arrest Dumont, but on his return from the plains it was no longer considered necessary. The métis " President " expressed his regret and offered to make reparation. In view of his obvious loyalty, and the law-abiding character of the people, no further action was deemed necessary.[13]

Notwithstanding this reverse, the colony of St. Laurent continued to grow in numbers. In 1878 the settlement was given the name of Grandin by the Government, and Father Leduc, in a report on the diocese of St. Albert, gave the population as 750, spread over an area of thirty miles.[14] New parishes sprang up within the old as the settlement was augmented by arrivals from Red River and from the plains. In 1878 Father André founded the parish of Sacré Coeur at Duck Lake, about seven miles from Grandin, to serve a growing community of 250 souls.[15] Several years later the original colony of St. Laurent branched out across the south fork of the Saskatchewan river. Here, in 1881, Père Végreville established the parish of St. Antoine de Padoue, which, as Batoche, became famous as the headquarters of the métis during the North-West Rebellion of 1885 ; while further down the river the parish of St. Louis de Langevin gradually took permanent shape during the early 'eighties.

The settlement of the North-West territory was by no means confined to the mixed bloods. An insatiable hunger for land and a restless westward surge were the central feature of North-American history during the latter half of the nineteenth century. Attracted by the great spaces and the fertile lands to be had for the asking, thousands of immigrants poured into the Western States of America. Canadian development was slower. Nevertheless, the fifteen years following the transfer of the Hudson's Bay Company territory to Canada saw the beginning of the transition of the old North-West into modern Western Canada.

The first white settlement of importance in the Saskatchewan country was Prince Albert. Established in 1866 by the Reverend James Nisbet as a Presbyterian mission to the Cree Indians and English half-breeds, it soon became the most progressive settlement in the Territories.[16] During the early years Prince Albert drew most of its inhabitants from the old villages of Manitoba. Many of the employees of the Hudson's Bay Company also settled there. From 1874 this small community developed rapidly. Every summer saw the arrival of new settlers, the staking of claims and the erection of new buildings. " Within the last five years," wrote the editor of the *Saskatchewan Herald* in 1878, "the settlement of which Prince Albert forms the centre has been making giant strides towards the goal of civilization and agricultural improvement. The buffalo hunter is rapidly giving way to the farmer, and the Indian trader to the merchant."[17] Business enterprise marked Prince Albert as a characteristically English Canadian village. In his *Journal* Bishop Grandin, Bishop of St. Albert, commented upon its progress :[18]

" Le 18 août j'arrivais au Prince Albert, véritable ville anglaise qui s'élève dans mon diocèse à 15 ou 25 lieues de St. Laurent de Grandin. Il y a là deux usines à vapeur ; j'y ai vu pour la première fois dans ce pays des constructions en briques. L'agglomération n'est pas encore considérable, mais les anglais, écossais et canadiens anglais qui s'y rencontrent sont tous des hommes entreprenants et décidés à faire fortune."

Up the Saskatchewan river, about 160 miles from Prince Albert, another white settlement was founded. In 1874 the surveyors for the telegraph line established their headquarters on the Battle river near its junction with the North Saskatchewan. The name given to this place was Telegraph Flat, but it was later changed to the more attractive name of Battleford. In 1877 this site was selected as the capital of the North-West. This was due, probably, to the geographical advantages of its central position in relation to the growing population of the Saskatchewan from Prince Albert to Edmonton ; for, in development, it was behind Prince Albert. In the *Journal* quoted above Bishop Grandin wrote :[19]

" Battleford est la capitale du Nord-Ouest, c'est là que réside le gouverneur avec son entourage et les autorités du pays. On appelle Battleford une ville, mais vainement y ai-je cherché des maisons ; à part les habitations du gouverneur, des magistrats et des soldats, il n'y a pas une seule maison convenable. Le bureau du télégraphe, celui du journal (*Saskatchewan Herald*) sont de misérables baraques en bois. L'Eglise catholique et la mission sont en parfait accord avec la pauvreté de la cité naissante."

In spite of this unfavourable comment, Battleford differed little from many western villages which developed into thriving communities.

Still further west, Fort Edmonton was a centre of settlement. Although it was described by Paul Kane in 1846 as " a large establishment "[20] of forty or fifty men and their families, chiefly in the service of the Hudson's Bay Company, Edmonton made little progress until the late 'seventies and early 'eighties. In 1879 the Dominion Land Surveyor reported that " the Edmonton Settlement extends along the Saskatchewan about eight miles, principally on the north bank " and commented favourably upon its agricultural prospects.[21]   A year later a newspaper appeared, the second to be published in the North-West Territories.[22]   A small sheet, five by seven inches called *The Bulletin*, published under the editorship of Frank Oliver, was issued on December 6th, 1880.   By 1883 the population of the Edmonton district numbered over one thousand, and was, in consequence, the first electoral district to be set up in what is now the Province of Alberta.

The southern part of the territories had, until the arrival of the railway, little attraction for the prospective settler.   With the exception of the perambulating métis parish of St. Florent, which ultimately became attached to Wood Mountain, a few Mounted Police Forts and several trading posts and missions, there were no settlements south of the North Saskatchewan valley.   Not only were the northern settlements deemed more suitable for agriculture, but they were also more accessible.   The main trails led overland from Red River to the Hudson's Bay Company post at Fort Ellice, through the Touchwood Hills via Gabriel's or Batoche's Crossing to Fort Carlton, and then westward to Battleford, Fort Pitt and Edmonton, or north-eastward to Prince Albert and Fort à la Corne.[23]   The remaining territory was more or less uncharted ground.   Moreover, the inauguration of water transport from Winnipeg to the North-West, via Lake Winnipeg and the Saskatchewan river, opened up great possibilities for northern development. In 1874 the steam vessel *Northcote* made the first successful passage to Fort Carlton, and Chief Commissioner Grahame of the Hudson's Bay Company was enthusiastic over the possibilities of ascending the river even beyond Edmonton.[24] The prospective immigrants and travellers were not slow to take advantage of this new means of transportation. In 1877 " The Report of the Working of the Steamer *Northcote* " read :[25]

" As many applications for passage by the *Northcote* were made during the past season which could not be granted on account of the accommodation being limited to the requirements of the crew, I think that an addition to the cabin should be made next season, which can be done at small expense. Passenger travel up and down the Saskatchewan will always be on the increase, and if our boats are to run regularly and to connect at Grand Rapids with the *Colville* I see no reason why we should not carry all the passengers who travel over the route."

The final outcome was the formation, in 1880, of the North-West Navigation Company, with a fleet of five vessels, for the transport of freight and the carriage of passengers between Manitoba and the settlements on the Saskatchewan.[26]

Settlement in the north was also stimulated by the proposed route laid out for the Canadian Pacific Railway by Sandford Fleming. The original plan was to run the road north-west from the Lake of the Woods, across the Red River at Selkirk and thence to the North Saskatchewan. To gain all the advantages and reap all the profits of settlement along the line of the proposed railway, squatters, traders, speculators and *bona-fide* settlers rushed into the north and augmented the growing populations of Prince Albert, Battleford and Edmonton.

To meet the pressing demands of British Columbia for a trans-continental railway and the economic considerations of a road in closer proximity to the American border, the Canadian Pacific Railway determined, in 1881, to build their line, not to the North Saskatchewan, but westwards in a direct line from Winnipeg to the Kicking Horse Pass via the Assiniboine, Qu' Appelle and Bow valleys. The adoption of this southerly route was one of the most significant events in the history of the Territories. The water routes had hitherto determined the location of the settlements. Henceforth the railway line became the artery of immigration.   The North Saskatchewan settlements were side-tracked.   Settlers now came in along the southern route, and towns sprang up all along the new path of the Canadian Pacific Railway; Moosomin, Regina, Moose Jaw, Maple Creek, Medicine Hat and Calgary.   Prince Albert and Battleford were left in the backwaters of neglect, while the current of population turned southwards.   This was emphasized in 1883 by the removal of the capital of the North-West Territories from Battleford to Regina.

Settlement by voluntary immigration was, however, a slow development, and an attempt was made to stimulate it by means of colonization companies.   In 1882 the Government was authorized to enter into agreements with chartered companies to colonize and settle certain tracts of land.   Two plans were proposed.   Under the first plan, blocks of townships outside the railway belt might be granted to applicants upon certain terms. The companies were obliged to pay two dollars an acre for the odd-numbered sections and to colonize their tracts within five years.   In this event they were to be allowed a rebate of half the purchase price or $120 for every *bona-fide* settler.   Colonization was to consist of placing two settlers on every section irrespective of whether it was odd or even-numbered.   The other plan provided for the sale of all the sections in the townships, excepting those, four in number, reserved by the Government for special purposes, at two dollars an acre with the same provisions for rebate.[27]   If the plans were meant to attract speculators and capitalists they were amply fulfilled ; but as instruments of colonization they were both failures.   The old settlers viewed them with mistrust, and feared that their holdings might be endangered if included in the companies' grants.   The new-comers disliked the apparent restriction of their choice of home-steads.   One company succeeded in arousing the apprehensions of the métis of St. Laurent, others became involved in disputes with squatters, and some failed to bring in even a single settler. In Saskatchewan, where the companies were particularly active, the Temperance Colonization Company founded the town of Saskatoon, but only seven companies placed more than fifty settlers upon the land.[28]   Finally, after four years, the majority of the colonization companies were dissolved and none remained in operation after 1891.

On the whole, the growth of the North-West Territories during the first fifteen years was slow when contrasted with the rapid development of the western territories of the United States. In the Dakota Territory the population increased from 2,576 in 1850, to 12,887 in 1870, and 133,147 in 1880 :[29] while in the North-West Territories, during a similar stage of development, the population increased from upwards of 1,000 in 1870, to 6,974 in 1881, and about 50,000 in 1891.[30] This comparatively slow development of the Canadian North-West was due to several causes. The plains of the United States were more accessible before 1885 than the prairies of Canada, their immigration agents were more energetic, and the prospects held out more alluring. To reach Manitoba settlers had to travel by American railway lines and then overland by wagon or stage. The all-Canadian, or Dawson Route—a series of wagon and river transportation over the route followed by Wolseley from Lake Superior to the Lake of the Woods—involved unnecessary hardship when contrasted with the American journey by train. Notwithstanding the sums spent upon the Canadian route by the Government, it never proved popular. From Red River to the Saskatchewan valley the only means of transport were the Red River cart and the America " democrat." If favourable weather prevailed Prince Albert might be reached in one month. To reach Edmonton was just as far again. Railway development came slowly. The monopoly clause in the charter of the Canadian Pacific Railway forbade the building of competitive lines, and the railway itself was not completed from Eastern to Western Canada until 1885. Moreover, little assistance was given to foreign immigration during this period. It was not until after the Second Riel Rebellion had advertised the country, and Sifton had inaugurated his vigorous campaign of immigration propaganda, that the prairies became dotted with those alien settlements which have provided a problem of racial assimilation for Canada to solve. The land policy, too, was not a popular one. Liberal as the terms were, the constant changes in the Dominion land regulations and the large areas of land withheld from the operation of the homestead law, discouraged prospective immigration and retarded the spontaneous growth of village communities.

The land policy of the Dominion Government, inextricably bound as it was to the problem of settlement, deserves detailed consideration. Upon the transfer of Rupert's Land and the North-West to Canada in 1870, the Canadian Government announced that, pending the passage of the necessary legislation and the prosecution of the surveys, all rights to land acquired in advance of the survey would be duly recognized. The survey had been commenced late in 1869, but was, as we have seen, suspended during the disturbances at Red River. In 1871 the surveying of the North-West was undertaken seriously. The system of survey adopted was similar to that which Louis Riel and the half-breeds had so vigorously opposed at Red River. The unit was the township, consisting of thirty-six sections of one mile each, with road allowance of one chain in width. Each section consisted of 640 acres, and was subdivided into quarter sections. The survey began at the international boundary, the meridians numbering from east to west and the townships from south to north. The whole country was thus arbitrarily laid out in squares in a manner which made location and reference very simple. The survey progressed rapidly. By June 1873, 4,792,292 acres or 29,952 quarter sections had been surveyed. The period of Mackenzie's administration saw a retardation in the rate of survey, but from 1879 the work was pushed forward with vigour. By June 1883, 61,863,772 acres had been surveyed in the North-West, providing for 380,399 homesteads, which, on the basis of three people to the homestead, would provide for an agricultural population of 1,141,197.[31]

The homestead regulations were liberal. Every immigrant of twenty-one years of age and upwards, who chose to go to the North-West to settle on the land, was entitled to take up a quarter section (160 acres) as a free homestead. A fee of ten dollars at the time of application was all that was required in the way of payment. Cultivation, improvement and three years' settlement entitled the homesteader to a patent for the original quarter. Anyone who did not wish to homestead could purchase un-appropriated Dominion lands to the extent of 640 acres at the nominal price of one dollar per acre without condition of residence or improvement.[32] These regulations were modified from time to time. The age of claimants was reduced to eighteen years or over and the privilege of pre-empting an adjoining quarter section was conceded to homesteaders. Contrasted with the United States, the Canadian regulations appear to have offered the more favourable terms for settlement. Prior to 1879, American immigrants were allowed only eighty acres of land as a homestead, and could acquire only eighty acres by pre-emption. The price of the latter was fixed according to location at $1.25 or $2.50 per acre. In 1879 Congress extended the homestead and pre-emption privilege to 160 acres, the price remaining the same. Five years residence was required in the United States as compared with three in Canada, and cash for pre-emption compared with credit.

The quantity of land withheld from the privileges of free homestead and pre-emption to a great extent nullified these advantages. In Manitoba 1,400,000 acres, or approximately one-seventh of the province, were reserved for the half-breeds and original white settlers by the Manitoba Act. In the remaining territory of the North-West one-twentieth of all the land south of the North Saskatchewan was set aside for the Hudson's Bay Company in accordance with the terms of the transfer. This involved the reservation of two of the even-numbered sections, 8 and 26, in every township of thirty-six sections. To provide a fund to meet the cost of education in the territories, sections 11 and 29 were reserved as school lands. To add to the discouragement of settlement, all odd-numbered sections were reserved as public lands, to be disposed of only by sale. Moreover, the railway policy of both political parties, although at variance on the question of public or private ownership, had one common feature, namely, the defraying of the cost of the road by the sale of public lands in the North-West Territories. Mackenzie's administration set aside for railway purposes large blocks of land, twenty miles on each side of the proposed route, in which settlement was absolutely forbidden. The change of government in 1878 brought a change in the letter but little in the spirit of the existing law. For the barren railway reserves were substituted a series of " land belts," extending one hundred and ten miles on each side of the assumed line of the Canadian Pacific Railway, in which homesteads were limited to eighty acres in alternate sections, with descending rates of pre-emption and purchase.[33] A few months later the homestead privilege was increased to 160 acres and the price of the purchasable lands slightly reduced.[34] Other changes followed in 1881 and 1882,[35] until finally the Government reserved all the odd-numbered sections throughout the west for railway purposes, and threw open the remaining even-numbered sections for homestead purposes. The result was that of the thirty-six sections in a township, only eight were open to homesteads, the remainder being reserved for pre-emption, the Hudson's Bay Company, school and railway purposes.

It is interesting to note that the land policy, in relation to colonization, was based upon the incentive of free land. The Government did not attempt to link the disposal of land by sale with a policy of immigration, after the economic abstractions of Gibbon Wakefield. The colonization companies were, perhaps, an exception to this rule, but they were little more than speculative efforts. The land policy of the Dominion in Western Canada was a modified reproduction of that policy in the United States for which Durham had expressed great praise. It was, however, open to criticism. The large reserves discouraged settlement, and the position of the free grant areas led to unnecessary dispersion.

In 1870 the little province of Manitoba was granted a responsible government, complete with bicameral legislature and all the dignity and power necessary to maintain law and preserve order. There was, however, no intention of imposing such a burden upon the remainder of the North-West. The Territories in 1870 were wholly without government of any form. The institutions of law and order, as understood in civilized communities, were non-existent. The passing of the Hudson's Bay Company as a political body left the country without executive organization and destitute of any means to enforce authority. Despite this anarchic beginning, the North-West, during the next thirty-five years, passed through all the stages of political evolution from the passive rule of a chartered company to the active responsibility of a provincial government. This development presents an interesting parallel with that of old Canada, in all its forms, conciliar, representative, and responsible government. Moreover, the exasperating delay of " Mr. Mother-country," of Eastern Canadian history was repeated, in the North-West with similar strife and bitterness. This parallel cannot be pushed too far, for the rebellion of 1885, like that of 1869–70, was a struggle for racial survival and not, like that of 1837, a fight for responsible government. The history of responsible government in the North-West is, however, beyond the limits of this treatise. The years from 1870 to 1885 saw only the first steps in that evolution, the establishment of a conciliar and its gradual transition to a representative form of government.

By the Manitoba Act of 1870 the North-West was to be governed by the Lieutenant-Governor of Manitoba, as *ex-officio* Governor of the North-West Territories, and a council of not exceeding fifteen or less than seven members appointed by the Governor-General.[36] A spirit of procrastination and delay, however, attended the actions of the Federal Government in their dealings with the North-West. Two years elapsed before any action was taken to appoint a council under this Act. Lieutenant-Governor Archibald had, in October 1870, taken it upon himself to appoint an emergency council of three, representing " the three great interests of the West, the English, the French and the Hudson's Bay interest,"[37] but his action was undeniably irregular.[38] In December 1872, the Honourable Alexander Morris succeeded Archibald as Lieutenant-Governor of Manitoba and the North-West Territories, and a properly constituted council was appointed to assist him.

To keep pace with the progressive development of the Territories, the Dominion Government took several steps during the next few years, for the better establishment of law and order, the federal supervision of the North-West, and for the extension of the privileges and responsibilities of self-government. In accordance with the reports of Lieutenant W. F. Butler in 1871,[39] and Colonel Robertson Ross in 1872,[40] and the urgent solicitations of the North-West Council in 1873,[41] a corps of mounted riflemen, known as the North-West Mounted Police, were formed and despatched to the prairies. The affairs of the Territories were then entrusted to a new department of state, the Department of the Interior. The final step was the passing of the North-West Territories Act of 1875,[42] which reorganized the North-West Council and provided for the appointment of a separate Lieutenant-Governor for the North-West.

With the passing of this Act began the second stage of the conciliar period, the gradual transition from an appointed council to a representative assembly. With a few minor alterations, the North-West Territories Act of 1875 remained the basis of federal policy for the next twelve years. It provided for the appointment of a Lieutenant-Governor and council of five with power to pass ordinances relative to taxation for local purposes, property and civil rights in the Territories, the administration of justice, public health, highways and other matters of merely local or private nature. It is important to note that the administration of Indian affairs and the control of the Mounted Police remained with the federal authorities. The Dominion Government also reserved the right to disallow ordinances of the North-West Council. The most important innovation of the Act was the provision made for the progressive introduction of elected members to the council. When any region, not exceeding one thousand square miles, was found to contain a population of not less than one thousand inhabitants of voting age, such a district might be formed into an electoral district by a proclamation of the Lieutenant-Governor. The first district to be thus formed was that of Prince Albert and St. Laurent which was erected into the electoral district of Lorne in 1880. Edmonton, Qu'Appelle, Broadview, Regina and Moose Jaw followed in 1883, Calgary and Moose Mountain in 1884, and others in 1885, 1886 and 1887. The steady growth in territorial population thus increased the elective element in the council until it was transformed into a Legislative Assembly. The North-West Territories Act of 1875 had provided for this contingency when the elected members should reach twenty-one in number. In 1888, although this number had not yet been attained, the Legislative Assembly came into being, and full representative—although not yet responsible—government became an accomplished fact.

In 1882 a new development took place. The Territories were divided into four provisional districts, Assiniboia, Saskatchewan, Alberta and Athabaska. Although a few optimists saw in this portents of great political changes at an early date,[43] the divisions were made for the convenience of the postal authorities, and not for the facilitation of provincial status. It signalized, however, the shifting of the centre of population from the north to the south. This was emphasized by the removal of the capital in the following year.

Such is the picture of the development of the Canadian North-West—exclusive always of the Province of Manitoba—during the formative period from 1870 to 1885. During these years the foundations were laid for the settlement, security, and administration of the vast region ceded to Canada by the Hudson's Bay Company.   The half-breeds abandoned their nomadic existence, and immigrants from Eastern Canada and elsewhere settled upon the free lands of the " last west."   A system of government was established, and provision made for the maintenance of law and order.   It was, moreover, the period of transition.   The old North-West disappeared, the new was born.   In 1870 the plains were covered with buffalo.   The Indian was monarch of all he surveyed.   In 1885 prosperous towns and villages stood where only a few years before the Indian had pitched his teepee. Domestic cattle replaced the untamed buffalo and the railway pushed the Red River cart into antiquity.   All these changes brought with them a sociological problem of great magnitude, the reconciliation of the needs of a primitive native society with the demands of a modern civilization.   To the white man this transitional period in Western Canadian history opened new horizons of adventure, but to the red man it brought disaster and decline.

CHAPTER X

THE gravest problem presented to the Dominion of Canada by the acquisition and settlement of Rupert's Land and the North-West, was the impact of a superior civilization upon the native Indian tribes. Again and again, in different places and in different ways, this problem has unfolded itself at the contact of European and savage. Too often the advent of the white man has led to the moral and physical decline of the native. In Africa, Australia, Melanesia and America, the clash of peoples in different stages of development has spelled disaster to the weaker. The European, conscious of his material superiority, is only too contemptuous of the savage, intolerant of his helplessness, ignorant of his mental processes and impatient at his slow assimilation of civilization. The savage, centuries behind in mental and economic development, cannot readily adapt himself to meet the new conditions. He is incapable of bridging the gap of centuries alone and unassisted. Although white penetration into native territories may be inspired by motives of self-interest, such as trade and settlement, once there, the responsibility of " the white man's burden " is inevitable.

Different methods have been adopted by different peoples in dealing with primitive races. Some, in search of slaves or gold, proceeded by right of conquest and expropriation. This policy governed the actions of Spain in the New World. But Ferdinand and Isabella and their successors only shared the theory of conquest held in common by all the sovereigns of their day, namely, that the vanquished races had no rights save those conceded by the victors. The result, in most cases, was the exploitation and extermination, partial or complete, of the native races. The realization of this fact brought about the first suggestion of what might be dignified by the name of native policy. Fearing that the unrestrained mingling of Indians and Europeans might effect the destruction of the former, Spain devised a plan of native segregation. The plan failed, but the policy of segregation became the dominant feature, not only of American, but later of South African native administration. Amalgamation, the policy of Sir George Grey, has been a third method pursued in relation to the aboriginal races, with a considerable degree of success in New Zealand. The last, and perhaps the most enlightened in a country where the natives predominate in numbers, is the policy of indirect rule and the adaptation of native primitive institutions to the changing conditions consequent upon the advent of an alien civilization.

In Canada, the history of native policy passed through three phases, conquest, segregation and amalgamation. The early French discovery meant conquest as far as the Indian rights to land were concerned. This was followed by Sir William Johnson's policy of native negotiations and the settlement of the Indians in segregated areas. From 1830 British native policy in regard to the Canadian Indians was designed to break up their tribal organization by making them amenable to the laws of the land and by providing means for their ultimate enfranchisement. Like that of Sir George Grey in New Zealand, the object of Canadian policy from the middle of the nineteenth century was the amalgamation of the native and the European races. A clear statement of this purpose is found in the Report of the Deputy Superintendent-General of Indian Affairs for 1871, in which he stated that the policy of the Government was " designed to lead the Indian people by degrees to mingle with the white race in the ordinary avocations of life."[1] In the North-West, however, while political and social assimilation or amalgamation remained the ultimate object of native policy, the Canadian Government followed in the footsteps of the Johnson tradition by negotiating treaties with the Indians and by setting aside inalienable reserves for their use.

In order to understand more fully the native policy adopted by the Dominion of Canada, and also the part played by the Indian chiefs in the Second Riel Rebellion, a short outline of the Indian character is necessary.[2] The Indians of the North-West were divided—as we have observed in Chapter I—into three linguistic groups which were again divided into tribes and bands. Although these groups differed in language and customs, there were prominent characteristics which marked all of them in common. All belonged to a purely nomadic type of culture.

The North-West Indians were essentially races of hunters, existing wholly or largely by the chase. Accordingly, simplicity was the central feature of their organization.

In each Indian community every man was his own master. Nevertheless, each tribe had its civil and military organization, and gradations of rank and influence. At the head of the tribe was the civil chief. His position was, to a limited extent, hereditary ; his authority was only advisory or influential. The Indians resented anything that savoured of absolute authority or assumption of superiority. Thus, while the head chief could influence the conduct of his tribe, his word was not necessarily regarded as a command. He was assisted by his councillors, the minor chiefs and headmen. The Indian chiefs, in accordance with the principles of their savage democracy, never set themselves in opposition to the will of the tribe. The war chief was independent of the civil chief. He held his position by virtue of his physical prowess and military reputation, and might, at any time, gather a number of young men around him, set up a " soldiers' lodge " and make forays against hereditary foes.

The strength of this simple society lay in the Indians' respect for, and inflexible adherence to tradition and custom. Like the savage folk of other lands, the life of the Indian was full of inhibitions and ceremonies. Theirs was a world peopled with spirits, voices, and mysterious influences. Ancient usages and primitive taboos governed their whole existence. But the essential Indian characteristics never became subordinated to their social organization. A wild love of freedom and intolerance of restraint lay at the basis of Indian character and fired their whole existence.

The largest tribe in the North-West were the Crees. In pre-European times their numbers were small, but, with the introduction of horses and firearms, they spread in all directions over the greater part of the North-West. The Blackfeet were the strongest and most warlike of the western tribes. Together with the Bloods, Piegans and Sarcees, they evolved a mild form of military confederation, which, however, never approached in thoroughness and complexity that of the Six Nations in Eastern Canada. The sworn enemies of the Crees and Assiniboines, they were the " Ishmaels of the prairie," and lived in a state of desultory warfare with their neighbours. Their home covered what is now central and southern Alberta. The other principal tribe, the Assiniboines, although scattered throughout the Cree country, lived largely in Southern Saskatchewan in the neighbourhood of the international boundary.

For centuries the western prairies were the " happy hunting grounds " of these Indian tribes. Numberless herds of bison moving over the plains provided them with all the necessaries of their simple life ; food, clothing and shelter. From the Rio Grande to the Peace River, the plains trembled beneath the heavy tread of these wild cattle. It was the golden age of Indian freedom. In the Canadian North-West the red men lived in savage opulence, wandered over the plains, hunted the " thundering herds " and warred among themselves. The passing years brought little change to their mode of life. But, with the coming of the white man, undismayed by demons or distance, all this underwent a change.

The first Europeans in the North-West were the servants of the Hudson's Bay Company. Friendship and harmony marked their relations with the Indian tribes. The basis of this friendship lay in the policy of the Company towards the natives with whom they came in contact. Inspired though they may have been by prudence and self-interest, rather than by enlightened motives of native welfare, their dealings with the Indians were marked by a sense of trusteeship and strict integrity. The Indian learned to respect the " Kingchauch " man as the representative of a superior civilization and the embodiment of fair dealing; a fact which, during the Indian rising of 1885, saved several white men from the horrors of an Indian massacre. The Standing Rules of the Fur Trade summarized the policy of the Company.

" 40th. That the Indians be treated with kindness and indulgence, and mild and conciliatory means resorted to in order to encourage industry, repress vice, and inculcate morality ; that the use of spirituous liquors be gradually discontinued in the very few districts in which it is yet indispensable ; and that the Indians be liberally supplied with requisite necessaries, particularly with articles of ammunition, whether they have the means of paying for it or not, and that no gentleman in charge of district or post be at liberty to alter or vary the standard or usual mode of trade with the Indians, except by special permission of council."[3]

The result of this policy was apparent in the peaceful history of the Company. While the Indians south of the border were fighting for life and revenge against the white men, in the Canadian North-West the employees of the Hudson's Bay Company were able to build little stockaded forts in the midst of thousands of warlike natives, to carry on their trading operations without serious disturbance, and to pass freely and without fear throughout the Indian country.

The policy of the Hudson's Bay Company was not, however, an unmixed blessing to the Indian. Not only did the Fur Trade tend to draw the Indian away from his tribal organization and to make him into a " Company Indian," but the introduction of the white man's manufactures destroyed the natives' self-reliance and independence. Long before 1870 the white man's blankets, knives, guns and powder, had displaced the skins, bows and arrows of an earlier period. The one time luxuries became necessities, and the hapless Indian, forgetting the weapons and usages of his fathers, henceforth became dependent upon the white man for his homely needs and even for life itself.

It was not until after 1870 that the Western Indians felt the full force of white expansion. The few Canadians who penetrated to the Red River Settlement prior to that date exerted no economic pressure upon the prairie tribes, and, in spite of Dennis' enlistment of fifty mission Saulteaux and McDougall's alleged dealings with a few wandering Sioux, the Indians took no part in the first Riel insurrection. After that event, white settlement spread rapidly over the North-West plains and the Canadian Government were, accordingly, brought face to face with that problem of disorganization which is produced among a primitive people when they are suddenly brought into contact with a more complex civilization.

As long as the Hudson's Bay Company retained their trade monopoly and political status, the Indian was free to live as he wished. But, with the introduction of free trade in furs and the passing of the Company as the governing power of the North-West, the lot of the Indian became an unhappy one. Whatever may be said against the Hudson's Bay Company monopoly, it was essential for the preservation of the Indians' sense of value, and the maintenance of a policy of justice and integrity. The policy of the free trader was a short-sighted one. Unlike the

Company man, the free trader cared nothing for the future ; the continuance and well-being of the native was no concern of his as long as he could get possession of the furs which the Indian had to barter. New and reprehensible practices in trade were introduced. Competition was keen. Trader outbid trader and upset the century old values fixed by the Hudson's Bay Company.[4] Alcoholic spirits, discontinued by the Company in the Saskatchewan for many years, now poured in from Red River and from across the border. In southern Alberta, American whisky runners from Montana introduced the lawless spirit of the American frontier. Contemptuous of Canadian authority, they built forts in Canadian territory, and debauched the Indians with alcohol.[5] In 1872 Colonel Robertson Ross reported upon the fearful results of this nefarious traffic :

" The demoralization of the Indians and injury resulting to the country from this illicit traffic are very great. It is stated upon good authority that during last year (1871) eighty-eight (88) of the Blackfeet Indians were murdered in drunken brawls amongst themselves, produced by the whisky and other spirits supplied to them by those traders. At Fort Edmonton during the present summer whisky was openly sold to the Blackfeet and other Indians trading at the post by some smugglers from the United States who derive large profit thereby, and on these traders being remonstrated with by the gentleman in charge of the Hudson's Bay Post, they coolly replied that they knew very well that what they were doing was contrary to the law of both countries, but as there was no force there to prevent them, *they would do just as they pleased.*"[6]

In May 1873[7] occurred a most bloodthirsty event. A band of American desperadoes crossed the frontier with a large quantity of whisky, which they traded to a band of Assiniboines in the Cypress Hills. When their supplies had been bartered and the Indians were in the midst of their orgy, the traders accused the natives of horse stealing and opened fire upon them. Over thirty Indians, men, women, and children, were killed. The remainder took to the hills for cover. The liquor itself was murderous enough without such massacres as these.[8]

Conditions in the Saskatchewan valley were little better. Alcoholic spirits and wild rumours were fed to the credulous natives by evilly disposed traders. Threats, insubordination, and violence became common. No attempt was made to assert the supremacy of the law and serious crimes were allowed to pass unpunished. Hardly a year passed without several murders and crimes of the most serious nature being committed with comparative impunity. The Hudson's Bay Company influence rapidly dwindled. The officer in charge of Fort Pitt assured Colonel Robertson Ross that " of late the Indians have been overbearing in manner, and threatening at times. Indeed, the white men dwelling in the Saskatchewan are at this moment living by sufferance, as it were, entirely at the mercy of the Indians. They dare not venture to introduce cattle or stock into the country, or cultivate the ground to any extent for fear of Indian spoliation."[9] The situation was critical. Even as early as 1871 Lieutenant Butler wrote in his Report :

" As matters at present rest, the region of the Saskatchewan is without law, order, or security for life or property ; robbery and murder for years have gone unpunished ; Indian massacres are unchecked even in the close vicinity of Hudson Bay Company's posts, and all civil and legal institutions are entirely unknown."[10]

Debauchery and demoralization were the result of the contact of the native and the trader : starvation was the result of the advent of the settler. As settlement advanced, the chase, the Indians' sole means of subsistence, rapidly diminished. The buffalo and antelope withdrew before the activity of the hunt. Game became scarce, and everywhere, throughout Manitoba and the North-West, this scarcity became a serious problem to the Indians. Even as early as 1871 Lieutenant Butler traversed the plains from Red River to the Rocky Mountains without seeing a single buffalo in twelve hundred miles of prairie. A few years later the mission post of St. Paul des Cris, founded in 1853, was abandoned, both by the missionaries and the Indians, because of the withdrawal of the chase from that region.[11] Grey Owl, a modern half-breed Indian writer, describes the destruction wrought by the white man in the North-West in the following picturesque terms :[12]

" His coming changed the short springy carpet of buffalo-grass that covered the prairie into a tangle of coarse wild hay, shoulder high. The groves of the forest became dismal clearances of burnt and blackened skeleton trees, and the jewelled lakes were damned and transformed into bodies of unclean water, bordered by partly submerged rampikes, and unsightly heaps of dead

trees, where, in the event of a sudden storm, landing was dangerous if not impossible. Fish died in the pollution, and game of all
kinds migrated to other regions."

This scarcity of their means of subsistence the Indians were not
slow to attribute to the presence of the white men, and dissatisfaction and discontent were rampant among them.

But the coming of the white settler involved a more serious
problem than the diminution of the wild life, namely, the
occupation of the Indians' land. This problem hardly arose in
the Canadian North-West before the 'eighties, but the gruesome
experience of their kinsmen in the United States was not lost upon
the Canadian Indians in the North-West Territories. From
early times a chronic state of hostility existed between the whites
and Indians in the United States. Land hungry frontiersmen,
defiant of Indian rights and federal prohibition, and predisposed
to hostility by a conflict of economic interests, squatted upon
Indian lands. Friction with the natives followed. Extermination was the frontiersman's policy,[13] and to it, by force of circumstances, the American Government became an unwilling ally.
Obliged to protect their citizens against Indian retaliation, the
United States were involved in a series of Indian wars. To the
natives this meant ultimate extinction but they fought with
desperation.

During the spring of 1870 a particularly bloody attack was
made upon a band of Piegans not far from the Canadian frontier,
in which 170 Indians were massacred in a few moments.[14]
Occurrences such as these, especially in view of the alliance of the
Piegans with the Canadian Blackfeet, and the presence in Canada
of refugee Indians from the United States, must inevitably have
communicated a feeling of apprehension to the Canadian Indians
concerning the white newcomers. Psychological rather than
material pressure was at the basis of their fears.

Moreover, the events at Red River during 1869 and 1870 had
been unsettling to the native mind. Although the Indians
had not participated actively in Riel's insurrection, a few savages,
drawn by the prospects of war, had been appealed to by Dennis
and Monkman for support, and, from fear or recklessness, had
received promises impossible to fulfil. Beyond the limits of
Red River stories of rebellion and pillage, of change of
governments and capture of forts, magnified and distorted by

H

the distance and the telling, found ready credence among the suspicious natives. The westward migration of the half-breeds, crowded out of their country and cheated out of their holdings, impressed the minds of the Indians. They readily believed that white expansion would do the same to them. This belief was justified. Immigration implied the occupation of land for agricultural purposes, thus depriving the Indians of those means of living which had been theirs and their forefathers for centuries. It is not surprising, therefore, that the Indians, interrupted in the peaceable possession of those hunting grounds which they considered their own inalienable patrimony, regarded the white intruders with unfriendly eyes.

Unscrupulous traders and resentful half-breeds made no efforts to reassure the Indians. Having everything to lose and nothing to gain by the establishment of a strong, vigorous Canadian administration in the Territories, they plied the Indians with rum and spread stories of faithlessness and probable extermination among the natives. The Government was painted in repulsive colours. Wild tales of the calamities which would befall them should the Canadians come were propagated, and many Indians were wrought to such a pitch that they would spit at the very name of Canada![15] Thus, with their minds unsettled, their lands threatened, and their beliefs, convictions and mode of life rudely shaken, the North-West Indians were thoroughly disquieted at the white man's presence.

The Canadian Government was fully alive to the danger which threatened both the Indian races and the peace of the country. Butler, Robertson Ross, and the North-West Council reported upon the rampant lawlessness, and recommended the establishment of a military force in the North-West Territories. Archibald, Christie and French,[16] described the Indian unrest and urged the necessity of a clear statement of policy and the opening of negotiations for the extinction of the Indian title. The Federal Government at Ottawa followed both of these recommendations.

Early in 1873 Sir John A. Macdonald introduced a Bill " Respecting the Administration of Justice, and for the Establishment of a Police Force in the North-West Territories,"[17] and in the autumn of the same year the first steps were taken to organize the force which became famous as the North-West Mounted Police. The organization of the force was in many ways a military one and an Imperial Officer, Captain G. A. French, R.A., was accordingly placed in command. Its object was the maintenance of order in the vast territory west of the settled parts of Manitoba; especially as between the white settlers and the Indian tribes. The massacre at the Cypress Hills hastened matters, and on July 10th, 1874, a small force of 275 men set out for the unknown North-West.[18] One division was despatched north to Fort Edmonton, but the main body pushed westward to the foothills where the chief danger lay. Their purpose was to strike directly at the lawlessness from across the frontier. Fort Macleod was built in the closing months of 1874, and other posts were established at Calgary and at Fort Walsh in the Cypress Hills.

No time was lost in rounding up the whisky runners. Fort Whoop-Up was visited in October, but was found empty of liquor or ruffians. Outlying detachments were placed at Stand-Off and Fort Kipp, and, after a few arrests, the country was deserted by the erstwhile bravoes who saw in the Mounted Police determined adversaries.

The Indians, in spite of their passion for liquor, were not slow to express their appreciation of the benefits which the Mounted Police had brought to them. One year after the coming of the force, the Blackfeet and Piegans spoke highly of " the great satisfaction they derived from the presence of the Mounted Police in their country, the security and peace that had succeeded to anarchy, disorder, and drunkenness, the prosperity which had replaced poverty and want."[19] The chiefs themselves testified to this effect upon the occasion of Treaty 7. Addressing the Commissioner, Button Chief declared:

" The Great Mother sent Stamixotokon (Colonel Macleod) and the Police to put an end to the traffic in fire-water. I can sleep now safely. Before the arrival of the Police, when I laid my head down at night, every sound frightened me; my sleep was broken; now I can sleep sound and am not afraid."[20]

And Crowfoot, the head chief of the Blackfoot nation:

" If the Police had not come to the country, where would we be all now? Bad men and whisky were killing us so fast that very few, indeed, of us would have been left to-day. The Police have protected us as the feathers of the bird protect it from the frosts of the winter."[21]

But the establishment of the North-West Mounted Police did not solve the problem of economic contact. The aim of the European settler was the acquisition of land for cultivation, that of the native was to preserve his hunting grounds. The Indians always jealously guarded their lands, but they felt that sooner or later the ancient Indian prophecy would come true, " The Paleface shall trick the Indian out of his land till there is nothing left."[22] They were apprehensive of the future and anxious for some arrangement with the Canadian Government in the form of a treaty. Thus, so long as the Indian title remained unextinguished, so long remained the danger of a possible native rising.

It was early apparent that the Indians would oppose the extension of settlement in the North-West, unless certain guarantees were given by the white settlers or the Canadian Government. In 1870 it had been deemed necessary to despatch two agents to inform the Indians of the Government's intention to send troops to Red River, and to arrange with them a right of way through their country. At a pow-wow with Colonel Wolseley at Fort Frances, the Indian chief, Crooked Neck, refused to accept the presents offered him, gaudy red shirts, coats and caps, and declared " Am I a pike to be caught with such a bait as that ? Shall I sell my land for a bit of red cloth ? We will let the pale-faces pass through our country, but we will sell them none of our land, nor have any of them to live amongst us."[23] Other bands expressed similar views. " We believe what you tell us when you say that, in your land, the Indians have always been treated with clemency and justice . . . but do not bring settlers and surveyors amongst us, to measure and occupy our lands, until a clear understanding has been arrived at, as to what our relations are to be in the time to come."[24] " These," declared the Government agent in his memorandum, " were the views which seemed generally to prevail among the Indians. Next spring they will look for a clear definition of the policy which is to be adopted toward them."[25]

Similar demands were made by Indian tribes in other parts of the North-West. No sooner had Archibald been installed as Lieutenant-Governor than a large number of Manitoba Indians demanded an interview. To calm their excited spirits and to secure their peaceable dispersion he gave them presents and promises, engaging " to see them in the spring and conclude a

Treaty with them of some kind."[26]   The Saskatchewan Indians, too, anxiously awaited a statement of the Government's native policy.   In January 1871, the Reverend John McDougall and Richard Hardisty forwarded a petition from Seenum's Crees at Victoria and Whitefish Lake.[27*] Amongst other things the petition stated :

" We, as loyal subjects of Our Great Mother the Queen whom Your Excellency represents, wish that our privileges and claims of the land of our fathers be recognized by Commissioners whom Your Excellency may hereafter appoint, to treat with the different tribes of the Saskatchewan, whereas at the present time, many of our fellow Crees entertain strange and wrong ideas regarding the way Your Excellency's Government is to treat with the different tribes of this country for their laws (sic).   We are taught by our Missionary that the British Government has never taken advantage of the ignorance of any tribe of Indians with whom they have treated.   We therefore hope that our rights shall be recognized."

From Edmonton came the following petition from Sweetgrass,[28] one of the leading Cree chiefs :

" Great Father,—I shake hands with you, and bid you welcome.—We heard our lands were sold and we did not like it; we don't want to sell our lands ; it is our property, and no one has the right to sell them.

" Our country is getting ruined of fur-bearing animals, hitherto our sole support, and now we are poor and want help—we want you to pity us.   We want cattle, tools, agricultural implements, and assistance in everything when we come to settle—our country is no longer able to support us.

" Make provision for us against years of starvation.   We have had great starvation the past winter, and the small-pox took away many of our people, the old, young, and children.

" We want you to stop the Americans from coming to trade on our lands, and giving firewater, ammunition and arms to our enemies the Blackfeet.

" We made a peace this winter with the Blackfeet.   Our young men are foolish, it may not last long.

" We invite you to come and see us and to speak with us.   If you can't come yourself, send some one in your place.

" We send these words by our Master, Mr. Christie, in whom we have every confidence.—That is all."

From these demands it was obvious that some measures had to be taken to reassure the Indians. Real or fancied encroachments might be resisted by force. Accordingly, in 1871, the Secretary of State recommended the immediate appointment of a Commissioner to undertake negotiations with the Indians of the North-West.[29]

Although the Canadian Government were not without experience in the management of native affairs, the North-West Indian problem presented new and difficult angles. In Eastern Canada the natives and whites had been in contact with each other for centuries. The early settlers were few in number and dependent upon the goodwill of the natives for their lives and security. Life was simple, and the manner of existence of white and red man not dissimilar. There was no overwhelming difference in progress to bridge. The advance of settlement was slow, and the Indians continued to hunt over and enjoy, in many cases for years, the lands for which they were receiving yearly payment. Thus, over a period of two centuries, the Indians were able to adapt themselves and to merge themselves into the new civilization. In the North-West, however, the natives felt the full pressure of the white invasion within the short space of two decades. Scarcely were the embers of the treaty fire cool, when engineers began to survey the railway line. Here was no gradual, imperceptible change. The problem of centuries in Eastern Canada had to be solved in as many decades in Western Canada, if the Indian was to be saved from extinction. The problem of readjustment was made all the more difficult by the mechanical progress and industrial complexities of nineteenth-century civilization. There was no room in it for a people that had little to contribute. The whole social and economic framework of native development had, therefore, to be rebuilt in a few years, lest the primitive Indian society be wrecked beyond all hope of salvation.

The policy followed by Canada in the North-West was a continuation of that which had governed the relations between the whites and the Indians since the days of Sir William Johnson. Western Indian history was merely the application of these well-founded principles to a new problem, the acknowledgment of the Indian title, and the formal negotiation for the surrender of the same.

The French régime in Canada had recognized no native title to the soil, or any rights which could possibly occasion a Treaty or negotiation. Special tracts of land were set aside for the Indians, such as those granted to the Jesuits at Lac St. Louis in 1680 and to the Seminary of St. Sulpice at the Lake of Two Mountains in 1717.[30] But these grants, although made for the benefit of the Indians, flowed only from the clemency of the Crown; any acknowledgment of an aboriginal Indian title was scrupulously absent.

In direct contrast to this policy was that adopted by the British Crown. Following the example of the Dutch, who concocted the legal function of an aboriginal title to counter the English claim of prior discovery,[31] the British adopted the practice of voluntary purchase of native lands as a matter of prudence and justice. This practice was continued in Canada after the American Revolutionary War, and Governor Simcoe secured the surrender by the Indian tribes of Upper Canada of large tracts of that province, sometimes by direct purchase, and on other occasions for an annuity. The transference in 1860 of the control over native affairs from the Imperial to the Colonial authorities brought about no change in policy. The Colonial Government of the province of Canada continued to follow the Johnson tradition and to cultivate the goodwill of the Indians.

There was an important difference between the Indian surrenders in Eastern Canada and the treaties in Western Canada. The latter were more formal, ceremonious, and imposing; the areas to be ceded were larger; and the number of Indians to be treated with more numerous and warlike. Moreover, the early negotiations involved only a simple surrender for cash or annuities, with, perhaps, the promise of a reserved area. The later treaties contained, not only the details of the cession, but the expressed obligation of the Canadian Government to make provision for the instruction, health and civilization of the native tribes.

The earliest treaty, as distinct from a mere surrender or cession of land, was that made by Lord Selkirk with the Saulteaux and Crees of Red River in 1817. This implied a recognition of the Indian title, and the Earl and his successors undertook to pay an annual quit rent of 100 pounds " of good and merchantable tobacco."[32] Although not permanent, for the same area had to be treated for in 1871, it is noteworthy as the precedent upon which were based the negotiations of the 'seventies. Other early treaties were made in 1850 and 1862 with certain tribes of Western Ontario; but the first official treaty with the North-West Indians was that made by Simpson and Archibald at Lower Fort Garry in 1871.

In April 1871, the Honourable Joseph Howe, then Secretary of State for the Provinces, in view of " the necessity of arranging with the Bands inhabiting the Tract of Country between Thunder Bay and the Stone Fort, for the cession (subject to certain reserves such as they should select) of the lands occupied by them,"[33] recommended the appointment of Mr. W. M. Simpson as Commissioner to negotiate with the Indians. The need for such an appointment was pressing. The Indians had already " interfered with emigrants, warning them not to come on the ground outside the Hudson's Bay Company's surveys," even posting a notice on the door of the church at Portage la Prairie " warning parties not to intrude on their lands, until a Treaty should be made."[34] Accordingly, Archibald wrote:

" With this anxiety and uneasiness among the Indians, with a feeling of danger on the part of emigrants seeking lands and ready to commence work, but subjected to enforced idleness by the danger of entering against the will of the Indians, you will easily understand that I awaited with much anxiety and hailed with much pleasure the arrival of Mr. Simpson."[35]

Immediately upon his arrival in Manitoba the Indian Commissioner took the necessary steps to conduct the negotiations. With the assistance of Lieutenant-Governor Archibald and the Honourable James Mackay, a prominent Scotch half-breed, proclamations and invitations were issued calling upon the Indians to meet the Commissioner at Lower Fort Garry and Manitoba Post in July. About a thousand Indians attended. On July 27th, Lieutenant-Governor Archibald opened the negotiations with all the dignity, formality, and precaution, appropriate to the occasion. His address to the assembled natives outlined the Government's proposals and stressed the inevitability of a change in their mode of life:

" Your Great Mother, the Queen, wishes to do justice to all her children alike. She will deal fairly with those of the setting sun, just as she would with those of the rising sun. She wishes order and peace to reign through all her country, and while her arm is strong to punish the wicked man, her hand is also open to reward the good man everywhere in her Dominions.

"Your Great Mother wishes the good of all races under her sway. She wishes her red children to be happy and contented. She wishes them to live in comfort. She would like them to adopt the habits of the whites, to till land and raise food, and store it up against a time of want. She thinks this would be the best thing for her red children to do, that it would make them safer from famine and distress, and make their homes more comfortable. . . . Your Great Mother, therefore, will lay aside for you ' lots ' of land to be used by you and your children forever. She will not allow the white man to intrude upon these lots. She will make rules to keep them for you, so that as long as the sun shall shine, there shall be no Indian who has not a place that he can call his home, where he can go and pitch his camp, or if he chooses, build his house and till his land."[36]

At first a short delay occurred owing to the presence of " a cloud before them which made things dark."[37] On inquiry the " cloud " turned out to be the imprisonment of four Indians convicted of a breach of contract with the Hudson's Bay Company. The Lieutenant-Governor, as a diplomatic gesture, ordered the release of the four, a favour which cleared the sky, and in a serene atmosphere Treaty 1 was brought to a successful conclusion after eight days' deliberation.

There was some difficulty experienced in making the Indians understand the significance of the terms of the treaty. They demanded an area fully two-thirds the size of the Province as a segregated area, a demand which clearly demonstrated their misunderstanding of the purpose of the reservations. In the end, the Indians had to be content with much less. The treaty stipulated the complete surrender of an area roughly approximating the Province of Manitoba ; the setting aside of inalienable reservations at the proportion of 160 acres for a family of five ; the prohibition of intoxicating liquors ; the maintenance of a school on each reserve ; an initial present of three dollars a head and an annuity at the same rate, payable in " blankets, clothing prints (assorted colours), twine or traps . . . or . . . if Her Majesty shall deem the same desirable . . . in cash " ; and finally, the strict observance of the terms of the treaty and the maintenance of " perpetual peace " between the Indians and the white settlers.[38]

Treaty 1 was the forerunner of a series of treaties which involved the surrender of the whole of the organized territories of the North-West. By 1877 the only unceded land lay far to the north, where settlement, if at all, would be slow to penetrate. On the whole, the negotiations and terms of the subsequent Treaties, 2, 3, 4, 5, 6 and 7, resembled those of Treaty 1. There were, however, several important additions or modifications which we shall examine.

Treaty 3 was one of considerable importance. Not only did it " tranquillize " a large native population holding a strategic position on the proposed route of the Canadian Pacific Railway, but it fixed the type of subsequent treaties by granting greater concessions in the way of annuities and reserves than had been granted by Treaties 1 and 2,[39] and in promising practical assistance to encourage the adoption of agriculture by the Indians. The Indians of Treaty 3 drove a harder bargain with the Commissioner than had those of the previous Treaties. In spite of their poverty and isolation, they were fully aware of the value of their country. " The sound of the rustling of the gold is under my feet where I stand ; " declared one chief, " we have a rich country ; it is the Great Spirit who gave us this ; where we stand upon is the Indians' property, and belongs to them. If you grant us our requests you will not go back without making the treaty."[40] Perhaps the most significant demand was made by the Lac Seul chief :

" We are the first that were planted here ; we would ask you to assist us with every kind of implement to use for our benefit, to enable us to perform our work ; a little of everything and money. We would borrow your cattle ; we ask you this for our support ; I will find whereon to feed them. The waters out of which you sometimes take food for yourselves, we will lend you in return. . . . If you give what I ask, the time may come when I will ask you to lend me one of your daughters and one of your sons to live with us ; and in return I will lend you one of my daughters and one of my sons for you to teach what is good, and after they have learned, to teach us. If you grant us what I ask, although I do not know you, I will shake hands with you. This is all I have to say."[41]

THE INDIAN TREATIES
N.W.Ts 1871~1877

HUDSON BAY

NELSON R.

HEIGHT OF LAND

3 1873

OJIBWAYS

SWAMPY CREES

BERENS R.

L. WINNIPEG

OJIBWAYS

1 1871

CREES

OJIBWAYS

LAKE OF THE WOODS

5 1875

SAULTEAUX

2 1871

CREES

OJIBWAYS

4 1874

CREES

SAULTEAUX

ASSINIBOINES

N. 6 1876

CREES

SASKATCHEWAN R.

BATTLE R.

ASSINIBOINES

S. SASKATCH ~ EWAN R.

SAULTEAUX

ASSINIBOINES

CHIPEWYANS

CREES

RED DEER R.

7 1877

BOW R.

BLACKFEET

ROCKY MOUNTAINS

Miles 100   0   100   200   300   Miles

The resultant treaty set aside reserves at the increased proportion of one square mile, 640 acres, per family of five; granted an initial present of $12 a head to extinguish all previous claims; and promised to maintain schools and to prohibit the introduction of alcoholic liquors on the reserves. The Government also promised to supply any bands desiring to cultivate the soil, with a fixed number of hoes, spades, scythes, axes, saws, files, grind-stones, ploughs, harrows, etc., and also with a box of carpenter's tools, a yoke of oxen, a bull and four cows, "all the aforesaid articles to be given once for all for the encouragement of the practice of agriculture among the Indians." In addition, the annuities to the ordinary Indians were increased to $5, while the chiefs and headmen, officially recognized in the treaties for the first time, were to receive $25 and $15 annually with suitable clothes every three years, and medals and flags at the close of the treaty.

These concessions shaped the terms of the following treaties. During the negotiations for Treaty 4, the Qu'Appelle Indians, having learned the terms of the previous treaty, demanded similar provisions. "We want the same Treaty you have given to the North-West Angle. This I am asking for," declared Kamooses, voicing the wishes of the Southern Crees and Saulteaux to Lieutenant-Governor Morris.[42] Accordingly, the terms of Treaty 4 were similar to those of Treaty 3. The conditions of Treaty 5, covering what is now northern Manitoba, were also similar.

Treaty 6, which involved the surrender by the Plain and Wood Crees of the North Saskatchewan region, was, with the possible exception of Treaty 7 with the Blackfeet, the most important treaty negotiated in the North-West. The area treated for was vast and extensive. The Indians were wild, warlike, and determined to allow no white invasion of a country to which immigration had already turned for settlement.[43] From 1871 urgent requests to conclude a treaty with the North Saskatchewan Indians had been forwarded to the Canadian Government, but met with no immediate response. The Indians, as a result, showed a hostile face to the white settlers. In 1875 Colonel French reported that the Indians had turned back a party of the Geological Survey, and interrupted the progress of the telegraph.[44] He pointed out, at the same time, that the force under his command was insufficient to take any action, and urged that " the only moral force that could be brought to bear would be an assurance that the Government purposed having a Treaty with the Crees at some definite period."

As a result of the importunities of the officers of the Hudson's Bay Company, the inhabitants of the settlement of Prince Albert, the North-West Council, and the Mounted Police, the federal authorities took action.   The Reverend George McDougall, a missionary much beloved by the Indians, was despatched in the autumn of 1875 to calm the excited spirits of the aborigines and to assure them that commissioners would be sent the following year to conclude a treaty with them.[45]   McDougall's mission was successful, but the attitude of the wilder spirits boded trouble. Big Bear, who later became the leader of the malcontent Indians against the Treaty, distrusted McDougall's overtures :

" We want none of the Queen's presents ; when we set a fox-trap we scatter pieces of meat all round, but when the fox gets into the trap we knock him on the head ; we want no bait, let your Chiefs come like men and talk to us."[46]

The Treaty was signed at Fort Carlton on August 23rd, and at Fort Pitt on September 9th, 1876.   It contained, in addition to the usual terms, the slight—" more onerous," the Minister of the Interior called them—[47] concessions of a horse, harness and wagon to each chief, a few additional agricultural tools, a medicine chest for the band, and a grant of $1,000 for three years for the purchase of provisions for those Indians who settled down and actively engaged in agriculture.   The most important clause was one providing for aid and rations to the Indians in the event of " any pestilence " or " general famine."   The officials of the Indian Department were fully aware of the implications of this promise. In his Annual Report, the Minister of the Interior referred to this provision as one which

" I greatly regret should have been agreed to by the Commissioners, as it may cause the Indians to rely upon the Government instead of upon their own exertions for sustenance, especially as their natural means of subsistence are likely to diminish with the settlement of the country."[48]

The Minister was justified in his fears.   The fulfilment of this famine clause became a fruitful source of discord between the

Indians and the Government on the disappearance of the buffalo several years later.

In 1877 the seventh treaty was concluded with the tribes inhabiting the foothill reaches of the Rocky Mountains. It was a treaty of great importance. The Blackfoot Confederacy included the most warlike Indians of the plains, and Crowfoot, their head chief, was the ablest of his race. On this occasion the Indians, true to their warlike propensities, requested that an issue of rifles might be included in the treaty. But martial exploits were viewed with disfavour by a Government endeavouring to promote pastoral pursuits, and, with the exception of the present of a few Winchester carbines to the chiefs, as an act of diplomatic courtesy, the Indians had to be content with the terms of the previous treaties, and the promise of a few additional agricultural implements and cattle.

In general, the treaty system, as a method of governing the relations between savages and civilized peoples, has not been an unqualified success. Native treaties, intended to preserve native rights, maintain peaceful relations and promote harmony between natives and frontier settlers, have been attended in North America, as well as in South Africa and New Zealand, by misunderstanding, racial hostility and, oftentimes, bloodshed. Hobson's Treaty of Waitangi with the Maoris, Stockenstrom's with the Kaffirs and those with the American Indians, although designed to meet different conditions, were all based upon the common assumption of free consent and the equality of the contracting parties. This assumption was unsound. The natives seldom understood the full implications of the contract. The disparity in power and interests between the signatories reduced the treaties to mere grants of such terms as the weaker people might accept without active resistance, and such treaties were, accordingly, rather the preparatives and apology for disputes than securities for peace.

Nevertheless, the Canadian treaty system has worked reasonably well. Only one breach occurred in the faithful observance of the Indian Treaties. Although the system was abandoned with few regrets in the United States in 1871, it has remained, to the present time, the basis of Canadian native policy. Treaties 8, 9, 10 and 11 have been negotiated since 1877. As late as 1929–30, tribes in the neighbourhood of Hudson Bay formally signed their adhesion to Treaty 9. In comparison with the terms granted in the United States, those of the Canadian treaties have not erred on the side of liberality; the monetary considerations have been less and the reserves smaller. But strict honesty, justice and good faith have marked the administration of Indian affairs in Canada. The treaties have not only been mutually observed, but have been supplemented by the Government in the interests of the native. There have been no wars of extermination or compulsory migrations. On the whole, Canada has followed the tradition of the Imperial Government in its relations with native tribes, and has endeavoured to deal fairly with her aboriginal wards.

At the same time it is only fair to note that, when contrasted with the United States, Canada has had two advantages over her southern neighbour; namely, the absence of a lawless frontier class and the invaluable assistance of the half-breeds. The fighting plainsman of American history found no counterpart in Canada. The "roaring days" of "the last wild west," the crude, lawless population of miners and aggressive adventurers, the romantic exploits of Boone and Cody, were peculiar to the American frontier. In Canada the frontier was peopled by peaceful, law-abiding settlers, ranchers, farmers and government-fostered settlements. The effect upon Indian policy was important. The white settler looked to the Government and to the Mounted Police for his protection against the Indian, and not to the rifle over his door. Nor did he defy the law and trespass upon the native reserves. The Indian question in Canada was one of keeping the red man in order, not the white.[49]

To the half-breeds the Dominion owes much. They were indispensable at the negotiation of every treaty, and to their influence was due in a large part the peaceful relations which existed between the Indians and the whites in the North-West. The American consul at Winnipeg, ever fearful of an outbreak in Canada of the native troubles which marked his own country, bore witness to this fact in a letter to Washington:

"If an Indian war with all its attendant horrors is avoided, it will be attributable to a circumstance peculiar to the region so long occupied by the Hudson's Bay Company and without parallel in the Western Territories of the United States. I refer to the extensive intermarriage of the English, Scotch and French residents—prominently the officers and employees of the Hudson's Bay Company—with the Indian women, diffusing over the whole country in the lapse of several generations a population of métis or mixed bloods equal in number to the Indians and exerting over their aboriginal kindred a degree of moral and physical control which I find it difficult to illustrate, but which I regard as a happy Providence for the Dominion of Canada."[50]

Thus by 1877 the Ottawa Government had opened its relations with the Indians of the North-West with every hope of success. The policy of paternalism and justice inaugurated by the Hudson's Bay Company passed on to Canada no hereditary hatreds and no traditions of broken faith and unfulfilled promises. The treaties had been concluded in that spirit which had ensured the friendliness of the Indians of old Canada. It now remained to determine a policy which would ensure a continuance of these peaceful relations, convince the Indians of the Government's good faith, and assist them over the difficult transition from savagery to civilization.

CHAPTER XI

THE INDIAN PROBLEM—THE RESERVES

" THERE are two modes wherein the Government may treat the Indian nations who inhabit this territory," wrote Indian Superintendent Provencher in 1873, " Treaties may be made with them simply with a view to the extinction of their rights, by agreeing to pay them a sum, and afterwards abandon them to themselves. On the other side, they may be instructed, civilized and led to a mode of life more in conformity with the new position of this country, and accordingly make them good, industrious and useful citizens."[1] Under the first " mode " or policy, the Indians would have remained in ignorance and inferiority. As soon as the growth of settlement should have deprived them of their hunting and fishing grounds, they would have been forced to seek refuge beyond the civilized frontier in the hinterland of savagery, or to become helpless dependents and degenerate mendicants. Under the second, the Indians might be enabled to take their place in the white man's society, to share the advantages of civilization, and eventually to participate with him in the conduct of national affairs.

In Parliament the Indian question excited little interest. With the exception of short discussions when the departmental estimates were submitted, debates upon matters of Indian policy were few. Following his return to power in 1878, Sir John A. Macdonald took over the titular headship of the Indian Department, but the conduct of the Department was left largely in the hands of his friend and deputy, Mr. Lawrence Vankoughnet. Vankoughnet was a man with a very high sense of duty. He considered himself the permanent head of the Department, and the Ministers as mere passing politicians. He, more than any other man, was responsible for the policy which was adopted during the years covered by this study.

Civilization and enfranchisement were, like those of Sir George Grey's amalgamation policy, the ultimate aims of Canadian native policy. But to throw the uncivilized red man

into the struggles and competitions of life with his white neighbour, without sufficient preparation, care and guidance, would
have been the greatest cruelty and paramount error. The
Canadian Government had, therefore, not only to recognize its
duty to protect Indian rights by treaties, but to remember that,
during the period of transition from savagery to civilization, the
Indian stood in need of consideration and guidance.

The period of transition is a critical one. It is a period of
hope and fear, of promise and danger. The impact of a more
complex civilization which imposes its alien elements upon a
primitive society, inevitably involves the complete disorganization of the weaker culture. The whole basis of native life is
almost forcibly altered. Christian missionaries use their powerful
influence against the " uncivilized " aspects of native culture
and oppose the spiritual sanctions and religious taboos of savage
life. The establishment of white political authority means the
curtailment or abolition of the powers of the native authorities.
Regular chiefs and tribal councils become institutions of the
past. The ancient customs disappear and the thread of tradition
is broken. The Indian enters upon new conditions of life,
strange and unfamiliar. He acquires the vices as well as the
virtues of civilization. He is susceptible to evil as well as to
beneficent influences. His savage self-reliance gives way to a
childlike dependence, and he is overwhelmed with a feeling of
helplessness. To him the new order means the complete
overthrow of his system of religion, government and law, and
the attempt to transform his individual nature.[2]

To guide the Indian over this difficult period, the Canadian
Government followed three lines of action : the placing of the
Indians upon their reserves, the developing of an interest in
labour, and their training in the white man's means of self-
support. " The best means," wrote the Indian Superintendent,
" to break them of their roving habits, to elevate and assure their
position, is to attach them to agriculture."[3] This was no easy
task. A traditionally nomadic existence was a poor preparation
for an agricultural life and the Indians were, on the whole,
unresponsive to the Government's policy. Ill success accompanied their efforts at " nursing food out of sand and rocks " and
with their hopes depressed the Indians threw aside their tools
and longed for the " good old days." In the end, however,

many responded vigorously to the new life ; others, submitting with reluctance to compulsory agriculture and stock raising, never recovered from the social and economic revolution which civilization had brought.

At first little effort was made to prepare the Indians for the inevitable change. During the negotiations for Treaty 1, Lieutenant-Governor Archibald distinctly stated that they would not be forced to adopt the white man's ways. Treaties 3, 4, 5, 6 and 7 all contained clauses guaranteeing to the Indians the right to live their old life as they wished. The following section from Treaty 3 was typical :[4]

" Her Majesty further agrees with her said Indians, that they, the said Indians, shall have the right to pursue their avocations of hunting and fishing throughout the tract surrendered as hereinbefore described, subject to such regulations as may from time to time be made by her Government of her Dominion of Canada, and saving and excepting such tracts as may from time to time be required or taken up for settlement, mining, lumbering or other purposes, by her said Government of the Dominion of Canada, or by any of the subjects thereof duly authorized therefor by the said Government."

The Indians, of course, had no desire to settle down. As long as the herds of bison tramped the prairies and the antelope sped across the plains, they were loth to abandon the thrilling life of the chase for the tedious existence of agriculture. The Commissioners sent to negotiate Treaty 4 reported that few tribes wished to adopt civilization :

" Many of the Bands have no desire to settle and commence farming, and will not turn their attention to agriculture until they are forced to do so on account of the failure of their present means of subsistence by the extermination of the buffalo."[5]

The extermination of the buffalo was not far distant. Only four years were to elapse after these words were written when the great herds were to be seen no more upon the Canadian prairies. The effect upon the Indians was disastrous. In the space of a few years they were transformed from lords of a barbaric wilderness into miserable dependents upon mission and state charity. The surrender of their lands was the first wrench ; the disappearance of the buffalo completely severed the Indian from his historic past. " What shall we do ? " asked a young Sioux of an American officer, "what shall we do ? The buffalo is our only friend. When he goes, all is over with the Dacotahs."[6]

It is not surprising that the Indians regarded the buffalo as their " only friend." They depended upon the buffalo for all the essentials of life, food, fuel and raiment. Its hide supplied them with their moccasins, clothing, harness, tents, cradles and shrouds. Its sinews were their bow strings, its horns their powder flasks, and its dung their fuel. The flesh of the buffalo supplied the Indian with his staple article of food, and with pemmican during the lean days when fresh meat could not be found. To the Indian the buffalo was the manifestation of the Great Spirit's care for his red children, and its disappearance meant the complete destruction of their livelihood and morale.

Even prior to the coming of the white settlers the buffalo had been diminishing in numbers. Although Paul Kane wrote during 1846 :

" During the whole of the three days that it took us to reach Edmonton House, we saw nothing else but these animals covering the plains as far as the eye could reach, and so numerous were they, that at times they impeded our progress, filling the air with dust almost to suffocation."[7]

and Lieutenant-Colonel Lefroy declared in 1857 before a parliamentary committee that " the buffaloes swarm " in the neighbourhood of Red River ;[8] other travellers found the Indians full of complaints at the diminution of the once mighty herds. The Stonies told Dr. Hector in 1859 " that every year they find it more difficult to keep from starving, and that even the buffalo cannot be depended on as before."[9] Southesk found the natives in the Saskatchewan valley " almost starving,"[10] and Milton and Cheadle wrote in 1862 that Fort Carlton had ceased to be one of the most profitable establishments " as the fur-bearing animals have decreased in the woods, and the buffalo are often far distant on the plains."[11]

With the introduction of modern firearms and the increase in population and settlement, the destruction of the buffalo proceeded apace. The repeating rifle and the farmer's plough spelled the doom of the prairie bison.[12] The hunts were transformed from a search for food into a thrilling sport, which attracted Indians, métis and whites from far and near. The plains of North America became strewn with rotting carcasses and bleaching bones.   In 1848 Father de Smet wrote :

" Last year 110,000 buffalo robes . . . and 25,000 salted tongues were received in the warehouses of St. Louis.   This may give you an idea of the extraordinary number of buffaloes killed, and of the extent of the vast wilderness which furnishes pasturage to these animals."[13]

The completion of the first transcontinental railway in the United States split the once universal herd in two.   It was as a great steel knife thrust through the heart of the buffalo.   Not only did it bring the crowds of hunters anxious to emulate the destructive exploits of Comstock and Cody, but it brought with it the surveyor, the rancher and the farmer.   The continued existence of the buffalo as a range animal was incompatible with white settlement.   The buffalo, like the Indian, was native to the wilderness ;   settlement and civilization without conservation meant its extermination.

In Canadian territory the same wicked and senseless slaughter proceeded.   The Red River buffalo brigade assumed considerable commercial proportions.   It is stated that even as early as 1840 1,210 carts were sent from Red River to the plains at a cost of £24,000.[14]   Cows were destroyed merely for their tongues and bosses, and the carcasses, which should have gone to form the food of their slaughterers, were left to rot upon the plains. Although in 1872 the Hudson's Bay Company reported that the buffalo were apparently still " numerous " in the Saskatchewan district,[15] and Grant was informed that they were " in swarms " in the Qu'Appelle valley,[16] the days of the bison were numbered. Father Leduc wrote from St. Albert in 1874 that the buffalo would probably disappear in the near future,[17] and in the following year Father André at St. Laurent considered that five years only remained to the buffalo unless some governmental action was taken.[18]   The end came even more quickly.   In 1877 and 1878 traders reported a rapid falling off in the numbers of the buffalo, and the complete failure of the provision trade.   In 1879 the Chief Commissioner of the Hudson's Bay Company wrote to London concerning the problems arising out of " the total disappearance of buffalo from British territory this season."[19] In his autobiography another Company servant sadly relates that, having dined upon buffalo steak at Qu'Appelle in the winter of

1879, " It was the last buffalo fresh meat I ever had the pleasure of eating, . . . although we had lots of pemmican, dry meat and marrow fat bladders for several years following."[20] The extermination was complete. While 150,000 skins were disposed of in the market of St. Paul, U.S., in 1883, the supply in 1884 did not exceed 300 ; and the Game Report for 1888 stated that of all the countless thousands which had roamed the prairies, only six animals were then known to be in existence ! [21]

A belated effort to restrict the appalling slaughter was made in 1877. Father André had urged the necessity of such a course two years previously. Pointing out the " rapidité effrayante " with which the buffalo were disappearing, and the " rage de destruction " which possessed the hunters, he suggested to Colonel French of the Mounted Police several measures for conservation :[22]

" 1. Que la chasse ne soit tolerée pour les métis et les blancs que du 1er juin jusqu'au premier novembre.

" 2. Défense absolue sous peine de 500 piastres d'amende et confiscation de toutes leurs robes d'hiverner dans la prairie.

" 3. Défense d'aller à la chasse pendant l'hiver, que les sauvages seuls aient liberté de vivre dans la prairie en hiver et de chasser le buffalo, mais que cette liberté soit interdite aux métis.

" 4. Peut-être une mesure plus sure ; que le gouvernement ·impose une haute taxe sur les robes des vaches tuées en hiver. Il faut prendre une mesure radicale si on veut arrêter l'extinction totale de la race des buffalos."

Colonel French was impressed by the necessity for some drastic action. He considered André's suggestions " worth serious consideration," and wrote to the Minister of Justice " I think this matter should be legislated on as soon as possible."[23]

The Indians, too, were alive to the danger which threatened them. Those of Qu'Appelle, early in 1875, demanded flour and pemmican from the Government owing to the scarcity of buffalo. The Crees of Treaty 6, taking time by the forelock, secured the promise of assistance in the event of " being overtaken by any pestilence, or by a general famine." Crowfoot's words in 1876 were prophetic of the distress to come : [24]

" We all see that the day is coming when the buffalo will all be killed, and we shall have nothing more to live on, and then you will come into our camp and see the poor Blackfeet starving. I know that the heart of the white soldiers will be sorry for us, and they will tell the Great Mother, who will not let her children starve."

The urgency of the question was fully pressed upon the officials of the Indian Department. On the occasion of the treaty payments at Qu'Appelle in 1876, not only every chief, but each headman, separately begged the Government to do something to prevent the entire extermination of the buffalo. Writing to the Minister of the Interior M. G. Dickieson declared :[25]

" In all my previous intercourse with the Indians I have never seen this course adopted. In discussing other matters a spokesman is generally chosen who speaks for all, the others merely signifying their assent, but in this case it was evident they considered something more was necessary and adopted this method to impress the gravity of their position upon me."

The question of the impending extinction of the buffalo was discussed in the Federal Parliament at Ottawa. During the session of 1876, Dr. Schultz, a Manitoba representative, moved for copies of all correspondence between the Canadian Government and the Lieutenant-Governor of the North-West relative to North-West affairs, including suggestions as to the preservation of the buffalo. The matter was dismissed with the formal response that " the preservation of the buffalo in the Western Prairies had occupied a large share of the attention of the Government for a considerable time."[26]   At the next session Schultz again raised the question. In the course of debate he urged that a closed season, such as Père André had suggested, should be enforced from November to May, while the killing of calves should be prohibited at all times. Other western members gave their support to these recommendations. The end of the matter, so far as the Federal Government was concerned, was contained in the reply of the Minister of the Interior ; the preservation of the buffalo was a question for the local Government of the North-West which " could probably devise a cheaper and better plan than this parliament, it being on the spot, and more familiar with the matter."[27]

The suggestions of André, French, and Schultz, were finally embodied in an Ordinance passed by the Council of the North-West Territories on March 22nd, 1877.[28]   The use of " pounds," and the running of the buffalo over steep banks or precipices were forbidden. Slaughter " from the mere motive of amusement, or wanton destruction, or solely to secure their tongues, choice cuts or peltries " was prohibited. The using of less than one half of the flesh of the animal was to be considered as evidence of the violation of this section. A closed season was declared on cows between November 15th and August 14th, and no calves were to be killed under the age of two years. The Indians, however, were granted certain concessions during the winter months, and " in circumstances of pressing necessity " others might kill the buffalo " to satisfy . . . immediate wants." Severe penalties were provided for the violation of the Ordinance, and half of the fine was to go to the informer.

The Ordinance was not a successful one. Although it was passed in the interests of the natives of the plains, it met with considerable opposition on their part. The métis took offence at the discrimination against them, while the Indians resented the attempt of the white man to forbid the killing of the buffalo which the Great Spirit had provided for the red man. A pregnant comment on the enactment came from the refugee Sioux chief, Sitting Bull. " When," he is reported to have asked, " did the Almighty give the Canadian Government the right to keep the Indians from killing the buffalo ? "[29] Owing to this opposition, and perhaps to the fact that it had been passed too late to achieve its purpose, the Buffalo Ordinance was repealed at the following session of the North-West Council. The buffalo were left to their unhappy fate, and in a few years nothing remained to attest the existence of the countless thousands of former years but their bleaching bones and a maze of tracks growing fainter every day.

The extermination of the buffalo brought with it a crisis in native affairs. Many Indians pressed further and further south after the receding buffalo. Unaccustomed to hunting small game in the forests, like the Wood Crees and Saulteaux of Treaties 3 and 5, the plains Indians had no alternative but to follow the buffalo or starve. This southward trek began even prior to 1876. In that year the Blackfeet complained to the Mounted Police that the northern Crees were crowding them out of their country ;[30] and in the three years following, Indians of every tribe and band congregated in the neighbourhood of the Cypress Hills, Fort Walsh, Wood Mountain and elsewhere along the boundary, where the few remaining buffalo were to be found.

The presence of Sitting Bull's band of refugee Sioux in the same district only served to aggravate an already critical situation. The few buffalo were hardly proportionate to the needs of so many natives and the presence of the Sioux was regarded by the Canadian Indians with resentment. " If you will drive away the Sioux," declared Crowfoot to the Indian Commissioner in July 1879, "and make a hole so that the buffalo may come in, we will not trouble you for food."[31]   Driven southwards by the on-coming Indians, and hemmed in by the selfish actions of the Americans,[32] the buffalo remained south of the frontier in the region of the Missouri and the Judith Basin.   Faced with the alternative of starvation, thousands of Canadian Indians, Crees, Assiniboines, Blackfeet, Bloods and Piegans, crossed the boundary line hopelessly seeking the great herds of the past.

The withdrawal of the buffalo from the prairies brought destitution in its train.   Throughout the North-West, poverty, want, privation and distress reigned supreme.   The Indians who remained in Canadian territory were faced with the spectre of famine.   The years 1878, 1879 and 1880 were, perhaps, the worst in Indian history.   Crees, Assiniboines, Blackfeet, Sarcees and Sioux were all in a like condition.   Even the small game seemed to have followed the buffalo from the barren plains.   " Not even a rabbit track is to be seen anywhere," wrote the Hudson's Bay Company Factor from Fort Carlton.[33]   The once intrepid hunters and warriors were reduced to killing their horses and dogs, to feeding on gophers and mice, and even to picking over the putrid carcasses of dead and rotting animals.[34] Almost anything, dead or alive, provided food for the wretched Indians.

The reports of missionaries, traders and police from every quarter told the same tale of famine and hardship.   In the far north the Hudson's Bay Company reported that the Indians had been " starving all winter,"[35] and that " the means of living are *now* more difficult to obtain than they have been at any time since the advent of the Company in the north."[36]   At Battleford and Fort Pitt, Indians of the prairie country gathered in hundreds to beg for assistance.   The whites had nothing but flour to give them, and only limited quantities of that.   From Carlton the Factor wrote gloomily :[37]

" The winter has been most trying to us, the whole of the Indians on the five reserves about Carlton have been in a state of semi-starvation, causing me great care and anxiety at times. The summer is now upon us and instead of our prospects improving the outlook is still more gloomy, and the future really looks desperate . . . I foresee that this is only the beginning of the end."

Similar reports were received from the Touchwood Hills. In Alberta the situation was equally bad. Father Leduc at St. Albert even reported an instance of cannibalism among the wretched savages.[38] At Blackfoot Crossing many of the old people and children, unable to help themselves and abandoned by their friends, died of want. At Fort Macleod seven thousand were fed every other day upon what scanty rations the Mounted Police were able to dole out.[39] " Quel changement depuis l'automne précédent ! " declared Father Doucet of the Blackfeet, " J'avais peine à reconnaître dans ces victimes de la faim, amaigries et décharnées, sans vigeur et sans voix, les magnifiques sauvages, véritables colosses que j'avais vus autrefois . . . Ce n'étaient plus des hommes mais des squelettes ambulants."[40]

The situation was critical. Starvation bred desperation. Throughout the North-West men went about with the constant fear of an Indian rising before them. The Commissioner of the Hudson's Bay Company wrote to London :[41]

" The Government are not only rousing themselves to throw in provisions to feed the starving Indians, but are also taking steps to increase their force of Mounted Police throughout the North-West in case of any outbreak, which I hardly think there is any real fear of, although it is hard to say what starving people may do."

Cattle thieving became prevalent. The starving red men were often forced to seize upon the ranchers' stock. In June 1879 a show of force was made against Fort Qu'Appelle. A large stock of flour and provisions had been left over from the previous treaty payments, and these the Indians regarded as their own. The officer in charge unfortunately displayed a lack of discretion in dealing with natives, and the Indians, desperate with starvation, and driven to extreme measures, broke into the Government stores.[42] Several months later an ominous event occurred. In November the first Mounted Police constable was murdered by unknown Indians, and many believed that it was merely the forerunner of worse to come.

The Canadian Government were scarcely prepared to meet the

problems brought about by the Indian famine.   Although they had been aware, for several years, of the impending extinction of the buffalo, few believed that the crisis was so near at hand. When the treaties were made it was thought that the buffalo might last for many years, and that the Indians would continue, partially at least, to live by the chase.   The survey of the reserves was not yet complete and few of the Indians had settled down.   A suitable policy of social, moral, and economic advancement had not yet been developed, nor were there sufficient provisions on hand to relieve distress in the event of " any pestilence " or " general famine " overtaking the Indians as provided for in Treaty 6.   The Government were, accordingly, faced with the double necessity of feeding the Indians, while encouraging them to settle upon their reserves and training them, by agriculture or otherwise, to sustain themselves.   Their policy was primarily one of expediency.

In view of the alarming reports which reached Ottawa of the distressing condition of the aboriginal population in the North-West Territories, the Canadian Government took prompt action. An Indian Commissioner was hastily despatched to the territories of Treaty 7, where the need was greatest and the tomahawks the sharpest.   Food supplies were rushed to Fort Walsh and Fort Macleod, and other provision made to meet the requirements of the emergency.   In addition to the treaty supplies, the Government forwarded 500 head of beef cattle, 91,000 pounds of bacon, 100,000 pounds of beef, 20,000 pounds of pemmican and 806 sacks of flour to relieve the immediate distress.   The Indians were, however, carefully informed that the Government regarded these circumstances as " entirely exceptional," that the relief was only " for the time being," and that " after they might become either through the reappearance of the natural food supply or by their individual efforts in farming or otherwise able to procure their own subsistence."[43]

During the summer of 1879 a conference was held at Battleford, consisting of the Lieutenant-Governor, the Commissioner of the Mounted Police, the Indian Commissioner and other Government officials.   The object of this meeting was to advise the Federal Government as to the relief necessary, and the steps to be taken to prevent starvation during the winter.   Certain recommendations were made and forwarded to Ottawa, but owing to the absence of Pascal Breland, a prominent half-breed member of the North-West Council, the conference met again at a later date. Breland, with a more thorough appreciation of the situation, urged the necessity of more liberal provisions. His recommendations were accepted by the conference, and further requisitions were sent to the Federal Government for additional supplies.[44]

The supplies sent into the North-West as a result of this meeting soon proved, as Breland had predicted, insufficient for the needs of the destitute Indians. Provisions were accordingly bought from the merchants of the Territories, and contracts let for additional supplies for the following year. The total sum expended upon Indian provisions for the year ending June 1880, amounted to $157,572.22. Of this, $66,448.04 was devoted to the relief of destitute Indians, the remainder being dispensed on the occasion of treaty payments.[45] In spite of this assistance, only the fact that so many Canadian Indians had pursued the rumours of buffalo herds across the frontier, into the United States, prevented dire distress and wholesale starvation.

To meet the now pressing needs of native affairs, the system of Indian administration in the North-West was reorganized. Several changes had already been made since the acquisition of the territories in 1870. For the first few years an attempt was made to conduct Indian affairs by correspondence with the Secretary of State for the Provinces at Ottawa, but the attempt was unsuccessful. Devolution was then essayed. In August 1873, a Board of Indian Commissioners for Manitoba and the North-West was appointed. Their duties were to arrange for and negotiate the treaties, and to suggest the general principles upon which the Indians were to be administered. This board, however, was never given an adequate trial. Too many departments still retained a hand in the conduct of Indian affairs. The Bureau of Indian Affairs, the Land Bureau, and the Indian Commissioners each acted independently of the others, with little or no effort at co-operation. The result was a diversity of action which led to unfortunate embarrassments and unnecessary delays which a more regular administration might have prevented. Accordingly, in 1876, the Minister of the Interior recommended the abolition of the Board and the substitution of Superintendencies and resident local agents similar to that machinery which had been found to work so well in Eastern Canada. This recommendation was adopted the following year with the appointment of J. A. N. Provencher and the Honourable David Laird as Indian Superintendents of Manitoba and the North-West Territories respectively. The superintendencies, however, remained comparatively unorganized, a fact which illustrated the lack of interest taken in the Indian problem. In 1878 David Laird, finding that his duties conflicted with those devolving upon him as Lieutenant-Governor, resigned, and in the same year Provencher was dismissed. The Indian administration was hence in a state of disorganization when the crisis of the Indian famine of 1879 was precipitated. Realizing the impossibility of dealing with the situation from the office of the Indian Department at Ottawa, the Government appointed the Honourable Edgar Dewdney as Indian Commissioner, and despatched him at once to the North-West Territories. He was invested with broad discretionary powers, and was instructed to direct the operation of the various agencies " in such a manner as to ensure the carrying out of all treaty stipulations and covenants in good faith and to the letter."[46]   In the following year the Department of Indian Affairs, hitherto a sub-department of the Ministry of the Interior, was established as a separate entity—a development which clearly indicated the increasing importance of native affairs.

The next step was to get the Indians on the reserves. The Government recognized that for the time being the Indians would have to be fed at the expense of the country, but hoped that, once they were on their reserves, they would take to agriculture and eventually be able to support themselves. Few of the Indians had, up to 1879, expressed any wish to go upon their reserves. Only those bands, particularly in Manitoba, upon whom the influence of the missionaries had been the most impressive, had made any effort to settle upon agricultural lands. The others clung to the old gods and to the old ways of life. The insistence of the Indians at the treaty negotiations on their right to pursue the old life as long as they desired, was illustrative of the general native response to the offers of civilization ; but, as long as the Indians were scattered over the plains, or huddled together outside the walls of the trading posts, nothing could be accomplished in the way of social and economic advancement.

The famine crisis of 1879–80, however, brought the necessity for some radical modification in their mode of life forcibly to the Indian mind, and the Government, taking advantage of the situation, made every effort to induce them to go upon their reserves. Commissioner Dewdney travelled over the North-West, meeting the Indians at various points, explaining the policy of the Government, and urging them to select their lands and settle down. Offers were made of assistance and instruction in cultivation. Alluring prospects of food and plenty were held out to the doubting natives. The Indians were not wholly convinced, but the promise of rations was a powerful lever in prizing them loose from adherence to the nomadic culture of their fathers, and, during the summer of 1879, many expressed their willingness to settle down and learn to farm. Two recalcitrant Cree chiefs, Little Pine and Lucky Man, were prevailed upon to sign their adherence to Treaty 6. Others, with their followers, reluctantly started off for their reserves. At Blackfoot Crossing Dewdney was presented with an address of welcome and a promise to cultivate the soil.[47]

" Honourable Sir :—We, the chiefs of the Blackfoot nation welcome you to our country and in our midst. Our great need and the dire calamity that has befallen our nation lately, is our best claim to your sympathy and care. In our name please to express our gratitude to the Dominion Government, for the prompt assistance rendered to our wants, and of their wisdom in sending you to our remote country for the special care and control of our affairs.

" The beneficial measures you have proposed to us in the name of the Government, we all accept, and guided by your advice and care we hope to fulfil them to the satisfaction of the Government.

" Our ancestors were tillers of the soil, but our warlike and nomadic habits have unfitted us for their ancient calling and industry ; however, we hope with patience and time that our children may get the benefit of honest labour, and enjoy the more secure means of existence than the precarious mode of living of a hunter of the wild.

" In the meantime we, the chiefs, assure you of our hearty co-operation for the execution of all your orders and advice, to promote the wise measures of the Government amongst our respective clansmen :—

    " CROWFOOT, Head Chief of the South Blackfeet
    " OLD SUN, Head Chief of the North Blackfeet
    " HEAVY SHIELD, Head Chief of the Middle Blackfeet

" Eagle Tail, Head Chief of Piegans
" Running Rabbit
" Calf Robe
" Big Plume
" Bear's Child   } Minor Chiefs
" Calling Eagle
"Only Chief
" Council House,
  " Blackfoot Crossing,
    " Bow River.
      " 19 July 1879."

Few of the North-West Indians accepted the new mode of life as willingly as the Blackfeet. Many of the plains Indians remained, beggarly and destitute, about Fort Walsh in the Cypress Hills. Several thousand more were living from hand to mouth in the United States. During the winter of 1879–80, 500 to 600 Indians were rationed at Fort Walsh by the Mounted Police. Provisions were scarce, and Superintendent Crozier made every effort to help the Indians to reach the buffalo country and to assist them with fishing nets and tackle. In the spring the Indians began to come in from the plains and from the United States, where they had wintered, to receive their treaty money. In every instance they were starving. Men and teams were constantly on the road with provisions to meet and feed the starving camps as they arrived. Five thousand Indians gathered about Fort Walsh. The Mounted Police endeavoured to convince them of the advisability of moving on to their own country and settling upon their reserves, but without success. Those who came in from the south were unfit for further travel, while those who had remained all winter about Fort Walsh invariably returned after a few days absence full of excuses and demands for food.[48] About June, several camps were despatched north, but only by the Mounted Police sending trains of provisions to be doled out to the hungry natives daily by their Police escort. Autumn, however, saw hundreds of the Indians who had started north to their reserves, voluntarily or involuntarily, back in the Cypress Hills. The rumour of buffalo at Fort Belknap on the Milk River had spread over the country by moccasin telegraph and many of the wilder Indians returned south once more.[49]

Thousands of Canadian Indians remained south of the frontier

CROWFOOT

during the year 1881. In his Report to the Superintendent-General of Indian Affairs in January 1882, Dewdney stated that over half of the Indians of the North-West Territories were not as yet settled upon their reserves. Of Treaties 4, 6 and 7, 11,577 Indians were on the plains. About 5,000 were in the neighbourhood of Fort Walsh, and 4,000 were in American territory.[50]

The outlook for 1882 was one of grave uncertainty. The Canadian Indians in the United States encountered the hostility of the American authorities and the American red men, and, driven back by force of arms they were forgathering with other malcontents in the Cypress Hills. These, the wildest, most fearless and independent Indians of the North-West, with no desire to abandon the old ways of life, clinging desperately to the adventurous nomadic existence of former days, yet reduced by force of economic circumstances to poverty, want and starvation, were a formidable host for the meagre forces of the Mounted Police to ration and control. "They are," wrote the Indian Commissioner, "the most worthless and troublesome Indians we have, and are made up of Big Bear's old followers and Indians belonging to different bands in the north; when they arrive they will be joined by all the other Indians in the southern part of Fort Walsh District, and will rendezvous at some central point, I think Qu'Appelle; they will number over 7,000."[51]

Early in January the Indians began to straggle into Fort Walsh in a state of utter starvation. Superintendent McIllree was compelled to issue supplies, and, in the course of a few weeks, all the Indians that could reach Fort Walsh had collected to receive rations. "It is hard to realize," he wrote, "the destitution that prevails in an Indian camp during the winter now that the buffalo are gone. I began by issuing a ration of about three-quarters of a pound to each individual. I soon found that I had to increase this ration, as, on complaint from the chiefs, I went round the camps, and found that rations intended to last four days were finished in less than half that time."[52] Early in April the northern Crees arrived from the Missouri. Little Pine came in with 300 followers, and a few days later Long Lodge, with the Assiniboines. Others followed, and soon the bands of Jack, Little Child, Sparrow Hawk, Piapot, Bear's Head, Poor Man, Big Bear and others were camped in the Cypress Hills.

The dangers of such a large gathering of wild and destitute

Indians in close proximity to the border were manifold. The Indians had discovered the peculiar propensities of the " medicine line," as they called the international boundary, namely, that the white soldiers could not pursue them across it, and horse stealing raids became the brightest feature of Indian life. Incursions by one tribe, however, provoked reprisals by another with unhappy results to each. These hunting and stealing expeditions into the United States were much resented by the American authorities, and the mails were filled with protests against " alleged depredations by Canadian Indians in American territory."[53] Although the privilege of crossing the border had been exercised by the Indian tribes of both countries as far back as their separate history extended, and the traversing of an imaginary boundary line by nomadic bands in search of subsistence was not an offence against international law, nevertheless, the presence of Canadian Indians on American soil and in large encampments on the frontier constituted a potential source of international discord. The impossibility of preventing incursions over so extended a frontier was obvious. Even the United States with their thousands of troops had been unable to prevent Sitting Bull and his followers from crossing the boundary line to seek refuge in Canada. The small numbers of the Mounted Police could hope to accomplish but little in this regard, and the American authorities, in spite of wordy protests, were slow to co-operate.[54] The removal of the Indians from the neighbourhood of the border was the only practical solution. As long as the buffalo existed in the United States, and the Mounted Police remained at Fort Walsh, the Indians would continue to make the Cypress Hills the base of their incursions into the United States, returning to Canadian territory for treaty payments and provisions.

Apart from considerations of international policy, the presence of the Indians at Fort Walsh was objectionable for social and economic reasons. Proximity to the boundary afforded the Indians too many opportunities of living in the old way ; of rushing away from their reserves on rumours of buffalo herds, or of indulging in horse-stealing raids and other Indian irregularities. Six years in the Cypress Hills had convinced the Mounted Police that the district was unsuited for cultivation. If the Indians were to be profitably employed and instructed in agriculture, reserves would have to be found elsewhere. Colonel

Macleod had suggested the possibility of abandoning Fort Walsh as early as 1879.[55] Superintendent Crozier, Inspector Denny, and Colonel Irvine also urged the abandonment of Fort Walsh as the best solution of the Indian problem in the Cypress district. Finally, in 1882, the Government determined to move all the Indians in that neighbourhood north of the projected line of the Canadian Pacific Railway, and to carry out the recommendations of the Police with regard to Fort Walsh.

As the Indians congregated about Fort Walsh during the spring months of 1882, the Mounted Police officers urged upon them the necessity of leaving for their own country. " I had orders," wrote Superintendent McIllree to Indian Commissioner Dewdney, " that the express wish of the Government was to get all Indians on reservations north of the C.P.R. I used my utmost endeavour to carry out this order, and day after day, from the time I took over the agency until I left Walsh, I talked to the Indians and endeavoured to persuade them to leave. There was but a small percentage promised me to go, but I talked to them so much on the subject, that, from utterly refusing to think of the proposition in the beginning, from hearing so much about it they got familiarized with the subject, and in the end promised me that after seeing Colonel Irvine on his return from Canada, they would give me their final answer."[56] On April 8th Irvine arrived.   Day after day councils were held by the Indians and the police officers.   Finally, the Indians submitted. The Assiniboines first, and then the Cree chief Piapot, agreed to move.[57] These, of all the Indians at Fort Walsh, were the only ones who could claim the Cypress Hills as their own country.   The remainder were largely Crees from the Saskatchewan valley.   On May 7th the first band of Indians left Fort Walsh.   " They were very loth to go," wrote McIllree, " but did start according to promise, consisting of the following chiefs and their bands, Long Lodge, Jack, Little Child, Sparrow Hawk, and some independent bodies of Indians going to join their respective chiefs in the vicinity of Qu'Appelle."[58]   Other bands followed in June and July, until the greater part of the Indians had been removed from the Cypress Hills.

The policy of placing the Indians upon their reserves during 1882 was only partially successful.   Prompted by rumours of buffalo and encouraged by the retention of Fort Walsh by the

Mounted Police, the greater number of those who had been
dispatched north eventually returned to the Cypress Hills.   The
Assiniboines, who had taken a reserve at Indian Head, became
restless and impatient towards the time of treaty payments.
They complained that they could not live on bacon, and demanded beef.   Beef was provided, but after the annuities had
been paid, the Indians quietly gave up their tools and announced
that they intended to return south.   The request for a reserve in
the Cypress Hills was refused.   Long Lodge then left without a
word   to   the   Department.   The   Man-Who-Took-the-Coat
declared that, while they were content with the treatment accorded
them by the Government, they did not like the north ; they
wished to be where their dead were buried and their friends were
living.   To add to the Government's difficulties, Piapot, the
leading Cree chief of the Qu'Appelle district, put forward impossible demands and made their refusal the excuse to return to
the Cypress Hills.[59]   The result was a repetition of the history of
former years.   The Canadian Indians, expecting an old-time
buffalo hunt, found at Fort Walsh only starvation and destitution.
   The winter of 1882–3 was no less critical than that of former
years.   By October 290 lodges were gathered about Fort Walsh
in a starving condition.[60]   In spite of a previous determination to
pay treaty money only upon reserves, the Government were
forced, by the deplorable condition of the natives, to waive the
point and make the payments at Fort Walsh.   As the winter
drew nigh, the wretched Indians increased in number.   In
December, Dewdney reported about 5,000 under Big Bear,
Little Pine, Lucky Man, Piapot, Long Lodge, Foremost Man and
other chiefs.[61]   The expense of maintaining these Indians was
considerable.   During the month of December 44,825 lbs. of
beef, 353,000 lbs. of flour, 170 lbs. of tea, 70 lbs. of sugar and
124 lbs. of tobacco[62] were consumed on "starvation allowance."[63]
The Mounted Police Inspector in charge at Fort Walsh reported
a condition of abject misery :[64]

   " There is a great deal of misery in all the camps owing to the
old women and children being housed in wretched cotton lodges,
which are no protection whatever in cold weather, their clothing
is poor and the only means they have of living is the small issue
of food they are at present receiving from the Government.   I
might add for your information, that at present I am issuing

about 90 sacks of flour per week to these Indians; were a regular issue of flour made, this quantity would last but two days; with regard to the meat, I am giving them about a similar allowance, so that they are receiving two days food to last them for seven days."

The effect upon the Indians of their sojourn at Fort Walsh during the winter of 1882-83 was conclusive. The severe cold, the mass starvation, and the persistent urging of the Mounted Police convinced the disheartened Indians that their only hope of survival lay in settling upon their reserves. In December 1882, Inspector Norman reported that Piapot was ready to talk about returning to his reserve, and in the same month Big Bear, after months of objections and excuses, signed his adhesion to Treaty 6.[65] In April 1883, the Assistant Indian Commissioner, Hayter Reed, added his arguments to those of the patient police. Long conferences were held. Weeks of delay followed. The Indians advanced all manner of excuses for not quitting the locality. Interested traders whispered discreditable falsehoods into the ears of the natives to defeat the efforts of the Indian Department. The Indians requested arms and ammunition for one last telling raid into the United States for as many horses and scalps as possible. The negotiations hung fire until Dewdney's arrival. Finally, after months of bickering, talking and urging, the Indians abandoned their opposition to the Government's wishes, and the greater portion, under Big Bear, Lucky Man, and Piapot, left for their respective neighbourhoods in the Saskatchewan and Qu'Appelle valleys. Some, of course, soon returned. Lucky Man, full of complaints that the promises made to him were not carried out, retraced his steps as far as Maple Creek. But the Indian Department were determined to tolerate no further delays. Assistant Commissioner Reed was authorized to call upon the Mounted Police to use force if necessary. This prompt action had a salutary effect. Not only the reluctant Lucky Man, but the dilatory Little Pine, and all the Saskatchewan Indians south of the Canadian Pacific Railway, were obliged to proceed north under Mounted Police escort. Fort Walsh was abandoned, and by the end of the summer, " not a single teepee belonging to the northern districts is to be found south of the railway track." " Thus," wrote Dewdney to Ottawa, "may be considered solved one of the greatest problems which has had to be encountered for some years past, and the Indian Department has to congratulate itself on so easy a solution of the difficulty of preventing incursions from our side into the neighbouring territory."[66]

The passing of the old days of the North-West cannot be related without a word of sympathy for the Indians. To them the old life meant independence and liberty ; the new, restriction and bondage. It is a matter of no wonder that a strong stand was made against the Government's efforts to make them leave their old haunts, places associated with the memories of freedom and plenty. To leave behind the tawny hills and treeless prairie, was to break for ever with the scenes of their happiest thoughts, and to destroy the last hope, to which they had so fondly clung, of once more being able to live by the chase.

The placing of the Indians upon their reserves was only the first step in the policy of civilization. The interests of the Indians and the State alike, required that every effort should be made to assist the red man to lift himself out of his condition of tutelage and dependence, to prepare him for a higher civilization, and to encourage him to assume the privileges and responsibilities of full citizenship. With this aim in view, a policy of instruction in agriculture and stock raising was inaugurated.

In Manitoba the Indians quickly settled down upon their reserves after the treaties were concluded, and with the assistance of the missionaries and the help of the Government, undertook to cultivate the soil. Writing in 1877, the Indian Agent at Lake Manitoba stated that his Indians were " quiet and inoffensive and well satisfied with their position and treatment. They all appear very desirous of imitating the Whites in their mode of life, habit, education and religion. It would be too much to expect the older generation to adapt themselves speedily.to a new mode of life, but they are eager, and their children much more so, that they should be taught the rudiments of civilization by competent persons."[67] In the North-West Territories the Indians, for the most part, continued to follow their nomadic life until forced upon their reserves by economic pressure. A few, however, settled upon their reserves soon after the conclusion of the treaties. During the spring of 1877, seed barley and potatoes were furnished by the Government to Indians at Fort Ellice, Qu'Appelle, Touchwood Hills, Pelly and Shoal River, and a man hired to help them plant and cultivate. At Fort

Carlton one band is reported as having as many as 100 acres under cultivation.[68]

The extermination of the buffalo hastened the adoption of a definite farming policy by the Government. In his Annual Report for 1878 Vankoughnet, the Deputy Superintendent-General of Indian Affairs, outlined the policy which subsequently governed federal relations with the Indians of the North-West:[69]

" . . . it becomes incumbent upon the Government to adopt early and energetic measures to prepare them for the change in their mode of living and sustaining themselves and families, which must inevitably take place, when they can no longer kill sufficient buffalo and fish wherewith to feed themselves and families.

" Instruction in farming, or herding and raising cattle (as the character of the country inhabited by the different Tribes may indicate to be best) should be furnished to the Indians, and in such manner as will effectually accomplish, within the shortest period, the object sought for, namely, to make them self-supporting.

" The Indians should be encouraged by precept, and, when necessary, by pecuniary aid to erect houses and barns. The use of the tent and wigwam should be discouraged as much as possible, and every effort should be made to induce them to abandon their old habits of life and to adopt those of the White man.

" Their Reserves should be subdivided into lots and each head of a family should receive a location ticket, covering the land to which he is entitled (which land, of course, as stipulated under the Treaties is non-transferable).

" A school should be established on each of the Reserves, on which one has not already been established, as soon as there is a sufficient number of families settled thereon to warrant it ; and competent teachers should be appointed to these schools, who should possess, besides their other attainments, a knowledge of farming, or of herding and raising cattle (as the circumstances of the country may require), and this knowledge should be utilized for the instruction of the Indians in either occupation.

" There is . . . nothing to prevent operations towards this much-to-be-desired end being initiated and vigorously prosecuted in the North-West Territories and in the Province of Manitoba, under the supervision of competent and reliable men, who, in turn, should have over them an Inspecting Officer, possessing the very best attainments, and of unimpeachable integrity, whose duty, among other matters, it would be to go from one Reserve to another and mark the progress being made by the Indians in their industries, and see that the men employed to instruct the Indians in farming or herding and raising stock attend to their duties.

" The Inspecting Officer should also be the medium for the purchase of cattle, seed, implements, etc., for the Indians, and he should regulate the points and dates at which the payment of annuities shall be made. The dates of payment might be so arranged that the Inspecting Officer could be present at each point to hear any complaints that the Indians might have to make, see that everything was conducted properly, and, if possible, settle any differences that might arise and, if this were not possible, he could report the particulars to the Superintendent-General of Indian Affairs for decision."

The expediency of encouraging the Indians to cultivate the soil or to raise cattle had been urged by Indian Superintendent Laird, who recommended the appointment of permanent agricultural instructors for each reserve or group of reserves. The Government acted promptly. In 1879 a number of farming agencies, nineteen in all, were established throughout the Territories, and M. G. Dickieson was appointed as Inspector.[70]

The agricultural policy was not, however, an unqualified success. The promise of the first few years was not borne out by subsequent development. The system of rationing begun on the occasion of the treaty payments and expanded during the buffalo famine was never wholly abandoned. Relief continued to be afforded to working Indians, and many years were to elapse before the Indian bands could be considered as self-supporting. At the outset many, by a display of energy, gave every promise that ere long they might free themselves from dependence upon public assistance. The official reports were full of confident prophecies of Indian self sufficiency. But the very character of the Indians militated against a rapid advance. An Indian once declared to Sir John Macdonald, " We are the wild animals ; you cannot make an ox of a deer."[71]   The sanguine expectations and optimistic reports of Sir John A. Macdonald and Edgar Dewdney were not based upon an understanding of Indian character, or a thorough appreciation of the distance which the primitive Indian had to travel to reach the white man's scale of proficiency. The character moulded by centuries could not be transformed in a few years. Restlessness was inherent in the Indian disposition. His dislike of uncongenial labour was proverbial. The difficulty of handling the wild Indians is illustrated in the following episode. A band of non-treaty Indians camped near a reserve in the Battleford district. The reserve Indians, unable to resist the temptation, quietly joined the strangers in nightly raids upon their own plots of potatoes and turnips, thereby causing great loss to those who had been prevailed upon to cultivate. " I am forced," admitted the Agent for Treaty 6 in 1881, " to the belief that it will be long ere aid, either in kind or through the watchful eye of officials, can be discarded by the Government as with the present generation it is merely by constant urging that headway is made or even a *status quo* maintained."[72]

The farming system was itself open to criticism. It had been the policy to establish a number of " home farms," in the close vicinity of the reserves, under the care of the Farm Instructors, which were to serve as models for the Indians. The actual practice left much to be desired. The Instructors, instead of teaching the individual Indians to do the work and showing them how it was done, preferred to dispense with the unappreciative native labour and work the farms themselves. Little attention was paid to the preservation of the Indians' implements, and few of the Instructors went about the reserves at all.[73] After several years Reed reported unfavourably upon the working of the farm policy, and Sir John Macdonald admitted in Parliament that the home farms " were an experiment ; and I do not think that, on the whole, they have been successful—some have turned out well, others the reverse."[74] Accordingly, the less successful farms were sold and the Instructors were placed upon the reserves, not upon separate and distinct farms, to see that the Indians were properly instructed in their work, that they engaged in agricultural pursuits and contributed something towards providing themselves with the necessities of life.

The Indian schools were also ineffective. Each treaty had expressly stipulated that the Government would grant assistance in the erection and maintenance of schools upon the Indian reserves. The policy adopted was not one of establishing state Indian schools, but of granting monetary aid to various religious foundations. There were several of these in Manitoba prior to the treaty, and the number rapidly increased after the treaties were concluded with the Indians. These schools were, for the most part, unsatisfactory. The salaries were small and many of the teachers incompetent.[75] The attendance was irregular, and the Indian parents either indifferent or hostile. In 1878 the question of Indian education was reconsidered. The Deputy Minister of the Interior drew up a lengthy memorandum on the native problems of the North-West,[76] and submitted his recommendations to the ecclesiastical dignitaries of the Territories. At the same time N. F. Davin was sent to the United States to report upon the subject of Indian Industrial Schools and the applicability of the American system to the North-West.[77] The result was the adoption of a new policy. A thorough and systematic inspection of schools was inaugurated, and teachers were required to hold certificates of competency and character.[78] Annual bonuses were granted in addition to salaries to the most successful instructors and prizes were presented to deserving pupils. In order to teach the Indian youth a useful trade, to dissociate him from the baneful influence of the reserve and to place him in an entirely new environment, residental industrial schools were founded in 1883. One was established at Battleford under Protestant control, and the others at Qu'Appelle and High River under the Roman Catholics.

Instruction in agriculture and practical education were accompanied by the gradual destruction of the tribal organization. In 1878 circulars were sent to the Indian Superintendents and Agents asking them to report whether the bands under their supervision were sufficiently enlightened to justify the inauguration of a simple form of Indian municipal government, such as existed in Eastern Canada. Both Laird and Macdonald were convinced of the desirability of substituting some new system for the rule by the tribal chiefs.[79] Macdonald outlined his scheme in the Annual Report of the Superintendent-General in 1880 :

" . . . a council, proportionate in number to the population of the band, elected by the male members thereof, of twenty-one years and over, and presided over by a functionary similar to the Reeve of a Township, might answer the purpose ; or in its initiatory stage the council might be presided over, with better results, by the local Indian Superintendent or Agent."[80]

This body was to be empowered to pass laws embracing fences, ditches, roads, trespass of cattle, suppression of vice and other matters of purely local interest. The western Indians were, however, not sufficiently advanced for such a system, and the framework of tribal authority was retained. The power of the chiefs was from the first merely nominal. The treaties expressly stated that the Indians must obey the white man's laws, and be amenable before the white man's courts of justice. Local affairs were regulated by the Indian Agent and not by the tribal councils. Resistance on the part of the old conservative chiefs was resented by the Government and denounced as noxious and heathenish. Moreover, the fact that the Government had assumed the power to depose chiefs by refusing them recognition as such under the treaties, militated against any attempt to exercise the traditional influence which alone attached to their position. The chiefs and headmen became mere names, archæological expressions.

Many of the time-honoured practices and primitive customs were gradually abandoned. As early as 1882 efforts were being made to suppress the customary dances. " One cause of unsettling the Indians," wrote the Assistant Indian Commissioner, "and taking them from their reserves, and at times when their presence was urgently required, has been their annual dances, at which all who are in a position to attend come from far and near. As they are of heathenish origin and more or less tend to create a spirit of insubordination among the young men of the bands, I have this year discountenanced them as much as in my power lay, in which I was ably seconded by Lieut.-Col. Herchmer, commanding the Mounted Police at this post ; and owing to the difficulties experienced this year on the part of the Indians and my positive refusal to aid them by any gift of provisions, as has been the case heretobefore, I am under the impression that in future they will be guided in the matter by the dictates of the agent."[81] Discouraged by the Government, frowned upon by the missionaries, and shorn of the ancient glamour, the traditional customs lost their interest to the Indians. The young men no longer came forward to undergo the torture required of them as " braves," and regarded with indifference the functions of their tribe.

The reserve policy of the Canadian Government in the North-West stands out in contrast to that adopted south of the boundary. American policy, until the later 'seventies, was to gather the Indians on a few large reserves where they could be kept out of contact with the whites and where their peaceful and orderly conduct might be guaranteed by a few military posts. In pursuance of this policy, various Indian bands were removed from the lands which they occupied to the new native areas. It was hoped that, by the consolidation of a great " Indian Territory," and the removal of the natives from the dangers of collision with the white men, there would be an end to Indian disturbances. The plan of large segregated native areas was an ideal ; but it failed to take into consideration the evils and dangers arising from the penetration of the Indian territory by the irresistible tide of westward expansion. The prairie schooner, the Mormon pushcart, the flat-bottomed river boat and the railway, shattered the dream of an exclusive Indian state. The maintenance of large native areas was, in the face of white expansion, impracticable. Disturbances and wars were the result. In Canada, the creation of a large native territory in the far north where the Indians might live their own life and not impede settlement was, on several occasions, advocated in the Canadian Parliament. Sir John A. Macdonald toyed with the idea[82] but, fortunately, it was never adopted. Canada profited by the experience of the United States. With the one exception of the Cypress Hills the Indians were allowed to choose their reserves in that part of the country to which they belonged. It was not only in accordance with the tradition of British justice, but a matter of wise expediency to respect their home attachments. They were accordingly left on the lands of their fathers, provided such lands were suitable to agricultural or pastoral pursuits, and not, as in the United States, gathered together in large native areas bearing no Indian tradition.

On the whole, the reservation policy met the needs of the moment. Although it limited their ability to sustain themselves by the chase and made them dependent upon the whites—" pensioners upon the Public Treasury " one Minister of the Interior called them[83]—it probably saved the Indians from the fate of the buffalo. In the face of universal famine, the Indians could not have withstood the westward march of Canadian expansion. Wars of extermination and ceaseless strife might have followed, until the Indian, like the buffalo, had been driven from the plains by the rifles and ploughs of the incoming settlers.

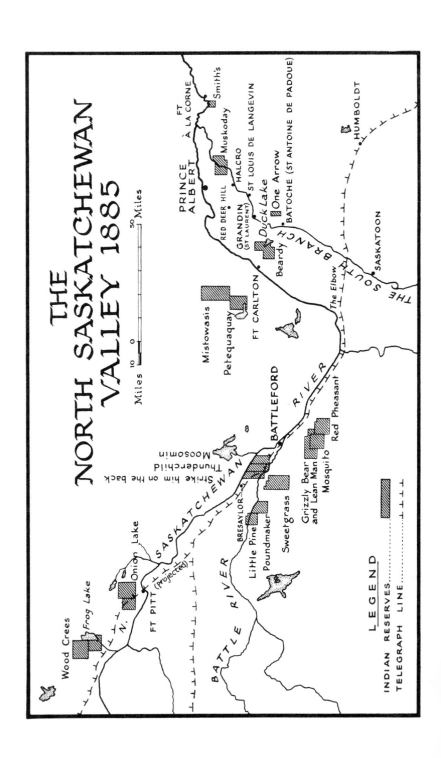

THE
NORTH SASKATCHEWAN
VALLEY 1885

Miles
10   0   50
                              Miles

PRINCE
ALBERT

FT
À LA CORNE

Smith's

Muskoday

HALCRO

RED DEER HILL

ST LOUIS DE LANGEVIN

One Arrow

GRANDIN
(ST LAURENT)

Duck Lake

BATOCHE (ST ANTOINE DE PADOUE)

Beardy

HUMBOLDT

SASKATOON

THE   SOUTH   BRANCH

The Elbow

Mistowasis

Petequaquay

FT CARLTON

RIVER

BATTLEFORD

Moosomin

Thunderchild

Strike him on the back

SASKATCHEWAN

Red Pheasant

Grizzly Bear
and Lean Man

Mosquito

Sweetgrass

N.

Onion Lake

FT PITT
(Projected)

BRESAYLOR

Little Pine

Poundmaker

BATTLE   RIVER

Wood Crees

Frog Lake

LEGEND

INDIAN RESERVES..............

TELEGRAPH LINE..............

CHAPTER XII

THE Indians were not the only people in the North-West Territories whose social and economic life was disorganized by the
advent of the white men ; the half-breeds, too, were unable to
withstand the impact of the new civilization. In 1869–70 the
half-breeds, through their political leaders and clerical advisers,
had viewed the transfer of the Hudson's Bay Company Territories
to Canada with the fear that their primitive society would be
trampled upon by the march of an intolerant and superior
civilization. The rising under Louis Riel had been an effort
upon their part to secure legislative safeguards for the preservation of their race. But, although politically successful, the half-
breeds were doomed to economic absorption. No treaty or
Act of Parliament could alter hard economic fact and in a few
years the feeble barriers erected by the Manitoba Act were
swept away by the flood of newcomers. Some accepted the new
order with the philosophy of defeat, but many, as we have
observed, spurred by the same determination which inspired the
Boers in South Africa, trekked to the Saskatchewan and Qu'
Appelle valleys, where life was still free and European civilization
had not yet penetrated. For a few years they were able to revive
the old order. But the march of westward expansion was
inexorable, and the days of the " New Nation " were numbered.
Without the protection of the Government the métis were
unable to preserve either their primitive economy or their racial
identity, and, forced back by the advancing frontier of settlement,
they made their last stand on the banks of the Saskatchewan.
The Dominion Government repeated the blunders of 1869. No
consistent effort was made to win the confidence of the half-breeds
nor serious consideration given to their alleged grievances, and
in 1885 the métis rose again under their old leaders to fight once
more the battle for economic and racial survival.

The events of 1869–70 had one important result, at least, as far as the métis were concerned ; they led to the voluntary recognition by the Canadian Government of the half-breed claim to share in the aboriginal title to the soil.   Section 31 of the Manitoba Act stated :

" . . . it is expedient, towards the extinguishment of the Indian Title to the lands in the Province, to appropriate a portion of . . . ungranted lands, to the extent of one million four hundred thousand acres thereof, for the benefit of the families of the half-breed residents."[1]

The reason for this grant is obscure.   Neither the métis " List of Rights " nor the delegates of Riel's Provisional Government made any such demand.   Archbishop Taché suggested in 1889 that the grant was made to compensate for the refusal to give the newly-formed Province of Manitoba control over its public lands.[2]   Whether or not this was the case, the grant of 1,400,000 acres of land was obviously intended to conciliate the métis who had risen in arms and to remedy one of their principal grievances— the uncertainty of the position of their lands—but was not intended as a formal acknowledgment of a legal right on the part of the métis to share in the extinction of the aboriginal title.[3]   This, however, was the way in which the métis interpreted the concession, and it became the basis of their claim for preferential treatment in the North-West Territories.

The history of the half-breed grant in Manitoba was one of ministerial incompetence, parliamentary indifference and administrative delay.   Instead of being a measure of conciliation, the grant proved to be a source of constant irritation to the half-breeds.   Although a census was taken in 1870 and a plan of allotment adopted in 1871, slow progress was made in the distribution of the lands.   The first delay occurred when the law officers decided that the half-breed heads of families were not entitled to the land reserve.   This reduced the number of participants, and the Government agreed to grant 190 acres to each child resident in Manitoba at the time of the transfer, i.e., July 15th, 1870.   Upon this basis the allotment was begun in the summer of 1873.   The second delay resulted from the change of government in the autumn of the same year.   By an Act in 1874 the claims of the half-breed heads of families were recognized ; these claims to be extinguished by the concession of 160 acres of land or an issue of money scrip to the value of $160 to every father and mother.[4] The land grant to the children was also altered. Archibald's census was disregarded. Many of the métis had been absent on the plains during the enumeration and their claims were not registered. Accordingly the Mackenzie Government ordered a new enumeration and appointed two commissioners, Ryan and Machar, to undertake the regulation of the half-breed grant. The Report of the commissioners was submitted to the Governor-General in Council in the spring of 1876. It showed about 5,088 persons entitled to share in the land reserve, but admitted that this enumeration was incomplete. The Dominion Land Agent was authorized to continue the enumeration, and on August 10th he reported 226 additional claimants. To allow a sufficient margin the Minister of the Interior concluded that, perhaps, 500 more claimants might appear, and fixed the grant at 240 acres. The preliminary allotment which had been made in several of the parishes on the basis of 190 acres was cancelled and the final allotment was made on the basis of 240 acres. By 1879 the whole of the 1,400,000 acres set apart by the Manitoba Act had become the property of the half-breeds whose claims had been approved and nothing was left for those, equally entitled to a share in the land grant, who filed their claims after that date. This question was not settled until 1885 when an Order in Council finally fixed May 1st, 1886, as the last date on which claims would be received.[5]

The delay in the settlement of this question occasioned much dissatisfaction among the half-breeds. White immigration had rushed into Manitoba after the Red River Rebellion, and the métis soon found that a new order had descended upon them, sweeping aside their old methods of life and leaving them helpless. Their usual occupations, hunting, freighting or farming in a small way were no longer profitable, or even possible. Trading was out of the question to those who had neither the goods to sell nor the credit to obtain them. Despairing of ever receiving their land patents, many disposed of their rights for a mere song.[6] Some gladly sold their scrip for trifling sums to smooth-tongued speculators, packed up their few possessions and trekked across the plains to the Saskatchewan to live again the old life of freedom. Others, who had been absent hunting during both enumerations, remained upon the plains, receiving neither the scrip nor the land to which they were entitled.

Although the claim to share in the extinction of the Indian title was recognized in 1870 in Manitoba, no such claim upon the part of the half-breeds beyond the boundaries of that province was recognized until 1885. The half-breeds of the North-West Territory were ignored. As early as 1873, however, the North-West métis petitioned for a recognition of their land claims. In that year John Fisher and ten others of Fort Qu'Appelle petitioned through Lieutenant-Governor Morris for " lands in compensation of our rights to the lands of the country as métis."[7] Other petitions followed from different quarters. In 1874 John Mackay informed the North-West Council of the anxiety of the English and Scotch half-breeds of Prince Albert and the métis of St. Laurent to have the land question settled ;[8] and in the same year Father Décorby wrote to the Minister of the Interior on behalf of the métis of Lac Qu'Appelle.[9]

The question, however, did not become urgent until the late 'seventies. There were few surveys and little settlement in the Territories. But, as white immigration increased, a new order of things pressed itself upon the attention of the native races. With the influx of settlers from Eastern Canada, the métis became more insistent upon their aboriginal rights. At the same time the numbers of the mixed bloods were increased by the arrival of the discontents from Manitoba, and a formal agitation began to take shape. 1878 saw petitions from all parts of the Territories. On the last of February, Gabriel Dumont, the leader of the St. Laurent métis, sent a petition to Lieutenant-Governor Laird, asking :

" that there be granted to each half-breed head of a family, and to their children, who have not participated in the distribution of scrip and lands in the Province of Manitoba, a like amount of scrip and like land grants as in Manitoba."[10]

Dumont's petition was circulated among the other métis settlements, and petitions from St. Albert, the largest of the métis colonies,[11] and from the Cypress Hills,[12] reinforced the demand for recognition of the half-breed Indian title.

The French half-breeds were not alone in making these demands. Their English and Scotch kindred of Prince Albert also forwarded to the Governor-General a petition which contained, among others, this paragraph :

" Lastly, your petitioners would humbly represent that

whereas a census of the half-breeds and old settlers was taken in the Province of Manitoba shortly after the organization of that Province, with a view to the distribution of scrip, etc., said scrip having since (been) issued to the parties interested, and whereas, at the time this census was taken many half-breeds, both minors and heads of families, resided in the Territories and were not included in the said census.

" Your petitioners would humbly represent that their rights to a participation in the issue of the half-breed or old settlers' scrip are as valid and binding as those of the half-breeds and old settlers of Manitoba, and are expected by them to be regarded by the Canadian Government as scrupulously as in that Province. And with a view to the adjustment of the same, your petitioners would humbly request that a census of said half-breeds and old settlers be taken, at as early a date as may conveniently be determined upon, with a view to apportioning to those of them who have not already been included in the census of Manitoba their just allotments of land and scrip."[13]

The urgency of the question was fully appreciated by the Lieutenant-Governor who wrote, when forwarding the Cypress petition :

" I feel it my duty to ask you to urge upon the Dominion Government the necessity of taking early action with respect to the claims set forth by the half-breeds of the Territories . . . I may remark from what information is within my reach I have no doubt the half-breeds of the Territories, who think they have as good a claim to consideration as their compatriots in Manitoba, will be very much dissatisfied unless they are treated in a somewhat similar manner."[14]

These petitions, however, received nothing more than formal acknowledgments from Ottawa and promises of future consideration.

With the accession to power of Sir John A. Macdonald, the half-breed question was taken up with more vigour. Macdonald himself took over the portfolio of the Interior. In December the Deputy Minister presented a long memorandum to the new head of the Department. It frankly admitted the métis claim " to favourable consideration," the only question being " how is that claim to be satisfied, so as to benefit the half-breeds, and, at the same time, benefit the country ? "[15] The memorandum discountenanced the making of treaties as with the Indians and disapproved of the issue of scrip as in Manitoba, but advanced certain suggestions for inducing the métis to settle down and for assisting them in farming. This memorandum was forwarded to Archbishop Taché and other ecclesiastical and civil authorities in the North-West for their advice, and N. F. Davin was instructed to report upon the working of the American system of native industrial schools. To enable the Government to carry out whatever policy they might determine upon, the Dominion Lands Act of 1878 delegated authority to the Governor-General in Council:

" To satisfy any claims existing in connection with the extinguishment of the Indian title, preferred by half-breeds resident in the North-West Territories outside the limits of Manitoba, on the fifteenth day of July, one thousand eight hundred and seventy, by granting land to such persons, to such extent and on such terms and conditions, as may be deemed expedient."[16]

Thus, although they had not yet determined upon the precise form of their policy, the Canadian Government granted a quasi-recognition of the principle of the métis claim to an aboriginal title, and asked Parliament for a *carte blanche* in negotiating for the extinction of such a title. The admirable energy which the Government had hitherto displayed seemed to vanish at this point, and from 1879 to 1885, nothing further was done to carry the recognition into effect.

The agitation continued unabated. In the spring of 1880 the Scotch half-breeds of Manitoba Village forwarded a petition with the usual demand for scrip.[17] At the same time the French métis forwarded an identical petition from Edmonton—a fact which showed the existence of an effective collaboration among all the mixed blood population from one end of the Territories to the other, and one which, owing to the lack of educated leaders among them, can only be explained by the supposition of ecclesiastical support. The Government acknowledged both of these petitions promising " due consideration " to each.[18] But, unfortunately, they were under " consideration " until 1885 ! More petitions followed in 1881. On June 6th and 7th, the District of Lorne, having secured representation in the North-West Council, placed the half-breed case before the Council through their representative, Chief Factor Lawrence Clarke. Clarke's memorial[19] was forwarded to Ottawa by the Lieutenant-Governor, who urged that it should be brought to the notice of the Governor-General in Council " at an early day."[20] In reply the Deputy Minister prepared a file of correspondence on the North-West question, and submitted it to the Honourable David Macpherson,[21] Acting Minister of the Interior during Macdonald's absence. Unfortunately, the evidence available gives no clue as to the opinion of the Government on this matter, but, in any event, no action was taken.

Later in the year the people of Prince Albert tried again to draw the attention of the Government to the half-breed question. A large meeting was held on October 8th, 1881, and a series of resolutions was passed, the third of which read :[22]

" Whereas the Indian title in this district or Territory has not become extinct, and the old settlers and half-breed population of Manitoba were granted scrip in commutation of such title, and such allowance has not been made to those resident in this Territory—Resolved, that the Right Hon. the Minister of the Interior be requested to grant such scrip to such settlers, thus placing them on an equal footing with their *confrères* in Manitoba."

Lawrence Clarke was instructed to forward a copy of these resolutions to the Federal Government and to " obtain a reply." Clarke accordingly proceeded to Ottawa to press the half-breed demands. The Acting Deputy Minister acknowledged receipt of the resolutions, but remarked :

" Resolution No. 3. As by treaty with the Indians their title to any portion of the territory included within the District of Lorne has been extinguished, this resolution would need explanation."[23]

In reply Clarke fully outlined the half-breed claim to an aboriginal title, and cited in detail the various Acts of Parliament from 1870 to 1879 which constituted a recognition of this title. " It will be seen, therefore," he concluded, " that from the first enactment, in 1870, to the last, in 1879, the rights in the soil of the half-breed have been recognized by the Government and provision made for the extinguishment of their title."[24]

Petitions continued throughout 1882, 1883 and 1884, demanding land grants and scrip as granted in Manitoba in commutation of the half-breed Indian title. In the spring of the last-named year John Turner and other English half-breeds complained that they had forwarded five petitions to the Federal Government, but their efforts had been without result.[25] In autumn the North-West Council, in a memorial to the Governor-General, referred to the half-breed demand for scrip and stated, " this Council cannot too strongly impress upon Your Excellency's Government the urgent necessity of an immediate settlement of the question."[26]   Nothing, however, developed from these demands.   The only official reference to any Government action during this period is contained in the Annual Report of the Minister of the Interior presented on February 15th, 1882 :[27]

" The condition of the Half-Breed population of the Territories, and the claims which have been preferred on their behalf
to be dealt with somewhat similarly to those of the Half-Breeds
of the Red River, have been receiving careful consideration, with
a view to meeting them reasonably."

The " careful consideration " was fruitless.   No report was apparently made by any Minister, or any action taken until, under the pressure of imminent rebellion, the Government hastily appointed a commission and rushed scrip to the rebellious métis in March 1885.

Side by side with the dissatisfaction produced among the half-breeds by the failure to concede scrip, developed a feeling of irritation over the working of the land law, and an alarm at the insecurity of their holdings.   The experience of their kindred at Red River was fresh in the minds of the half-breeds.   The absence of patents, which would secure their titles to the lands upon which they had squatted, at once became a matter of grievance.   In the year 1874, Lieutenant-Governor Morris enclosed a statement concerning the feelings of insecurity at St. Laurent and Prince Albert.[28]   In December 1876, Inspector Walker of the Mounted Police reported an increasing number of land disputes and complaints against encroachments.[29]   Forward-ing this letter to the Department of the Interior,[30] the Lieutenant-Governor urged that the survey should be pushed forward with vigour and that means should be adopted to facilitate the granting of patents to those who had already settled upon their lands :

" There is another question which will doubtless present itself.
Should settlers who have located before the transfer be obliged
to enter their lands under the homestead provision of the Dominion Lands Act, and consequently be required to wait three
years after the survey before they receive their patents such a
requirement would seem to be harsh to those who have been
many years in the country."

This matter, it is important to note, was to prove a source of irritation among the white settlers, no less than among the métis.

This letter was referred to the Surveyor-General, who replied to the Minister of the Interior urging the prosecution of the survey as demanded, but declared that the question of patents was " a question of policy . . . for the Minister to consider " and would require special legislation by Parliament.[31]

The justice of the métis case cannot but be admitted. They were the first settlers in the North-West Territories. Some had abandoned their nomadic life even before 1872 and squatted upon small plots of land. Others settled at a later date. In these instances the métis considered it a grievance to be obliged to enter their holdings as homesteads and wait until the expiration of three years for their patents. Moreover, those who remained on the prairie until forced to settle down by the economic transformation of the country, regarded the North-West as their patrimony. They resented the terms of the Dominion Lands Act, and refused to pay for lands taken up subsequent to the survey upon odd-numbered sections, Hudson's Bay Company or school lands. The Government Land Regulations were regarded as a legitimate grievance, but the real force underlying this grievance was the feeling of insecurity.

As in the case of the agitation for scrip, the agitation in regard to patents and surveys developed rapidly after 1877. Petitions were numerous in 1878. A petition from Prince Albert in February complained of the " many disputes and disagreements . . . now arising among the settlers, concerning alleged encroachments upon each other's boundaries."[32] Another from St. Albert expressed similar complaints and demanded surveys and patents. On February 1st a public meeting was held by the métis of St. Laurent under Gabriel Dumont. Amongst the resolutions presented in the form of a petition was the following:[33]

" That it is of the most urgent necessity that the Government should cause to be surveyed, with the least possible delay, the lands occupied and cultivated by the half-breeds or old residents of the country, and that patents therefor be granted to them."

In forwarding this petition to Ottawa, Lieutenant-Governor Laird added his word of advice :[34]

" It is important that the land policy of the Government towards old settlers and others living for many years in the

Territories should be declared. It appears to me that they have a claim to some more speedy means of acquiring a title for settlement purposes than the homestead provisions of the Dominion Lands Acts.

" To prevent disputes between neighbors, it is highly desirable that the survey of lands settled upon along the principal rivers should be prosecuted with all convenient speed."

The Minister of the Interior, the Honourable David Mills, replied to the petition in March. After promising to submit the petition to the Governor-General in Council, he informed Lieutenant-Governor Laird that the survey would be pushed forward as rapidly as the funds at the disposal of the Government would permit, but stated, regarding the question of patents :

" The propriety of passing an Act to secure for the half-breeds some more speedy means of acquiring a title for settlement purposes than under the provisions of the present Homestead and Dominion Lands Act, has for sometime past engaged my attention."[35]

Although the Minister's attention was cut short by the fall of the Mackenzie administration, his successor in office, Sir John A. Macdonald, took no immediate steps to remedy this grievance.

Illustrative of the dilatoriness which characterized the actions of the Canadian Government in the North-West, was the delay which attended the opening of the land office at Prince Albert. Not only were the métis prevented from obtaining their patents by the operations of the. Dominion land regulations, but they were unable, until late in 1881, even to register their claims ! This delay was not only without justification, but was detrimental to the interests of the settlement, and contributed to the feelings of anxiety and discontent already prevalent among the métis and the English half-breed population.

In June Father André presented a petition to the Lieutenant-Governor and the North-West Council, containing a vivid statement of the unsettled condition of the land question in the North-West Territories. He himself had been the victim of an unscrupulous claim jumper—a practice which was, in the absence of land office or patents, becoming only too common—and wrote :

" In presenting this petition to your honorable body, allow me to observe that I came to Battleford, urged not only by my own grievances, but by the entreaties of the half-breed population about Duck Lake and St. Laurent, and they join their earnest prayers to mine to call your special attention to the unsatisfactory state of the lands question in the country. Disputes and difficulties are continually arising, touching the limits and rights of property of landholders in the country, and there is no proper authority to settle these questions, however conducive to the peace and tranquillity of the country. The land has almost entirely been surveyed in the electoral district of Lorne for now over two years, and a land office has been in existence at Prince Albert for nearly four years, but as the land agent is not authorized to enter claims or to issue patents, the settlers have no way to secure the lands they hold in possession, and which they have improved through considerable expense and much exertion ; and besides, as the stipendiary magistrates seem not invested with the legal authority to try cases of boundary between neighbors on lands for which no entry is made, the anxiety of the people of the part of the country where I am living is very great, and calls for your immediate consideration."[36]

At the same time, Lawrence Clarke, the elected member of the North-West Council for the district of Lorne, sent to that body a memorial—referred to previously—stressing the dangers of insecurity, and asking for the opening of a land office at an early date. On June 14th the Lieutenant-Governor transmitted both petition and memorial to Ottawa, urging, that in view of the constant disputes and unsettled condition of the country, they should receive " early consideration."[37] Finally, as a result of these petitions, after an interval of two years from the time of the survey, the Land Office was ordered to be opened at Prince Albert in August 1881.[38]

The opening of the Land Office did not wholly solve the question of insecurity. The settlers, métis and white, who had long been settled upon their claims, were still unable to receive their patents except through the working of the homestead law. Some, who had found themselves squatted upon lands reserved by law for schools or allotted to the Hudson's Bay Company, were anxious about their holdings. Others, who had purchased lands from early settlers in good faith, shared the prevailing feeling of insecurity. The question was thoroughly discussed at the meeting at Prince Albert in October 1881. Among the resolutions which this meeting forwarded to Ottawa was one which read :

" Whereas many persons have been settled on land in this district for three years and more, and have performed the homestead duties required by law ; and many persons have bought land from such settlers, depending on the good faith of the Government for security in their holding such land—Resolved, that the Right Hon. the Minister of the Interior be requested to grant patents to such persons with as little delay as possible."[39]

Again, as in the previous year, the Lieutenant-Governor pressed for " early action."[40] He pointed out that the delays were complicating settlement and enclosed a letter from a local settler at Prince Albert to that effect.

In September 1882 the métis of St. Antoine de Padoue— better known as Batoche—a newly formed settlement near St. Laurent, petitioned for exemption from the operation of the homestead law:

" Having so long held this country as its masters and so often defended it against the Indians at the price of our blood, we consider it not asking too much to request that the Government allow us to occupy our lands in peace, and that exception be made to its regulations, by making to the half-breeds of the North-West free grants of land."[41]

The feeling engendered by a disregard of these claims was such that on October 25th the Land Agent at Prince Albert reported to the Minister of the Interior that to date no settlers had made application for a patent in view of the regulations of 1879, which counted occupation only from the date of entry.[42]

During 1882 the Government took a step towards removing this grievance. In April the Department of the Interior informed Lawrence Clarke that an amendment to the Dominion Lands Act, to provide for the issue of patents to those who had fulfilled the settlement requirements of the homestead regulations prior to entry, would be proposed in Parliament.[43] Unfortunately, this amendment was withdrawn at the last moment.[44]

The question remained in this state of uncertainty and confusion. The agitation continued. Meetings were held, resolutions passed, and memorials forwarded to Ottawa. But the machinery of the Government moved slowly. It was not until 1884 that an investigation of the situation was undertaken. Late in 1882 Macdonald signified his intention of sending Lindsay Russell, then Deputy Minister, who was familiar with French and several Indian tongues, to investigate the land claims in the North-West Territories; but in February 1883 Russell met with an accident, and after waiting several months was unable, in the end, to undertake the task.[45]   Finally, during the early months of 1884, W. Pearce, the Inspector of Dominion Lands, carried out an investigation of the white and English-speaking half-breed claims at Prince Albert.   He examined each claim individually and forwarded his recommendations to Ottawa in March.   This report was approved by the Government, and in April the Minister of the Interior ordered the settlement of the claims upon the basis of Pearce's recommendations.   Unfortunately for the peace of the country, the French-speaking parishes and their métis population were not embraced in this report.   Pearce was unable to attend personally to the matter " as the greater portion of the claimants spoke only French, and I would have required an interpreter,"[46] and delegated the task to the Dominion Land Agent at Prince Albert.   In May the Agent proceeded to St. Laurent and St. Antoine, but his report was not submitted until October.   In Ottawa it was apparently buried among the departmental files until February 1885, when, in view of the alarming reports of a possible métis rising, the Government hastily approved the report and instructed the Agent to give effect thereto.[47]   This concession came too late : the métis were on the eve of rebellion.

Another cause of insecurity among the mixed blood population was to be found in the system of survey imposed upon the métis settlements.   In the North-West the métis, as at Red River, took up their land in long narrow strips running back a mile or two from the river.   In this way they were able to preserve the community life upon which their society was based.   The attempt to impose an unfamiliar, and, to the métis, unsatisfactory system of survey, and thus deprive them of their river frontages and destroy their village community life, invited armed resistance. The fear of losing their lands had been one of the principal causes of the métis disturbances at Red River in 1869–70.   The cause of the rising on the Saskatchewan was similar.   In both instances the township survey proved to be a direct cause of that general feeling of insecurity, which, directed by Louis Riel, broke out into open rebellion.

With the lesson of 1870 fresh in their memories the Canadian Government did not, at first, insist upon the square survey along the rivers of the North-West Territories.   When the métis demanded the right to hold their lands as they had taken them,[48] the Government conceded the principle of river lots without delay.   In March 1877 the Surveyor-General wrote :

"It is proposed, in all cases where settlements have been formed along the rivers in the Territories, to adopt the surveys of the farms accordingly, that is to say, giving an average (where practicable) of 10 or 20 chains frontage on the river and letting the lots run back far enough to make 160 acres each, the lines between lots (as a rule) to be made to conform to the direction of the section lines in the regular survey adjoining."[49]

Hence, during 1877 and 1878, special surveys were made of the settled districts at Prince Albert and St. Laurent on the river frontage principle.

Beyond the settled districts the township survey was carried out as originally intended.   This fact was responsible for much of the bitterness and misunderstanding which followed.   Many of the métis had not yet settled down at the time of the survey of the parish of St. Laurent.   Thus, when they came to choose their permanent locations, they had no choice but to settle upon land which had been wholly or partially laid out upon the township principle, or which was designated for the square survey. These métis, together with their immigrant kindred from Red River, the bulk of whom settled in the Saskatchewan valley subsequent to 1878,[50] completely disregarded the existing square or sectional survey.   They took up their lands after the old fashion and settled upon the long river lots to which they had been accustomed.   As a result the Land Agent at Prince Albert informed the Surveyor-General in 1882 that :

". . . in view of the difficulty likely to be experienced in this office in adjusting the boundaries of these claims in accordance with the section survey, I have, at the request of several of the settlers so situated, the honor to request information as to the possibility of re-surveying these sections into river lots on a similar plan to that adopted in Prince Albert settlement, none of these claims having as yet been entered in this office."[51]

With the delay which marked their actions in the North-West Territories, the Department of the Interior replied six and a half months later :

"I have the honor, by the direction of the Minister of the

Interior, to acknowledge the receipt of your letter of the 11th of March last . . . and to inform you that it is not the intention of the Government to cause any re-surveys to be made."[52]

This insistence upon the square survey brought about unlimited confusion. The township survey disregarded the meandering of the river and it was impossible to know the numbers or to adjust the frontages, depths or improvements. Not a métis farm outside the special survey made in 1878 fitted into the new system. A petition[53] in January 1883 from Father André protested :

" I cannot understand, Sir, why your surveyors should have two different methods of parcelling the public domain ; one for Prince Albert, ten chains in width by two miles in depth, which we approve, and which we claim as a right, seeing you have granted it to Prince Albert ; the other, of blocking out the land in squares of forty chains, without taking the river nor location of the settlers into consideration. The latter method we protest solemnly against, all of us and humbly pray, Sir, that you order a new survey, and thus validate our request.

" Already the people of this colony have addressed to you a petition on this subject,[54] but the answer, given under your directions, is not one calculated to inspire them with the hope that you would right the wrong of which they complain.[55]

" Knowing the difficult situation in which our people are placed, I have resolved to make another effort, which I trust will bring happy results, and I dare to hope that you will accede to their just request, and no later than next summer order a new survey of the lands on the south branch of the Saskatchewan.

" By your kindly concurrence in this matter you will do an act of justice to our people and render them a service for which they will ever be thankful."

This letter was apparently passed on by Macdonald to Macpherson, the Minister of the Interior, who referred it to his Deputy, asking :

" How is it these difficulties recur so often, when it is the rule of the Department to survey around the old surveys without disturbing the occupants ? "[56]

There is no record of further correspondence relative to André's letter and the question remained unsolved.

The same insistence upon the township survey in the métis settlement of St. Albert led to considerable discontent and threats of violence.[57]   Finally, calmer counsels prevailed and a meeting was held at which Father Leduc and M. B. Maloney were delegated to go to Ottawa to lay the métis case before Sir John A. Macdonald.   Edmonton and Fort Saskatchewan also joined St. Albert in contributing to the expenses of the delegation. The demands put forward by the delegates at Ottawa included among others the questions of scrip and patents, and also river lots for St. Albert and along the Saskatchewan valley from Edmonton to Fort Saskatchewan.   The mission was successful. The demands of the delegation were, for the most part, conceded.[58] Unfortunately, however, the concessions so readily granted to St. Albert were not extended to the settlements at St. Laurent. This was probably due to the fact that in the Edmonton district half-breed settlement had preceded the survey, while at St. Laurent, with the exception of the " old settlement belt " on the left bank of the South Branch, the greater part of the half-breed population had settled upon land after the square survey had been begun.   In the latter instance the Government were unwilling to go to the trouble and expense of a re-survey.

In January 1884 another letter of protest was sent to the Department of the Interior.   Writing on behalf of the parishes of St. Antoine de Padoue and St. Louis de Langevin, Father Végreville renewed the demands for a river survey.

" Be good enough, Sir, to consider the consequences of a painful delay.   The settlers have made settlements, and are making them day by day, without knowing where the lines of their future properties are to pass.   These inflexible limits, right-lines and parallels will traverse fields, pass through houses, cut off farm houses from the fields connected with them.   This must inevitably occur where parties have already put up buildings, and wherever buildings are erected, until the survey is made.   What serious hardships, what deplorable results must flow from all this ! Three-fourths of these miseries might have been avoided had the survey been made when asked for and promised."[59]

The Chief Inspector of Surveys suggested to the Ministry of the Interior that legal subdivisions of the sectional survey would provide river lots without the necessity of a re-survey;[60] but this conveyed little meaning to the métis.   When Inspector Pearce endeavoured to explain the proposed substitute, the answer he invariably received was :

" That is plain enough to you, as a surveyor, but it is Greek to us. Those parties are *bona fide* settlers, as such have or will acquire title, and if they wish their land laid off in a certain way, why should the Government object ? In fact, it is the duty of the Government to survey it, as requested."[61]

Pearce urged that one of two courses should be adopted ; a rough traverse should be made so that entries might be made by legal subdivisions, preserving, as far as possible, to each man his improvements ; or a re-survey should be granted. These were the suggestions of a man on the spot, who was acquainted with the country and the people, had discussed the question with the settlers and knew the facts and difficulties. They were not, however, acted upon.

It was beside the point for the Government to argue that the métis had settled upon lands which had been partially or wholly surveyed into squares.[62] It was not a question of legality, but one of expediency. The métis of the South Branch of the Saskatchewan were determined to have their river lots, government regulations to the contrary notwithstanding ; and it was an ill-advised policy to refuse them, especially in view of the concession of the principle of river lots elsewhere in the North-West Territories.

The question at once arises as to the reason for the complete negative passivity with which the Government apparently regarded these appeals from the half-breeds of the North-West. Macdonald's explanation to Parliament in 1885 was unsatisfactory. He replied to Blake's charge of indifference with *tu quoque*, declared that opinion in the North-West had been divided as to the wisdom of the proposals of the Deputy Minister in 1878, and defended his inaction on the grounds that " the Government knew, my honourable friend, Sir David Macpherson, the Minister of the Interior, knew that we were not acting in the interests of the half-breeds in granting them scrip, in granting him (sic) the land."[63] This fact, while it may have been true, did not, however explain the Government's procrastination in the question of patents and surveys. But if Macdonald's defence was weak, Macpherson's was even more so. He denied that half-breed grievances existed, making the following remarkable statement in the Senate in May 1885 :

" The half-breeds had no grievance whatever in relation to

their lands or any other matter.   No half-breed was ever disturbed or threatened with disturbance in the occupation of his
lands, not in one solitary case.   No half-breed delegation came
to Ottawa to complain of ill-treatment, or disturbance in relation
to their lands.   No complaint on behalf of half-breeds was ever
made on the floor of parliament.   No grievance existed. . . ."[64]

The answer to the question is, necessarily, a matter of conjec-
ture.   It may rest in the fact that Macdonald was essentially a
party leader rather than a departmental administrator.   In
no sphere of his administration is this more clearly shown than
in his conduct of the Ministry of the Interior.   Mackenzie, the
previous head of the Government, had neglected his work as
party leader and Prime Minister in the meticulous management
of his department.   Sir John was too astute a politician to run
into this error, but, in steering clear of Scylla, he was caught in the
clutch of Charybdis.   He consistently neglected the administration of his department, the Ministry of the Interior, in the
interests of the Prime Ministership.

Macdonald committed a blunder in taking the portfolio of
Minister of the Interior in 1878.   It would appear that he underestimated the importance of the office.   Sir John was not a
young man at the time.   He had never visited the North-West,
and was too busy with the larger task of governing the country
to pay much attention to the demands of a few thousand half-
breeds in the western wilderness.   When, finally, he relinquished
this office, Macdonald made an even more serious blunder in the
selection of his successor.   Sir David Macpherson, who assumed
the office of Minister of the Interior in October 1883, was lacking
in administrative experience, well advanced in years, and quite
ignorant of the North-West and its needs.   That he was not
inclined to give himself much trouble over the affairs of a few,
poor, ignorant half-breeds whom he had never seen, is shown by
his denial that the Government had ever been informed of the
existence of any grievances among these people.   The Department of the Interior should have been occupied by a younger man,
either thoroughly familiar with the North-West Territories, or
prepared to devote his whole time and energy to the task of
becoming acquainted with it.   Had Macdonald taken into his
Cabinet the Honourable John Norquay, the half-breed premier
of Manitoba, it is quite probable that the unfortunate disturbances

arising out of the indifferent administration of North-West affairs might have been avoided. As it was, this very important department, at this critical stage in North-West history, had neither an interested or capable head, nor a consistent North-West policy. The case against the Government is conclusive. In spite of Macdonald's defence in the House of Commons and Macpherson's in the Senate, one cannot escape the impression that the Federal Government were, in the words of Blake, guilty of " grave instances of neglect, delay and mismanagement in matters affecting the peace, welfare and good government of the country."[65]

<h2 style="text-align:center">SECTION II</h2>

The métis of St. Laurent were incapable of turning their agitation to political account unassisted. A poor, ignorant people, they had neither the education nor the political experience to do so. Nor did they have suitable leaders. Every agitation must have a dynamic personality as leader, and this essential the métis lacked. Gabriel Dumont, the acknowledged head of the settlement, in spite of his fame as a buffalo hunter and his natural military ability, had neither the executive qualities nor the rhetorical power to lead a political movement. Charles Nolin, a former Minister of the Crown in Manitoba, who was by experience and education the best fitted to lead the agitation, did not have the influence over the métis which his position warranted. Only one man could carry the métis with him, and that man was Louis Riel. In 1869–70 it had been Riel's personality and Riel's organizing ability which brought the métis movement to a successful conclusion ; but in 1884 Riel was in exile, and the métis were hesitant and uncertain how to proceed.

Odd as it may appear, the first effort to organize the half-breed and métis discontent into a political agitation was made by the white settlers. Throughout Manitoba and the North-West Territories discontent was widespread, particularly among the agricultural population. In the Western United States militant agrarianism was organized under the Patrons of Husbandry or the Grange, and a similar movement spread quickly into Manitoba. In Western Canada the conditions were ripe for an agrarian

K

movement.   The influx of immigrants and capital, which accompanied the rapid construction of the Canadian Pacific Railway, led to one of the periodic land booms which have been a common feature of the opening of new territories to settlement.   During 1881 and 1882 a " fever of speculation . . . came upon the country."[66]   Homesteaders hastened to obtain their titles in order to sell, and mortgaged their lands in order to make further purchases or second entries.   During 1882 the number of entries were nearly treble those of 1881.[67]   At the same time the Government and the numerous colonization companies issued attractive pamphlets, more or less exact, concerning the country and its unparalleled agricultural advantages.   As a result thousands emigrated into Manitoba, hoping there to find the promised land of plenty.   But instead of plenty they found only hardship and want.   The country was not ready to receive them. Loneliness, isolation and disappointment, so much the more felt because they were the less expected, were the unhappy results of this too hasty emigration.   The effects of the " ruinous speculative mania " in 1883 were serious.   " In almost every locality," reported the Land Commissioner in 1885, " one meets numerous homesteads, once under a fair state of cultivation, but now deserted ; the land that was once tilled being weed-grown and less easily cultivated than the virgin prairie ; the buildings fast decaying."[68]

The great frost of September 7th, 1883, served as a pretext for a large milling company of Montreal to cause a panic in the grain market, and to purchase the Manitoba crop at nominal prices.   The price of wheat fell to fifty and forty cents a bushel and oats to fifteen cents.[69]   The high cost of railway transportation together with the fall in the price of grain, placed the farmers in a difficult position.   Moreover, this unfortunate state of affairs coincided with one of those periods of general depression, characteristic of the nineteenth century, as a result of which producers of staple commodities were then, as they are now, more affected by economic conditions than the producers of secondary manufactured products.   More particularly in Manitoba, where wheat was the principal crop, were the effects of the frost, the depression, and the collapse of the land boom of 1882, most severe.   The farmers, burdened with debts, were in many instances unable to meet their obligations.   The result was a feeling of discontent and animosity towards the Federal Government. In this we have the first manifestation of that struggle between the West and the East which has marred the growth of Canadian unity and which has even led to ill-considered threats of secession, namely, the struggle between an agricultural area forced to sell its produce in a world market and an industrial area disposing of its goods in a protected market. As in 1921 and 1930, this economic distress on the Canadian prairies led to an agitation, and political action was heralded as the instrument by which wrongs, real and imagined, might be righted.

On December 19th and 20th, 1883, a farmers' convention was held at Winnipeg. Sixty-six delegates from all parts of the province were present, and also five members of the Manitoba Rights League. In addition there were some fifty to sixty unaccredited delegates. A series of resolutions were passed and a constitution drawn up for the organization of the Manitoba and North-West Farmers' Union.[70] The members of the convention complained that they had been induced by the representations of the Dominion Government to emigrate to the North-West where they had endured only hardship and expense, and that the price of grain did not cover the cost of subsistence. They discussed the causes of " the present depression in agricultural and commercial industries," and drew up a " Declaration of Rights " as to what they believed the causes to be ; " oppressive duty upon agricultural implements," " the monopoly of the carrying trade enjoyed by the Canadian Pacific Railway," and the " vexatious methods employed in the administration of the public lands of Manitoba." They declared that they were denied " the rights of free British subjects " and demanded the right for the local government to charter railways, provincial control of public lands, the removal of the customs duties on agricultural implements and building materials, and the modification of other duties on goods of ordinary consumption, representation in the Dominion Cabinet and the construction of a railway to Hudson Bay to provide an outlet to the European market.[71] Three delegates were appointed to wait upon the Dominion Government and present their " Declaration of Rights." The petition was considered by the Government, but the answer was " not of that satisfactory nature which the importance of our mission demands," and the delegates returned to Manitoba with threats that " unless remedial measures of relief are at once provided serious results will be inevitable."[72]

In the North-West Territories similar conditions prevailed. Even as early as 1882 a local resident of Prince Albert complained that " there is no quantity of money in the settlement . . . and therefore trade is carried on under disadvantageous conditions. Farmers live entirely on credit, and consequently have to pay much higher prices for goods than would be the case if they had cash."[73]   The unfortunate crop conditions which had led to the disappointment and discontent in Manitoba had the same distressing results in the North-West Territories.   In addition to this were the number of disappointed speculators who had purchased land at inflated prices for speculative purposes in anticipation of the railway, and who, when the Canadian Pacific changed their proposed route from the Saskatchewan valley to the southern part of the Territories, were left with areas of unsaleable property.[74]   White discontent in the North-West was also increased by the unpopular land regulations of the Government, and by the lack of representation of the Territories in the Federal Parliament.[75]   Here was a fertile field for a political agitation, and, following the example of Manitoba, settlers' and farmers' organizations were formed throughout the North-West Territories.

The centre of the political agitation in the Territories was the District of Lorne in Saskatchewan.   Here was the largest population in the Territories.   The people of this district, too, had suffered more from the economic conditions than those of other districts.   Business at Prince Albert was stagnant.   The collapse of the land boom and the change in the railway line ruined the land speculators, while the failure of the crops had impoverished the farmers.   The merchants accordingly suffered with them.   Here, too, were the discontented English half-breed and French métis settlements.

Advantage was quickly taken of these circumstances by those anxious to turn the prevailing discontent against the Government. Meetings were convened throughout the autumn and winter of 1883–84 among the white and English half-breed parishes in the neighbourhood of Prince Albert.   On October 17th a mass meeting was held at Prince Albert, at which strong resolutions were passed.   In January 1884 a meeting was held by the settlers of St. Catherine's to discuss grievances.   A committee composed

MERELY A HUM-BUG-BEAR!

(*Grip*, Nov. 24th, 1883)

of James Isbister, a prominent English half-breed, W. Kennedy and T. Swain, was appointed to draw up a petition and to co-operate with committees in other parts of the country. The petition outlined the usual white and half-breed grievances, including the demand for scrip. In the same month a meeting was held at the Lindsay School House, Red Deer Hill, which endorsed the resolutions passed at the St. Catherine's meeting. On January 29th, 1884, a meeting of settlers was held at Halcro, on the South Branch, at which the resolutions of the two previous meetings were read and adopted. A committee under Andrew Spence was appointed to draft a memorial to the Government, and hopes were expressed that the agitation would increase. At this meeting an important step was taken. A Mr. Jackson was appointed to obtain the co-operation of the French métis in carrying out the resolutions which had been passed at the various meetings of the whites and English half-breeds.[76]

The platform of the new movement was formally adopted at a meeting at the Colleston School House on February 25th.[77] The resolutions adopted at this meeting subsequently formed the basis of the " Bill of Rights " which was forwarded to Ottawa in December by Louis Riel and the Settlers' Union. It was well calculated to win both white and half-breed support. Tariff reduction, representation of the Territories in the Federal Government, and a Hudson Bay Railway were the white demands. To these were added protests against the land regulations, the obnoxious timber dues, and the non-issue of scrip, grievances largely half-breed in character.

At Ottawa the growing unrest in Manitoba and the Territories was regarded with complacency. In March 1884 the North-West grievances were brought before Parliament by M. C. Cameron, but the ensuing discussion was short and excited little interest in the House. Only Cameron and Cartwright spoke for the Opposition, attacking the Government's railway and tariff policies. The essential grievances were, however, ignored. Tupper replied for the Government, and Cameron's motion that :

" This House do resolve itself into a Committee of the Whole, to consider the condition, complaints and demands of Manitoba and the North-West Territories, with a view to devise means for remedying any well-founded grievances and complying with any reasonable demands,"[78] was negatived by a vote of 116 to 57. Accordingly, no further debate took place and whites and half-breeds were left to carry on their agitation undisturbed.

The Prince Albert newspaper backed the movement with its influence. On March 21st a bombastic editorial on " Our Grievances " read as follows :

" We presume that the descendants of men who wrested from the hands of grasping monarchs the safe-guards of their rights and liberties contained in the Magna Charta, Bill of Rights, Grand Remonstrance, Habeas Corpus, Act of Settlement, must be fully alive to what their constitutional rights consist of ; and when they remember that the stroke of the axe which deprived King Charles I of his head, ended the theory of the Divine Right of Kings in our fathers' land, and the attempt to tax without a Parliament, it is not likely that we will long submit to taxation without representation."[79]

On May 10th the *Prince Albert Times* printed an article which was translated into French, and distributed among the métis of the district. The following is an extract :

" The people of Manitoba and the North-West Territories have for a long time past been struggling by every legitimate means in their power to impress upon the Eastern Provinces the fact that they have been treated with deliberate and gross injustice, and that however anxious they may be to avoid extreme measures, they will not shrink, should the worst come to the worst, from taking any steps absolutely necessary for the vindication of their rights. The more patiently they have suffered the more determined have they become, and it is with feelings of joy they now see the immediate commencement of the battle thrust upon them in the full assurance that God will defend the right. The Dominion Government, possibly compelled by the people of the East to act against its better judgement, occupies the contemptible position of a greedy, grasping, overbearing bully, who has, however, totally misjudged the fighting power of the subject it has chosen to oppress."

The article concluded with the ominous words :

" Where they get the information which induces them to believe the people likely to submit much longer, we do not know ; but we can answer them that they need not look for their friends among the Canadians, half-breeds or Indians, as they are likely soon to be made aware of in a manner at once startling and unpleasant."[80]

During the spring of 1884 the agitation was in full flame throughout the District of Lorne, the bellows being assiduously applied from Prince Albert. Meetings were held and grievances discussed, the principal agitators being whites. Early in May a large meeting was held at the Pocha School House. A working committee was formed and a list of complaints—non-representation, non-recognition of the half-breed claims, and alleged discrimination against residents of the North-West Territories in the filling of public offices—was drawn up. "They seem," wrote the *Times*, "to be fully alive to the fact that the farmers' interests are all alike and that union is strength."[81]

The most important development, however, was the co-operation between the English and the French-speaking elements. An article in the local newspaper of May 23rd said :

"We have every reason to believe that the half-breeds have only been restrained hitherto from very active measures to enforce redress of . . . grievances peculiarly their own, by a doubt as to whether they carried with them the sympathy of the rest of the population. But as they are now fully confident of this, they do not intend to tamely submit much longer. The Government must remember that to the numerical strength of this party must be added the power at any moment to stir into a flame the slumbering embers of discontent smouldering in the breasts of our Indians."[82]

For the purpose of adopting a common policy a meeting was held in the Lindsay School House on May 6th.[83] Whites, English half-breeds, and French métis were present. The resolutions passed were similar to those agitated during the winter. The most important point of discussion was, however, the advisability of consulting Louis Riel ! Objection was raised to this by some of the English half-breeds, but some, at least, of the whites present appear to have sided with the French. The Chairman, Andrew Spence, criticized the English half-breed attitude and the matter was finally referred to a committee. The result was the adoption of the following resolution :

"We, the French and English natives of the North-West, knowing that Louis Riel has made a bargain with the Government of Canada, in 1870, which said bargain is contained mostly in what is known as the ' Manitoba Act,' and this meeting not knowing the contents of said ' Manitoba Act,' we have thought it advisable that a delegation be sent to said Louis Riel, and have his assistance to bring all the matters referred to in the above resolutions in a proper shape and form before the Government of Canada, so that our just demands be granted."[84]

The invitation determined upon, a delegation of four was chosen and a collection taken to defray the expenses of the journey to Riel. It was indicative of the support that the whites were giving to the movement that one of the " Canadians from Ontario " took " the lead in opening his purse when subscriptions were called for."[85]   The delegation was composed of James Isbister, an English half-breed, Michael Dumas, Gabriel Dumont and Moïse Ouellette, French métis. Several days after this meeting they set off upon their historic ride to Montana, seven hundred miles distant, to seek out the quondam President of the Provisional Government of Red River, and to invite him to champion, once more, the alleged rights of the people of the North-West.

CHAPTER XIII

WITH increasing discontent manifest among the half-breeds it behoved the Canadian Government to use the utmost caution in dealing with the Indians of the North-West over whom the mixed bloods were known to exercise great influence. The Indians had only just entered upon the reservation phase of their transition and were still in a state of flux. Sympathetic understanding and generous assistance were more than ever necessary to help the Indians bridge the gap between the old and the new order. But instead came a cruel policy of financial retrenchment which almost wrecked the whole Indian experiment at a moment when delicate handling was required, and which aggravated the native distrust when their confidence was needed most. There can be no doubt that the policy of economy adopted in 1883 and 1884 was the major cause which led to the active participation of the Indian tribes in the Second Riel Rebellion.

Following the accession to power of Sir John A. Macdonald and the introduction of the " National Policy " in 1878, economic conditions in Canada showed a great improvement over the dark days of the 'seventies. Prices rose strongly, the index number mounting from 79.8 in 1878 to 93.1 in 1882.[1] The last quarter of 1882, however, saw a turn in the economic tide. 1883 was a period of recession. Business activity slackened. Prices, both of stocks and commodities, declined and confidence was shaken. This decline continued until 1886. During this period the general price level declined from 93.1 in 1882 to 75.3 in 1886. At the same time the value of exports fell from $101,766,110 in 1882 to $85,194,783 in 1886,[2] owing to the depressed economic conditions in Great Britain and the United States, Canada's two principal customers. These unfavourable conditions were reflected in the finances of the country. The large surpluses of the early 'eighties were followed by a sharp decline and heavy deficits in 1884, 1885 and 1886. To meet this situation a reduction in controllable expenditure was necessary and the Indian Department estimates were among those which were reduced.

To reasons of national economy were added reasons of local policy. When Vankoughnet, the Deputy Minister of Indian Affairs, returned from his tour of the North-West in 1883, he was convinced of the advisability of cutting down upon Indian expenditure. Writing to the Prime Minister, the titular head of the Indian Department, in December 1883, Vankoughnet declared :

" I sent you down the estimates to-day. You will observe that in the N.W.T. we propose making a reduction of $140,000, which I think may safely be done. There has been too much reliance placed in the past upon *agents'* reports on requisitions as to the necessary expenditure. Careful consideration after personally visiting localities has convinced me that there has been much needless expenditure which works detrimentally in more ways than the intrinsic money value involved, although that is serious enough."[3]

Accordingly Vankoughnet ordered wholesale dismissals of clerks, assistants and other employees of the Department in the North-West, and a stricter supervision over the issue of rations to the Indians.[4]

The same parsimony was carried out in the Indian Industrial School at Battleford. The rations were cut down from a pound and a half of beef to a quarter of a pound per pupil per day. The result was an outbreak of petty kitchen thieving.[5] On the reserves the rations were cut to the minimum. The Government's policy could be summed up in six words : feed one day, starve the next.

To ensure a more rigid control over the expenditure, a policy of greater centralization was enforced by the Indian Department. Vankoughnet was firmly convinced that, prior to his visit to the North-West, " the contractors and agents had, in some instances, suspicious relations with one another "[6] and was determined to put an end to any danger of peculation arising out of the free exercise of local authority. Accordingly, the discretionary powers of the Indian Agents, Farm Instructors, and even of the Indian Commissioner were greatly diminished. Provisions were to be issued only in return for work, and all vouchers were to be approved by the Indian Commissioner before payment. The result was, in some cases, greater inefficiency rather than greater effectiveness. On one occasion an Agent complained that the cost of stationery purchased for use in his office was charged to his private account, in spite of the fact that he had requisitioned it and had to make up his monthly account; while on another occasion the Government storehouse at Fort Pitt went two months without a padlock because the sub-agent had to write to Agent Rae for authority to make the purchase, and Rae had to refer the matter to Regina for approval. It was impossible for the Commissioner to supervise everything, and merchants repeatedly complained of the " vexatious delay," " the endless procrastination " and the " dangerous and unsatisfactory way in which the Government do business."[7]

For the Indians the application of this policy only increased the distress and hardship which the tribes were experiencing. The condition of the Stonies, in particular, was deplorable. Even in 1883 Rae had described them as " mere skeletons." " I thought," he wrote, " my Carlton Indians were badly off, but they are as kings in comparison with these Indians."[8] There is little wonder that the Stonies proved to be the most implacable enemies of the whites during the rebellion of 1885. At Qu' Appelle the conditions were equally bad. There was a high death rate among the miserable natives, " accelerated," wrote the medical inspector, " if not immediately caused by the scant supply of food served out."[9] From the Touchwood Hills the Interpreter reported a similar state of starvation: " I beg to inform you that the Indians around here are starving very badly . . . I fear that many of these people will not see spring."[10] It had been to escape these very conditions of hunger, disease, destitution and want, that the Indians had submitted to being placed upon reserves, but an unthinking Department with its economy, and an inconsiderate climate with its drought and frost[11] only added to the Indian misery.

The Dominion Government were fully warned as to the inadvisability of their policy. Opinion in the Territories was unanimous in its condemnation. The Indian Agents on the spot remonstrated. The Indians were far from self-supporting and constant oversight was necessary. Herchmer at Birtle, A. McDonald at Indian Head, and Anderson at Edmonton urged upon the Department the inexpediency of the proposed course.

272 THE BIRTH OF WESTERN CANADA

Rae at Fort Carlton even went as far as to write a private letter to the Prime Minister, stating :

"If Agents cannot be trusted to carry on their Districts, new ones should be appointed ; but it is nonsense to think that Mr. Vankoughnet or anyone else can run Indian affairs in this country without having previously had a thorough knowledge of Indians."[12]

C. E. Denny, the Agent for the Blackfeet, tendered his resignation:

"I beg to inform you I cannot undertake to do this work, and I therefore think it best to notify you of the same, as I have always, and shall always, do my work thoroughly, and I do not see my way clear to doing so in this instance. The work of a clerk in my office takes all his time from one week's end to the other and I cannot do this and look after my Treaty. My work has been difficult since I came here but I am glad to say that I have everything in the Treaty now in perfect order and do not wish, while I am here, to see it upset. I therefore beg that I be allowed to resign my position as Agent of this Treaty as soon as convenient to the Department."[13]

It was illustrative of the extent to which the Department were prepared to carry out their economy policy that Denny's resignation was accepted, in spite of the fact that he had been one of the Department's most successful agents.

The Indian Commissioner, Dewdney, also bitterly complained of Vankoughnet's action, stating in a letter to Sir John A. Macdonald that Vankoughnet had come to the North-West "with his mind made up to make several changes which I deemed most unwise and impracticable, if we wished our work to be done satisfactorily."[14] Dewdney also charged the Deputy Super-intendent-General with acting over his head. Writing to Macdonald he stated that he had, on more than one occasion, issued instructions to Agents which could, at their discretion and in exceptional circumstances, be broken ; only to learn that Vankoughnet had issued instructions which not only conflicted with these, but were of such a positive nature that the Agents' powers were curtailed more and more.[15] "Allow," he wrote, "a much larger share of responsibility to be exercised by the acknowledged head in the country, but demand, if need be, full explanations at all times for any deviation from the acknowledged rules and you will find that matters will run smoothly ; just in the same manner as I would not bind too tightly the hands of the Agents, or they the hands of the Instructors . . . but when mistakes are made pitch into the Officials, this has been found to work well."[16]

The officers of the Mounted Police argued likewise, advising their headquarters that the local authorities should " be given discretionary power to some extent, at least, to feed and thereby humour the unsettled Indians."[17] Superintendent Crozier, in particular, was keenly sensitive of the defects of the Government's economy policy and saw in it the seeds of rebellion :

" Considering all that is at stake, it is poor, yes, false economy to cut down the expenditure so closely in connection with the feeding of the Indians, that it would seem as if there was a wish to see upon how little a man can work and exist, and to refuse those little presents of tea and tobacco so welcome to an Indian. The Indian Department should congratulate itself upon the splendid progress the Indians have made towards living a civilized people, and having done so well they should be humoured a little. . . . Do not in any case be too economical at once, for such a policy will be far the most expensive in the end. My firm conviction is, if some such policy as I have outlined is not carried out, there is only one other and that is to fight them."[18]

The diminutive weekly press attacked the Government's policy with all the vigour of a metropolitan daily :

" Does it not seem the most sensible view . . . to suppose that the Agents who are in daily contact with the Indians should be better acquainted with their requirements and when to feed them and when to stop their rations. Their suggestions should be promptly acted upon and not laughed at, criticized or treated with contempt. . . . Give the Agents fair scope to execute the general policy of the Department, but do not hamper them at every step in the performance of their duty."[19]

In spite of the manifest unpopularity in all quarters of the North-West of the economy cuts, they were persisted in. The Indian expenditure which had reached $1,106,961 in 1882, was reduced in 1883 to $1,099,796, and in 1884 to $1,025,675.[20] The reduction in 1884 was greater than would appear from these figures ; for, while the net cut was $74,121, the gross reduction in the amount spent upon Indian provisions, annuities, education and farm instruction was $111,649, the difference being made up by an increase of $37,528 in the expenses of administration and the Commissioner's house and office. For 1885 the estimate after much " boiling down " remained " about the same as was voted for the current year."[21] That such a course should have been persisted in in the face of the warnings which the Department had received was indeed ill-advised : Sir John A. Macdonald and the Indian Department either considered the reports of their western officers as unduly alarmist, or they were convinced that such a course was necessary to force the Indians to settle down upon their reserves and devote some of their energies to practical agriculture. But, whatever the reason may have been, this insistence upon strict economy was attended with disastrous results. Economy may have been financially sound, but it was politically inexpedient. The Indians were passing through the crisis of their transition to the new order. Once this difficult period was passed, they would be able to stand upon their own feet and Government assistance might be dispensed with, but, for the time being, such a niggardly policy was short-sighted.

This becomes the more apparent when it is remembered that discontent was inherent in the situation in which the Indian found himself. The experience of the Western United States was not without a lesson for Canada. There the military had had no trouble with the Indians until the white settlers appeared upon the scene. As long as the Indians were regarded by the whites as partners in the chase and sale of furs, there were no racial conflicts. The Sioux, when dealing with Kittson, Rice, Choteau and the Missouri Fur Company, boasted that they had never shed the white man's blood. It was a different matter when immigrant trains crowded the Californian trails, and the buffalo fled before the surveyor and the settler. Similarly in Western Canada, trouble began with the coming of the white immigrants. " The settlers," wrote Colonel Irvine, urging an increase in the Mounted Police force in 1880, "unaccustomed to the Indian manner and habits, do not make due allowances and .exhibit that tact and patience necessary to deal successfully with Indians."[22]

The newcomers looked upon the aborigines with contempt. In November 1877 a surveyor on the South Branch wrote to Ottawa that " there is constant enmity between the Indians and white settlers."[23] Illustrative of the difficulties and tension arising out of the contact of the Indians with contemptuous white settlers was an incident described by the Commissioner of the Mounted Police in 1880. In September of that year a settler living near Fort Walsh struck an Indian in the face because he found him leaning against his garden fence. This so enraged the Indians of the tribe to which the assaulted man belonged, that, notwithstanding the fact that the settler had been fined, they proceeded in a body to his garden which they began to uproot; " and, but for the timely arrival of the Police . . . much more serious consequences would have followed. Had this happened, it is hard to tell where it would have ended."[24] Acts of scorn and contempt such as this were unspeakably humiliating to the haughty spirit of the Indians. Colonel Irvine was seriously apprehensive of the effect of a rapid influx of immigrants, ignorant and disdainful of the natives, and feared that such incidents as this might lead, in the long run, to outbreaks and native wars.

To add to the Indian resentment against the whites, a realization of their fundamental error as to the real meaning of the treaties began to penetrate the Indian mind. In few cases had they understood the full import of the treaties to which they had so readily affixed their totems. To them, as to many savage tribes, the western notion of private property in land was entirely foreign. Among the Indians the idea prevailed that the white men had come to " borrow " their land, not to buy it. Remarkable evidence of this fact is afforded by the following Indian statement made at an Indian council in 1884 :[25]

" The Indian was blind in regard to making the treaty. He understood not the treaty when he heard of it. He did not see what use he had for it. He was then rich, he had plenty to eat. His food and clothing were in his hand. He could do what he liked with it. The country was free to him wherever he wanted to go. That was why the Indian thought himself rich. While he was enjoying these things, a human, a Government came to him without invitation. The Government makes the Indian understand that he could make the Indian live better than he was doing. If that was all we would not have been persuaded. We looked further.

" He first called the Great Spirit to witness the treaty. He then invoked the name of the Queen. He thirdly mentioned himself the Governor. After mentioning all these names, we made a treaty, not for the sake of this Government, but on account of God and the Queen. The Governor Morris comes and tells the Indian we are not coming to buy your land. It is a big thing. It is impossible for a man to buy the whole country, we come here to borrow the country, to keep it for you. I want my children to come here and live at peace with you, to live like two brothers.

"The Indians therefore understand that the country is only borrowed not bought."

When the meaning of the treaty became clear to the Indians they denied ever having sold their land. An emphatic assertion of this denial is contained in a letter written in broken English by a Cree Indian to Louis Riel in March 1885. The letter contained the names of twenty Cree, Stoney and Saulteaux chiefs from the Qu'Appelle, Crooked Lakes, Touchwood Hills and File Hills districts, who declared that they had made " no bargin by the white skin folks for their native country. . . . Even we did not heard them our dicease parents to make bargin with them by such a thing, neither our Grand Fathers. . . . And again the same way to Hudson's Bay Company use and Fathers and Grand Fathers they did not make any kind bargin for our native country. We can make oath that we did never such a thing. Government of Canada I wonder they do not ashamed to going on this matters of this our native country."[26] This misunderstanding between the native and white conception of land tenure was one of the underlying causes of the Indian discontent which broke out in 1885 into open rebellion.

Further disillusion followed the efforts to civilize the Indians by weaning them from the chase to the cultivation of the soil. Only the threat of starvation and the attractive promises of the Government induced the nomadic Indians of the plains to abandon their old life and settle upon reserves. In their innocence the Indians were led to believe that self-sufficiency and food in plenty from the soil were only a matter of a few years ; that agriculture held more for them than the chase.[27] But their inherent restless disposition unfitted them as tillers of the soil. They were, for the time being, unable to stifle their longing for the " good old days." Only the hope of escape from starvation kept their inexpert hands at work. The results were disappointing. The Indian crops were poor, and the Government rations insufficient. The optimistic forecasts of success which marked the early reports of the Indian Agents remained unfulfilled, and the Government finally admitted that some of the means taken for the advancement of the Indians " have not been attended with as much success as one would desire."[28]   On the other hand, the Indians regarded the failure of the Government to advance them " to an equal footing with my children," as obvious evidence of the non-fulfilment of the terms of the treaties by the whites, an opinion which was confirmed by the application of economy to Indian rations in 1883 and 1884. Bishop Grandin, who had spent many years among the Indians, feared that this disappointment would lead to trouble.

" Bien que le gouvernement ait fait de grandes dépenses pour faire ces sauvages autant de colons, je doute beaucoup du succès ; je sais même pertinemment que dans la plupart des réserves, les résultats ne répondent point à ces sacrifices.   Les sauvages, ceux des prairies surtout, ne peuvent se résoudre au travail ; ils ne savent s'y résoudre que pressés par la faim, et la raison en est qu'ils ne voient pas en cela comme dans la chasse, le résultat immédiat de leurs efforts ; cela les décourage.   Ainsi, travaillant peu et mal, ils consomment en quelques mois, et souvent en quelques semaines, les patates qui sont leur principale récolte, et alors, souffrant de la faim, ils ont recours aux agents du gouverne-ment, aux missionaires, à tout le monde.   Comme ils reçoivent rarement assez pour satisfaire leur appétit, ils se plaignent, accusent les blancs et le gouvernement d'être la cause de leurs maux . . . et qui sait si le besoin ne pourrait pas les pousser à des excès regrettables."[29]

Symptomatic of the growing unfriendliness of the Indians towards the whites and the Canadian Government was the increasing boldness of their front towards the Mounted Police. The days when a Mounted Policeman might apprehend an Indian single handed were rapidly disappearing.   Defiance became more pronounced and rebuffs more numerous.   The Indian Commis-sioner viewed this with alarm.   " The mind in reference to the Police," he wrote, " is changing so rapidly that no arrest should be made unless it could be enforced by an efficient force."[30]

As early as 1882 the Mounted Police met with a serious reverse. In January of that year Inspector Dickens[31] at Blackfoot Crossing, accompanied by a sergeant and two constables, attempted to arrest Bull Elk, a minor Blackfoot chief, for firing upon a white man.   They succeeded in making the arrest, but the Indians gathered in large numbers urging resistance.   " Come, what are you afraid of, they are only four policemen," cried the insolent young braves.[32]   Squaws with axes and knives and men with

carbines appeared. The police were jostled, tripped up, and
their rifles snatched from them, while the Indians shouted and
fired their guns. Attracted by the confused din, police reinforcements, numbering nine men, arrived upon the scene, and
with great difficulty succeeded in lodging the struggling prisoner
in the neighbouring fort. The Indians, however, were determined that Bull Elk should be released. Seven hundred well-
armed, truculent braves surrounded the police quarters and cut
off the occupants from food and water. Dickens was helpless.
His party were greatly outnumbered and without adequate
defence. To have defied the Indians would have been sheer
bravado and suicide. Dickens finally sent for Crowfoot, the
head chief. Crowfoot arrived, declared Bull Elk innocent, and
stated meaningly that " some of the white men had treated the
Indians like dogs."[33]   In the end Crowfoot agreed to guarantee
the prisoner's appearance when wanted for trial, and announced
to his excited tribesmen that Bull Elk was free : " Such discharge
of firearms and such yelling was never heard."[34]   A week later
Crozier and a strong body of police secured the prisoner again and
carried him off to Fort Macleod for trial. A show of arms and
determination for the moment overawed the Indians, but the
moral effect of the previous failure had left its impression upon
the Indian mind.

An outbreak at Crooked Lakes in February 1884 was another
ominous event. It was the direct outcome of the Government's
policy of economy. Up to December 1883 the Crooked Lakes
Indians had received adequate supplies from the Government to
meet their needs. Five hundred and sixty-seven out of nine
hundred and twenty Indians upon the reserve were in receipt of
Government rations.[35]   Consequent upon the adoption of the
new policy the Department expressed the opinion that " provisions
had been for a length of time issued much too freely,"[36] and orders
were accordingly sent to the Farm Instructor to cut down upon
the issue of rations, and to feed only the aged and infirm. The
Hudson's Bay Company trader on the reserve protested against
this ill-conceived order. " For God's sake," he declared to
Farm Instructor Keith, " do not reduce their rations any lower, or
there certainly will be trouble."[37]   These fears were amply
justified. The Indians were in reduced circumstances. The
winter of 1883–84 had been severe. Rabbits were scarce, and

those Indians who had left the reserve to hunt, returned with little or nothing. They were, moreover, in an unsettled frame of mind owing to the dismissal of their previous Instructor.[38] Throughout the month of January continual grumbling was heard among the Indians and in February the matter came to a head.

On February 18th, Yellow Calf and twenty-five armed Indians came to Farm Instructor Keith and demanded an interview. They talked " in a most vicious manner," and threatened, unless supplies of flour and bacon were given them, to break open the storehouse and help themselves. The exercise of a little discretion might have obviated the difficulty, but Keith felt himself bound by his instructions. The Indians contemptuously refused his offer of ammunition and rushed upon the warehouse. In the mêlée Keith was knocked down, kicked and stabbed, barely escaping with his life.[39]

On hearing of the attack upon the Government storehouse and the assault upon the Farm Instructor, Inspector Deane and ten men were despatched to the reserve. Deane soon discovered that the Indians were in an ugly temper and wired for reinforcements which arrived quickly under Superintendent Herchmer. On the reserve the Indians gathered inside their dance house and awaited the arrival of the police. A stake was driven about six paces from the door, and when Herchmer appeared, he was warned that if he passed the stake the Indians would open fire upon his men. Herchmer tried to bluff the Indians in the approved Mounted Police fashion, but the Indians were in earnest. As the police approached, an Indian sentry presented his rifle full in Herchmer's face, and every loop-hole " literally bristled with muzzles."[40] Observing the determined attitude of the Indians, Herchmer hesitated. " Another step forward," he later declared, " would have drawn their fire and I do not believe one of us would have escaped."[41] A colloquy ensued. The Indians were still very excited and " one would undoubtedly have fired into the police force had not Yellow Calf held his gun."[42] The parleys continued, but little progress was made. The Assistant Indian Commissioner pointed out to the Indians the gravity of their offence in resisting the Queen's authority, but the Indians argued they were justified in taking what they considered was their own when they were starving.

Yellow Calf informed Herchmer that "when they stole the provisions their women and children were starving . . . and that they were well-armed and might just as well die then as be starved by the Government."[43]   Not until a week had elapsed after the raid upon the storehouse was an agreement arrived at. In the end four Indians voluntarily surrendered themselves. The charge against the chief, Yellow Calf, was diplomatically dropped, and the others, after pleading guilty, were discharged on suspended sentence.   This was a satisfactory ending to a difficult situation, which, for the moment, threatened to develop into an Indian war.   Farm Instructor Keith had no illusions as to the cause of the trouble.   "The instructions I received from Mr. Assistant Indian Commissioner Reed," he reported to Dewdney, "more especially the cutting down the rations to such a fine point, so suddenly, then only to be given to a few, I fear accounts for the raid . . . I fear if something's not done to punish the offenders they will try the game again ; they are very determined."[44]

That Vankoughnet was fully cognizant of the cause of this outbreak is shown by a letter to Macdonald on March 12th, in which he stated that the previous Instructor had been "too lavish" with his issue of supplies, and that the trouble was probably due to "the too sudden reduction in the supplies made to the Indians."[45]

The outbreak proved to be a most dangerous precedent.   The Police, numbering about forty, had been successfully defied by a similar number of Indians.   The customary bluff had failed, and the Police had lost in a large measure their most valuable asset, their prestige.   The news of the successful resistance spread like a prairie fire through every Indian camp and wigwam in the North-West, and there is no doubt that it contributed greatly to the unrest and turbulent spirit displayed by Big Bear and the North Saskatchewan Indians later in the summer.

Big Bear !   The name already had a sinister ring in the ears of white men throughout the Territories.   Big Bear was a Cree, a native of the Carlton district.   In the early 'sixties he moved from Fort Carlton to Fort Pitt, where, as a result of his natural ability, determined resolution, self-reliance and native cunning, he became the headman of a small band of twelve lodges.   He was never recognized as a chief until the occasion of Treaty 6, when he assumed the leadership of those stubborn Indians who refused

BIG BEAR

to sign away, for what seemed to them a few illusory promises, the
territorial rights of their forefathers. His objection to the
Treaty offered in 1876 was, oddly enough in view of the subsequent Indian rising of 1885, that the Commissioners would not
promise him immunity from hanging. Annual attempts to
persuade him to adhere to the Treaty were met with many excuses.
He did not think that the buffalo would disappear so quickly ; he
was afraid that the Treaty did not furnish enough for the Indians
to live on ; he wished to see if the Government would abide by
the terms of the Treaty, and other reasons. Like Crowfoot he
recognized that the red man's day of untrammelled freedom was
drawing to a close, but unlike Crowfoot, he was unwilling to
accept the consequences of the inevitable change. He sought
to postpone as long as possible the break with the past ; and then
to secure better terms for his people than the Government had
been willing to grant to other Indian tribes. From the moment
of his refusal to accept the Treaty, Big Bear and his small band
were joined by the most independent Indians of the plains. His
lodge became the rallying point for the " die hards " of every
band. While he may have lacked the diplomacy of Brant, the
bravery of Tecumseh, or the military genius of Sitting Bull or
Joseph, Big Bear was, nevertheless, one of the great Indians of
Canadian history.

Big Bear and the main body of recalcitrant Crees arrived at
Battleford during the course of the summer of 1883, a date which
coincided with the introduction of the Government's economy
cuts. The year being too far advanced for the Indians to begin
farming, Big Bear and his satellites, Little Pine and Lucky Man,
remained in the North Saskatchewan doing as little work as
possible, and subsisting upon the rations which the Government
doled out to them. Little Pine and Lucky Man accepted
their reserves upon the Battle river, but Big Bear remained
obdurate. He refused, for the time being, to select his reserve,
and spent his time in travelling from one place to another, in
complete defiance of the wishes of the Government. With such
a spirit of sullen independence and unrest prevalent among the
newcomers, it required all the tact and firmness of the Indian
Agents to maintain even the ground which they had gained with
the bands upon the reserves. The settled Indians were jealous
of the newcomers. They demanded why the recalcitrants should

be fed in idleness, while they, who had acceded to the Government's requests, should have to labour for their rations. The bold actions of these newcomers also prompted the settled Indians to make new and unwarranted demands upon the Government. The result was to neutralize much of the good that had been accomplished during the previous years. Crops were neglected, the work of the Department was reduced to confusion, and murmurs of discontent and unfulfilled promises were heard around every Indian camp-fire and council. The local press was very apprehensive of impending native troubles and urged the Government to show a strong hand towards the malcontents :

" The importance of a speedy adjustment of existing difficulties or differences cannot be over-estimated. Every unsettled question is made an excuse for interfering with the bands already settled, and trouble is always made by the new men prompting the settled ones to resist the authority of those placed over them. The unsettled bands always have a stock of grievances and a list of what they call unfulfilled pledges to complain of. If promises have been made, they must be kept ; if none are left unfulfilled, the grumblers must be taught that there are obligations on their part as well as on that of the Government, and they must in all things conform to the rules laid down for their guidance. The bands already settled in this district have learned this lesson, and it would be inflicting a grievous wrong to let it appear that unreasonable or unjust demands would be conceded to the new bands merely because they insisted upon them."[46]

Vankoughnet was of the same opinion. During his visit to the North-West in 1883 he met Big Bear at Fort Pitt and gave him to understand that the Government had done more for him than it had agreed to do. Big Bear was plainly informed that he must go upon his reserve before November 1st, otherwise all rations would be withheld ; that he would get only what assistance he was entitled to receive ; and that no amount of begging or stubborn behaviour would extort a bribe to fulfil his share of the treaty obligations.[47] Big Bear was not slow to take up the challenge. He regarded Vankoughnet's ultimatum as an insult to his position and refused peremptorily to go upon his reserve at the date set.

During the winter of 1883–84 the disaffected Indians from the south, distributed as they were among the settled bands of the north, kept up a continual agitation. Runners were despatched throughout the Territories with the object of bringing about a large gathering of Indians in the spring, to make demands upon the Government, which they knew would not be acceded to while they remained scattered upon their several reserves.[48] Previous attempts at concentration had been unsuccessful. In 1881 dissatisfaction with the treaties led to several attempts to bring about a united front, but nothing developed from them.[49] The Indians at that time lacked the leaders with the prestige necessary to secure a combined action, and the timely presence of the Governor-General in the North-West allayed, for the moment, the general discontent. With the arrival of Big Bear these efforts were renewed. Big Bear was fully aware of the fate which threatened the Indian race, but he did not, like many of his people, entertain the absurd idea that the red men could drive out the white men by force of arms. He, therefore, adopted the only plan consistent with reason, a concentration of all the Indian tribes of the North-West in one demand for better treaty terms.

Closely associated with Big Bear in his efforts to secure better terms was the Cree chief, Poundmaker. Although his band numbered only about 165 followers, Poundmaker was, perhaps, the most influential chief in the North Saskatchewan district. He had been adopted as a son by Crowfoot, and with the prestige accompanying that position, acquired a considerable reputation as a mediator and negotiator. He was physically a magnificent specimen of his race, " tall and good looking, slightly built and with an intelligent face, in which a large Roman nose was prominent ; his bearing was so eminently dignified and his speech so well adapted to the occasion as to impress every hearer with his earnestness and his views. Indeed, for the time being, I believe, he impressed himself."[50] Poundmaker had taken a part in the negotiations of Treaty 6, and signed his adhesion as a headman of Red Pheasant's band. When Red Pheasant settled upon his reserve in the Eagle Hills, Poundmaker remained upon the plains. He gathered about himself a band of truculent young braves and joined the increasing number of discontents in the Cypress Hills. Poundmaker, however, was one of the first of those who clung to the old life to recognize the necessity of accepting the new, and in 1879 he settled voluntarily upon a reserve on the Battle river. He did not long remain quiet.

The crops were poor, the assistance inadequate, and the outlook dismal. In 1881 Poundmaker made an effort to secure a large Indian gathering to press demands upon the Government for further concessions. This proving a failure he again turned his attention to the Cypress Hills. But conditions about Fort Walsh were much worse than he had expected and he willingly returned to his reserve the same year.[51]

In 1883 Poundmaker again assumed the leadership of an Indian agitation. He stopped work, left his reserve, and endeavoured to persuade others to do likewise. He resented the treatment meted out to him by the officials of the Indian Department, and demanded, in deference to his position, that complete control of matters upon the reserve should be turned over to himself and his councillors. The Government refused. Poundmaker was not sufficiently advanced to be entrusted with the supervision of Indian agriculture, nor was it the Government's policy to strengthen the hands of the chiefs. The only reply he received was that rations would be withheld from any of his band who refused to work.[52]

As the summer progressed Poundmaker's unrest increased. He repeatedly declared that he had fulfilled his share of the compact entered into when he left the plains, but that the Government had not fulfilled theirs.[53] The arrival of Big Bear, Lucky Man, and Little Pine added fuel to the growing unrest and the Government's drastic reduction in rations and supplies gave force to his complaints. The Indians regarded the contraction of their supplies as a deliberate deception upon the part of the whites, and everywhere the charge was made that the Government had not kept faith with the red man. The conditions were ripe for united action. Indian runners were sent to all the chiefs of the Territories. Piapot, who had been with Big Bear at Fort Walsh, received a letter early in September asking:

" Are you, Piapot, treated in the same way, not getting what was promised you? I suppose we will all meet again. The Indian is not to blame. The white man made the promises and now does not fulfil them."[54]

Crowfoot in southern Alberta, and Peccan at Edmonton, also received messengers from Big Bear. Everywhere plans were laid for " when the grass grows."

The Indians concealed their designs with the dissimulation of

POUNDMAKER

their race, but their actions, nevertheless, aroused the suspicions of the Department. In December 1883 the Assistant Indian Commissioner reported :

" Big Bear and his followers were loth to settle on a reserve and from what I could gather, and judging by the Indian nature, I am confident these Indians have some project in view as yet undisclosed, and it would not surprise me to find that they are making efforts to procure a large gathering from East and West at Battleford or adjacent thereto in the spring, in order to test their powers with the authorities once more."[55]

To forestall any concerted action upon the part of the natives, he urged that the numbers of the Mounted Police in the North Saskatchewan district should be augmented, that the Agents should remain constantly among their charges, and, if the slightest pretext offered, that the ringleaders among the Indians should be arrested. " The law," declared Reed, " might have to be strained a little to meet a particular case, but in the interests of the country at large, as well as the Indians themselves, such a course, I think, would be advisable."[56] In accordance with this advice, Vankoughnet requested the Comptroller of the Mounted Police at Ottawa to increase the force in the Battleford area, and to patrol " such localities in the Territories as may be deemed proper by the Indian Commissioner for the North-West Territories with a view to prevent Indians from congregating in large numbers during the coming spring, as there seems to be an indication on their part to hold a meeting, with the object, it is thought, of concerting plans with a view to discuss their relations with the Government and of making larger demands."[57]

In June the Indians began to assemble. The annual " Thirst Dance " was the pretext for the gathering. A spot near the northern boundary of Poundmaker's reserve was named as the meeting place, and by the middle of the month nearly two thousand Indians had pitched their teepees in the neighbourhood.[58] Indians from every reserve in the district were present, Big Bear, Poundmaker, Little Pine, Lucky Man, Moosomin, Strike-Him-on-the-Back, and Red Pheasant. Only the Stonies, Lean Man and Mosquito do not appear to have attended. Seldom before had there been gathered so many fighting men for a dance. The situation was pregnant with danger. The hysteria of the dance, the thrill of the throbbing drums and the exciting reiteration of the glories of their past would work the natives into a state of emotional intoxication. Rae, the Indian Agent, took what precautions he might, and requested that a detachment of police should be hastened to the reserve. However, before the detachment had arrived, a crisis was precipitated by a most untoward event.

On June 18th, Kahweechetwaymot, a member of Lucky Man's band, assaulted Farm Instructor Craig. The trouble arose over the question of rations. The Indian requested an issue of flour. Craig refused; his instructions were precise, to give out no rations except " to the old and to the sick and to no others unless they work." Kahweechetwaymot was bitter in his reply. " I suppose if a dog came along you would give to him rather than to me," he said to Craig.[59] Under the circumstances a refusal was impolitic; the Indians were excited and Kahweechetwaymot was a visitor of prestige. Craig, unfortunately, displayed a complete lack of appreciation of the situation. He may have understood farming but he did not understand Indians. Kahweechetwaymot was not only refused his flour, but was " pushed " out of the storehouse " on a spot where I was sore."[60] In a burst of anger the Indian seized an axe handle and struck the Farm Instructor over the arm. Craig was more frightened than injured, but the matter was immediately reported to the Mounted Police.

The handful of police, who had arrived upon the scene in accordance with Rae's request, were too few in number to make an arrest. The chiefs refused to give up Kahweechetwaymot at their request, and the attitude of the Indians was so threatening that the corporal in charge reported the difficulty to Superintendent Crozier at Battleford. Crozier, accompanied by the Indian Agent, the Police Surgeon and twenty-five men, proceeded at once to the reserve where the Thirst Dance was by now in full progress. In view of the frenzied excitement of the Indians it was deemed advisable to wait until the dance was over before attempting to make an arrest; meanwhile Crozier sent for reinforcements and proceeded to fortify the Agency buildings on Poundmaker's reserve. All night the police worked, and all night the overwrought Indians danced and shouted to the heavy thud of the tom-tom. On the 20th the dance was finished. With his force now numbering about 86, Crozier moved towards the Indian camp. In the town of Battleford preparations were made for all eventualities ; a Home Guard was formed of the local inhabitants and the neighbouring settlers crowded inside the little fort for protection.[61] The situation was precarious. Although they did what they could to persuade Kahweechet-waymot to give himself up quietly, the chiefs frankly admitted that their influence was insufficient to induce the turbulent young braves to consent to such a course, and warned Crozier that any attempt upon the part of the police to use force would result in bloodshed. It was obvious that the moral prestige of the police was waning, and that the Indians were inspired with a new intensity of antagonism against white authority. Many were convinced that the " Indians meant war," and Crozier was extremely apprehensive of the outcome. Writing to Colonel Irvine he declared :

" I had no doubt as to the result so far as the force under my command was concerned, for I had taken the advantage of position and had my supplies and spare ammunition well protected ; but what made me most anxious to avoid a collision was the fear that the first shot fired would be a signal for an Indian outbreak with all its attendant horrors. . . . From tribe to tribe would the disaffection have spread until the whole Indian population was against the white population."[62]

Finally the chiefs agreed to bring the prisoner to the Mounted Police quarters, provided his trial should take place upon an open plateau on the reserve. On reaching a point about half a mile from the improvised fort the Indians halted. Another parley followed; Crozier and the chiefs argued for several hours. Losing patience with the dilatory proceedings, Crozier made a bold move. Ordering his troops to advance, Crozier and the Interpreter went forward, seized the surprised Kahweechet-waymot and dragged him struggling into their midst. In an instant the police were surrounded with a whirling circle of " intensely excited " braves, " making the most threatening and indescribable noises." In the background Big Bear vainly shouted " Peace ! Peace ! "[63] while the Indians rushed upon the whites. Poundmaker, clad only in a breech cloth, and armed with a large club from which protruded three ugly knives, made for Inspector Antrobus, crying " I will kill you now."[64] Antrobus was hastily pulled back into the ranks and Poundmaker was covered with three or four rifles. The uproar increased. The Indians rode at the police, charged their ranks, jostled the men and stabbed their horses. Poundmaker and several others laid hold of a Mounted Policeman, who had become separated from the others, threw him down and stripped him of his arms. Every imaginable effort was made to provoke the police into firing in self-defence ; but no shot was fired. With great difficulty the struggling police column, with their prisoner still in their midst, reached the little fort. Once inside they hurled provisions of beef and flour over the walls to the howling Indians outside. The effect was immediate ; the noise and angry clamour ceased as if by magic, and the hungry Indians forgot their grievance in an unexpected abundance of food. Under cover of this new excitement the crestfallen Kahweechetwaymot was hurried off to Battleford to stand his trial.[65]   " It is yet incomprehensible to me," wrote Crozier in his report of this event, " how some one did not fire, and it is more than fortunate they did not. Had a shot been fired by either the police or Indians, I fear it would have been the signal for an engagement, and when that had taken place, it is hard to foretell what the consequences to the country would have been."[66]

This episode ended, for the time being, the proposed Indian council. Big Bear had not anticipated an outbreak of this nature, and, assisted by Lucky Man and Little Pine, made every effort to restrain the wilder spirits among the hot-headed young braves. Big Bear did not want an Indian rising. He knew the power of the whites and realized that the Indians had all to lose and nothing to gain by fighting. His efforts had been directed to bringing about an Indian union and to force concessions by a potential threat rather than by actual hostilities. On June 25th he invited Crozier and Rae to the reserve and expressed his regret for the unfortunate turn which events had taken. " The chiefs and their bands who had taken part in this affair," wrote the Indian Agent after this meeting, " seem very much frightened at what they have done, and I feel sure that if the proper power is placed in my hands and supplies given me so that I can deal liberally with these bands, there will be no more trouble, but I do not think that Big Bear or any others are going to submit to be *starved* out, and there is no doubt that these men are particularly hard-up. If, on the other hand, the Department are bound to stick to their present orders, then full preparations should be made to fight them, as it will sooner or later come to this, if more liberal treatment is not given."[67]

The idea of an Indian Council was not, however, abandoned. Following the arrival of Louis Riel in the North Saskatchewan district in July, and the rapid growth of a political agitation among the métis and the discontented whites, proposals for Indian action were once more revived. The Indians were well acquainted with Riel's reputation as an agitator and Big Bear was not long in taking advantage of his presence. Towards the end of July he and several of the chiefs of the Carlton district interviewed Riel at Duck Lake.[68] What transpired at this meeting is not known, but it may be presumed that Riel encouraged Big Bear in his determination to continue with his plans for another council. In any event, Big Bear sent messengers among the neighbouring tribes with invitations to attend a council of the chiefs at Duck Lake. Once more the Indians became excited. Rae declared pessimistically :

" I . . . never saw the Indians mean business before, the thing has to be looked at seriously and precautions taken before it is too late."[69]

The warnings of Cassandra never fell upon deafer ears. Even the Indian Commissioner added his voice to those of the Agents by asking that a show of force should be made to prevent the Indians from moving about as they pleased ; but Vankough-net maintained that this " would be the initiation by the Government of a policy which has not hitherto been applied towards any of our Indians—that of preventing them from moving about at will throughout the Territories."[70] He was apparently convinced that Rae's reports were unduly alarmist—a state of mind which was encouraged by the reports of the Assistant Indian Commissioner that the Indians were no more excited than in previous years and that Rae was " inclined to look upon the worst side of things."[71] Accordingly no action was taken by the Government to prevent the gathering of the Indians at Duck Lake.

The long-planned Council finally began on July 31st, 1884. On that day several chiefs visited the office of the Indian Agent at Fort Carlton, informed him of their intention of holding a council, and demanded food.[72] This demand was refused, but the Indians, nevertheless, continued to assemble. Although rumours that Piapot from Qu'Appelle and Little Pine from Battleford were to be present proved false, in addition to Big Bear and Lucky Man,[73] all the chiefs of the Carlton district were there, Beardy, Okemasis, One Arrow, Mistowasis, Ahtacka-koop, Petequaquay, John Smith, James Smith, Badger and others.

The speeches were full of disillusion, disappointment and resentment. Big Bear delivered a scathing denunciation of the lack of good faith of the whites and urged united Indian action :

" Yes, I am willing to speak. Since the leaves have begun to come it is why I have been walking, walking, trying to make myself understood. It is why I have come to Duck Lake. To show you why I have been so anxious, it is because I have been trying to seize the promises which they made to me, I have been grasping but I cannot find them. What they have promised me straightway I have not yet seen the half of it.

" We have all been deceived in the same way. It is the cause of our meeting at Duck Lake. They offered me a spot as a reserve. As I see that they are not going to be honest I am afraid to take a reserve. They have given me to choose between several small reserves but I feel sad to abandon the liberty of my own land when they come to me and offer me small plots to stay there and in return not to get half of what they have promised me. When will you have a big meeting. It has come to me as through the bushes that you are not yet all united, take time and become united, and I will speak. The Government sent to us those who think themselves men. They bring everything crooked. They take our lands, they sell them and they buy themselves fine clothes. Then they clap their hands on their hips and call themselves men. They are not men. They have no honesty. They are an unsightly beast. Their faces are twisted from the appearance of honest men."[74]

Perhaps the most remarkable suggestion made at this Council, —and one which had been possibly inspired by Louis Riel—was that of choosing an Indian representative every four years to act as intermediary between the Indians and the whites.

" He has done. I wish to speak. I wish to stay on the land that God has given me. I wish all the world to make my claim good. I see clearly the one who cheats me. I wait for the day when we are united when I can speak to him straight. It is good in one way that I am cheated for it is only now that I know what a great good God has given me, how I appreciate the kindness of

God. They play too much on me when they say 'you don't know anything.' . . . It's an idea that I have, if the whites would choose an Indian from all the tribes to simplify the question, in understanding that one they would understand all the rest.

" During four years that Indian could make the understanding progress all the time between the Indians and the white man. Let us work that good work every day without stopping as long as earth will appear before us and we have a spirit. The sun he has a spirit and he works every day, why ? to enlighten the world. Let us do the same. Let our spirits work constantly to enlighten those who are in the same land as we are.

" . . . Don't allow any man to poison my words. The choice of our representative ought to be given to us every four years. Crowfoot is working for the same thing as I am."[75]

After several days the Council took on a new development. On the morning of August 6th, two of Beardy's men arrived at Fort Carlton and informed the Agent, J. A. Macrae, that the chiefs required provisions. He replied that, as the Government knew nothing of the object of their meeting, and as the Indians were holding it entirely upon their own account, no food would be supplied. The next day Mistowasis and Ahtackakoop renewed the request in more respectful terms. Macrae acted wisely. Instead of driving the Indians to exasperation, he informed them that if they would move the Council to Fort Carlton and lay their grievances openly before the Government, provisions would be provided.[76] The Indians hesitated. But a surfeit of speeches did not fill empty stomachs and the chiefs finally accepted Macrae's offer, the whole Council moving to the new location. The Indians were then supplied with food and their complaints were fully aired before the Agent. Several days later the Agent declared the Council at an end, and the Indians, their grievances ventilated and their appetites satisfied, returned to their reserves, temporarily pleased with what they had accomplished.

The general tenor of the complaints was indicative of the Indian reaction to the Government's native policy. The Indians declared that the terms of the treaties were inadequate for the needs of the aboriginal population and that, moreover, they had not been faithfully observed by the Government. They complained that the cattle given them were both insufficient to gain a livelihood with and that they were too wild and intractable to be cared for ; that many of the tools and waggons were of inferior quality and should be replaced ; and that certain other provisions of the treaties had in no way been complied with. Other grievances were that the Government had failed to maintain schools, to grant " liberal assistance " in time of distress, and to place the Indian " in the same position as the white man," as promised by the treaties. They declared that " at the time of the treaty they were comparatively well off " but " were deceived by the sweet promises of the Commissioners," and that their subsequent requests for redress of grievances had been ignored. The Council concluded with a threat. The chiefs stated that " while they are glad that the young men have not resorted to violent measures . . . it is almost too hard for them to bear the treatment at the hands of the Government after its sweet promises," and that they would only " wait until next summer to see if this council has the desired effect, failing which they will take measures to get what they desire."[77]

Although the Indian Department considered that " the Indians have no good grounds for serious complaint in any respect " and instructed Dewdney " to keep this constantly before the minds of the Indians, impressing them, as far as possible, with the fact that they have been most generously treated by the Government and far beyond any expectations that they could have entertained under the most liberal interpretation that could be put upon the treaties made with them,"[78] there was much justification for the complaints formulated at this council. Some of the treaty promises had been only partially fulfilled, not through oversight or corruption, but because the Indian Department considered that the Indians were not sufficiently advanced to make the best use of the promised tools, livestock or schools.[79] It does not appear that the implements and waggons were of inferior quality, but, owing to the hard usage anything in the hands of the Indians received, an article had to be particularly strong to withstand the wear and tear. In regard to the treaty cattle and oxen, the Assistant Indian Commissioner admitted that many were " of a wild nature, and anything but easily managed by the Indians."[80] The complaints relative to the parsimonious issue of rations, too, were not without their justification in fact as well as in theory. The Commissioners negotiating the treaties had painted pictures of prosperity and contentment for the Indians—"sweet promises" the Indians called them—which, through faulty interpretation or misunderstanding, the Indians construed into meaning Government maintenance. Unfortunately the demands of the economic situation outweighed considerations of native policy, a fact which, as we have observed, aroused the fears of the Indians, and gave force to the charge that treaty promises were being disregarded. Too great an emphasis was laid upon the letter of the law and too little foresight was applied to the larger political aspects of the Indian problem.

The Carlton Council witnessed the partial success of Big Bear's efforts. A year before he had stood practically alone, but by the close of 1884 the Indians from Fort Pitt to Fort à la Corne had united under his influence to back his demands. The Craig affair in June had ruined the first Council at Poundmaker's, but the Duck Lake–Carlton Council proved the unanimity of opinion among the Indians of the North Saskatchewan district. "An answer in detail is expected by the Council," wrote the Indian Agent, "which declared itself to be a representative one of the Battleford as well as Carlton Crees. No doubt need be entertained that the Indians regard it as such."[81]

The next step lay with the Government. Following the receipt of Macrae's letter containing the Indian demands, the Department ordered the Assistant Indian Commissioner, Hayter Reed, to report upon them. Reed minimized the effect of the Government's policy upon the Indians and the determination of the aborigines to secure better terms. In his report he admitted that a few of the grievances were justified, but expressed it as his opinion that " many of the Indians, although they have endorsed the list of complaints formulated on their behalf, would not, if closely questioned by an official, feel inclined to assert that all these were real ground of grievances." He attributed the gathering of the Indians to the agitation of Big Bear and to the subversive influence of Louis Riel :

" Big Bear is an agitator and always has been, and having received the moral support of the half-breed community, he is only too glad to have an opportunity of inciting the Indians to make fresh and exorbitant demands.

" There are Indian as well as white agitators and the hard times make one and all, good and bad, only too prone to give any assistance they can towards procuring more from the authorities without having to work for it.   Riel's movement has a great deal to do with the demands of the Indians, and there is no possible doubt but that they, as well as the half-breeds, are beginning to look up to him as one who will be the means of curing all their ills and obtaining for them all they demand."[82]

This view of the situation was a short-sighted one and misled the Government into a false sense of security.   Believing that the Indian demands could be ignored and the policy of economy carried on with impunity, Vankoughnet merely requested Dewdney to inquire into the question of the wild cattle, and to continue to impress upon the Indians " that they have really received much more than the Government was, under the Treaty, bound to give them."[83]

In the meantime, the Indians did not pause in their activity. Plans were developed for a greater and still more representative council during 1885, at which the Government's answer to their demands would be considered and a course of action resolved upon.   Early in the winter messengers and invitations were again sent out among the different tribes.   Little Pine was to visit the Blackfeet and Little Poplar the Stonies, neither of whom had attended the previous gatherings.[84]   Big Bear himself considered going to Duck Lake and Qu'Appelle,[85] and in January messengers were reported by Superintendent Crozier to be on their way to Red Pheasant and Edmonton.[86]

But, before the council could gather, time and circumstances had taken the control of events out of the hands of the Indian chiefs.   1885 saw, not an Indian council, but an Indian rebellion.

CHAPTER XIV

By the spring of 1884 unrest was general throughout the Saskatchewan valley. The Indians, as we have observed, were restless and discontented ; the half-breeds, English and French, were in a similar state of disquietude ; and the white settlers were dissatisfied with their political and economic conditions. To co-ordinate these three groups and to bring about a united political action was the task to which Louis Riel addressed himself.

The events of 1869–70 had proven Riel's remarkable influence over the half-breeds. Although he was not himself a fighter, he had the power to stir others to fight. His hold over the métis was extraordinary. To the present day the personal magnetism which enabled this strange megalomaniac to command the support of the métis in two uprisings still commands the admiration of their descendants. Others, too, felt the power of his personality. After meeting Riel for the first time in 1884, a priest in the North-West wrote of him :

" C'était la première fois que je voyais Riel ; je fus enchanté de sa conversation et de son bon esprit ; j'admirai la foi qui respirait dans toutes ses paroles, la douceur qui caracterisait sa physionomie et son élocution. Et cependant ce visage, ou se peignent la bonté, l'humilité, et la modestie, s'anime parfois tout à coup et s'enflamme d'un feu terrible, et cela surtout quand on fait quelque opposition aux idées exprimées par l'orateur. Les droits de sa nation sont pour lui sacrés, et il jure de les défendre jusqu'à la mort. Dans ces moments d'exaltation ce n'est plus le même homme. Son regard de feu, l'éclat de sa voix, l'agitation de son épaisse chevelure, lui donnent un aspect qui vous effraie, et tout dans sa personne trahit l'éloquence. On ne peut s'empêcher de dire : ' Voilà un homme convaincu.' "[1]

Nevertheless, Riel was, in 1884, totally unfit to undertake the task for which he had been recalled. His career as a leader of the half-breeds had culminated with his election to the Dominion

Parliament in 1874, and his appearance at and flight from the Commons Chamber at Ottawa. For the next ten years he wandered aimlessly in the United States, bitter, disillusioned and mentally unbalanced as a result of the events of 1869–70 and the persecution which ensued. During 1876 and 1877 he spent twenty months in the mental asylums of Longue Pointe and Beauport in the Province of Quebec, after which he drifted to Montana, where he became a trader and subsequently a school teacher. Obsessed with the idea of his " mission "[2] he sought to assume the role of leader of the half breeds of that state, hoping to consolidate them into a political force. His political efforts in Montana were, however, without success. His egotism and his lack of ballast handicapped him everywhere. But in spite of this apparent lack of stability in his character, throughout Riel's actions and writings there is one constant theme, the furtherance of the métis cause.

It is not surprising, therefore, that Riel kept himself informed as to the progress of the agitation in the Canadian North-West. In 1882 Philip Garnot of St. Laurent, while visiting a brother-in-law in Montana, discussed North-West politics with Louis Riel.[3] It has been alleged that Riel also met Napoléon Nault in St. Boniface in 1883 and arranged for his recall to the Saskatchewan,[4] but there is no corroborative evidence. In the spring of 1884 Riel received a letter from the troubled area, notifying him of the delegation sent to invite his return and outlining the métis view of the agitation:

" Hence, my dear cousin, we may say that the part of the North-West in which we are living is Manitoba before the troubles, with the difference that there are more people, that they understand things better, and that they are more determined ; you will form an idea as to the conditions upon which the people base their claims, for the reason that there are many people in the North-West whom the Government have recognized less than Indians ; and yet it is these poor half-breeds who have always defended the North-West at the price of their blood and their sacrifices for a country which is stirring up the whole world to-day. They have been petitioning for the last ten years. I suppose the Government have looked upon the matter as mere child's play ; despite formal documents and Acts of Parliament as a guarantee, the whole matter has been a farce ; the honor of Parliament and of the Government has been trampled under foot when justice was to be done to the poor half-breeds. My dear cousin, I think the solemn moment has come. For my part, I have closely watched the people of the North-West, as well as the Indians, and the one cry resounds from all, it is the spark over a barrel of powder. It is late, but it is the time now more than ever, for we have right and justice on our side. Do not imagine that you will begin the work when you get here ; I tell you it is all done, the thing is decided ; it is your presence that is needed. It will, in truth, be a great event in the North-West ; you have no idea how great your influence is, even amongst the Indians. I know that you do not like the men much, but I am certain that it will be the grandest demonstration that has ever taken place, and the English are speaking about it already. Now, my dear cousin, the closest union exists between the French and English and the Indians, and we have good generals to foster it. . . . The whole race is calling for you ! "[5]

On June 4th the delegation, which had been appointed by the meeting in the Lindsay School House on May 6th, arrived at St. Peter's Mission in Montana, and consulted Riel. They informed him of the state of the country and invited him to return to the North-West. A refusal was hardly to be expected. Riel was not only devoted to the métis cause, but he loved the adulation of the crowd, and felt, moreover, that he had a claim upon the Canadian Government for a share in the half-breed land grant in Manitoba in which he had not participated. He was, also, probably influenced by the assurance of the complete unanimity of feeling in the North-West Territories among the métis, the whites and the Indians, a situation which he had striven for but failed to bring about during the insurrection of 1869–70. Accordingly, on June 5th, 1884, Louis Riel accepted the invitation to lead the agitation in the North-West, with the qualification that he would like to return to the United States " sometime in September."[6]

Riel's arrival on the banks of the Saskatchewan was hailed by both the French and the English half-breeds. On July 1st, Louis Schmidt, ex-secretary of the Provisional Government of Red River and now secretary of the settlers' committee which had sent for Riel, wrote enthusiastically to the French newspaper at St. Boniface :

" J'ai appris hier soir que M. Louis Riel devait se rendre aujourd'hui à St. Laurent. Vous savez peut-être, qu'après les assemblées de ce printemps, une délégation des métis français et anglais était partie pour se rendre auprès de l'ex-président du Gouvernement Provisoire de la Rivière Rouge, alors au Montana, pour lui exposer les besoins de ses nationaux (puisqu'il est métis) et le prier de venir au milieu d'eux. Il faut croire que la délégation a réussi au moins jusqu'à ce point. On dit que M. Riel arrive avec sa famille. Que n'a-t-il la bonne idée de se fixer irrévocablement au milieu de nous. Cet homme ne peut faire que du bien à ses compatriotes, et il est le seul qui réunirait tous les suffrages dans n'importe quel contestation. Son nom est grand parmi les métis français ou anglais, et il est incontestable que son influence, bien dirigée, leur sera d'un secours immense. Le peuple devait hier se rendre en foule à sa rencontre."[7]

On July 8th a meeting was held at the house of Charles Nolin at Batoche. The delegation to Riel presented their report and expressed their entire confidence in his leadership. Riel himself made a speech which " fit une grande impression," although his insistence upon a peaceful agitation disappointed some of the more belligerent métis " dont les indispositions hostiles à l'égard du governement leur auraient fait désirer une charge à fond contre ce même gouvernement."[8]

Riel began his task of co-ordinating the white, half-breed and Indian discontent on July 11th, by holding a large meeting in the English-speaking settlement of Red Deer Hill.[9] He addressed the people in both French and English and outlined the difficulties under which the North-West was labouring. W. H. Jackson, the Secretary of the Settlers' Union, Thomas Scott and other white settlers also spoke, condemning the administration of the Federal Government in the North-West. The meeting then proceeded to organize the agitation for the summer. Representative committees were chosen for each district whose duties were to call local meetings and to draw up lists of grievances which would be embodied in one general petition to be forwarded by the central committee to the Dominion House of Commons. The meeting was orderly throughout, and the impression left upon the whites and the English half-breeds present was entirely favourable to Riel.[10] He had spoken with moderation and restraint, and made it perfectly clear that his agitation would be conducted upon constitutional lines.

As a result of this meeting, Riel was invited to address a mass meeting of the white settlers at Prince Albert. Riel hesitated.

He was keenly sensible of the feeling which the execution of Scott in 1870 had aroused among the English-speaking Canadians, and felt that his appearance in a town which was inhabited predominantly by settlers from Ontario, might stir up opposition to the popular movement. Replying to the invitation he wrote :

" Gentlemen, I know that as your guest I would be perfectly safe from anything like discourtesy ; and with such a respectable body of men as those who have signed the invitation I would feel far above any insult that could be offered to me. But for the sake of avoiding even the slightest trouble, in order to allow no germ of division to weaken our basis of action, I beg leave to be excused. Please consent to put off the meeting."[11]

The people of Prince Albert were not disposed to accept a refusal. A petition pressing Riel to hold the meeting was drawn up and signed by eighty-four people representative of all walks of life, only five or six being half-breeds.[12] Father André, the Superior at Prince Albert, also added his word of insistence :

" The opinion here is so pronounced in your favor ; and you are so ardently desired, that it will be a great disappointment to the people of Prince Albert if you do not come. So you must absolutely come ; you are the most popular man in the country, and with the exception of four or five persons every one awaits you with impatience. I have only to say to you come, come quickly."[13]

Pressed from all sides Riel consented, and on July 19th he addressed a large gathering at Prince Albert. The meeting was well attended. Riel was nervous, but defended his actions with vigour. He pointed out the constitutional nature of the agitation, stressed the necessity for concerted action among the people, and, to win the support of the white settlers, urged responsible government as the panacea for the ills of the North-West Territories.[14] Messrs. Miller, Slater, T. Scott and Jackson, the leaders of the white agitation and the Settlers' Union, also spoke, and Riel concluded the meeting by replying to questions. The meeting was a complete success. Those who had come in from the surrounding country returned home " struck with the quiet and gentle way he spoke to them."[15] There had been no hint of violence. The result was to give a stimulus to the progress of the movement among the white settlers.

The work of carrying on and organizing the white agitation was largely in the hands of William Henry Jackson, the Secretary of the Settlers' Union.   Jackson was a young man, a graduate of Toronto University, and a staunch partisan.   His father and brother, also living at Prince Albert, were Liberals in politics and strong opponents of Sir John A. Macdonald.   From the outset, the Jacksons, William Henry in particular, were the foremost protagonists of the North-West agitation and spared no effort to make Louis Riel acceptable to the discontented white settlers. It was difficult at first, owing to the prejudice engendered by the events of 1869-70 ; but, when they realized that without Riel they could not hope to secure the co-operation of the half-breeds and Indians, they made a virtue of necessity and professed, even if they did not feel, an admiration for and willingness to follow the former insurrectionary leader.   Jackson and others, including Isbister and Scott, visited the various districts, organized local committees, and secured the election of local delegates to the central committee of the Settlers' Union.   There appeared to be no lack of funds for the agitation.[16]   On July 23rd Jackson reported his activities to Riel :

" To-day, I shall finish up work in town, and to-morrow start for the Lower Flat, etc.   I will try and get out to your place towards the end of the week.   Please be working up the petition into shape, and we will get it in neat form before the committee is called to endorse or alter it, as they see fit. . . . There is a big work for us while the petition is waiting an answer, but I think we will be ready for a stiff campaign when the answer does come. A number of trimmers are waiting to see if the current in your favor will last.   By the time they are satisfied it will be too late for them to bother us much, if disposed to do so."[17]

The progress of the movement was sufficient to alarm the adherents of the Government, and the Prince Albert Conservatives considered the advisability of adopting Riel's platform under their party colours.[18]   Perhaps with the object of forestalling such a move, W. H. Jackson issued a manifesto on July 28th,[19] giving a clear statement of the object and purposes of the Riel agitation and calling upon the people for their political support.

" To the Citizens of Prince Albert :

" GENTLEMEN—We are starting a movement in this settlement with a view to attaining Provincial Legislatures for the North-West Territories and, if possible, the control of our own resources, that we may build our railroads and other works to serve our own interests rather than those of the Eastern Provinces.   We are preparing a statement of our case to send to Ottawa as a matter of form. We state the various evils which are caused by the present system of legislation showing :

" 1. That they are caused by the facts that the Ottawa legislators are responsible to Eastern constituents, not to us, and are therefore impelled to legislate with a view to Eastern interests rather than our own ; that they are not actually resident in the country and therefore not acquainted with the facts that would enable them to form a correct opinion as to what measures are suitable to North-West interests, consequently liable to pass legislation adverse to North-West interests even when not favorable to their own ; lastly that they have not the greater part of their immediate private interests involved in the interests of the said Territories, and are therefore liable to have their judgement warped by such private interests.

" 2. That the legislation passed by such legislators has already produced great depression in agricultural, commercial, and mechanical circles, and will continue to increase that depression unless the system is revised ; that is to say, unless our legislators are chosen by and responsible to ourselves actually resident in the country and having the bulk of their private interests involved in the interests of the country.

" We give the complete list of our grievances, but instead of asking the redress of each of them separately, we ask the remedy to the root of the evil, i.e., Provincial Legislatures with full control over our own resources and internal administration, and power to send a just number of representatives to the Federal Legislature whatever and wherever that may ultimately lie. Possibly we may settle up with the East and form a separate federation of our own in direct connection with the Crown.

" Louis Riel of Manitoba fame has united the half-breed element solidly in our favour. Hitherto it has been used largely as the tool of whatever party happened to be in power in the East, but Riel has warned them against the danger of being separated from the whites by party proposals. The general impression is that Riel has been painted in blacker colors than he deserves ; that in regard to his public attitude it is better to accept his services as long as he works for us ; while as to his private record it would be well to suspend judgement until his side of the case has been heard, especially as his general bearing is frank and straightforward, indicating sincerity of purpose and assurance of his convictions. As long as both elements work on the square, doing justice to each other, there will be no clash, but a marked advance toward our end, i.e., justice in the North-West.

"It is by force of right that we hope to win our cause and any inconsistency on our part will greatly damage our cause, as it will lose us the moral support of Great Britain and the United States. Restrain any tendency toward the forcible taking charge of our own affairs before we have used all constitutional means.

.   .   .   .   .

"We are in communication with other parts of the North-West Territories, and we hope to hold a general convention of the North-West before Autumn, in order to arrange a common basis with Manitoba, and join with her in taking the matter to the Privy Council.

"Our local press is not to be relied on. It is in the hands of a few governmental favorites who inspire its editorials which are anonymous. It is, accordingly, circulating wild reports about impending rebellion and Indian troubles, seeking a pretext for placing the country under martial law and so goad the people into a false step. Riel will do more toward pacifying Big Bear than could be accomplished by twenty agents in a month of Sundays. Had the Eastern Government looked at *our interests*, they would have shown such fair play toward the decent Indians that the turbulent ones would have had no moral sympathy as pretext, and would have caused us no apprehension. However, there is no danger of Indian troubles as long as we can keep Riel in the country.

"WILLIAM H. JACKSON,
Secretary, Executive Committee."

As stated in the manifesto above, Riel exercised a strong influence over the Indians. They regarded him as "a man skilled in obtaining what he desires from the Government by means of agitation,"[20] and the Indian Agent at Carlton was correct in believing that "to a greater or lesser extent their future action will depend upon the counsel that he may see fit to give them."[21] The discontented aborigines were not slow to seek his advice. On July 26th, Sir John A. Macdonald was informed by telegram that Big Bear had left Battleford to see Riel at Duck Lake. An interview was held between Riel and the Indian chiefs, and the demands of the Duck Lake–Carlton Council showed unmistakably the influence of the métis leader. It was also reported that Indians from Qu'Appelle, including Piapot, were coming north to consult Riel, but a deputation of Saskatchewan Indians persuaded them to return so as not to prejudice white opinion.[22]

The northern Indians, however, kept in close touch with Riel. Another interview between the leader of the North-West agitation and Big Bear was reported in August. On the 21st, Sergeant Brooks of the N.W.M.P. wrote to Superintendent Crozier that Big Bear and Riel had met at Jackson's house at Prince Albert.[23] T. E. Jackson, later describing the interview, stated that Big Bear complained that the conditions of the treaty had been violated by the Dominion Government and asked that when the whites and half-breeds had secured their rights they would assist the Indians to win theirs.[24] That Riel and Jackson agreed to do so is shown by the fact that more liberal treatment for the aborigines became one of the principal planks of the North-West party's platform. On August 10th, Riel stated at Batoche that " the Indians' rights should be protected as well as their own "[25] and later Jackson, speaking before a meeting which included whites as well as half-breeds, declared that the North-West belonged to the Indians and not to the Dominion of Canada.[26]

Assured of white and Indian support, Riel then turned his attention to the métis. His object was to consolidate them into a single political force by the formation of a national métis society, after the model of the St. Jean Baptiste Society of the French Canadians. The idea was not a new one. At Red River he had seriously considered the founding of a similar organization to bear the name " L'Union Saint Alexandre " in honour of his benefactor, Archbishop Taché, but the opportunity to do so passed. Early in September 1884, Riel revived the project, and taking advantage of Bishop Grandin's presence at St. Laurent, secured episcopal approval of his plan. The Bishop suggested St. Joseph as the patron saint ; the new organization hence took the name, " L'Union Métisse de Saint Joseph."[27] The inauguration was conducted on September 24th at St. Antoine de Padoue (Batoche), Riel utilizing the occasion to address a gathering, which included almost the entire population of the métis settlement of St. Laurent, upon North-West politics.

The métis continued to give evidence of affection for their leader. They looked upon him, remarked Father Fourmond in December, as " un Josué, un prophète, et même un saint."[28] On January 6th, 1885, a public banquet was held in his honour at St. Antoine. All the neighbouring parishes were represented. The banquet was presided over by the Honourable Charles Nolin, who emphasized the debt which the métis owed to Riel and reproached the Canadian Government for their treatment of the ex-president of the Provisional Government of Red River. During the course of the banquet Riel was presented with a small purse of money as a token of the métis esteem. Riel replied in a moderate tone, which gave no hint of the troubles to come, declaring only that " Dieu m'a donné une cause à défendre."[29]

Although Prince Albert and St. Laurent were the centres of Riel's political actions among the whites, métis and Indians, other sections of the North-West Territories were also carrying on an agitation for North-West rights. At Qu'Appelle a " Settlers' Rights Association " had been pressing for the reform of the land laws and for legislation in the interests of the settlers. During the summer of 1884 a series of meetings were held throughout Assiniboia to discuss the commercial and political situation of the Territories. Demands were forwarded to Ottawa for representation in the Dominion Parliament and for the construction of a railway to Hudson Bay. In December a meeting was held at the town of Wolseley, and a committee appointed to take the necessary steps to organize a deputation to press their case personally before the Dominion Cabinet. Commenting on this meeting the *Nor'Wester* of Calgary declared that it was a " war-whoop which it was determined should be heard in Ottawa," while the Edmonton *Bulletin* added ominously, " If that particular whoop is not heard, its echoes, or other similar whoops evidently will be. All along the C.P.R. line in the Territories mass meetings are being held which unanimously and emphatically adopt the principle " of North-West rights.[30] In Alberta similar meetings were held, Frank Oliver and his *Bulletin* contributing to the growing agitation. On November 1st Oliver outlined his demands in a leading article entitled " Our Platform," namely : provincial status, the abrogation of the Canadian Pacific Railway monopoly and construction of the Hudson Bay Railway, the reduction of the tariff, the modification of the terms of Confederation in the interests of complete provincial autonomy, and a toleration of the British connexion only " as long as it is found profitable and generally advantageous as at present, with a view to independence when that connection shall be dissolved."[31]

Even beyond the boundaries of the North-West Territories

the manifestations of discontent must have encouraged Louis Riel and his co-agitators in the Saskatchewan valley. In Manitoba the Farmers' Union, disappointed in its efforts to secure redress of alleged grievances, indulged in fiery memorials and wild threats of annexation, secession and rebellion![32] In other provinces the depression brought out inevitable expressions of discontent with the Government. At a meeting in St. John, New Brunswick, a number of business men advocated annexation to the United States as the only means of escaping financial ruin. The Edmonton *Bulletin* related the details of this meeting and, with manifest satisfaction, attributed it to the same policy which was allegedly oppressing the North-West.

Economic conditions in the North-West showed no improvement during 1884, and the repeated crop failure in the autumn proved a useful ally to the agitators. Conditions were particularly bad in the neighbourhood of Prince Albert. The Hudson's Bay Company reported to London that many farmers were cutting for fodder the acres which had been under crop. The métis of St. Laurent were in a desperate condition, and the Mounted Police authorities viewed the situation with apprehension :

" The crops here are almost a total failure and everything indicates that the half-breeds are going to be in a very straitened condition before the end of the coming winter, which, of course, will make them more discontented, and will probably drive them to an outbreak, and I believe that trouble is almost certain before the winter ends unless the Government extends some aid to the half-breeds during the coming winter."[33]

Although this prediction of a half-breed rising proved premature, the fears of the Mounted Police were well founded. The métis and Indians were discontented, and many whites likewise. But, up to the present, there had been no open advocacy of violence by any of the discontented elements. The leaders had always stressed the peaceful character of their agitation and Riel had only sought to unite all parties in one common purpose, the constitutional redress of grievances. That his efforts were not without success is shown by a letter from T. Getting Jackson to the Toronto *Globe* :

" there is a thorough understanding between the French and the English half-breeds and Canadian settlers, and all are pledged to unite in one common brotherhood until all grievances are redressed."[34]

The first tangible result of the combined efforts of the white and half-breed discontents was the forwarding of the long-agitated petition to Ottawa. On December 16th, 1884, W. H. Jackson addressed the following letter[35] to the Honourable J. A. Chapleau, Secretary of State for the Dominion of Canada.

" SIR,

" I have the honour to transmit to you herewith for the consideration of His Excellency in Council, a copy of the petition which the people of this district have decided to forward under present circumstances. From your knowledge of the matter referred to, you will perceive that the petition is an extremely moderate one. I may say, in fact, that, to the Canadian and English wing of the movement, a more searching exposition of the situation would have been more satisfactory. The opinion has been freely expressed that our appeal should be directed to the Privy Council of England and to the general public, rather than to the federal authorities, on the ground not only that our previous petitions would appear to have gone astray, but that even the benefit of federal representation might be largely neutralized by the placing of obstacles in the way of our choice of leaders, or the disregard of those leaders even when elected, as was done in the case of Manitoba.[36]

" It is, therefore, to be hoped that His Excellency and advisers will not fail to appreciate the attitude which our people have adopted on the assurances of the more moderate councillors, and that a speedy and satisfactory response will be accorded to our present appeal.

" I have, etc.
" W. H. JACKSON, Secretary General
Committee.
" By order of
" ANDREW SPENCE, Esq., Chairman.

" District of Lorne,
" Grandin P.O.,
" St. Laurent,
" North-West Territory,
" December 16, 1884."

The petition[37] embodied the grievances of all parties in the North-West Territories. It demanded more liberal treatment for the Indians : scrip and patents for the half-breeds : responsible government, representation in the Dominion Parliament and Cabinet, provincial control of natural resources, modification of the homestead laws, vote by ballot, a railway to Hudson Bay and reduction in the tariff for the white settlers. It also contained a long complaint, obviously prepared by Louis Riel himself, of the treatment of the North-West delegates in 1870 and the non-promulgation of the promised amnesty. In view of the above letter and this petition, it is interesting to note that Sir John A. Macdonald boldly declared in the Dominion Parliament in March 1885 that no North-West " Bill of Rights " had ever been " officially, or indeed in any way, promulgated so far as we know, and transmitted to the Government."[38] The Government not only received the petition and forwarded it to the Colonial Office, but apparently acknowledged the receipt of the petition, for, on January 27th, Jackson wrote to Riel that the reply from the Under-Secretary of State was a " good sign " in view of " the bold tone of my letter, and our audacious assumption that we are not yet in Confederation, an assumption which, it seems to me, they have conceded in their letter . . . It is evident that they are prepared to communicate with us on something like equal terms."[39] In anticipation of an invitation to send delegates to negotiate at Ottawa, as had been done in 1870, Jackson advised Riel to postpone the meeting of the central committee, and in the meantime to forward another letter to the Government " hinting at the nature of the document we will address to Parliament, and thus place in the hands of the Opposition as a weapon if they do not treat with us in earnest." " That, I think," he wrote, "will fetch them to terms, for there is every prospect of a stormy session."

The agitation which led to the drafting of this petition had not been carried on without considerable opposition. The North-West movement had assumed a definite party tone with the adhesion of professed Reformers like the Jacksons and others, and the supporters of the Macdonald Government became suspicious of its bona fides. Against the agitation was directed the full force of the pro-government press in the Territories. The Prince Albert *Times*, which had, up to the recall of Riel, openly espoused the demands of the settlers, made a sudden *volte-face*.[40] It denied ever having expressed sympathy with the Colleston School House programme and condemned, in no uncertain terms, Riel's leadership of the new movement.   Doubts were cast upon Riel's pacific professions, and it was suggested that " he has been merely trying to feel the public pulse, and would, did he find the symptoms favourable, proceed to raise a row."[41] The *Times* also turned its journalistic batteries upon the Jacksons and other white leaders, calling them " cranks and rebels," whose " frothy utterances must inevitably ruin all our hopes of sympathy from those who have the power to help us."[42]   At Battleford the *Saskatchewan Herald* was equally denunciatory of the agitation. An editorial of August 9th stated :

" Instead of sending a deputation to a foreign country to bring in an alien demagogue to set class against class, and to mar the harmony between the races under which the country was growing prosperous and happy, they should have sent a representative to Ottawa to lay before the Government a statement of their claims ; and, as the complaints of her citizens have always been listened to in the past, so would they be now.   But we cannot believe the Government will seriously entertain any claims or propositions put forward by or through Riel."[43]

The *Herald*, however, failed to remember that the very measures suggested had been attempted and that the indifference of the Federal Government to the settlers' demands was responsible for Riel's presence in the country.

Of greater significance than the subsidized denunciations of a partisan press, was the reluctance of many, who were in genuine sympathy with the demands of the settlers, half-breed and white, to accept the leadership of Louis Riel.   The bitter racial and religious passions engendered by the execution of Scott during the Red River Rebellion had not subsided, and Riel's name was anathema to many of the English-speaking whites.   Some were able to sink racial prejudice in a common struggle, but many remained aloof.   Frank Oliver, who had been the leading expo-nent of North-West rights for several years, and who had urged through the columns of the Edmonton *Bulletin* the same demands put forward by Riel and the Settlers' Union, was frankly doubtful of the advisability of the selection of Riel as leader of the North-West movement.   Writing to Jackson, he said :

" I am glad to hear that Prince Albert is likely to shake loose from the ring control henceforth.   But I fear you are too forward with your preparations for the forthcoming elections and that the ardour of to-day may cool before June next. . . . A word privately about Riel.   He may be a man of the greatest influence and the most high-minded patriotism but he is political dynamite, or may be a political boomerang.   In endorsing Riel you will be held up as endorsing his whole course, and your enemies will have thus put in their hands the best possible weapon they can have against you.   I don't say don't endorse him, you must judge for yourself as to that, but I warn you that it is a ticklish thing to do, and one that I would not from my slight acquaintance with the case, care about doing until he has done something to wipe out the blot that stands against him."[44]

The most serious opposition, however, with which Riel had to contend came from the Roman Catholic clergy.   From the beginning they had been opposed to Riel.   Father André believed that Riel ought not to have been allowed to cross the frontier, and Bishop Grandin wrote to Macdonald in June expressing his regret that the métis had been associated in the movement to bring Riel into the country.[45]

On his arrival in the North-West Riel made every effort to secure the influence of the Church in the support of his movement, but without success.   Although he impressed André for a short time with his peaceful demeanour, it is evident that the Roman Catholic clergy at St. Laurent were by no means in sympathy with the growing agitation, fearing, possibly, that it might get beyond their control.   In September the métis openly charged the clergy with opposition to their movement and expressed a failing confidence in their leadership.   Bishop Grandin replied that the Church had always been the foremost advocate of the métis cause, but refused to countenance the secrecy with which Riel cloaked his actions among them.   The breach was temporarily patched, but Bishop Grandin remained apprehensive concerning the future.   " Je ne puis m'empêcher," he said of Riel, " de redouter l'influence de cet homme, et de craindre pour l'avenir."[46] The bishop's fears were justified.   Relations between the Catholic clergy and the malcontents became more strained as time went on.   Father André was branded as " a man sold to the Government,"[47] and discussions between Riel and the priests were marked by bitter passages.

Realizing that their influence was rapidly waning and that the movement might assume a less moderate tone once their restraining influence was removed, the clergy endeavoured to secure

Riel's removal from the country. Father André wrote to this effect to Lieutenant-Governor Dewdney :

"Now, Governor, I think it is really the duty of the Government to get Riel out of mischief as soon as possible. As I told you from the beginning there has never been any fear of an outbreak, but the presence of that man in the country will be a source of anxiety to the Government, and we do not know what may happen at last . . . Riel and some other agitators are the only ones who have interest to excite the mind of the people. Riel disappearing everything will quiet down."[48]

Like the clergy, the Government of the Territories were inclined to view Riel's actions with suspicion. Lieutenant-Governor Dewdney had endeavoured to forestall Riel's return by visiting St. Laurent early in June, but his efforts met with an " uncordial reception."[49] Following the arrival of the métis leader in the Territories the local Government took precautionary measures to prevent any possible outbreak. The Mounted Police force at Prince Albert was reinforced and a detachment was stationed at Fort Carlton. No attempt was made to interfere with Riel's freedom of movement, but a close watch was kept upon the progress of the agitation throughout the summer.

In September alarming rumours reached Dewdney that a rising of the métis and Indians was imminent. The Lieutenant-Governor hastily despatched Charles Rouleau, the French-speaking stipendiary magistrate, and Hayter Reed, Assistant Indian Commissioner, to the scene of the expected trouble. They found that the report was grossly exaggerated, but Rouleau wrote that Riel " cannot be relied upon, he is a hot-headed individual who has nothing to lose and everything to gain . . . he can do a great deal of harm to this part of the country if the half-breed reclamation is not settled."[50] Another report upon the agitation was made by Amédée Forget, Clerk of the North-West Council. Forget accompanied Bishop Grandin to St. Laurent in September, and observed the situation carefully. He wrote that the métis were determined to protect Riel from arrest, that the clergy were rapidly losing the confidence of their people, but that, nevertheless, there appeared to be little danger of a rising. It is interesting to note that Forget considered the principal danger to the peace lay with Riel's white supporters :

" The agitation is not, at present, as noisy as in the beginning, but none the less serious, I believe. It comprises nearly all the French and English half-breeds and a number of unprincipled white settlers at Prince Albert. These latter are opponents politically of the present party in power and would delight in causing troubles that might embarrass the present Government. . . . Mr. Riel, while in conversation with me defending his conduct said, that were it not for his presence there, serious complications would already be existing, and added having received that very day a letter from a certain party in Prince Albert reproaching him with being too slow and casting suspicion upon his intentions."[51]

In December Father André renewed his efforts to bring about Riel's withdrawal from the North-West. Accompanied by D. H. MacDowall, member of the North-West Council for the District of Lorne, he interviewed Riel on the 22nd to persuade him, if possible, to quit the country. Riel admitted that he had originally intended to return to Montana, but argued that he had just claims of his own against the Canadian Government " which he hoped to press at the same time as he advocated the claims of the British half-breeds."[52] He stated that in the autumn of 1873, the Reverend J. B. Proulx had been sent by Sir John A. Macdonald to offer him $35,000 to leave the country, and that when Mackenzie came into office the same offer was renewed through Father Lacombe and Dr. Fiset of Rimouski. Mac-Dowall was convinced by this meeting that governmental action was necessary and urged upon Dewdney that to grant Riel a small indemnity in satisfaction of his claim would be the best way to conciliate the half-breeds. Riel's claims amounted to the large sum of $100,000, " but he will take $35,000," wrote MacDowall, " . . . and I believe myself that $3,000 to $5,000, would cart the whole Riel family across the border."[53] Father André's advice relative to Riel was similar :

" He has certainly certain claims against the Government and those claims must be settled in some way . . . he has much influence for good or bad with the half-breeds . . . obtain for him four or five thousand dollars and I am bold in saying Mr. Mac-Dowall and I will make him agree to any conditions."[54]

In January MacDowall again pressed upon the Government the urgency of satisfying Riel's personal claims. Writing to the Lieutenant-Governor on the 28th he stated :

" If red tape can be abolished for one month, I can tell you how to settle the whole of this half-breed row at the expense of some $6,000.   Get the Government to give you full power as commissioner and I can have all cut and dried, but I must have $5,000 for Riel, one thousand more will do for the rest."[55]

No action was taken to carry out this advice, and Louis Riel was left to use his powerful influence over the métis for good or evil as circumstances should decide.

Not only were Riel's personal claims ignored ; the petition, upon which the discontented elements of the Saskatchewan had pinned their hopes of redress, met a similar fate.   The optimistic anticipation expressed by Jackson, that the Government would yield to their threats and invite delegates from the North-West, was not borne out in fact.   As a result, the half-breeds became more exasperated than ever at Federal indifference.   On February 2nd, MacDowall telegraphed to the Lieutenant-Governor :

" Riel and leading half-breeds have been here to hear intention of Government respecting Breeds matter—great discontent at no reply to representation.   Nolin and Lépine have been compelled by Riel's supporters to withdraw tender for telegraph poles on Battleford line at great personal sacrifice. . . . I anticipate no immediate danger but urge Government to declare intention immediately."[56]

Superintendent Crozier of the Mounted Police also telegraphed, " I urge immediate action in the matter and settlement if possible."[57]   On February 6th, André reported " great indignation " on the part of the half-breeds at the Government's silence, and expressed his fears that " such excitement might easily lead them to extreme acts."[58]

These warnings fell upon deaf ears.   The utmost the Government did was to inform Dewdney on February 4th that they had decided to investigate the claims of those half-breeds who had not participated in the Manitoba scrip.   But statements such as this had been made as early as 1878, and the half-breeds, seeing no evidence to support the statement, put little faith in the Government's promise.   Their attitude was such that Dewdney wrote to Macdonald relative to Pearce's proposed visit to the North Saskatchewan : " I don't anticipate a very cordial reception for him unless he has power to go into all their grievances at the South Branch."[59]

It is not surprising, therefore, that when Louis Riel suggested to the métis that he should return to Montana, they protested, and prevailed upon him to continue to champion their rights. On February 24th Riel laid this question before the métis at Batoche. He claimed that, having completed the task for which he had been summoned to the country by drawing up and forwarding the petition to Ottawa, he desired to return to the United States. The meeting clamoured for him to remain.[60] The same proposal was put before a gathering of the English half-breeds on March 2nd, with the same result, an emphatic demonstration of personal loyalty to Riel. Following the meeting at Batoche Superintendent Crozier sent the following confidential warning to Lieutenant-Governor Dewdney :

" I have the honour to request that matters concerning the half-breeds be settled without delay—could not a surveyor be sent *now*, if it is intended to allow the half-breeds their land as they wish to have it laid out in place of the regular blocks as surveyed throughout the country.

" Then there is the question of the half-breeds being allowed scrip as granted in Manitoba. I must strongly urge that these and other matters already reported upon be attended to at once. Delay causes uneasiness and discontent which spreads not only among the half-breeds but the Indians. There are, as you well know, among the latter those who are only waiting for any opportunity, no matter how unimportant or unreasonable, they can get, to do all in their power to unsettle the working of affairs and bring a repetition of the unpleasantness of last summer, or even a condition of things worse, with its attendant evil consequences in the country.

" It would be only wise then, in face of former experience, to have all causes that may predispose to discontent or agitation removed from among the half-breeds if at all possible. If such causes were removed I anticipate but little trouble in the other quarters or in this section of the country, but if an effort is not soon made and settlement come to one way or the other, that is, either as they wish or the contrary, then it would not be surprising if the whole country were kept in a continual commotion, if not worse, during the coming spring and summer. What is required is a settlement so that there may be no misunderstanding as to the intention of the Government."[61]

Crozier's warnings might have been redoubled had he realized the mental change which had come about in Louis Riel since the

early days of the agitation. By the end of February 1885 Riel
was fully determined to hold no longer to constitutional methods.
The constitutional agitation and the petition had been an acknowledged failure, and the only possible hope of arousing the
Government's attention seemed to be in the adoption of a bold
policy. Accordingly Riel decided to follow the tactics which he
had employed in 1869 and 1870.[62]   He determined to form a
Provisional Government for the Saskatchewan, take possession
of the country and force the Canadian Government to revise the
terms of the entry of the North-West into Confederation.   It
was the scheme of a mad man, but Riel was no longer sane.   The
obsession of his " mission," the turmoil of the agitation and the
disappointment at the ineffectiveness of his political efforts,
brought on a return of the mental trouble which had sent him to
Longue Pointe and Beauport in 1876.   He suffered from
delusions of greatness, and his mind was dazzled by the memory
of his former success in Manitoba.   The methods which had
proved so successful there could not fail to work in Saskatchewan.
Riel had no intention of fighting the Dominion with arms ;   it
had not been necessary in 1869 ;   it would not be necessary in
1885.   Philip Garnot, the Secretary of the Provisional Government of 1885, stated in his evidence that the half-breeds had only
risen to force the attention of the Government to their needs,
that every day they expected that the Dominion of Canada would
send commissioners to negotiate with them.[63]   But instead of
commissioners came troops.   Riel, in his weakness, made one
great mistake ;   the situation in 1885 was vastly different from
that of 1869.   In 1869 the North-West had not belonged to
Canada, there were no military forces in the country, and Red
River was effectively isolated from Canada by the formidable
barrier of geography.   In 1885 everything had changed.   The
North-West had been transferred to Canada and was now
Canadian territory, there was a strong force of Mounted Police
in the country, and the barrier of geography, which had made the
North-West the " Great Lone Land," had been penetrated by the
Canadian Pacific Railway.

There had been rumours as early as September 1884, that
something more than constitutional action was being advocated
by the North-West party.[64]   It was not, however, until after the
failure of the petition that the movement definitely assumed an

unconstitutional character. On March 2nd, Louis Riel, in one of his constantly recurring moments of excitement, urged upon Father André the necessity of an immediate formation of a Provisional Government. Father André refused, and the matter ended in a dispute between the priest and the demagogue. On the following day a meeting was held in the English half-breed settlement of Halcro. Riel attended the meeting accompanied by sixty armed men. He stated that the police wished to arrest him, but, pointing to the men with him, declared " These are the real police."[65] Two days later Riel and Dumont interviewed Charles Nolin and informed him, " We are going to take up arms for the glory of God, the honour of religion and for the salvation of our souls."[66] They showed him a document with nine signatures attached and requested his,[67] but he refused. He urged, instead, that a Novena, nine days of special prayers, should be held in the Catholic Chapel, to learn the will of God in the matter. This proposal was discussed at Riel's house on March 6th. Napoléon Nault considered that two days of prayer should suffice, but finally Nolin's suggestion was adopted. The Novena was then fixed for March 10th, to carry on until the 19th, the celebration of the feast of St. Joseph.

It was on March 18th that Riel resolved to form a Provisional Government. The Novena was not yet completed, but Riel probably realized that the métis, as a whole, were not disposed to go to extremes, and that Nolin's influence might be sufficient to destroy the necessary unanimity of opinion among them. Therefore, following the precedent of 1869, he determined to take time by the forelock by securing hostages and immediately setting up a Provisional Council. On the same evening Riel's men made several arrests among the inhabitants of the neighbouring settlement, including among others the Indian Agent and the Farm Instructor from Beardy's and One Arrow's reserves. They had hoped to secure Inspector Gagnon of the Mounted Police, but a mistake was apparently made in his identity.[68] These arrests were carried out by a small determined minority led by Riel and Dumont. It is doubtful if the majority of the French métis had any idea as to what was happening.

On the following day, March 19th, the métis met at St. Antoine (Batoche). It was an occasion of importance. Not only was it the feast of their patron Saint, St. Joseph, but it concluded the Novena, and was to be celebrated by the baptism of W. H. Jackson into the religious faith which now inspired Louis Riel. The métis were armed ; a volley was to be fired at the conclusion of the proceedings in honour of St. Joseph. The moment was opportune for a bold action and Riel took advantage of it. With all the fire and spirit of his eloquence, which so fascinated his hearers, Riel declared to the assembled multitude that a strong force of Mounted Police were on their way to the settlement to attack the métis.[69] The métis were aware of the movement of the Mounted Police and of Crozier's efforts to raise volunteer troops at Battleford, and feared the worst. The alarm spread like a prairie fire and preparations were made for an immediate defence. Riel took prompt advantage of the panic. A Provisional Government was immediately proclaimed, Riel nominating the members and the people signifying their approval. Pierre Parenteau was elected President ; Charles Nolin, Commissaire ; Gabriel Dumont, Adjutant-General ; and Bapt. Boyer, Donald Ross, Damase Carrière, Amb. Jobin, Norbert Delorme, Moïse Ouellette, Bte. Parenteau, David Tourond, Pierre Gariepy, Maxime Lépine, Albert Monkman, Bte. Boucher, members of the Council ; and Philip Garnot, secretary. The Council chosen, one of the first acts of the newly-formed " Provisional Government of the Saskatchewan " was to place Gabriel Dumont " à la tête de l'armée " with Joseph Delorme and Patrice Tourond as his assistants.[70]

By this time Riel had definitely broken with the Roman Catholic clergy. His religious unorthodoxy had long been suspect. Even prior to his return to Canada, he had given evidence of religious peculiarities. In the Saskatchewan his proposals to change the Mass and the liturgy and to establish Archbishop Bourget as the Pope of the New World, added to the growing violence of his agitation, gained him the complete disapproval of the clergy. Finally the priests met together and decided that Riel was *non compos mentis* and therefore should not be admitted to the sacraments.[71] On March 1st, Father Fourmond preached against Riel, who replied with the accusation that " the priests are spies of the Police."[72] During the Novena Father Fourmond declared that the sacraments would be withheld from any who took up arms, a proposition which led to another dispute between Riel and the clergy. Notwithstanding the efforts of the clergy to win over the métis they continued to remain loyal to Riel.

On March 15th the clergy made a determined effort to bring about a division in the métis ranks. Charles Nolin, who had fostered the agitation in the beginning but who was not in favour of a recourse to arms, was selected to counter Riel's inflammatory agitation. Nolin met with no success. On the 19th, when the Provisional Government was formed, Riel felt strong enough to demonstrate his authority. He seized the Catholic Church as his headquarters and ordered the arrest of Nolin. Towards midnight Nolin was brought before the Council and charged with discouraging the movement to take up arms. He defended himself with vigour and accused Riel of working more for his own ends than for those of the métis. In the end he was acquitted but the counter movement had been broken, and Nolin, to save himself, promised to throw in his lot with the Provisional Government.[73]

More significant to Riel than the alienation of the clergy was the attitude of neutrality now assumed by the English half-breeds and white settlers. From the beginning Riel had been assured of their co-operation.[74] They not only contributed to the agitation which brought about Riel's return from the United States, but openly supported him and acknowledged his leadership of the new political movement on the prairies. Jackson's letter to Chapleau even implied that the English-speaking elements were only holding themselves back from more radical action. Had the Settler's Union not encouraged Riel by their attendance at his meetings, their collaboration in drawing up the petition to Ottawa, and by supplying him with money, thus misleading him into the belief that the whole of the white population of the North Saskatchewan was behind him, his actions might have been restrained and the rebellion avoided. But in spite of the fact that they had encouraged Riel politically and financially, it is questionable whether any of the whites or English half-breeds anticipated for a moment that their agitation would end in a resort to arms. They were disinclined to proceed to extremes, and although many continued to sympathize with Riel, the majority regarded desperate actions with apprehension.

With the English-speaking element hanging in the balance, both the rebels and the police made every effort to win them to their

respective sides.   Following a meeting at the Lindsay School
House on March 20th, at which a delegation had been appointed
to interview the French half-breeds, Riel addressed the following
appeal to the English half-breeds and white settlers for their
co-operation[75] :

"DEAR BROTHERS IN JESUS CHRIST :—

"The Ottawa Government has been maliciously ignoring the
rights of the original half-breeds during fifteen years.   The
petitions which have been sent to that Government on that
matter and concerning the grievances which our classes have
against its policy are not listened to : moreover, the Dominion
has taken the high handed way of answering peaceable complaints
by dispatching and reinforcing their Mounted Police.   The
avowed purpose being to confirm in the Saskatchewan their
Government spoliation and usurpation of the rights and liberties
of all classes of men, except their resident oppressors the Hudson's Bay Company and land speculators, by threatening our
liberty and our lives.   The aboriginal half-breeds are determined
to save their rights or to perish at once.   They are supported
with no doubtful energy by a large number of able half-breeds,
who have come to the Saskatchewan, less as emigrants than as
proscripts from Manitoba.   Those of the emigrants who have
been long enough in this country to realize that Ottawa does not
intend to govern the North-West so much as to plunder it, are
in sympathy with the movement.   Let us all be firm in the support of right, humane and courageous, if in him to fight, just
and equitable in our views, thus God and man will be with us,
and we will be successful.

"Dear Brothers, the Council of the French Canadian half-
breeds, now under arms at St. Anthony, and in the Saskatchewan,
have been most happy to receive your friendly communications
through your Messrs. Scott, Ross and William D. . . .

"Justice commands to take up arms."

On March 22nd another meeting of the English-speaking
settlers was held at the St. Catherine's Church.   The meeting was
instigated by Superintendent Crozier with the object of counter-
acting the influence of Riel's sympathizers among the English
half-breeds.   The meeting was undoubtedly sympathetic to
Riel,[76] and resulted in the adoption of a series of resolutions
which stated "that the members of this meeting continue to
sympathize, as they have always done, with the French half-

breeds in their desire to obtain their legal rights, by all constitutional means," but that " they do not approve of the resort to arms or the rising of the Indians, and wish to remain neutral."[77]

Riel replied with another request for assistance.[78]

" GENTLEMEN :—The Councillors of the half-breeds now under arms at St. Anthony have received your message of the 22nd of March, 1885. They thank you for the sympathy with which you honor them, even in this crisis, and of which you have given ample proof before. Situated as you are, it is difficult for you to approve immediately of our bold, but just uprising, and you have been wise in your course. Ottawa has followed with us neither the principles of right nor constitutional methods of government. They have been arbitrary in their doings. They have usurped the title of the aboriginal half-breeds to the soil, and they dispose of it at conditions contrary to equity in every manner, and which are already weighing very hard on all classes of the North-West people. They deprive their own emigrants of their franchises, of their liberties, not only political, but even civil, and as they respect no right, we are justified before God and man to arm ourselves, to try and defend our existence, rather than to see it crushed.

" As to the Indians, you know, Gentlemen, that the half-breeds have great influence over them. If the bad management of Indian affairs by the Canadian Government has been fifteen years without resulting in an outbreak, it is due only to the half-breeds who have up to this time persuaded the Indians to keep quiet. Now that we ourselves are compelled to resort to arms, how can we tell them to keep quiet ? We are sure that if the English and French half-breeds unite well in this time of crisis, not only can we control the Indians, but we will also have them weigh on our side in the balance.

" Gentlemen, please do not remain neutral. For the love of God help us to save the Saskatchewan. We sent to-day a number of men with Mr. Monkman, and help to support, as it is just, the cause of the aboriginal half-breeds. Public necessity means no offence. Let us join willingly. The aboriginal half-breeds will understand that if we do so much for their interests we are entitled to their most hearty response. We consider it an admirable act of prudence that you should have sent copies of your resolutions to the Police in Carlton and to the men of St. Anthony. If we are well united our union will cause the Police to come out of Carlton as the hen's heat causes the chicken to come out of the shell. A strong union between the French and

English half-breeds is the only guarantee that there will be no bloodshed."

On the 23rd another meeting was held at the Lindsay School House, to hear the report of the delegates. Riel had been assured that the people were prepared to join him and sent Monkman and Nolin to enrol recruits. The English half-breeds were not convinced that every constitutional measure had been exhausted, and addressed a petition to the authorities expressing their sympathy with the métis and urging " the Government to do justice to the settlers, treat with them and save the effusion of blood."[79]   Immediately following this meeting Scott sent the following letter to Riel :[80]

" At a meeting held at the Lindsay School to-night, which was largely attended, the voice of every man was with you, and we have taken steps which I think will have a tendency to stop bloodshed and hasten a treaty.   We will communicate with you inside of forty-eight hours after you get this.   Notify us of any step, if any is liable to take place."

Riel was disappointed.   The success of his plans depended upon the active assistance of those English-speaking settlers who had hitherto supported him.   In desperation Riel sent a final plea to his erstwhile adherents.

" If the police could be isolated from the people at Prince Albert, we would make them surrender easily.   I think we could keep them as hostages until you join us, without endorsing our taking up arms if you feel too much repugnance to do it ; but send us delegates to meet ours, we will discuss the conditions of our entering into confederation as a province.

" Let us unite in those interests which are common to the English and French half-breeds and to the emigrants and we will celebrate in peace and in success the 24th of May.

" But if we cannot unite, the struggle will grow.   Indians will come in from all quarters ; and many people will cross the line early this Spring ; and perhaps our difficulties will end in an American fourth of July."[81]

This last appeal, however, met with no greater response than previous appeals.   The great majority of the English half-breeds and white settlers who had participated in the political agitation held aloof from the Provisional Government, unwilling to assume the responsibilities which Riel's plans involved.

In the meantime the authorities had been taking precautions. Ever since Riel's arrival in the North-West the Mounted Police had kept a close watch upon him and his adherents. Riel's movements were the subject of numerous reports, the police headquarters being kept constantly informed as to the progress of the agitation. Moreover, during the course of the year, the numbers of the police in the North Saskatchewan District were increased from 78 to 200.[82] The force at Battleford was doubled owing to the Indian unrest and new posts were established at Frog Lake and Carlton. Crozier wrote constant warnings to the Government during 1884. He urged the advisability of redressing the half-breed grievances and the necessity of sending additional Mounted Police, " or some other force," into the Saskatchewan. " Nothing," he wrote early in July, " but seeing a large force in the country will prevent very serious trouble before long. If matters are allowed to drift, or if it is felt that no greater, or only a slight increase to the force at present here is made, I am strongly of the opinion we shall have the Manitoba difficulties of 1869 re-enacted with the addition of the Indian population as allies to the half-breeds."[83] Owing to the manifest unrest in February 1885 at the failure of the long-agitated petition, the Government seriously considered adding to their armed forces in the Territories. Commissioner Wrigley of the Hudson's Bay Company was informed at Ottawa, " that more Mounted Police were to be sent to Carlton," and that " the Government would ask for the possession of Fort Carlton for a longer time than the year for which it was leased."[84]

On March 10th the first report that Riel was definitely planning a resort to arms was forwarded from Duck Lake. On that date Inspector Gagnon sent two telegrams to the Commissioner of the N.W.M.P. The first read :[85]

" Half-breeds excited. Moving about more than usual. Preparing arms, do not know cause nor object of these preparations."

and the second :[86]

" Reported that half-breeds purpose preventing supplies coming in from 16th inst."

On the 11th Superintendent Crozier sent an alarming report from Fort Carlton :[87]

" Half-breeds greatly excited. Reported they threaten attack on Carlton before 16th.   Half-breeds refuse to take freight or employment from Government.   Will stop all freight coming into the country after 16th of this month.   Getting arms ready. Leader will not allow people to leave home as they may be required.   Origin of trouble I think because letter received stating Riel not recognized British subject.   They expect arms from the States.   Have ordered 25 men from Battleford and one gun to come here at once.   Some whites I think favourable to movement."

Dewdney was alarmed at the sudden turn which events had taken.   He privately informed Sir John A. Macdonald of the " disquieting " telegrams, and, although he considered it might possibly be " the first part of a game of bluff they are playing," he urged an increase in the force in the North Saskatchewan :

" If the half-breeds mean business the sooner they are put down the better.   They are like Indians, when they gather and get excited it is difficult to handle them, but if they are taken unawares there is little difficulty in arresting the leader."[88]

Macdonald replied that the responsibility for maintaining the peace of the Territories rested with the Lieutenant-Governor, but asked if a visit to the troubled centres by Father Lacombe or Father Hugonard would be of any value.[89]   This suggestion was not adopted, but it is doubtful whether the two priests, in spite of their influence over the métis, could have prevailed against Louis Riel.   On the 13th Crozier reported that a half-breed rebellion was " liable to break out any moment " and called for reinforcements.   Hence, on the 15th, Commissioner Irvine, at Regina, was instructed to proceed north as quickly as possible with all available men up to one hundred.

Crozier made every preparation for the trouble which he so accurately foretold.   At Battleford he organized a body of volunteers, or special constables, to defend the town and took with him to Carlton fifty men of the regular force, one gun and the arms of the disbanded Prince Albert militia.   On March 15th he proceeded to Prince Albert where he arranged with Captain Moore, a former militia officer, to sound quietly the feeling of that settlement and report if, in the event of an emergency, a volunteer force could be readily enrolled.   The association of Prince Albert with the Riel movement had caused Crozier some uneasiness, but Moore's report was favourable, and four days later Crozier appealed for assistance.   Riel had made his arrests, cut the telegraph wire and formed his Provisional Government. His men were now patrolling the country in armed bands seizing stores. The citizens of Prince Albert responded to the call. A mass meeting was held, eighty men enrolled in a volunteer corps and immediately set off to join Crozier at Fort Carlton ; others formed a home guard and stationed sentries about the town as a precaution against a surprise attack.

Crozier had no desire to precipitate hostilities. He was not yet certain of the feeling of the English half-breeds of the surrounding country, and desired to await the arrival of Colonel Irvine with reinforcements from the depot division. Therefore the next few days were occupied with last minute efforts to bring about a peaceful solution of a very critical problem.

On March 18th, Hillyard Mitchell, a trader at Duck Lake, interviewed Riel. He was a recognized friend of the half-breeds and told them " I have come over here as a friend . . . not as a spy, but to give you all some good advice. For God's sake don't go any further. It's going to be something terrible if you go on with this."[90] Riel replied with a long account of the métis grievances and declared that he " would bring Sir John Macdonald down at his feet yet." Mitchell tried to reason with him, but without success. Mitchell, however, wrote to Crozier to make no move :

" In my opinion there is no cause for alarm as long as these fellows are not interfered with, but the presence of a few Police just now would have the same effect as waving a red flag at an enraged bull, and I am afraid would cause trouble with the Indians who so far (except a few) have kept aloof."[91]

On the 20th Mitchell again saw Riel and the métis council. His arguments were fruitless. Riel was determined to capture the police, and told Mitchell, " If we take Fort Carlton we will be able to bring the Government to terms and get our rights."[92] He was, however, willing to meet Crozier or Gagnon and to discuss the situation with them. Mitchell therefore returned to Carlton, made his report to Crozier, and set out again for the rebel headquarters accompanied by a Scotch half-breed, Thomas McKay. At Duck Lake they met two French half-breeds bearing a letter from W. H. Jackson, who expressed himself as neutral but desirous of bringing about a pacific understanding between the " participators of the present movement " and

M

"Inspector Crozier as representing the Canadian Government." His terms were hardly a basis for compromise :

"I must state that the only understanding possible between Major Crozier and the leaders of the movement is the prevention of bloodshed by an immediate surrender."[93]

Ignoring this letter Mitchell and McKay continued on their way to Batoche. On meeting McKay, Riel became violent. He accused the English-speaking half-breed of being a traitor and threatened that if hostilities should break out, his would be the first blood shed. Riel then dictated his reply to Crozier's mission :[94]

"MAJOR :—The Councillors of the Provisional Government of the Saskatchewan have the honor to communicate to you the following conditions of surrender :—You will be required to give up completely the situation which the Canadian Government have placed you in, at Carlton and Battleford, together with all Government properties.

"In case of acceptance, you and your men will be set free, on your parole of honor to keep the peace. And those who will choose to leave the country will be furnished with teams and provisions to reach Qu'Appelle.

"In case of non-acceptance, we intend to attack you, when to-morrow, the Lord's Day, is over ; and to commence without delay a war of extermination upon all those who have shown themselves hostile to our rights. Messrs. Charles Nolin and Maxime Lépine are the gentlemen with whom you will have to treat.

"Major, we respect you. Let the cause of humanity be a consolation to you for the reverses which the governmental misconduct has brought upon you."

A postscript added :

"To MESSRS. CHARLES NOLIN and MAXIME LÉPINE.

"GENTLEMEN :—If Major Crozier accedes to the conditions of surrender, let him use the following formula, and no other : 'Because I love my neighbour as myself, for the sake of God, and to prevent bloodshed, and principally the war of extermination which threatens the country, I agree to the above conditions of surrender.' If the Major uses this formula and signs it, inform him that we will receive him and his men, Monday.

"Yours,

"LOUIS 'DAVID' RIEL,

"Exovede."

It is possible that had Crozier's force surrendered in accordance with this demand, he and his men would have suffered the fate of the Portage party in 1870, arrest and imprisonment as hostages. But Crozier was not the man to be intimidated by a threat. McKay and Captain Moore met Nolin and Lépine and replied to Riel's terms with the demand that the leaders and instigators of the rebellion should be delivered up to the police ; this done an amnesty would be granted to the rank and file of the métis.

Thus the matter rested until the morning of March 26th. Riel had not attacked. He was still far from his " war of extermination " and his own situation, in view of the defection of the English half-breeds and the approach of Colonel Irvine, was daily becoming more impossible. The police had refused to walk into his trap, and the possibility of repeating the success of 1870 was rapidly disappearing. On the 26th, however, circumstances almost gave Riel the opportunity which he was awaiting. On that day Crozier despatched a small party, under Thomas McKay and Sergeant Stewart, to secure a quantity of provisions and ammunition which were stored at Mitchell's trading establishment at Duck Lake. About three miles from Duck Lake they were stopped by Dumont and a band of mounted métis. The rebels " behaved in a very overbearing and excited manner," and Dumont demanded the surrender of the party. McKay refused. The métis endeavoured to provoke the police party into firing and a few Indians present jeered and shouted, " If you are men, now come on." Nevertheless the police refused to be drawn into unequal combat. The métis were afraid to press the engagement and the police retired to Fort Carlton.[95]

Crozier was thus placed upon the horns of a dilemma. To remain at Fort Carlton would mean the acquisition by the rebels of much needed supplies and ammunition, and a fall in the prestige of the Mounted Police among the wavering Indian tribes. To risk an encounter at possibly unfavourable odds when Colonel Irvine was only a few hours distant was equally inadvisable. Crozier did not hesitate to take the bolder course. His men were eager for " the picnic " as it was termed, and unwarranted insinuations of cowardice roused his Irish blood.[96] Moreover, Crozier fully believed that the few hours were " of vital importance."[97] Hence, with an impetuous nature fortified by a reasonable excuse he gave the order to sound the " Boots and Saddles."   Preparations were quickly made and Superintendent Crozier with " Inspector Howe, Surgeon Miller, 53 non-commissioned officers and men (N.W.M.P.) with one 7-pounder gun, Captains Moore and Morton, and 41 Prince Albert Volunteers,"[98] marched out of Carlton on Thursday, March 26th, to assert the authority of the Dominion of Canada in the North Saskatchewan valley.

CHAPTER XV

GABRIEL DUMONT and his men returned to Duck Lake after their meeting with McKay's party ; but scarcely had they dismounted when the cry " Voilà la Police " was heard. Springing to their saddles Dumont and twenty-five horsemen dashed forward, followed more slowly by a number of men on foot, to meet the force which Crozier was leading through the crusted snow.

The two forces met at a point about a mile and a half from Duck Lake. From the half-breed point of view the position was decidedly favourable. Crozier's line of march was commanded from two angles. Across the road extended three elevations of land separated from each other by dips of varying degrees of steepness. On the one side the hollow behind the centre elevation extended to the left of the road and then bent around running parallel in the same direction. On the other side a small ravine offered a natural cover for a flanking force. In addition ample shelter was afforded by thick clumps of brush and willow.

As Crozier's party advanced, they were unaware of the position of the métis until they had descended the first hill and were within one hundred and fifty yards of the second. The advance scouts gave the first warning as they galloped back closely pursued by the half-breeds, and Crozier immediately gave the order to halt. At that moment an Indian accompanied by Isidore Dumont, Gabriel's brother, approached waving a white blanket. Croziei, believing that the half-breed wished to hold a parley, advanced with his interpreter to meet them. In the meantime, the small force of half-breeds, which had been joined by a few Indians from the neighbouring reserves of Beardy and One Arrow, extended under cover of the trees and high ground to outflank the Government force. At the same time the Mounted Police constructed a barricade across the road with their sleighs, withdrew their horses to the rear, and prepared for hostilities. As the parley began the Indian seized the interpreter's rifle. A short hand to hand struggle ensued. Crozier, who had watched with apprehension the movements of the half-breeds upon his flank, became convinced that the parley was merely an excuse to place him in an impossible position, and gave the order to "Fire away, boys!"[1] Isidore Dumont and the Indian who had advanced to parley were immediately shot and the firing became general.

On the right the rebels had taken possession of a log house, which, partly obscured from view by the banks of snow and brushwood, was an excellent point of vantage. From it they poured a hot fire upon the Prince Albert Volunteers who had extended their formation to the right and were without cover of any description. To relieve the pressure upon that flank, Crozier ordered the cannon to be directed upon the brush, but, owing to the position of the volunteers, this was impossible.[2] The gun was accordingly trained upon another section of the field, but with little result, the shots "flying far over the enemies' heads."[3] To make matters worse, after several discharges a shell was rammed home before the powder charge was inserted, which rendered the cannon useless for the remainder of the engagement.

Finally, after thirty or forty minutes, Crozier, recognizing the inevitable, gave the order to retire. His position was untenable. The half-breeds had all the advantage of position and, Crozier believed, of numbers.[4] The casualties in the small Government force had been heavy. Ten men lay dead upon the field; two more were at the point of death and eleven had been wounded. All but surrounded, exposed to the fire of an enemy they could not see, and with five of their transport horses killed or disabled, retreat was the only sensible move. Under fire the remaining horses were brought to the sleighs. Confusion reigned everywhere; nevertheless the retreat was effected. The métis were anxious to complete the rout of their enemies, but Riel, who had viewed the battle armed only with a crucifix, declared, "Pour l'amour de Dieu de ne plus en tuer . . . il y a déjà trop de sang répandu."[5] Accordingly the shattered column, thus saved from annihilation, slowly made its way back to Fort Carlton, leaving behind nine of their dead and a trail of blood-sodden snow.

Crozier's defeat was a great shock to Colonel Irvine who arrived at Fort Carlton with 108 men shortly after the defeated column returned to the Fort. He had covered the distance between Regina and Carlton, over three hundred miles through the heart of the enemy country, in eight days, and had informed Crozier from Prince Albert of his approach. A few hours' delay upon Crozier's part would have meant all the difference between victory and defeat. " I cannot but consider it a matter of regret," wrote Colonel Irvine in his official report, " that with the knowledge that both myself and command were within a few miles of and *en route* to Carlton, Superintendent Crozier should have marched out as he did, particularly in the face of what had transpired earlier in the day. I am led to the belief that this officer's better judgment was overruled by the impetuosity displayed by both the police and volunteers."[6]

The question which now demanded Colonel Irvine's attention was the defence of Fort Carlton. The fort had been built for trading purposes and as a military post was quite indefensible. Immediately behind the fort was a bank three hundred feet high, which commanded everything in the square of the fort from two sides. The slope of the hill was thinly covered with scrub brush and on the top at the south side with heavy timber. Moreover, the line of retreat passed through a country which provided ample opportunity for an enemy ambush. To make matters more difficult, the ground was still covered with snow, and progress could only be made by proceeding in file.

The Volunteers were anxious to return to Prince Albert. With a number of its men and nearly all its arms at Carlton, the settlement was defenceless. Irvine, too, was in favour of the evacuation of Fort Carlton. Prince Albert was the strategical centre of the Territory of Saskatchewan, while Carlton was of little importance, either from the point of view of situation or supplies. Moreover, Prince Albert, surrounded as it was by the English half-breed settlements of St. Catherine's, Red Deer Hill and Halcro, which had been centres of the Riel agitation during 1884, was believed to be in danger of attack from the victory-flushed rebels. To discuss this question, Colonel Irvine called a council of the commissioned officers of the Police and Volunteers. The decision was unanimous in favour of evacuation and the destruction of such stores as could not be taken away.[7]

The evacuation was carried out during the night of the 27th and the morning of the 28th. Every available vehicle was loaded with goods. Those supplies which could not be taken were sunk beneath the ice in the river or emptied into the snow. While these preparations were in progress a fire broke out in the quarter occupied by the non-commissioned officers, some hay used in making mattresses for the wounded men having been scattered in too close proximity to the stove. The fire spread with great rapidity, and after the first few moments, no effort was made to extinguish it. This fire, of course, destroyed the secrecy of the evacuation, which was pushed forward with all possible speed. By 4 a.m. the last sleigh had left Carlton. They drove half-way before stopping to water the horses, and then, without waiting to feed them, pushed on to Prince Albert, where they arrived about eight o'clock in the evening.[8] The evacuation was thus speedily and effectively carried out; but it must be admitted that, had the métis attacked under cover of the darkness and during the confusion of the fire, nothing could have saved the police column from annihilation.

At Prince Albert Irvine's force was received with expressions of relief and welcome. Wild rumours had been circulating throughout the settlement, and the fear of an Indian or half-breed attack had caused great alarm. Following the news of Riel's victory at Duck Lake, no time was lost in putting Prince Albert into a position to withstand attack. A stockade was erected around the Presbyterian Church and the nearby buildings, into which the people from the surrounding countryside were packed. Father André in his daily journal gives an interesting account of the situation.

"C'était une confusion et un encombrement dont il serait difficile de se faire une idée. L'Evêque anglais était là avec sa famille et ses ministres et le danger rapprochant les coeurs, l'union et l'accord régnaient parmi tous les membres des diverses religions. L'Evêque anglais me pressait affectueusement les mains et me remerciait avec émotion, cet après-midi, de l'intérêt que je lui avais témoigné dans ses anxiétés. Voilà deux nuits que nous n'avons pas dormi. Nous nous attendions à être attaqués à chaque moment par Riel et ses alliés, les sauvages."[9]

The arrival of Irvine's force inspired the settlers with confidence, and many returned to their homes outside the improvised walls. Nevertheless, on the first rumour of the approach of the enemy, the whole settlement was thrown into a panic. Nothing was too wild to be credited as truth. The following incident, related by

André, is vivid testimony of the fears which pervaded the whole of the North Saskatchewan as a result of the métis rising.

" On a renoncé à se refugier de nouveau au fort. Nous étions assis tranquillement, Ambroise Fisher, Damase, mon jeune homme et moi, et nous nous réjouissions ensemble de nous voir sortis de cette situation critique, lorsqu'en regardant par la fenêtre, je vois un cavalier et une bande de chevaux se précipi-tant comme poursuivis par l'ennemi. Je sors pour demander la cause de ce mouvement ; les hommes arrivent pâles et les yeux hagards et passant devant moi ils me crient : ' Come on ! they are coming, the French and the Indians ! ' Aussitôt de dehors je crie aux Soeurs de sortir au plus vite et de se sauver car l'ennemi arrive. Les pauvres Soeurs étaient au lit, et pendant qu'elles s'habillaient je courus vers le fort pour chercher un wagon. J'arrive hors d'haleine au fort où déjà M. Clarke commande un wagon pour elles. Le plus grand désordre et la plus grande confusion régnaient dans la ville. Les familles, tout éplorées et affolées de terreur, sortaient de leurs maisons. Ce n'étaient partout que des cris de terreur et de désespoir. J'attendais les Soeurs ; elles arrivent à moitié habillées et tremblantes de peur. Il est difficile de tracer une peinture exacte du spectacle que nous avions sous les yeux : les hommes commes les femmes étaient dans les transes et s'attendaient à voir les sauvages et les métis fondre sur nous pour nous égorger et mettre tout à feu et à sang ... peu à peu les esprits se réassurèrent en voyant que l'ennemi ne paraissait pas ; mais quelle terrible nuit les femmes passèrent dans le fort, pressées et serrées qu'elles étaient les unes contre les autres ! Sous l'influence de la chaleur et de la peur les mal-heureuses tombaient sans connaissance, plusieurs furent sérieusement malades, cinq femmes accouchèrent ; les Soeurs me racontant le lendemain les impressions de cette nuit horrible me disaient qu'il s'était passé des scènes déchirantes. . . . Ce dimanche il n'y eut aucun service public dans aucune église à Prince Albert. On était trop fatigué pour prendre part aux offices."[10]

Thus in the space of three days and with the loss of only five men [11] the métis had defeated the Mounted Police in a pitched battle, captured what remained of Fort Carlton and its supplies after its evacuation, completed the destruction of the fort[12] and forced the terror-stricken whites to seek shelter behind the improvised stockade at Prince Albert.

Nevertheless Riel's plans had not met with complete success.

He had hoped to forestall actual hostilities by capturing Crozier's whole force and holding them as hostages. It was with this purpose that the half-breeds had surrounded Crozier at Duck Lake while engaging him in a parley. Riel's plan was defeated by the fact that Crozier observed the métis' movements and ordered his men to open fire. Evidence that such was Riel's intention is afforded by his statement to Captain George Young after Batoche. Riel declared "that his object had been to capture Major Crozier and his force and then say to the Canadian Government, consider the situation. As he was attempting to surround Crozier, Crozier fired, he then said, in the name of God the Father who made us reply to that, and his men fired."[13] The fact was that Riel was drawing too largely upon his experience in 1870, and thought that with Crozier and his men prisoners he could force the Canadian Government to negotiate with the insurrectionists. Garnot, the Secretary of the Provisional Government, agreed at the trial of White Cap that there had been no "serious expectation that they would be able to drive the Dominion Government out of the country," but that they rose to "force the Dominion Government to attend to them" and expected daily that "some one would come from the Government and treat with them."[14]

The métis were in no position to conduct a successful rebellion. At the most Riel could only call upon four or five hundred métis, many of whom were definitely opposed to fighting and took up arms only under pressure. Moreover, they were poorly armed, and smooth bore shot-guns were no match for service rifles. Supplies, too, were insufficient and ammunition was scarce. Riel was not blind to these disadvantages but staked his all upon the coup which he had planned. Thus Duck Lake, while a tactical success was, from Riel's point of view, a strategical failure.

The immediate effect of the métis victory was to bring the Indians into the rebellion. No better occasion for a native outbreak could have been selected by Riel than the early spring. The winter had been severe, and in any event the Indians were always in a more desperate condition in the spring than at other times. This was the season when the Agency supplies were most likely to fall short and the uncongenial spring work was about to begin. Moreover, the Indians were in an ugly mood owing to the indifference displayed by the Government towards the petition which they had put forward on the occasion of Big Bear's council in August.

As we have noted earlier, the Indians had taken advantage of Riel's presence, as early as July and August 1884, to consult him upon their grievances. His advice had been moderate in character and the Indians had proceeded by constitutional methods to place their demands before the Federal Government. Thenceforward they continued to look to Riel for guidance. In January 1885 Crozier wrote confidentially to the Indian Commissioner that many of the Indian bands were prepared to follow Riel's leadership :

" Some of the half-breeds report that the Indians are quite in accord with them, even the Sioux, and will act at any time and manner they wish. I do not, however, believe that there is universally with the Indians such an understanding, though there are undoubtedly bands and individuals among other bands who look to Riel and the half-breeds as their champions, and who, I think, have promised to join or act with them as they bid, and the greater the chances may be of the half-breeds and malcontent Indians accomplishing whatever object they have in view so many Indians proportionately would join them."[15]

Throughout the spring of 1885 Riel was in constant touch with the Indians of the North-West, and his runners were despatched to every reserve. The Indians placed implicit confidence in the métis chief, so much so that one Indian, Antoine Lose Brave, wrote to Riel stating that his son was at the Mission School at Qu'Appelle and asked " I want you to tell me, if I done good or wrong, and if I done wrong I will go and him out (sic)." The letter also gave a list of the Crooked Lakes, Qu'Appelle, File Hills and Touchwood chiefs who denied that they had ever made " a bargin by the white skin folks " for their country, and asked " now we want from you to open us thouroly or make us clear understand to us which way you are going to commence at present, because we want to let them understand all our Kine Tribe, and therefore we want to open us everything what is going to be after this."[16] Typical of the means used by Riel to incite the Indians were those employed by his runners among the Battleford Crees and Stonies. William Lightfoot, a Cree of Red Pheasant's band, stated that Trottier and another half-breed came to the reserve with tobacco from Riel and Dumont, and declared that those Indians who would not join them would be forced to do so.   They told Red Pheasant that Riel was a god and was in communication with heaven.[17]   The same emissaries informed the Indians on the Stoney reserves that Riel " said if we smoked the tobacco he wanted us to join him, that he had lots of soldiers and if we did not join him he would send them after us, that the Americans were going to help him."[18]   On another occasion Riel wrote to the métis of Battle River and Fort Pitt instructing them to " rouse up the Indians.   Do what you can to put the Police of Fort Pitt and Fort Battle in an impossible position."[19]

As a result of their own grievances and these incitements the Indians were wrought to a dangerous pitch of excitement.   Into this electric atmosphere came the shock of the victory of the half-breeds and the Indians at Duck Lake.   The police had been defeated in battle !   Upon several occasions during 1884 the Indians had been upon the point of rebellion ;   only their fear of the white men's power had restrained them.   This fear was now removed and the exciting news spread like a quick grass-fire across the prairie.   Scarcely more than twenty-four hours elapsed before the Indians at Frog Lake, two hundred miles from the scene of the battle, were aware of the result.   From one end of the North-West to the other the possibility of an Indian rising was imminent.

One of the principal points in danger was the town of Battle-ford.   Situated in close proximity to the disaffected bands of Poundmaker, Little Pine, Red Pheasant and the Stonies, it was an obvious point of attack.   That Riel urged the Indians to assault the fort is shown by the following letter :[20]

" DEAR BRETHREN AND KINSMEN—Since we wrote to you many important things have taken place.   The Police came to attack us.   We met them and God gave us the victory.   Thirty métis and five Indians sustained the combat against one hundred and twenty men, who, after thirty-five or forty minutes' fighting, took flight.   Praise God with us for the success He has granted us.   Arise.   Face the enemy.   If you can take Fort Battle, destroy it.   Save all the merchandise and provisions, and come and join us.   Your number will probably permit you to send us a detachment of forty or fifty men.   Whatever you do, do for the love of God.   Under the protection of Jesus Christ, the

Blessed Virgin, St. Joseph and St. John the Baptist, and be certain that faith works wonders.

" LOUIS ' DAVID ' RIEL, Exovede."

On March 27th, following the repulse of the whites at Duck Lake, vague rumours began to float about of impending trouble and that there was likely to be a rising of the Indians,[21] and on the following day word was received at Battleford that the Indians of Poundmaker, Strike-Him-on-the-Back and Little Pine were on their way to make demands upon the Indian Agent. Great excitement prevailed in the town. In spite of the fact that the local magistrate considered " the Riel business " would prove to be only " a bit of political bluster,"[22] many of the settlers abandoned the unprotected town and sought shelter behind the walls of the Mounted Police barracks upon the north side of the Battle River. On the 29th the Indians camped about seven miles from the town, having brought with them only a sufficient number of squaws to do camp drudgery—a significant indication as to their hostile intent. That evening the remainder of the citizens took refuge in the fort. During the night a few of the Indians raided several of the abandoned farms and houses, and on the following day two hundred savages belonging to the bands of Poundmaker and Little Pine arrived at Battleford " all armed and in war paint."[23]

Indian Agent Rae agreed to meet the Indians half way between the barracks and their camp, but, as he and the Farm Instructor approached, they were fired upon.[24] Rae then returned to the fort, while the Indians made known their demands to William McKay, an officer of the Hudson's Bay Company. They expressed a willingness to return to their reserves if their demands for clothing, sugar, tobacco, powder and shot were complied with. Rae immediately telegraphed to Dewdney urging that he be given " full authority to deal with them as we are not in a position at present to begin an Indian war . . . Answer at once as answer must be given to-night."[25] Dewdney immediately replied :

" You have full authority to deal with Indians. Use discretion and ask Poundmaker to meet me Swift Current with copy of any arrangements you make. He can bring a couple of his best Indians with him. His expenses will be paid and I guarantee his safety."[26]

This overture came too late. The Indians, their cupidity

aroused by the unprotected stores, had broken into and pillaged the Hudson's Bay Company and the other buildings in the town.[27]

On the following day the Stonies of the Eagle Hills joined Poundmaker before Battleford. The latter, probably, had not contemplated anything more than a show of arms to force concessions from the Department; but the Stonies, who had already murdered their Farm Instructor and a white settler, set up a "soldiers' lodge" over which the civil chief exercised little authority. No assault was, however, attempted against the fortified barracks. The Indians were not accustomed to that mode of warfare and were content to play a waiting game. As a result they concentrated on Poundmaker's reserve, while small war parties prowled about the neighbourhood of the town to ambush patrols from the fort. From the end of March until the relief of Battleford by Colonel Otter late in April, the Indians were practically in possession of the town, and the police and settlers to the number of five hundred were besieged in the barracks.[28]

The most serious situation arose at Frog Lake, a small hamlet situated about thirty miles from Fort Pitt. It had been established in 1883 as a trading post and was at this time not only the centre of a Roman Catholic mission, but also a sub-agency of the Indian Department. Here, in the neighbourhood of a Wood Cree reserve, Big Bear passed the winter of 1884–5.

Big Bear's band was in a wretched condition, destitute of both food and clothing. Even their horses were suffering, and in February the Indian Agent reported that they had only twenty miserable animals which were rapidly dying.[29] No game was to be found at Frog Lake, and to satisfy the barest needs of existence the Indians were compelled to submit to the Government's dictum of "no work no food." Hence, in January 1885 Inspector Dickens wrote to the Officer commanding at Battleford :

"I have the honour to report that Big Bear's Indians are working being engaged in drawing logs, cutting wood, etc. As long as they work they will receive rations, all quiet at present."[30] In view of their wretched condition and the scarcity of game, it was indeed an ominous sign that the Indians had for some time past been buying ammunition. This did not pass without notice from the Mounted Police. After arresting a half-breed for selling ammunition without a Government permit, Sergeant

Martin at Fort Pitt notified Inspector Dickens that Big Bear's band "had a large quantity of fixed ammunition in their possession," and declared his opinion that "considering the unsettled state in which this band is at present, it would be advisable not to sell or to allow them to obtain so much ammunition, as I believe it to be dangerous to the public peace for them to have such large quantities in their possession."[31] Inspector Dickens added his word of warning in a report to Superintendent Crozier :

"This ammunition has not been used for hunting as there has been no big game killed near Frog Lake this winter. The cartridges have been hoarded by the Indians and are still in their possession. These Indians do not require fixed ammunition ; powder and shot are all that they want for killing rabbits and ducks in the spring ; and considering the untrustworthy and fickle character of these Indians I think that the issue of these permits should at once be put a stop to."[32]

This recommendation had been voiced as early as the spring of 1884 after the Crooked Lakes affair, but it was not until late in February 1885 that the Government realized the urgency of these solicitations and printed two hundred copies of a proclamation forbidding the sale of fixed ammunition or improved weapons to the Indians. These were forwarded to Commissioner Dewdney, who distributed them throughout Treaty 6 early in March. But, like Macdonald's proposal to the Indians in 1882 to exchange their rifles for fowling pieces, the proclamation was ignored.

Notwithstanding his warlike preparations, Big Bear finally capitulated to the Government's ultimatum. In February he definitely promised Indian Agent Quinn that he would take his reserve in the spring. Quinn attributed this change of front to the fact that "ever since I offered to let Indians from his band join other bands in the District they are stirring themselves about a reserve. The chief asked me not to try to break up his band by allowing them to join other bands because I (sic) will go on a reserve."[33] On March 18th the site was chosen at Dog Rump Creek, but Big Bear, still loth to abandon his former freedom, expressed his intention of seeing the Commissioner once more before settling down. The outbreak of the half-breed rebellion, however, took the control of events from Big Bear and thrust it into the hands of the extremists.

Throughout the winter, Big Bear's authority over his band had been diminishing. The old chief had consistently striven to better the lot of his people by peaceful methods, fully realizing that the Indians had nothing to gain and all to lose by fighting the white man ; but, unfortunately, at this critical moment, his authority, never more than influential, was undermined by the activities of Wandering Spirit, the war chief, Little Poplar, an Indian agitator, and Imasees, Big Bear's eldest son.[34] Riel's agents had been at work among these Indians, and, when the news of the métis rising was received, the wilder spirits among them, led by the war chief, were ready to take any action. To make matters worse, Big Bear, who alone might have exercised any moderating influence over his men, was absent on a hunting trip during the critical days of the latter part of March, and the more turbulent element held full sway.

On March 28th Big Bear's Indians were decidedly restless and engaged in a council with the Wood Crees. W. B. Cameron, the Hudson's Bay Company agent at Frog Lake, observed the meeting and was apprehensive of its meaning :

" The talk was of ' news.' Wandering Spirit, the war chief, rose and spoke earnestly in his low, impassioned voice and with that transfixing look in his dark eyes that I have never seen in those of any other Indian. Then he drew his shirt over his head and presented it to Longfellow, brother to a Wood Cree chief. Longfellow followed, and he in turn handed his shirt to Wandering Spirit. And all the while the camulet of compact continued to pass from mouth to mouth around the circle. Big Bear's band, it was evident, was making proposals of some kind to the Wood Crees. . . . As I walked home . . . I had a premonition of evil days at hand and I felt uneasy and depressed."[35]

The " news " which had excited the Indians reached the white population at Frog Lake on March 30th. On that day Inspector Dickens at Fort Pitt received word from the Indian Agent at Battleford that the country was in a state of rebellion, with the request that every effort should be made to prevent Big Bear's Indians from joining Poundmaker. Inspector Dickens at once informed Indian Agent Quinn at Frog Lake of the situation and advised him to come to Fort Pitt at once " if he considered that there was serious danger." Quinn replied that the Indians were " perfectly quiet," and that " he felt perfectly confident that he could keep them at Frog Lake by feeding them well and treating

IMASEES

them kindly."[36] Nevertheless, it was deemed advisable by the whites at Frog Lake to dispense with the small Mounted Police detachment at that post as their numbers were too few to be any protection in the event of an outbreak and their presence only tended to exasperate the Indians.[37] The police were despatched from Frog Lake to Fort Pitt on March 31st. The following day passed without any hint of future disturbance : but the attempt of Imasees to murder the Indian Agent during the night[38] was an ominous portent of what was to follow.

On the morning of April 2nd the Indians appeared in full war paint, having forestalled any possibility of escape or resistance on the part of the white people by the removal of their horses and rifles. At the Hudson's Bay Company shop a number of Indians demanded ammunition. Cameron asked them for the required permit from the Agent, but received instead the reply, " This is no time for idle talk ! If you don't give it to us we'll break the shop open and take it." The Indians then proceeded to take complete possession of the village and ordered the whites to proceed to the Indian encampment as prisoners. Quinn, the Agent, refused. Whereupon Wandering Spirit, addressing him in an insolent tone, shouted, " Kapwatamut, you have a hard head. You boast that when you say no you mean no. To-day, if you love your life, you will do as I tell you. Go to our camp." Quinn again refused. Wandering Spirit repeated the order. " My place is here," Quinn replied, " Big Bear has not asked me to leave. I will not go." The war chief then raised his rifle, "I tell you—go!" he shouted, and fired point blank at the Agent.[39] This was the signal for an outbreak of shooting, Wandering Spirit shouting to the Indians to kill all the whites. Big Bear, hearing the crack of the rifles, rushed upon the scene, shouting " Tesqua ! Tesqua ! (Stop ! Stop !) " It was too late ; the smouldering embers of racial hatred had burst into flame and a general massacre was but the work of a few moments. The Indian Agent, the Farm Instructor, two priests and five others including a French half-breed, were shot down in cold blood. Only Cameron of the Hudson's Bay Company and two women escaped death, to be taken prisoners by the Indians. Another white man, Henry Quinn, having been warned by a friendly Indian only a few minutes before the shooting, escaped to carry the news of the tragedy to Fort Pitt.

Throughout the winter Inspector Dickens at Fort Pitt had been aware of the unrest and uneasiness prevalent among the Indians, but was scarcely prepared for an Indian rising. In the middle of February he wrote to Crozier assuring him that such a contingency was extremely unlikely. " It is evident," the letter read, " that these Indians have no intention at present of committing any hostile act. In the summer when their horses are fat and the lakes are covered with ducks, they may give trouble on some of the reserves as they did last year."[40]   On March 20th, however, W. J. McLean of the Hudson's Bay Company intimated to Dickens that the situation on the reserves was becoming very grave indeed. He urged that all the Government employees and white people should be ordered to take refuge in the fort. Dickens and Quinn treated the matter lightly, remarking that the Indians were no more aggressive than in previous years.[41] The news of Duck Lake and the Indian rising at Battleford and on the South Branch of the Saskatchewan quickly aroused the people to a sense of their dangerous position. Dickens hastily warned the whites in the neighbourhood and posted extra guards about the fort. On March 31st the police detachment from Frog Lake arrived, and on April 2nd, the date of the massacre, rumours were prevalent, " about something having happened at Frog Lake."[42]   Early on the morning of the 3rd, the Farm Instructor and his wife, from the Onion Lake reserve in the immediate vicinity, reached Fort Pitt, having been warned by friendly natives " that Big Bear's Indians were close at hand." They brought " the dreadful news that the Indians were up in arms, and had massacred all the white people at Frog Lake and that it would be only a matter of a few hours until they would be upon us ; "[43] news which was fully confirmed by the arrival of Henry Quinn a few hours later.

The inhabitants of the fort, civil and military, immediately set to work to strengthen their defences. The windows and doors were barricaded with sacks of flour, of which there was a large quantity in the fort. Outlying buildings, which might possibly afford shelter to the Indians, were torn down. Every available civilian was sworn in as a special constable, and even the women took their turn at sentry duty. In spite of these efforts the position of the fort was, from the point of view of undergoing a siege, a weak one. Battleford was already beleagured, and little assistance could be hoped for from that quarter. The fort itself stood four hundred yards from its water supply, which was fully exposed to the enemy. Food supplies were abundant, but ammunition was short, only sufficient to distribute forty rounds to each Mounted Policeman and eighteen rounds to every civilian. Moreover, the total population of the fort numbered only about seventy, twenty-four of whom formed the police garrison. The defenders had no illusions as to their ability to withstand a siege; if anything, they underestimated their strength. Thus, recognizing that retreat might become necessary, the defenders began the construction of a large scow on April 11th.[44] During the ten days following the news of the massacre of Frog Lake the inhabitants of Fort Pitt went about their tasks " in constant fear of being attacked at any moment."[45]

On April 7th Little Poplar and nine teepees arrived from Battleford. Their appearance was not of a hostile character, but the police, mistrustful of their pacific professions, ordered them not to cross the river towards the fort or they would be fired upon. The Indians remained quiet, and it was not until the 13th that Big Bear and his men arrived from Frog Lake.[46] On the morning of that day, Dickens, who had been without news of Big Bear's whereabouts for ten days, despatched three police scouts to locate the Indians. McLean and others protested against this action, the former pessimistically prophesying that " the Indians would add three horses and as many rifles and revolvers with a quantity of fixed ammunition to their strength whilst we would be weakened to that extent, besides the almost certainty of the loss of three men."[47] McLean's words proved to be correct. Scarcely had the scouts disappeared by one road than Big Bear's band, numbering about 250, appeared by another.

On their arrival at Fort Pitt the Indians peremptorily demanded that the police surrender their arms and ammunition and give up the fort. Dickens refused, but considered it advisable to placate their tempers by acceding to their demands for tea, tobacco, clothing and kettles. A blanket was also sent to Big Bear who had declared that " he was very cold." The Indians, believing that an assault upon the fort might prove too costly, thereupon adopted fresh tactics. Towards evening three of the leading Indians sent a message to McLean who went out to parley with them. At the same time Little Poplar, who had remained upon the opposite bank since the 7th, crossed over the river, ostensibly to assist McLean.[48]   The result of the parley was an agreement upon the part of McLean to resume the parley the following day, the Indians undertaking not to attack the fort during the night.   On returning to the fort, McLean discussed the question with Dickens and others, and with their approval,[49] went out to continue the negotiations with the Indians on the following day. The Indians reiterated the usual grievances, grievances which were, unfortunately, only too real to them.   McLean described the parley as follows :

" Their chief spokesman was then directed to come forward and speak.   He commenced by telling me that they were all very much dissatisfied with their conditions since the Government had taken them in hand, and, that owing to the changes that were going on in the country, they regarded their own future and that of their children with great alarm.   He referred to the extermination of the buffalo that they relied so much upon for their support and that the influx of white men would lead to the extermination of many other animals and fish which helped them to live.   He said that the Government had made many promises to them, which were not productive of any good, and that instead of their conditions improving they were becoming worse every year since the Government people came into the country, and, very much excited, he said that they had now arrived at a determination to drive the Government and the white people out of the country, and for which they would get plenty of help as there were twenty ox trains loaded with rifles and ammunition with ten thousand Americans to join them, and they also had all the half-breeds to fight with them.   Continuing he said that they did not want to drive the Hudson's Bay Company people away, as they and their forefathers before them had been receiving many useful supplies and help from the Company and their people, and they did not want them to leave the country under any circumstances. . . . He was frequently applauded during the harangue."[50]

McLean pointed out to them that " any endeavour on your part to drive the Government and the peaceable white men out of the country is not only a hopeless but a most dangerous undertaking for you to attempt," but Wandering Spirit was in no mood to listen to advice.   Loading his gun as he spoke, the war chief replied, " You have spoken enough.   We are in a hurry . . . you have said too much about the Government, we do not want to hear anything about him. . . . We are tired of him and of all his people and we are now going to drive them out of our country."

At this moment the police scouts, who had been despatched the previous day, returning, suddenly came upon the Indian encampment. The Indians at once gave chase. One scout was killed, another wounded, but the third managed to escape, only to fall into the hands of the Indians the following day. McLean attempted to reach Fort Pitt during the *mêlée*, but was prevented from doing so by the Indians, who not only made him a prisoner but ordered him to write to the fort urging the civilians to throw themselves upon the mercy of the savages and informing Inspector Dickens that unless the police withdrew from the fort the Indians would attack it. Dickens was placed in a difficult position. The police were prepared to fight, but the civilians preferred to accept the Indians' offer. Hence, with the responsibility for their protection removed from his shoulders, Dickens ordered the abandonment of the fort.[51] The evacuation was carried out under adverse conditions. The police destroyed what arms they could not remove, collected their ammunition, and embarked in the leaky scow upon their perilous and indefinite journey down the river; perilous because they might be attacked from the banks by hostile Indians, and indefinite because they had no idea how long it would be before they reached safety. Finally, after seven days of hardship and suffering from the cold and water, Dickens' detachment arrived at Battleford on April 22nd. In the meantime the Indians pillaged the fort and, after removing everything of value, set fire to it.

Frog Lake and Fort Pitt marked the culmination of the rebel successes. Nearly half of the Indians who eventually surrendered, joined Big Bear after the fall of Fort Pitt. Had it been possible to hold this fort it is more than probable that the whole campaign north of the Saskatchewan would have been unnecessary, and that Big Bear's following would have melted away at the first determined show of force. It was the surrender of Fort Pitt which provided the Indians with the supplies to carry on, and which finally destroyed any lingering doubts as to the invincibility of the white men. The fame of these exploits spread throughout the North-West and Big Bear's name carried terror wherever it went. Following Big Bear's success many of the Indian bands in the Territories demonstrated the insincerity of their professions of loyalty by sporadic raids upon isolated trading posts where resistance on the part of the whites was unlikely.

The first of these minor outbreaks occurred at Battle River Crossing between Calgary and Edmonton. The news of the métis rising at St. Laurent arrived in this region about the end of March and the Indians immediately became excited and restless. To add to their excitement came rumours that the Frog Lake, Saddle Lake and Lac la Biche Indians had risen for Riel.[52] There is no doubt that the chiefs of this district were in communication with Big Bear. Bobtail had sent messengers to all the bands in the vicinity, and, the Indian Agent reported, had received promises of support from the Stonies at Lac Ste. Anne and Rivière qui Barre. Feeling that the situation warranted the step, the Indian Agent finally abandoned the reserve on April 8th, to seek safety at Edmonton. On the 9th the remaining whites, with the exception of the Roman Catholic priest, followed his example on the advice of friendly Indians.[53]

Many of the Indians, including the chief Ermine Skin, were only lukewarm in their sympathies with the Indian rising, but, as had occurred at Frog Lake, the more turbulent spirits took matters into their own hands. The flight of the whites only increased their assurance. They " supposed the white men had bad news."[54] A pow-wow was held, followed by a dance, and on the 11th, the Indians led by Ringing Sky raided the Hudson's Bay Company store at Battle River and took possession of the buildings and property abandoned by the whites. The lack of support from other bands, added to the non-appearance of Big Bear and the failure of the southern Blackfeet to rise, dampened their ardour for rebellion, and a few days later they expressed their regret for what they had done. Nevertheless there was reason to fear that further trouble might arise. The Indian Agent wrote to Dewdney :

" As it now stands the Bears' Hills Indians are afraid of the consequences of their actions and will not move until they are joined by Indians from Battleford, the Blackfeet or Stonies from Lake St. Ann's. Should they receive help from these sources they will be joined by most of the Indians in this District, except perhaps Peccan of White Fish Lake, who may remain quiet. I have no confidence in the promises made by Bears' Hill band. Ermine Skin admits that he cannot even control his own men."[55]

At Lac la Biche, north-west of Frog Lake and north-east of Edmonton, another raid was carried out. As the rumours of the Indian and half-breed rising reached the Indians about Lac la Biche they became restless. They complained of want of food and declared that they had not been furnished with their usual spring supply of seeds.[56] The people in the neighbourhood were terrified at their insolent attitude, and everywhere rumours spread that Big Bear was on his way to the fort. A meeting was held of the whites and half-breeds of the district. " Tous ces messieurs étaient terrifiés," wrote Mgr. Faraud, " et leur visage était decomposé par la peur."[57] Young, the Hudson's Bay Company clerk, pointed out that Big Bear was on the war path and had on two occasions urged Peccan to attack Lac la Biche. The métis present agreed to defend the fort and the mission, while Young offered to go to Edmonton to see what could be done to secure supplies for the Indians.

Young departed on April 19th. At Edmonton he was appointed Deputy Indian Agent and received a supply of food for the Indians. On the eve of his return, however, his freighters, having heard of the atrocities at Frog Lake and the fall of Fort Pitt, refused to go north. Young accordingly returned alone to find the post completely gutted of its goods and furs and the buildings wrecked.[58]

Several days after Young's departure from Lac la Biche, emissaries from Big Bear arrived at Beaver Lake. They quickly persuaded the Crees of that district to take up arms, and on April 26th, Ka-Qua-Nam and the Beaver Lake Crees raided the post at Lac la Biche. The raid was carried out with typical Indian strategy. At first the Indians asked the Hudson's Bay Company employee, whom Young had left in charge of the post, if they might remove the goods to " protect them from Big Bear's men." This offer being refused, one of the Indians then asked for a little " debt "[59] in order that he might go on a hunting expedition. As the trader opened the door of the buildings, the Indians crowded inside and helped themselves to the goods on the shelves. Mgr. Faraud described the scene :

" Il s'ensuivit une scène indescriptible : hommes, femmes et enfants se précipitèrent dans le magasin, envahirent la maison. En moins d'un quart d'heure il ne restait pas une épingle. Objets de commerce, comestibles de toutes sortes, fourrures, tout avait disparu. Puis à l'instar de tous les révolutionaires, ils brisèrent les vitres, les portes, les tables ; les chaises volaient en morceau sous la hache ; les livres de toutes sortes, déchirés en mille pièces, étaient emportés par le vent. Les femmes s'amusaient à déchirer les tapisseries et à se partager les robes de Mme Young, coupées au préable avec des ciseaux. Ils avaient ordre de ne pas brûler, ils ne brûlèrent donc pas ; mais tous ceux qui ont vu ce petit fort après cet exploit disent qu'il présente l'image de la plus grande désolation."[60]

During the evening two large fires were built, and the Indians passed the night dancing, singing and firing their rifles.

On the following day one of Big Bear's Indians in full war regalia arrived at the mission which was situated a short distance from the fort. The place was defended by some thirty métis. The Indians demanded that they should join the rebels, but the métis, restrained by their clergy, refused. Then, with the threat that Big Bear would march against them in a week's time, the Indians departed, leaving the inhabitants of the mission in a state of terror. The métis garrison had expended their courage in their bold reply and a panic became general. Everybody fled to the woods : " Tous affolés par la peur," wrote Mgr. Faraud, " partaient sans savoir où ils allaient, sans provisions, sans secours d'aucune sorte, abandonnant leurs maisons aux voleurs, ne pensant plus à leurs semences." Such was the universal terror which Big Bear's name inspired. The next few days were " journées pénibles " for the mission. Finally, on April 30th, Young returned bringing the news of the advance of the Government troops. After several days he managed to bring together twenty-seven men to guard the mission, while the Indians, their boldness evaporating, came in with regrets for their part in the pillage. As the month of May advanced the settlers began to doubt the probability of Big Bear's appearance, but precautions were not relaxed. A false rumour of the 17th almost precipitated another panic ; a sense of security was not restored until the news of Big Bear's flight had reached the settlement.

Green Lake, north-west of Prince Albert, was the scene of another Indian raid. Here the news of the rebel outbreak on the Saskatchewan reached the post about the middle of April through a priest accompanied by two métis deserters from Riel's ranks. The trader in charge of the post at once began to move the

ammunition and the stores from the post to a cache on the
Beaver River.   This action was well advised.   Riel's agents had
been active among the neighbouring Indian bands and Green
Lake was an important post as the half-way station to the far
north.   Once in command of it, the rebels would be in possession
of the only store of arms and provisions north of the Saskatchewan river.   At Prince Albert the Chief Factor realized the danger
in which Green Lake stood and wrote to Colonel Irvine to send
a force of men to protect the stores.   " We have at Green Lake,"
he stated, " the complete outfits for the Districts of Athabaska
and Mackenzie River, there are in this outfit over two hundred
stand of arms, and a very large amount of gunpowder, ball and
shot, as well as fixed ammunition, together with a large quantity of
provisions.   If these goods are taken by the rebels it will very
much add to their resources, as well as give them a free access by
the Beaver River to Ile à la Crosse.   Riel's success at Green Lake
would prove to the Indians to the north that he had taken possession of the whole country and create a very undesirable
impression."[61]   Irvine, however, refused to send any force to
Green Lake.   He believed that Prince Albert was still in danger
of a half-breed assault, and was unwilling to risk weakening the
garrison for the sake of a few stores.

On April 26th, the greater part of the stores having been cached,
the whites at Green Lake prepared to abandon the post.   But no
sooner had they embarked in their boats when the Indians
appeared.   The savages were intent upon plunder rather than
slaughter and, without molesting the whites, only forced the
Hudson's Bay Company trader to open the Company's shop.
The Indians then gave themselves over to pillage while the trader
escaped to overtake the bateaux with their terrified human
cargoes.   Constantly fearing an attack the bateaux pushed on
until they arrived at Ile à la Crosse, over one hundred miles
distant.   An attempt was later made by an armed party from Ile
à la Crosse to return to Green Lake, but reports of the presence
of large numbers of hostile Indians quickly dissuaded them.   At
the same time Lawrence Clarke at Prince Albert despatched a
small volunteer force to the Lake, but it found the post looted
and the Indians in command of the situation.   To make matters
worse the party from Prince Albert were made prisoners by a
band of Indians from Fort Pitt.   They were, however, soon

released, the Indians keeping only their horses while the discomfited relief party made their way back to Prince Albert on foot.[62] In the meantime the looting continued. The outpost at Waterhen Lake was raided and the trader made prisoner. Taken to Green Lake he was forced to open a depot at the north end of the Lake and supplies amounting to over $40,000 were lost to the Company. Fortunately few of the arms and little of the ammunition was discovered by the raiders.

These minor events, while they were strategically unimportant, did demonstrate the general temper of the Indians. There were few bands in Treaty 6 who did not long for a return to the old days and the old ways ; who did not desire to see the pale-skinned strangers driven from the land ; and who did not take advantage, in some way or another, of the half-breed rising to strike a blow against the white man. Those on the plains waged a war of revenge ; those in the woods, less warlike and less affected by the revolutionary social and economic changes of civilization, confined themselves to raids upon small trading posts. But in each case the underlying desire was the same ; to recover their freedom, their independence and their country.

Thus the situation stood during the month of April. The rebels had met with surprising success at every hand. At Duck Lake, Carlton, Frog Lake, Fort Pitt and elsewhere the métis and Indians had defeated the white men and the Mounted Police. The line of the North Saskatchewan was practically in their hands and the white men were beleagured in Prince Albert and Battleford. These successes had been entirely spontaneous efforts. There had been no clearly devised plan of action. Indeed Riel had hoped to carry everything by one spectacular coup at Duck Lake and, supported by the potential threat of an Indian rising, to force the Canadian Government to accede to his demands. Instead, he brought an Indian rising with all its attendant horrors of pillage and murder upon a virtually defenceless country. Riel's position was now desperate. The half-breeds were unable to carry on a prolonged war, while the Indians, held together by no strong principle of cohesion and with no central authority to combine their strength, were incapable of sustained effort, and could act with little efficiency against the disciplined force which the Government was sending against them. Had Riel been a student of English history, he might have repeated the words of the Duke of Manchester, the pessimistic leader of the Parlimentary forces during the Civil War, with a much greater degree of truth :

" If we beat the King ninety-nine times yet he is King still, and so will his posterity be after him, but if the King beat us once we shall all be hanged and our posterity made slaves."

CHAPTER XVI

On the evening of March 27th the people of Eastern Canada were startled by the news that the Mounted Police had been defeated in battle by a mixed force of métis and Indians. That the Riel agitation should have developed into a serious rebellion was totally unexpected. During 1884 few of the complaints from the North-West plains had filtered into Old Canada. News of Riel's reappearance was announced, but not discussed, of so little importance was it deemed. Throughout the winter the embers of discontent smouldered unsuspected. Early in March a few despatches and private letters, referring to the growing discontent among the half-breeds, Indians and whites, appeared in the eastern press, but the possibility of revolt was never seriously considered. Following the news of the seizure of certain stores and the retention of prisoners by the métis the *Gazette* of Montreal expressed the general feeling when it wrote :

" That this rebellion will assume any serious proportions or cause any difficulty in its suppression is not for a moment to be supposed . . . the incident cannot attain proportions of serious significance, being merely local in its character and of no more consequence than a petty riot in any well settled part of old Canada."[1]

The Government, however, had already taken steps to suppress the incipient rising by force. On March 14th, following the information that the half-breeds intended preventing settlers from entering the country after the 16th, the Prime Minister telegraphed to the Lieutenant-Governor : " You must assume responsibility for peace of District as Governor." He also suggested that the Lieutenant-Governor, or Hayter Reed, the Assistant Indian Commissioner, should visit the locality, and asked " Would Lacombe or Hugonard be of any service ? "[2] Five days later a reinforcement of police was despatched to Prince Albert under Colonel Irvine, but as the situation appeared to grow worse, Dewdney appealed to the Prime Minister for military support.

On March 22nd, four days before the disaster of Duck Lake, Dewdney wired Macdonald :

" Situation looks very serious. Think it imperative able military man should be on staff in event of militia going north."[3]

Macdonald replied with a promptitude which had scarcely characterized his previous dealings with the North-West Territories :

" General Middleton to proceed to Red River to-night. Order sent to Winnipeg Militia to be ready to move."[4]

In accordance with this order Major-General Frederick Middleton, commanding the militia of Canada, at once departed for the North-West. On the 25th, one company of the 90th militia battalion of Winnipeg proceeded to Troy and two days later the remainder of the battalion followed with the Major-General. March 28th, 29th and 30th were spent in arranging the transport and commissariat services, and by April 2nd the whole force had reached Qu'Appelle which had been chosen as the base of operations.

In the meantime the métis victory had altered the whole situation. What had been up to Duck Lake little more than a riotous assembly, then became open rebellion against constituted authority. Middleton, realizing that the Mounted Police were insufficient in number to cope with a rebellion which threatened to develop into a general native rising, asked for an immediate force of 2,000 men. Troops were accordingly summoned from every province of the Dominion. Eastern Canada provided 3,324 men, composed of the following :

Quebec.—" A " Battery, 120 ; the Cavalry School, 48 ; the 9th Voltigeurs, a French-speaking regiment, 230, from Quebec City ; the 65th Rifles, a French-speaking regiment, 315 ; and the Montreal Garrison Artillery, an English-speaking regiment acting as infantry, 299, from Montreal—Total, 1,012 men.

Ontario.—" B " Battery, from Kingston, 120 ; the Infantry School, 92 ; the Queen's Own Rifles, 280 ; and the Royal Grenadiers, 265, from Toronto ; the 7th Fusiliers from London, 263 ; a company of Sharpshooters from Ottawa, 51 ; two composite regiments drawn from different parts of the province, the Midland Regiment, 382, and the York and Simcoe Battalion, 346 ; the Governor-General's Bodyguard of cavalry, 80 ; and the

Dominion Land Surveyors Intelligence Corps, 50. Total— 1,929 men.

Nova Scotia.—the Halifax Battalion, 383.

Western Canada furnished 2,011 troops, exclusive of the Mounted Police. Winnipeg alone provided a small cavalry corps, 32, and a field battery, 62, in addition to the infantry regiments, the 90th, 317; the 91st, 432; and the Winnipeg Light Infantry, 327. In the North-West, mounted units were formed at Qu'Appelle—the Moose Mountain Scouts, French's Scouts and Boulton's Scouts; Calgary—the Rocky Mountain Rangers and Steele's Scouts; and St. Albert—the St. Albert Mounted Riflemen. Infantry units were organized at Yorkton, Birtle and Battleford. In addition to these there were numerous companies of "home guards." The total number of soldiers officially mobilized during the North-West Rebellion amounted to 5,334, added to which were 2,648 Staff, Transport, Commissariat, Medical and other corps, totalling in all 7,982 men.[5] The Mounted Police, who are not included in this total, numbered about 500. The artillery consisted of nine guns and two machine guns.

The eastern regiments were despatched to the North-West with great rapidity considering the time of year, the absence of a standing force, and the lack of stores and equipment for the citizen soldiery. Moreover, the Canadian Pacific Railway line was not yet completed from east to west. North of Lake Superior there were several gaps in the line, aggregating nearly one hundred miles, over which men and supplies had to be transported by sleighs. Nevertheless "A" and "B" Batteries, the only corps constituting a permanent military force in Canada, arrived at Winnipeg on April 5th, ten days after the battle of Duck Lake. Several militia regiments followed within a few days, having been mobilized, equipped and despatched over two thousand miles, in less than a fortnight.

While the mobilization was being carried out precautions were taken to guard against the possibilities of incursions by Indians or half-breeds sympathetic to the rebels from south of the international boundary. The Governor-General immediately put himself into communication with the British Minister at Washington, requesting that the necessary steps be taken to prevent men or munitions of war being sent across the frontier.[6] In contrast to 1869–70, the Government of the United States, in this instance, co-operated loyally with the British authorities. Secretary of State Bayard at once replied to Sackville-West's request :

" I shall use every endeavour to obtain the earliest knowledge in relation to the revolt in Winnipeg (sic) and this Government will take all available precautions to prevent the dispatch of hostile expeditions, or of arms and munitions of war, from within the jurisdiction of the United States to aid the insurgents in the North-West provinces."[7]

Thus, although there were constant rumours of Fenian invasions and Indian incursions, nothing ever came of them. On April 11th Bayard assured the British Minister that the military authorities in Dakota discredited the truth of reports of movements towards Canada by hostile Indians, stating :

" The Commanding General adds that he has enjoined the utmost vigilance upon the commanders of the posts along the boundary, and that the reports which he has received indicate that they are zealously carrying out their instructions."[8]

Constant vigilance was thus maintained throughout the rebellion by the American authorities, and Canada, protected from the danger of any serious attack from the south, was free to concentrate her efforts in the north.

The seriousness of the rebellion lay not in the actual numbers which the rebels were able to bring into the field against the forces of the Federal Government, but in the potential danger of a general native rising. Although the rebels who took up arms numbered scarcely over 1,000, the number of Indians in Treaties 4, 6 and 7, totalled about 20,000. There were, moreover, numerous métis settlements scattered throughout the North-West from Wood Mountain to St. Albert, which might easily provide nuclei for revolt. The first object of the Government was, therefore, to localize the rebellion. This was accomplished by the immediate despatch of men to Qu'Appelle, even prior to the fight at Duck Lake. The rapidity with which these and subsequent troops were thrown into the North-West from Eastern Canada kept quiet the disaffected Indians and métis in the Qu'Appelle valley who might otherwise have joined the insurgents after their initial success. The early and rapid movement of the troops was one of the decisive actions of the campaign ; it practically settled the issue of the rebellion before it had fairly begun.

At the same time the Government took steps to remove the grievances of those who had not yet risen in arms. Extra supplies were immediately rushed to the wavering Indian bands. Two car loads of flour and 15,000 pounds of bacon were ordered to Indian Head. The allowances of rations were increased. Tea and tobacco were given to working Indians and requests for oxen and cattle complied with. The cost was considerable, but the Indian Commissioner realized that the extra expense would probably prevent a general Indian rising. " We are impressing upon all our officials," he wrote to Macdonald, " the necessity of economy, but at this time it is essential that the Indians be kept busy and contented, and it would be false economy to be too sparing of provisions and other articles that tend to that end."[9] It was to be regretted that the wisdom of this advice had not been recognized during 1883 and 1884 and the unfortunate Indian rising of 1885 thus, possibly, avoided.

As far as the half-breed claims to patents and scrip were concerned, the Government, having ignored the métis petitions for ten years, virtually admitted their culpability for the rebellion by hastily appointing a Commission to investigate these claims. The Commission had been decided upon as early as January 1885,[10] but it was not until eleven days after Riel had formed his " Provisional Government of the Saskatchewan," that Messrs. Street, Forget and Goulet, the last-named a métis from Manitoba, were instructed to report upon the claims preferred by the North-West half-breeds, and not until April 6th, that the Commissioners were authorized to issue scrip in extinguishment of the half-breed title.[11] Had this action been taken during 1884 or earlier, it is more than probable that the métis rising would never have been precipitated. But belated justice though it may have been, it was an expedient move to localize the half-breed rising to the district of St. Laurent, by removing elsewhere the grievances which had contributed so powerfully to Riel's rising on the North Saskatchewan.

The object of localization achieved, the second object was to crush the armed resistance of the métis and the Indians by military force. The original intention of the Major-General had been to move against St. Antoine or Batoche, the rebel head-

THE NORTH WEST TERRITORIES

MILITARY COLUMNS
MIDDLETON
OTTER
STRANGE
N.W.M.P
LOCAL SCOUTS

ATHABASCA

SASKATCHEWAN

PROVINCE OF MANITOBA

ASSINIBOLA

ALBERTA

MONTANA

DAKOTA

Lac la Biche

Lac la Ronge

Green Lake H.B.C.

St. Albert
EDMONTON
Frog L.
Ft. Pitt
Frenchmans Butte
Cut Knife
BATTLEFORD
Ft. Carlton
PRINCE ALBERT
Batoche
Fish Creek
Duck L.
SASKATOON

WINNIPEG
BRANDON
R'L'Y
REGINA
Ft. Qu'Appelle
Qu'Appelle

PACIFIC
CANADIAN
Swift Current
MEDICINE HAT
Ft. Macleod
CALGARY

quarters, with two separate columns, but with the rising of Poundmaker and Big Bear it was deemed advisable to despatch three different columns against the three principal centres of disaffection, Batoche, Battleford and Fort Pitt. The three bases of operations were fixed at Qu'Appelle, Swift Current and Calgary. From the first General Middleton planned to take Batoche, thus relieving Prince Albert; from Swift Current Colonel Otter was to relieve Battleford; and from Calgary General Strange was to move against Big Bear via Edmonton and the valley of the North Saskatchewan, effecting a junction with Middleton at Fort Pitt.

The general strategy of the campaign was well conceived but poorly carried out. The movements of the troops were slow, their disposition inadequate, and their principal success fortuitous. The General in command had seen service against the Maoris in New Zealand and in the Indian Mutiny, but, in spite of the plaudits heaped upon him at the time, his management of the North-West campaign was marked by undue deliberation and hesitancy. His was not the nature to descend to consultation and his lack of confidence in his men was apparent at every engagement. Trained in the theory of the impregnable British square he relied entirely upon infantry, thus forfeiting the advantage of mobility in a country which lent itself to rapid movement. His cavalry were stationed in the rear to protect the line of communications when they should have been at the front. Moreover, when cavalry were finally summoned to the front they were ordered there in inverse order of training! For mounted troops Middleton relied solely upon local corps, such as French's Scouts and Boulton's Scouts; even summoning to the critical centre at Batoche a hastily improvised mounted corps known as the Dominion Land Surveyors Intelligence Corps in preference to the Governor-General's Body-Guard—a well-trained cavalry corps under the command of Colonel G. T. Denison, one of the foremost cavalry officers of this time—the Quebec Cavalry School or the Winnipeg Cavalry, who remained in the rear doing the work ordinarily allotted to infantry. Had it not been for the fact that Riel overruled Dumont's plan to take advantage of the superior mobility of the métis, Middleton's lack of horse might have proved an expensive blunder.

On April 6th Middleton set out from Fort Qu'Appelle, having

halted there four days " to enable the 90th Battalion to fire blank and ball ammunition, as I found that many of the men had never pulled a trigger."[12] The march proceeded slowly. The weather was unfavourable. The winter snow was beginning to melt and the nights were " fearfully cold." On the first evening " the thermometer . . . fell tremendously, and at sunrise it was 23 degrees below zero, and all the tent pegs had to be cut out of the ground with axes next morning."[13] Moreover, Middleton's column was not yet complete in numbers, and the transport services, having been hastily improvised, left much to be desired. Finally, on the 17th Middleton reached Clarke's Crossing on the South Branch of the Saskatchewan river, about forty miles from the rebel headquarters, having covered approximately 180 miles in eleven days. Here he was overtaken by the Royal Grenadiers, bringing the total strength of the column to about 800 men.

At this point Middleton halted, and the next few days were spent in executing what later turned out to be an unnecessary and inadvisable manœuvre. The force was divided into two columns, the second of which was transported with difficulty across the river to march parallel with the first column down the South Branch towards Batoche. Middleton was perfectly acquainted with the geographical position of Batoche, and the policy of dividing a small force on approaching the enemy country and placing an effective barrier between the two wings was, to say the least, questionable. If the left division was intended to carry out a flanking movement against the rebel stronghold its action would have been rendered useless by the impossibility of effective co-operation across an unbridged river. This move, in the end, not only served to delay the advance of Middleton's force thus giving valuable days to Riel to strengthen his position, but it deprived Middleton of the service of nearly half of his troops at the battle of Fish Creek on April 24th.

In the meantime the métis were making every preparation to resist the troops. They had been in touch with Middleton's force ever since it had left Fort Qu'Appelle, by means of Indian and half-breed scouts, one of whom, Jérome Henry, accompanied the troops as a Government freighter ![14] In view of their reports Dumont, the métis military leader, determined to harass the infantry column by a series of attacks under cover of the darkness. In his account of the campaign Dumont wrote :

" Une vingtaine de jours après,[15] on a appris, par nos éclaireurs qui étaient allés jusqu'à Qu'Appelle, à 260 milles environ de Batoche, que Middleton était en marche.

" Nous étions alors 350 hommes en tout, dont 200 étaient armés. J'ai proposé d'aller au devant des troupes et de les harceler pendant la nuit, en les empêchant surtout de dormir, persuadé que c'était un bon moyen de les démoraliser et de leur faire perdre tout courage. Mais Riel n'y a pas consenti, disant que c'était trop sauvage et que d'ailleurs on s'exposait ainsi à tirer sur nos amis canadiens. Moi, j'aurais été déterminé à le faire sans scrupule, et même j'aurais volontiers fait sauter les chemins de fer, car je ne considérais pas comme des amis ceux qui s'unissaient aux Anglais, pour nous tuer et nous piller. Riel me disait ; si vous les connaissiez, vous ne chercheriez pas à les traiter ainsi.

" Quoiqu'il en soit, nous avons dû renoncer au projet d'aller rencontrer les ennemis sur un terrain avantageux pour nous, et j'en suis sûr, nous les aurions tellement abrutis qu'au bout de trois nuits ils se seraient entretués les uns les autres."[16]

Thus, in spite of his better judgment, Dumont gave in to Riel, such was his confidence in the former President of the Provisional Government :

" J'ai cédé au conseil de Riel, quoique persuadé que humainement mon dessein était meilleur ; mais j'avais confiance dans sa foi et dans ses prières, et que Dieu l'exaucerait."[17]

Riel, however, feared to weaken Batoche by allowing Dumont to carry out his plan of night attacks. The Mounted Police under Colonel Irvine were stationed at Prince Albert only forty miles north of Batoche, and constituted, in Riel's mind, a constant threat to the métis capital. Riel had, moreover, been shaken by the fact that Dumont had been wounded at Duck Lake, and was loth to permit his military leader to expose himself unduly to danger. In a memorandum on the defence of Batoche, written on April 22nd, Riel stated :

" If anything happened to Dumont, it would not only be a misfortune for his friends, but an irreparable loss for the army and to the nation. If my Uncle Gabriel were cured of his wound I should be more willing to see him start on an expedition of this kind. If we get reinforcements I might change my opinion, I think, to a certain extent. Under present circumstances, I know, I understand, that it would be of great benefit to us to go and attack and harass the Mounted Police on the other side of the river, at Clarke's Crossing ; but that would weaken us here, and I am afraid that in the meantime there might come from Prince Albert or elsewhere a force which would take all ours to repel."[18]

Such advice, although not unreasonable under the circumstances, was fatal to the métis cause.   Their chief hope of military success lay in taking advantage of Middleton's immobility by a series of rapid demoralizing thrusts against an untried column of infantry, not in the attempted defence of a single position against unfavourable odds.

Finally, however, Dumont could no longer be restrained. He informed Riel " que je ne pouvais plus suivre ses conseils humanitaires, et que j'étais decidé d'aller tirer sur les envahisseurs, et en cela, j'étais approuvé par mes gens."[19]   On April 23rd, with a mixed force of two hundred métis, Crees, Saulteaux and Sioux, he advanced towards Middleton's position.   Riel accompanied the force, conducting religious services during the halts. No sooner had they proceeded a few miles from Batoche when the news reached them that the Mounted Police from Prince Albert were on their way to make a sortie against the rebel headquarters. Riel at once returned with fifty men to reinforce the small garrison which had been left at Batoche.   On the following morning Dumont with twenty men advanced to within half a mile of Middleton's camp. The main body, numbering 130, he stationed in a small ravine or coulée known as Fish Creek, which cut directly across Middleton's road and emptied into the river on his left.   Dumont's plan was to draw the troops into the coulée and then to fire on them from behind the shelter of the trees. " Je voulais les traiter comme on traite les buffles," he declared.[20]

In many respects the half-breed tactics were similar to those used by the Boers.   The rolling prairie, like the South African veldt, offered extensive cover to the defending force which invariably appeared to be much stronger than it really was.   Like the Boers, the métis kept to the valleys, coulées and hollows, thus placing their adversaries against the skyline whenever they attempted to advance down the slopes.   Silhouetted against the sky the troops were admirable targets for the métis marksmen, many of whom were old buffalo hunters and all of whom were familiar with every foot of the ground upon which they fought. The wonder is, not that the small numbers of half-breeds and

GABRIEL DUMONT

Indians were able to check Middleton and Otter, but that the casualties of the citizen militia were not more numerous.

On the morning of the 24th General Middleton broke camp and resumed his deliberate progress towards Batoche. As the troops were entering what was recognized to be the enemy country, added precautions against surprise were taken. Boulton's Scouts were thrown out well in advance of the main body. Middleton, attended by his staff officers, accompanied them. As they approached the ravine the scouts discovered traces of camp fires ; at the same time some of the métis among Dumont's advance party betrayed their presence by firing upon the scouts. Boulton's men dismounted and returned the fire, while Dumont's force hastily retreated towards the edge of the coulée.[21] Middleton ordered the troops to advance and a heavy fire was exchanged. Although they had lost the inestimable advantage of surprise, the métis had, nevertheless, the advantage of position. From behind the trees and brush of the ravine they were able to fire upon the enemy as they came over the horizon. As the battle progressed, however, the métis became hard pressed. They attempted to drive back the troops by setting fire to the prairie but without success.[22]   The pressure of numbers and the heavy fire of the soldiers, particularly from the artillery, discouraged many of Dumont's men and deserters from the métis ranks became numerous. At the conclusion of the engagement the métis numbered only fifty-four men.[23]   Nevertheless, they were able to check effectively Middleton's advance, and at the end of the day remained in possession of the coulée. The half-breed success was due largely to the unorthodox tactics employed ; although, according to Maxime Lépine, " We prayed all the day, and I think prayer did more than the bullets."[24]

On the whole the result of the battle was indecisive. Middleton was by no means defeated but he had failed to gain a victory. Only the eagerness of the half-breeds had prevented him from walking into a serious ambush. Had Middleton's left wing been in a position to participate in the battle and turn the métis flank, in place of remaining helpless within the sound of the guns on the opposite side of the river, it is possible that Dumont's force might have been surrounded and captured. Instead, Dumont was given the opportunity to administer a severe check to Middleton which delayed for over a fortnight the attack upon Batoche.

While the first column under Middleton was thus engaged against the métis on the South Saskatchewan, the second column under Colonel Otter succeeded in relieving the town of Battleford. Superintendent Herchmer of the Mounted Police had been ordered as early as March 29th to proceed north, but, unfortunately, the ice in the river having given way at Saskatchewan Landing, no further progress was possible for the time being. Herchmer then proceeded to Medicine Hat, where the steamer *Northcote* was being prepared to carry troops to the troubled area. On April 11th Colonel Otter, the Officer commanding the second column of militia, was ordered to relieve Battleford " with as little delay as possible."[25]   Herchmer then joined Otter, and the combined Mounted Police and Militia force, numbering 543 men with three guns, left Swift Current on the 13th. Considerable difficulty was experienced in crossing the river at Saskatchewan Landing and it was not until the 18th that the march was definitely begun. The progress made by Otter's column was rapid and contrasted favourably with Middleton's deliberate movements. The country traversed in each case was rolling prairie presenting no serious obstacles ; but Otter added a waggon train of some 200 men to his force and was thus able to provide transport for the greater number of his troops. The column averaged over thirty miles per day, and on April 23rd, five days after leaving Saskatchewan Landing, Otter camped within three miles of his destination. On the following day the troops marched into Battleford amid the shouts of welcome of five hundred inhabitants who had been, for nearly a month, pent up inside an enclosed stockade some two hundred yards square.

The object of the third column, which was formed at Calgary, was to overawe the Indians of Alberta, to protect the outlying settlements, and to move via Edmonton and the North Saskatchewan valley against Big Bear. The protection of southern Alberta was important. Here the Blackfoot confederacy, composed of the strongest and most warlike tribes of the North-West, held the balance of peace and war. If these Indians elected to join the rebels, a general Indian rising from Manitoba to the Rocky Mountains was not an improbability. Although the Blackfeet were treated with greater consideration on account of their warlike tradition, they too, like the other Indians of the plains, were embittered by the grim experience of civilization.

As early as 1877-8 the head chief had been in communication with Louis Riel in the United States.[26] During 1884 the Indian Agent reported that Riel's half-breed emissaries were again among the Blackfeet Indians, and that, as a result, their former friendly demeanour had given way to one of sulkiness and hostility. A half-breed, suspected of inciting the aborigines, was arrested by the Mounted Police but managed to escape and sought refuge in Crowfoot's lodge. The man was re-arrested but only in the face of manifest hostility of Crowfoot and the Blackfeet chiefs.[27]

When the news of the rebellion reached Ottawa the Canadian Government, realizing the absolute necessity of placating the southern Alberta Indians, acted promptly. On March 24th, two days before Duck Lake, Macdonald telegraphed to Father Lacombe, a missionary greatly beloved by the Indians, asking him to see Crowfoot and endeavour to ensure the loyalty of the Blackfeet.[28] Lacombe went to the reserve, and on the 31st, replied to the Prime Minister that Crowfoot " promised me to be loyal no matter how things may turn elsewhere."[29] To assist Father Lacombe in his efforts, and to remove any possible cause for complaint among the Indians, Macdonald advised Dewdney that extra rations should be issued to the Indians.[30] In addition to complying with this request, Dewdney also recalled Agent Denny, who had resigned as a result of the economy cuts, and himself visited Blackfoot Crossing for assurance as to the sincerity of Crowfoot's professions. On April 12th he forwarded the following message from the Blackfoot chief :

" On behalf of myself and people I wish to send through you to the Great Mother the words I have given to the Governor at a Council held, at which my minor chiefs and young men were present. We are agreed and determined to remain loyal to the Queen. Our young men will go to work on their reserve, and will raise all the crops we can, and we hope the Government will help us to sell what we cannot use.

" Continued reports are brought to us, and we do not know what to believe, but now that we have seen the Governor and heard him speak, we will shut our ears and only listen to and believe what is told us through the Governor.

" Should any Indians come to our reserves and ask us to join them in war we will send them away. I have sent messengers to the Bloods and Piegans who belong to our treaty to tell them what we are doing, and what we intend to do about the trouble. I want Mr. Dewdney to be with us and all my men are of the same mind. The words I sent by Father Lacombe I again send. We will be loyal to the Queen whatever happens. I have a copy of this, and when the trouble is over will have it with pride to show the Queen's officers, and we leave our future in your hands.

" We have asked for nothing, but the Governor has given us a little present of tea and tobacco. He will tell you what other talk we had at our Council; it was all good, not one bad word."[31]

It was not, however, a deep sense of loyalty which inspired these words, but rather the fact that the Indians, realizing their powerful position, were determined to use it to extort concessions from the Government. Father Lacombe, who had lived for many years among them, and who fully understood Indian character, wrote confidentially after the rebellion was over :

" For my own part what I have seen of the Blackfeet and their kindred since last spring makes me believe, that, if they have been quiet and have made loyal promises during the Cree rebellion, it was purely out of self-interest in order to get more and more out of the Department. From the beginning of the war any one who knows the Indian character could very early perceive that they were not pleased when told of the victories of the whites ; on the contrary they were sorry and disappointed. Crowfoot received into his camp and fed for months many Cree families, and was very much displeased when we tried to send away these Crees, and it was very generally believed that a great many of our soldiers were killed by their Cree friends."[32]

To discourage any inclination upon the part of the Blackfeet to go back on their word and to reassure the panic-stricken settlers, troops were quickly despatched to southern Alberta. Calgary had already formed a troop of scout cavalry and a home guard under the command of Major-General Strange, a retired Artillery officer ranching near the town, and on April 8th Strange was appointed to command the third column to move against the rebels. The local force was soon reinforced by the arrival of the 65th Rifles of Montreal, the Winnipeg Light Infantry and the 9th Voltigeurs of Quebec. Provision was made for the defence of the southern part of the territory by volunteer companies and later by the 9th Voltigeurs, and on April 20th Strange proceeded north to Edmonton with the first division of his force.

Every precaution was taken against attack. Father Lacombe

and the Reverend John McDougall of Morley went in advance of the troops to reassure the Indians, and to inform the settlers at Edmonton that the troops were advancing with all speed. The cavalry scouts under the command of Major Steele were detailed to protect the convoy. Nothing that caution could dictate was neglected.

The march was not without its difficulties. The horses, with few exceptions, had seldom been ridden and bucked whenever mounted. At Red Deer Crossing the river was in flood and only one small skiff available as a ferry. To cross the swollen ford the waggon boxes had to be raised to prevent the supplies from getting wet and their contents damaged, and some of the carts were swept away. The cannon presented the most formidable problem. Finally a raft was constructed to carry the gun with picket ropes to serve as a ferry cable. The cable parted and the raft was salvaged with the greatest difficulty.[33]

On May 1st the first division of the column reached Edmonton, having covered about 210 miles in ten days. The other divisions followed in the course of the next few days. Small garrisons were placed on the line of communications at Red Deer and at Government Ford near Edmonton. Another force was sent to overawe the Indians on the Bears' Hill reserve, while the remainder advanced down the North Saskatchewan towards Big Bear and Fort Pitt.

While Otter and Strange were leading their respective columns against the Indians on the line of the North Saskatchewan, Louis Riel was endeavouring to bring about a concentration of those who had taken up arms against the Government. The check administered to Middleton at Fish Creek enabled Riel and Dumont to despatch urgent appeals for help to Poundmaker and Big Bear. Immediately after the engagement, runners were despatched to the reserves to urge upon the Indians the necessity of joining the métis force at Batoche. McLean stated in his *Reminiscences* that towards the end of April Big Bear received a letter from the half-breeds asking him to join Poundmaker without delay and promising, in the event of his agreeing, to send 100 waggons and horses to assist him to move quickly. This junction was to be followed by an assault upon Battleford, after which the combined forces of the Indians would join Riel at Batoche.[34]

This plan was excellent strategy.   The union of the three
rebel forces would have brought their numbers to nearly 1,000
and would have enabled Riel to prolong the rebellion, if not to
inflict a decisive defeat upon the Canadian troops under Middleton.
It was, however, rendered ineffective by the procrastination and
lack of purpose which characterized the Indians as a fighting
force.   The demands of their savage democracy rendered them
incapable of rapid decision and much valuable time was lost in
factional disputes.

Big Bear's band, it will be remembered, was composed of the
allied forces of the Wood Crees and the Plain Crees. The former,
less warlike and less affected by the advent of the white man, were
well satisfied to have secured a large quantity of provisions in
the pillage of Frog Lake, Cold Lake and Fort Pitt.   The Plain
Crees, harbouring a greater resentment against the whites, were
determined to carry on a war of extermination.   Thus the latter
were anxious to move towards Battleford to join forces with
Poundmaker, while their allies consistently opposed the plan.
In this they were abetted by the white prisoners in the camp who
fully realized the importance of preventing the junction.   The
result was a continual bickering and disputation after the Indian
fashion.   The Plain Cree chiefs, however, made every effort to
preserve the alliance and to convince their reluctant allies of the
advantage to be gained from the half-breed proposal, and finally,
about May 1st, Big Bear's camp began to move, by short marches,
from Frog Lake towards Fort Pitt and Battleford.

In Poundmaker's camp a similar dissension prevailed.   The
chief himself, like Big Bear, was by no means heart and soul in the
rebellion ;[35] but the Assiniboines or Stonies, who had murdered
their Farm Instructor and a neighbouring farmer before joining
the Crees at Battleford, were inveterate in their hatred of the
whites.   Like Big Bear's Plain Crees they were strongly in favour
of joining the métis. Poundmaker was unwilling to move from
his reserve. He suspected that all was not well in the métis camp.
The early messengers had conveyed the impression that Riel
would carry all before him but now they asked for help.   Moreover, nothing had been heard of the assistance which Riel had
promised would be forthcoming from the United States. Poundmaker accordingly temporized.   He replied to Riel's overtures
with the statement that " he would send to Fort Pitt, to Big

Bear's camp, and he would wait for him a while before he would go down to Riel."[36]   On April 29th Poundmaker addressed a long letter to Riel.   He informed him of the progress of the Indian rising, but instead of promising to join Riel at Batoche he asked the métis leader to send men and ammunition to Battleford.   His doubts as to Riel's position are apparent from this letter :

" I want to hear news of the progress of God's work.   If any event has occurred since your messengers came away, let me know of it.   Tell me the date when the Americans will reach the Canadian Pacific Railway.   Tell me all the news that you have heard from all places where your work is in progress. . . . Here we have killed six white men.   We have not taken the barracks yet, but that is the only entire building in Battleford.   All the cattle and horses in the vicinity we have taken.   We have lost one man, Nez Percé killed, he being alone, and one wounded. Some soldiers have come from Swift Current, but I do not know their number.[37]   We have here guns and rifles of all sorts, but ammunition for them is short.   If it be possible, we want you to send us ammunition of various kinds.   We are weak only for the want of that.   You sent word that you would come to Battleford when you had finished your work at Duck Lake.   We wait still for you, as we are unable to take the fort without help.   If you send us news send only one messenger.   We are impatient to reach you.   It would give us—encourage us much to see you, and make us work more heartily.   Up to the present everything has gone well with us, but we are constantly expecting the soldiers to visit us here.   We trust that God will be as kind to us in the future as he has in the past."[38]

Riel was not in a position to assist Poundmaker; rather he needed Poundmaker's assistance.   Riel, therefore, replied in a fulsome strain telling the Indians of the " victory " at Fish Creek at which " nos volontaires . . . se conduisèrent . . . je ne dirai pas seulement commes des braves mais commes des héros."   The letter, however, betrayed the critical position of the métis when it asked :

" Nous vous demandons au nom du Bon Dieu de nous envoyer aussitôt que vous pourrez et si vous le voulez entre deux à deux cent cinquante hommes et même trois cent s'il se peut, afin que non seulement nous puissions venir à bout de Middleton mais que nous puissions même après avoir anéanti, par la puissance de Dieu, une partie de son armée, faire prisonnier l'autre moitié ;

et la tenant en otage amener le gouvernement d'Ottawa à traiter avec nous, et à lui faire reconnaître et respecter nos droits, les droits des métis et des sauvages, Courage! Venez-vous en tous."[39]

This message was not received by Poundmaker until after his Indians had been attacked by Colonel Otter at Cut Knife Hill.

The engagement at Cut Knife was a failure. Otter's object was to prevent, if possible, the junction of Big Bear and Poundmaker and their union with Riel.[40] Although Poundmaker had made no deliberate assault upon the fort at Battleford, his men had raided and fired the town, murdered several white men and waylaid a Mounted Police patrol several days before Otter's arrival. That Poundmaker's intentions were by no means pacific is shown in his letter to Riel—quoted above—in which he asked for assistance to take the fort. Moreover, the Assiniboines in his camp had set up a "soldiers' lodge," and under the influence of a half-breed agitator, were anxious to join the métis at Batoche. Otter was therefore justified in an attack, which, had it been successful, would have been considered as a master stroke rather than a blunder.

Otter did not consult General Middleton as to the advisability of the attack upon Poundmaker.[41] Instead he telegraphed to the Lieutenant-Governor for his approval, a breach of military etiquette that may be explained by the mistaken belief that it was necessary to consult the civil authority responsible for the administration of Indian affairs before launching the attack. On April 26th, two days after his relief of Battleford, Otter wired to Dewdney:

"I would propose taking part of my force at once to punish Poundmaker, leaving one hundred men to garrison Battleford. Great depredations committed. Immediate decisive action necessary. Do you approve?"[42]

Dewdney wired his approval on the same day, adding a note of warning:

"Think you cannot act too energetically or Indians will collect in large numbers. Herchmer knows country to Poundmaker's reserve. Sand hills most dangerous ground to march through. Be sure to secure good reliable scouts."[43]

Otter therefore despatched his scouts to reconnoitre. They reported on the 29th that some two hundred Crees and Assiniboines were camped near Poundmaker's reserve, about thirty-eight miles from Battleford. Otter informed Dewdney on the 30th that he was prepared to move and on the afternoon of the following day set out with a force of 325 men, 48 waggons, 2 seven-pounder guns and a Gatling machine gun.[44] They pushed forward during the night hoping to surprise the Indians at sunrise on May 2nd.

The Indians were encamped on the western slope of Cut Knife Hill where Poundmaker and the Crees had, many years before, defeated the Sarcee warrior, Cut Knife. Poundmaker was daily anticipating an attack from the troops and had obviously chosen his position accordingly. The surprise which Otter had planned was, therefore, only partial. An Indian camp can scarcely ever be said to be asleep, and Otter's column was discovered at daybreak as it was descending the hill opposite and preparing to cross Cut Knife Creek. At once the troops and the Indians raced towards Cut Knife Hill. As the Mounted Police and the gunners gained the crest of the hill the Indians fell back into the coulées surrounding it. Taking advantage of the cover thus afforded by the trees and shrubbery, they worked their way around until they had practically surrounded the troops and from their concealed position poured a rapid cross-fire upon the soldiers as they lay exposed upon the hill. For seven hours the fight continued. Finally, with his men exhausted by the all-night march and the hunger and fatigue of the engagement, and realizing that his position would become more and more untenable as the darkness descended, Otter gave the order to retire. The line of retreat was cleared by a charge, and the column, under cover of fire from the cannon and machine gun, made its way over the creek and up the hill on the opposite side. The retreat might easily have developed into a rout. Poundmaker, however, held back his victorious warriors and prevented them from cutting the retreating column to pieces.[45]

Although the troops outnumbered the Indians by three to two and acquitted themselves nobly under fire, Otter's force accomplished nothing. It is possible that, had Otter taken advantage of the surprise, and hurled his few cavalry directly at the Indian camp, instead of being awed by a few casualties, the Indians might have surrendered in order to save their women and children. The Indians' weakest point was their anxiety to keep the fighting as far as possible from the camp, but they were allowed to choose their own fighting ground. The battle of Cut Knife taught the Indians a lesson ; but not the lesson which Otter had hoped to teach them. Had he succeeded he would have put an end to any possibility of the junction of the Indian with the half-breed force. Instead his failure rendered it more probable.

On the same or following day the messengers arrived from Batoche with Riel's appeal for help, and with the war party in the ascendant, Poundmaker's Indians began to move towards the half-breed headquarters. On May 14th the Indians, having reached the Eagle Hills, intercepted a supply train en route to Battleford. They were thus able to renew their stock of provisions and took twenty-two prisoners. Later in the same day a skirmish occurred between a small party of Indians and a scouting party from the fort. The scouts suffered one killed and one wounded and beat a hasty retreat to Battleford.[46] Three days later a messenger arrived with the news that the métis and the soldiers were engaged in a battle at Batoche and with another urgent appeal for assistance from Riel. The Indians, however, did not begin to move until it was too late. On May 19th Poundmaker learned that the métis had been defeated by the troops after a three days' engagement and that Riel and Dumont were fugitives.[47]

Following the check at Fish Creek, Middleton remained for nearly a fortnight in camp at that place. He had to make provision for his wounded and hesitated to advance without reinforcements. The division which had been so laboriously transported to the left bank of the river at Clarke's Crossing now rejoined the main column and two companies of the Midland Battalion, the Surveyors' Intelligence Corps and a Gatling gun were ordered to join the General's force. It is difficult to understand why Middleton did not order up either the Governor-General's Body-Guard or the Quebec Cavalry from the Qu' Appelle trail : both of these were better mounted and better trained than the improvised Surveyors' Corps.

On May 7th Middleton began to move towards Batoche, his force numbering approximately 850 men.[48] On board the steamer *Northcote*, which had brought the reinforcements from Swift Current, were placed thirty-five men from the Infantry

Canadian Artillery in Action at Batoche

School. The steamer had already been fortified, the object being to use her in a combined attack upon Batoche. On the 9th the troops advanced slowly towards their objective. It had been previously arranged that the *Northcote* should drop downstream to co-operate in the attack which had been scheduled to begin at eight a.m. The General, however, either miscalculated the marching speed of his column or misunderstood the proposed course of action, as the troops, unfortunately, did not arrive until nine a.m., one hour after the *Northcote* had opened fire on the rebels.[49] Hence the advantages of co-operation were lost. The steamer drifted down the river, her mast and funnels carried away by the steel ferry cable which had been lowered by the half-breeds to stop her, and was soon out of range of the battlefield.

Middleton found the rebel position well chosen and strongly entrenched. On the left the South Saskatchewan river flowed westerly for about three-fourths of a mile, then turning sharply it ran almost due north. The bank on the easterly side was bold and steep and well covered with timber and undergrowth. Nearing Batoche it gradually flattened out, rising again lower down the river. The approach to the village was defended by a line of rifle pits or trenches along the edge of the bank. These extended down the river for nearly a mile and were placed at short intervals from each other. The main position of the rebels extended along the edge of a range of hills running parallel with the river and forming the eastern slope of the valley. The slopes of these hills were fairly well wooded and cut by several coulées which afforded excellent protection to the defending force. Independent of the main line of rifle pits, which extended along the brow of the hill, were many others, placed at various points on the face of the hill, which might possibly become a commanding position. The pits were admirably constructed for their purpose. They were about three or four feet deep with breastworks of earth and logs channelled for the rifles. From these pits a constant fire could be directed against the enemy with more or less impunity. The effectiveness of these fortifications is shown by the fact that the métis sustained no serious casualties during the first three days of the engagement. Middleton himself declared " on inspecting the scene of action after it was over, I was astonished at the strength of the position and at the ingenuity and care displayed in the construction of the rifle pits."[50]

On the first day of the battle Middleton received a definite check. The rebels kept up a steady fire from their trenches as the troops and batteries approached the crest of the hill. Only the rapid fire from the machine gun offered any covering for the movements of Middleton's force. The rebels, it will be observed, were using the same tactics as at Fish Creek and Cut Knife, namely, firing from naturally protected hollows upon an enemy advancing over an unsheltered horizon ; unorthodox tactics but eminently successful. Towards evening Middleton's men retired into a zareba which had been formed about a mile to the rear of the battlefield. The same operation was repeated the following day and again on the 11th.[51]   The troops, under cover of an artillery barrage, advanced to the edge of the hill, engaged in skirmishes with the rebels, suffered a few casualties and then retired into the fortified zareba for the night.

This policy of delayed action had two important results. In the first place it wore down the resistance of the métis. They were not prepared to undergo a long siege. The majority of the half-breeds were armed, not with rifles, but with smooth-bore shot guns. On the second day the Brigade Surgeon stated that the rebels were using slugs and duck shot in their shot guns. On the third day their fire became noticeably less, and Bishop Grandin later stated that they were reduced to using small stones and nails for ammunition.[52]   It must be remembered, moreover, that many of the métis were only half-hearted in their resistance, having been forced to take up arms by the militant party amongst them.

But while Middleton's persistence discouraged the métis, his inaction irritated the troops. The militia officers felt that the General had no confidence in his men and they began to lose confidence in him. The men were indignant at the constant rumours that British Regulars would have to be sent for, but saw little hope of redeeming themselves by Middleton's tactics. It was, therefore, with a feeling of restlessness that the battle was resumed the following day.

On May 12th Middleton planned a great combined movement. Following a reconnaissance on the previous day, he determined to move around to the north-east of Batoche with 150 men, one cannon and the Gatling machine gun, in order to engage the line of rifle pits to the right of the village. In the meantime the main body of troops under Colonel Van Straubenzie were to attack from the south. Owing to a misunderstanding, however, Van Straubenzie remained quiet, waiting to hear Middleton's force engaging the enemy on the right. The misunderstanding turned out to be a fortunate one. The silence on the left apparently convinced the métis that Middleton's move was genuine and that the main attack would come from that direction. They were, therefore, unprepared for what happened.

Middleton was thoroughly displeased and the Midlanders and the Grenadiers were sent to take up their old position on the left flank as on the previous day. But upon this occasion there was no holding the men. Led by Colonels Williams and Grassett they advanced with a cheer, driving the enemy out of the first line of rifle pits. Pushing on they dashed down the slope towards the village of Batoche scattering the métis before them. In the meantime the General rushed forward his support. The 90th, Boulton's Scouts, the Surveyors, the machine gun and the batteries followed the charging line, and in a few moments Batoche had fallen. The métis fled to the woods ; any hope of a further resistance was at an end.[53]

On May 15th Riel was taken prisoner. He had communicated with Middleton during the course of the last day of the battle relative to the position of the non-combatants, and indicated his anxiety for negotiations by scribbling upon the envelope of his despatch " I do not like war " and threatening to put to death his white prisoners " If you do not retreat and refuse an interview."[54] The infantry charge put an end to any possibility of carrying out this threat. On the 13th Middleton wrote to Riel inviting his surrender :

" I am ready to receive you and your council and protect you until your case has been decided upon by the Dominion Government."[55]

This message was borne to Riel by a métis prisoner who undertook the mission at the General's request. Riel replied on the 15th :

" General, I have received only to-day yours of the 13th instant. My council are dispersed. I wish you would let them go quiet and free. I hear that presently you are absent. Would I go to Batoche, who is going to receive me ? I will go to fulfil God's will."[56]

Gabriel Dumont was definitely opposed to surrender, returning the answer to Middleton that " J'ai encore quatre-vingt-dix cartouches à dépenser sur ses gens."[57]   Riel accordingly gave himself up, surrendering to two scouts, while Dumont fled over the frontier into the United States.

Middleton, having taken Batoche and received the surrender of Riel, proceeded to Prince Albert where Colonel Irvine and his force of Mounted Police had remained inactive since the fall of Fort Carlton.   Irvine's inaction threw the police open to considerable criticism and press diatribes.   The appellation of " gophers " was freely applied to them.   This criticism was not only uninformed ; it was unjust.   Irvine was under Middleton's orders and for weeks he was without news of any description, from his superior officer.   In his report Irvine stated that he suggested to Middleton that a combined movement on Batoche might be a good plan, but received only the command " not to attack but to look out for flying half-breeds."[58]   Subsequent communications contained no counter order ; indeed, throughout the whole campaign Irvine was kept in ignorance as to the General's movements.   Had he been ordered to attack from the north while Middleton commanded the assault from the south, the task of reducing Batoche might have been rendered much simpler.

From Batoche Middleton continued, on board the *Northcote*, to Battleford.   Here, on the 23rd he received Poundmaker's submission.   The chief had long favoured negotiations with the whites but had been overruled by the war party ; therefore, upon receipt of the news of Riel's defeat, he at once sent a letter to Middleton asking for terms.[59]

" I am camped with my people at the east of the Eagle Hills, where I am met by the news of the surrender of Riel.   No letter came with the news, so that I cannot tell how far it may be true. I send some of my men to you to learn the truth and the terms of peace, and hope you will deal kindly with them.   I and my people wish you to send us the terms of peace in writing, so that we may be under no misunderstanding, from which so much trouble arises.   We have twenty-one prisoners whom we have tried to treat well in every respect.   With greetings,

" POUNDMAKER."

Middleton was in no mood to negotiate terms and demanded an unconditional surrender.   He replied to Poundmaker :[60]

The Surrender of Poundmaker

" I have utterly defeated the half-breeds and Indians at Batoche, and have made prisoners of Riel and most of his Council. I have made no terms with them, neither will I make terms with you. I have men enough to destroy you and your people or, at least, to drive you away to starve, and will do so unless you bring in the teams you took and yourself and Councillors, with your arms, to meet me at Battleford on Monday, the 26th. I am glad to hear you have treated the prisoners well and have released them."

On the 26th Poundmaker and his men came in, " the most pathetic and picturesque procession I have ever seen," wrote an observer.[61] Middleton, fresh from his victory, refused to take the Indian chief's hand in greeting, disarmed his followers, lectured them severely, and imprisoned Poundmaker and his head men.

With the surrender of Riel and Poundmaker, the only remaining rebel in the field was Big Bear. Having decided to effect a junction with Poundmaker, he had left Frog Lake on May 1st and proceeded as far as Frenchman's Butte, a high conical hill, about twelve miles east of Fort Pitt. Here the Indians determined to hold a Thirst Dance in order to restore harmony between the Plain and the Wood Crees. The feeling between the two bands had become so strained that they no longer camped together but in separate groups, and Big Bear's chiefs saw the necessity of averting the impending rupture between the two factions and restoring their fighting zeal. Messengers were sent to Poundmaker; they returned, not with the expected greetings, but with the news that " the earth was trembling at Battleford with soldiers and horses."[62] Nevertheless the Thirst Dance continued. On May 25th the Indians observed an unfavourable omen. The large Hudson's Bay Company flag which they carried with them was inadvertently raised upside down, a sign of ill-fortune which rendered them very uneasy. On the 26th the alarming news was received that troops were close at hand, at Fort Pitt! It was General Strange with the third column descending the North Saskatchewan to join Middleton in a combined action against Big Bear.

The whole camp was thrown into a panic. The Indians immediately prepared for flight and battle. The Thirst Dance was abandoned, tents were struck, and the camp moved to the north bank of the Red Deer Creek to take up a position on French-man's Butte, thus securing a favourable ground for battle and an open line of retreat.   Here the Indians determined to make a stand.   Old men and women dug themselves pits and covered them with green logs for protection, while the warriors threw up earthworks and sighted their rifles.   At the same time a small scouting party was sent to observe the movements of the troops. This party came into contact with Strange's advance guard under Steele at Pipestone Creek, a few shots were exchanged, two Indians were killed and the others quickly retired to French-man's Butte.[63]

Strange attacked the Indians on May 28th from the south bank of Red Deer Creek.   The Indian position was well suited for defensive purposes.   They occupied " an impregnable position in the forks of the Red Deer and Little Red Deer, presenting a salient with a natural glacis crowned with brush and rifle pits along the crest.   The Red Deer River, which expands into a muskeg, covering the front and flanks of the position which extended about three miles."[64]   Although his force numbered only 195, Strange did not hesitate to attack this natural strong-hold.   Practically no headway was made in a frontal attack, and as it was found impossible to turn the enemy's flank, Strange decided to withdraw.   This was an unfortunate decision in view of the fact that the cannon had finally secured the range of the Indian trenches and the terrified savages were flying from the field at the very moment when Strange gave the order to retire. Finding that the attack was not followed up the Indians returned, picked up their wounded and hastily abandoned property, and rejoined their camp.   It is possible that the Indians might have awaited a second attack, but their ammunition was short and the shrapnel shells had taken the edge off their fighting enthusiasm. Moreover, they were weighed down with the full impedimenta of an Indian camp and the prisoners which they had taken at Frog Lake and Fort Pitt, a circumstance which would make rapid flight impossible in the event of another attack.   They therefore took advantage of the withdrawal of Strange and set off as rapidly as possible towards the north.

Strange made no effort to follow up the retreating enemy.   In fact he was totally unaware that the Indians had taken flight, and was afraid to move without reinforcements.   The news of Otter's

reverse at Cut Knife made Strange over cautious.   As he often
said, he had no intention of " committing Custer."   Furthermore
Strange had not yet established communication with General
Middleton.   There appears to have been a mutual jealousy and
lack of co-operation between the two commanders.   Strange
later declared that he had repeatedly urged upon Middleton the
advisability of proceeding up the Saskatchewan river in order to
catch Big Bear in the rear.   Upon three different occasions couriers
were sent by Strange to the Commander-in-Chief, but like the
ravens of the ark, they never returned, and instead of the reinforcements asked for came a letter calling upon Big Bear to
surrender.   Strange waxed sarcastic :   " General Middleton's
letter addressed to Big Bear, for various reasons—among others
the deficiency of pillar post boxes—failed to reach that gentleman."[65]   After the news of Strange's check at Frenchman's
Butte, Middleton acted with more vigour and, accompanied by
several companies of the 90th, the Midland Battalion, and the
Grenadiers, together with Boulton's, Herchmer's, Brittlebank's
(late French's) and the Surveyor Scouts, he joined General
Strange at Fort Pitt on June 3rd.

   In the meantime the Indians were cutting their way through the
wooded country north of the Saskatchewan in the direction of
Loon Lake.   Their progress was slow owing to the nature of the
country, the size of the camp, the number of prisoners and the
shortage of horses.   It is more than likely that Strange could
have overtaken the Indians and inflicted a defeat upon them had
he taken the risk of a rapid pursuit.   The hardships of the
prisoners were great.   Often they had to wade over swollen
streams up to their waists, to march through mud and rain, and
sleep in drenched clothes.[66]   A certain number had managed to
escape during the confusion of the engagement at Frenchman's
Butte through the connivance of the Wood Crees, but the Plain
Crees kept a close watch upon the remainder and forced them to
keep up with the fleeing camp.

   Several days after the engagement at Frenchman's Butte,
Strange despatched Steele and his Scouts to learn the whereabouts
of the Indians.   Steele, with his mounted force, soon overtook
them at Loon Lake and a skirmish ensued.   Under cover of a
rearguard action the Indians succeeded in transporting their
whole camp over a ford, sixty yards in width, which joined two

branches of the lake. Steele realized the futility of attempting to force a passage over the ford in the face of the Indian opposition, so, lacking the men to attempt a flanking movement, he rejoined the main body of troops.[67]

Upon hearing of this skirmish Middleton at once set out to join Steele. At the same time Strange was ordered to move parallel with Middleton's force in order to intercept the Indians should they turn westwards towards Beaver River. Middleton ignored Colonel Irvine's offer of 175 Mounted Police to follow up Big Bear, preferring to rely upon the militia which had proven itself at Batoche.[68] This was a mistake. The Mounted Police were able to travel twice as fast as the troops, they knew the country, and the habits of the people against whom operations were being conducted. Steele's Scouts had demonstrated the advisability of a mounted force when in pursuit of the Indians, but Middleton ignored this and, like the famous Duke of York, marched his men through the woods and over the rocks and muskegs of Northern Saskatchewan, carrying with them travois and pack saddles in their waggons, and then marched them back again. The troops reached Loon Lake but the Indians forestalled further pursuit by crossing a dangerous morass impassable for Middleton's heavy transport. On June 9th Middleton ordered the pursuit to cease and the troops returned to Battleford. Strange's column reached the Beaver river but failed to locate Big Bear. They were ordered to return on June 24th.

In the meantime Big Bear's camp became divided when the Wood Crees finally determined to break with their allies. A meeting was held and the Wood Crees, concealing their plans with the dissimulation of their race, suggested that they should join Louis Riel, a proposal which was readily accepted by the Plain Crees who were unaccustomed to the wooded country and were becoming disheartened at the persistent pursuit. On the following morning Big Bear and his followers departed eastward. The Wood Crees feigned to follow, but after travelling a short distance along an arm of Loon Lake struck north-west as fast as the nature of the country would permit. The prisoners were taken with the latter who hoped to use them in negotiations with the whites. The Wood Crees had always been less inclined than their Plain kindred to carry on the war and when McLean offered to arrange terms of peace for them, his offer was readily

The Surrender of Miserable Man

accepted. It was, nevertheless, striking evidence of the Indians' distrust of the Government that they commanded McLean to have no dealings with the Government but " to write to our Great Mother, the Queen, and ask her to stop the Government soldiers and Red Coats from shooting us."[69] McLean acquiesced and the prisoners, numbering twenty-seven in all, were released. Provided with a few provisions, some new moccasins, and many good wishes, they set out on a 140 miles journey to Fort Pitt after sixty-two days of captivity. At Loon Lake they overtook the troops and arrived at Fort Pitt on June 24th.

Eight days later, on July 2nd, Big Bear surrendered. His camp had broken up in a general *sauve qui peut*, and the old chief, evading all the columns sent to intercept him by turning in his tracks, travelling almost alone and covering his trail, made his way to Fort Carlton where he gave himself up to Sergeant Smart of the Mounted Police, one of the few men who had not been sent in pursuit of Big Bear's band !

With the surrender of Big Bear the rebellion was at an end. From the military point of view it reflected considerable credit upon the Government. In fifty days the Honourable Adolphe Caron, the Minister of Militia, called into the field five thousand organized Volunteer troops, with four hundred horses ; furnished them with transportation to the seat of the rebellion two thousand miles distant ; pushed forward three columns widely separated to points hundreds of miles from the railway ; kept the troops supplied ; and covered an immense military front so that from the moment the troops arrived the rebellion was localized in the North Saskatchewan, and the rebels were able to strike only at scattered posts. It was not the least important feature of the campaign that it was carried through under the direction of the Minister of Militia practically without the aid of any Regular Army organization.

On the other hand, the campaign displayed many weaknesses. The military leadership, on the whole, exhibited undue hesitancy. The transport service was extravagant,[70] and the hospital service inadequate.[71] Supplies existed only in sufficient quantity for the very small permanent force and the great bulk of the stores of war material, camp equipment, clothing and other necessaries, had to be purchased from private contractors. Hence much of the ammunition was poor[72] and the saddles despatched to

Strange's corps were condemned as unserviceable by a board of officers.[73]   To add to the difficulties of the supply problem, the troops were furnished with three different makes of rifles.   The total cost of the rebellion amounted to over $5,000,000.

The rebellion was followed by the trial of the principal leaders. Riel was condemned to death for treason, and eighteen of his half-breed associates were sentenced to various terms of imprisonment ranging from one to seven years, for treason-felony. Eleven Indians were condemned to hang for murder, but three were ultimately reprieved. Big Bear and Poundmaker were given prison sentences on the charge of treason-felony.   Imasees, Little Poplar, Lucky Man and others managed to avoid capture and escaped over the frontier into Montana.   Two white men, W. H. Jackson and Thomas Scott, were also tried for complicity in the rebellion but were discharged.

Such an outcome to the rebellion was inevitable.   Louis Riel staked the peace of the country and the fate of his people in a gamble that held no chance of success.   The métis were not only defeated ; as a distinct national and political group they were annihilated.   With their homes burned and looted and their property destroyed, many of the métis had no option but to seek entrance into the Indian treaties by virtue of their Indian blood. Others migrated to the Peace River in order to escape the pressure of a merciless civilization.   Those who did not join the rebels were granted the scrip and patents which they had demanded— a procedure which admitted the justice of the métis cause and the culpability of the Federal Government for the rebellion.   But as had occurred in Manitoba, the métis disposed of their scrip to eager purchasers, often at ridiculous prices, content to live for the present at the sacrifice of the future ; and unable to compete with the white men as farmers or artisans, they sank in the social scale, their life, society and national spirit crushed and destroyed.

The Indians suffered less from the rebellion than did the métis. To the loyal bands the Government granted extensive concessions and numerous presents in the form of cattle, sheep, blankets and other useful articles.   The chiefs were rewarded with special gifts of tea, tobacco, blankets and even money.   The rebel Indians were punished but not with vindictive severity.   They were deprived of their annuities until the destruction wrought by the rebellion had been made good, and their horses and arms were taken from them. Strict regulations were enforced in regard to the sale of ammunition, and an effort was made to restrict the movement of the Indians to and from their reserves. The Deputy Superintendent-General also recommended the abolition of the tribal system " in so far as is compatible with the Treaty ; i.e., in all cases in which the Treaty has been broken by the rebel tribes ; by doing away with chiefs and councillors, depriving them of medals and other appurtenances of their offices."[74]   This was, however, only partially carried out. The remnants of Big Bear's band were merged with other bands, thus destroying the principal nucleus of Indian agitation. In 1886 a general amnesty was proclaimed to all who were not actually under sentence and who had not committed murder save in the actual engagements of the war. In the following year Poundmaker and Big Bear were liberated from prison, but neither long survived his freedom. Thus the Indians quickly resumed normal relations with the white men and the Government. In 1896 negotiations were undertaken with the United States for the return of those Indians who had fled to Montana after the rebellion, and on June 2nd, the refugees re-crossed the frontier to return to their old reserves. Among them were Lucky Man and Big Bear's son, Imasees, who, with Wandering Spirit, had been responsible for the Frog Lake Massacre.

THE North-West Rebellion was far more important in its results than in itself. The actual armed conflicts which took place and the numbers of men involved were small by contrast with modern warfare, but they left behind them a religious and racial feud which jeopardized, for the time being, the very foundations of Confederation, and which led, eventually, to a drastic change in the relationship of the two political parties to the racial elements of Old Canada.

The politico-racial crisis of 1885 was, perhaps, the most serious crisis in the early history of Canada. The Dominion had weathered, in 1870, the storm over the Riel troubles in Manitoba, but the ideal of unification and national consciousness was by no means accomplished; and the racial and religious tension which had marked the relations of French and English prior to Confederation, and which had bedeviled the amnesty issue after the Red River insurrection, was renewed by the métis rebellion on the Saskatchewan. In one way the rebellion contributed to national unity. All parts of Canada had rallied to the call to arms, and troops from Nova Scotia, Quebec, Ontario and Manitoba had participated in a common endeavour. But this gain was offset by the bitter racial and religious antagonism which developed, as a result of the rebellion, between the French and English-speaking peoples of the Dominion. This antagonism, for the moment, threatened to wreck the work of Confederation and to destroy for ever its founders' ideal of national unity. The English Canadians of Ontario saw in the North-West Rebellion only a half-breed and Indian outbreak led by a French Catholic rebel, the murderer, in 1870, of an Ontario Orangeman. The French Canadians of Quebec saw in Riel another Papineau leading men of French blood in a struggle against English domination and political oppression. Thus the English clamoured for the punishment of the " rebels " and the French for the pardon of the " patriots." The resultant racial crisis was fortunately tided over, but there remained a wound which only mutual forbearance and goodwill have served to heal. Later crises have arisen, but they have become rarer and less bitter as the ideal of Cartier, two peoples united in a common allegiance and purpose, has taken the uppermost place in the minds of the people of Canada.

But not only did the racial and sectarian dissension try the strength of the federal union ; it also altered the whole course of Canadian politics by destroying the Conservative supremacy in the Province of Quebec upon which Sir John A. Macdonald and Sir George Cartier had built up the Conservative party. As a result of the crisis of 1885 the most conservative province in Canada swung over to the Liberal party, a position which was consolidated by the selection of a French Canadian, Wilfrid Laurier, as leader of that party in 1887. This shifting of the political weight of Quebec, not as a result of any fundamental change in political outlook but under the stress of a powerful racial emotion, brought about a new orientation in Liberal policy and philosophy. It forced the abandonment of the radical tradition and brought to that party a conservative outlook.[1] At the same time the Province of Ontario shifted from a more or less traditional Reform or Liberal allegiance to become a political counterbalance to Quebec. " Le tocsin sinistre de la cloche qui accompagna Riel à l'échafaud," wrote L. O. David, the French Canadian nationalist, " a été le glas funèbre du parti conservateur. Ce grand parti illustré par tant d'hommes éminents, avait cessé de représenter le sentiment national des Canadians-français, une tache de sang ineffaçable souillait son drapeau."[2]

Upon the outbreak of hostilities in the North-West, the people of Ontario responded at once to the call to arms. Many in Quebec, however, were apprehensive of the meaning of the rebellion and expressed their suspicion of the warlike zeal displayed by the sister province. As early as March 31st, L'Etendard, a Conservative clerical journal, expressed its opinion that commissioners, rather than troops, should be sent to the North-West adding :

" Dans l'Ontario surtout l'on manifeste une grande ardeur guerrière. Partout on brûle à courir sus à Riel, sans doute pour soutenir l'honneur de notre drapeau et maintenir l'autorité du gouvernement canadien, mais aussi, nous en sommes convaincus, pour venger sur le chef rebelle l'exécution du malheureux Scott."

On the following day the same newspaper made the first appeal to

race and religion. It has been said that two things only are
able to arouse public opinion in Quebec, a financial crisis or a
question involving French Canadian nationality, and of the two
the latter is the more powerful. National sentiment rather than
materialistic considerations govern French Canadian politics and
life, and *L'Etendard* struck Quebec's most sensitive chord when it
appealed to " la voix du sang."

" Il ne nous est pas permis d'oublier quel rôle la constitution,
les lois d'équité, la voix du sang, nous assigne vis à vis les minor-
ités des autres provinces, notamment celles qui sont nos co-
religionnaires et nos soeurs d'origine."

Arguing that while the métis revolt might not be justifiable, it
was obviously excusable, *L'Etendard* continued :

" On les haït peut-être pour leur origine française, et leur foi
catholique ; il n'est pas même impossible qu'on les ait persécutés
à cause de nous ; deux raisons qui nous feraient un devoir
d'honneur et de loyauté d'accepter une part de solidarité dans
leur situation."[3]

As a result, the mobilization of the French Canadian regiments
met with a certain amount of opposition from the extremists.
Propaganda was spread among the troops that they were being
sent against " nos frères, à des français comme nous."[4]   Certain
newspapers joined in the campaign of misrepresentation. *Le
Nouvelliste* of Three Rivers in an article of several columns
declared " que l'on envoie des canadiens français pour égorger
leurs compatriotes."[5]   *La Verité*, rather belying its name, even
doubted whether Riel was in reality at the head of the métis
movement and stated that the rebellion was the result of

" le fanatisme orangiste qui voudrait l'extermination des métis
français dans le Nord-Ouest, et qui a dû travailler à fomenter
ces troubles afin d'avoir une raison de sévir contre la race détestée.
C'est ainsi que la Russie procède en Pologne."[6]

while on May 2nd *Le Métis*, which appeared in Montreal as
" L'Organe des Populations du Nord-Ouest " declared that every
Ontario volunteer carried with him a piece of rope with which to
hang Riel ![7]

This unfortunate appeal to race prejudice was not confined to
the French Canadians. In Ontario the anti-French and anti-
Catholic extremists made full use of their opportunity to launch
another crusade against " French Domination." On April 20th

the Toronto *Evening News* published a violent slander against the 65th Rifles, a French Canadian Regiment from Montreal. Referring to them as a " mutinous, reckless, disorderly gang . . . no discipline, no spirit, no nothing except drinking whisky and grumbling," the *News* declared that, as they would not fight, the Government was seriously considering disbanding the regiment. This was followed by an article on " French Aggression " which urged the ejection of Quebec from the Canadian Confederation. The following quotation illustrates the tone of the fanatical English press :

" Ontario is proud of being loyal to England. Quebec is proud of being loyal to sixteenth century France. Ontario pays about three-fifths of Canada's taxes, fights all the battles of provincial rights, sends nine-tenths of the soldiers to fight the rebels, and gets sat on by Quebec for her pains. Quebec, since the time of Intendant Bigot, has been extravagant, corrupt and venal, whenever she could with other people's money, and has done nothing for herself or for progress with her own earnings. Quebec now gets the pie. Ontario gets the mush, and pays the piper for the Bleu carnival. . . .

" If we in Canada are to be confronted with a solid French vote, we must have a solid English vote. If Quebec is always to pose as a beggar in the Dominion soup kitchen she must be disfranchised as a vagrant. If she is to be a traitor in our wars, a thief in our treasury, a conspirator in our Canadian household, she had better go out. She is no use in Confederation. Her representatives are a weakness in Parliament, her cities would be nothing but for the English-speaking people, and to-day Montreal would be as dead as the city of Quebec but for the Anglo-Saxons, who are persecuted and kept down by the ignorant French. . . . We are sick of the French Canadians with their patriotic blabber and their conspiracies against the treasury and the peace of what without them might be a united Canada. . . . With Quebec holding the balance of power Canada isn't safe a moment. The constitution, or the British North America Act which is our alleged constitution, must be altered so as to deprive these venal politicians of their powers or else Confederation will have to go. As far as we are concerned, and we are as much concerned for the good of Canada as anyone else, Quebec could go out of the Confederation to-morrow and we would not shed a tear except for joy. If Ontario were a trifle more loyal to herself she would not stand Quebec's monkey business another minute."[8]

The *World* published articles in the same key while the Toronto *Evening Telegram* made no effort to hide its hostile feeling for anything French or French Canadian. Articles of this nature did great harm and the English Canadian press like the French Canadian press, by appeals to prejudice, fomented discontent and fanned into life the embers of racial conflict just at a time when moderation and mutual understanding were essential for the maintenance of national unity.

But the racial fanaticism which was displayed at the beginning and during the rebellion was only the first gust of the storm which followed the trial and execution of Louis Riel.

Riel was tried at Regina during the latter part of the month of July before a stipendiary magistrate and an English-speaking jury of six. A committee was formed in Quebec, the Riel Defence Committee, to provide for the legal defence of the métis leader, and François Lemieux, Charles Fitzpatrick, J. N. Greenshields and T. C. Johnstone were sent to Regina to represent Riel. The Crown was represented by C. Robinson, B. B. Osler, G. W. Burbidge, D. L. Scott and T. C. Casgrain. The Crown charged Riel " as a false traitor " with the full responsibility for the rebellion, and with inciting the Indians to revolt. The defence replied contesting the jurisdiction of the court and basing their case upon a plea of insanity.

That Riel was insane would not, at the present time, be seriously contested. He had entered the asylum of Longue Pointe at Montreal during 1876 and was later transferred to the provincial asylum at Beauport for a period of twenty months from May 20th, 1876, to January 23rd, 1878. One cannot read his political and religious writings, even prior to his return from the United States, without realizing that they were the work of an unbalanced mind. His " mission " was his obsession, and it developed, under the strain and excitement of the agitation of 1884, into a form of mania. Riel saw himself as the " prophet of the new world," he cast aside the doctrines of " la vieille Rome " for those of his own creation. Even with the roar of Middleton's cannon in their ears, Riel and his Council were to be found discussing, not the problem of defence, but new names for the days of the week and acknowledging Riel's divine mission.[9]

Riel himself, however, vigorously repudiated the plea of insanity. In two addresses to the jury he destroyed his only possible defence. He insisted that he was not a madman but a prophet and a patriot; that he had seen the injustices and evils under which his people suffered, and that he had determined to remove them. He argued that the rebellion had been the logical consequence of Crozier's attack upon the métis at Duck Lake, and demanded that he be tried by a special tribunal for his part in the events of 1869–70 as well as for those of 1885. The medical evidence on his behalf was not conclusive and the jury returned a verdict of guilty, adding a recommendation to mercy. Riel was sentenced to suffer the extreme penalty of the law by hanging on September 18th. An appeal was lodged before the Court of Queen's Bench of Manitoba, but the jurisdiction of the lower court was confirmed and the judgment upheld. The Judicial Committee of the Privy Council, to whom Riel then petitioned, declined leave to appeal.

In the meantime Riel was reprieved from September 18th to October 16th, and again to November 12th. A third reprieve was granted to November 16th in order that a commission might further inquire into the state of the condemned man's mind.

The commission was not an expert one, and their official instructions virtually nullified their mission. They were instructed to inquire " not as to whether Riel is subject to illusions or delusions but whether he is so bereft of reason as not to know right from wrong and as not to be an accountable being."[10] Although the commission was unable to agree upon a common report, the tenor of their individual reports was similar, namely that while Riel obviously suffered from delusions of greatness upon political and religious questions, on other points he appeared to be quite sensible and able to " distinguish right from wrong."[11] Hence, on November 16th, 1885, Louis Riel was hanged.

The passing of the sentence of death upon Riel brought forth protests from all parts of the world. Petitions for clemency poured into the Government from the French Canadian parishes of Quebec, Ontario, Manitoba and the North-West Territories. From the United States came petitions from New York, Chicago, St. Louis and elsewhere. The International Arbitration and Peace Association of London urged the remission of the death sentence. Lord Clifford forwarded a petition from the English Catholics and a certain Dr. Lockyer wrote three letters to the

o

Colonial Office requesting their intervention for " this poor daft enthusiast." Petitions were also sent to the Governor-General from France, and one was addressed to the Queen from Le Syndicat de la Presse Coloniale Française. Riel himself also addressed a petition to President Cleveland of the United States.

Riel, as an American citizen, had already written to the American consul at Winnipeg during the autumn of the previous year. He assured him of " the peaceable, constitutional and energetic movement which is taking place in the Saskatchewan District,"[12] and enclosed a copy of the petition which the Settlers' Union were preparing to forward to the Canadian Government. After his arrest Riel wrote again to the consul, declaring that he was not guilty of treason, that the court was incompetent to try him, and appealing " to the Government of my adopted country for help through you."[13] In August he sent another appeal for assistance and in September addressed a petition to the President of the United States.[14] The American consul expressed his sympathy with the case, and petitions from different regions urged the American Government to intervene to save Riel on the ground that he was an American citizen. The American Government maintained an attitude which was strictly correct under the circumstances. The Secretary of State replied to a petition from Rochester, New York, that " such citizenship . . . even if beyond doubt, would not secure the possessor any immunity from Canadian law, when, as it is definitely certified to the Government in the . . . present instance, the offense was committed within the territory of the Dominion."[15]

The British Government also maintained an attitude of official silence. Following a different course from that pursued in regard to the amnesty question the Colonial Government made no attempt to shift the responsibility of deciding upon the question to the Home Government. In fact, Macdonald endeavoured to reduce the status of the rebellion to that of a domestic riot and thus preclude any possibility of Imperial intervention. Writing to the Governor-General he urged that " this North-West outbreak was a mere domestic trouble, and ought not to be elevated to the rank of a rebellion."[16] Lansdowne, however, pointed out that Macdonald's view was untenable. " The outbreak," he replied, " was, no doubt, confined to our own territory and may therefore properly be described as a domestic trouble, but I am afraid we have all of us been doing what we could to elevate it to the rank of a rebellion, and with so much success that we cannot now reduce it to the rank of a common riot."[17]

The British Government had been kept informed as to the progress of the rebellion, but there is no evidence that any correspondence passed between the Colonial Office and the Dominion relative to the punishment of the leaders. Nor was such desirable. If Canada was to attain nationhood she had to accept the responsibility of the solution of her own internal problems and racial disputes. Moreover the precedent of non-interference had been firmly established by the refusal of the Home Government to promulgate an amnesty for the Manitoba insurrectionists in 1870. It is, however, interesting to note that the advisability of a commutation of the death sentence passed upon Riel was discussed by several members of the Imperial Cabinet. Lord Carnarvon was definitely in favour of such a course. Writing privately to the Prime Minister he said, " It is a matter of grave doubt in my mind whether this is not a case for exercise of Royal Clemency under proper conditions."[18] The reply was definite. The Riel question was purely a matter for the Canadian Government to decide upon.

" My dear Carnarvon,

" I received your message from Ashbourne, and brought before our colleagues the question of Riel. We are of opinion that there should be no interference on our part with the course which the Canadian Government may think it their duty to pursue, and I am informed that at the present time we have received no intimation that we shall be asked to support a commutation of sentence.

" It is not felt to be right to volunteer to the Canadian Government any statement that we should be willing to assent to a commutation, but, if appealed to, we should certainly not take a more severe view than that of the Government at Ottawa, who must best know what duty and policy necessitate.

" I may add that our colleagues appeared to be unanimous in this decision.

" Yours very truly,

" Fred. Stanley."[19]

Carnarvon persisted. He replied to the above letter with another outlining his own views :

" MY DEAR STANLEY,

" Thanks for your letter. I think you must have somewhat misunderstood my ideas as to Riel. I never thought of an interference with the Canadian Government, it would be very imprudent for us formally and unsolicited to recommend any new course to them. But the situation might easily and in the shortest space of time become most critical, and I think it might be desirable that the Canadian Government should know in *complete confidence* that we are ready to assist them if the difficulty is likely to overtax their strength. Beyond this I never dreamt of going : but up to this I think you may with perfect security venture. Such a communication may be absolutely confidential and need not of course extend to more than one or two individuals.

" My opinion of Sir J. Macdonald is an extremely high one, and I have known him intimately for many years ; but it must be remembered that he is now an old man and that his Lower Canada friends and surroundings are not what they once were. I see some danger in this.

" He may be strong enough to hang Riel—who richly deserves it—but I *know* that it will be an act that will severely strain the relations of parties and men in Canada, and I feel sure that it must add a fresh element of irritation to an already dangerous heap of combustibles.

" I have no doubt that there are many R.C. priests and laymen who are content to see Riel hung, but there are many more, I am afraid, who will bitterly resent it.

" I would venture earnestly to press on you the importance of not only jealously watching the progress of the matter, but of not hesitating to assume any responsibility if the crisis should unfortunately (as I trust it may not) become acute.

" I hope also you will forgive me for thus pressing my opinion upon you. I should not do so if I did not know personally and intimately many of the persons and if I had not a very lively sense of the dangerous elements with which we are dealing in this matter."[20]

The British Government were not prepared to adopt this line of action, although the evidence shows that conversations were held privately on the question with certain Canadian officials.[21] Finally, on November 13th, Lord Lansdowne transmitted a long memorandum on the Riel affair to the British Government. This memorandum stated the determination of the Canadian Government that the sentence upon Riel should be carried into effect and outlined the reasons which prompted this decision.[22]

On receipt of this memorandum Carnarvon noted on the margin of his copy, " I still think the execution was hazardous and a strain on the relations of Quebec and Ontario."

Carnarvon's misgivings were well-founded. The social and economic factors which had led to the rebellion were completely lost sight of in the maze of political, religious and racial controversy which followed the condemnation of Riel. From August to December the racial agitation continued to increase in intensity. Quebec called for pardon and Ontario for punishment.   Passion mounted on each side until it threatened the very foundations of the federal union.   The sentence of death brought forth a storm of protest from the French Canadians and a storm of approval from the English Canadians.   *La Patrie, La Presse, L'Etendard, La Verité, L'Electeur* and other journals heaped their praises upon the métis chief and hurled anathemas upon the " Orangistes." From *L'Electeur* came the following eulogy of Riel :

" L'Histoire te consacrera une page glorieuse et ton nom sera gravé dans le coeur de tous les vrais canadiens-français. . . . Tes fautes personnelles s'effacent devant la sainteté de la noble cause dont tu t'es fait le champion.   Jeanne d'Arc ! Napoléon ! Chénier ! Riel ! C'est avec le plus profond respect que l'on prononce vos noms sacrés.   Chénier a son monument, Riel tu auras le tien."[23]

From the English press came the opposite view :

" We consider that such lives as that of Riel are blots and stains on our humanity which ought to be summarily removed by the hand of justice in like manner as the dangerous cancer is removed from the human body by the hand of the surgeon."[24]

In September the *Orange Sentinel* hinted at the break up of Confederation :

" The French are as much French now as before Wolfe vanquished Montcalm upon the Heights of Abraham.   The dividing line is sharply drawn, and although upon many previous occasions differences of race and religion have been made strongly apparent, never before was the demarcation as distinct as over the present Riel imbroglio.   The signs of the times point to the fact that this artificial nationality cannot last much longer."[25]

So vital an issue as this could not but raise questions of party attitude.   During the progress of the rebellion the Liberal Opposition in the Federal Parliament had acted with moderation.

It had recognized the urgent necessity of the moment, the suppression of the rebellion, and confined the party battle to occasional sniping at the Government's conduct of the campaign. The moment, however, that Batoche had fallen and the leaders of the insurrection were in prison, the Liberals opened fire upon the Government. A preliminary barrage was fired on May 21st, when Edward Blake, now Leader of the Opposition, speaking on the adjournment, accused the Government of criminal negligence and responsibility for the rebellion.[26] On July 6th Blake opened the attack in earnest, moving :

" That in the administration of North-West affairs by the present Government, prior to the recent outbreak, there have occurred grave instances of neglect, delay, and mismanagement, in matters affecting the peace, welfare and good government of the country."[27]

This speech was a powerful indictment of Sir John's administration but it was injured by excessive detail and exceeding dullness. The speech took six hours to deliver and, if we may believe the Montreal *Gazette*, " By the end of the first hour no less than fifteen of his own followers were fast asleep, among them Mr. Watson of Marquette who slept so soundly that he had actually to be shaken by the shoulders to wake him up."[28] Macdonald replied with *tu quoque*. He accused Blake of gratuitously furnishing a brief for the counsel for Louis Riel, and stated, with some truth, that the whole object was to make a case against the Government rather than to obtain justice for the North-West. He denounced the Liberal administration of Mackenzie for their neglect of the half-breeds and the North-West during their term of office, contended that the half-breeds had no claim to any special treatment different from the whites, and argued that the Government had conceded the demands of the insurgents before the rebellion had actually broken out. Wilfrid Laurier seconded Blake's motion and Girouard, another French Canadian, replied for the Government. Other speakers followed. On the whole the dialectic honours rested with the Opposition. Their case against the Government was conclusive, but party lines prevailed and Blake's motion was defeated by 105 votes to 49.[29]

In the province of Quebec the Liberals at once grasped the opportunity which the métis rebellion afforded for political capital against the Conservative party. Visiting the sins of the federal Conservatives upon their provincial colleagues, the Liberals moved a resolution of censure in the Legislative Assembly on April 15th, even while the French Canadian regiments were on their way to the front! Amongst other things this resolution declared :

" That this House, while again asserting its loyalty to the Crown, deeply regrets the troubles in the North-West, and that its members, as citizens, solemnly protest against the Federal Government which they hold responsible for the blood which has been shed, and, in particular for the culpable neglect of the Minister of the Interior, who, it might be said, has driven the half-breeds to take up arms, and for the incapacity of the Minister of Militia which seriously exposes the lives of our volunteer soldiers."[30]

The Government replied with the following amendment :

" This House regrets the unfortunate events which have occurred in the North-West but admires the courage and loyalty of the volunteer officers and men of this Province, who, listening only to the voice of patriotism and duty have, without hesitation, abandoned their occupations and their families to reach the scene of the insurrection.

" That through motives of loyalty, of patriotism and of prudence, this House cannot discuss at the present moment the facts which may have led a portion of the inhabitants of the North-West to sedition and to forget their duty towards the constituted authorities ; but that it deems it its duty to express its confidence, that the Government of *Canada* will neglect no legitimate means to prevent as much as possible the shedding of blood, and will promptly restore tranquillity and peace."[31]

This resolution and the amendment were hotly debated, but on April 21st the Government amendment was carried on a party vote of forty-one to fifteen. This resolution was both mischievous and premature. The North-West question was outside the realm of provincial politics and the Government were justified in avoiding entanglements in a matter of purely federal concern. The Liberal resolution was not prompted by any real sympathy for the métis, but was obviously designed to excite racial prejudice against the Conservative Government in Quebec by striking at it through the shortcomings of Macdonald's administration at Ottawa.

Macdonald himself was in a quandary. The Riel issue

threatened to disrupt the diverse elements of which the federal Conservative party were formed. Hitherto Macdonald had depended upon the unnatural alliance of the Orangemen of Ontario and the Roman Catholics of Quebec. In his Cabinet sat Mackenzie Bowell, the Grand Master of the Orange Order, and Sir Hector Langevin, the Ultramontane leader of the French Catholics. Under the stress of the Riel agitation this alliance broke down and Macdonald was faced with the alternative of pardoning Riel to retain the support of the French Catholics, or of allowing the law to take its course to please the Orangemen. On the one hand the Orange party of Ontario had always been, not merely Conservative, but Tory to the backbone. The pardon of Riel would force them into the Liberal camp, or, at the very least, to refrain from voting. On the other hand, if Riel were not pardoned the French Canadian Conservatives, upon whom Macdonald had been able to rely for support since the days of Cartier, might secede in a body, thus placing the Ministry in an impossible position.

There is no doubt that considerable pressure was brought to bear upon Macdonald by the French Canadian supporters of his party. Till the day of Riel's execution they felt that their influence would save the métis leader. Recognized Bleu papers, such as *Le Canadien*, *L'Etendard*, *Le Monde*, and later *La Minerve*— the latter two the official organs of Sir Hector Langevin and Adolphe Chapleau—loudly demanded clemency for Riel and assured the people that the Bleus would not let Riel hang. The appointment of the Insanity Commission on October 31st was the result of French Canadian pressure and *Le Monde* was the first to announce the appointment. Chapleau even went as far as to prepare a memorandum for his resignation from the Cabinet.[32]

The last few days prior to the execution were critical days for the Government. Langevin and Chapleau were wavering on the brink of resignation in the face of the universal disapproval expressed by the French Canadians ; Caron alone remained firm in his support of the Government, but he now carried little weight in Quebec as a result of his vigorous suppression of the Riel Rebellion. The rank and file of the French Conservative members of Parliament were openly rebellious.[33] On November 12th several members met in Montreal to decide upon a course of action. The movement was inaugurated by D. Girouard,

M.P. for Jacques Cartier, and was supported by Senators Lacoste and Trudel, the latter the director of the pro-Riel newspaper, *L'Etendard*. A committee was formed to interview Langevin to learn the intention of the Government regarding Riel. Langevin's lips were sealed by his oath as Privy Councillor so he at once telegraphed to Macdonald :

" Coursol, Desjardins, Girouard and Vanasse, met me here and say they and all others object to execution and will act accordingly."[34]

Macdonald replied :

" Keep calm resolute attitude—all will come right."[35]

In the meantime the rebellious Conservatives sent telegrams to all the members from Quebec inviting them to meet in caucus at Montreal. Eleven responded and many others sent telegrams expressive of sympathy with the object of the meeting. The presence of the eleven country members with the Montreal members brought the caucus to twenty-one in number including three Conservative senators. It was first proposed to send a telegram to Macdonald to the effect that if Riel were hanged it would be impossible for them to justify the Government before their constituents, and that they would have no other recourse, remaining consistent with themselves, but to go into opposition. Ouimet[36] and Fortin refused to subscribe to such a course on the ground that it was unconstitutional to threaten a ministry before it had officially announced its decision. After further discussion the following telegram was despatched to Macdonald bearing the signatures of sixteen members, the two above mentioned declining to sign.

" Dans les circonstances l'exécution de Louis Riel serait un acte de cruauté dont nous repoussons la responsibilité."[37]

Three other French Conservatives who were not present sent a similar message. On November 14th Macdonald was inundated with further telegrams from the various Conservative constituencies in Quebec, expressing their approval of the position taken by the " bolting Bleus." That this pressure was organized is shown by the fact that virtually every telegram took the following form :

" Les soussignés électeurs de . . . déclarent approuver cordialement la position prise par les députés conservateurs de la

Province de Québec dans le télégramme qu'ils vous ont addressé hier le 13 courant et ils vous prient de bien vouloir agir en conséquence dans les meilleurs intérêts de la paix et de l'avenir de la Confédération."[38]

Chapleau was also interviewed by the " bolters " but to no avail. Chapleau had already made his decision to retain office and " to fight and to fall in the old ship and for the old flag."

To add to Macdonald's worries, threats were hurled at him from every side. From one correspondent, who preferred to remain anonymous, he received the following :

" BEWARE OLD MAN. The death of Riel by hanging would be your own death. I give you fair warning so beware. And if Riel is hanged prepare to appear before your Creator without further notice. You will be liable to fall at any moment. Remember that this is no snake story."[39]

From the " Sister of an Ontario Volunteer " came a letter to the effect that if Riel were pardoned, it would be an " outrage on the country and a great calamity " ; that Riel was not only a " double-died " but also a " cold-blooded murderer " ; that nothing had moved " the rebel monster " to mercy in the case of " poor Scott " so that he himself deserved none ; that " hundreds of Reformers " would support Macdonald " if Riel gets his deserts" ; but if he was pardoned owing to the " machinations of the Romish Clergy " he would only " lay another lot of our noble volunteers under the sod."[40] From Valleyfield, Quebec, came the following missive[41] accompanied by a sketch of a revolver :

" Monsieur. Il y a devant nous une *question* qui faits *boucoups* de *troubles* parmi la *population canadiennes*. Sur le sort de Riel. Si vous lui *accorder* pas son pardon nous avons *désidé* de vous *paser* une *palle* dons la *tête*, et c'est *moi* qui *suis* rester charger de cette affaire. Je vous avertis dy voir sans délai, il vous reste a *choisire*, la pendéson de Riel *vous cosera* votre *mort certeine*, j'ai déjà le *troue à l'oeuil* sur votre *fron*. J'ai prefaire vous *avertire* afin que je soit *claire devant Dieu*. Je suis pas pour vous donnez de long *détaille*, à un renord qui cant *le ferre, rappelle vous* de *McGille*. Il est désidé de vous le même sort certin.

" *Attantion   Attantion*
" Je suis un
" (sketch of a revolver)   " *National Nelliste*
"Ce qui est prais."

From an Ontario barrister came a warning of a different nature, but one to which Macdonald, the politician, would pay more attention :

"Ontario is not going much longer to be sat upon by those Frenchmen and the priesthood. Quiet people here are beginning to talk savagely. The Anglo-Saxons will turn some day and make them ' go halves ' or drive them into the sea. The latter would be the best place."[42]

Throughout the raging tide of agitation Macdonald stood firm. In his eyes Riel was twice guilty of rebellion. His offence was therefore doubly unpardonable and Macdonald cried " He shall hang though every dog in Quebec bark in his favour."[43] Political expediency probably dictated the same decision, for Macdonald was always an astute politician. He fully appreciated the feeling in Ontario and possibly felt that he stood to gain more in Ontario than he would lose in Quebec. A by-election in East Durham in August must have reinforced this opinion. The seat was carried by the Government in a campaign in which the Riel question was the dominant issue. During the campaign the Government candidate wrote to Macdonald :

"During my canvass I have found that the Riel matter has, before any other question, engaged the attention of the farmers, and many of the very strongest of our friends have not hesitated to declare, that, if the Rebel is not hung, they will never again vote on the Conservative side. They are very much in earnest over this question and evidently quite determined to carry out their threat to desert the party in the event of a reprieve being granted by the Government . . . as one old farmer told me, ' Well the election is coming on at a rather bad time, but I'm glad it is before the 18th of September for I can give John A. Macdonald one more vote, but God help him next time if he don't hang Riel.' "[44]

As far as Quebec was concerned Macdonald probably felt that the political storm would soon blow itself out. He had retained the support of the French Canadian Ministers, and Quebec was, after all, fundamentally conservative. Moreover, the Roman Catholic clergy, owing to Riel's apostasy, were opposed to the agitation. Nevertheless Macdonald underestimated the intensity of the racial feeling in Quebec and, by throwing in his lot with Ontario, he practically wrecked the French Conservative party and threw an outraged French Canada into the arms of Mercier and Laurier.

The position of Langevin, Chapleau and Caron as the representatives of French Canada in the " pendard " Cabinet was exceedingly difficult. Their natural sympathies, as we have observed, were with their nationality. Under the circumstances resignation was the obvious course. Only the fear of what such a course might lead to restrained them. In his letter to Macdonald on November 12th, Chapleau outlined his reasons for remaining in Cabinet in spite of his disagreement with the Government's policy relative to Riel.[45]

" MY DEAR SIR JOHN,

" I spent the greatest part of the night in preparing my memorandum in support of my disagreement in the Riel case. Just as I was sending it this morning, I hesitated, in the face of the terrible responsibility of an agitation on such a question where national animosities would surely meet to fight their battle, and after a long meditation I have decided not to incur that great responsibility.

" I believe in the guilt of the prisoner. His mental delusions would be the only extenuating point against the full application of the law in his case.

" In the state of doubt in which I am with regard to that point, I prefer giving the benefit of the doubt to the law than to the deluded criminal.

" We may be called upon to suffer, my Quebec colleagues and myself, I more than others,[46] at the hands of our people, owing to the intense feeling which exists in our Province. (It is a further reason with me not to abandon my colleagues, as it would look like desertion at the hour of danger.)

" However, I prefer the risk of personal loss to the national danger imminent, with the perspective of a struggle in the field of race and religious prejudices. We will have to fight, and perhaps to fall. Well, I prefer, after all, to fight and to fall in the old ship and for the old flag.

" I would prefer in this case, that the minute of last evening's Council would record my assent to the decision of the Council."

" Yours faithfully,
" J. A. CHAPLEAU."

Caron and Langevin likewise realized the fact that only by remaining loyal to the Government could they hope to avoid the worst evils of a racial conflict.

At the same time it may have been that Macdonald played upon the mutual jealousies of his French Canadian ministers. It has been said that Macdonald followed the precept of *divide et impera* with his Quebec colleagues ; that the frequent changes in their Cabinet representation were more policy than accident. Certainly the jealousy of Langevin and Chapleau was ill-concealed and the latter's strong ambition to step into the shoes of Cartier as leader of the French Conservatives was well-known. *La Presse* stated, perhaps with a certain amount of truth, that Macdonald held his ministers in his Cabinet during this crisis by playing one against the other :

" A Sir Hector le vieux renard dit : si vous résignez Chapleau deviendra le chef des conservateurs et vous redeviendrez GROS JEAN. A M. Chapleau il dit : Avec Langevin je m'arrangerai toujours pour avoir une majorité et vous serez sacrifié inutilement. Quant à M. Caron, il ne se donne pas la peine de feindre ni de faire aucune diplomatie, il lui donne le mot d'ordre et lui dit : Allez."[47]

But whatever motives may have inspired the three French Canadians to retain their posts, there is little doubt that their action modified the Riel agitation and saved Canada from the most serious consequences of a bitter racial struggle. Knowing well the danger of Anglo-French antagonism they feared that if it were unrestrained the unity of the Dominion would be endangered. They endeavoured, therefore, to prevent the formation of parties divided according to race and creed. A united French Canada opposed to a united English Canada was the one development to be avoided at all costs if the Confederation were to be preserved. By refusing to sacrifice the future of the Dominion to the popular but irresponsible clamours of the moment, Langevin, Chapleau and Caron earned for themselves the temporary ill-will of many of their compatriots but the lasting regard of those who have placed the ideal of Canadian national unity before racial prejudice and sectional antagonism.

The outbreak of national resentment in Quebec proved to be a gift from the political gods to the Liberal party. Since Confederation the provincial Liberal party had tasted the sweets of office for only eighteen months in 1878–9 and they welcomed the opportunity to advance their party interests. Honoré Mercier was then the leader of the party. He was a man of great energy, brilliant, bold and inflammatory, and unequalled as a political orator. He hurled himself at once into the midst of the Riel agitation and within a year brought about the downfall of the Conservative régime in Quebec.

On November 22nd, following the execution of Riel, a great public meeting was held on the Champ de Mars in Montreal. Every effort was made to " boom " the gathering, and *La Patrie* invited " a hundred thousand free citizens to be there, so that their voices might be heard, from the shores of the Atlantic to those of the Pacific, in protestation of the execution of Riel."[48] The result was a political demonstration such as Montreal had never before seen.   Thousands of people thronged the square. Three platforms were erected and decorated with the Tricolour and the Union Jack.   Thirty-seven speakers addressed the multitude, among them Mercier, Laurier and Marcil representing the Liberals, and Coursol, Desjardins and Tarte, hitherto supporters of Sir John Macdonald. Everywhere appeals were made to political prejudice and racial passion.   Laurier declared that " there never had been a people who had suffered such gross injustice as the métis," and that " if he had lived on the shores of the Saskatchewan he would have taken up a rifle himself to defend his property."[49]   Tarte, who with his organs *Le Canadien* and *L'Evénement* was soon to return to the Conservative fold only to desert it again, cried, " may the hand wither that holds the pen of the man on *Le Canadien* who would not defend the rights of the French Canadians."   Coursol declared that the Conservatives of Quebec would no longer support Macdonald " who had declared a war of injustice on the French people " and denounced Langevin, Chapleau and Caron " who were not only cowards, but they were something worse than cowards—they were traitors."   Senator Trudel compared Riel to Joan of Arc who had been burnt at the stake " by the ancestors of the men who hanged Riel."   Mercier was even more extreme in his comparison.   He began his speech by saying " Our poor brother is dead.   He has been sacrificed to the fanaticism of the Orangemen and the three traitors of the race are still in the Macdonald Cabinet holding portfolios," and continued by stating that Riel had died upon the scaffold, a hero given to his country, " who like Christ forgave his enemies." By hanging Riel, Mercier claimed that the Conservatives had struck a blow at justice and humanity, and that Liberals and Conservatives had now joined together in Quebec " to weep for the man whose death raised a cry of pity from the hearts of all civilized people." Henceforth there were to be no more Liberals or Conservatives. All differences of party and creed were to be submerged in one common effort to overthrow the Macdonald Government at Ottawa and the Ross Government at Quebec.

The direct outcome of this agitation and the meeting on the Champ de Mars was the formation of " Le Parti National." Such a development was the inevitable result of the defection of the nineteen Bleus and the appeal for a united French Canadian party. The Conservative Senator Lacoste and later J. A. Chapleau were offered the leadership of the " national " party, but both were unwilling to accept the responsibility and finally the choice fell upon Honoré Mercier.

The new Parti National soon met with obstacles which prevented it from becoming a permanent force in Canadian politics. The old jealousies and the old rivalries could not be smothered. The Ultramontanes could not unite permanently with the Rouges whom they had attacked for years. The most important factor, however, was the knowledge that an exclusively French party would result in an exclusively English party, and a passionate struggle in which race would be pitted against race and creed against creed. Ever since the union of the two Canadas, French Canadians had recognized the folly of constructing parties on racial lines and Langevin and his colleagues were only following a sane tradition when they refused to countenance such a project with their resignations. The fact that the three French Canadian Ministers and three-fifths of their following continued to support the Conservative party, in spite of the popular outcry, prevented the formation of a really " national " party built on racial lines as a consequence of Riel's execution. Thus Le Parti National, composed of a small number of dissentient Bleus and led by the official leader of the Liberal party, was doomed to failure as a distinct party. It was significant that the Liberals did not leave their party to join Le Parti National as did the Conservatives. Thus the " nationalists " were eventually absorbed into the Liberal party fold, while those who were unable to reconcile themselves to the new Grit-Rouge-Bleu alliance returned to their old allegiance. But in this we anticipate our story.

In Ontario racial passions kept pace with those in Quebec. The news of the execution met with the general approval of the people.   Parades and demonstrations were held and everywhere Riel was burned in effigy.   In Ottawa, Sherbrooke and elsewhere conflicts between the anti-Riel English and the pro-Riel French demonstrators led to many broken heads and much ill-feeling. As the agitation increased in intensity in Quebec so it did in Ontario.   The formation of Le Parti National led at once to the suggestion that a similar party should be formed by the English-speaking people of the Dominion.   The Toronto *Mail*, which had been calm enough in July to admit that " the métis had good grounds for complaint " and to agree with Blake's charge that the Government's negligence " was gross and inexcusable and contributed to bring about the insurrection,"[50] cried in November :

" the French Canadians are now seeking to compel us to recognize their right to suspend the operation of the law whenever a representative of their race is in the toils.   But let us solemnly assure them again that, rather than submit to such a yoke, Ontario would smash Confederation into its original fragments, preferring that the dream of a united Canada should be shattered forever than that unity should be purchased at the expense of equality."[51]

And again :

" if the overthrow of the present Cabinet is to be followed by the planting of French ascendancy—and such in effect is Mr. Mercier's programme—then as Britons we believe the Conquest will have to be fought over again, and Lower Canada may depend upon it, there will be no Treaty of 1763."[52]

There is little doubt that in these inflammatory and irresponsible utterances the *Mail* expressed the dominant feeling in Ontario. Here, as well as in Quebec, the intense racial antagonism threatened to undo all that had been accomplished in the way of national consolidation.

But while the Liberals had made the most of the Riel agitation in Quebec, in Ontario it redounded to the benefit of the Conservatives.   From the outbreak of trouble in the North-West both Liberals and Conservatives had been one in demanding the punishment of Louis Riel.   The Toronto *Globe* had vied with the *Mail* in stating that " to allow those who incited the rebellion, and the Indians who have imbrued their hands in the blood of the peaceful settlers and of women and children, to go unwhipt of justice would be neither just nor politic."[53]   In fact the Liberal press in Ontario endeavoured to take advantage of the prevailing public feeling by suggesting that the French Conservatives would never allow Riel to hang and that Sir John : " will shelter himself behind Her Majesty, will reprieve Riel, will 'wish to God he could catch him,' will point to the *Globe* in order to show that he tried very hard to convict Riel, and every Tory politician in the land will be satisfied."[54] During the East Durham by-election the Liberal candidate stated openly that " the sentence passed upon Riel will not be carried out because Sir John is afraid of the Bleus."[55]

It was accordingly a great blow to the party when the Liberal leader, Edward Blake, showed a disposition to raise the question of Riel's mental condition. Blake was obviously convinced that Riel was *non compos mentis*, but he failed to realize the unfavourable reaction the advocacy of such a view would have upon his party in Ontario. The Liberals had, for many years, been nourished on the anti-French Canadian tradition of George Brown and the *Globe*, and Blake himself had been foremost in 1870 in condemning Riel for the " murder" of Scott. His defence of Riel in 1885 was, therefore, a political blunder. The Liberal party accepted the change of front unwillingly, although the *Port Hope Guide*, which had written in August " It has come to a pretty pass indeed when a red-handed rebel can thus snap his fingers at the law," with easy inconsistency stated after Riel's execution " It has come to a pretty pass indeed that in the noontide glare of the nineteenth century political offenders must suffer death if they dare to assert their just rights."[56] The Conservatives gloated over the Liberal discomfiture :

" That Ontario Reformers, whose politics for forty years has been one long cry against French domination in the ordinary affairs of the country, should now consent to recognize French domination in so sacred a domain as that of the administration of law, is a phenomenon only to be accounted for by the depth and profundity of their desire for office."[57]

Blake was, however, unable to carry the majority of his followers with him, and when Parliament opened in the spring of 1886 the Liberals were divided between those of Ontario who, on the whole, believed Riel's execution to be justifiable and those of Quebec who denounced it as a " judicial murder."

This absence of unity among the Opposition forces proved to be a fortunate circumstance for the Federal Government and one of which they took full advantage.   On March 11th, Philippe Landry, a French Conservative, moved :

" That this House feels it its duty to express its deep regret that the sentence of death passed upon Louis Riel, convicted of high treason, was allowed to be carried into execution."[58]

Whether or not this motion was sincere is open to question. Certainly the available evidence would imply that it was merely an adroit political manœuvre to force a debate on the question of Riel's execution upon a divided Opposition.   In any event Macdonald took full advantage of it.   Langevin was instructed to take the floor immediately after Landry and move the previous question.[59]   This prevented the moving of any amendment and forced the Liberals to debate a question upon which they had no common view, instead of upon the question of the Government's North-West policy upon which they and the " bolting Bleus " might have united.   The result was that, when the division was finally taken, the Government, supported by a large number of Ontario Liberals, was sustained by the largest majority of the session.

The debate was long and hotly contested.   Macdonald was absent from the House for the first few days, and the management of the debate was left in the capable hands of Sir Hector Langevin. Langevin's tactics were to move each day to make the Landry motion the first order of the day until disposed of.   For thirteen days the debate continued.   The Ontario Liberals largely refrained from speaking.   Blake inflicted upon the House a seven-hour dissertation on Riel's insanity which had taken him three months to prepare.   J. C. Rykert, a Conservative speaker, regaled the Government benches with specimens of Liberal inconsistency culled from his scrap book.   Malcolm Cameron accused the Government of casting dice over Riel's body and then finally yielding to Orange pressure.   Langevin's speech was brief and formal.   The best orations were those of Laurier for the Opposition and Thompson for the Government.   Laurier's in particular was a brilliant effort and earned for him the epithet of " the silver tongued Laurier."   The debate was of high order throughout, moderate in tone and distinctly superior to the rantings of the press and platform.   On March 24th the question was put to a vote.   Seventeen French Conservatives voted against the Government, a defection which was offset by twenty-three Liberal votes from Ontario, including those of the former Prime Minister, Alexander Mackenzie, and his Minister of Finance, Richard Cartwright. The final division was 146 to 52.[60]

The federal Conservative Government had thus manœuvred itself out of difficulty, but its provincial protégé was by no means so fortunate. In Quebec the Riel agitation had continued unabated under the stimulus of party politics. The Liberal and " Nationard " press whipped up any waning enthusiasm. Riel Clubs were formed and Riel Masses said. In the provincial Parliament the following resolution was moved by a " National " Conservative :

" That the Members of this House, without wishing to interfere in questions which are not within the scope of Provincial Legislatures, deem it their duty, nevertheless, to take advantage of their being assembled together to give a more public and solemn expression to the regret and sorrow which the people of this Province, whom they are elected to represent, universally manifested on the occasion of the deplorable execution of *Louis Riel*, which execution was carried into effect even after the recommendation of the jury to mercy, and in despite of all the reasons, in favour, from a humane point of view, of a commutation of the sentence."[61]

The Government were thus confronted with a dilemma. They could not accept the motion without forswearing their allegiance to the federal Conservative party with whom they had always maintained a close alliance, nor could they refuse it without incurring the displeasure of a racially conscious electorate. Therefore they tried to sidestep this political trap by arguing that " this House has no jurisdiction in these matters, which appertain exclusively to the Federal authorities," and that " this House . . . should not . . . express any opinion upon the execution of *Louis Riel*."[62] This was the strictly correct position to take, but it brought upon the Quebec Government all the unpopularity which a direct refusal of the motion would have involved. As the summer progressed the trend of opinion in Quebec became more pronounced. Four by-elections—two provincial and two federal—went against the Conservatives and the position of the Ross Government thus became more and more unsteady. Even Chapleau referred to it as " the sick man " which " like Turkey, lives on the strength of the *Great Powers*."[63]   Finally, on September 11th, Ross dissolved the provincial Parliament.

In the ensuing election the Riel question, although hardly a legitimate issue in local politics, was, nevertheless, the dominant issue of the electoral campaign. Questions of provincial politics were forgotten in appeals to race and religion. Mercier stumped the whole province. He addressed hundreds of meetings and inflamed the French Canadians with the fire of racial patriotism. One contemporary wrote of Mercier's agitation, " On se serait cru reporté aux jours où Papineau, revendiquant nos libertés attirait au pied des tribunes populaires tous les vrais patriotes."[64] Laurier also gave his assistance by addressing various meetings. Everywhere the Ross Government was linked with the " pendards " of Ottawa. One popular lithograph appeared showing Riel hanging, the federal Ministers pulling the rope and Ross standing by giving his approval. The Conservatives defended themselves with vigour. Ross took the stand that the Riel issue was outside the realm of provincial politics. The federal Conservatives took a hand in the campaign and did all they could to carry the day. Public works were instituted in several constituencies to defeat the Nationalists and to assist the Ministerial candidates. Chapleau actively supported Ross and money flowed freely. The Conservative press denounced the Parti National as a mere Liberal election dodge, to which *La Verité* replied :

" Lorsqu'il s'agit de tuer une vipère on ne regarde pas trop à l'instrument dont on se sert ; on prend le premier bâton qui se trouve sous la main."[65]

Considering everything the Conservatives felt reasonably confident of their success. Chapleau wrote privately to Macdonald :

" . . . the 14th will tell the fate of the two parties in Quebec for the next ten years. A prominent Liberal told me he would sign the Conservative pledge for his lifetime if he were beaten this time. If we are prudent and liberal during the next four days, we can be imprudent and despotic, if we wish, for another ten years' lease of power."[66]

The election was a victory for the Nationalists. It threw the balance of power into the hands of Le Parti National. Of twenty-six candidates who had adhered to the programme of *L'Etendard* eleven were returned. Of these, eight were National

Conservatives, and three National Liberals.   *L'Etendard* received the results with manifest satisfaction.

"Nous croyons qu'un ministère Mercier est tout à fait dans l'ordre des choses. . . . Une chose certaine, cependant, c'est que ni M. Mercier ni M. Ross ne pourront gouverner sans le concours de nos amis.   A eux donc de se concerter, de se tenir unis et d'exiger du parti auquel ils pourront donner leur appui indépendant les plus sérieuses garanties d'économie, de bonne administration. . . . Ils devront également insister . . . sur la rupture de toute alliance entre le gouvernement de Québec et celui des Chevaliers de la Corde qui siège à Ottawa."[67]

Although *La Minerve* and *Le Monde* claimed that the Conservatives had gained the day, and Langevin wrote hopefully to Macdonald that the Ross Government would stand " unless the Nationalist Conservatives vote with the Liberals to overthrow it which is not likely,"[68] the Conservative ascendancy in Quebec was at an end.   Ross struggled along until January when he resigned on the 19th, advising the Lieutenant-Governor to call upon L. O. Taillon to form a ministry.   Taillon's ministry lasted only eight days.   On January 26th, Mercier arrived at Quebec city.   The public ovation tendered him sounded the death knell of Taillon's minority Conservative Government.   On the following day the Government was defeated on the election of the Speaker and Taillon resigned.   Mercier was then called upon to form a Government, and on January 29th a coalition ministry of Liberals and Nationalists entered into power in Quebec.

Mercier's triumph was due almost wholly to his appeal to French Canadian nationalism.   The Province of Quebec was swept from its traditional political allegiance as nothing but a race and religion issue could have swept it, and the Provincial Government was punished because it refused to join in the condemnation of the Federal Government for allowing the law to take its course in the case of Louis Riel.   With the ascendancy of Mercier the day of Le Parti National as an independent force in Quebec politics was at an end.   It had served its purpose in defeating the Conservative Government and opening the way for a Liberal victory.   The bitter comment of *Le Canadien* was true :

"Ils ont fait mal au parti Conservateur, mais ils n'ont tiré autre résultat que celui d'accroître la force du parti Liberal."[69]

The Nationalist press reluctantly admitted this fact.   But, while

406 THE BIRTH OF WESTERN CANADA

regretting that the Nationalists had not remained a distinct and separate group free from party trammels, the Nationalist organ, *La Justice*, boldly declared :

" The exigencies of the hour made it an absolute duty to put a stop to the political crisis and to assure the existence of a ministry which should help pull down the Federal Government."[70]

On the heels of the provincial election came the federal election. On January 15th, 1887, the Dominion Parliament was dissolved. Everything pointed to the possibility of a Liberal victory. Nova Scotia, New Brunswick, Quebec and Ontario had returned Liberal administrations during the course of 1886. In Quebec the Riel issue and the anti-Catholic fulminations of the Toronto *Mail* were counted upon to win seats for the Opposition. Moreover, the Government forces were paralysed by a recrudescence of the old feud between Langevin and Chapleau, the latter being prevailed upon only at the last moment to withdraw his resignation by Macdonald's acquiescence in his demands.[71] Under these circumstances the jubilant tone of the Liberal press is scarcely surprising.

The fate of the Government naturally turned upon the results in the Provinces of Quebec and Ontario. In the latter the Riel issue was dead. It had played no part in the provincial election of December 1886, largely owing to the fact that Ontario Liberals generally, in spite of Blake's position, approved of the execution of Riel. In Quebec, however, the success of Mercier had kept the issue very much alive, and *L'Etendard* greeted with delight the prospect of a straight fight between " les patriotes " and " les gens de la corde." Once more the ghost of Riel stalked across the political stages of Quebec, appealing to the people to " revenge his foul and most unnatural murder."

On February 22nd the voting took place. In the Province of Quebec substantial Liberal gains were recorded. Here the Government held only twenty-nine seats of the sixty-five allotted to that province ; ten seats went to the Nationalists and Independents and the remainder to the Liberals.[72] During the course of the session the Nationalists were absorbed into the two old parties, some returning to their old allegiance and the others aligning themselves permanently with the Liberals. The ultimate result was a net loss of fifteen French Canadian seats to the Government. This development was significant. Up to this time Quebec had been the key province of political conservatism; Macdonald had always been able to count upon forty-five to fifty seats in Quebec; now his supporters numbered about thirty-three. The national feeling aroused by the métis rebellion and the execution of Riel had brought about a fundamental change in the political outlook of the French Canadians. The casualties in the ranks of the French Conservatives in 1887 only foreshadowed the political rout which the Liberals, themselves led by a French Canadian, were to force upon that party in subsequent elections. The Riel agitation gave Laurier his opportunity, and with the unswerving loyalty of his compatriots, he established a Liberal ascendancy in Quebec which has remained unshaken to the present day.

Such were the political results of the Second Riel Rebellion. Statesmanship and national unity were subordinated to the selfish interests of race and party. It is doubtful whether the agitation would have reached the intensity it did had it not been stimulated by politicians. In both provinces the racial cry was used for party ends. In Quebec the Liberals reaped the advantage, and in Ontario, the Conservatives. But, though passion and demagogism marked the political crisis, reason and conciliation ultimately prevailed: the French Canadian Ministers in 1885 refused to encourage the alliance of their people with a racial faction, and in succeeding years Laurier's greatest service to his country was to break down racial prejudice in English-speaking Canada. A nation divided against itself cannot stand. Only in the realization of national unity can the ideal of the Fathers of Confederation survive.

BIBLIOGRAPHICAL NOTE

A COMPLETE bibliography of the Riel Rebellions would be a long one. There are few general histories or works relating to Western Canada without some reference, however slight, to Louis Riel. Such a bibliography would be impressive, but not, in the author's opinion, of great value. Most, if not all the books bearing on the subject, have been examined during the preparation of this work; few have been used. For the most part it has been written from original materials and those books which have been used are indicated in the list of notes which follows.

In the main the sources of original material have been three; London, Ottawa and Washington. In the Public Record Office the correspondence between the British and the Canadian Governments is to be found in the series *C.O.* 42 and *C.O.* 43; a few references to Wolseley's expedition are to be found in *W.O.* 33/21 and *W.O.* 33/22; and the opinion of British statesmen on the execution of Louis Riel in *G.D.* 6/130. At the Hudson's Bay Company* the *Correspondence with the Colonial Office*, the *London Inward Correspondence*, the *Winnipeg Inward Correspondence*, and certain post journals and letter books as well as separate folios on the Riel Rebellions and a manuscript account of his experiences by W. J. McLean, have been of great value.

At Ottawa the sources are three in number; the Public Archives, the Department of Indian Affairs and the Royal Canadian Mounted Police. In the Archives are collections of papers and correspondence of the first importance; in particular, the *Confidential Papers Relative to the Trial of Louis Riel (Department of Justice)*, the *Macdonald Papers* and the *Dewdney Papers;* of lesser importance are the *Caron Papers*, the *Buell Papers* and the *Drummond Letters*. The papers at the Department of Indian Affairs are difficult of access, owing to the absence of suitable catalogues. Those which were consulted are given in the

---

* All references from this source are published by permission of the Governor and Committee of the Hudson's Bay Company.

notes. They are of particular value as regards the Government's Indian policy and the growth of Indian discontent. There is little material at the Royal Canadian Mounted Police which cannot be found in the Sessional Papers.

At Washington the *Consular Despatches from Winnipeg* and the *Notes to and from the British Legation* are obtainable at the State Department.

The printed papers bearing on the Riel Rebellions are to be found in the recognized sources, the *Journals* and *Sessional Papers*, in certain *Colonial Office Confidential Prints* and British *Blue Books* relating to Canada (see notes) and in the *Debates of the House of Commons* and the *Debates of the Senate*; also in *Les Missions de la Congrégation des Missionaires Oblats de Marie Immaculée : Les Annales de la Propagation de la Foi :* Oliver, E. H., *The Canadian North-West, its Early Development and Legislative Records*, 2 vols., Ottawa, 1915 ; *Indian Treaties and Surrenders 1680–1890*, 2 vols. Ottawa, 1905 ; Morris, Hon. A., *The Treaties of Canada with the Indians of Manitoba and the North-West Territories*, Toronto, 1880 ; Pope, Sir J., *Correspondence of Sir John Macdonald*, Toronto, 1921.

It would have been almost impossible to write the history of the Riel Rebellions without consulting the newspapers of the time, not only on matters of political opinion, but also on matters of fact. Those to which greatest reference was made (others are indicated in the notes) include *The New Nation* (Fort Garry) ; *The Prince Albert Times : The Saskatchewan Herald* (Battleford) ; and *Le Manitoba* (St. Boniface) of Western Canada : *The Globe* (Toronto) ; *The Mail* (Toronto) ; *The Gazette* (Montreal) and *The Star* (Montreal) ; *L'Opinion Publique* (Montreal) and *L'Etendard* (Montreal) of Eastern Canada.

The Riel agitation produced a spate of pamphlets. The best collection of these is to be found at the Dominion Archives. For the most part they are propagandist works written in the heat of controversy and are of little value except in so far as they illustrate the intensity of racial feeling of the time.

ABBREVIATIONS

C.O.	Colonial Office papers, Public Record Office, London.
C.S.P.	Canada Sessional Papers.
F.O.	Foreign Office papers, Public Record Office.
G.D.	Gifts and Deposits, Public Record Office.
H.B.C.	Hudson's Bay Company, London.
I.D.	Department of Indian Affairs, Ottawa.
Missions des O.M.I.	Missions of the Oblates of Mary Immaculate.
P.A.C.	Public Archives of Canada, Ottawa.
R.C.M.P.	Royal Canadian Mounted Police, Ottawa.
W.O.	War Office papers, Public Record Office.

NOTES

CHAPTER I

THE OLD ORDER OF RED RIVER

[1] The Royal Charter for incorporating the Hudson's Bay Company A.D. 1670 : *Charters, Statutes, Orders in Council relating to the Hudson's Bay Company*, pp. 3–21.

[2] In 1857 Sir George Simpson estimated the number of Indians living in Rupert's Land at 42, 840 : Evidence of Sir George Simpson, 993, Report from the Select Committee on the Hudson's Bay Company (P.P. 1857 (Session 2) xv, 224, 260), p. 57.

[3] The Royal Charter.

[4] A Journal of a Voyage and Journey undertaken by Henry Kelsey through God's assistance to discover and bring to a commerce the Naywatame Poets in Anno 1691 : *The Kelsey Papers* (The Public Archives of Canada) Ottawa, 1929. For a discussion of the route taken by Kelsey see C. N. Bell, *The Journal of Henry Kelsey* (The Historical and Scientific Society of Manitoba Transaction No. 4, New Series) Winnipeg, 1928.

[5] Burpee, *The Search for the Western Sea*, p. 235.

[6] Harmon, *A Journal of Voyages and Travels in the Interior of North America*, pp. 49–50.

[7] Ross, *The Fur Hunters of the Far West*, Vol. I, p. 296. Alexander Ross is a contemporary writer of importance. He entered the service of the fur trade in 1810, and in 1825 settled at Red River. From 1836 to 1850 he was a member of the Council of Assiniboia and from 1839 to 1850, sheriff. He was, therefore, well acquainted with the people of the North-West and their customs. He died at Red River in 1856.

[8] Southesk, *Saskatchewan and the Rocky Mountains, A Diary and Narrative of Travel, Sport, and Adventure during a Journey through the Hudson's Bay Company's Territories in 1859 and 1860*, pp. 360–1.

[9] *Ibid.*, p. 359.

[10] Milton and Cheadle, *The North-West Passage by Land, being the Narrative of an Expedition from the Atlantic to the Pacific undertake.. with the view of exploring a route across the continent to British Columbia through British Territory, by one of the northern passes in the Rocky Mountains*, pp. 43–4.

[11] Ross, *The Red River Settlement : Its Rise, Progress and Present State, with some account of the Native Races and its General History, to the Present Day*, p. 193.

[12] *Ibid.*, p. 250.

[13] *Ibid.*, p. 196.

[14] Milton and Cheadle, *op. cit.*, pp. 42–3.

[15] McLean, *Notes of a Twenty-Five Years Service in the Hudson's Bay Territory* (Publications of the Champlain Society), p. 374.

[16] Milton and Cheadle, *op. cit.*, p. 44.

[17] McLean, *op. cit.*, p. 378.

[18] Le Dernier Mémoire de Louis Riel : Ouimet, *La Verité sur la Question Métisse au Nord-Ouest*, p. 78.

[19] Selkirk Papers 1468 : Martin, *Lord Selkirk's Work in Canada*, p. 108.

[20] " Chanson écrite par Pierre Falcon," is printed with an explanatory note in Hargrave, *Red River*, Appendix A, pp. 485–91.

[21] Grant of Assiniboia to Lord Selkirk by the Hudson's Bay Company, June 12th, 1811 : Martin, *op. cit.*, Appendix B, p. 204.

[22] Oliver, *The Canadian North-West, its Early Development and Legislative Records* (Publications of the Canadian Archives No. 9), Vol. I, p. 267, note 1.

[23] Hind, *Narrative of the Canadian Red River Exploring Expedition of 1857 and of the Assiniboine and Saskatchewan Exploring Expedition of 1858*, Vol. I, p. 177.

²⁴ Census Returns 1871 : Canada Sessional Papers 1871, Vol. V, No. 20.

²⁵ Ross, *op. cit.*, p. 244. For a discussion of the Red River Hunt, see Roe, *The Red River Hunt* (transactions of the Royal Society of Canada, 3rd series, 1935, Vol. XXIX, pp. 171–218).

²⁶ A Statistical Account of Red River Colony taken on May 20th–24th, 1856 : Report from the Select Committee on the Hudson's Bay Company. Appendix 2B, p. 363.

²⁷ Gunn to Vankoughnet, March 6th, 1857, Statistics of the Red River Colony : Report from the Select Committee etc., Appendix 7, p. 383.

²⁸ *Ibid.*, p. 382.

²⁹ Evidence of Sir George Simpson, 1207–1223 : Report from the Select Committee, etc., pp. 67–8. Leasehold was not the only system of land tenure. There are some instances of land being granted in fee simple. See Martin, *The Hudson's Bay Company Land Tenures*, Chapter iv.

³⁰ Hudson's Bay Company Land Deed : Report from the Select Committee, Appendix 2A, pp. 361–2.

³¹ Evidence of Sir George Simpson, 1769 : *op. cit.*, p. 92.

³² *Ibid.*, 1861, p. 96.

³³ Hind, *op. cit.*, Vol. I, p. 190.

³⁴ The Hudson's Bay Company continued after 1836 the system of survey inaugurated by Peter Fidler and William Kempt during the Selkirk period, and in 1836-7-8, George Taylor made a complete survey of the Settlement for the Company. The original of this plan is to be found in the Record Department of the Hudson's Bay Company, London.

³⁵ Taché to Dallas, December 15th, 1862 : Enc. in Dallas to Fraser, December 20th, 1862, London Inward Correspondence from Winnipeg, 1862, H.B.C. Taché expressed a similar opinion in his *Esquisse sur le Nord-Ouest de l'Amérique*, p. 45.

³⁶ Anderson to Dallas, December 22nd, 1862 : London Inward Correspondence from Winnipeg, 1862, H.B.C.

³⁷ Oliver, *op. cit.*, Vol. I, pp. 76–83.

³⁸ *Ibid.*, Vol. I, pp. 87–90.

³⁹ 43 Geo. III c. 138 : *Charters, Statutes, Orders in Council Relating to the Hudson's Bay Company*, pp. 87–90.

⁴⁰ 1 and 2 Geo. IV, c. 66 : *ibid.*, pp. 93–102.

⁴¹ MacBeth, *The Romance of Western Canada*, p. 95.

CHAPTER II

THE END OF COMPANY RULE

¹ Smith, *An Inquiry into the Nature and Causes of the Wealth of Nations*, Vol. II, p. 137.

² Evidence of Edward Ellice, 5391 : Report from the Select Committee 1857, p. 341.

³ Stephen to Le Marchant, July 25th, 1837 : C.O. 43/86 ; also Report from the Select Committee, Appendix 11, No. 4, p. 423.

⁴ Report from the Select Committee, p. ii.

⁵ Evidence of Sir George Simpson, 702–2125 : *op. cit.*, pp. 44–108.

⁶ The Committee included among others the Rt. Hon. Henry Labouchere, Sir John Pakington, Lord John Russell, Lord Stanley, Viscount Goderich ; W. E. Gladstone and J. A. Roebuck represented the anti-Company element, while Edward Ellice watched over the Company's interests.

⁷ Stephen to Hume, August 15th, 1837 : Report from the Select Committee, Appendix 11, No. 6, p. 424.

⁸ Quoted in Dent, *The Last Forty Years*, Vol. II, p. 349.

⁹ Evidence of Draper, 4062 : Report from the Select Committee, pp. 212–3.

¹⁰ Minute of the Council, January 17th, 1857 : Journals of the Legislative Assembly 1857, Vol. XV, Appendix 17.

[11] Ross, *op. cit.*, pp. 339–340.

[12] Petition to the Canadian Legislature for annexation of the Red River Settlement and the North-West Territory to Canada, April 24th, 1862 : P.P. 1870, L. 443, pp. 3–4.

[13] Evidence of Isbister 2449 : Report from the Select Committee, p. 124.

[14] Evidence of Draper 4102 : *ibid.*, p. 218.

[15] The question of westward communications is thoroughly discussed in Trotter, *Canadian Federation, its Origins and Achievement*, Chapters XIX and XX.

[16] P.P. 1864, XLI, 530, p. 19.

[17] Simpson to Shepherd, March 14th, 1857 : Enc. in Shepherd to Labouchere, March 16th, 1857, H.B.C. Correspondence with the Colonial Office 1856-8.

[18] Evidence of Ross, 73 : Report from the Select Committee, p. 7.

[19] Journals of the Legislative Assembly 1857, Vol. XV, p. 41.

[20] *Ibid.*, p. 207, See also Report from the Select Committee, Appendix 12, p. 435.

[21] Evidence of Draper, 4122–3 : *op. cit.*, p. 221.

[22] Meredith to Draper, February 20th, 1857 : Journals of the Legislative Assembly 1857, Vol. XV, Appendix 17.

[23] Memorandum of the Honourable Joseph Cauchon, Commissioner for Crown Lands, Canada, 1857 : *ibid.*

[24] Bethell and Keating to Labouchere, July 1857 : Report from the Select Committee, Appendix 9, p. 403.

[25] Labouchere to Head, January 22nd, 1858 : Journals of the Legislative Assembly 1858, Vol. XVI, Appendix 3.

[26] Merivale to Shepherd, January 20th, 1858 : H.B.C. Correspondence with the Colonial Office 1856-8.

[27] Berens to Lytton, July 27th, 1858 : *ibid.* This letter outlines the conversation which Lytton had with Shepherd and Berens on the previous day at the Colonial Office.

[28] Joint Address to the Queen from the Legislative Council and Legislative Assembly of Canada, August 13th, 14th, 1858 : Journals of the Legislative Council, 1858, pp. 513–4.

[29] Berens to Lytton, October 12th, 1858 : H.B.C. Correspondence with the Colonial Office 1856-8.

[30] Carnarvon to Berens, November 3rd, 1858 : *ibid.*, 1858-60.

[31] Kelly and Cairns to Lytton, December 16th, 1858 : Journals of the Legislative Assembly 1859, Vol. XVII, Appendix 7.

[32] Joint Address of the Legislative Council and Assembly of Canada to the Queen, April 20th, 1859 : *ibid.*, pp. 454–5.

[33] Fortescue to Berens, confidential, May 5th, 1860 : H.B.C. Correspondence with the Colonial Office 1858-60.

[34] Berens to Newcastle, May 30th, 1860 : *ibid.*, 1860-3.

[35] Watkin, *Canada and the States, Recollections 1851-1886*, p. 65.

[36] Berens to Newcastle, May 19th, 1862 : H.B.C. Correspondence with the Colonial Office 1860-3.

[37] Watkin, *op. cit.*, p. 120.

[38] *Ibid.*, p. 123.

[39] Berens to Dallas, confidential, March 20th, 1863 : H.B.C. Locked Letter Book 1860-3.

[40] Head to Newcastle, July 3rd, 1863 : H.B.C. Correspondence with the Colonial Office 1863-8.

[41] Head to Rogers, August 28th, 1863 : *ibid.*

[42] Head to Rogers, November 11th, 1863 : *ibid.*

[43] Fortescue to Head, March 11th, 1864 : Fortescue to Head, April 5th, 1864 : *ibid.*

[44] Head to Fortescue, April 13th, 1864 : *ibid.*

[45] Rogers to Head, June 6th, 1864 : *ibid.*

[46] Head to Rogers, November 11th, 1863 : *ibid.*

[47] Head to Fortescue, March 15th, 1864 : *ibid.*

[48] Report of the Canadian Delegates to England, July 12th, 1865 : Journals of the Legislative Assembly, 1865, Vol. XXV, p. 12.

[49] Watkin, *op. cit.*, p. 17, 421–6 ; Macdonald, *Canadian Public Opinion on the American Civil War*, pp. 199–200.

[50] *Congressional Globe*, 39 : 1, p. 3548 ; see also Watkin, pp. 227–35.

[51] New York *Tribune*, April 1st, 1867 : Quoted in Oberholtzer, *A History of the United States since the Civil War*, Vol. I, p. 543.

[52] Callahan, *An Introduction to American Expansion Policy* (West Virginia University Studies), p. 32.

[53] Russell, *Canada : Its Defences, Condition, and Resources*, p. 329. See also Blegen, *James Wickes Taylor, a Biographical Sketch* (Minnesota History Bulletin, Vol. I, No. 4)

[54] St. Paul, *Daily Press*, February 27th, 1868.

[55] Taylor to Seward, March 13th, 1868 : MSS. Despatches Winnipeg Special Agent, 1867–70, Department of State. Taylor wrote, " I . . . availed myself of the opportunity to obtain from the Minnesota Legislature, resolutions requesting Congress to confirm by requisite legislation the annexation of Alaska and presenting other views of national policy in respect to North-West British America."

[56] U.S. Miscellaneous Documents, 68, 40th Congress 2nd Session, Serial 1319.

[57] Taylor to Chase, December 17th, 1861 : House Executive Documents 146, Serial 1138.

[58] McEwen to Head, January 18th, 1866 : H.B.C. Correspondence with the Colonial Office 1863–8.

[59] Taylor to Kittson, May 15th, 1869 : London Inward Correspondence 1868–9, H.B.C.

[60] Extracts from speeches by Holton and Macdonald in the Canadian Parliament, enc. in Head to Buckingham and Chandos, January 25th, 1868 : Journals of the House of Commons, Canada, 1867–8, Vol. I, p. 374.

[61] Buckingham and Chandos Minute of interview with Lampson, February 5th, 1868 : Buckingham and Chandos (Stowe Collection) H.B.C.

[62] Kimberley to Adderley, May 13th, 1868 : H.B.C. Correspondence with the Colonial Office, 1868–70.

[63] Original draft by the Duke of Buckingham and Chandos, May 1868, Buckingham and Chandos (Stowe Collection) H.B.C. This letter was not sent to the Hudson's Bay Company and it was not until August 7th that Rogers informed Kimberley that the Company's terms could not be accepted and suggested a personal interview. This delay was probably due to the passage of the Rupert's Land Act in July.

[64] 31–32 Vic. c. 105.

[65] Northcote to Rogers, January 13th, 1869 : H.B.C. Correspondence with the Colonial Office, 1868–70.

[66] Monk to Buckingham and Chandos, telegram, September 9th, 1868 : C.S.P. 1869, Vol. V, No. 25.

[67] Willson, *The Great Company*, Vol. II, pp. 289–90.

[68] Rogers to Northcote, February 22nd, 1869 : H.B.C. Correspondence with the Colonial Office 1868–70.

[69] Cartier and McDougall to Rogers, confidential, February 8th, 1869 : *ibid.*

[70] Rogers to Northcote, March 9th, 1869 : *ibid.*

[71] *Ibid.*

[72] Cartier and McDougall to Northcote, March 15th, 1869 : *ibid.*

[73] Court of April 9th, 1869 : H.B.C. General Court Minute Book, 1866–76.

[74] In their letter of February 8th, 1869, Cartier and McDougall stated that although Buckingham's terms had not been made at their instigation, they had informed him that if the Company accepted them the Canadian Government might also be prepared to accept them. Buckingham's terms offered the Company one-fourth the receipts of land sales and one-fourth export duty on gold and silver, both conjointly to total £1,000,000, and a land grant of five lots in every township in addition to blocks about the various Company posts (see Adderley to Kimberley, December 1st, 1868 : H.B.C. Correspondence with the Colonial Office 1868–70).

[75] Rose to Young, confidential, July 23rd, 1869 : C.O. 42/677.

[76] Dom. Stat. 32–33 Vic. c. 3.

[77] *Correspondence and Papers connected with Recent Occurrences in the North-West Territories*, C.S.P. 1870, Vol. V, No. 12.

CHAPTER III

HALF-BREED UNREST IN THE RED RIVER SETTLEMENT

[1] Pelly to Palmerston, May 24th, 1837 : F.O. 5/319. Enclosed with this letter is one from " Brigadier-General " John George McKenzie addressed to Cuthbert Grant, September 12th, 1836, urging him to rouse the half-breeds and lead the forces of " liberation " in Red River.

[2] Simpson to the Governor and Committee, June 20th, 1845 : Public Correspondence, Simpson, 1845-6, H.B.C.

[3] Ibid.

[4] Various documents relative to this dispute are printed in Begg, op. cit., Vol. I, pp. 261-5.

[5] Simpson to Metcalfe, November 6th, 1845 : Public Correspondence op. cit.

[6] K. Mackenzie to McDermott and McLaughlin, March 14th, 1845 : Enc. in Simpson to the Governor and Committee, November 11th, 1845, ibid.

[7] The documents relative to this petition are printed in P.P. 1849, XXXV (227) and P.P. 1850, XXXVIII (542).

[8] Thom to Ballenden, June 5th, 1849 : Winnipeg Inward Correspondence 1823-71, H.B.C.

[9] Simpson to the Governor and Committee, June 21st, 1844 : Public Correspondence, op. cit., 1844.

[10] MacBeth, The Making of the Canadian West, Being the Reminiscences of an Eye-Witness, p. 14.

[11] Minutes of a Meeting of the Governor and Council of Assiniboia, October 25th, 1869 : C.S.P. 1870, Vol. V, No. 12.

[12] Ibid.

[13] Dallas to Fraser, January 28th, 1864 : London Inward Correspondence from Winnipeg, 1864, H.B.C.

[14] Mactavish to Fraser, December 18th, 1866 : Mactavish Letter Book 1865-7. See also Hargrave, Red River, p. 402.

[15] Mactavish to Smith, March 31st, 1868 : London Inward Correspondence from Winnipeg, 1868.

[16] Mactavish to Fraser, November 27th, 1866 : Mactavish Letter Book 1865-7.

[17] Hargrave, op. cit., pp. 285-7.

[18] Hargrave (pro Mactavish) to Smith, January 20th, 1868 : London Inward Correspondence from Winnipeg 1868. See also Hargrave Red River, pp. 424-26.

[19] Hargrave, op. cit., p. 413.

[20] The Nor'Wester, January 14th, 1860 : Quoted in Martin, The Red River Settlement, Canada and its Provinces, Vol. XIX, p. 67.

[21] Bannatyne to " Ellis," July 1st, 1863 : London Inward Correspondence from Winnipeg, 1863.

[22] Mactavish to Smith, April 14th, 1868 : ibid., 1868. See also Bannatyne, deposition, Report of the Select Committee on the Causes of the Difficulties in the North-West Territory in 1869-70 : Journals of the House of Commons, Canada 1874, Vol. VIII, Appendix No. 6.

[23] Hargrave to Lampson, February 8th, 1870 : London Inward Correspondence from Winnipeg, 1870.

[24] Taché, L'Esquisse sur le Nord-Ouest de l'Amérique, p. 46.

[25] Taché to the Nor'Wester, August 11th, 1868 : reprinted in the Toronto Globe, September 4th, 1868.

[26] Young to Sandford, November 27th, 1868 : The Toronto Globe, December 19th, 1868.

[27] The Times, September 26th, 1868.

[28] Lampson to Rogers, December 22nd, 1868 : H.B.C. Correspondence with the Colonial Office, 1868-70.

[29] Cartier and McDougall to Rogers, January 16th, 1869 : ibid.

[30] " Justitia " to the Globe, November 10th, 1869 : The Toronto Globe, December 2nd, 1869. See also Gouldhawke to the Owen Sound Times, May 2nd, 1869 : The Globe, June 28th, 1869 : Bannatyne, deposition op. cit. ; Begg, The Creation of Manitoba or a History of the Red River Troubles, p. 17.

[31] Hargrave to Lampson, February 8th, 1870 : *op. cit.*

[32] Mactavish to Smith, September 7th, 1869 : London Inward Correspondence from Winnipeg, 1869.

[33] *The Globe*, December 14th, 1868 ; December 27th, 1868 ; January 4th, 1869.

[34] Hargrave, *Red River*, p. 455.

[35] Dugas, *Histoire Véridique des Faits qui ont préparé le mouvement des Métis à la Rivière Rouge en 1869*, pp. 27–8.

[36] Spence, deposition : Report of the Select Committee, 1874, *op. cit.*

[37] Mactavish to Fraser, July 27th, 1860 : London Inward Correspondence from Winnipeg, 1860.

[38] Taché, deposition : Report of the Select Committee, 1874. See also Begg, *op. cit.*, p. 17.

[39] Dennis, deposition : *ibid.*

[40] Mactavish to Smith, August 10th, 1869 : London Inward Correspondence from Winnipeg, 1869.

[41] Dennis to McDougall, August 21st, 1869 : C.S.P., 1870, Vol. V, No. 12.

[42] Dennis to McDougall, August 28th, 1869 : *ibid.*

[43] Braun to Dennis, October 4th, 1869 : *ibid.* It is only fair to mention that McDougall himself was not at Ottawa when Dennis' warnings were received.

[44] Dennis, Memorandum of Facts and Circumstances Connected with the Active Opposition of the French Half-Breeds in this Settlement to the Prosecution of the Government Surveys : *ibid.*

[45] Hind, *op. cit.*, Vol. I, p. 179.

[46] Mactavish to Smith, October 12th, 1869 : London Inward Correspondence from Winnipeg, 1869.

[47] Garrioch, *First Furrows, A History of the Early Settlement of the Red River Country, including that of Portage la Prairie*, p. 198.

[48] *The New York Times*, December 28th, 1869.

[49] Bryce, *The Remarkable History of the Hudson's Bay Company*, p. 460.

[50] Taché to the Governor-General, May 7th, 1870 : Quoted in Benoit, *Vie de Mgr. Taché*, Vol. II, p. 75.

[51] Lecompte, *Sir Joseph Dubuc, 1840–1914*, p. 41.

[52] Malmros to Davis, September 11th, 1869 : MSS. Consular Despatches from Winnipeg, Vol. I, Department of State.

[53] Malmros to Davis, November 6th, 1869 : *ibid.*

[54] Fish to Taylor, December 30th, 1869 : Instructions to Special Missions 1852–86, Department of State. Taylor's appointment was kept secret; his instructions stated " All your proceedings under this commission are to be strictly confidential, and under no circumstances will you allow them to be made public. This injunction includes the fact of your appointment."

[55] U.S. Senate Executive Documents 33, 41st Congress, 2nd session, Serial 1405.

[56] Bryce, *op. cit.*, p. 460.

[57] Taché to Cartier, October 7th, 1869 : Benoit, *op. cit.*, Vol. II, p. 17.

[58] Bunn, deposition : Report of the Select Committee, 1874.

[59] Mair, *Insurrection in Red River* ; in Denison, *Reminiscences of the Red River Rebellion of 1869*, pp. 1–8.

[60] Extract from a private letter of Governor Mactavish, June 9th, 1868 : London Inward Correspondence from Winnipeg, 1868.

[61] Joseph McDonald to McDougall, December 8th, 1869 : C.O. 42/684.

[62] Machray to the Governor-General, March 18th, 1870 : C.O. 42/685.

[63] Dennis, Despatch on the State of Public Opinion, October 27th, 1869 : C.O. 42/677. Printed in *Correspondence and Papers connected with Recent Occurrences in the North-West Territories*, C.S.P., 1870, Vol. V, No. 12.

[64] Martin, *op. cit.*, p. 63.

[65] Pope, *Memoirs of the Right Honourable Sir John Alexander Macdonald*, Vol. II, p. 50.

[66] Machray, *Life of Robert Machray, Archbishop of Rupert's Land and Primate of All Canada*, p. 168.

[67] McArthur, *Causes of the Rising* (Manitoba Historical Society Publication, 1882, Vol. I, No. 1). McArthur accompanied Mactavish on his return to Red River. He was later imprisoned by Riel with Schultz's party of Canadians.

[68] Taché, deposition, *op. cit.*

[69] *Ibid.*

[70] Howe to Macdonald, October 16th, 1869 : Pope, *op. cit.*, Vol. II, p. 51.

[71] Extract from a private letter of Governor Mactavish, October 13th, 1869 : London Inward Correspondence from Winnipeg, 1869.

[72] McDougall, *The Red River Rebellion, Eight Letters to the Honourable Joseph Howe*, p. 6.

[73] *The Globe*, January 17th, January 23rd, January 26th, 1870.

[74] Mactavish to McDougall, November 9th, 1869 : London Inward Correspondence from Winnipeg, 1869.

[75] *The Globe*, August 31st, 1869.

[76] McArthur, *op. cit.*

[77] Taché, deposition.

[78] Minute, December 16th, 1869 : C.O. 42/677. " The Canadian Government have certainly much to answer for. Sir A. Galt told me that he had suggested the appointment of Mactavish as Governor thus making the transfer as easy as possible. McDougall had unfavourable antecedents as regards the natives."

CHAPTER IV

THE RED RIVER REBELLION. PART ONE

[1] Schmidt, *Mémoires de Louis Schmidt*, published in *Le Patriote de l'Ouest*, Duck Lake, Saskatchewan, 1912. Further references will be to the date of the newspaper. This quotation is to be found in the issue of January 25th, 1912. Schmidt was a half-breed of English descent, although brought up as French speaking. He was one of those sent to school in Montreal by Bishop Taché, but owing to ill health he returned to Red River after a short period. Schmidt later became secretary of the Provisional Government of Red River but took no part in the events of 1885.

[2] *Ibid.*

[3] Mousseau, *Une Page d'Histoire*, p. 9.

[4] Schmidt, *Le Patriote*, February 8th, 1912.

[5] Oscar Malmros, the American consul at Winnipeg, reported to Washington on September 11th, 1869, that " the mass of settlers are strongly inclined . . . to get up a riot to expel the new Governor on his arrival here about the 15th of October." MSS. Consular despatches from Winnipeg, Vol. I, Department of State.

[6] Dennis, Memorandum of Facts and Circumstances connected with the Active Opposition by the French Half-Breeds in the Settlement to the prosecution of the Government Surveys, October 11th, 1869 : C.S.P., 1870, Vol. V, No. 12. See also Prud'homme, *André Nault*, Transactions of the Royal Society of Canada, 3rd Series, Vol. XXII, 1928.

[7] A French half-breed magistrate and a member of the Council of Assiniboia.

[8] Dennis, *op. cit.*, October 12th, 1869.

[9] *Ibid.*, October 21st, 1869.

[10] Unpublished Memoirs of Rev. Mr. Giroux, who was present at the interview : Morice, *History of the Catholic Church in Western Canada*, Vol. II, p. 25.

[11] Evidence of John Bruce, *Preliminary Investigation and Trial of Ambroise D. Lépine*, 1874, p. 62.

[12] Schmidt (*Le Patriote*, February 1st, 1912) stated that the métis took counsel from " personnes sages et plus exerimentées qu'eux." Martin Jérome, one of the half-breeds who escorted McDougall from Canadian soil, wrote in his *Souvenirs d'Autrefois* (p. 18), " M. Ritchot, l'esprit dirigeante des métis qui dans sa jeunesse avait eu une certaine expérience des différentes régimes operées sur les bords du St. Laurent fut celui qui donna le premier signal. ... Louis Riel, qui avait un talent irréfutable et une haute éducation, quoique possédant très peu d'expérience, son jugement sain uni à la sagesse de M. Ritchot, devenaient une force pour le bien des métis." See also Dennis, Despatch on the State of Public opinion, October 27th, 1869.

[13] Minutes of the Council of Assiniboia, October 25th, 1869 : C.S.P., 1870, Vol. V, No. 12.

[14] Minutes of the Council of Assiniboia, October 30th, 1869 : *ibid.*

P

[15] Mactavish to McDougall, October 30th, 1869 : C.O. 42/677 : C.S.P., 1870, Vol. V, No. 12. The C.O. reference is to the copies of the originals which were sent to the Colonial Office by the Governor-General. Both the Canadian and the Imperial Government published Blue Books on the Red River Insurrection, the former being C.S.P., 1870, Vol. V, No. 12, and the latter P.P., 1870, L. (C. 207). Both the C.O. and the Blue Book references will be given as far as possible.

[16] Extract of Private Correspondence, November 2nd, 1860: C.O. 42/678; P.P., 1870, L. (C. 207).

[17] Mactavish to Smith, November 2nd, 1869 : London Inward Correspondence from Winnipeg, 1869. See also Cowan, deposition : Report of the Select Committee, 1874.

[18] McDougall to Howe, November 20th, 1869 : C.O. 42/678 ; C.S.P., 1870, Vol. V, No. 12.

[19] Riel and Lépine to Morris, January 3rd, 1873 : Report of the Select Committee, 1874. This letter is printed with notes by de Trémaudan in the *Canadian Historical Review*, June, 1926, pp. 137-60.

[20] Provencher to McDougall, November 3rd, 1869: C.O. 42/677 ; C.S.P., 1870, Vol. V, No. 12.

[21] C.O. 42/678 ; C.S.P., 1870, Vol. V, No. 12.

[22] Extract from a letter reputed to be from a Hudson's Bay Company man to the *Globe*, December 1st, 1869.

[23] The account of the first Convention given here is taken, except where otherwise noted, from a Riel manuscript published with an introduction by C. A. Harwood in the *Canadian Antiquarian and Numismatic Journal*, 3rd Series, 1909, Vol. VI, Nos. 1 and 2.

[24] Mactavish to Smith, November 23rd, 1869 : London Inward Correspondence from Winnipeg, 1869.

[25] *Ibid.*

[26] McDougall to the Secretary of State for the Provinces, October 31st, 1869 : C.O. 42/677 ; C.S.P. 1870, Vol. V, No. 12.

[27] Howe to McDougall, October 31st, 1869 : *Red River Insurrection, Hon. William McDougall's Conduct Reviewed*, p. 15. This pamphlet, which is a vigorous criticism of McDougall, was reputedly the work of Howe.

[28] McDougall to the Secretary of State for the Provinces, October 31st, 1869 : *op. cit.*

[29] " Spectator " to the *St. Paul Press*, November 4th, 1869 : U.S. Senate Documents, 33, 41st Congress, 2nd Session, Serial 1405.

[30] McDougall to Mactavish, November 2nd, 1869 : C.O. 42/677 : C.S.P., 1870, Vol. V, No. 12.

[31] Mactavish to McDougall, November 9th, 1869 : C.O. 42/678 : C.S.P., 1870, Vol. V, No. 12.

[32] Snow to McDougall, November 9th, 1869 : *ibid.*

[33] Mair to McDougall, November 8th, 1869 : *ibid.*

[34] McDougall to Mactavish, November 2nd, 1869 : *op. cit.*

[35] McDougall to Mactavish, November 7th, 1869 : *ibid.*

[36] McDougall to Howe, November 13th, 14th, 1869 : C.O. 42/678 ; C.S.P., 1870, Vol. V, No. 12.

[37] McDougall to Howe, November 25th, 1869 : *ibid.*

[38] McDougall to Howe, November 29th, 1869 : *ibid.*

[39] McDougall to Howe, December 2nd, 1869 : *ibid.*

[40] Howe to McDougall, November 19th, 1869 : C.O. 42/677 ; C.S.P., 1870, Vol. V, No. 12.

[41] Macdonald to McDougall, November 20th, 1869 : Pope, *op. cit.*, Vol. II, pp. 52-3.

[42] Macdonald to McDougall, confidential, November 27th, 1869 : C.O. 42/678.

[43] Young to Granville, telegram, November 26th, 1869 : C.O. 42/677 ; P.P., 1870, L. (C. 207).

[44] Granville, Minute, November 25th, 1869 : C.O. 42/683. Granville was first notified officially of Canada's refusal to complete the transaction by a telegram from Young dated the 23rd. This was followed by another telegram dated the 26th.

[45] Granville to Young, November 30th, 1869: C.O. 43/156; P.P., 1870, L. (C. 207).

[46] Collier and Coleridge to Granville, December 10th, 1869: C.O. 42/679.

[47] Copy of a Report of the Privy Council, Canada, December 16th, 1869: C.O. 42/678: P.P., 187○, L. (C. 207).

[48] Granville, Minute, December 10th, 1869: C.O. 42/679.

[49] Howe to McDougall, December 24th, 1869: C.O. 42/684; C.S.P., 1870, Vol. V, No. 12.

[50] McDougall to Howe, December 6th, 1869: C.O. 42/678; C.S.P., 1870, Vol. V, No. 12.

[51] Commission of Colonel Dennis, December 1st, 1869: C.O. 42/684; C.S.P., 1870, Vol. V, No. 12.

[52] Dennis to Schultz, December 4th, 1869: *ibid.*

[53] J. McDonald ("Guide") to McDougall, December 8th, 1869: *ibid.*

[54] Dennis Proclamation, December 6th, 1869: *ibid.*

[55] Notes by J.W. between November 4th and 22nd, 1869: C.O. 42/678; C.S.P., 1870, Vol. V, No. 12.

[56] Dennis, Record of Proceedings under Commission from Lieutenant-Governor McDougall, December 1st, 1869: C.O. 42/684; C.S.P., 1870, Vol. V, No. 12.

[57] Dennis, Proclamation, December 9th, 1869: *ibid.*

[58] Howe to McDougall, December 24th, 1869: *ibid.*

[59] Dennis, Record of Proceedings, etc., *op. cit.*

[60] Woodington, *Diary of a Prisoner in the Red River Rebellion* (Niagara Historical Society Publications, 1913, No. 25), p. 37.

[61] Boulton to Dennis, December 4th, 1869: C.O. 42/684; C.S.P., 1870, Vol. V, No.12.

[62] Machray to Dennis, December 6th, 1869: *ibid.*

[63] Mactavish to Smith, December 11th, 1869: London Inward Correspondence from Winnipeg, 1869.

[64] Schmidt, *Le Patriote*, February 15th, 1912.

[65] It has been said that Riel promised the besieged Canadians that they should be set at liberty if they surrendered. (See Boulton, *Reminiscences of the North-West Rebellions*, p. 83; Young, *Manitoba Memories*, pp. 110-1; Bryce, *History of Manitoba*, p. 156.) The bulk of contemporary evidence disproves this charge. Riel's note to Schultz (Begg, *op. cit.*, Vol. I, p. 414) gave no promise save that "Their lives will be spared should they comply." Three of the prisoners have written that the surrender was unconditional. (O'Donnell, *Manitoba as I Saw It*, pp. 34-5; Stewart Mulkins in the Toronto *Globe*, January 28th, 1870: Woodington, *op. cit.*, pp. 39-40). Woodington's *Diary* reads: "December 7 . . . A despatch was brought in by Mrs. Black from Colonel Dennis ordering us to surrender and make the best terms we could. Said he had been out all night in the Scotch Settlement to get men to come to our relief, but out of six hundred men was surprised on reaching the Fort to find none—and McArthur were sent to Riel to get permission to retire with our arms,—being the one selected to negotiate, the result being most disastrous to us,—having agreed to an unconditional surrender, with the stipulation that our lives be spared, without asking McArthur's opinion."

[66] C.O. 42/684; C.S.P., 1870, Vol. V, No. 12.

[67] Macdonald to McDougall, confidential, November 27th, 1869: *op. cit.*

[68] Copy of a Report of the Privy Council, Canada, December 16th, 1869: *op. cit.*

[69] Collier and Coleridge to Granville, December 21st, 1869: C.O. 42/679.

[70] Schmidt, *op. cit.*

[71] McDougall to Mactavish, December 16th, 1869: C.O. 42/684; C.S.P., 1870, Vol. V, No. 12.

[72] Mactavish to Smith, December 25th, 1869: London Inward Correspondence from Winnipeg, 1869.

[73] Orders of the Provisional Government of Rupert's Land, January 8th, 1870: Oliver, *The Canadian North-West, Its Early Development and Legislative Records*, Vol. II, pp. 913-4.

CHAPTER V
THE RED RIVER REBELLION. PART TWO

[1] Granville to Young, telegram, November 25th, 1869 : C.O. 42/678.

[2] Sir John Young Proclamation, December 6th, 1869 : C.S.P., 1870, Vol. V, No. 12.

[3] Young to Granville, November 25th, 1869 : P.P., 1870, L. (C. 207).

[4] Young to Granville, December 9th, 1869 : C.O. 42/678 ; P.P. 1870, L. (C. 207).

[5] Smith to Howe, November 24th, 1869 : C.S.P., 1870, Vol. V, No. 12.

[6] Macdonald to Stephen, December 1st, 1869 : Pope, *Correspondence of Sir John Macdonald*, pp. 110-1.

[7] Stephen to Macdonald, December 10th, 1869 : *ibid.*, p. 112.

[8] Macdonald to Stephen, December 13th, 1869 : *ibid.*, p. 112.

[9] Howe to Smith, December 10th, 1869 : C.O. 42/678 ; C.S.P., 1870, Vol. V, No. 12.

[10] Preston, *The Life and Times of Lord Strathcona*, p. 14.

[11] Thibault to Howe, March 17th, 1870 : C.O. 42/685. This was printed as Thibault's Report in C.S.P., 1870, Vol. V, No. 12.

[12] Mactavish to W. G. Smith, December 25th, 1869 : London Inward Correspondence from Winnipeg, 1869 ; P.P., 1870, L. (C. 207).

[13] Tupper to Macdonald, December 30th, 1869 : Pope, *op. cit.*, pp. 115-6.

[14] Thibault's Report.

[15] Smith to Howe, April 12th, 1870 : This is Smith's Report on his mission to Red River. It is printed with a few slight omissions in C.S.P., 1870, Vol. V, No. 12. There is a copy of the original in C.O. 42/685.

[16] Smith to Macdonald, December 28th, 1869 : Pope, *op. cit.*, pp. 114-5.

[17] Smith's Report.

[18] Smith, deposition : Report of the Select Committee, 1874.

[19] Malmros to Davis, January 15th, 1870 : MSS. Consular Despatches from Winnipeg, Vol. I, Department of State.

[20] Smith's Report.

[21] *Ibid.*

[22] Smith to Macdonald, January 18th, 1870 : Pope, *op. cit.*, p. 120.

[23] *The New Nation*, January 21st, 1870, Vol. I, No. 3. Although the *New Nation* was published under the editorship of an American, Major Robinson, and had, therefore, strong annexationist sympathies as well as a political bias in favour of the insurgents, the accuracy of its reports is vouched for by D. A. Smith. The account given above of the Mass Meetings and the proceedings of the Second Convention are taken from the *New Nation* except where otherwise noted.

[24] Riel, *L'Amnistie, Mémoire sur les Causes des Troubles du Nord-Ouest et sur les Négociations qui ont amené leur Règlement Amiable*, p. 8.

[25] *The New Nation*, January 21st, 1870.

[26] Thibault to Howe, January 22nd, 1870 : C.O. 42/684.

[27] Lestanc to Riel, January 26th, 1870 : Riel Papers, P.A.C.

[28] Smith's Report.

[29] Lestanc to Riel, January 26th, 1870 : *op. cit.*

[30] Macdonald to Rose, February 23rd, 1870 : Pope, *op. cit.*, pp. 127-9.

[31] Hargrave to Lampson, February 8th, 1870 : London Inward Correspondence from Winnipeg, 1870.

[32] Mactavish to W. G. Smith, February 12th, 1870 : *ibid.*

[33] Smith's Report.

[34] *The New Nation*, February 18th, 1870.

[35] Evidence of Sutherland and Pagée, *Preliminary Investigation and Trial of Ambroise Lépine*, p. 80, p. 75. See also *The New Nation*, February 18th, 1870.

[36] *The New Nation*, February 18th, 1870.

[37] Martin in *Canada and its Provinces* (Vol. XIX, p. 85) states that no formal resolution was passed forming the Provisional Government. From the evidence which I have examined it would appear that the Convention as a body accepted the Provisional Government and that Pagée's motion was a formal resolution to that

effect. It is doubtful whether Riel would have accepted anything less. For this account I have relied upon the *New Nation* of February 18th, and upon a document in the archives of the Hudson's Bay Company which appears to be a précis of the sittings of the Convention with the various motions, discussions and divisions. There is no clue as to the writer.

[38] Thibault to Langevin, February 6th–8th, 1870 : C.O. 42/684.

[39] MacBeth, *op. cit.*, pp. 59–60.

[40] *The New Nation*, January 21st, 1870. The *Globe*, February 26th, 1870, launched a vigorous attack against Commissioner Smith for not making the release of the prisoners the *sine qua non* of negotiations.

[41] *The New Nation*, February 18th, 1870.

[42] *Ibid.*

[43] Boulton, *Reminiscences of the North-West Rebellions*, pp. 100–1.

[44] Boulton is silent about this, but Begg (*The Creation of Manitoba*, p. 277) states that they were informed of the impending release of the prisoners and advised to return home. This is corroborated by Charles Mair, one of the Portage party in a public address at Toronto in April, 1870, reported in the *Globe*, April 7th, 1870.

[45] Boulton, *op. cit.*, pp. 110–1 ; Young, *Manitoba Memories*, p. 124 ; Schofield, *Story of Manitoba*, Vol. I, p. 271.

[46] Riel to "Fellow Countrymen," February 16th, 1870 : Begg, *op. cit.*, p. 287 ; Boulton, *op. cit.*, pp. 115–6.

[47] Taché to Howe, confidential, March 11th, 1870 : C.O. 42/685.

[48] Machray, *Life of Archbishop Machray*, p. 201.

[49] X.Y.Z. to the *Globe*, February 22nd, 1870 : The *Globe*, March 28th, 1870.

[50] *The New Nation*, February 18th, 1870.

[51] Boulton, *op. cit.*, p. 117.

[52] Macdonald to Rose, March 11th, 1870 : Pope, *Memoirs of the Right Honourable Sir John Alexander Macdonald*, Vol. II, p. 62.

[53] Smith's Report.

[54] Boulton, p. 123. MacBeth (*op. cit.*, p. 80) gives another version. " It has not been generally known, but the fact is that Boulton's life was finally spared at the intercession of Mr. (now Senator) and Mrs. Sutherland, of Kildonan, who had known Riel from his childhood, and who had come almost direct from the grave of their slain son to plead for the life of the condemned man. Riel was by no means without heart, and when he saw their earnestness as well as the grief of the parents, who had been so recently bereaved but who in their sorrow were thinking of others, he said, placing his hand on the shoulder of the mother, ' It is enough—he ought to die, but I will give you his life for the life of the son you have lost through these troubles." Sutherland's son had been killed by a French half-breed who had been taken prisoner by the Schultz party at Kildonan on suspicion of being a spy of Riel. A. H. de Trémaudan says " this . . . version is the one current among the Métis to this day " (*Canadian Historical Review*, June, 1926, Vol. VII, No. 2, note 1, p. 147). The version in the text is taken from Smith's Report and from the letter of Riel and Lépine to Lieutenant-Governor Morris, January 3rd, 1873 : Report of the Select Committee, 1874.

[55] MacBeth, *The Romance of Western Canada*, p. 156.

[56] Snow to the Minister of Public Works, October 6th, 1869 : C.S.P., 1870, Vol. V, No. 12.

[57] Mactavish to W. G. Smith, October 12th, 1869 : London Inward Correspondence from Winnipeg, 1869.

[58] Riel, *Affaire Scott* (*The Canadian Historical Review*, September, 1925, Vol. VI, No. 3, pp. 222–36). Edit. de Trémaudan.

[59] Riel, *L'Amnistie*, etc., p. 13.

[60] Taché to Howe, confidential, March 11th, 1870 : *op. cit.*

[61] Riel, *Affaire Scott*, p. 230 ; Begg, *op. cit.*, 302.

[62] Riel, *Affaire Scott*, p. 231 ; *L'Amnistie*, pp. 14–5 ; Smith's Report.

[63] Evidence of Joseph Nolin at the trial of Lépine as reported in *Le Métis* : enc. in Taylor to Cadwalader, February 4th, 1875 : MSS. Consular despatches from Winnipeg, Vol. IV, Department of State. See also Nolin's evidence in *Preliminary Investigation and Trial of Ambroise D. Lépine*, pp. 120–1. There has been much loose

writing concerning the trial and execution of Scott.   Joseph Nolin was the secretary
of the tribunal which condemned Scott and therefore speaks with authority.

[64] Smith's Report.

[65] Riel, *Affaire Scott*, p. 233.

[66] *The New Nation*, March 11th, 1870.

CHAPTER VI

THE MANITOBA ACT

[1] *Cf. Supra* p. 64.   Macdonald wrote of this to Rose, November 23rd, 1869 :
Pope, *Correspondence of Sir John Macdonald*, p. 106, " and to add to our troubles,
Cartier rather snubbed Bishop Taché when he was here on his way to Rome."

[2] Taché, deposition.   Except where otherwise noted, the documents and depositions cited in this chapter are to be found in the Report of the Select Committee,
1874, Journals of the House of Commons, Canada, Vol. VIII, Appendix 6, 1874.

[3] Taché to Mme Dugas, January 4th, 1870 : Benoit, *Vie de Mgr. Taché*, Vol. II,
p. 52.

[4] Bishop Langevin to Sir Hector Langevin, telegram, January 11th, 1870.

[5] Northcote to Granville, January 22nd, 1870 : C.O. 42/694.

[6] Macdonald to Rose, February 23rd, 1870 : Pope, *op. cit.*, p. 127.   This letter
stated that Taché " is strongly opposed to the idea of an Imperial Commission,
believing, as indeed we all do, that to send out an overwashed Englishman, utterly
ignorant of the country and full of crotchets, as all Englishmen are, would be a
mistake."

[7] Young to Taché, February 16th, 1870 : C.O. 42/684, P.P. 1870, L. (C. 207) ;
Macdonald to Taché, private, February 16th, 1870 ; Howe to Taché, February 16th,
1870 : *ibid*.

[8] Smith to Macdonald, February 26th, 1870 : Pope, *op. cit.*, pp. 129-30.

[9] Benoit, *op. cit.*, Vol. II, p. 59.

[10] Malmros to Davis, March 12th, 1870 : MSS. Consular Despatches from
Winnipeg, Vol. I, Department of State.   This mark of suspicion on the part of
Riel who had been one of Taché's protégés caused the Bishop some grief. (Morice,
History of the Catholic Church in Western Canada, Vol. II, p. 56.)

[11] Taché to Howe, confidential, March 11th, 1870.

[12] Malmros to Davis, March 12th, 1870 : *op. cit.*

[13] *The New Nation*, March 11th, 1870.

[14] Schmidt, *Le Patriote*, April 11th, 1912.

[15] *The New Nation*, March 11th, 1870.

[16] Taché, deposition.

[17] Begg, *op. cit.*, p. 315.

[18] Macdonald to Taché, private, February 16th, 1870.

[19] Howe to Taché, telegram, February 25th, 1870.

[20] *The New Nation*, March 18th, 1870.

[21] Black to Riel, February 16th, 1870 : Riel Papers, P.A.C.

[22] Taché, *The Amnesty Again*, p. 11.

[23] Malmros to Davis, March 12th, 1870 : *op. cit.*

[24] C.O. 42/685 ; P.P. 1870, L. (C. 207).   There is a copy printed in French
dated March 23rd in the Riel Papers.   P.A.C.

[25] Taché to Cartier, April 7th, 1870 : Benoit, *op. cit.*, Vol. II, p. 65.   Thibault
likewise wrote to Langevin on February 6-8th (*op. cit.*), " Ceux qui sont à la tête
des affaires veulent absolument que le pays entre de suite comme province dans la
Confédération.   Selon moi et bien d'autres plus entendus que moi dans ces sortes
d'affaires, je me permettrais, Monsieur, de vous dire que pour éviter plus tard des
troubles encore plus grands, que ceux qui existent aujourd'hui, si vous le pouvez,
accordez cette demande."

[26] This clause is given in the List cited by Benoit, *op. cit.*, Vol. II, pp. 67-9.

[27] The existence of this so-called secret list was not made known until 1874 when Ritchot, at the trial of Lépine, produced it during his evidence as the list which was used during the negotiations which led to the Manitoba Act. This list was printed in *Le Métis*, a copy of which was forwarded by Consul Taylor to Washington on February 4th, 1875 (MSS. Consular Despatches from Winnipeg, Vol. IV, Department of State). It escaped notice at the time and nothing more was heard of it until 1889 when it was published by Archbishop Taché at the time of the Manitoba School controversy. (Taché to the Editor of the *Free Press*, December 22nd, 1889 ; January 24th, 1890.) There is a certified copy of Ritchot's list at Ottawa. (See Benoit, Vol. II, p. 66, note 3.)

[28] Dufferin to Carnarvon, December 10th, 1875 : C.O. 42/730 ; C.S.P., 1875, Vol. VII, No. 11.

[29] Bunn to Ritchot, March 22nd, 1870.

[30] Denison, *The Struggle for Imperial Unity, Recollections and Experiences*, p. 22. The author of this book was himself one of the leading spirits of the Canada First Group.

[31] *The Globe*, April 7th, 1870. For other demonstrations see Ottawa *Free Press*, April 13th, and Ottawa *Times*, April 14th, 1870.

[32] Parliamentary Debates, Canada, 3rd Session, Vol. I, 1870, p. 898.

[33] *Ibid.*, p. 901.

[34] *Ibid.*, pp. 983-6.

[35] Memorandum of the Minister of Justice, April 21st, 1870 : C.O. 42/685 ; P.P. 1870, L. (C. 207).

[36] Ritchot to Young, April 20th, 1870 : C.O. 42/685.

[37] Young to Granville, telegram, (rec'd) April 19th, 1870 : *ibid.* The printed version omits to mention the fact that Canada retained counsel for the prisoners.

[38] Schultz, Lynch and Fletcher endeavoured to secure official recognition as delegates of the North-West and were supported in their efforts by Mackenzie and the Liberal Opposition.

[39] Rogers, Minute, April 8th, 1870 ; " Agreement with the delegates is hardly possible." Minute, April 30th, 1870 ; " It seems to me doubtful whether after the murder of Scott the Canadian Government is right in entering into any relation with the other Scott and Ritchot." C.O. 42/685.

[40] Granville to Young, telegram, March 30th, 1870 : C.O. 42/685.

[41] Young to Granville, confidential, February 27th, 1870 : C.O. 42/684.

[42] Taylor to Fish, April 23rd, 1870 : MSS. Despatches Winnipeg Special Agent, 1867–70, Department of State. J. W. Taylor, the Special Agent appointed by the American Government to watch the progress of the Red River insurrection, was at Ottawa during the negotiations and conversed upon several occasions with the North-West delegates. He was therefore well informed as to what was going on.

[43] Howe to Ritchot, Black and Scott, April 26th, 1870.

[44] Young to Granville, confidential, April 21st, 1870 : C.O. 42/685.

[45] Taylor to Fish, April 29th, 1870 : MSS. Despatches Winnipeg Special Agent, 1867–70, Department of State.

[46] Parliamentary Debates Canada, 3rd Session, Vol. I, 1870, p. 1302.

[47] *Ibid.*, p. 1296.

[48] *Ibid.*, p. 1528.

[49] Memorandum of Sir John A. Macdonald, December 29th, 1870 : C.O. 42/696 ; C.S.P., 1871, Vol. V, No. 20.

[50] 34 & 35 Vic. c. 28.

[51] Willison, *Sir Wilfrid Laurier and the Liberal Party, a Political History*, Vol. I, p. 159.

[52] Thibault to Howe, March 20th, 1870 : C.O. 42/685.

[53] Pope, *Memoirs of the Right Honourable Sir John Alexander Macdonald*, Vol. II, p. 64.

[54] Rose to Granville, May 4th, 1870 : P.P. 1870, L. (C. 207).

[55] Printed in *Charters, Statutes, Orders in Council Relating to the Hudson's Bay Company*, pp. 171–200 ; and in Oliver, *op. cit.*, Vol. II, pp. 939 ff.

[56] *The New Nation*, April 8th, 1870. See also Begg, *op. cit.*, pp. 330-1. It is interesting to note that these resolutions were largely the work of the English-speaking delegates to the Provisional Government.

[57] Riel to Mactavish, March 28th, 1870 : Papers on the Riel Rebellion, folio 1, H.B.C. This is the original in Riel's handwriting. The English copy is printed in P.P. 1870, L. (C. 207).

[58] Robinson to Davis, May 10th, 1870 : MSS. Consular Despatches from Winnipeg, Vol. I, Department of State.

[59] Prud'homme, *André Nault* (Transactions of the Royal Society of Canada, 3rd Series, 1928, Vol. XX, p. 99).

[60] Begg, *op. cit.*, p. 343.

[61] Robinson to Davis, April 4th, 1870 : MSS. Consular Despatches from Winnipeg, Vol. I, Department of State.

[62] Robinson to Davis, June 7th, 1870 : *ibid.*

[63] Taché to Howe, June 9th, 1870.

[64] *The New Nation*, July 1st, 1870.

[65] Bunn to Howe, June 24th, 1870 : C.O. 42/687.

[66] *The New Nation*, July 1st, 1870.

[67] Ritchot, deposition. "I then asked Sir George who was to govern the country, pending the arrival of the Lieutenant-Governor, and if he was to name somebody to do so. He answered, 'No, let Mr. Riel continue to maintain order and govern the country as he has done up to the present moment.' He asked me if I thought that Riel was sufficiently powerful to maintain order. I said I thought he was. Then he answered, 'Let him continue till the Governor arrives.'"

CHAPTER VII

THE MILITARY EXPEDITION, 1870

[1] *The National Republican*, Washington, March 5th, 1870.

[2] *The Daily Globe*, Washington, April 23rd, 1870.

[3] Notes on the Routes from Lake Superior to the Red River and on the Settlement itself, compiled from the Reports by Capt. Palliser, Professor Hind, Colonel Crofton, etc., confidential, 1870 : W.O. 33/21. Colonel Crofton wrote from first hand knowledge of the métis, having spent several years in Red River in command of the troops despatched there in 1846.

[4] Riel, *The Fort Garry Convention* (*Canadian Antiquarian and Numismatic Journal*, 3rd Series, Vol. VI, Nos. 1, 2, 1909).

[5] See Todd, *Parliamentary Government in the British Colonies*, p. 296.

[6] Hansard Debates, Vol. CCXIV, p. 1531 ; Todd, p. 297.

[7] Collier and Coleridge to Granville, December 21st, 1869 : C.O. 42/679.

[8] Granville, Minute, December 25th, 1869 : *ibid.*

[9] The *Globe*, January 24th, 1870.

[10] Braun to Dawson, January 12th, 1870 : C.S.P., 1870, Vol. V, No. 12.

[11] Extract from a letter of Sir John A. Macdonald, January 26th, 1870 : C.O. 42/695.

[12] Confidential Minute of the Privy Council, Canada, February 1870 : C.O. 42/684.

[13] Granville to Young, telegram, March 5th, 1870 : P.P. 1870, L. (C. 207).

[14] Michel, Memorandum on the Military and Political Question of Sending British Troops in Conjunction with Canadian Militia to the Red River Settlement, April 10th, 1870 : W.O. 33/21.

[15] Extract of a private letter of Sir John Michel, April 27th, 1870 : *ibid.*

[16] Lindsay to the War Office, May 27th, 1870 : *ibid.* ; Correspondence relative to the Red River Expedition is printed in P.P., 1871, Vol. XLVIII (C. 298).

[17] Lindsay to the War Office, April 15th, 1870 : *ibid.*

[18] Granville to Young, telegram, May 6th, 1870 : C.O. 43/157 ; P.P. 1870, L. (C. 207).

[19] Official Journal of the Red River Expedition : W.O. 33/21 ; P.P., 1871, Vol. XLVIII (C. 298).

[20] Denison, *The Struggle for Imperial Unity, Recollections and Experiences*, p. 33. Robertson Ross had been responsible for the organization of the Canadian Militia.

[21] Lindsay to the War Office, May 27th, 1870 : *op. cit.*

[22] Taylor to Fish, April 27th, 1870 : MSS. Despatches Winnipeg Special Agent, 1867–70, Department of State.

[23] Parliamentary Debates, Canada, 3rd Session, 1870, Vol. I, pp. 1147, 1560.

[24] Young to Granville, May 12th, 1870 : C.O. 42/686.

[25] Parliamentary Debates, Canada, 3rd Session, 1870, Vol. I, p. 1573.

[26] Report of a Committee of the Privy Council, June 3rd, 1870 : C.O. 42/686.

[27] Young to Thornton, telegram, May 14th, 1870 : *ibid.*

[28] The *Globe*, May 28th, 1870. " A more pitiable exhibition was surely never presented to the world by an ambassador of Great Britain."

[29] Thornton to Young, telegram, May 17th, 1870 : C.O. 42/686.

[30] Dawson to Braun, January 17th, 1870 : C.S.P., 1870, Vol. V, No. 12.

[31] Dawson, Report on the Red River Expedition of 1870 : C.S.P., 1871, Vol. VI, No. 47.

[32] See Wolseley's *Narrative of the Red River Expedition* in Blackwood's Edinburgh Magazine, December, 1870, January, February, 1871.

[33] Huyshe, *The Red River Expedition*, p. 143.

[34] *Ibid.*, p. 145.

[35] Butler, *The Great Lone Land, a Narrative of Travel and Adventure in the North-West of America*, p. 168.

[36] Begg, *op. cit.*, p. 386.

[37] Wolseley, *The Story of a Soldier's Life*, Vol. II, p. 212.

[38] Steele, *Forty Years in Canada, Reminiscences of the Great North-West*, p. 26.

[39] *Narrative of the Red River Expedition*, Blackwood's Edinburgh Magazine, January, 1871, p. 54 ; Wolseley, *op. cit.*, Vol. II, pp. 197–8.

[40] Wolseley, Vol. II, p. 217.

[41] Huyshe, *op. cit.*, pp. 195–6.

[42] Cartier to Taché, private and confidential, July 5th, 1870 : Report of the Select Committee, 1874.

[43] Official Journal of the Red River Expedition : *op. cit.*

[44] Begg, *op. cit.*, p. 383.

[45] This section was later deleted upon Lindsay's orders.

[46] Butler, *op. cit.*, p. 134.

[47] Young to Granville, June 8th, 1870 : C.O. 42/686.

[48] McTavish to Taché, July 31st, 1870 : Report of the Select Committee, 1874.

[49] *Ibid.*

[50] Taché to Riel, n.d. (July) 1870 ; Taché to Riel, August 5th, 1870 : Denison, *op. cit.*, pp. 46–7.

[51] Willson, *Lord Strathcona, The Story of His Life*, p. 107.

[52] Archibald to Howe, December 31st, 1870 : C.O. 42/696.

CHAPTER VIII

THE AMNESTY QUESTION

[1] Siegfried, *Le Canada, les Deux Races*, p. 1.

[2] Macdonald to Rose, March 5th, 1872 : Pope, *op. cit.*, p. 165.

[3] Proclamation of Sir John Young, December 6th, 1869 : C.S.P. 1870, Vol. V, No. 12.

[4] Taché, deposition. Except where otherwise noted the depositions and documents quoted in this chapter will be found in the Report of the Select Committee 1874, Journals of the House of Commons, Canada, Vol. VIII, Appendix 6, 1874.

[5] Taché, *Notes sur les Troubles de la Rivière Rouge fournies à l'honourable A. Dorion, novembre* 1874 : Benoit, *op. cit.*, Vol. II, p. 55.

[6] Macdonald to Rose, February 23rd, 1870 : Pope, *op. cit.*, p. 127.

[7] Taché, deposition.

[8] Young to Taché, February 16th, 1870 : C.O. 42/684 ; P.P. 1870, L. (C. 207).

[9] Macdonald to Taché, February 16th, 1870. Macdonald attached a virtually impossible condition to the promise of the general amnesty in his letter. Taché, however, declared that this condition was never mentioned in the conversations. The fact is that the Government misunderstood the situation at Red River. They had only a vague idea concerning the Provisional Government, while in Red River the existence of this government was the fact which dominated all others.

[10] Taché to Howe, June 9th, 1870.

[11] *Ibid.*

[12] Howe to Taché, July 4th, 1870.

[13] Cartier to Taché, private and confidential, July 5th, 1870.

[14] Ritchot, deposition.

[15] Taylor to Fish, April 28th, 1870 : MSS. Despatches Winnipeg Special Agent 1867–70, Department of State.

[16] Ritchot, deposition.

[17] Taylor to Fish, May 2nd, 1870 : MSS. Despatches Winnipeg Special Agent 1867–70, Department of State.

[18] Ritchot, deposition.

[19] Lisgar to Kimberley, April 25th, 1872.

[20] Cartier to Macdonald, February 23rd, 1873.

[21] Ritchot, deposition.

[22] Taché, deposition.

[23] *Ibid.*

[24] *Ibid.*

[25] Cartier, secret memorandum, June 8th, 1870.

[26] Ritchot and Scott, Petition to the Queen, February 8th, 1872.

[27] Taylor to Fish, May 3rd, 1870 : MSS. Despatches Winnipeg Special Agent, 1867–70.

[28] Royal, deposition.

[29] Girard, deposition.

[30] Cartier to Taché, private and confidential, July 5th, 1870.

[31] Denison, *op. cit.,* p. 37.

[32] Lynch to the Governor-General, June 29th, 1870 : C.O. 42/687. Lynch was a member of the Canadian Party of Red River.

[33] Journals of the Legislative Assembly of Ontario, Session 1870-1, Vol. IV, p. 105.

[34] The *Globe*, July 13th, 1870.

[35] Quoted in the *Globe*, February 13th, 1871.

[36] *Ibid.,* March 13th, 1871.

[37] *La Minerve*, Montreal, March 1st, 1871.

[38] Taché to Howe, May 7th, 1870.

[39] *L'Opinion Publique*, Montreal, April 9th, 1870.

[40] *Le Nouveau Monde*, Montreal, April 9th, 1870.

[41] *L'Opinion Publique*, September 8th, 1870.

[42] *Le Nouveau Monde*, Montreal, April 14th, 1870.

[43] Cartier, confidential memorandum, July 23rd, 1870 : C.O. 42/687.

[44] Egerton, *A Short History of British Colonial Policy*, p. 316.

[45] Hammond to the Under Secretary of State for the Colonies, May 18th, 1870 : C.O. 42/691.

[46] Rogers, Minute, May 19th, 1870 : *Ibid.*

[47] Granville to Young, confidential, May 26th, 1870 : C.O. 43/157.

[48] Young to Granville, secret, June 1st, 1870 : C.O. 42/718.

[49] Granville to Young, confidential, June 30th, 1870 : C.O. 43/157.

[50] Kimberley to Young, confidential, July 18th, 1870 : *ibid.*

[51] Young to Kimberley, July 21st, 1870 : C.O. 42/687.

[52] Kimberley, Minute, n.d. : *ibid.*

[53] Cartier, confidential memorandum, July 23rd, 1870 : *ibid.*

[54] Kimberley to Young, July 28th, 1870 : C.O. 43/157.

[55] Kimberley to Young, August 11th, 1870 : *ibid.*

[56] Kimberley, Minute, July 22nd, 1873 : C.O. 42/722.

[57] Archibald to Cartier, September 3rd, 1870.

[58] For a discussion of the Fenian Raid of 1871 see Pritchett, *The Origin of the so-called Fenian Raid on Manitoba in* 1871 (*Canadian Historical Review*, Vol. X, No. 1, March, 1929).

[59] Archibald, deposition.

[60] Hill, *Manitoba, History of its Early Settlement, Development and Resources*, p. 587.

[61] Judge Johnson to Archibald, December 6th, 1870: C.O. 42/698. The correspondence relative to Goulet and Tanner is printed in C.S.P. 1871, Vol. V, No. 20.

[62] The *Globe*, December 19th, 1870; *The Manitoban*, Winnipeg, December 10th, 1870.

[63] The *Globe*, March 15th, 1871; Prud'homme, *André Nault, op. cit.*, p. 105.

[64] Archibald, deposition.

[65] Riel, Lépine and Parenteau to Archibald, October 7th, 1871.

[66] Girard, deposition; Archibald, deposition. Riel has been accused of waiting until the defeat of the Fenians was assured before offering the services of the métis to the Government. (See McMicken, *The Fenian Raid in Manitoba*, Manitoba Historical Society Publications, No. 32, 1888, p. 10; Young, *op. cit.*, pp. 220–1; Hill, *op. cit.*, p. 347.) The documents edited by de Trémaudan in the *Canadian Historical Review*, Vol. IV, No. 2, June 1923, pp. 132–144, prove conclusively that the decision of the métis and the organization of their brigades was begun before the date of O'Donoghue's invasion. Moreover it must be remembered that the Government did not believe that all danger had passed. Major Irvine, commanding the force sent against the Fenians, wrote on October 8th, " There is no doubt the Fenians intend making a raid between this and to-morrow night. . . . I shall require reinforcement *at once*; 150 *men*" (Irvine to Archibald, October 8th, 1871). Archibald also declared " I am perfectly satisfied that the prevailing impression, as well among the French as among the English, was, that there was to be a fresh raid, and that the action of the French was not based on the idea that the affair was over, but on the idea that the difficulty still continued."

[67] Archibald to Ritchot, October 5th, 1871.

[68] Ritchot, deposition.

[69] Macdonald to Archibald, telegram, September 4th, 1872.

[70] Macdonald to Archibald, telegram, September 12th, 1872.

[71] Archibald to Cartier, February 24th, 1872.

[72] C.O. 42/706. See also Journals of the Legislative Assembly of Manitoba, 1872, pp. 37–8.

[73] Macdonald to Lisgar, April 20th, 1872 : Pope, *op. cit.*, p. 168.

[74] Holland, Minute, May 18th, 1872 : C.O. 42/706.

[75] Kimberley to Lisgar, secret, May 28th, 1872 : C.O. 42/718.

[76] Langevin, deposition.

[77] Masson, deposition.

[78] Journals of the House of Commons, Canada, Vol. VIII, 1874, p. 64.

[79] *Ibid.*, pp. 68–71.

[80] Journaux de l'Assemblée Législative de la Province de Québec, 1874-5, Vol. VIII, pp. 46–7.

[81] Dufferin to Carnarvon, December 10th, 1874: C.O. 42/730; C.S.P. 1875, Vol. VII, No. 11.

[82] *Ibid.*

[83] Carnarvon to Dufferin, January 7th, 1875 : *ibid.*

[84] The Hamilton *Spectator*, January 26th, 1875.

[85] The Montreal *Gazette*, January 26th, 1875.

[86] The Ottawa *Citizen*, January 27th, 1875.

[87] Hansard Debates, Great Britain, 1875, Series 3, Vol. CCXXIII, p. 1071.

[88] *Ibid.*, p. 1076.

[89] Blake to Carnarvon, July 1st, 1876 : C.S.P. 1877, Vol. VII, No. 13.

[90] Debates of the House of Commons, Canada, 1875, Vol. I, p. 50.

[91] *Ibid.*, pp. 135–6.

[92] Laflamme, Memorandum of the Minister of Justice, September 20th, 1877: C.O. 42/749 : C.S.P. 1878, Vol. XI, No. 55.

BOOK TWO
THE NORTH-WEST REBELLION
CHAPTER IX
THE GROWTH OF SETTLEMENT IN THE NORTH-WEST

[1] Butler, *The Great Lone Land*, preface, p. v.

[2] Butler, Report on the North-West, March 10th, 1871, Appendix A : C.O. 42/698

[3] Décorby to Lacombe, November 1st, 1879 : *Missions des O.M.I.*, Vol. XVIII, 1880, p. 193.

[4] Fourmond letter, December 15th, 1879 : *ibid.*, p. 261.

[5] Légeard to Martinet, June 7th, 1872 : *ibid*, Vol. XII, 1874, p. 42.

[6] *Souvenir du Pèlerinage de N.D. de Lourdes à St. Laurent*, 1925, p. 2.

[7] Leduc to T.R.P. Supérieur-Général, January 3rd, 1874 : *Missions des O.M.I.*, Vol. XII, 1874, pp. 524–5.

[8] *Copie des Lois et Régulations Etablies pour la colonie de St. Laurent sur la Saskatchewan* : P.A.C. This document takes the form of a letter written by Father André to Inspector Fréchette of the Mounted Police in 1875 to explain the nature of Dumont's Provisional Government.

[9] This may have been due partly to the political experience of the Red River métis who formed the majority of the colony, but more probably to the guidance of Father André. In the *Lois et Regulations* he wrote, " Otez le prêtres, les lois et les règlements seront lettre morte, comme l'expérience ne le prouve que trop."

[10] Clarke to Morris, July 10th, 1875 : R.C.M.P. file 333. 1875.

[11] Winnipeg *Daily Free Press*, July 21st, 1875.

[12] French to the Minister of Justice, telegram, August 7th, 1875 : R.C.M.P. file 333.

[13] Crozier to French, September 8th, 1875 : *ibid.* Correspondence with the Colonial Office relative to Dumont's Provisional Government may be found in C.O. 42/737.

[14] Leduc, Rapport sur le Vicariat de St. Albert : *Missions des O.M.I.*, Vol. XVII, 1879, p. 445.

[15] *Ibid.*, pp. 445–7.

[16] Further accounts of the early white settlements in Saskatchewan as distinct from the half-breed settlements may be found in Oliver, *The Beginnings of White Settlement in Northern Saskatchewan* (Transactions of the Royal Society of Canada, Vol. XIX, 1925, pp. 83–129) and *The Settlement of Saskatchewan to 1914* (*ibid.*, Vol. XX, 1926, pp. 63–87).

[17] *The Saskatchewan Herald*, December 16th, 1878 : Oliver, *The Beginnings of White Settlement in Northern Saskatchewan*, p. 89.

[18] Mgr. Grandin, Journal de Voyage, June 13th, 1880 : *Missions des O.M.I.*, Vol. XIX, 1881, p. 270.

[19] *Ibid.*, pp. 271–2.

[20] Kane, *Wanderings of an Artist among the Indians of North America*, p. 136.

[21] King to Russell, January 16th, 1879 : C.S.P. 1878, Vol. VI, No. 7.

[22] The first newspaper published in the N.W.T. was the *Saskatchewan Herald*, first published at Battleford by P.G. Laurie in 1878.

[23] Oliver, *op. cit.*, pp. 96–8.

[24] Grahame to Armit, September 21st, 1874 : London Inward Correspondence, 1874.

[25] Report on the Working of the Steamer *Northcote*, Season 1877. G. S. Mactavish, November 1st, 1877 : *ibid.*, 1877.

[26] Brydges to Grahame, November 25th, 1880 : *ibid.*, 1880.

[27] C.S.P. 1882, Vol. IX, No. 30h.

²⁸ Oliver, *The Settlement of Saskatchewan* to 1914, p. 65.

²⁹ Tenth Census of the United States, 1880, Population, Washington, 1883, p. 383.

³⁰ *Canada Year Book*, 1905, 2nd Series, Ottawa, 1906, p. 11.   The numbers given above are exclusive of the Indians.   The census for 1891 gives 66,799 but does not give racial origins ; the Indians of Treaties, 4, 6, 7 numbered about 16,000 hence the figure 50,000.

³¹ Burgess to Macpherson, February 29th, 1884 : C.S.P. 1884, Vol. VII, No. 12. For a short history of the surveys see C.S.P. 1892, Vol. IX, No. 13.

³² The Dominion Lands Act, 35 Vic. c. 23.

³³ Regulations for the Disposal of Public Lands, July 9th, 1879 : C.S.P. 1882, Vol. IX, No. 30h.

³⁴ *Ibid.*, October 14th, 1879.

³⁵ *Ibid.*, May 25th, 1881 ; January 1st, 1882.

³⁶ 33 Vic. c. 3.

³⁷ Archibald to the Secretary of State for the Provinces, October 22nd, 1870 ; C.O. 42/689.

³⁸ Owing to the outbreak of smallpox in the Territories, Archibald appointed this emergency Council in order to take legislative action to delimit the area of infection.   His papers had, unfortunately, been delayed in the post and Archibald relied solely upon his memory in making the appointments.   Joseph Howe hastened to inform him of the unconstitutionality of his actions and pointed out that the Council must number no less than seven and be appointed by the Governor-General.   Archibald then submitted a list of names of suitable persons but no action was taken and in the meantime the ordinances of the emergency body were treated as perfectly legal and valid.   For this correspondence see Oliver, *The Canadian North-West, its Early Development and Legislative Records*, Vol. II.

³⁹ Butler, Report, *op. cit.*

⁴⁰ Robertson Ross, Report on the North-Western Provinces and Territories, December 10th, 1872 : C.O. 42/715.

⁴¹ Minutes of the North-West Council, March 10th, 1873 : Oliver, *op. cit.*, Vol. II, p. 994.

⁴² 38 Vic. c. 49.

⁴³ *The Saskatchewan Herald*, September 30th, 1882.

CHAPTER X

THE INDIAN PROBLEM. THE TREATIES

¹ Spragge to Howe, February 2nd, 1871 : C.S.P. 1871, Vol. V, No. 23.

² A detailed account of the nature and customs of the Indians of Canada may be found in Jenness, *The Indians of Canada* (National Museum of Canada, Bulletin 65).

³ Report from the Select Committee on the Hudson's Bay Company, Appendix No. 2 (D.1) : P.P. 1857 (Session 2) XV, 224, 260, p. 368.

⁴ Grahame to Armit, June 1st, 1876 : London Inward Correspondence, 1876. " The country is getting over-run with traders who all have greater or less stocks of goods and recklessly give ruinous prices for furs."

⁵ Begg, *History of the North-West*, Vol. II, p. 237.

⁶ Robertson Ross, Report, *op. cit.*

⁷ Steele (*op. cit.*, p. 55) is in error when he gives the date as 1872.   The American consul at Winnipeg gives the date as May 1873 in his report on the massacre to the Assistant Secretary of State.   (Taylor to Cadwalader, September 22nd, 1875 : MSS. Consular Despatches from Winnipeg, Vol. V, Department of State.)

⁸ In March 1874 the North-West Council recommended " that steps be taken to secure the arrest of the murderers at Cypress Hills of unoffending Indians, if in our territory, or their extradition if in the United States." (Minutes of the North-West Council, March 16th, 1874 : Oliver, *op. cit.*, Vol. II, p. 1021.)   In co-operation with the Montana civil authorities the murderers were arrested and application was made for their extradition. They were, however, discharged for lack of evidence.

Subsequently three of the men involved were arrested at Fort Macleod and Cypress Mountain. Although Taylor believed that the trial would go against the prisoners, as " the authorities propose holding a treaty with the Indians in the vicinity of Cypress Hills this summer, and hope for a favourable result of their negotiations, if the prisoners are condemned to death," (Taylor to Cadwalader, June 8th, 1876 : MSS. Consular Despatches from Winnipeg, Vol. V, Department of State): the three men were finally discharged.

[9] Robertson Ross, Report.

[10] Butler, Report.

[11] Lestanc to Aubert, July 30th, 1879 : *Missions des O.M.I.*, Vol. XVIII, 1880, p. 168.

[12] Grey Owl, *The Men of the Last Frontier*, p. 215.

[13] Illustrative of the frontier adage that the only good Indian was a dead one was the offer once made to exterminate the Indian races in the United States at $300 per scalp. (See *Indian Extermination or Civilization*, The Republic, a Monthly Magazine devoted to the Dissemination of Political Information, Vol. II, No. 5, May 1874.) One American newspaper suggested the introduction of small-pox as the best means to destroy the Indians ! It is only fair to note, however, that while this may have represented the extreme frontier view, opinion in the eastern United States was favourable to the Indians. The suggestion in question was denounced in the Washington *National Republican*, October 26th, 1877, in an article entitled " Who are the Savages ? "

[14] Butler, Report. See also Butler, *The Great Lone Land*, p. 269.

[15] Cunningham, speech in the House of Commons, March 31st, 1873 : enc. in Taylor to Davis, May 21st, 1873, MSS. Consular Despatches from Winnipeg, Vol. III, Department of State. Cunningham was member of the Federal Parliament for the constituency of Marquette, Manitoba, and editor of *The Manitoban*. There were no copies of the Parliamentary debates printed during 1873 and 1874. Précis reports were published during 1870–1–2. The verbatim reports were not begun until 1875.

[16] Christie was the Hudson's Bay Company Factor at Fort Edmonton and French was Commissioner of the North-West Mounted Police.

[17] 36 Vic. c. 35.

[18] Haydon, *The Riders of the Plains*, p. 25.

[19] Selby Smythe to the Minister of Justice, November 27th, 1875 : C.O. 42/741.

[20] Morris, *The Treaties of Canada with the Indians of Manitoba and the North-West Territories, including the negotiations on which they are based and other information relating there to*, p. 270. The Honourable Alexander Morris who compiled this work was Lieutenant-Governor of Manitoba from 1872–7, and himself negotiated Treaties 3, 4 and 5.

[21] *Ibid.*, p. 272.

[22] Barbeau, *Our Indians* (Queen's Quarterly, Vol. XXXVIII, No. 4, 1931, pp. 692–3.)

[23] Huyshe, *The Red River Expedition*, p. 146. Cf. *supra* p. 136.

[24] Dawson, Memorandum in Reference to the Indians, December 19th, 1870 : C.O. 42/698.

[25] *Ibid.*

[26] Archibald to the Secretary of State for the Provinces, September 17th, 1876 : C.O. 42/689.

[27] McDougall, Hardisty, Whitford and others to Archibald, January 10th, 1871 : C.O. 42/697 ; James Seenum, Cree Chief and others to Archibald, January 9th, 1871: *ibid.*

[28] Messages from the Cree Chiefs of the Plains to His Excellency, Governor Archibald, our Great Mother's Representative at Fort Garry, Red River Settlement, enc. in Christie to Archibald, April 13th, 1871 : C.S.P. 1872, Vol. VII, No. 22.

[29] Howe, Memorandum, April 17th, 1871 : *ibid.*

[30] *Indian Treaties and Surrenders from 1680 to 1890*, Vol. I, pp. 12–3, 13–4.

[31] Macleod, *The American Indian Frontier*, p. 195.

[32] The Selkirk Treaty, July 18th, 1817 : Morris *op. cit.*, Appendix pp, 299·300.

[33] Howe Memorandum, *op. cit.*

[34] Archibald to Howe, July 19th, 1871 : C.S.P. 1872, Vol. VII, No. 22.

[35] *Ibid.*

[36] Morris, *op. cit.*, pp. 28–9.

[37] *Ibid.*, pp. 30–1.

[38] The terms of the Treaties from 1 to 7 inclusive are to be found in *Indian Treaties and Surrenders from* 1680 *to* 1890, Vol. I, pp. 282–321, Vol. II, pp. 16–62 ; and Morris *op. cit.*, Appendix, pp. 313–75.

[39] In 1875 owing to the wide dissatisfaction among the Indians of Treaties 1 and 2, as a result of the failure of the Government to fulfil certain verbal promises made on the occasion of the negotiations of the treaties, and the more liberal terms granted in Treaties 3 and 4, the Government revised Treaties 1 and 2 by fulfilling the promises made, and by increasing the annuities to $5 per head, with $25 to each chief, and a suit of clothing to each chief and headman every three years.

[40] Morris, *op. cit.*, p. 62.

[41] *Ibid.*, p. 63.

[42] *Ibid.*, pp 119–20.

[43] McDougall reported the following story to Morris as illustrative of the Indian attitude to the settlers : " A few weeks since, a land speculator wished to take a claim at the crossing on Battle River and asked the consent of the Indians, one of my Saulteaux friends sprang to his feet, and pointing to the east, said : ' Do you see that great white man (the Government) coming ? ' ' No,' said the speculator. ' I do,' said the Indian, ' and I hear the tramp of the multitude behind him, and when he comes you can drop in behind him and take up all the land claims you want ; but until then I caution you to put up no stakes in our country,' " McDougall to Morris, October 23rd, 1875 : Morris, *op. cit.*, p. 174.

[44] French to the Minister of Justice, August 6th, 1875 : R.C.M.P. file 333 ; C.O. 42/737.

[45] Laird to Dufferin, January 31st, 1876 : C.S.P. 1876, Vol. VII, No. 9.

[46] McDougall to Morris, October 23rd, 1875 : *op. cit.*

[47] Mills to Dufferin, January 15th, 1877 : C.S.P. 1877, Vol. VII, No. 11.

[48] *Ibid.*

[49] The problem underlying most of the Indian difficulties in the United States was indicated by a question put to the Canadian Minister of the Interior while on a visit to Washington, " How do you keep your whites in order ? " Mills, confidential Memorandum, August 23rd, 1877 : C.O. 42/749.

[50] Taylor to Seward, March 26th, 1878 : MSS. Consular Despatches from Winnipeg, Vol. V, Department of State.

CHAPTER XI
THE INDIAN PROBLEM. THE RESERVES

[1] Provencher to the Minister of the Interior, December 31st, 1873, C.S.P. 1875, Vol. VII, No. 8.

[2] " Left to his own devices in civilization the Indian is a child let loose in a house of terrors. As a solace he indulges in the doubtful amusements of those only too ready to instruct him, and lacking their judgment, untrained in the technique of vice, he becomes a victim of depravity. Unable to discern the fine line between the evasions and misrepresentations with which civilized man disguises his thoughts, and downright dishonesty, he becomes shiftless and unreliable. The few words of English he learns consist mainly of profanity, so we have the illuminating object lesson of a race just emerging from a state of savagery turning to the languages of the white men for oaths that their own does not contain. Some few have been brought out to the front and partially educated, but almost invariably they return to the tent or the teepee, and the crackling wood fires, to the land of endless trails, tumbling water and crimson sunsets." Grey Owl, *op. cit.*, p. 211.

[3] Provencher to the Minister of the Interior, December 31st, 1873 : *op. cit.*

[4] Morris, Appendix, p. 323.

[5] Christie and Dickieson to the Minister of the Interior, October 7th, 1875 : C.S.P. 1876, Vol. VII, No. 9.

[6] Butler, *The Wild Northland, Being the Story of a Winter Journey, with Dogs, across Northern North America*, p. 56.

[7] Kane, *op. cit.*, pp. 130–1.

[8] Evidence of Lefroy, 199 : Report from the Select Committee 1857, *op. cit.*

[9] Journals, Reports, etc., of the Palliser Expedition, 1857–60, p. 145.

[10] Southesk, *Saskatchewan and the Rocky Mountains*, p. 255.

[11] Milton and Cheadle, *The North-West Passage by Land*, p. 59.

[12] The suddenness of the disappearance of the buffalo has led to the theory that their extermination was the result of some form of epidemic disease. This question is discussed by Roe, *The Extermination of the Buffalo in Western Canada*, Canadian Historical Review, Vol. XV, No. 1, March 1934. Roe concludes that the buffalo were exterminated by man and not by natural causes.

[13] *Life, Letters and Travels of Father Pierre-Jean de Smet, S. J.*, 1801–73, Vol. II, pp. 635–6.

[14] Begg, *History of the North-West*, Vol. I, pp. 299–300. *Cf. supra*, note 25. p. 412.

[15] Mactavish to Armit, January 26th, 1872 : London Inward Correspondence. 1872.

[16] Grant, *Ocean to Ocean, Sandford Fleming's Expedition Through Canada in 1872*, p. 108.

[17] Leduc to T.R.P. Supérieur-Général, January 3rd, 1874 : *Missions des O.M.I.*, Vol. XII, 1874, p. 525.

[18] *Lois et Règulations Etablies pour la Colonie de St. Laurent, cf. supra*, Chap. IX, note 8.

[19] Grahame to Armit, August 5th, 1879 : London Inward Correspondence 1879.

[20] McKenzie, *The Men of the Hudson's Bay Company*, p. 72.

[21] Meakin, Canada's Own, Chap. XX : MacInnes, *In the Shadow of the Rockies*, p. 145.

[22] *Lois et Régulations Etablies pour la Colonie de St. Laurent*.

[23] French to the Minister of Justice, September 14th, 1875 : R.C.M.P. file 333.

[24] Denny to Irvine, July 18th, 1876 : C.O. 42/744. Denny was then sub-Inspector of the N.W.M.P. stationed at Fort Macleod. He later became Indian Agent for Treaty 7.

[25] Dickieson to the Minister of the Interior, October 7th, 1876 : C.S.P. 1877, Vol. VII, No. 11.

[26] Debates of the House of Commons, Canada, 1876, p. 731.

[27] *Ibid.*, 1877, p. 993.

[28] Journals of the Council of the North-West Territories of Canada, Session 1877, p. 25 ; Ordinances of the North-West Council 1877 : C.S.P. 1878, Vol. XI, No. 45.

[29] Taylor to Seward, March 21st, 1878 : MSS. Consular Despatches from Winnipeg, Vol. V, Department of State.

[30] Denny to Irvine, July 18th, 1876 : *op. cit.*

[31] Dewdney to the Superintendent-General of Indian Affairs, January 2nd, 1880 : C.S.P. 1880, Vol. III, No. 4.

[32] In 1879 a series of prairie fires " were started at different points almost simultaneously, as if by some preconstructed arrangement, and the country north of the boundary line was burnt from Wood Mountain on the east to the Rocky Mountains on the west, and nearly as far north as the latitude of Qu'Appelle." (Dewdney to the Superintendent-General, December 31st, 1880 : C.S.P. 1881, Vol. VIII, No. 14.) The Hudson's Bay Company Commissioner stated concerning these fires that " the general impression is that the fires were kindled by the Americans to keep the buffalo south." (Grahame to Armit, December 4th, 1879 : London Inward Correspondence, 1879.) At the same time General Miles placed himself between the boundary and the buffalo, and drove back the Canadian Indians who were going south to hunt. This action was the subject of a strong protest on the part of the Canadian Government. (Campbell, Memorandum, August 13th, 1879 : enc. in Lorne to Hicks Beach, September 4th, 1879 : C.O. 42/757.) Lord Lorne had a personal conversation on September 11th, 1879, with Mr. Evarts, the American Secretary of State, on this matter and asked him to reconsider Miles' action, stating that " It seemed to be his object to prevent the buffalo from coming north.

NOTES

433

thought it would be fair to ask that no impediment should be placed on the migration of the buffalo herds." (Memorandum of conversation between Lord Lorne and Mr. Evarts, September 11th, 1879 : Enc. in Lorne to Hicks Beach, confidential, September 29th, 1879 : C.O. 42/757.)

[33] Clarke to McTavish, February 17th, 1878 : Winnipeg Inward Correspondence, 1878.

[34] Doucet to T.R.P. Supérieur-Général, February 24th, 1880 : *Missions des O.M.I.*, Vol. XVIII, 1880, p. 155.

[35] Camsell to Grahame, March 26th, 1879 : London Inward Correspondence, 1879.

[36] MacFarlane to Grahame, March 10th, 1879 : *ibid.*

[37] Clarke to Grahame, July 2nd, 1879 : *ibid.*

[38] Leduc, December 29th, 1879 : *Missions des O.M.I.*, Vol. XVIII, 1880, p. 158.

[39] Winder to Macleod, January 3rd, 1880 : C.S.P. 1880, Vol. III, No. 4.

[40] Doucet to T.R.P. Supérieur-Général, February 24th, 1880 : *op. cit.*

[41] Grahame to Armit, August 28th, 1879 : London Inward Correspondence, 1879.

[42] A. McDonald to Grahame, June 16th, 1879 : *ibid.*; Dickieson to Macdonald, July 21st, 1879 : C.S.P. 1880, Vol. III, No. 4.

[43] Macdonald to Lorne, n.d. : C.S.P. 1880, Vol. III, No. 4.

[44] Vankoughnet to Macdonald, December 31st, 1879 ; Dewdney to the Superintendent-General, January 2nd, 1880 : *ibid.*

[45] General Account, Indians of Manitoba and the North-West, " A " to " I," Appendix : C.S.P. 1881, Vol. VIII, No. 14.

[46] Macdonald to Lorne, n.d. : C.S.P. 1880, Vol. III, No. 4.

[47] Dewdney to the Superintendent-General, January 2nd, 1880 : *ibid.*

[48] Crozier to the Commissioner of the N.W.M.P., December 1880 : C.S.P. 1881, Vol. III, No. 3.

[49] Dewdney to the Superintendent-General, December 31st, 1880 : C.S.P. 1881, Vol. VIII, 1881.

[50] Dewdney to the Superintendent-General, January 1st, 1882 : C.S.P. 1882, Vol. V, No. 6.

[51] *Ibid.*

[52] McIllree to Dewdney, December 2nd, 1882 : I.D. file 29506-3.

[53] See Evarts to Thornton, November 3rd, November 14th, 1879 : (C.O. 42/758) ; Evarts to Thornton, January 4th, 1881 : (C.O. 42/766) ; Blaine to Thornton, May 10th, May 26th, June 11th, 1881 ; Blaine to Drummond, August 25th, 1881 : (C.O. 42/767) ; Frelinghuysen to West, March 29th, March 31st, April 1st, 1882 : (C.O. 42/771). Other despatches and enclosures are to be found in C.O. 42/769, 772, 773, 774.

[54] In view of the American protests, the Canadian Government expressed the desire to " willingly join the Government of the United States in some concerted plan of action to prevent the recurrence (as far as possible) of such migrations." (Report of a Committee of the Privy Council, June 3rd, 1881 : C.O. 42/767.) No action was, however, taken by the Americans and several months later the Hon. A. Campbell, acting Minister of the Interior, stated that, although the Canadian authorities always expressed readiness to take concerted action with the United States, no response to this offer had ever been received from the United States Government, nor had any evidence been produced of any overt acts by the Canadian Indians. (Report of a Committee of the Privy Council September 16th, 1881 : *ibid.*) An American response was made in February 1882, when they offered to instruct their military to compel all American Indians to remain on their side of the border if Canada would do likewise. The Canadian Government replied that it would be impossible to prevent the Indians from travelling, due to their ties of blood, but suggested that a system of permits should be adopted in order that each individual Indian might be held responsible for his own conduct and not the government of the country concerned. They also suggested the mutual surrender of Indians for trial. (Report of a Committee of the Privy Council, April 24th, 1882 : C.O. 42/771.) In April 1883, the United States, preferring force to policy in dealing with Indians, urged upon Canada the advisability of destroying the property of foreign Indians and the reciprocal crossing of the frontier by the troops of both

nations in pursuit of refractory Indians. The suggestions were considered " unwise " by the Canadian Government. It was contrary to Canadian policy to fight the natives and hence there was no value in continuous pursuit. In the meantime the Canadian Indians were being sent north and, as a result, the Indian raids quickly ceased. (Dewdney, Memorandum on the Correspondence from the United States re Indian raids, April 1883 : Report of a Committee of the Privy Council, July 24th, 1883 : C.O. 42/774.)

[55] Macleod to Macdonald, n.d. : C.S.P. 1880, Vol. III, No. 4.

[56] McIllree to Dewdney, December 2nd, 1882 : op. cit.

[57] Piapot's agreement to leave Fort Walsh and settle upon his reserve was much resented by the more recalcitrant Indians, and a strong guard had to be posted about his camp every night until some means of transport could be provided for his band. Ibid.

[58] Ibid.

[59] Dewdney to the Superintendent-General, December 15th, 1882 : C.S.P. 1883, Vol. IV, No. 5.

[60] Hourie to A. McDonald, October 18th, 1882 : I.D. file 29506–3.

[61] Dewdney to the Superintendent-General, December 15th, 1882 : op. cit.

[62] Monthly Return of Provisions for Indians at Fort Walsh, December 31st, 1882 : I.D. file 29506–3.

[63] " Indians at Walsh are to be kept on starvation allowance." Vankoughnet to Dewdney, December 6th, 1882 : ibid.

[64] Norman to Dewdney, December 27th, 1882 : ibid.

[65] Irvine to Macdonald, telegram, December 12th, 1882 : ibid.

[66] Dewdney to the Superintendent-General, October 24th, 1883 : ibid.

[67] Martineau to the Superintendent-General, n.d. : C.S.P. 1878, Vol. VIII, No. 10.

[68] Laird to the Superintendent-General, November 18th, 1877 : ibid.

[69] Vankoughnet to Macdonald, December 31st, 1878 : C.S.P. 1879, Vol. VI, No. 7.

[70] Macdonald to Lorne, n.d. : C.S.P. 1880, Vol. III, No. 4.

[71] Debates of the House of Commons, Canada, 1880, p. 1991.

[72] Reed to the Superintendent-General, November 7th, 1881 : C.S.P. 1882, Vol. V, No. 6.

[73] Reed to the Superintendent-General, July 9th, 1881 : ibid.

[74] Debates of the House of Commons, Canada, 1884, p. 1450.

[75] McColl to the Superintendent-General, December 31st, 1878 : C.S.P. 1879, Vol. VI, No. 7.

[76] Dennis to Macdonald, confidential, December 20th, 1878 : C.S.P. 1885, Vol. XIII, No. 116.

[77] Dennis to Davin, January 28th, 1879 : ibid.

[78] Macdonald to Lorne, n.d. : C.S.P. 1881, Vol. VIII, No. 14.

[79] Extract of a letter from Laird to the Superintendent-General, November 11th, 1878 : C.S.P. 1879, Vol. VI, No. 7.

[80] Macdonald to Lorne, n.d., op. cit.

[81] Reed to the Superintendent-General, August 1st, 1882 : C.S.P. 1883, Vol. IV, No. 5.

[82] Debates of the House of Commons, Canada, 1880, p. 1696.

[83] Ibid., 1882, p. 1186.

CHAPTER XII

THE GROWTH OF POLITICAL DISCONTENT IN THE NORTH-WEST TERRITORIES

[1] 33 Vic. c. 3.

[2] Taché, letter, *Winnipeg Free Press*, December 27th, 1889 ; Martin *The Natural Resources Question*, p. 47.

[3] " Whether they had any right to those lands or not was not so much the question as it was a question of policy to make an arrangement with the inhabitants of that

Province, in order, in fact, to make a Province at all—in order to introduce law and order there, and assert the sovereignty of the Dominion." Macdonald, *Debates of the House of Commons, Canada,* 1885, p. 3113.

[4] 37 Vic. c. 20.

[5] Burgess to White, February 23rd, 1886 : C.S.P. 1886, Vol. VI, No. 8.

[6] Begg, *op. cit.,* Vol. II, p. 85.

[7] Petition, John Fisher and others to Lieutenant-Governor Morris, May 5th, 1873 : C.S.P. 1885, Vol. XIII, No. 116. Except where otherwise stated the sources upon which this chapter is based will be found in this collection of documents.

[8] Mackay, Memorandum, n.d.: enc. in Morris to the Minister of the Interior, June 9th, 1874.

[9] Décorby to Laird, October 1st, 1874.

[10] Dumont and Fisher to the Lieutenant-Governor, February 1st, 1878.

[11] Petition, the French Canadians and Half-Breeds of St. Albert to the Lieutenant-Governor : enc. in Laird to the Minister of the Interior, April 10th, 1878.

[12] Petition, David Laverdure and others : enc. in Laird to the Minister of the Interior, September 30th, 1878.

[13] Petition, George McKay and others to the Governor-General : acknow. Dennis to Moore, February 23rd, 1878. The office of Deputy Minister of the Interior was held by E. A. Meredith to 1878, J. S. Dennis the Surveyor-General succeeded him from 1878 to 1881. Dennis was followed by Lindsay Russell, then Surveyor-General and by A. M. Burgess, Secretary to the Department in 1883.

[14] Laird to the Minister of the Interior, September 30th, 1878.

[15] Dennis to Macdonald, confidential, December 20th, 1878.

[16] 42 Vic. c. 31.

[17] Petition, Charles McKay and others to Sir John A. Macdonald : acknow. Russell to McKay, May 10th, 1880.

[18] Russell to Charles McKay, May 10th, 1880 ; Russell to Thomas McKay, July 10th, 1880.

[19] Clarke, Memorial to the Lieutenant-Governor in Council, June 6th, 1881.

[20] Laird to the Minister of the Interior, June 14th, 1881.

[21] Dennis to Macpherson, July 22nd, 1881.

[22] Resolutions passed at a Meeting representing the District of Lorne, Prince Albert, October 8th, 1881.

[23] Russell to Clarke, November 22nd, 1881.

[24] Clarke to Russell, January 25th, 1882.

[25] Petition, John Turner and others to Macpherson n.d. : acknow. April 8th, 1884 : Macdonald Papers, Vol. II.

[26] Memorial, North-West Council to the Governor-General in Council, August 2nd, 1884 : Macdonald Papers, North-West Territories.

[27] Macdonald to Lorne, February 15th, 1882 : C.S.P. 1882, Vol. VIII, No. 18.

[28] Morris to the Minister of the Interior, June 9th, 1874.

[29] Walker to Laird, December 29th, 1876.

[30] Laird to the Minister of the Interior, February 12th, 1877.

[31] Dennis to the Minister of the Interior, March 14th, 1877.

[32] Petition, George McKay and others to the Governor-General : acknow. Dennis to Moore, February 23rd, 1878.

[33] Dumont and Fisher to the Lieutenant-Governor, February 1st, 1878. The copy of this petition in C.S.P. 1885, Vol. XIII, No. 116 does not include this clause. The copy printed in C.S.P. 1886, Vol. XII, No. 45b does include it.

[34] Laird to the Minister of the Interior, February 13th, 1878.

[35] Mills to the Lieutenant-Governor, March 18th, 1878.

[36] Petition, André to the Lieutenant-Governor : enc. in Laird to the Minister of the Interior, June 14th, 1881.

[37] Laird to the Minister of the Interior, June 14th, 1881.

[38] Russell to Duck, August 2nd, 1881. Duck was the Dominion Land Agent at Prince Albert.

[39] Resolutions passed at a meeting representing the District of Lorne, Prince Albert, October 8th, 1881.

[40] Dewdney to Macdonald, March 27th, 1882.

[41] Petition, Dumont and others to Sir John A. Macdonald, September 4th, 1882.
[42] Duck to the Minister of the Interior, October 25th, 1882.
[43] Burgess to Clarke, April 14th, 1882.
[44] Burgess to Dewdney, June 16th, 1882.
[45] Memorandum on the North-West half-breeds, n.d. : Macdonald Papers, Vol. II. See also Burgess to Macpherson, January 20th, 1885: C.S.P. 1885,VolVII, No. 13.
[46] Pearce to Walsh, October 31st, 1884 : C.S.P. 1885, Vol. VII, No. 13.
[47] Macpherson Memorandum, April 18th, 1885 : Macdonald Papers, Vol. II. See also Debates of the House of Commons, 1885, pp. 3109–10.
[48] Décorby to Laird, October 1st, 1874.
[49] Dennis to the Minister of the Interior, March 14th, 1877. This proposal was approved by the Minister of the Interior, Meredith to Laird, March 26th, 1877.
[50] Of 99 claimants at St. Laurent, only 6 held their land in 1872, and less than 20 had settled by 1880, Macpherson Memorandum, April 18th, 1885 : op. cit.
[51] Duck to the Surveyor-General, March 11th, 1882.
[52] Burgess to Duck, September 21st, 1882.
[53] André to Macdonald, January 16th, 1883.
[54] Petition, Dumont and others to Macdonald, September 4th, 1882.
[55] " I am directed to request you to inform the petitioners that when the proper time arrives the case of each bona fide settler will be dealt with on its own merits ; but as regard the surveying of the land in question, that all lands in the North-West Territories will be surveyed according to the system now in force." Russell to Nolin, October 13th, 1882.
[56] Macpherson to Russell, April 23rd, 1883.
[57] " Notre population est paisible, calme, soumise ; mais si elle était victime d'une semblable injustice, si les habitants devaient être traités comme un peuple conquis, s'ils ne recevaient pas à ce titre de justice ce qui a été accordé à Edmonton, à Prince Albert, et dans la province du Manitoba ils protesteraient et ne cederaient qu'à la force ouverte." Leduc, letter, April 5th, 1883 : Missions des O.M.I., Vol. XXII, 1884, p. 18.
[58] Ibid., p. 22.
[59] Végreville to Deville, January 19th, 1884.
[60] Deville to Burgess, February 14th, 1884.
[61] Pearce to the Minister of the Interior, March 19th, 1884.
[62] Macpherson, Memorandum, April 18th, 1885 : op. cit.
[63] Debates of the House of Commons, Canada, 1885, p. 3117.
[64] Debates of the Senate, Canada, 1885, p. 1022. In his memorandum Macpherson also stated " If they have grievances, no statement of these grievances has ever reached the Government."
[65] Debates of the House of Commons, Canada, 1885, p. 3110.
[66] Smith to White, October 31st, 1885 : C.S.P. 1886, Vol. VI, No. 8.
[67] The entries during 1881 totalled 5,819 and during 1882, 16,740. The number of acres of land involved were 1,057,519 and 2,699,145 respectively (Russell to Macdonald, March 24th, 1883 : C.S.P. 1883, Vol. X, No. 23). The 1882 total was not passed until several years after the rebellion.
[68] Smith to White, October 31st, 1885 : op. cit.
[69] For this statement of the economic conditions in Manitoba I have drawn upon Taché, La Situation au Nord-Ouest, and more particularly upon a long letter upon the Manitoba situation by the Honourable Joseph Royal, dated May 17th, 1884, published in Le Manitoba, June 19th, 1884. Royal was at that time member of the Federal Parliament for the District of Provencher, Manitoba.
[70] There is no mention of the Farmers' Union in Wood's, A History of Farmers' Movements in Canada. The account above is taken from several letters in the Macdonald Papers, and from a pamphlet published by the Manitoba and North-West Farmers' Union, Brandon, 1884.
[71] Purvis to Macdonald, February 4th, 1884 : Macdonald Papers, North-West Territories.
[72] Martin, Mutchmor and Purvis to Macdonald, February 9th, 1884 : ibid.
[73] Extract from a letter from D. H. McDowall : enc. in Dewdney to Macdonald, March 27th, 1882 : C.S.P. 1885, Vol. XIII, No. 116.

[74] Taché, *op. cit.*, pp. 7–8. See also the Toronto *Mail*, March 31st, April 2nd, June 1st, 1885. Sir John A. Macdonald also attributed much of the responsibility for the agitation to disappointed white speculators, Debates of the House of Commons, Canada, 1885, pp. 3117–8.

[75] The newspapers of the Territories were one in demanding representation of the Territories in the Federal Parliament. See Edmonton *Bulletin*, November 1st, 1884; January 10th, 1885; *Saskatchewan Herald*, November 14th, November 24th, December 22nd, 1884: Prince Albert *Times*, July 10th, 1885; *Regina Leader* (in *Saskatchewan Herald*, June 22nd, 1885. The three latter papers were supporters of the Macdonald Government.

[76] Debates of the House of Commons, Canada, 1885, p. 3107.

[77] Prince Albert *Times*, February 29th, 1884.

[78] Debates of the House of Commons, Canada, 1884, p. 1147.

[79] Prince Albert *Times*, March 21st, 1884.

[80] *Ibid.*, May 10th, 1884.

[81] Debates in the House of Commons, Canada, 1885, p. 3084.

[82] Prince Albert *Times*, May 23rd, 1884.

[83] *Ibid.*, May 30th, 1884.

[81] Resolutions in re Sending a Delegation to Louis Riel: C.S.P. 1886, Vol. XII, No. 43h.

[85] Prince Albert *Times*, May 30th, 1884.

CHAPTER XIII
THE GROWTH OF DISCONTENT AMONG THE INDIANS

[1] Taylor and Mitchell, *Statistical Contributions to Canadian Economic History*, Vol. II, p. 56. 1913 is used as base 100. Upon the basis of 1900 as 100 the index numbers above would be 103.2 and 120.3.

[2] *The Canada Year Book*, 1934–5, p. 554.

[3] Vankoughnet to Macdonald, December 4th, 1883: Macdonald Papers Vankoughnet to Macdonald 1882–3.

[4] Vankoughnet to Rae telegram, November 24th, 1883; Dewdney to Anderson, December 15th, 1883; Dewdney to Pocklington, December 13th, 1883; Dewdney to Rae, December 17th, 1883; Dewdney to Denny, December 13th, 1883: I.D. file 9843. Dewdney's letter to Denny stated "I beg to advise you that it has been found necessary in the interests of economy to dispense with the services of some of the employees at our farms and reserves at your agency."

[5] *The Saskatchewan Herald*, March 20th, 1885.

[6] Vankoughnet to Macdonald, private, February 10th, 1885: Macdonald Papers, Vol. IV.

[7] Grahame to Armit, April 4th, 1884: London Inward Correspondence from Winnipeg, 1884, H.B.C.

[8] Rae to Reed, January 17th, 1883: I.D. file 5307.

[9] Dr. Edwards to Reed, February 7th, 1884: I.D. file 11175.

[10] Hourie to A. McDonald, January 11th, 1884: I.D. file 10845.

[11] "The Indians during the past summer suffered materially from bad crops— this fact would naturally alarm the better conducted ones, but the ill-disposed and lazy were only too glad of such a pretext to urge upon the authorities a grant of extra aid in the way of food supplies, and matters not looking so bright for the well-conducted portion of the Indian community as, no doubt, they were led to believe in their innocence, at the time of the treaty they would be, they are therefore only too prone to be led away by the more designing ones." Reed to the Superintendent-General, January 23rd, 1885: I.D. file 10645. See also Wadsworth to Vankoughnet, November 30th, 1884: I.D. file 16894.

[12] Rae to Macdonald, private, July 5th, 1884: Macdonald Papers, Vol. IV.

[13] Denny to Dewdney, January 14th, 1884: I.D. file 9843. During the rebellion the Government were obliged to call upon Denny's services to pacify the Blackfeet.

It was a tribute to his popularity among the Indians and the work which he had accomplished in Treaty 7 as Indian Agent.

[14] Dewdney to Macdonald, private, n.d. 1884 : Macdonald Papers, Vol. IV.

[15] Proof that this charge was not unfounded is contained in a letter from Reed to the Indian Department, April 14th, 1884 (I.D. file 9843) in which he pointed out that he had received conflicting instructions in regard to the employment of instructors in the Battleford District. Vankoughnet admitted the charge to Macdonald, but denied that any serious complications had arisen from his action. At the same time he alleged that Dewdney was not giving his support to Inspector Wadsworth in the discharge of the latter's duties. (Vankoughnet to Macdonald, private, February 10th, 1885 : Macdonald Papers, Vol. IV.) The correspondence on several other occasions shows that the working of the Indian Department was by no means harmonious.

[16] Dewdney to Macdonald, private, n.d. 1884 : *op. cit.*

[17] Crozier to White, June 25th, 1884 : I.D. file 13990.

[18] *Ibid.*

[19] *The Saskatchewan Herald*, March 20th, 1885.

[20] Debates of the House of Commons, Canada, 1885, p. 3143.

[21] Vankoughnet to Macdonald, February 14th, 1885 : Macdonald Papers. Vankoughnet to Macdonald, 1884–5.

[22] Irvine to the Minister of the Interior, December 29th, 1880 : C.S.P. 1881, Vol. III, No. 3.

[23] A. L. Russell to Assist. Surveyor General, November 24th, 1877 : C.S.P. 1878, Vol. VIII, No. 10.

[24] Irvine to the Minister of the Interior, December 29th, 1880 : *op. cit.*

[25] These words were evidently part of a speech delivered at an Indian Council at Carlton in August 1884 (*cf. supra* p. 290). The memorandum of the speech is on rough paper and bears no clue as to the writer. It may have been the work of a half-breed as it is to be found among the Riel papers in the Confidential Papers of the Department of Justice relative to the Trial of Louis Riel, P.A.C.

[26] Antoine Lose Brave to Mr. Louis Real, March 13th, 1885 : Confidential Papers, etc.

[27] In the Indian speech previously referred to the speaker continued. "The Governor then said, I want first to help you to advance to an equal footing with my children, then after you attain that you will be free to shift for yourself, and the Government will not need to help you any more. Meantime the Government will do all in its power to help you to reach the same footing. I will make you equal." The Assistant Indian Commissioner also wrote " matters not looking so bright for the well-conducted portion of the Indian community as, no doubt, they were led to believe in their innocence, at the time of the treaty they would be, they are therefore only too prone to be led away by the more designing ones." (*cf. supra*, note 11.)

[28] Macdonald to Lansdowne, January 1st, 1884 : C.S.P. 1884, Vol. III, No. 4. Treaties 4, 6 and 7 were the critical areas. By 1884 the Indians of Treaties 1, 2, 3 and 5 were " almost self-supporting." This was not the result of the Government's agricultural policy so much as the fact that the Indians of these treaties lived in wooded country and had never been solely dependent upon the buffalo as had the plains tribes. Settlement had not yet penetrated the areas covered by Treaties 3 and 5, while the Indians of 1 and 2 were able to support themselves partly by agriculture and partly by fishing and hunting small game and also by working in survey parties, lumber shanties, farms and on the steamboats.

[29] Grandin, Les Missions Sauvages du Nord-Ouest : *Missions des O.M.I.*, Vol. XXI, 1883, pp. 126–7.

[30] Dewdney to the Superintendent-General, February 12th, 1885 : I.D. file 17936; Dewdney to the Superintendent-General, June 30th, 1884 : I.D. file 29506–4.

[31] A son of the famous novelist.

[32] Sergeant Howe to Crozier, January 4th, 1882 : C.S.P. 1882, Vol. VIII, No. 18.

[33] Dickens to Crozier, January 3rd, 1882 : *ibid.*

[34] Howe to Crozier, January 4th, 1882 : *op. cit.*

[35] A. McDonald to Dewdney, January 6th, 1884 : I.D. file 10181.

NOTES

[36] Reed to the Superintendent-General, February 21st, 1884 : *ibid.*

[37] McKenzie, *The Men of the Hudson's Bay Company*, p. 116.

[38] " They all expressed the same feeling towards having Mr. Setter retained as Instructor. They think his removal and the appointment of a new man meant starvation to them." McDonald to Dewdney, January 6th, 1884 : *op. cit.*

[39] Keith to Dewdney, February 19th, 1884 : I.D. file 10181.

[40] Reed to the Superintendent-General, February 27th, 1884 : *ibid.*

[41] Herchmer to White, February 26th, 1884 : *ibid.*

[42] Reed to the Superintendent-General, February 27th, 1884.

[43] Herchmer to White, February 26th, 1884.

[44] Keith to Dewdney, February 19th, 1884 : *op. cit.*

[45] Vankoughnet to Macdonald, March 12th, 1884 : Macdonald Papers, Vankoughnet to Macdonald, 1884-5.

[46] *The Saskatchewan Herald*, May 26th, 1883.

[47] *Ibid.*, September 29th, 1883.

[48] Dewdney to Macdonald, June 14th, 1884 : Macdonald Papers, Vol. IV.

[49] Dewdney to the Superintendent-General, January 1st, 1882 : C.S.P. 1882, Vol. V, No. 6.

[50] Jefferson, *Fifty Years on the Saskatchewan* (Canadian North-West Historical Society Publications, Vol. I, No. 5), p. 103. Jefferson speaks with authority having served as a school teacher on Red Pheasant's reserve from 1878 to 1883, and as Farm Instructor on Poundmaker's in 1884. He was kept a prisoner in Poundmaker's camp throughout the rebellion.

[51] Dewdney to the Superintendent-General, January 1st, 1882 : *op. cit*

[52] Macdonald to Lansdowne, January 1st, 1884 : C.S.P. 1884, Vol. III, No. 4.

[53] *The Saskatchewan Herald*, June 9th, 1883.

[54] S. Macdonald (Farm Instructor Treaty 4) to Dewdney, September 5th, 1883 : I.D. file 29506-3.

[55] Reed to Dewdney, December 28th, 1883 : I.D. file 10644.

[56] Reed to the Superintendent-General, April 12th, 1884 : *ibid.*

[57] Vankoughnet to White, March 20th, 1884 : *ibid.*

[58] Jefferson, *op. cit.*, p. 108.

[59] *The Saskatchewan Herald*, July 12th, 1884.

[60] *Ibid.*

[61] Rae to Dewdney, June 21st, 1884 : I.D. file 13990.

[62] Crozier to Irvine, June 25th, 1884 : R.C.M.P. file 1137d ; Irvine to Macdonald, n.d. 1884 : C.S.P. 1885, Vol. XIII, No. 153.

[63] *Ibid.*

[64] Rae to Dewdney, June 21st, 1884 : *op. cit.*

[65] Cameron, *The War Trail of Big Bear*, pp. 39-40.

[66] Crozier to Irvine, June 25th, 1884 : *op. cit.*

[67] Rae to Dewdney, June 28th, 1884 : I.D. file 13990.

[68] Rae to Dewdney, July 29th, 1884 ; Macrae to Dewdney, August 5th, 1884 ; Reed to Dewdney telegram, August 23rd, 1884 : Macdonald Papers, Vol. IV.

[69] Rae to Dewdney, July 29th, 1884 : *op. cit.*

[70] Vankoughnet to Macdonald, July 12th, 1884 : I.D. file 29506-4.

[71] Reed to Dewdney, September 4th, 1884 : Macdonald Papers, Vol. IV.

[72] Macrae to Dewdney, August 25th, 1884 : I.D. file 15423. J. A. Macrae was Indian Agent at Fort Carlton.

[73] It does not appear that Poundmaker was present. Although Rae wrote to Dewdney on August 2nd, that the Indians were " bringing down Poundmaker and other chiefs to the Council " (Macdonald Papers, Vol. IV) Macrae makes no mention of his name in his report of the Council.

[74] This speech is transcribed on a rough sheet of paper with no clue as to the writer or speaker. The content would indicate that it was made at the Duck Lake Council and that the speaker was Big Bear who was the only well-known chief without a reserve. This document, like that mentioned in note 25, is to be found among the Confidential Papers of the Department of Justice relative to the Trial of Louis Riel.

[75] *Ibid.* The reference to Crowfoot might suggest Poundmaker who was an

adopted son of the Blackfoot chief, but there is no proof that he was present at this Council.

[76] Macrae to Dewdney, August 25th, 1884 : *op. cit.*

[77] *Ibid.*

[78] Vankoughnet to Dewdney, December 21st, 1884 : I.D. file 15423.

[79] It was the practice to issue to the Indians only such tools and implements as the Agent considered might be used to advantage and not in the numbers demanded by the Indians. If the latter course had been adopted " everything they were entitled to receive would be broken or lost before the band knew how to handle them properly." Reed to the Superintendent-General, January 23rd, 1885 : *ibid.* Schools were erected on the reserves of Ahtackakoop, Mistowasis, Petequaquay and John Smith, but the attendance was poor especially on John Smith's reserve where the teacher found it difficult to live on the per capita allowance received. There was no school on the reserves of One Arrow or Chakastaypasin as their bands were too small.

[80] Reed to the Superintendent-General, January 23rd, 1885 : *ibid.*

[81] Macrae to Dewdney, August 25th, 1884 : *op. cit.*

[82] Reed to the Superintendent-General, January 23rd, 1885 : *op. cit.*

[83] Vankoughnet to Dewdney, February 4th, 1885. I.D. file 15423.

[84] Ballendine to Dewdney, January 2nd, 1885 : I.D. file 17936.

[85] Rae to Dewdney, December 27th, 1885 : *ibid.*

[86] Crozier to Dewdney, January 14th, 1885 ; *ibid.*

CHAPTER XIV

THE RETURN OF RIEL AND THE DEVELOPMENT OF THE AGITATION.

[1] Fourmond to T.R.P. Supérieur-Général, December 27th, 1884 : *Missions des O.M.I.*, Vol. XXIII, 1885, p. 276.

[2] Archbishop Bourget wrote to Riel " God who has always directed and assisted you up to this time will not abandon you in your worst troubles, for he has given you a mission which you will have to accomplish in all points." (Draft letter, Riel to Mgr. Bourget, February 1884 : Dewdney Papers, Vol. VIII.) This idea of a " mission " became Riel's obsession, and it motivated his subsequent conduct. His belief in his " mission " was reaffirmed at the time of his trial. Addressing the court Riel said, " I believe that I have a mission, I believe I had a mission at this very time. What encourages me to speak to you with more confidence in all the imperfections of my English way of speaking, it is that I have yet and still that mission." Queen vs. Riel : C.S.P. 1886, Vol. XII, No. 43 c.

[3] Garnot, Statement, September 7th, 1885. Except where otherwise stated the documents cited in this chapter are taken from the Confidential Papers relative to the Trial of Louis Riel, P.A.C.

[4] Queen vs. Parenteau and twenty-five others : C.S.P. 1886, Vol. XIII, No. 52.

[5] N.C.W. to Louis Riel, May 18th, 1884 : Macdonald Papers, Vol. III. See also C.S.P. 1886, Vol. XII, No. 43.

[6] Riel to Isbister, Dumont, Ouellette, Dumas, June 5th, 1884.

[7] *Le Manitoba*, St. Boniface, July 17th, 1884.

[8] *Ibid.*, July 24th, 1884.

[9] The Prince Albert *Times*, July 18th, 1884.

[10] *Le Manitoba*, July 24th, 1884.

[11] Riel to the Gentlemen who kindly invite me to hold a public meeting in Prince Albert, July 18th, 1884.

[12] T. G. Jackson to the *Globe*, August 19th, 1884 : The *Globe*, September 4th, 1884.

[13] André to Riel, n.d. : Dewdney Papers, Vol. VIII. It has been generally assumed that this letter was addressed to Riel by Father André in support of the invitation extended by the métis and whites to return to Canada and lead the agitation (See Begg, *op. cit.*, Vol. III, p. 187 ; Black, *A History of Saskatchewan and*

the Old North-West, p. 259; Longstreth, *The Silent Force*, p. 137 ; Boulton, *op. cit.*, p. 171). This view is difficult to reconcile with André's professed opposition to Riel's return. Both André and Clarke believed that if Riel was " not allowed to enter the country, the influence we can bring to bear on the body of the people will counteract the influence of that section of them who are leaders in this movement." (Clarke to Grahame, May 20th, 1884 : Macdonald Papers, Vol. II.) I am personally inclined to believe that this letter was written by André after Riel's return. André's opposition was greatly modified for a time after Riel's return owing to Riel's moderation. The reference to " the people of Prince Albert " would also appear to support this view.

[14] The Prince Albert *Times*, July 25th, 1884.

[15] André to Dewdney, July 21st, 1884 : Macdonald Papers, Vol. II.

[16] " I think I see our way clear to raising all the funds we want." Jackson to Riel, July 23rd, 1884 : *ibid.*

[17] *Ibid.*

[18] " T. J. Agnew proposed to Maclise that the Conservatives should take counsel together, and adopt your platform, under their party name." *Ibid.*

[19] Jackson to the Citizens of Prince Albert, July 28th, 1884.

[20] Macrae to Dewdney, August 5th, 1884 : Macdonald Papers, Vol. IV.

[21] *Ibid.*

[22] T. E. Jackson, Statement, Evidence Books.

[23] Brooks to Crozier, August 21st, 1884 : Macdonald Papers, Vol. II.

[24] T. E. Jackson, *op. cit.*

[25] Crozier to Irvine, August 14th, 1884 : C.S.P. 1885, Vol. XIII, No. 116.

[26] Keenan to Crozier, September 7th, 1884 : *ibid.*

[27] *Le Manitoba*, September 25th, 1884.

[28] Fourmond to T.R.P. Supérieur-Général, December 27th, 1884 : *Missions des O.M.I.*, Vol. XXIII, 1885, p. 277.

[29] *Le Manitoba*, February 19th, 1885.

[30] The Edmonton *Bulletin*, December 6th, 1884.

[31] *Ibid.*, November 1st, 1884.

[32] Indicative of the extremes to which some members of the Farmers' Union were prepared to go, is the following letter addressed to the Secretary :

" Dear Sir.—I think there has not been since the commencement of the agitation a better time to strike than the present. Everything seems ripe for it. I am certain seven-eighths of the people of Winnipeg are in our favour, and I am certain four or five hundred good men will accomplish our object without any difficulty whatever. The fact of the matter is this, we have nothing to resist us, the military here is nothing more than a pack of boys, and we have easy access to the store rooms. We had a small meeting to-night, and the parties present were unanimous in favour of making a strike at once. Now I think that if we delay we will only be losing ground and the thing will never be accomplished. I would like to know the possible number of men who can be got from the country to assist in the scheme. I hope you will come to some definite conclusion at your council meeting. Believe me I am in perfect sympathy with you, and I am ready at any time to take part in the active part of the business and see if we can't get the people their rights. Kindly let me hear from you in the matter at your earliest convenience and oblige,

" Yours fraternally,
" MACK HOWES."

" George Purvis, Esq.,
" Brandon, Secretary,
" Farmers' Union."

This letter was forwarded to Macdonald by Premier Norquay of Manitoba (Norquay to Macdonald, private, June 24th, 1884 : Macdonald Papers, Vol. II), who stated that he had set detectives on Purvis and Howes. Nothing, however, developed from this letter. The letter is printed in C.S.P. 1886, Vol. XIII, No. 52c and in Black, *op. cit.*, p. 260.

[33] Keenan to Crozier, September 25th, 1884 : Macdonald Papers, Vol. II.

[34] Jackson to The *Globe*, August 19th, 1884 : *op. cit.*

[35] Jackson to Chapleau, December 16th, 1884 : C.O. North America 113, Correspondence respecting the Rising in the North-West Territory, Confidential, September 1885.

[36] This refers to the expulsion of Louis Riel from the House of Commons in 1874 after his election for the county of Provencher in Manitoba.

[37] The petition is found in C.O. North America 113, *op. cit.*

[38] Debates of the House of Commons, Canada, 1885, p. 693.

[39] Jackson to Riel, January 27th, 1885.

[40] This volte face may be explained by the following letter from Lieutenant-Governor Dewdney to Sir John A. Macdonald. " I forget whether I told you that I have arranged to secure the Prince Albert paper, so if any little patronage can be sent them from below it will be appreciated." Dewdney to Macdonald, July 23rd, 1884 : Macdonald Papers, Dewdney to Macdonald, 1884-5.

[41] The Prince Albert *Times*, September 19th, 1884.

[42] *Ibid.*, September 26th, 1884.

[43] *The Saskatchewan Herald*, August 9th, 1884.

[44] Oliver to Jackson, October 22nd, 1884.

[45] Grandin to Macdonald, June 13th, 1884 : Macdonald Papers, Vol. II.

[46] Fourmond to the Directeur de l'Oeuvre de la Propagation de la Foi, May 24th, 1885 : *Les Annales de la Propagation de la Foi*, Vol. LVII, 1885, p. 374.

[47] Forget to Dewdney, September 18th, 1884 : Macdonald Papers, Vol. IV.

[48] André to Dewdney, n.d. : *ibid.*

[49] Grandin to Macdonald, June 13th, 1884 : *op. cit.* ; Dewdney to Macdonald private, June 14th, 1884 : *ibid.*, Vol. IV.

[50] Rouleau to Dewdney, September 5th, 1884 : *ibid.*

[51] Forget to Dewdney, September 18th, 1884 : *ibid.*

[52] MacDowall to Dewdney, December 24th, 1884 : *ibid.*

[53] *Ibid.*

[54] André to Dewdney, n.d. : *ibid.*

[55] MacDowall to Dewdney, January 28th, 1885 : Macdonald Papers, Macpherson to Macdonald, 1885-91.

[56] MacDowall to Dewdney, telegram, February 2nd, 1885 : Dewdney Papers, Vol. I.

[57] Crozier to Dewdney, telegram, February 3rd, 1885 : *ibid.*

[58] André to Dewdney, February 6th, 1885 : Macdonald Papers, Vol. IV.

[59] Dewdney to Macdonald, February 13th, 1885 : *ibid.*

[60] Riel to Fiset, June 16th, 1885. Nolin stated at Riel's trial that Riel had prepared this meeting to make it appear as if the people desired him to remain in the country. There is no other evidence on this point but it does not seem likely that the métis, in view of the personal hold which Riel had over them, would have consented to his leaving at this particular time. Moreover, Nolin was strongly prejudiced against Riel and his evidence may be coloured by his bias.

[61] Crozier to Dewdney, confidential, February 27th, 1885: Dewdney Papers, Vol. I.

[62] A significant prayer in Riel's Journal illustrates this determination. " Seigneur . . . accordez-nous . . . la grâce de prendre durant ce mois de mars en l'année mille huit cent quatre vingt cinq, la position de 69, et de la maintenir de la façon la plus glorieuse à votre souverain domaine."

[63] Garnot, Evidence, Trail of White Cap : C.S.P. 1886, Vol. XIII, No. 52.

[64] Sergeant Keenan reported to Crozier on September 25th, 1884 (C.S.P. 1885, Vol. XIII, No. 116) that at a meeting at Baptiste Boyer's Nolin had suggested that they should take up arms if their demands were not complied with.

[65] Nolin, Evidence, Queen vs. Riel.

[66] Nolin, Statement, Evidence Books.

[67] Riel's Journal contained the following entry :
" Nous les sous-signés nous engageons de propos délibéré et de bonne volonté à faire tout ce qui dépendra de nous
" 1.—pour sauver nos âmes en nous efforcant jour et nuit de vivre saintement en toutes choses et en tout lieu.
" 2.—pour sauver notre pays de la mauvaise gouvernment en prenant les armes qu'il le faut.

"Que Dieu le Père Tout Puissant nous soit en aide. Jésus, Marie, Joseph, Saint Jean Baptiste, intercédez pour nous ! Priez pour nous sans cesse afin que nous remportions des à présent toujours et jusqu'à la fin, vos succès, vos victoires, vos triomphes qui sont le succès, les victoires, les triomphes de Dieu même.

"Nous nous engageons particulierement à lever nos familles saintement et à pratiquer sans cesse la plus grande confiance en Dieu, en Jésus, Marie, Joseph, en Saint Jean Baptiste et en nos saints patrons. Nous prenons pour notre drapeau celui des commandements de Dieu et de l'église et la croix encourageante de Jésus Christ notre sauveur.

"JOSEPH OUELLETTE, GABRIEL DUMONT, PIERRE GARIEPY, ISIDORE DUMONT, JOHN ROSS, PHILIPPE GARIEPY, AUGUSTIN LAFRAMBOISE, MOISE OUELLETTE, CALIXTE LAFONTAINE, NAPOLÉON NAULT."

[68] Ness, Evidence, Queen vs. Riel.

[69] Riel in his letter to Fiset (June 16th, 1885) stated that Lawrence Clarke, a Hudson's Bay Company Factor, when passing St. Antoine, declared that 500 Mounted Police were coming to disperse them and to imprison Riel. Clarke denied this. In a letter to the Hudson's Bay Company Commissioner on July 6th, 1885 (H.B.C. folio on the Riel Rebellions) Clarke gave a detailed account of his movements on the day in question and said "Between meeting Lépine twelve miles on the other side of the South Branch and Fort Carlton, I did not meet a single halfbreed, nor with those that I did meet on the way had I one word of conversation about anything connected with Riel or his movements." Nevertheless the other view was prevalent at the time. Hillyard Mitchell, who acted as intermediary between Crozier and Riel wrote to Crozier on March 20th, that he had learned " that Mr. L. Clarke of the H.B.C. is the cause of the whole excitement, viz. on Wednesday he, on driving from Grey, stopped at the Settlement on the South Branch, and told the people that the Government were sending up 500 Police from Troy to fight the half-breeds. The people, of course, got excited and said they were going to fight the said 500 men. And they are now waiting at Batoche expecting them to arrive." Another version is put forward in an unfinished letter dated April 3rd, 1885 from Prince Albert (Confidential Papers, etc.). " During the day in question and before the meeting took place, several English half-breeds, who were in town on business, went home having heard the various rumours relative to the intentions of the Police. Knowing that Riel had done nothing worthy of arrest, and feeling that as they were responsible for his safety, they sent the news on to the lower end of the French Settlement, and as these things always grow by rehandling it reached the French in the form of a statement to the effect that the citizens of Prince Albert were arming to assist the Police to arrest Riel." Whichever version may be true the important fact is that Riel took advantage of the panic to form the Provisional Government.

[70] Minutes of the Provisional Government, March 19th, 1885.

[71] André, Evidence, Queen vs. Riel.

[72] Nolin, Statement.

[73] Ibid.

[74] T.Z. to Riel, May 20th, 1884. This letter was written by Régnier, the schoolteacher, for Maxime Lépine, the initials being used to cloak identity in the event of letter falling into the hands of their opponents : Régnier Statement.

[75] Riel to the English half-breeds of Red Deer Hill, St. Catherine's and St. Paul, March 21st, 1885.

[76] " they sympathized very strongly with the French half-breeds, as being acquainted with them, and many of them near relations." Craig, Evidence ; Trial of Scott, C.S.P. 1886, Vol. XIII, No. 52. Craig was the secretary of the meeting.

[77] Copy of the Minutes at a Public Meeting held at St. Catherine's Church on the evening of March 22nd, 1885. E. Matheson, Chairman, W. Craig, Secretary.

[78] Riel to the English half-breeds at St. Andrews and St. Catherine's, March 23rd, 1885.

[79] Resolutions passed at Lindsay School, March 23rd, 1885. T. F. Miller, Chairman ; W. Miller, Secretary.

[80] T. Scott to Riel, March 23rd, 1885 : Trial of Scott. C.S.P. 1886, Vol. XXIII, No. 52.

[81] Riel to the English-speaking people of Prince Albert re uniting in action.

[82] In March 1884 the Mounted Police were distributed as follows : Battleford, 47 ; Prince Albert, 12 ; Fort Pitt, 19 ; total, 78. (White to Vankoughnet, March 8th, 1884 : I. D. file 10644.) In December 1884 the force was distributed as follows : Battleford, 103 ; Prince Albert, 23 ; Fort Pitt, 20 ; Frog Lake, 5 ; Fort Carlton, 49 ; total, 200. (Appendix, Report of the Commissioner of the N.W.M.P. 1885 : C.S.P. 1885, Vol. XIII, No. 153.)

[83] Crozier to Irvine, July 13th, 1884 : R.C.M.P. file 1137d.

[84] Wrigley to Armit, February 20th, 1885 : London Inward Correspondence, 1885. H.B.C.

[85] Gagnon to Irvine, telegram, March 10th, 1885 : R.C.M.P. file 2527.

[86] Gagnon to Irvine, telegram, March 10th, 1885 : *ibid.*

[87] Crozier to Irvine, telegram, March 11th, 1885 : *ibid.*

[88] Dewdney to Macdonald, private, March 11th, 1885 : Macdonald Papers, Vol. IV.

[89] Macdonald to Dewdney, telegram, March 14th, 1885 : *ibid.*

[90] Mitchell, Statement.

[91] Mitchell to Crozier, March 20th, 1885.

[92] Mitchell, Statement.

[93] Jackson to Mitchell, March 20th, 1885.

[94] Riel to Crozier, March 21st, 1885.

[95] Irvine to Macdonald, April 1st, 1885 : C.S.P. 1886, Vol. VI, No. 8.

[96] A letter from a correspondent at Prince Albert to the Winnipeg *Sun* (June 2nd, 1885) stated that Lawrence Clarke had accused Crozier of being afraid of the half-breeds. Black (*op. cit.*, pp. 281-2) accepted this statement and it is the traditional view at Prince Albert to-day. Crozier made no mention of this and Irvine only stated that Crozier's " better judgment was overruled by the impetuosity displayed both by the police and volunteers." Irvine to Macdonald, Part II, December 31st, 1885 : C.S.P. 1886, Vol. VI, No. 8.

[97] Crozier to Irvine, May 29th, 1885 : *ibid.*

[98] Irvine to Macdonald, April 1st, 1885 : *ibid.*

CHAPTER XV

THE NORTH-WEST REBELLION. PART ONE

[1] The official version of the engagement has it that the métis fired the first shot. (Irvine to Macdonald, April 1st, 1885 : *op. cit.*) This is supported by various statements by Sergeant Ramsey, Sergeant Smart and Corporal McPherson (Confidential Papers relative to the trial of Louis Riel, Department of Justice). On the other hand Dumont maintained that the Government force fired the first shot. (*Le Récit de Dumont*, in Ouimet, *La Verité sur la Question Métisse*, p. 123.) Riel also stated that while he was attempting to surround Crozier, Crozier fired, and then he said, " In the name of God the Father who made us, reply to that." (Young, Statement; Confidential Papers ; Lash, Astley, Tompkins, evidence, Queen vs. Riel, *op. cit.*) Black (p. 277) accepts the half-breed version stating that he had it on the authority of Joseph Mackay, the interpreter that the Police fired first. The evidence is inconclusive as regards the first shot, but it is certain that the Police and volunteers fired the first volley.

[2] Crozier to Irvine, May 29th, 1885 : *op. cit.*

[3] Brass, *Narrative of John Brass* : MSS. folio on the Riel Rebellions, H.B.C. Brass was guide to Colonel Irvine.

[4] Crozier believed that the force opposed to him numbered between 300 to 400 men. (Crozier, to Irvine, May 29th, 1885.) This estimate is accepted by MacBeth, *Policing the Plains*, p. 112, and Longstreth, *The Silent Force*, p. 152. Crozier, however, greatly overestimated the numbers of his opponents. The métis fought from

behind cover and Crozier was not in a position to make an accurate estimate. Dumont declared that he began the engagement with 25 horsemen and " un certain nombre d'hommes à pied " (Dumont, *op. cit.*, p. 123). The account of the engagement in the Prince Albert *Times*, July 10th, 1885, confirms the métis statement that they began the fight with small numbers although reinforcements steadily came in from Duck Lake. Another report in the Toronto *Mail*, April 13th, 1885, states that " there were two hundred armed half-breeds within earshot of this firing, but when they arrived at the scene Crozier was in full retreat."

[5] Dumont, *op. cit.*, p. 125.

[6] Irvine to Macdonald, Part II, December 31st, 1885 : *op. cit.*

[7] *Ibid.*, See also Clarke, Statement : Rebellion Losses Claims, Fort Carlton, H.B.C.

[8] Brass, *op. cit.*

[9] André, Journal, March 28th, 1885 : *Missions des O.M.I.*, Vol. XXIII, 1885, p. 292.

[10] *Ibid.*, pp. 293-4.

[11] Four métis and one Indian were killed at Duck Lake, Dumont, *op. cit.*, p. 125; Garnot, Memorandum : Confidential Papers, Department of Justice.

[12] The losses of the Hudson's Bay Company at Fort Carlton amounted to $52,540.78; Statement of Claims of the Hudson's Bay Company against the Government of the Dominion of Canada for Compensation for Pillage, Loss and Destruction of Goods, Property and Effects at various Posts in the North-West Territories in the Insurrection in the Spring and Summer of 1885. H.B.C.

[13] Young, Statement : Confidential Papers, Department of Justice.

[14] Garnot, Evidence, Trial of White Cap : C.S.P. 1886, Vol. XIII, No. 52.

[15] Crozier to Dewdney, confidential, January 7th, 1885 ; Macdonald Papers, Vol. II.

[16] Antoine Lose Brave to Mr. Louis Real, March 13th, 1885 : Confidential Papers, Department of Justice.

[17] Lightfoot, Declaration, May 31st, 1885 : Macdonald Papers, Vol. IV.

[18] Hay Moza (Stoney), Declaration, May 31st, 1885 : *ibid.* This was corroborated by declarations by Right and Left and Mah-to-Pah.

[19] Riel to the métis at Battle River and Fort Pitt ; Dewdney Papers, Vol. VIII.

[20] Riel to the métis of Battle River and Fort Pitt, April 8th, 1885 : *ibid.* The French version of which this is a translation is to be found in the Macdonald Papers, Vol. IV.

[21] A Diary of Events, March 27th, 1885 : *The Saskatchewan Herald*, April 23rd, 1885.

[22] *Ibid.*, March 28th, 1885.

[23] Rae to Vankoughnet, telegram, March 31st, 1885 : I.D. file 19950.

[24] A Diary of Events, March 30th, 1885 : *op. cit.*

[25] Rae to Dewdney, telegram, March 30th, 1885 : Dewdney Papers, Vol. VIII.

[26] Dewdney to Rae, telegram, March 30th, 1885 : *ibid.*

[27] The Hudson's Bay Company losses at Battleford amounted to $22,969.61. Statement of Claims of the Hudson's Bay Company against the Government of the Dominion of Canada for Compensation, etc., H.B.C.

[28] Of the 500 who took refuge in the Fort, 300 were women and children. Inspector Morris to Herchmer, April 1st, 1885 : Appendix B, C.S.P. 1886, Vol. VI, No. 8.

[29] Quinn to Dewdney, February 28th, 1885 : I.D. file 29506-4.

[30] Dickens to the O.C. Battleford, January 12th, 1885 : *ibid.*

[31] Martin to Dickens, February 13th, 1885 : I.D. file 11582.

[32] Dickens to the O.C. Battleford, February 15th, 1885 : *ibid.*

[33] Quinn to Dewdney, February 28th, 1885 : *op. cit.*

[34] Neither W. B. Cameron, the sole male survivor of the Frog Lake Massacre, nor W. J. McLean, who was taken prisoner by Big Bear's Indians at Fort Pitt believed Big Bear was responsible for the actions of the Indians and attributed the Frog Lake Massacre to the evil influence of Wandering Spirit and Imasees. As for Little Poplar, although he was not present at the massacre, the Assistant Indian Commissioner considered him " the worst Indian we have to contend with, and is capable of any

overt act." (Reed to the Superintendent-General, January 16th, 1885 : I.D. file 17936.) Vankoughnet suggested that Little Poplar should be arrested if there was sufficient evidence to warrant it, but no action was taken in this regard. Further evidence in Big Bear's favour is supplied by a letter from Father Rémas to Mgr. Grandin, August 25th, 1885 : Missions des O.M.I. Vol. XXIII, 1885, pp. 432-4.

[35] Cameron, *The War Trail of Big Bear*, p. 48.

[36] Dickens to the Commissioner of the N.W.M.P., June 8th, 1885 : Appendix H, C.S.P. 1886, Vol. VI, No. 8.

[37] *Ibid.* It is only fair to note that the corporal in charge of the detachment at Frog Lake refused to leave without the women until he was ordered to do so by Agent Quinn.

[38] Cameron, *op. cit.*, p. 58.

[39] *Ibid.*, pp. 72-3.

[40] Dickens to Crozier, February 15th, 1885 : I.D. file 11582.

[41] McLean, *Reminiscences of the Tragic Events at Frog Lake and in Fort Pitt District with some of the Experiences of the Writer and his Family during the North-West Rebellion of* 1885. MSS., H.B.C., p. 2.

[42] Dickens to the Commissioner of the N.W.M.P., June 8th, 1885 : *op. cit.*

[43] McLean, *op. cit.*, p. 2.

[44] *Diary of Francis Dickens*, edit. V. Lachance (Bulletin of the Departments of History and Political and Economic Science in Queen's University, Kingston, No. 59, 1930), p. 17.

[45] McLean, *op. cit.*, p. 4. McLean wrote that he slept on an average of only two hours in every twenty-four for ten days.

[46] Cameron (*op. cit.*, p. 111) is in error when he gives the date as April 14th. *Dickens Diary*, p. 17, gives the 13th as the date, likewise McLean, p. 6.

[47] McLean, p. 6.

[48] *Diary of Francis Dickens*, p. 17.

[49] In his report to the Commissioner, June 8th, 1885, Dickens wrote, " Mr. McLean, without telling me of his intention, and in spite of the warning of his interpreter and friends, went out again, and was taken prisoner." Other evidence, however, shows that McLean acted with Dickens' knowledge. See McLean, p. 7 ; Rev. Quinney, Statement, Rebellion Losses Claims, Fort Pitt, H.B.C. ; F. S. Simpson, Statement, *ibid.* Both Quinney and Simpson were present at the discussions as to what McLean should do. It seems probable that Dickens was endeavouring to throw the onus of the responsibility for the abandonment of Fort Pitt upon McLean.

[50] McLean, pp. 8-9.

[51] Dickens to the Commissioner, N.W.M.P., June 8th, 1885 : *op. cit.*

[52] Scollen to Dewdney, April 12th, 1885 : Macdonald Papers, Vol. IV.

[53] Lucas to Dewdney, April 15th, 1885 : I.D. file 19550-2.

[54] McDonnell to Dewdney, April 16th, 1885 : *ibid.*

[55] Lucas to Dewdney, April 15th, 1885 : *op. cit.*

[56] Young, Statement, Rebellion Losses Claims, Lac la Biche, H.B.C.

[57] Mgr. Faraud to T.R.P. Supérieur-Général, June 6th, 1885 : *Missions des O.M.I.*, Vol. XXIII, 1885, p. 322.

[58] Young, *op. cit.*

[59] An issue of goods on credit.

[60] Mgr. Faraud to T.R.P. Supérieur-Général, June 6th, 1885 : *op. cit.*, pp. 325-6. The total net loss of goods at Lac la Biche amounted to $9798.38. A certain number of the furs, etc., were later recovered.

[61] Clarke to Irvine, April 25th, 1885 : Clarke, Statement, Rebellion Losses, Green Lake, H.B.C.

[62] *Ibid.*

CHAPTER XVI

THE NORTH-WEST REBELLION.   PART TWO

[1] The Montreal *Gazette*, March 25th, 1885. The Toronto *Mail* of March 24th stated, " It is a monstrous exaggeration to say that rebellion is afoot. Riel, who is never happy except when he is posing as the hero of some desperate cause, has talked war for months ; but no one acquainted with the ex-President will credit him with either the courage or the capacity to make serious trouble." The Winnipeg *Times*, March 23rd, 1885, expressed a similar view.

[2] Macdonald to Dewdney, telegram, March 14th, 1885 : Macdonald Papers, Vol. IV. Fathers Lacombe and Hugonard were Roman Catholic priests with great influence over the Indians and the métis.

[3] Dewdney to Macdonald, telegram, March 22nd, 1885 : Dewdney Papers, Vol. V.

[4] Macdonald to Dewdney, telegram, March 23rd, 1885 : *ibid.*

[5] Jackson, Report on Questions Relative to the Suppression of the Insurrection in the North-West Territories in 1885, December 24th, 1886 : C.S.P. 1887, Vol. VIII, No. 9c.

[6] Sackville-West to Bayard, March 28th, 1885 : Notes from the British Legation, Vol. CXI, MSS. Department of State.

[7] Bayard to Sackville-West, March 28th, 1885 : Notes to the British Legation, Vol. XIX, *ibid.*

[8] Bayard to Sackville-West, April 11th, 1885 : *ibid.*

[9] McGirr (pp. Dewdney) to Macdonald, April 24th, 1885 : I.D. file 19550-1.

[10] Report of a Committee of the Privy Council, January 28th, 1885 : C.S.P. 1885, Vol. XIII, No. 116.

[11] Burgess to Street, March 30th, 1885 ; Macpherson to Street, telegram, April 6th, 1885 : *ibid.* Oliver is in error when he writes " it was after the granting of the scrip in March 1885 . . . that Riel formed his provisional government " (Oliver, *Saskatchewan and Alberta, General History* 1870-1912, Canada and its Provinces, Vol. XIX, p. 210) Riel's government was formed on the March 19th. The Commission was not appointed until the 30th nor the issue of scrip authorized until April 6th.

[12] Middleton, Special Report upon the Military Operations in the North-West, December 30th, 1885 : C.S.P. 1886, Vol. V, No. 6a.

[13] *Ibid.*

[14] Henry, Report, April 23rd, 1885 ; Carrière, Report, April 22nd, 1885 : Dewdney Papers, Vol. VIII. Carrière reported that the troops had three cannon " and another machine with a handle that fires 100 shots a minute."

[15] After the engagement at Duck Lake.

[16] Dumont, *op. cit.*, p. 127.

[17] *Ibid.*

[18] Riel, Advice on the defence of Batoche, April 22nd, 1885 : Dewdney Papers, Vol. VIII.

[19] Dumont, *op. cit.*, p. 130.

[20] *Ibid.*, p. 131.

[21] Boulton, *op. cit.*, pp. 225-6 ; Dumont, *op. cit.*, p. 132.

[22] Middleton, Report on the Engagement at Fish Creek, May 1st, 1885 : Appendix A, C.S.P. 1886, Vol. V, No. 6a.

[23] Middleton stated in his Report on the Engagement at Fish Creek that the métis numbered 280 men. Begg, *op. cit.*, Vol. III, p. 213, basing his account on Middleton gives the same figure. According to Dumont, the métis reached Fish Creek with 150 men. Dumont then went ahead with 20 and stationed 130 in the coulée. At the end of the engagement Dumont had only 54 men when Edouard Dumont arrived with a reinforcement of 80 horsemen. (Dumont, p. 134.) This is corroborated by reports by Maxime Lépine and Charles Trottier on the engagement. Trottier stated that he counted 48 men and then 6 more came out of the wood, making a total of 54. Dumont's casualties consisted largely of deserters from the métis ranks. As Middleton had no means of telling the exact numbers of his opponents his estimate is very likely exaggerated.

[24] Lépine, Report on the Battle of April 24th : Dewdney Papers, Vol. VIII.

[25] Otter to Major-General Middleton, May 26th, 1885: Appendix E, C. S.P. 1886, Vol. V, No. 6a.

[26] L'Heureux, Report, November 1st, 1886: Macdonald Papers, Vol. VII. L'Heureux was the interpreter on Crowfoot's reserve.

[27] Steele, *Forty Years in Canada*, pp. 183-4.

[28] Macdonald to Lacombe, telegram, March 24th, 1885: I.D. file 19550-1.

[29] Lacombe to Macdonald, telegram, March 31st, 1885: *ibid.*

[30] Macdonald to Dewdney, telegram, April 1st, 1885: *ibid.*

[31] Dewdney to Macdonald, April 12th, 1885: *ibid.*

[32] Lacombe to Dewdney, confidential, July 11th, 1885: Macdonald Papers, Dewdney to Macdonald. Steele of the N.W.M.P. also shared this distrust of Crowfoot, Steele, *op. cit.*, p. 185.

[33] Strange, Report of Operations of Alberta Field Force from March 1885, to July 2nd, 1885: Appendix G., C.S.P. 1886, Vol. V, No. 6a; Perry to Irvine, August 19th, 1885: Appendix F, C.S.P. 1886, Vol. VI, No. 8; Steele, p. 214.

[34] McLean, *op. cit.*, p. 20.

[35] On May 14th Indian Agent Macrae wrote to Dewdney:
" I learn that that chief has twice been serious of sending a messenger to us—once to treat—and subsequently to desire the garrison to leave the country. It would seem . . . that his camp has been divided into a peace and war party ; if this is so, it is to be greatly regretted that we have been unable to cause a separation of the two." I.D. file 19550-3.

[36] Desjardins, Evidence, The Trial of Poundmaker: C.S.P. 1886, Vol. XIII, No. 52. See also Jefferson's evidence.

[37] This was Otter's force.

[38] Poundmaker to Riel, April 29th, 1885: Confidential Papers, Department of Justice. See also Trial of Poundmaker, *op. cit.*

[39] Riel to Poundmaker, May 1st, 1885: *ibid.*

[40] Otter, Report on the Engagement at Cut Knife Hill, May 5th, 1885: Appendix B, C.S.P. 1886, Vol. V, No. 6a.

[41] Middleton disclaimed any responsibility for the attack. " The movement which led to the engagement was made without my orders, though Lieutenant-Colonel Otter had the approval of Lieutenant-Governor Dewdney, to whom however he should not have applied on such a purely military matter." Middleton, *Suppression of Rebellion in the North-West Territories* (The United Service Magazine, January 1894, p. 380).

[42] Otter to Dewdney, telegram, April 26th, 1885: Dewdney Papers, Vol. II.

[43] Dewdney to Otter, telegram, April 26th, 1885: *ibid.*

[44] Otter, Report, *op. cit.*

[45] Bigonnesse, letter, June 7th, 1885: *Missions des O.M.I.*, Vol. XXIII, 1885, p. 336; Jefferson, *Fifty Years on the Saskatchewan, op. cit.*, p. 143; Cochin, *Reminiscences of Louis Cochin* (Canadian North-West Historical Society publications, Vol. I, No. 2, 1927, pp. 17-8). Both Jefferson and Father Cochin were prisoners in Poundmaker's camp.

[46] Otter to Middleton, May 26th, 1885: *op. cit.*

[47] Cochin, *Reminiscences, op. cit.*, p. 19.

[48] Middleton, Special Report, December 30th, 1885: *op. cit.*

[49] Captain Smith, who was in charge of the *Northcote* stated in his Report, May 13th, 1885 (Appendix C.1, C.S.P. 1886, Vol. V, No. 6a), that Middleton ordered him to reach Batoche at " the hour named by you, 8 a.m." Middleton, on the other hand, stated in his report (Report on the Capture of Batoche and the Surrender of Riel, May 31st, 1885 ; Appendix C, *ibid.*) that the time was fixed at 9 a.m. The only other testimony on this point is that of Colonel Houghton, Deputy Adjutant General, who stated in a letter to the Montreal *Gazette* (*The Gazette*, March 31st, 1894) that the steamer was under orders to be at Batoche at 8 a.m., and that its failure to connect with the troops was due to the fact that Middleton was an hour late in reaching the point of attack.

[50] Middleton, Report on the Capture of Batoche, *op. cit.*

[51] In his account of the fighting of May 11th, Middleton wrote, " though as yet we had not made much progress I resolved, to use a historical expression, ' to peg

away ' until I succeeded in my object of taking Batoche, which I was sure I should do."

[52] Mgr. Grandin to T.R.P. Supérieur-Général, October 17th, 1885 : *Missions des O.M.I.*, Vol. XXIV, 1886, p. 23.

[53] The responsibility for the charge at Batoche has been a matter of considerable dispute. Middleton in his Report and Van Straubenzie (Van Straubenzie to the Montreal *Gazette*, July 22nd, 1885 : the *Gazette*, July 27th, 1885) both claimed to have ordered the charge. Other evidence seems to show that the charge was a spontaneous development and was led by Colonel Williams of the Midland Battalion. In the first place, as Colonel Denison points out (*Soldiering in Canada*, p. 297), General Middleton was at lunch, the 90th and the two mounted units as well as the machine gun and batteries were resting in the zareba. Only 260 men were opposite the enemy, while the remainder, about 470, were behind the lines. "But who ever heard," wrote Denison, " of a General commencing an action with one-fourth or one-third of his men, with only thirty rounds of ammunition each, and with his artillery and cavalry unharnessed and unsaddled ! " Denison attributed the charge to Williams. Captain Kirwan, Assistant Transport Officer (Montreal *Gazette*, July 8th, 1885) and W.P.E., a member of the Surveyors' Intelligence Corps, (Toronto *Mail*, June 6th, 1885) support this statement. Colonel Houghton, Deputy Adjutant General, declared that the Canadian militia officers charged the rifle pits on their own initiative. " Had they been unsuccessful, they would have been tried by court-martial and shot, but being in close touch with their men, and knowing their metal, they drove the rebels from cover and broke the back of the rebellion " (Black, *op. cit.*, p. 322).

The half-breed tradition of the charge at Batoche is interesting. The half-breeds claim to have run out of ammunition and "in a bravado gesture of defiance they drove home their last charge of powder into their muzzle-loaders and fired their ramrods at the troops. Some of the militia, seeing these rods flying amongst them, guessed that the ammunition of their enemies was exhausted and advanced with more boldness. The movement spread along the line and developed into the final spontaneous charge that broke the rebel defence." (Jefferys, *Fifty Years Ago*, Canadian Geographical Journal, June 1935, Vol. X, No. 6.)

[54] Riel to Middleton, May 12th, 1885 : Confidential Papers, Department of Justice ; Exhibit No. 4, Queen vs. Riel.

[55] Middleton to Riel, May 13th, 1885 : *ibid.*

[56] Riel to Middleton, May 15th, 1885 : *ibid.* Exhibit No. 19.

[57] Dumont, *op. cit.*, p. 142.

[58] Irvine to Macdonald, Part II, December 31st, 1885 : *op. cit.*

[59] Poundmaker to Middleton, May 19th, 1885 : Middleton, Special Report.

[60] Middleton to Poundmaker, May 23rd, 1885 : *ibid.*

[61] Kennedy, *The Book of the West*, p. 112.

[62] McLean, *op. cit.*, p. 33.

[63] Strange, Report on Encounter with Big Bear, May 28th, 1885 : Appendix D, C.S.P., 1886, Vol. V, No. 6a ; Steele, *op. cit.*, p. 221.

[64] *Ibid.*

[65] Strange, *Gunner Jingo's Jubilee*, p. 468. This book was Strange's autobiography. Strange later wrote to the press that his official report had not been published in its entirety, but had been truncated and altered. (*La Presse*, July 26th, 1885.) Strange also related these incidents in a private letter to his wife (see Mrs. Strange to Caron, June 2nd, 1886 : Caron Papers) and stated that upon one occasion one of his messengers, who had reached Middleton with great difficulty, asked the Major-General for a pistol to replace one lost en route. Middleton replied " ' pouf,' you don't need a pistol, you could walk through the country where General Strange is with a good stick." This illustrates the lack of good feeling between the two generals.

[66] McLean, *op. cit.*, p. 40.

[67] Steele, *op. cit.*, p. 225-6.

[68] Irvine to Macdonald, Part II, December 31st, 1885 : *op. cit.* The Assistant Indian Commissioner considered this to be an error. " For the purpose of chasing Indians young active officers are required, that will run through the country with

what they can carry on their horses' backs and not with a waggon for nearly every man." Reed to Dewdney, June 23rd, 1885 : Macdonald Papers, Vol. IV.

[69] McLean, *op. cit.*, p. 43.

[70] The Commission on War Claims investigated claims for transport and supplies and stated in a Preliminary Report that " It cannot be denied, however, the people generally in that part of the country adhered to the time-honoured practice of getting all they possibly could out of the Government." Jackson, Whitehead and Forrest, Preliminary Report of the Commission on War Claims, February 25th, 1886 : Appendix IV, C.S.P. 1886, Vol. V., No. 6a.

[71] Bergin, Report of the Surgeon General, May 13th, 1886 : *ibid.* The following criticism was written to Caron by Army Surgeon Labat ; "Le service de l'intendance, de l'ambulance, et de la poste est ridiculement fait. Nous recevons ni lettres ni journaux depuis plus d'un mois, nous manquons souvent de viandes fraiches, toujours de tabac. Nos blessés n'ont aucun *medical comfort.* Pourquoi ne pas faire une razzia sur tous les spéculateurs d'ici et leur payer leur produits dix pour cent au dessus du cours ? Comme vous le voyez votre administration laisse beaucoup à désirer. " Labat to Caron, June 1st, 1885 : Caron Papers. See also Labat to Caron, May 7th, 1885 : *ibid.*

[72] Steele, *op. cit.*, p. 215.

[73] Strange, Report of Operations of Alberta Field Force : *op. cit.*

[74] Vankoughnet, memorandum, August 17th, 1885 : I.D. file 19550–4.

CHAPTER XVII

THE POLITICAL RESULTS OF THE NORTH-WEST REBELLION

[1] This idea is expressed in Dafoe, *Laurier* : *A Study in Canadian Politics*, pp. 17–19.

[2] David, *Laurier*, p. 39.

[3] *L'Etendard*, Montreal, April 1st, 1885.

[4] Beauregard, *Le 9me Bataillon au Nord-Ouest*, p. 11.

[5] *Le Nouvelliste*, April 1st, 1885.

[6] *La Vérité*, quoted in *L'Etendard*, April 4th, 1885.

[7] *Le Métis*, Montreal, May 2nd, 1885. Only two numbers of this sheet appeared.

[8] This article was the subject of a protest in the House of Commons by the French Canadians. See Debates of the House of Commons, Canada, 1885, pp. 1678–9.

[9] These are printed in C.S.P. 1886, Vol. XII, No. 43h. In one of Riel's strange writings we find the following :

"Dieu veut que le Nom du Zodiac soit changé, et qu'on le nomme désormais SON DIADEME ; Que ses signes ne soient plus nommés signes mais DIAMANTS ; et qu'ainsi au lieu de dire ' Les signes du Zodiac ' on dise et on écrive ' Les diamants de son Diadème.'

"Dieu veut qu'on donne au premier diamant de son Diadème, dans le calendrier et dans tous les écrits chrétiens le nom d'OXFORD. . ." (Confidential Papers, Department of Justice.)

[10] Macdonald to Lavell and Valade, October 31st, 1885 : Macdonald Papers, Vol. III.

[11] Valade to Macdonald, telegram, November 8th, 1885 : Lavell to Macdonald, telegram, November 8th, 1885. The reports of the Insanity Commission are printed in C.S.P. 1886, Vol. XII, No. 43, but these printed versions are misquoted. Valade's telegram laid stress upon the fact that Riel was " not an accountable being," which statement is omitted from the printed version. The original telegram read as follows :

"After having examined carefully Riel in private conversation with him and by testimony of persons who take care of him, I have come to the conclusion that he is not an accountable being, that he is unable to distinguish between wrong and right on political and religious subjects, which I consider well-marked typical forms of insanity under which he undoubtedly suffers, but on other points I believe him to be sensible and can distinguish right from wrong."

Dr. Jukes of the Mounted Police also submitted two reports, one to Dewdney and one to Macdonald. The former is printed but the following statement is omitted.

> " That Riel differs systematically from the large majority of mankind in the views he entertains respecting certain questions relating to religious subjects or rather to certain spiritual phenomena such as Inspiration, and Prophetic Vision in relation thereto, must be admitted ; on these subjects he cherishes illusions or hallucinations which vary materially in intensity under varying physical and mental conditions ; but diversities of opinion, I believe, upon these and kindred subjects do not properly constitute insanity.'

(Jukes to Dewdney, November 6th, 1885 : Macdonald Papers, Vol. III.) The Government were apparently unwilling to strengthen the hands of their opponents by printing the complete reports.

[12] Riel to Taylor, October, 1884 : MSS. Consular Despatches from Winnipeg, Vol. VI, Department of State.

[13] Riel to Taylor, July 21st, 1885 : *ibid.*

[14] Riel to President Cleveland, n.d. : enc. in Taylor to Porter, September 12th, 1885 : *ibid.*

[15] Bayard to Choquet, October 27th, 1885 : Senate Executive Documents. No. 1, 51 Congress Special Senate Session, Serial 2613.

[16] Macdonald to Lansdowne, August 28th, 1885 : Macdonald Papers, Vol. III.

[17] Lansdowne to Macdonald, August 31st, 1885 : *ibid.*

[18] Carnarvon to Salisbury, private, October 22nd, 1885 : G.D. 6/130.

[19] Stanley to Carnarvon, confidential, October 23rd, 1885 : *ibid.*

[20] Carnarvon to Stanley, private, October 25th, 1885 : *ibid.*

[21] " In spite of Tupper and of other Colonial authorities I have great misgivings as to hanging Riel." Carnarvon to Herbert, November 11th, 1885 : *ibid.* Tupper was High Commissioner for Canada.

[22] Lansdowne to Stanley, confidential, November 13th, 1885 : *ibid.* This despatch is also printed in North America, 116, Colonial Office Confidential Print.

[23] *L'Electeur*, June 25th, 1885.

[24] *The Selkirk Herald*, quoted in the Toronto *Mail*, December 5th, 1885.

[25] *The Orange Sentinel*, quoted in the Montreal *Star*, September 11th, 1885,

[26] Debates of the House of Commons, Canada, 1885, pp. 2030-40.

[27] *Ibid.*, pp. 3075-3110.

[28] The Montreal *Gazette*, July 7th, 1885.

[29] Debates of the House of Commons, Canada, 1885, p. 3213.

[30] Journals of the Legislative Assembly of Quebec, Vol. XIX, 1885, p. 123.

[31] *Ibid.*, p. 124.

[32] Chapleau to Macdonald, confidential, November 12th, 1885 : Macdonald Papers, Chapleau to Macdonald, 1873-85.

[33] The details of the defection of the French Canadian Conservatives are taken from the Montreal *Star*, November 14th, 1885, and *La Presse*, November 13th, 1885.

[34] Langevin to Macdonald, telegram, November 12th, 1885 : Macdonald Papers, Langevin to Macdonald, 1884-91.

[35] Macdonald to Langevin, telegram, November 13th, 1885 : *ibid.*

[36] Ouimet was Lieutenant-Colonel of the 65th Rifles and had served with the Alberta Field Force.

[37] Coursol and others to Macdonald, telegram, November 13th, 1885 : Macdonald Papers, Vol. V.

[38] Macdonald Papers, Vol. V.

[39] *Ibid.*

[40] *Ibid.*

[41] *Ibid.*

[42] O'Brien to Macdonald, August 21st, 1885 : *ibid.*

[43] Parkin, *Sir John A. Macdonald*, p. 244.

[44] Ward to Macdonald, August 26th, 1885 : Macdonald Papers, Vol. V.

[45] Chapleau to Macdonald, confidential, November 12th, 1885 : *op. cit.*

[46] Possibly because Chapleau had voluntarily defended Lépine in 1874. His refusal to assist Riel in 1885 centred much of the agitation upon him.

[47] *La Presse*, November 13th, 1885. The same idea is expressed in the Montreal *Star* of November 10th.

[48] *La Patrie*, quoted in the Toronto *Mail*, November 23rd, 1885.

[49] All quotations from speeches upon this occasion are taken from the Montreal *Gazette*, November 23rd, 1885.

[50] The Toronto *Mail*, July 8th, 1885.

[51] *Ibid.*, November 23rd, 1885.

[52] *Ibid.*, November 25th, 1885.

[53] The Toronto *Globe*, April 15th, 1885. Another Liberal Paper, the London *Times*, stated on April 3rd, " For the second time Riel has appealed to arms. His followers may have some excuse made for them. For Riel there can be no excuse, and if he is suffered a second time to escape condign punishment, we shall put it down as proof, not of the clemency, but of the culpable weakness of the Government."

[54] The *Globe*, July 24th, 1885.

[55] The *Mail*, August 21st, 1885. See also Brereton to Macdonald, August 22nd, 1885 : Macdonald Papers, Vol. V.

[56] Debates of the House of Commons, Canada, 1886, p. 160.

[57] The *Mail*, November 23rd, 1885.

[58] Debates of the House of Commons, Canada, 1886, p. 59.

[59] " I saw Sir Hector as requested and afterwards called on Chapleau. Sir Hector will do as you suggested. He will move the previous question and make his speech after Landry's motion." Caron to Macdonald, private, March 10th, 1886 : Macdonald Papers, Caron to Macdonald, 1886–91.

[60] Journals of the House of Commons, Canada, 1886, Vol. XX, pp. 73–4.

[61] Journals of the Legislative Assembly of Quebec, Vol. XX, 1886, p. 76.

[62] *Ibid.*, p. 77.

[63] Chapleau to Macdonald, private, October 7th, 1886 : Macdonald Papers, Chapleau to Macdonald, 1886–91.

[64] Langelier, *Souvenirs Politiques de 1878 à 1890*, Vol. I, p. 249.

[65] *La Vérité*, quoted in *L'Etendard*, August 7th, 1886.

[66] Chapleau to Macdonald, private, October 7th, 1886 : *op. cit.*

[67] *L'Etendard*, October 16th, 1886.

[68] Langevin to Macdonald, confidential, October 15th, 1886 : Macdonald Papers, Langevin to Macdonald, 1884–91.

[69] *Le Canadien*, October 15th, 1886.

[70] *La Justice*, quoted in the Montreal *Star*, February 4th, 1887.

[71] Chapleau to Macdonald, January 15th, 1887 : Macdonald Papers, Chapleau to Macdonald, 1886–91.

[72] *L'Etendard*, February 24th, 1887 ; Montreal *Star*, February 24th, 1887.

INDEX

A

Act of Parliament—
Act for the Temporary Government of Rupert's Land, 42 ; B.N.A. Act, 37, 120 ; B.N.A. Act 1871, 120 ; Dominion Lands Act, 250, 251, 252, 254 ; Manitoba Act, 119-20, 123, 124, 162, 189, 191, 243, 244, 245, 267 ; North-West Territories Act 1875, 191 ; Rupert's Land Act, 39, 78
Ahtackakoop, 290, 291
Alaska, 35, 37, 60
Alberta, 184, 192, 197, 199, 225, 284, 304, 360, 361, 362
Alexander, Fort, 139
Algoma, the, 129, 134
Americans—
Westward expansion of, 24-5 ; their interest in Canadian fur trade, 26, 46 ; their proposals to annex Canadian North-West, 35-6 ; encourage half-breed unrest, 45-6, 58 ; follow events in Red River, 58-60 ; offers of assistance from, 58, 123 ; their attitude towards Red River expedition, 126-7, 134 ; suppress Fenian invasion, 166 ; whisky runners, 199, 205 ; keep buffalo south of boundary, 224 ; their protests against incursions of Canadian Indians, 232 ; rebels hope for support from, 334, 342, 365 ; preserve neutrality during North-West Rebellion, 353 ; and execution of Riel, 386
Amnesty—
Promise of, 108 ; stipulated in List of Rights, 113 ; promised by Taché to Red River insurgents, 123, 140 ; stipulated in Bunn's letter to Ottawa, 124 ; controversy over alleged promise of, Chapter VIII ; Riel complains in 1885 of non-promulgation of, 307
Anderson, Wm., 271
André, Father Alexis—
Visits Duck Lake for first time, 179 ; guides formation of Dumont's Provisional Government, 180 ; founds Sacré Coeur, 182 ; his warnings re fate of buffalo, 220, 221-2 ; his petitions, 252-3, 257 ; his invitation to Riel, 299 ; his efforts to bring about Riel's departure from North-West, 309-10, 311 ; his fears of half-breed rising, 312 ; refuses to assist Riel form Provisional Government, 315 ; cited on situation in Prince Albert during the rebellion, 330-1.
Antoine Lose Brave, cited 333
Antrobus, Inspector, 287
Archibald, A.G.—
Appointed Lieutenant-Governor, 121 ; his arrival at Red River, 125, 141 ; forms new government, 142 ; cited on flight of Riel, 164 ; thanks Riel for offer of assistance against Fenians, 167 ; secures withdrawal of Riel's candidature, 168 ; appoints Council for North-West, 191 ; and the Indian treaties, 202, 204, 208, 218
Assiniboia, 15-7, 57, 58, 67, 111, 112, 113, 115, 121-2, 192, 304
Assiniboia, Council of—
Representative character of, 15-6 ; discuss Sayer case, 47 ; Riel's statement to, 48, 49, 70 ; refuse to appoint Schultz as member, 51 ; vote assistance during famine, 53 ; and half-breed rising 69-70, 73, 98 ; advise McDougall to return to Canada, 75.
Assiniboia, Governor of, 16, 45, cited 57 ; see also Mactavish, William
Assiniboine, River, 11, 68, 71, 100, 140, 143
Athabaska, 192, 347.
Athabaska, Lake, 5

B

Baby, L. F. G., 170
Badger, 290
Bannatyne, A. G. B.—
    Cited 52 ; intercedes for Canadians in Winnipeg, 84 ; seconds motion at mass
    meeting, 93 ; his powder appropriated by half-breeds, 102 ; seconds vote of
    thanks to Ritchot, 124.
Batoche—
    Founded, 182 ; petitions from, 254, 258 ; claims of reported on, 255 ; inaugur-
    ation of L'Union Métisse at, 303 ; provisional government established at,
    315-6 ; letters from half-breeds under arms at, 318, 319 ; Mitchell and McKay
    interview Riel at, 324 ; Middleton marches against, 354-6 ; Riel seeks aid for
    defence of, 363, 365, 366 ; fall of, 368-71, 373
Battleford—
    Founded, 183 ; development of 183-4, 185, 186 ; Indian distress at, 224 ; con-
    ference on Indian distress at, 226-7 ; Indian Industrial School at, 240, 270 ;
    arrival of Indians from south at, 281 ; rumours of Indian gathering at, 285 ;
    preparations at in event of Indian rising, 287 ; Indians from not present at
    Duck Lake Council, 290 ; Crozier raises volunteer troops at, 316, 322 ;
    Mounted Police at reinforced, 321 ; Riel demands surrender of, 324 ; Indians
    occupy, 334-6 ; Mounted Police from Fort Pitt retire to, 343 ; infantry units
    organized at, 352 ; relief of, 355, 360 ; Poundmaker asks for assistance against,
    365 ; Indians intercept supply train en route to, 368 ; Middleton proceeds to,
    372 ; Poundmaker's surrender at, 373 ; troops return to after pursuit of Big
    Bear, 376
Battle River, 183, 281, 283, 334, 335, 344
Battle River Crossing, 344
Bayard, T. F., American Secretary of State, 353
Beardy, 290, 291, 315, 327
Bear's Child, 230
Bear's Head, 231
Bears' Hills, 344, 363
Beauport, Riel confined in asylum at, 296, 314, 384
Beaver Lake, 345
Beaver River, 347, 376
Begg, Alexander, 65
Belknap, Fort, 230
Berens, J. N., Governor of the Hudson's Bay Company, 29, 30, 31, 32, 34 ; cited 32
Big Bear—
    His attitude to treaty negotiations, 212, 281 ; foregathers with Indians near
    boundary, 231, 234 ; signs Treaty 6, 235 ; leaves for north, 235 ; his character,
    280-1 ; becomes leader of malcontent Indians, 281 ; refuses to take reserve,
    281, 282 ; endeavours to bring about concentration of Saskatchewan Indians,
    282-5, 288, 289, 294 ; at Poundmaker's reserve, 285-8 ; interviews Riel, 289,
    302-3 ; at Duck Lake council, 290, 293 ; winters at Frog Lake, 336 ; his
    Indians gather ammunition, 337 ; dwindling authority of, 337-8 ; at Frog Lake
    massacre, 339 ; at Fort Pitt, 341-3 ; his emissaries to other bands, 344, 345-6 ;
    Strange marches against, 355, 360, 363 ; instructed to join Poundmaker, 363 ;
    factional disputes in his band, 364, 373 ; engagement at Frenchman's Butte,
    373-4 ; flight and pursuit of, 374-7 ; his surrender, 377 ; his imprisonment,
    387 ; his release and death, 379
Big Plume, 230
Bird, J. C., 94
Birtle, 271, 352
Black, Judge John—
    Secretary at mass meeting, 93 ; chairman of the Convention, 94 ; Red-River
    delegate to Canada, 99, 110, 114-5, 118 ; suggested as Lieutenant-Governor,
    121 ; conversation with Taylor re amnesty, 151
Blackfoot Crossing, 225, 229, 230, 277, 361

Blake, Edward—
His motion deploring death of Scott, 155-6 ; offers reward for apprehension of Riel, 167, 170 ; his mission to England regarding Governor-General's instructions, 173-4 ; charges Macdonald with neglect of half-breed claims, 259, 261, 390 ; raises question of Riel's sanity, 401, 402
Bobtail, 344
Bois Brulés, see Half-Breeds
Boucher, Bte., 316
Boulton, Major C. A.—
Supporter of Dennis, 81, 83, 84 ; leads the Portage expedition, 100, 101 ; condemned to death, 102-3 ; reprieved, 104 ; returns to Canada, 115 ; at Fish Creek, 359.
Boulton's Scouts, 352, 355, 359, 371, 375
Bourget, Archbishop Ignace, 316
Bow River, 185
Bowell, Mackenzie, 170, 392
Boyd, A. H., 99, 142
Boyer, Bte., 316
Boyne, River, 166
Brandon, House 11
Breland, Pascal, 227
British Columbia, 31, 33, 35, 49, 59, 185
British Government—
Its interest in colonization, 20 ; Select Committee on H.B.C., 21 ; and the H.B.C. charter, 29-30 ; and the purchase of assets of H.B.C., 32 ; renews H.B.C. licence of exclusive trade, 44 ; memorial and petition to, 46-7 ; Canada throws responsibility for transfer on, 78-80 ; conciliatory attitude of towards insurgents, 87 ; its observer at Red River negotiations, 117 ; not prepared to recognize insurgent claim to ratify agreement, 124 ; withdraws troops from Canada, 128, 143 ; authorizes use of British troops in Red River expedition, 129-30 ; refuses to assume responsibility for amnesty, 159-64, 169 ; favours partial amnesty, 169 ; and commutation of sentence of death passed on Lépine, 171-3 ; and the execution of Riel, 386-8 ; see also Colonial Office.
Brittlebank's Scouts, 375
Broadview, 192
Brooks, Sergeant 303
Brown, George, 23, 34, 156, 401
Bruce, John—
President of the Métis committee, 43, 69 ; appears with Riel before Council of Assiniboia, 70 ; willing to negotiate with Canada, 71 ; resigns presidency, 86
Bryce, Rev. George, cited 58, 60
Buckingham and Chandos, Duke of, 38, 39, 40, 42, 63
Buckingham, William, 51
Buffalo—
Importance of buffalo hunt, 13, 178 ; extermination of, 180, 193, 200, 218-224; importance of to Indians, 197, 219 ; Buffalo Ordinance, 222-3 ; effect of extermination of, 224 et seq., 342
Bull Elk, arrest of, 277-8
Buller, Captain Redvers, 138
Bunn, John, 15
Bunn, Thomas—
Member of Council of Assiniboia, sympathizes with Métis, 62 ; chairman of the mass meetings, 93 ; member of committee on rights, 94 ; secretary of the provisional government of Red River, 115 ; his letter to Howe ratifying agreement, 124, 161
Burbidge, G. W., 384
Butler, Captain W. F.—
His mission to Fort Garry, 136, 141 ; cited 177, 200 ; his report on conditions in the Saskatchewan, 191, 200, 202
Button Chief, 203

C

Calf Robe, 230
Calgary, 186, 203, 344, 352, 355, 360, 362
Calling Eagle, 230
Cameron, Captain D. R., 65, 75, 90
Cameron, J. H., 117, 156
Cameron, M. C., 170, 265, 402
Cameron, W. B., at Frog Lake, 338-9 ; cited 338
Canada First party, 115-7, 155
Canadian Government—
    Commissions Draper to watch Select Committee, 23 ; resolution in favour of
    transcontinental railway, 26 ; petitions to re acquisition of the H.B.C. terri-
    tories, 27 ; case against H.B.C. charter 27-30 ; rejects Watkins proposals, 34 ;
    delegation to England, 34-5 ; resumes negotiations, 37, 39-42 ; Fleming's
    petition to, 50 ; send road builders to Red River, 53 ; association of employees
    of with Schultz, 54 ; purchase of lands by employees of, 55 ; surveys in Red
    River, 56 ; ignores inhabitants of Red River during negotiations, 57 ; attitude
    of English-speaking inhabitants of Red River to, 62 ; warned of feeling in Red
    River, 63-4 ; Riel willing to negotiate with, 71, 73, 84 ; correspondence of
    with McDougall, 77-8 ; refuses to complete transfer, 78-80 ; alarmed at
    Dennis's actions, 82-3 ; stores of at Schultz's, 83 ; their fears of provisional
    government, 85 ; send emissaries to Red River, 87-90 ; invite delegates from
    North-West to Ottawa, 96 ; request assistance of Bishop Taché, 107-8 ;
    negotiations with Red River delegates, 114, 118-9, 124, 150-1 ; retain counsel
    for Ritchot and Scott, 117 ; conclude arrangements for transfer, 121 ; consider
    despatch of troops to North-West, 128-9, 131-3 ; protest against stopping of
    Chicora, 134 ; send emissaries to Indians, 135-6 ; state military expedition not
    punitive, 132, 133, 140 ; and question of amnesty, Chapter VIII ; send police
    to St. Laurent, 181 ; and colonization companies, 186 ; land policy of, 187-90 ;
    establishes government in North-West, 190-2 ; Indian policy of, re treaties,
    Chapter X, reserves, Chapter XI ; half-breed petitions to, Chapter XII ; pro-
    crastination of, 259-60 ; animosity to as result of depression, 262-3 ; farmers'
    delegation to, 263 ; policy of economy of in Indian affairs, 270-4 276-7 ;
    attitude to Indian grievances, 293-4 ; attacked by North-West agitators, 298,
    300-2, 304-5, 318 ; receive petition from North-West, 306-7 ; Riel's alleged
    claims against, 311-2 ; promise to investigate half-breed claims, 312 ; increase
    police in North Saskatchewan, 321 ; Riel hopes to force negotiations with,
    332 ; forbid sale of ammunition to Indians, 337 ; Indian distrust of, 342,
    377 ; take steps to suppress rebellion, 350-3 ; concede half-breed claims,
    354 ; secure loyalty of Crowfoot, 361 ; Indian policy after rebellion, 378-9 ;
    take responsibility for execution of Riel, 386-7 ; debate on execution of Riel,
    402 ; federal election, 406
Canadian Party—
    Antagonize half-breeds at Red River, 48 et seq. ; avoided by Howe, 65 ; in
    communication with McDougall, 76 ; responsible for Portage expedition, 100,
    103
Cardwell, Edward, 34, 35, 38
Carlton, Fort—
    Half-breeds settle near, 179 ; Mounted Police despatched to, 181-2 ; first,
    steamer to, 185 ; Treaty 6 signed at, 212 ; disappearance of buffalo from, 219,
    224 ; Big Bear native of, 280 ; Indian council at, 289-93 ; Mounted Police
    stationed at, 310, 321 ; half-breeds threaten, 321-2 ; volunteer troops sent to,
    323 ; Riel demands surrender of, 324 ; evacuation of 329-30, 331 ; Big Bear
    surrenders at, 377
Carnarvon, Earl of, 171, 173, 387-9
Caron, J. P. R. A., Minister of Militia, 377, 392, 396, 397, 398
Carrière, Damase, 316
Cartier, Sir George E.—
    Delegate to England, 34 ; negotiates transfer of H.B.C. territories, 39-41 ; snubs
    Taché, 64, 107 ; confers with Taché, 108 ; negotiates with Red River delegates,

118–9 ; introduces second reading of Manitoba Bill, 120 ; assures Ritchot Riel to carry on government, 125 ; Wolseley's charge against, 135 ; his ideal of confederation, 144, 381 ; his promise of an amnesty, 145, 149–54, 158, 161–3 ; cited 149–50, 153, 155, 162–3 ; attacked in Ontario, 156 ; his defeat in Montreal and election in Manitoba, 168 ; his death, 168

Cartwright, Sir R. J., 265, 403
Casgrain, T. C., 384
Cauchon, J. E., 28, 174
Chandler, Z., American senator, cited, 126–7
Chapleau, J. A.—
  His motion for pardon of Lépine, 171 ; petition of Settlers' Union addressed to, 306, 317 ; prepares memorandum for resignation from government, 392, 396 ; continues to support Macdonald Government, 394, 397, 398 ; cited, 396, 403–4 ; his jealousy of Langevin, 397, 406 ; offered leadership of Parti National, 399.

Cheadle, W. B., cited 7–8, 9, 219
Chicago, 385
Chicora, the, 129, 134, 159
Chouteau, Messrs., 46
Christie, Alexander, Governor of Assiniboia, 45
Christie, W. J., 202, 205
Clarke, Lawrence, 248–9, 253–4, 347
Clarke's Crossing, 356, 358, 368
Cleveland, Grover, President of the United States, 386
Clifford, Lord, 385
Cocking, Matthew, 4
Cold Lake, 364
Coldwell, William, 51, 94
Colleston School House, programme of the North-West agitation adopted at, 265, 307
Collingwood, 31, 133
Colonial Office—
  And the H.B.C. charter, 29–30 ; negotiations with the H.B.C. for the surrender of Rupert's Land, 30–4 ; negotiations with Canadian delegates, 34–5, 38–42 ; protest to from the minority of shareholders, 42 ; Fleming's petition to, 50 ; annoyance at refusal to accept transfer, 78 ; and the arrest of Ritchot, 117 ; and Red River negotiations, 117 ; and amnesty question, 145–6, 158, 161–4 ; and commutation of Lépine's sentence, 171 ; Settlers' Union petition forwarded to, 307 ; petitions sent to on behalf of Riel, 385–6 ; attitude of non-interference regarding execution of Riel, 387
Colonization—
  In Red River, 10 ; incompatible with fur trade, 12, 20 ; British interest in, 20–1, 22 ; Canadian interest in, 23 ; colonization companies in North-West, 186, 262
Colville, the, 185
Communications—
  Atlantic and Pacific Transit and Telegraph Company, 34 ; Canadian Pacific Railway, 185, 186, 187, 189, 210, 235, 262, 263, 264, 304, 314, 352, 365 ; Hudson Bay Railway, 263, 265, 304, 307 ; Lake Superior and Pacific Railway Company, 25 ; North-West Navigation Company, 185 ; North-West Transit Company, 31 ; North-West Transportation, Navigation and Railway Company, 26
Conventions—
  First Convention at Red River, 72–4, 80–1, 82, 128 ; Second Convention, 94–99, 100, 110, 113, 115, 142
Corbett, Rev. James, 51, 52
Corne, Fort à la, 178, 184, 293
Coureurs de Bois, 5, 9
Coursol, C. J., 393, 398
Coutu, 104
Cowan, Dr. Wm., 62, 68, 71, 95

Craig, John, Farm Instructor, 286, 293
Crofton, Colonel J. F., 47 ; cited 127
Crooked Lakes, 276, 278, 333, 337
Crooked Neck, 136 ; cited 204
Crowfoot—
    His appreciation of Mounted Police, 203 ; signs Treaty 7, 213 ; cited, 221, 224 ; promises to settle down, 229 ; and the arrest of Bull Elk, 278 ; contrasted with Big Bear, 281 ; his relation to Poundmaker, 283 ; messengers from Big Bear to 284 ; mentioned at Duck Lake council, 291 ; half-breed emissary to, 361 ; loyalty of during North-West Rebellion, 361-2
Crown Colony, 21, 22, 39, 42, 62
Crozier, Superintendent L.N.F.—
    His efforts to get Indians on reserves, 230 ; favours abandonment of Fort Walsh, 233 ; His opinion on Indian policy, 273 ; arrests Bull Elk, 278 ; and the Indian troubles at Poundmaker's, 286-8 ; reports Indian messengers on the move, 294 ; informed of meeting of Big Bear and Riel, 303 ; urges action on half-breed claims, 312, 313, 321 ; raises volunteers, 316, 322, 323 ; his efforts to win over English half-breeds and pro-Riel whites, 318 ; reports rising imminent, 321-2 ; his negotiations with Riel, 323-5 ; marches out of Carlton, 325-6 ; his defeat, 327-8, 332 ; fears Indian rising, 333 ; Dickens to, 337
Cumberland House, 178
Cummings, William, 99
Cut Knife, 367
Cut Knife Creek, 367
Cut Knife Hill, engagement at, 366-8, 375
Cypress Hills—
    Massacre at, 199 ; Indians gather in region of, 223, 230-4, 283-4 ; petition from half-breeds of, 246, 247

D

Dakota, 60, 187, 353
Dallas, A. G., Governor of Rupert's Land, 16, 32 ; cited, 50
Dawson, S. J., 129, 131, 135
Dawson, W. M., 27
David, L. O., cited, 381
Davin, N. F., 240, 248
Deane, Inspector R. B., 279
Décorby, Father, 246
Delorme, Joseph, 105, 316
Delorme, Norbert, 316
Denison, Colonel G. T., 155, 355
Dennis, Colonel, J. S.—
    His statement regarding Schultz's land purchases, 55 ; superintends surveys in Red River, 56-7 ; complains of stopping of survey, 68 ; his commission from McDougall, 81 ; his " call to arms," 82-4, 99 ; enlists Indians, 81, 198, 203
Denny, C. E., 233, 272, 361
Desjardins, A., 393, 398
Dewdney, Edgar—
    Indian Commissioner, 228, 229, 231, 234, 235, 238, 272, 280, 292, 294, 337 ; and Riel, 310-3 ; urges increase in military force in North-West, 322, 350-1 ; and Indian rising, 335, 344, 361, 366-7
Dickens, Inspector Francis—
    And Bull Elk episode, 277-8 ; his reports on Big Bear's Indians, 336, 337 ; advises Quinn to come to Fort Pitt, 338 ; and surrender of Fort Pitt, 340-3
Dickieson, M. G., 222, 238
Dickson, 44
Dog Rump Creek, 337
Donnelly, Ignatius, 36
Doucet, Father, cited, 225
Douglas, Fort, 11

Draper, Chief Justice, W. H., 23-7
Dreever, Mr., 116
Duck Lake—
  Métis settlement near, 179, 182 ; discontent of métis at, 253 ; Indian council at,
    289-94, 302 ; police warnings from, 321 ; Mitchell at, 323 ; skirmish near,
    325 ; engagement between half-breeds and police near, 327-8, 330, 332, 348,
    385 ; effect of engagement at, 334, 340, 351 ; Dumont wounded at engagement
    at, 357
Dufferin and Ava, Marquess of, 114, 171-4
Dulhut, D. G., 4
Dumas, Michael, 268
Dumont, Gabriel—
  President of Provisional Government of St. Laurent, 180-2 ; petitions of, 246,
    251 ; not good political leader, 261 ; delegate to Riel, 268 ; makes arrests
    and helps form Provisional Government of the Saskatchewan, 315-6 ; his
    skirmish with the Mounted Police, 325 ; defeats Crozier, 327-8 ; sends tobacco
    to Indians, 334 ; his plan of campaign, 356-7 ; overruled by Riel, 355, 357-8 ;
    wounded, 357 ; at Fish Creek, 358-9 ; his flight, 371-2
Dumont, Isidore, 327-8

E

Eagle Hills, 283, 336, 368, 372
Eagle Tail, 230
East Durham, by-election at, 395, 401
Edmonton, 178, 179, 187, 184, 185, 192, 199, 203, 205, 248, 258, 271, 284, 294, 344,
  345, 355, 360, 362, 363
Elgin, Earl of, 47
Ellice, Edward, 20
Ellice, Fort, 184, 236
England, 9, 34, 37, 40, 45, 46, 53, 57, 65, 79, 108, 130, 133, 143, 169, 173, 306
Ermatinger, Edward, 23
Ermine Skin, 344

F

Falcon, Pierre, "chanson" of, 12
Faraud, Bishop H. J., cited, 345, 346
Fenians, 123, 131, 133, 136, 164-6, 353
File Hills, 276, 333
Fiset, Dr., 311
Fish Creek, engagement at, 356, 358-9, 363, 365
Fish, Hamilton, American Secretary of State, 134
Fisher, John, 246
Fitzpatrick, Charles, 384
Fleming, Sandford, 26, 49-50, 185
Foremost Man, 234
Forget, A. E., 310, 354
Fortin, P., 393
Foster, W. A., 116
Fourmond, Father, cited on Riel, 303 ; preaches against Riel, 316
Frances, Fort, 136, 204
Fraser, John, 98
Fraser, River, 36
French, Colonel G. A.—
  His march to St. Laurent, 181-2 ; reports Indian unrest, 202, 211-2 ; first Com-
    missioner of the North-West Mounted Police, 203 ; reports diminution of
    buffalo, 221, 222
French Canadians—
  Western exploration by, 4, 28 ; marriage of with Indians, 5, 6 *et seq.* ; racial
    survival of, 60-1 ; appointment of F.C. emissaries to Red River, 88 *et seq.* ;
    oppose military expedition to Red River, 132, 133, 135 ; their attitude towards

execution of Scott, 157-8; they defeat Cartier, 168; threaten Macdonald Government 169; development of racial antagonism among after North-West Rebellion, Chapter XVII; change in party allegiance of, 381, 407; strength of national sentiment of, 382, 405; appeals in press to national prejudice of, 381-2, 389; their petitions for clemency for Riel, 385; their protest against Riel's execution, 389, 398-9; attitude of F. C. Conservatives, 392-4, 396-7, 398

Frenchman's Butte, engagement at, 373-5

French's Scouts, 352, 355, 375

Frog Lake—
Mounted Police detachment at, 321; Indians at hear of engagement at Duck Lake, 334; Big Bear winters at, 336-7; Indian massacre at, 337-9, 340, 348, 379; effect of news of massacre at, 344, 345; Big Bear moves east from, 373

Futvoye, Major G., 154

G

Gagnon, Inspector S., 315, 321, 323

Galt, Sir A. T., 34, 66

Gardiner, Rev., 139

Gariepy, Pierre, 316

Garnot, Philip, Secretary of the Provisional Government of the Saskatchewan, 296, 314, 316; cited, 332

Garrioch, A. C., cited, 58

Garrioch, W., cited, 106

Garry, Fort—
Withdrawal of troops from, 36; free trade in furs movement at, 44-5; prison at broken open, 51; Americans at, 58; taken by Riel and French half-breeds, 70-1; Convention called at, 72; McDougall to proceed to, 74; Cameron's attempt to reach, 75; imprisonment of Canadians in, 83-4; H.B.C. money at confiscated, 86; hostile feeling at towards Canadian emissaries, 90; arrival of Smith at, 91; mass meetings at, 92-3; opposition half-breeds ordered to leave, 95; escape of prisoners from, 99; release of prisoners from, 100, 101; Portage party imprisoned in, 102, 103; steam communication to demanded, 112; business resumed at, 122; Union Jack raised over, 123; military weakness of, 131, 166; Butler's visit to, 136; captured by Wolseley, 139-40; arrival of Lieutenant-Governor at, 141

Girard, Marc, 142, cited, 154

Girouard, D., 390, 392, 393

Gladman, George, 27

Gladstone, W. E., 22

Glenelg, Baron, 20, 22

Goulet, Elzéar, 105, 165

Goulet, Roger, 69, 354

Government Ford, 363

Grahame, J. A., 185

Grandin, village of, 182, 306

Grandin, Bishop V. J., cited, 183-4; 277, 303, 309, 310, 370

Grant, Cuthbert, 11, 15, 55

Grant, G. M., cited, 220

Grant, U. S., President of the United States, 37, 164

Granville, Earl of—
Colonial Secretary, and transfer of the H.B.C. territories to Canada, 40, 41, 78, 121; and the military expedition to Red River, 129, 131, 133; his correspondence relative to promise of an amnesty, 87, 146, 150, 152, 160-1

Grassett, Colonel, 371

Great Britain, 20, 25, 26, 28, 35, 36, 37, 40, 85, 144, 146, 159, 173, 269, 302; see British Government

Green Lake, 346-8

Greenshields, J. N., 384

Grey, Sir George, 195, 216
Grey Owl, cited, 200–1.
Gunn, Donald, 13–4, 98

H

Halcro, 265, 315, 329
Half-Breeds—
  Offspring of fur traders and Indians, 6 ; the " New Nation," 10; stirred up by
  North-West Company, 11–2 ; settle at Red River, 13 ; represented on Council
  of Assiniboia, 15 ; their simple life, 17–18 ; their unrest at Red River, Chapter
  III ; their opposition to political change in Red River, 48–9, 67 *et seq.* ; land
  reserve for, 119, 120, 189, 244–5 ; suitability as soldiers, 127 ; their discontent
  after Red River insurrection, 165, 245 ; settle in the North-West territories,
  178–9 ; abandon nomadic life, 193 ; their influence over Indians, 214–5 ; basis
  of their claims in North-West, 244 ; claims and petitions of in North-West,
  Chapter XII ; co-operate with white discontents, 264–8, 296–303 ; their
  petition to Ottawa, 306–7 ; exasperation of, 312, 313, 321 ; their demands
  conceded, 354
  French Half-Breeds—Origin and character of, 6–9 ; number of at Red River, 13 ;
  1847 petition of, 46–7 ; they release Sayer, 47 ; irritated by road builders, 54 ;
  object to surveys, 56–7, 68 ; national committee of, 69 ; organized by Riel, 70 ;
  take Fort Garry, 71 ; in the Convention, 72–4, 80–1 ; expel McDougall, 70,
  75 ; take Canadian prisoners, 83–4 ; masters of Red River, 86 ; Canadian
  emissaries sent to, 88 *et seq.* ; and Portage expedition, 102–3 ; try Scott, 105 ;
  Taché's influence over, 107 ; do not resist Wolseley, 139, 140, 141 ; and Fenians,
  165–7 ; their settlements in the North-West, 177, 178 ; they trek to North-
  West, 179, 245 ; form provisional government at St. Laurent, 180–2 ; their
  petitions, Chapter XII ; and the return of Riel, 265–8, 297–8, 303–4 ; their
  breach with clergy, 309 ; meet at Batoche, 315–6 ; defeat Crozier, 327–8 ;
  unable to carry out successful rebellion, 332 ; at Lac La Biche, 345–6 ; their
  engagements with troops, 356–9, 369–71 ; effect of rebellion upon, 378
  English and Scotch Half-Breeds—origin and character of, 9 ; their common
  feeling with French, 10, 166 ; less affected by the developments at Red River,
  62 ; some of co-operate with French during Red River Rebellion, 62, 71–2, 81,
  93 *et seq.* ; unwilling to form provisional government, 73–4 ; do not adopt
  Canadian cause, 76, 81–2, 112 ; participate in provisional government, 98–9 ;
  and Portage expedition, 103 ; their settlements in the North-West, 177 ; their
  petitions, 246–7, 248, 249 ; co-operate with French to bring back Riel, 266–8 ;
  their favourable attitude to Riel, 297, 298, 305–6, 311, 313 ; disapprove of
  recourse to arms, 317, 318, 320
Halifax, 128
Hardisty, Richard, 92, 205
Hargrave, J. J., cited, 52 ; 54, 72
Harmon, Daniel, cited, 6
Head, Sir Edmund, Governor of the Hudson's Bay Company, 34
Headingly, 101
Heavy Shield, 229
Hector, Dr. James, 219
Henday (also spelled Hendry), Anthony, 4
Henry, Jérome, 356
Herchmer, L. W., 271
Herchmer, Superintendent, 241, 279–80, 360, 366
High River, 240
Hincks, Sir Francis, 163
Hind, H. Y., cited, 13 ; 14, 27, 57
Holton, L. H., 38, 170
Homestead regulations, 188–9, 250–254
Howe, Joseph—
  Secretary of State for the Provinces, visits Red River, 64–5 ; meets McDougall en

route to Red River, 74-5 ; his correspondence with McDougall, 76, 77, 81, 82 ; condemns McDougall's actions, 80 ; his correspondence with Taché, 108, 110, 149, 155 ; his letter to Red River delegates, 118 ; clashes with McDougall, 120 ; Bunn's letter to, 124 ; Archibald to, 142 ; appoints commissioners to negotiate Indian treaties, 208

Howe, Inspector, 326

Hudson Bay, 3, 4, 13, 24, 28, 126, 131, 213

Hudson's Bay Company—
    Charter granted to, 3 ; exploration by, 4 ; organization of in the North-West, 5 ; view on intermarriage with Indians, 5-6 ; isolationist policy of, 10, 17, 20, 21, 23 ; grant to Selkirk, 10 ; union with North-West Company, 12 ; land policy of, 14 ; administers Red River, 15-7 ; licence of exclusive trade, 20, 21, 26, 30, 44 ; Select Committee on, 21-2 ; press attack, 23 ; negotiations with Colonial Office and Canada for the surrender of the H.B.C. territories, 27 *et seq.* ; adopt measures to cope with illicit trade in furs, 44-5 ; their monopoly attacked, 46-7 ; half-breeds generally contented with, 48, 70 ; weakened authority of in Red River, 50 *et seq.* ; their assistance during Red River famine, 53 ; protest against road workers, 53 ; grant permission for survey, 56 ; employees of not enthusiastic for transfer, 62 ; does not warn Canada, 63 ; forced to surrender public accounts, 73 ; Canada refuses to complete transfer with, 78-80 ; arms and money of confiscated, 83, 86 ; Riel moves all bargains with H.B.C. be deemed void, 95 ; reference to in List of Rights, 112, 113, 114 ; resumes business in Red River on Riel's terms, 122 ; transfer completed, 121, 177 ; employees of settle in North-West, 183 ; land reserve of, 189, 190, 251, 253 ; Indian policy of, 197-8, 200, 215, 342 ; report disappearance of buffalo, 220 ; report Indian distress, 224-5 ; report economic distress in North-West, 305 ; their posts pillaged, 335-6, 344-8

Hugonard, Father J., 322, 350

Huyshe, Captain G. L., cited, 136, 139-40

I

Ile à la Crosse, 347

Imasees, 338, 339, 378, 379

Indians—
    Linguistic stocks in Rupert's Land, 3 ; intermarriage with fur traders, 5-6 ; H.B.C. fur monopoly with, 14 ; apprehension of danger from, 87, 123, 133 ; emissaries sent to prepare way for Red River expedition, 129, 135-6 ; problem of contact with whites 194-5 ; character of, 195-6 ; their friendship with H.B.C., 197-8, 342 ; effect of white expansion upon, 198-202 ; their appreciation of Mounted Police, 203 ; treaties made with, 204 *et seq.* ; basis of Canadian Indian policy, 216-8 ; unwilling to settle, 218 ; distress of on disappearance of buffalo, 218-9, 223-5 ; Government feeds and endeavours to put on reserves, 226-36 ; training in agriculture, 236-9 ; schools for, 239-40 ; destruction of tribal organization of, 240-2, 379 ; effect of economy policy upon, 270-4 ; attitude to treaties, 275-6 ; growing unfriendliness of, 276-80 ; their agitation in Saskatchewan, 281-5 ; their council at Duck Lake, 289-91 ; grievances of, 291-3 ; and the Riel agitation, 303, 306 ; incited by half-breeds, 332-5 ; part played during rebellion, 335-48, 354, 360-2, 363-8, 372-7 ; effect of rebellion upon, 378-9 ; amnesty to, 379.
    Assiniboine, 3, 4, 196, 197, 199, 224, 231, 233, 234, 364, 366 ; Beaver, 3 ; Blackfeet, 3, 196, 199, 201, 203, 205, 211, 213, 221, 223, 224, 225, 229-30, 272, 277-8, 294, 344, 360-2 ; Blood, 3, 196, 224, 361 ; Chipewyan, 3 ; Cree, 3, 4, 183, 196, 205, 207, 211, 212, 221, 223, 224, 229, 231, 233, 234, 276, 280, 281, 283, 293, 333, 345, 358, 362, 364, 366-7, 373, 375, 376 ; Ojibway, 3 ; Piegan, 3, 196, 201, 203, 224, 361 ; Sarcee, 3, 196, 224 ; Saulteaux, 3, 81, 198, 207, 211, 223, 276, 358 ; Sioux, 3, 198, 218, 223, 224, 274, 333, 358 ; Stoney, 3, 219, 271, 276, 285, 294, 333, 334, 336, 344, 364

Indian Department, 212, 222, 227-8, 235, 236, 270, 271, 272, 273, 274, 278, 282, 284, 285, 288, 292, 336, 362 ; see Indians

Indian Head, 234, 271, 354
Indian Treaties—
   Negotiation of, Chapter X ; Indian misunderstanding of, 275-6, 291 ; half-breeds enter, 378 ; Selkirk's Treaty, 207-8 ; Treaty 1, 209-10, 218 ; Treaty, 2, 210 ; Treaty 3, 210-11, 218 ; Treaty 4, 211, 218, 231, 353 ; Treaty 5, 211, 218, 223 ; Treaty 6, 211-3, 218, 221, 226, 229, 231, 235, 239, 280-1, 283, 348, 353 ; Treaty 7, 213, 218, 226, 231, 353
International Financial Society, 32
Irvine, Colonel, A. G.—
   Commissioner of the North-West Mounted Police, negotiates with Indians, 233 ; apprehensive of contact of whites and Indians, 274-5 ; marches north, 322, 323, 325, 328-9 ; evacuates Carlton, 329 ; arrives at Prince Albert, 330 ; refuses to send force to Green Lake, 347 ; Riel fears, 357 ; Middleton and, 372, 376
Isbister, A. K., 25, 27, 46, 47
Isbister, James, 265, 268, 300

J

Jack, 231, 233
Jackson, 265
Jackson, T. E., 303
Jackson, T. G., cited 305-6
Jackson, W. H.—
   Secretary of the Settlers' Union, speaks for Riel, 298 ; organizes agitation, 299-300 ; his manifesto, 300-2 ; supports Indian grievances, 303 ; his letter to Chapleau, 306, 317 ; his letter to Riel, 307 ; baptism of, 316 ; demands Crozier's surrender, 323-4 ; trial and acquittal of, 378
Jobin, Amb., 316
Johnson, Sir William, 195, 206, 207
Johnstone, T. C., 384
Judith Basin, 224

K

Kahweechetwaymot, 286, 287, 288
Kaministiquia River, 135
Kamooses, 211
Kane, Paul, cited, 184, 219
Ka-Qua-Nam, 345
Keith, Farm Instructor, 278-80
Kelsey, Henry, 4, 5
Kennedy, W., 265
Kicking Horse Pass, 185
Kildonan, 12, 81, 83, 99, 101, 103
Kimberley, Earl of, 53, 146, 151, 161, 162, 163, 169, 173
Kingston, 351
Kipp, Fort, 203

L

Labouchere, Henry, 28, 29, 30
Lacoste, Senator Louis, 393, 399
Lac la Biche, 177, 344, 345-6
Lac Qu'Appelle, 246
Lac Ste. Anne, 177, 344
Lac St. Louis, 207
Lac Seul, 210
Lacombe, Father Albert, 322, 350, 361 ; cited, 362
Lagemonière, E., 105
Lagimodière, Julie, 67
Laird, David, 228, 238, 240, 246, 251, 252

Lampson, Sir Curtis, 38, 77
Lanark and Renfrew, Municipal Council of, 27
Landry, Philippe, 402
Langevin, Sir Hector L., 99, 107, 135, 169, 392, 393, 396, 397, 398, 399, 402, 405, 406
Langevin, Bishop J. P. F., 107
La Noüe, Z. R. de, 4
Lansdowne, Marquess of, 386-7, 388
Laurier, Wilfrid—
    Votes for conditional amnesty, 174; leader of Liberal Party, 381, 406; his speech on Blake motion, 390; his attitude on the Riel question, 398; his speech on Landry motion, 402; assists Mercier, 404
Law Officers, opinions of—
    On H.B.C. charter, 27, 28, 29, 30; on transfer, 38, 79; on Red River Rebellion, 85; on half-breed land reserve in Manitoba, 244
Lean Man, 285
Leduc, Father Hyppolite, cited, 180; 182, 220, 225, 258
Lee, John, 67
Lefroy, Colonel, J. F., 219
Légeard, Father, 179
Lemay, Pamphile, 157
Lemieux, Francois, 384
Lépine, Ambroise D.—
    Consults Mactavish, 98; arrests Portage party, 102; passes sentence of death on Scott, 105; interviewed by Taché, 109, 148; co-operates in defence against Fenians, 167; induced to leave Manitoba, 168; trial and condemnation of, 170, 171; his sentence commuted, 171-3; conditional amnesty for, 174
Lépine, J. B., 105
Lépine, Maxime, 312, 316, 324-5, 359
Lestanc, Father J. M., 69, 94, 104, 105, 153
Léviellé, Pierre, 92, 93, 95
Lightfoot, William, 333
Lindsay, Lieutenant-General, the Hon. James, 130-2, 134, 135
Lindsay School House, meetings at, 265, 267, 297, 318, 320
Lisgar, electoral district of, 170
Lisgar, Lord, see Sir John Young
Little Child, 231, 233
Little Pine—
    Signs Treaty 6, 229; at Fort Walsh, 231, 234; sent to North Saskatchewan, 235, 281, 284; assembles with others on Poundmaker's reserve, 285; tries to calm excited Indians, 288; at Duck Lake council, 290; expected to visit Blackfeet, 294; at pillage of Battleford, 334-5
Little Poplar, 294, 338, 341, 378
Lockyer, Dr., 385
London, 42, 50, 53, 56, 63, 78, 87, 121, 122, 169, 225, 305, 385
London (Canada), 351
Longfellow, 338
Long Lodge, 231, 233, 234
Longue Pointe, 296, 314, 384
Loon Lake, 375, 376, 377
Lorne, district of, 192, 248, 253, 264, 267, 306, 311
Lower Canada, 17, 22, 160, 388, 400
Lower Fort Garry, 81, 83, 208
Lucky Man—
    Signs Treaty 6, 229; at Fort Walsh, 234; sent to North Saskatchewan, 235, 281, 284; assembles on Poundmaker's reserve, 285; member of his band assaults Craig, 286; tries to calm excited Indians, 288; at Duck Lake council, 290; flight of, 378; his return to Canada, 379
Lynch, Dr., 116, 155
Lytton, Sir E. B., 29, 30, 34

M

MacBeth, Robert, 99
MacBeth, R. G., cited, 48
McCarthy, D'Alton, 156
McDermott, Andrew, 45, 46
McDonald, A., 271
Macdonald, Sir J. A.—
  Delegate to England, 34 ; his opinion on Canadian proposals to acquire H.B.C. territories, 38 ; warns McDougall, 77-8 ; disapproves McDougall's actions, 80, 84-5 ; appoints Smith as Commissioner to Red River, 89 ; cited on the half-breed insurrection, 95 ; disapproves of Portage expedition, 103 ; his letter to Taché, 108, 110, 148 ; negotiates with Red River delegates, 118-9 ; his memorandum on the Manitoba Act, 120 ; his choice for Lieutenant-Governor 121 ; prepares to send troops to Red River, 129-30 ; his compromise on amnesty, 144-5, 148, 151, 152, 153, 158, 161-2, 169 ; is condemned by Orangemen, 156 ; secures Riel's withdrawal from Provencher, 168 ; criticizes partial amnesty, 174 ; introduces Bill to establish Mounted Police, 202 ; head of Indian Department, 216 ; on Indian policy, 238, 239, 240, 242, 274, 337 ; Minister of Interior, 247 ; and half-breed grievances, 254, 258, 259-60 ; Prince Albert opponents of, 300 ; informed of meeting of Riel and Big Bear, 302 ; his attitude to North-West petition, 307 ; his alleged offer to Riel, 311 ; warned of growing discontent, 312, 322, 351 ; Riel's threat re, 323 ; his measure to secure Indian loyalty, 354, 361 ; on nature of North-West Rebellion, 386 ; answers Blake's charge of maladministration, 259, 390 ; his dilemma, 391-2, 395; and the bolting Bleus, 393 ; threats against, 394-5 ; retains support of French Canadian ministers, 396-7 ; and Landry motion, 402 ; and federal election, 406-7
Macdonald, J. S., 155, 156
Macdonnell, Allan, 25, 26
Macdonnell, Miles, 10, 11, 12
McDougall, Rev. George, 212
McDougall, Rev. John, 205, 363
McDougall, William—
  Urges acquisition of North-West, 23, 38 ; negotiates transfer of North-West, 39-42 ; his appointment as Lieutenant-Governor, 42-3, 65-6 ; métis warning to, 43, 69 ; Minister of Public Works, 56, 66 ; expulsion of, 59, 60, 70, 72, 75 ; his accusation against Howe, 64 ; half-breeds organize against, 69-71, 73 ; his instructions, 74 ; his meeting with Howe, 74-5 ; advised to return to Canada, 75 ; issues proclamation, 76-7 ; his correspondence with Government, 76-80, 84-5 ; his commission to Dennis, 81 ; returns to Canada, 86 ; criticizes Manitoba Bill, 119-20 ; his alleged dealings with Sioux, 198
MacDowall, D. H., 311-2
Machray, Bishop Robert, 63, 82, 83, 93, 102, 104
McIllree, Superintendent, cited, 231, 233
Mackay, James, 208
Mackay, John, 246
McKay, Thomas, 323-4, 325, 327
McKay, William, 335
Mackenzie, Alexander—
  Opposes negotiation with Red River delegates 116-7 ; criticizes Manitoba Bill, 119 ; his position regarding amnesty to Red River insurgents, 144, 170, 171, 174 ; surveys during administration of, 188 ; railway policy of, 189 ; and half-breed land grant, 245 ; compared with Macdonald, 260 ; his alleged offer to Riel, 311 ; his vote on execution of Riel, 403
Mackenzie, Kenneth, 101
Mackenzie River, 347
McLaughlin, 46
McLean, Archdeacon John, 104
McLean, John, cited, 9
McLean, W. J., 340-3, 363, 376-7

Macleod, Colonel J. F., 203, 233
Macleod, Fort, 203, 225, 226, 278
Macpherson, Sir David, 249, 257, 259–60, 261
Macrae, J. A., 291, 293
McTavish, J. H., 136–7, 141
Mactavish, William—
  Governor of Assiniboia, cited on causes of discontent in Red River, 54, 55, 56, 57 ; not informed of details of transfer, 57, 65 ; warns Canadian Government, 63–4 ; cited on Howe, 64 ; suggested as Lieutenant-Governor, 66, 121 ; and the métis, 69, 73, 76 ; his proclamation, 72 ; his correspondence with McDougall, 75, 85 ; co-operates with Smith, 89, 91, 92 ; cited on extent of opposition to Canada, 90 ; threatened by Riel, 95 ; his advice re provisional government, 98, 101 ; his negotiations with Riel, 122 ; supports amnesty, 148
Mair, Charles, 54, 55, 62, 76, 99, 116
Maloney, M. B., 258
Manchester School, 19, 23
Manitoba, 10, 21, 121, 140, 142, 149, 154, 156, 164, 168, 169, 170, 177, 182, 183, 185, 187, 189, 190, 191, 203, 208, 209, 211, 227, 228, 236, 237, 239, 244, 245, 246, 247, 249, 261–3, 264, 265, 266, 296, 302, 313, 314, 318, 321, 354, 378, 380, 385
Manitoba Lake, 236
Manitoba and North-West Farmers' Union, 262, 305
Manitoba Post, 208
Manitoba Rights League, 263
Manitoba Village, 248
Man-Who-Took-the-Coat, 234
Maple Creek, 186, 235
Marcil, Dr., 398
Martin, Sergeant, 337
Masson, L. F. R., 169, 174
Medicine Hat, 186, 360
Mercier, Honoré, 395, 397–9, 400, 404, 405, 406
Métis, see Half-Breeds (French)
Michel, Lieutenant-General Sir John, cited 130, 131
Michigan, 126
Middleton, Major-General Sir Frederick—
  Sent to the North-West, 351 ; his character, 355 ; marches north, 356 ; at Fish Creek, 358–9 ; not consulted regarding attack at Cut Knife, 366 ; captures Batoche, 368–71 ; receives surrenders of Riel and Poundmaker, 372–3 ; and Strange, 375 ; his pursuit of Big Bear, 376
Milk River, 230
Miller, Police Surgeon, 326
Miller, W., 299
Mills, David, 252
Milton, Viscount, 219
Minnesota, 10, 13, 24, 36, 37, 44, 58, 60, 131, 136
Missouri, 224, 231
Mistowasis, 290, 291
Mitchell, Hillyard, 323–4, 325
Monkman, Albert, 316, 319, 320
Monkman, Joseph, 116, 201
Montana, 199, 268, 296, 297, 298, 311, 313, 378, 379
Montreal, 4, 11, 67, 90, 116, 142, 168, 262, 351, 382, 392–3, 398
Moore, Captain, 322, 325, 326
Moosomin, Indian chief, 285
Moosomin, town of, 186
Moose Jaw, 186, 192
Moose Mountain, 192
Morris, Alexander, 191, 211, 246, 250, 275
Morton, Captain, 326
Mosquito, 285

Mousseau, J. A., 170, 171, 174
Murdoch, Sir Clinton, 117, 151, 152

N

Nault, André, 68, 105, 123, 165
Nault, Napoléon, 296, 315
New Brunswick, 35, 406
Newcastle, the Duke of, 30–3, 50
New France, 28
Newspapers—
    Bulletin, Edmonton, 184, 305 ; cited, 304
    Hamilton Spectator, 23 ; cited, 172
    Le Canadien, Quebec, 157, 392, 398 ; cited, 405
    L'Electeur, Quebec, cited 389
    L'Etendard, Montreal, cited, 381, 382, 405 ; 389, 392, 393, 404, 406
    L'Evénement, Quebec, 398
    Le Journal de Québec, 157
    La Justice, Quebec, cited, 406
    Le Métis, Montreal, 382
    La Minerve, Montreal, 392, 405
    Le Monde, Montreal, 392, 405
    Le Nouveau Monde, Montreal, 157; cited, 158
    Le Nouvelliste, Three Rivers, cited, 382
    L'Opinion Publique, Montreal, cited, 157
    La Patrie, Montreal, 389 ; cited, 398
    La Presse, Montreal, 389 ; cited, 397
    La Verité, Quebec, 389 ; cited, 382, 404
    Montreal Gazette, cited, 172, 350, 390
    Montreal Transcript, cited, 23
    Montreal Witness, cited, 156
    National Republican, Washington, cited, 126
    New Nation, Fort Garry, 85, 92, 94, 123 ; cited, 93, 102, 109
    New York Times, cited, 58
    New York Tribune, cited, 35
    North American, 23
    Nor'Wester, Calgary, cited, 304
    Nor'Wester, Fort Garry, 50, 51, 52, 53, 61, 85
    Orange Sentinel, cited, 389
    Ottawa Citizen, cited, 172
    Port Hope Guide, cited, 401
    Prince Albert Times, cited, 266, 267, 307, 308
    Red River Pioneer, Fort Garry, 85
    Saskatchewan Herald, Battleford, cited, 183, 308
    St. Paul Daily Press, cited, 36, 75
    The Times, London, 53
    Toronto Globe, 23, 54, 64, 116, 134, 156, 157 ; cited, 65, 102, 129, 305, 400, 401
    Toronto Mail, cited, 400 ; 406
    Toronto News, cited, 383
    Toronto Telegraph, 116, 157
    Toronto World, 384
New York, 385
Niagara, 153, 155
Nisbet, Rev. James, 183
Nolin, Charles—
    Member of committee on half-breed rights, 94 ; seconds motion for provisional
        government, 98 ; has not great influence, 261 ; Riel meeting at house of, 298 ;
        speaks in favour of Riel, 303–4 ; withdraws tender, 312 ; refuses to take up
        arms, 315 ; member of Riel's provisional government, 316 ; his quarrel with
        Riel, 317 ; sent to enrol recruits, 320 ; sent to demand Crozier's surrender,
        324–5

Norman, Inspector F., 235
Norquay, John, 101, 260
Northcote, the, 185, 360, 368-9, 372
Northcote, Sir Stafford, 39, 40, 41, 42, 108, 117
North-West—
　　Exploration of, 4 ; fur companies in, 5 ; first white settlement in, 21-2, 23 ;
　　　Canadian interest in, 23-7 ; danger to British rule in, 24-5, 35-7 ; transfer of to
　　　Canada, Chapter II ; warning to McDougall not to enter, 43 ; alleged suffering
　　　of people of, 51 ; difficult to rule, 63 ; arms sent to, 64 ; Canadian emissaries
　　　sent to, 88-90 ; Taché returns to, 108, 147 ; military expedition to, 119, Chapter
　　　VII ; the " Great Lone Land," 177 ; growth of settlement in, Chapter IX ;
　　　half-breeds trek to, 179, 243 ; transition of, 182, 192-3 ; capital of, 183, 186 ;
　　　survey of, 188 ; government of, 190-2 ; formation of Territories of, 192 ;
　　　Indians of, 196-7 ; Mounted Police sent to, 203 ; surrender of by Indians,
　　　206-16 ; fear of Indian rising in, 225 ; reorganization of Indian administration
　　　in, 227-8 ; regarded by half-breeds as their patrimony, 251 ; economic
　　　depression in, 264, 305 ; difference in position of in 1870 and 1885, 314 ; troops
　　　sent to, 351 *et seq.*
North-West Company, 5, 7, 11, 12, 20, 49, 55
North-West Council, 191, 192, 202, 212, 222, 223, 246, 248, 249-50, 252
North-West Mounted Police—
　　Sent to St. Laurent, 181-2 ; founded, 191, 202-3 ; appreciation of Indians for,
　　　203 ; urge treaty negotiations with Indians, 212 ; complaints of Blackfeet to,
　　　223 ; ration Indians, 225, 230, 234-5 ; first constable of murdered, 225 ; urge
　　　Indians to settle on reserves, 230, 233, 235 ; favour abandonment of Fort
　　　Walsh, 232-3 ; increasing boldness of Indians towards, 277 *et seq.* ; appre-
　　　hensive of rising in North-West, 305 ; force of augmented, 310, 321 ; alleged
　　　by Riel to be about to attack métis, 316 ; report rebellion imminent, 321 ;
　　　defeated at Duck Lake, 327-8 ; withdraw from Frog Lake and Fort Pitt, 339,
　　　340-1 ; numbers of insufficient to suppress rebellion, 351 ; and relief of
　　　Battleford, 360 ; patrol of waylaid by Indians, 366 ; at Cut Knife, 367 ;
　　　inaction of at Prince Albert, 372 ; their offer to pursue Big Bear refused, 376 ;
　　　Big Bear surrenders to, 377
North-West Territories, 184, 186, 187, 189, 190-2, 201, 202, 226, 227, 228, 231,
　　236, 237, 243, 244, 246, 248, 251, 252, 255, 256, 259, 260, 261, 264, 265, 266,
　　270, 271, 285, 297, 299, 300, 302, 304, 306, 310, 385 ; see North-West
Norton, Moses, 9
Nor'Westers, 11
Nova Scotia, 35, 57, 64, 121, 351, 380, 406
Noyon, J. de, 4

O

Oak Point, 55, 56
Oecumenical Council, 64, 107
O'Donoghue, W. B., 98, 102, 109, 123, 164-6, 174
Okemasis, 290
Old Sun, 239
Oliver, Frank, 184, 304, 308
O'Neill, " General," J., 165
One Arrow, 290, 315, 327
Onion Lake, 340
Only Chief, 230
Ontario, 54, 100, 115, 116, 118, 119, 123, 131, 132, 133, 145, 148, 153, 155, 156, 157,
　　158, 165, 168, 170, 171, 208, 299, 351, 380, 381, 382-4 ; 385, 389, 392, 395, 399,
　　400, 401, 402, 403, 406, 407
Oregon, 24, 126
Orkney Islands, 5
Osler, B. B., 384
Otter, Colonel W. D., 336, 355, 360, 363, 366-8, 374
Ottawa, 50, 63, 64, 77, 96, 107, 109, 110, 114, 115, 117, 118, 119, 123, 124, 131, 140,

147, 150, 152, 163, 169, 170, 215, 222, 226, 227, 228, 235, 247, 248, 249, 251, 253, 254, 255, 258, 260, 265, 274, 285, 296, 301, 304, 306, 307, 308, 313, 318, 321, 351, 361, 391, 399, 400, 404, 405 ; see Canadian Government
Ouellette, Moïse, 268, 316
Ouimet, J. A., 393

P

Pagée, Xavier, 98, 99
Pangman, Peter, 11, 55
Parenteau, Bte., 316
Parenteau, Pierre, 167, 316
Parti National, 399, 400, 404–5
Peace River, 378
Pearce, William, 255, 258–9, 312
Peccan, 284, 344, 345
Pelly, Fort, 178, 236
Pembina, 36, 43, 46, 60, 70, 75, 76, 81, 82, 86, 90, 92, 165, 166
Petequaquay, 290
Piapot, 231, 233, 234, 235, 284, 290, 302
Pipestone Creek, 374
Pither, R. J. N., 135
Pitt, Fort—
    H.B.C. post at, 178 ; trail to, 184 ; Treaty 6 signed at 212 ; Indians starving at, 224 ; economy at, 271 ; Big Bear from, 280 ; Big Bear meets Vankoughnet at, 282 ; half-breeds incite Indians against, 334 ; Quinn advised to retire to, 338 ; news of Frog Lake reaches, 339 ; Indians pillage and take prisoners at, 340–3, 345, 348, 364, 374 ; troops sent to, 355, 363, 373, 375 ; Indians' prisoners arrive at, 377
Pocha School House, 267
Poitras, Pierre, 124
Pope, Sir Joseph, cited, 63
Poor Man, 231
Portage Expedition, 100–3, 110
Portaging, method of, 138
Portage La Prairie, 100, 101, 104, 106, 119, 208
Portland, 108
Poundmaker—
    His character, 283 ; his unrest, 284 ; co-operates with Big Bear, 283, 284 ; Indian gathering on his reserve, 285–8 ; at pillage of Battleford, 334–6 ; proposed junction with Big Bear, 363–4 ; Riel appeals to for assistance, 364–6 ; factional disputes in camp of, 364 ; attacked by Otter, 366–8 ; his surrender, 372–3 ; imprisoned, 378 ; released, 379
Prince Albert—
    Founded, 177, 183 ; trail to, 184, 187 ; growing settlement at, 185 ; first electoral district in North-West ; 192 ; petitions from, 246, 249, 251, 254 ; feeling of insecurity at, 250 ; land office at, 252–3 ; claims investigated at, 255 ; special survey of, 256, 257 ; economic depression at, 264, 305 ; agitation at, 264, 267 ; Riel's meeting at, 298–9 ; Jackson's Manifesto to the people of, 300 et seq. ; Riel and Big Bear meet at, 303 ; Police reinforced at, 310 ; troops raised at, 322–3 ; Police retire to, 329, 330–1 ; party sent to Green Lake from, 347–8 ; Middleton marches to, 355, 372 ; Riel fears Police at, 357, 358
Prince Albert Volunteers, 326, 328, 329
Prince Arthur's Landing, 134, 141
Prince, Henry, 81
Privy Council, Judicial Committee of—
    And H.B.C. charter, 27, 29, 30 ; North-West agitators threaten appeal to, 302, 306 ; uphold sentence against Riel, 385
Proclamations—
    By Mactavish, 72, 75 ; McDougall, 76, 77, 78, 80, 86 ; Dennis, 82 ; Governor-General, 87, 88, 91, 108, 109, 146, 147, 150, 151, 153 ; Wolseley, 136, 140–1

Proulx, Rev. J. B., 311
Provencher, electoral district of, 168, 170
Provencher, J. A. N., 65, 71, 75, 90, 92, 216, 228
Provencher, Bishop J. N., 107
Provisional Governments—
  First at Red River, 73, 74, 84, 85–6, 91, 93, 95 ; second at Red River, 96–9, 100,
    101, 103, 104, 105, 106, 109, 110, 113, 114, 115, 121, 125, 132, 142, 148, 150,
    164, 165 ; " Legislative Assembly," 109, 110, 113, 121–2, 124, 141 ; Dumont's
    at St. Laurent, 180–2 ; of the Saskatchewan, 314, 316, 317, 320, 323, 324, 354

Q

Qu'Appelle, 192, 220, 222, 231, 233, 236, 271, 276, 294, 302, 304, 324, 333, 351,
    352, 353, 368
Qu'Appelle, Fort, 178, 225, 246, 355
Qu'Appelle, valley, 179, 185, 220, 235, 243
Quebec, 15, 118, 119, 131, 132, 133, 140, 145, 149, 156–7, 158, 169, 170, 171, 296,
    351, 362, 380–2, 383, 384, 385, 389, 390–1, 392, 393–4, 395, 396–400, 403–5,
    406, 407
Quinn, Henry, 339, 340
Quinn, T. T., 337, 338, 339

R

Rae, J. M., 271, 335 ; cited, 272, 286, 288, 289
Ramsey, Alexander, Governor of Minnesota, 36, 59, 164
Rat Portage, 139
Red Deer, 363
Red Deer Creek, 374
Red Deer Crossing, 363
Red Deer Hill, 265, 298, 329
Red Pheasant, 283, 285, 294, 334
Red River, 4, 10, 12, 22, 28, 31, 36, 37, 48, 49, 57, 71, 143, 185, 219
Red River Settlement—
  Attacked by Nor'Westers, 11 ; effect of union of two fur companies upon, 12 ;
    population of, 12–3 ; economic life of, 13–4 ; survey of, 15 ; government of,
    15–7 ; static nature of, 17–8, 47 ; agitation in against H.B.C. monopoly, 21,
    44–7 ; apprehension in regarding American expansion, 24–5 ; H.B.C. sur-
    render of, 22, 30, 33 ; lack of defensive force in, 36, 37, 41 ; half-breed unrest
    in, Chapter III ; famine in, 53 ; American interest in, 58–60, 126 ; insurrection
    in, Chapters IV, V ; Taché's return to, 108, 147 ; temper of people in, 109 ;
    refugees from, 116 ; administered by provisional government, 121 ; change of
    feeling in, 123, 125 ; routes to, 126 ; despatch of troops to, 129 et seq. ; Butler's
    visit to, 136 ; guides sent to Wolseley from, 139 ; Archibald takes census of,
    first provincial election in, 142 ; half-breed leaders return to, 164 ; feeling in
    generally favourable to amnesty, 168 ; half-breeds of trek to North-West, 178-9,
    182 ; route to Saskatchewan from, 184, 187 ; buffalo brigade from, 220 ; differ-
    ence in situation at and that in Saskatchewan, 314
Reed, Hayter, 235, 239, 280, 310, 350 ; cited, 285, 293
Reesor, David, 117
Regina, 186, 192, 271, 322, 329, 384
Richards, A. N., 65
Riel, Louis—
  On half-breed solidarity, 10 ; secretary of Comité National, 43, 69 ; on H.B.C.
    government, 48 ; on cause of rebellion, 49 ; character of, 67–8, 295 ; holds
    up survey, 68, 70 ; organizes métis, 70 ; takes Fort Garry, 70–1 ; invites
    English co-operation, 71–2 ; statements in Convention, 72–3, 80–1 ; forms
    provisional government, 73–4, 84–5 ; takes prisoners, 83–4 ; his aims, 71, 88,
    95, 96 ; assumes presidency, 85 ; and Canadian Commissioners, 90–2 ; and
    mass meetings, 92–3 ; and Convention, 94–6 ; forms second provisional

government, 96-9 ; and Portage expedition, 99-104 ; and Scott, 105-6 ; and Taché, 108, 109 ; demands provincial status, 95, 110, 113 ; formulates list of rights, 110, 113, 114 ; takes oath as president, 122 ; his negotiations with H.B.C., 122 ; his quarrel with O'Donoghue, 123, 164 ; his speech on ratification of Manitoba Act, 125 ; does not fear troops from Canada, 128 ; Butler's interview with, 136, 141 ; flight of, 140, 141, 164 ; Taché promises amnesty to, 148 ; Ritchot promises amnesty to, 152 ; President United States suggests amnesty for, 159 ; offers assistance against Fenians, 166-7 ; withdraws candidature in favour of Cartier, 168 ; his expulsion from parliament, 170-1 ; conditional amnesty granted to, 174 ; invited to return to North-West, 267-8 ; consulted by Indians, 289, 290, 302-3 ; unfit for his task, 295-6 ; informed of events in North-West, 296 ; his return and agitation in Saskatchewan, Chapter XIV ; mental change in, 313-4 ; forms provisional government in Saskatchewan, 315-6 ; appeals to English half-breeds, 318-20 ; negotiations with Mounted Police, 323-5 ; and engagement at Duck Lake, 328, 332, 348 ; incites Indians, 332-5 ; desperate position of, 348-9 ; overrules Dumont's plan of campaign, 357-8 ; appeals to Poundmaker for assistance, 364-6 ; his surrender, 371-2 ; trial of, 378, 384 ; insanity commission on, 385 ; execution of, 385 ; his petition to President Cleveland, 386 ; racial recriminations and political agitation over the death of, Chapter XVII

Riel père, Louis, 47, 67

Rights—
    First Bill of, 80, 82, 94, 114 ; Second Bill of, 94, 96, 110, 114, 118, Third List of, 110-3, 114, 150 ; Fourth List of, 114 ; Farmers' Union Declaration of, 263 ; Settlers' Union Bill of, 306, 307

Ringing Sky, 344

Ritchot, Janvier, 105

Ritchot, Abbé, J. N.—
    Assists half-breeds during Red River Rebellion, 61, 69, 70, 92, 93, 108 ; Red River delegate to Ottawa, 99, 110, 114, 115 ; his arrest, 117 ; negotiates with Canadian Government, 118-9, 150-1 ; returns to Red River, 123-4 ; and promise of amnesty, 150-2, 153 ; and Riel on occasion of Fenian invasion, 166

Rivière aux Ilets de Bois, 165-6

Rivière Qui Barre, 344

Rivière Sale, 69, 164

Rivière Seine, 104

Robertson Ross, Colonel, 132, 191, 202 ; cited, 199, 200

Robinson, Christopher, 384

Robinson, Major H. N., 58

Robitaille, Théodore, 169

Rochester, 386

Rogers, Sir Frederic, his memorandum on amnesty, 159 et seq. ; 161, 164

Rolette, J., 58

Roman Catholic clergy—
    Represented on Council of Assiniboia, 15-6 ; their part in the Red River Rebellion, 60-1 ; and the stopping of survey, 69 ; Thibault holds high position in, 88 ; at meeting of Convention, 94 ; separate schools in List of Rights, 114 ; oppose Riel's activity in Saskatchewan, 309-10 ; their breach with Riel, 316-7 ; opposed to Riel agitation in Quebec, 395

Rose, Sir John, 78, 121, 147

Ross, Alexander, cited, 8

Ross, Donald, 316

Ross, James, 52, 72, 73, 94, 96, 98

Ross, John, 26

Ross, John Jones, 399, 404, 405

Rouge, Fort, 4

Rouleau, Charles, 310

Royal Canadian Regiment, 36

Royal, Joseph, cited, 154

Running Rabbit, 230

Rupert's Land—
    Extent of, 3 ; early colonization in, 10 ; fur trade interests predominate in, 12 ;
    Recorder of, 16 ; isolation of, 20 ; boundary with Canada, 22, 29 ; H.B.C.
    willing to surrender portion of, 33 ; transfer to Canada of, 35, 37, 38-9, 41,
    121, 177 ; Council of, 45 ; half-breeds opposed to change in, 48 ; Public
    Notice to the Inhabitants of, 71-2 ; Declaration to the People of, 84 ; See also
    North-West
Russell, Lindsay, 254
Rykert, J. C., 402

S

St. Albert, 177, 179, 181, 182, 220, 225, 246, 251, 257-8, 352, 353
St. Antoine de Padoue, see Batoche
St. Boniface, 12, 67, 69, 107, 153, 167, 296
St. Catherines, 264, 265, 318, 329
St. Florent de Lebret, 181, 184
St. John, N. B., 305
St. Laurent—
    Founded, 179-80 ; Dumont's provisional government at, 180-2 ; becomes
    electoral district, 192 ; métis petitions from, 246, 251, 253 ; investigation of
    claims at, 255 ; survey at, 256 ; concessions to St. Albert not extended to, 258 ;
    Riel's return to, 297, 303 ; economic distress at, 305 ; visited by Grandin and
    Forget, 309, 310 ; rebellion localized at, 354
St. Louis, U.S., 220, 385
St. Louis de Langevin, 182, 258
St. Norbert, 43, 44, 69, 92
St. Paul, U.S., 13, 14, 24, 36, 37, 58, 59, 67, 75, 86, 113, 221
St. Paul des Cris, 200
St. Peter's Mission, 297
St. Vital, 57, 166
Sacré Coeur, 182
Sackville-West, Sir Lionel, 353
Saddle Lake, 344
Salaberry, Colonel Charles de, 88, 89, 90, 91, 92, 93, 95, 96, 115, 146, 148
Saskatchewan—
    Recommendation re surrender of, 22, 30 ; American interest in, 35, 59 ; first
    white settlements in, 183 et seq. ; colonization companies in, 186 ; Territory of,
    192 ; Indians in, 197, 205, 281, 283, 293 ; lawless conditions in, 199 et seq. ;
    buffalo in, 220 ; discontent in, 264 et seq. ; Provisional Government of,
    314-6 ; Riel on situation in, 318, 319 ; fears of people in, 331
Saskatchewan, Fort, 258
Saskatchewan Landing, 360
Saskatchewan River, 4, 28, 33, 36, 49, 185, 187, 199, 233, 235, 245, 256, 258, 264,
    295, 297, 305, 343, 347, 375
    North Saskatchewan, 179, 183 185, 186, 189, 211, 312, 326, 348, 355, 360, 363, 373
    South Saskatchewan, 179, 182, 257, 258, 259, 265, 274, 340, 356, 360, 369
Saskatoon, 186
Sault Ste. Marie, 129, 133, 134
Sayer, Guillaume, 47
Schmidt, Louis, cited, 67, 68, 297 ; 94, 109, 124
Schultz, Dr. J. C.—
    His agitation in Red River, 48, 50, 51, 52 ; Canadian Government employees
    associate with, 54 ; stakes land, 55 ; Howe avoids, 64 ; organizes resistance to
    Riel, 83 ; escapes from Fort Garry, 99 ; Riel's threat against, 100 ; joins
    Portage party, 101 ; member of " Canada First," 115 ; and agitation in Ontario,
    116 ; defeated by Smith in election, 142 ; votes for expulsion of Riel, 170 ; his
    recommendations re preservation of buffalo, 222
Scotland, 5, 9, 23
Scott, A. H., 99, 114, 115, 117, 118, 151, 154, 160, 169
Scott, D. L., 384

Scott, Hugh, 117
Scott, Thomas (Red River)—
    His escape from Fort Garry, 99, 100 ; imprisoned with Portage party, 104 ; his
        character, 104-5 ; his trial and execution, 105, 106 ; effect of his execution in
        Red River, 109 ; English Canadian and Ontario indignation at execution of,
        115, 116, 133, 145, 156 ; French Canadian and Quebec opinion regarding, 145,
        157 ; result of execution, 155
Scott, Thomas (Saskatchewan)—
    Supports Riel, 298, 299, 300, 318, 320 ; trial and acquittal of, 378
Seenum, 205
Siegfried, A., cited, 144
Selby Smythe, Major-General Sir Edward, 181-2
Selkirk, 185
Selkirk colony, 11, 35, 49, 59, 60 ; see Red River Settlement
Selkirk, Earl of, 10, 12, 13, 14, 15, 207
Semple, Robert, 11
Settlers' Union, 265, 298, 299, 300, 308, 317
Seven Oaks, massacre of, 11, 12, 15
Seward, W. H., American Secretary of State, 35, 36, 59
Shebandowan, Lake, 129, 135
Shellabarger, Mr., 36
Shepherd, John, Governor of the H.B.C., 29, 34
Sherbrooke, 400
Shoal River, 236
Simpson, Sir George, cited 14, 21-2, 26, 45, 46, 47
Simpson, W. M., 135, 208
Sinclair, James, 45, 46
Sitting Bull, cited, 223 ; 224, 232
Slater, J. C., 299
Smart, Sergeant, 377
Smet, Father de, cited, 220
Smith, Donald, A.—
    Canadian Commissioner to Red River, 89-94, 96, 146 ; invites delegates to
        Ottawa, 96, 99 ; disapproves of Portage expedition, 103 ; intercedes for
        Boulton and Scott, 104, 105, 106 ; considered as Lieutenant-Governor, 121 ;
        welcomes Wolseley, 139 ; administers Red River until Archibald's arrival, 142 ;
        defeats Schultz in election, 142
Smith, James, 290
Smith, John, 290
Snow, J. A., 53, 54, 55, 72, 76, 84, 104, 129, 137
South Branch ; see Saskatchewan River, South
Southesk, Earl of, cited, 7, 219
Sparrow Hawk, 231, 233
Spence, Andrew, 265, 267, 306
Spence, Thomas, 50, 123
Stand Off, Fort, 203
Stanley, Sir Frederick, cited on execution of Riel, 387
State Department, the, 59, 109
Steele, Major S. B., 138, 363, 374, 375-6
Steele's Scouts, 352, 363, 375, 376
Stephen, George, 89
Stephen, Sir James, cited, 22
Stone Fort, the, see Lower Fort Garry
Strange, Major-General, T. B., 355, 362-3, 373-6
Street, W. P. R., 354
Strike-Him-on-the-Back, 285, 335
Stuttsman, Enos, 58
Sulte, Benjamin, 154
Superior, Lake, 4, 5, 31, 112, 113, 127, 129, 133, 352
Sutherland, John, 94, 98

Swan River, 181
Swain, T. 265
Sweetgrass, 205
Swift Current, 335, 355, 360, 365, 368

T

Taché, Archbishop, A. A.—
    Bishop of St. Boniface, cited on Council of Assiniboia, 16 ; on Red River famine,
    53 ; on American influence during the Red River Rebellion, 58 ; on his fears
    regarding entry of North-West into confederation, 61 ; on amnesty, 147 ; his
    influence over the half-breeds, 54, 90, 107 ; warns Canadian Government,
    snubbed by Cartier, 64, 107 ; suggests Mactavish as Lieutenant-Governor, 66 ;
    sends Riel to Montreal, 67 ; absent during the insurrection, 69, 107 ; returns
    to assist pacification, 107-8, 147 ; his influence at Red River, 109-110, 123 ;
    and the List of Rights, 110, 113, 114 ; promises complete amnesty, 123, 140,
    148 ; his efforts to expedite arrival of Archibald, 141-2 ; confers with Canadian
    Government, 147-8 ; correspondence re amnesty 149-50, 155 ; his visit to
    Governor-General, 152-3, 155 ; requested to obtain withdrawal of Riel, 168 ;
    continues to agitate for amnesty, 169, 171 ; on the half-breed land grant in
    Manitoba, 244 ; consulted on half-breed policy, 248
Taillon, L. O., 405
Tanner, James, 165
Tarte, J. I., cited, 398
Taylor, J. W., 36, 37, 59 ; cited, 119, 151, 154, 214
Telegraph Flat, 183
Texas, 24, 48
Thibault, Very Rev. Grand Vicar J. B., 88-91, 93-96, 121, 146, 148 ; cited, 94, 99
Thibert, P., 99
Thompson, J. S. D., 402
Thornton, Sir Edward, 134
Thunder Bay, 141, 208
Toronto, 25, 26, 27, 31, 116, 117, 155, 157, 351
Touchwood Hills, 178, 184, 225, 236, 271, 276, 333
Tourond, David, 316
Tourond, Patrice, 316
Trottier, C., 333
Troy, 351
Trudel, Senator, 393, 398
Tupper, Sir Charles, 90, 265
Turner, Edward, 105
Turner, John, 249
Two Mountains, Lake of, 207

U

Union Métisse de St. Joseph, 303
United States, 13, 24, 25, 35, 36, 37, 43, 46, 53, 59, 60, 70, 78, 85, 126, 127, 128, 129,
    131, 134, 136, 148, 164, 187, 188, 189, 190, 199, 201, 213, 214, 220, 227, 230,
    231, 232, 235, 240, 242, 261, 269, 274, 296, 297, 302, 305, 313, 353, 361, 364,
    372, 379, 384, 385, 386 ; see also Americans and Washington
Upper Canada, 11, 17, 22, 119, 160, 207

V

Valleyfield, 394
Vanasse, Fabien, 393
Vancouver Island, 21
Vankoughnet, Lawrence—
    Deputy Superintendent General of Indian Affairs, 216 ; his memorandum on
    Indian policy, 237 ; his visit to North-West and his economy in Indian expendi-
    ture, 270 ; Dewdney's complaints re, 272 ; cited on outbreak at Crooked
    Lakes, 280 ; his ultimatum to Big Bear, 282 ; advises increase of Mounted

Police in North Saskatchewan, 285 ; refuses to restrict movement of Indians, 289 ; on Indian grievances, 294
Van Straubenzie, Colonel, 371
Vavasour, Lieutenant, 25
Végreville, Father, 182, 258
Vérendrye, P. G. Sieur de la, 4
Victoria, 177, 205

W

Walker, Inspector James, 250
Wallace, Major J., 65, 82
Walsh, Fort, 203, 223, 226, 230, 231, 232, 233, 234, 235, 275, 284
Wandering Spirit, 338, 339, 342, 379
Warre, Lieutenant, 25
Washington, 35, 36, 46, 59, 60, 119, 134, 154, 164, 214, 352
Water Hen Lake, 348
Watkin, Edward, 31, 32, 34
Webb, Captain, 56, 68
White Fish Lake, 177, 205, 344
Whoop-Up, Fort, 203
William, Fort, 11, 12, 31, 134, 135
Williams, Colonel A. T. H., 371
Winnipeg, 4, 51, 71, 81, 82, 83, 84, 104, 113, 115, 142, 184, 185, 263, 352
Winnipeg, Lake, 13, 37, 126, 127, 184
Winnipeg River, 136, 137, 139, 142
Wolseley, Colonel G. J.—
   Desires to accompany Smith, 89 ; suggested as Lieutenant-Governor, 121 ; leads Red River Expedition, 132 et seq. ; his charges against Canadian Ministers, 135 ; his request for road-workers, 136–7 ; cited on running rapids, 137–8 ; captures Fort Garry, 139–40, 153 ; his proclamation, 140–1, 165 ; requests Smith to administer settlement, 142 ; his pow-wow with Indians at Fort Frances, 136, 204
Wolseley, town of, 304
Wood Mountain, 184, 223, 353
Woods, Lake of the, 4, 53, 136, 137, 185, 187
Wrigley, Joseph, 321

Y

Yellow Calf, 279–80
York Factory, 5, 10
Yorkton, 352
Young, Captain, 135
Young, Captain George, 332
Young, Rev. George, 53, 84, 105
Young, H. S., 345–6
Young, Sir John—
   Governor-General of Canada, notifies Colonial Office of Canada's refusal to accept transfer, 78 ; his proclamation, 87–8, 146, 147, 148, 153 ; cited on Thibault, 88 ; his letter to Taché, 108 ; Lynch petition to, 116 ; Ritchot protests to, 117 ; and the military expedition, 131, 133 ; his protests against stopping of Chicora, 134 ; forwards Taché's correspondence to Colonial Office, 150 ; and the promise of amnesty to Red River insurgents, 151–3, 161, 169